Understanding Physical, Sensory, and Health Impairments

Characteristics and Educational Implications

Understanding Physical, Sensory, and Health Impairments

Characteristics and Educational Implications

Kathryn Wolff Heller
Georgia State University

Paul A. Alberto
Georgia State University

Paula E. Forney
Georgia Pines/INSITE Program,
Georgia Department of Education

Morton N. Schwartzman
Children's Rehabilitation Network

Brooks/Cole Publishing Company
I(T)P™ An International Thomson Publishing Company

Pacific Grove • Albany • Bonn • Boston • Cincinnati • Detroit • London • Madrid • Melbourne
Mexico City • New York • Paris • San Francisco • Singapore • Tokyo • Toronto • Washington

Sponsoring Editor: *Vicki Knight*
Marketing Team: *Carolyn Crockett and Jean Vevers Thompson*
Editorial Associate: *Lauri Banks Ataide*
Production Editor: *Laurel Jackson*
Manuscript Editor: *Mary P. O'Briant*
Permissions Editor: *Cathleen S. Collins*
Interior Design: *Jeanne Wolfgeher*
Interior Illustration: *John and Judy Waller*
Credits continue on page 429.

Cover Design: *Laurie Albrecht*
Cover Photo: © *Abraham Menashe*
Art Editor: *Lisa Torri*
Photo Editor: *Robert J. Western*
Indexer: *James Minkin*
Typesetting: *Graphic World, Inc.*
Cover Printing: *New England Book Components*
Printing and Binding: *Courier Westford, Inc.*

For more information, contact:

BROOKS/COLE PUBLISHING COMPANY
511 Forest Lodge Road
Pacific Grove, CA 93950
USA

International Thomson Publishing Europe
Berkshire House 168-173
High Holborn
London WC1V 7AA
England

Thomas Nelson Australia
102 Dodds Street
South Melbourne, 3205
Victoria, Australia

Nelson Canada
1120 Birchmount Road
Scarborough, Ontario
Canada M1K 5G4

International Thomson Editores
Campos Eliseos 385, Piso 7
Col. Polanco
11560 México D. F. México

International Thomson Publishing GmbH
Königswinterer Strasse 418
53227 Bonn
Germany

International Thomson Publishing Asia
221 Henderson Road
#05-10 Henderson Building
Singapore 0315

International Thomson Publishing Japan
Hirakawacho Kyowa Building, 3F
2-2-1 Kirakawacho
Chiyoda-ku, Tokyo 102
Japan

Printed in the United States of America

10 9 8 7 6 5 4 3 2 1

Library of Congress Cataloging-in-Publication Data
Understanding physical, sensory, and health impairments:
    characteristics and educational implications/by Kathryn Wolff
Heller . . . [et al.].
        p.   cm.
    Includes bibliographical references and index.
    ISBN 0-534-33913-1 (alk. paper)
    1. Physically handicapped children.   2. Child development
deviations.   3. Physically handicapped children—Education.
I. Heller, Kathryn Wolff, [date]
RJ137.U53 1996
618.92—dc20   95-9010
                                                  CIP

To all the children, families, teachers, and college students who have taught us so much over the years, and to our children and grand-children: Daniel Bryan, Megan Caitlin, Rhonda Beth, Paula Renée, Jon David, Harold Steven, Marissa Leigh, and Lauren Michele, from whom we've learned the most about growth and development and the learning process. Also, to the late Larry Thorne, whose teaching always reflected love and respect for children and their families.

About the Authors

Kathryn Wolff Heller, an assistant professor of educational psychology and special education at Georgia State University, coordinates graduate programs in orthopedic impairments, visual impairments, and deaf-blind. She also directs several projects, including a statewide technical assistance grant in the area of deaf-blindness, a technical assistance grant targeting communication for students with deaf-blindness, and a personnel preparation training grant that developed graduate programs in the areas of visual impairments and deaf-blind.

Dr. Heller, a registered nurse with experience in pediatric medicine, worked for five years in intensive care units and then went on to obtain master's and doctoral degrees in special education. She has worked as a classroom teacher of students with orthopedic impairments, mental retardation, traumatic brain injury, and visual impairments. In addition, Dr. Heller provided technical assistance to nine states and territories in the area of deaf-blindness as part of a national technical assistance grant. Dr. Heller has made numerous presentations, has served on several advisory boards, and has coauthored several articles pertaining to students with physical impairments, sensory impairments, and mental retardation. One of her primary interests is in providing effective educational instruction and health care for students with physical, sensory, and health impairments.

Paul A. Alberto, a professor of educational psychology and special education at Georgia State University, directs the teacher training program in multiple and severe disabilities. He also directs the Bureau for Students with Multiple and Severe Disabilities, a joint project with the Georgia State Department of Education, Division for Exceptional Students, to provide technical assistance to students, parents, teachers, and administrators. Previously, he was a classroom teacher of students with mental retardation.

Dr. Alberto has coauthored a college textbook on applied behavior analysis for teachers and has written numerous chapters and articles concerning students with multiple and severe disabilities, focusing on curriculum and instruction. In addition, he has directed funded projects in providing technical assistance to classroom teachers, for developing secondary and transition programs, for instructing students with profound disabilities, and for developing inclusive educational strategies for students with severe disabilities. Dr. Alberto also coordinated the southern region of a national technical assistance project to states for education of students with deaf-blindness. His primary interests include providing effective instructional strategies for students with severe disabilities and establishing transition services from school to adult settings.

Paula Forney, a therapy coordinator for the Georgia Pines/INSITE Program in Atlanta, Georgia, trains and supervises physical and occupational therapists throughout Georgia to provide home-based technical assistance services to families of young children with multiple disabilities and sensory impairments. Ms. Forney has a B.S. degree in physical therapy from Simmons College and an M.M.Sc. degree in pediatric physical therapy from Emory University and is certified in both pediatric neurodevelopmental treatment and sensory integration. In addition, she has over 20 years' experience in pediatric physical therapy, including development of school therapy and early intervention programs.

Ms. Forney has contributed to the authorship of the second edition of the INSITE Curriculum; has developed instructional videotapes on children with motor impairments; and has taught numerous courses and workshops on pediatric physical therapy, early intervention, and children with sensory impairments. She is also extensively involved with local and state interagency councils that serve young children with special needs and their families. Ms. Forney's major interest is in collaborative teaming in providing appropriate services to children with multiple disabilities and their families.

Morton N. Schwartzman, M.D., a pediatrician who specializes in pulmonary diseases, is the medical director of the Cystic Fibrosis Center affiliated with the Joe DiMaggio Children's Hospital at Memorial, Hollywood, Florida.

Dr. Schwartzman, whose previous experience includes working as a private practitioner for 29 years, was a medical consultant for the Health Rehabilitative Service Agency, Dade County, Florida. His responsibilities included caring for infants, children, and adolescents with chronic disease, such as neurological disorders, muscular dystrophy and myopathies, and chronic pulmonary diseases. He was also involved with the care and treatment of children with special needs, who resided in various group homes. In addition, he has served as medical director for a prescribed pediatric extended care facility for children with medical and physical impairments and has served on many advisory boards, medical boards, and boards of directors, including the American Lung Association of South Florida and the state of Florida. Dr. Schwartzman is a past president of the medical staff at Miami Children's Hospital in Miami, Florida, and a past president of the American Lung Association of Dade and Monroe County, Florida.

Dr. Schwartzman has lectured to students at local universities and to civic groups and professional organizations, and has coauthored several published articles in various medical journals. His interest lies in creating new avenues to improve care for children and adolescents with medical needs and with physical and mental impairments.

BRIEF CONTENTS

Contents

Preface

In this textbook, we describe various physical, sensory, and health impairments and their educational implications. Although each student who has one of these conditions is unique, school personnel need to understand the student's impairment in order to meet his or her unique needs and to provide an appropriate education. Because it requires a team of individuals to properly educate students with physical, sensory, or health impairments, a team of individuals wrote this book. Collectively, our backgrounds include education, medicine, nursing, physical therapy, and parenting a child with a physical impairment.

This book is divided into eight parts. Part I, which contains Chapters 1 through 3, lays a foundation for the rest of the book. Chapter 1 is a general introduction to physical, sensory, and health impairments and to members of the educational team. Chapter 2 provides an overall picture of typical and atypical motor development. Chapter 3 is an overview of learning and behavioral characteristics of students who have a physical, sensory, or health impairment. The learning and behavioral characteristics described form a framework of general characteristics. As they peruse other chapters, readers can fill in the framework with information regarding specific disabilities.

Parts II through VI describe major physical, sensory, or health impairments that are often found in the school-age population. In each of these chapters, we discuss the same major aspects of specific impairments. These aspects include description, etiology, dynamics, characteristics, detection, treatment, course, and educational implications. Each "educational implications" section is subdivided into the following types: meeting physical and sensory needs, meeting communication needs, meeting learning needs, meeting daily living needs, and meeting behavioral and social needs.

Part II, "Neuromotor Impairments," begins with a chapter on neuroanatomy that provides a foundation for the chapters that follow. The impairments described in these chapters include traumatic brain injury, seizure disorders, cerebral palsy, spinal cord injury, and spina bifida. Part III, "Degenerative Diseases," provides information on muscular dystrophy and spinal muscular atrophy. This part also contains information about issues related to death and dying. In Part IV, "Orthopedic and Musculoskeletal Disorders," we examine conditions that involve bones and muscles. These include curvatures of the spine, hip conditions, limb deficiency, juvenile rheumatoid arthritis, and musculoskeletal disorders. Part V, "Sensory Impairments," covers several types of visual and hearing impairments. In Part VI, "Major Health Impairments," we focus on several common health impairments, including congenital heart defects, blood disorders, asthma, cystic fibrosis, insulin-dependent diabetes mellitus, chronic renal failure, and childhood cancer. In Part VII, "Infectious Diseases," we discuss congenital and acquired infections, including AIDS. This section also contains information on how infection is transmitted and on the principles of infection control.

The last part of this book, Part VIII, is called "Meeting Educational Needs." The first chapter in this part, "Multiple Disabilities," contains descriptions of various types of multiple disabilities and includes an extended section on educational implications that can be applied to severe physical or sensory impairments discussed earlier in the book. Issues such as lifting and handling, medication monitoring, and physical health care procedures are discussed in this chapter. Chapter 28, "Classroom Adaptations," provides an overview of the types of adaptations that students with physical, sensory, or health impairments may need and contains information on how to select an appropriate adaptation. Chapter 29 centers on collaborative educational teams. In this chapter, we describe various types of teams and the team members' roles and responsibilities.

Acknowledgments

We are grateful to the many people who helped us prepare this textbook. We want to thank Harry Dangel, Sherri Williams, and Alison Stafford, who were coauthors of some of the chapters in this book. We want to extend a special thanks to the following individuals who assisted in reviewing select chapters, taking photographs, and providing support: Lee Wolff, Colleen O'Rourke, Virginia Bishop, Johnnie Hall, Janet Bowdin, Doug McJannet, Monica Werner, Leslie Sweatman, Michael Carroll, Jerry Adaskes, Kelly Lewis, Ann Williamson, Larry Forney, Marilyn Schwartzman, Eileen Wolff, Virgil Wolff, and Edward Heller.

We also appreciate our reviewers, who were selected by our editor and who provided meaningful feedback to assist in our effort to provide a comprehensive textbook on physical, sensory, and health impairments. These reviewers include Sherwood Best, California State University, Los Angeles; Dennis Cates, University of South Carolina–Columbia; Mary Kay Dykes, University of Florida; Joyce J. Fisher, Fresno Pacific College; and Rosanne K. Silberman, City University of New York, Hunter College.

Special thanks go to our managing editor, Vicki Knight, for her feedback and support, and to the rest of the staff at Brooks/Cole, including Lauri Banks Ataide, Cat Collins, Carolyn Crockett, Laurie Jackson, Kelly Shoemaker, Faith Stoddard, Jean Thompson, and Lisa Torri. We also wish to thank Laurie Albrecht, Mike Loomis, James Minkin, Mary O'Briant, Kathleen Olson, Susan Pendleton, John and Judy Waller, Bob Western, and Jeanne Wolfgeher for their work on this book.

Finally, we would like to thank all the graduate students who took our course on characteristics of severe physical and sensory impairments and who provided feedback regarding the need for a current, understandable textbook that would help them understand various physical, sensory, and health impairments and their educational implications. These students' comments over the years prompted the writing of this textbook. Further, students' feedback on draft chapters over the past two years have assisted us in providing an understandable, interesting, and meaningful textbook that we hope will provide a strong knowledge base for attaining an appropriate education for students with physical, sensory, and health impairments.

Kathryn Wolff Heller
Paul A. Alberto
Paula E. Forney
Morton N. Schwartzman

Understanding Physical, Sensory, and Health Impairments

Characteristics and Educational Implications

PART I

Implications of Physical, Sensory, and Health Impairments

Introduction to Physical, Sensory, and Health Impairments and Members of the Educational Team

What do you do if a child has a seizure? What accommodations must you make for a student with juvenile rheumatoid arthritis? What do you do when a child with muscular dystrophy says he's dying? What should you know about AIDS? Are children who are deaf and blind totally deaf and totally blind? Educators face questions like these every day, as students with a variety of physical, sensory, and health impairments are educated in their classrooms. Knowing the answers to these and to other such questions will help prepare teachers to better meet the needs of students with impairments.

To understand physical, sensory, and health impairments, the teacher must know not only about these impairments but also about their educational implications. Sometimes, the teacher should be prepared to provide adaptations for students with severe physical and sensory impairments. At other times, the teacher should be able to recognize signs and symptoms of distress and know what to do for students with health impairments. Knowing the course of diseases and ways of addressing concerns relating to dying are typically needed when dealing with students with degenerative diseases. Also, knowing about proper infection control helps a teacher maintain a healthy environment for all students, including those with infectious diseases.

This chapter is an introduction to the areas that educators should be familiar with if they are to meet the needs of students with physical, sensory, and health impairments. Each topic is discussed in the order in which it appears in the book. Because educational and medical personnel are vital to implementing the varying aspects of care, their roles are described at the end of this chapter. Discussions of these professionals will also appear throughout the book as their jobs relate to specific impairments.

Before learning about various types of physical, sensory, and health impairments, educators need to have a basic understanding of typical as well as atypical motor development (as described in Chapter 2). Knowledge of these characteristics helps teachers recognize various motor reactions or delays in motor development seen in such conditions as cerebral palsy or blindness. Knowing about the normal development of reflexes (such as primitive reflexes), reactions (such as postural, righting, and protective reactions), and early motor milestones (such as when the infant begins to sit) provides a basis for understanding atypical motor reactions. An educator who knows the implications of problems in motor development, as well as possible interventions, can do a much better job of addressing students' needs.

The effects of physical, sensory, or health impairments on students can extend beyond the physical nature of the impairments. Often, learning and social-emotional development is affected. Environmental variables, such as fatigue and use of adaptations, as well as psychological factors, such as motivation and self-concept, are intertwined with the characteristics of the impairment and can affect academic performance. Teachers can control many environmental variables and some psychological factors to create a supportive environment for students. (Chapter 3 describes some of these variables and factors and their possible effects on students with impairments.)

CHARACTERISTICS AND TYPES OF IMPAIRMENTS

The characteristics of individuals with physical, sensory, and health impairments differ greatly. Even individuals with the same impairment can be affected differently. Severity can range from an obvious, severe physical involvement to no noticeable impairment at all. Students with impairments also range from being gifted to being mentally retarded. In light of this range of intellectual abilities, teachers should never assume that students with severe physical or sensory impairments also have cognitive impairments. Students also differ in the type of curriculum they learn best (such as a regular aca demic or a functional curriculum), in the types of services they need (such as regular education only or support from special education), and in their optimal placement (such as in a regular classroom or a resource room).

There are several types and classifications of physical, sensory, and health impairments. In educational settings, children are classified differently in different states. One classification system that is based on medical characteristics and educational implications divides impairments in schoolchildren into six major categories:

1. Neuromotor impairments
2. Degenerative diseases
3. Orthopedic and musculoskeletal disorders
4. Sensory impairments
5. Major health impairments
6. Infectious diseases

Each of these categories constitutes a major section of this book.

Neuromotor Impairments

The first category, neuromotor impairments, includes disorders that affect both nerves and muscles. Impairments typically found in this category are **traumatic brain injury**, seizure disorders, **cerebral palsy**, and spinal cord disorders, including **spinal cord injury** and **spina bifida**. Traumatic brain injury (see Chapter 5) varies as to the severity of damage and permanency of the resulting impairments. Students with traumatic brain injury may have impairments in cognition, communication, physical ability, sensory input, and behavior. Educators should understand how pervasively this type of injury can affect the student and know specific ways to address the effects of the impairment (see Chapter 5).

Several types of **seizures** have varying characteristics and implications for the teacher. A seizure can occur as a blank stare (an absence seizure) in which the student might miss information in class; or a seizure can result in a stiffening and shaking motor movement, accompanied by a loss of consciousness (tonic-clonic seizures). Although seizures usually last from a few seconds to a few minutes, some seizures do not stop and require medical intervention. The educator must know what to do when these seizures occur, what constitutes a medical emergency that requires calling paramedics, and what requires only monitoring. Some seizures also require educational modifications to assist the student (see Chapter 6).

Some physical impairments have the potential to severely limit a student's movements and can hinder functional use of arms and legs. These conditions are cerebral palsy (Chapter 7), spina bifida (Chapter 8), and spinal cord injury (Chapter 8). The educator should have a good understanding of how motor movement can be affected and which secondary characteristics of these conditions can impair functioning. Also, problems such as ulcers and **contractures** can arise; the educator and members of the educational team should be alert for these problems and be prepared to provide appropriate intervention. When these conditions severely affect a student's functioning, there are usually many educational implications and adaptations that the teacher should be aware of and carry out to meet the student's needs.

Degenerative Diseases

The second category of impairments is **degenerative diseases**. Although these diseases are often forms of neuromotor impairments, a separate discussion of them is provided because of their physically deteriorating nature and the special educational considerations of having a student with a degenerative disease in the classroom. Although there are several types of degenerative diseases, **muscular dystrophy** (Chapter 9) and spinal muscular atrophy (Chapter 10) are two of the most common. Each has forms of the disease with initial onset in childhood. Students who have degenerative diseases are faced with a progressive loss of function. Educators should understand not only potential adaptations but also how children perceive death. Teachers can then address the concerns of students who are dying, as well as the concerns of those around them (see Chapter 9).

Orthopedic and Musculoskeletal Disorders

Many types of **orthopedic** disorders can occur singly or may be present in individuals with certain neuromotor impairments and degenerative diseases. Curvatures of the spine, such as **scoliosis** (see Chapter 11), often occur in such conditions as cerebral palsy, spina bifida, spinal cord injury, and degenerative diseases. Hip conditions, such as **dislocation** (see Chapter 12), may also occur in such conditions as cerebral palsy. Educators may encounter other types of orthopedic impairments and **musculoskeletal** disorders, including limb deficiencies (Chapter 13); **juvenile rheumatoid arthritis** (Chapter 14); osteogenesis imperfecta, also called brittle bone disease (Chapter 15); and **arthrogryposis**, or congenital multiple contracture (Chapter 15). Educators may need to refrain from making allowances, as with a student missing a limb from birth who compensates by using other limbs; or educators may need to make substantial modifications. For example, several types of adaptations may be required for a student with arthrogryposis.

Sensory Impairments

Sensory impairments, as presented in Part V, may require unique adaptations and considerations on the educator's part because the effect of having a major mode of sensory information limited or unavailable is so severe. Descriptions of some major types of **visual impairment** (Chapter 16) and **hearing impairment** (Chapter 17) will help educators gain a better understanding of the impairments' effects. As with other impairments, these may occur either separately or in combination with other disorders. Further, the lack of vision or hearing can affect not only a student's understanding of the material being presented, but also his or her ability to develop concepts. Educators need a basic understanding of how these impairments affect learning, which adaptations can be used, and how best to present educational material in a way that makes it accessible to students.

Major Health Impairments

Several types of impairment are typically not discernible by looking at the student. These impairments can be categorized as major health impairments. Major health impairments include a wide variety of disorders, ranging from those with no apparent symptoms when properly managed to those that result in death despite medical management. These impairments (discussed in Part VI) include congenital heart defects (Chapter 18); blood disorders, such as **hemophilia** and **sickle cell disease** (Chapter 19); **asthma** (Chapter 20); **cystic fibrosis** (Chapter 21); insulin-dependent diabetes mellitus (Chapter 22); **chronic renal failure** (Chapter 23); and childhood cancer (Chapter 24). Each of these

conditions has the potential to become a medical emergency under certain circumstances. It is crucial that the educator know the signs and symptoms that indicate the need for medical intervention. Also, in certain types of impairment, modifications in certain activities may be necessary due to the student's fatigue and lack of stamina.

Infectious Diseases

Several types of infectious diseases can be medically devastating to individuals who acquire them. Having a good understanding of these diseases, their means of transmission, and proper infection control will help teachers meet students' needs better.

Infectious diseases may be divided into two categories by time of onset (see Part VII): *congenital infections* (Chapter 25) and *acquired infections*, including acquired immune deficiency syndrome (AIDS) (Chapter 26). **Congenital** infections refer to infections that are transmitted from the mother to the fetus. Acquired infections refer to those contracted after birth. One group of congenital infections with the potential to cause severe, multiple impairments is referred to by the acronym **STORCH**, which stands for syphilis, **toxoplasmosis**, other, rubella, cytomegalovirus, and herpes. Understanding the significance and etiology of these infections will help educators understand the impact of the impairments they cause.

Besides congenital infections that sometimes cause severe impairment, several acquired infections can also cause impairment or death, such as those affecting the central nervous system (**meningitis, encephalitis**), hepatitis, and the virus that causes AIDS: the human immunodeficiency virus (HIV). Educators should know how infection is transmitted and how to maintain a healthy environment for all students, including those who have infections.

Teachers should have information about several aspects of each impairment in each category. In addition to a description of the impairment, knowledge about how a specific disorder affects or alters the anatomy and physiology of a specific bodily system will shed light on the disorder's characteristics. The chapters to follow provide this information.

Teachers also should know about the characteristics, detection, treatment, and course of impairments, as well as the specific educational implications of each impairment. Educational implications include meeting physical and sensory needs, communication needs, daily living needs, learning needs, and behavioral and social needs. Information about how best to meet these needs will follow.

MULTIPLE IMPAIRMENTS AND MEETING EDUCATIONAL NEEDS

Besides the specific educational implications for each impairment, some general educational implications apply to many impairments. These are provided in the last section of the book. For example, students with multiple impairments (Chapter 27) have unique educational needs due to the combined effects of several impairments. Students with such multiple disabilities as combined cerebral palsy and visual impairments present unique challenges. Further, several general educational implications that apply to many students with multiple impairments also apply to other impairments. Some of these implications include basic lifting and handling guidelines, use of assistive devices (including communication devices), and physical health care procedures (see Chapter 27).

Adaptation is usually needed to accommodate students with physical and sensory impairments. A description of adaptation strategies, such as the one in Chapter 28, provides information about several types of adaptations, as well as guidelines for selecting the proper type. To help make decisions regarding adaptations, as well as goals and objectives for students with impairments, the *educational team*—to be discussed in Chapter 29—will need to work together.

MEMBERS OF THE EDUCATIONAL TEAM

Several individuals in the educational setting help provide an appropriate education for students who have impairments. Members of the educational team and their areas of expertise are described here. The need for particular professional services varies from student to student.

Special Education Teacher

The special education teacher's role on the educational team is complex and encompasses a broad spectrum of responsibilities and skills. Tasks include working cooperatively with students, family members, and other team members to identify age-appropriate, functional activities and academic skills for instruction; consulting with regular classroom teachers about students' needs in integrated or mainstreamed activities; and coordinating the daily delivery of special education and related services.

In many states, special education teachers are certified in specific disability areas and have expertise in teaching students with those disabilities. The areas in which teachers may be certified vary greatly between states; some examples of specialties are orthopedic impairments, visual impairments, hearing impairments, mental retardation, learning disabilities, and behavior disorders.

Teachers who are certified in orthopedic impairments specialize in meeting the unique needs of students with physical disabilities. (See Figure 1-1.) Some specializations include expertise in: adapting instruction and instructional material to accommodate students' limitations in physical movement; selecting and implementing assistive devices; knowing the educational implications of physical impairments; training in physical health care procedures; promoting communication through the use of augmentative and alternative communication; using feeding, positioning, and handling techniques; and teaching nonacademic and academic skills.

Teachers certified in visual impairments know the educational implications of visual impairments and blindness, as well as appropriate teaching strategies for this population. (See Figure 1-2.) Some specialties include expertise in: adapting material and instruction to meet the needs of students with visual impairments and blindness; teaching braille; teaching the use of residual vision; conducting functional vision exams and learning media assessments; teaching concept development; teaching communication skills; teaching social skills; teaching the use of low-vision aids; and teaching nonacademic and academic skills.

Teachers certified in hearing impairments have specific knowledge of hearing impairments and deafness. (See Figure 1-3.) Some specialties include expertise in: teaching sign language; teaching concept

■ **FIGURE 1-1** Teacher certified in orthopedic impairments helping student with cerebral palsy to improve his writing skills in his regular classroom

■ **FIGURE 1-2** Teacher certified in visual impairments showing student a tactile map of Asia

■ **FIGURE 1-3** Teacher certified in hearing impairments signing a story

development; adapting materials and instruction; selecting and using assistive devices; teaching the use of residual hearing; and teaching academic and nonacademic subjects.

Special education teachers may be certified in mental retardation and gain unique knowledge of strategies for teaching students with mental retardation. Teachers also can gain specialized knowledge in assessment, academic and functional curricula (including such areas as daily living, vocations, leisure, and community skills), transition, and communication. Since students with mental retardation may also have sensory or physical impairments, the teacher specializing in mental

retardation (who may have had some training in these areas as well) will probably need the support of teachers in other specialty areas.

Special education teachers may be certified in other specialties, such as learning disabilities and behavior disorders. Teachers specializing in learning disabilities learn effective instructional strategies; those specializing in behavior disorders provide expertise in behavior management as well as effective instructional management strategies.

Orientation and Mobility Instructor

The orientation and mobility (O&M) instructor has specialized training in visual functioning as it relates to mobility and travel through specific environments such as home, school, community, work and leisure settings, and public transportation. (See Figure 1-4.) In this capacity, the O&M specialist plays an important role on the team, particularly when the student with visual impairment is making a transition to a new environment—a new school or a new work setting. The O&M specialist's role may overlap with those of the occupational therapist (OT) and the physical therapist (PT). Both assist students' development of perceptual concepts such as body awareness and spatial

■ **FIGURE 1-4** Orientation and mobility instructor teaching a student to cross the street safely

awareness. The vision and O&M specialists' roles may overlap in the areas of functional vision assessment and use of adapted devices to accommodate for visual loss.

Student and Family Members

The student and his or her family members make up another critical portion of the educational team. Not only is it the student's and the family members' legal right to be part of the assessment and planning process, but they have the most knowledge about the student and the greatest stake in the student's future. Age or intellectual functioning level may preclude some students' active participation in the team process, but family members should be given every opportunity to participate on whatever level they can.

The student's and family members' role includes working with other team members on choosing functional activities to be used for instructional purposes and planning the carryover of program activities into the home, work, or leisure settings. The student and family members have critical information and expertise in determining student motivators and functional activities for the development of communication, social, recreation, leisure, and self-care skills.

Teaching Assistant or Paraprofessional

The teaching assistant (associate or paraprofessional) usually plays a vital role in the daily functioning of the classroom and has important personal knowledge about students. In addition to helping teachers conduct instructional activities and construct or adapt materials, the assistant is often involved with handling and positioning students and meeting their daily physical needs.

Regular Classroom Teacher

The special education teacher and the other professionals on the team must work closely with regular classroom teachers who have contact with students with special needs. If students are to have a meaningful classroom experience, both educationally and socially, the classroom teacher must be trained to understand students' abilities and disabilities and to know how to adapt information, materials, and the environment to facilitate optimal student performance in the integrated classroom. The regular classroom teacher also brings important information to the team concerning age-appropriate curricular activities and social interaction.

Adapted Physical Education (PE) Teacher

The adapted PE teacher consults with physical educators, teachers, parents, and other team members regarding adaptations needed for students to participate in regular physical education classes, when that is possible, and in recreational and leisure activities. The adapted PE teacher may also provide specially designed PE programs for students who cannot participate in a regular PE program. This discipline's areas of expertise usually include knowledge of motor development and of ways to adapt motor activities, sports, games and recreation, and leisure activities for specific motor and sensory disabilities. The adapted PE teacher's participation on the educational team would also most likely include close cooperative planning with the occupational and physical therapists, teachers, and parents to develop and implement student programs.

Physical Therapist (PT)

The PT provides essential information to the team regarding optimal physical functioning in age-appropriate instructional activities, particularly as they relate to gross motor skills and mobility. The PT also consults with teachers, parents, and other team members, provides training to parents and other team members, and gives suggestions or constructs devices to facilitate necessary adaptations to the learning environment. (See Figure 1-5.)

The field of physical therapy, like most medical disciplines, is becoming more and more specialized. Training and experience in working with young and school-age children are essential for the PT working on an educational team.

The pediatric PT's expertise includes: understanding the typical and atypical development of motor skills (particularly gross motor and mobility); knowing the sensory factors related to posture and movement,

■ **FIGURE 1-5** Physical therapist adjusting an adapted chair

muscle tone, joint range of motion, muscle strength, physical endurance, postural alignment, balance and coordination, and automatic movement. The PT also has training in mobility, positioning and handling techniques, preventing acquired deformity, bracing lower limbs, splinting and inhibitive casting, using adaptive equipment and environments, and adapting tasks. The PT brings important medical knowledge to the team concerning terminology, etiology, postsurgical intervention and precautions, medical and health conditions, and so forth. With this knowledge, the PT can act as a liaison with physicians on the team.

Occupational Therapist (OT)

The OT's role on the educational team is also essential and, in some ways, is similar to that of the PT. (See Figure 1-6.) The OT provides information about optimal physical functioning in age-appropriate instructional activities, particularly as they relate to fine motor skills, visual-motor skills, and self-care activities. The OT also consults with teachers, parents, and other team members, provides training to parents and other team members, and gives suggestions or constructs devices to facilitate adaptations to the learning environment.

As with physical therapy, training and experience in working with young and school-age children are essential for the OT who is part of the educational team.

The pediatric OT's expertise includes: knowing the typical and atypical development of motor skills (particularly fine motor, visual-motor, and self-care skills); understanding the integration of sensory information and its effect on motor performance, balance and coordination and automatic movement, muscle tone, and joint range of motion; appreciating the psychological effects of disability; knowing how to position and handle children with impairments; knowing how to prevent acquired deformities; splinting upper limbs; and using adaptive equipment or environments and materials, particularly those relating to self-care activities, the classroom, work setting, and recreation and leisure settings. The OT also brings expert medical knowledge to the educational team and can act as a liaison with the medical community.

Speech and Language Pathologist (SLP)

The SLP contributes to the team with regard to communication programming in age-appropriate functional activities targeted for instruction. Other tasks include: consulting with teachers, family members, and other team members; providing training to family members and other team members when needed; and giving suggestions or constructing devices to facilitate a

FIGURE 1-6 Occupational therapist with adapted spoons, cup, and bowl

student's communication and socialization skills. (See Figure 1-7.)

The SLP's expertise includes: assessing environmental demands for communication; training students in methods of communication; instructing family members, teachers, and other team members in these methods; monitoring students' communication programs, and consulting with audiologists in cases of students with hearing impairments.

Experience and training in alternative augmentative communication (AAC) and oral motor and feeding skills can help the SLP contribute to the educational team, but not all SLPs have such a background.

Community Service Providers

Community service providers on the educational team may include community worksite representatives, therapists whom the child sees outside of school, and others. Pertinent information concerning students should be shared with these team members by the rest of the educational team so that a cohesive and appropriate program, with similar goals, can be carried out between a student's home, school, and community setting. In particular, when a student moves out into a community worksite, close communication between the team and the worksite representative is necessary if the student is to make appropriate task selections, understand any

■ **FIGURE 1-7** Speech and language pathologist programming a student's communication device

necessary adaptations (material or environmental), and maintain a functional communication system.

Psychologist

The role most often associated with the school psychologist is that of an evaluator of a student's intellectual and adaptive abilities and interpreter of the evaluation results for classroom programming. Psychologists may also be instrumental in designing strategies for reducing negative student behaviors and developing adaptive behavior programs for students who lack key social or self-regulatory behaviors. Psychologists also counsel students, and they may work with families and other professionals in times of stress or grief, such as when a student dies.

Social Worker

The school social worker may assist the educational team as a facilitator of access to services. This discipline's training and experience usually include knowledge of, communication with, and access to community services. In this capacity, the social worker can help the

educational team establish links between the school and community programs. The social worker may also act as an advocate for the student and family and can help make appropriate referrals when there are emotional or financial problems in the family. Social workers on some educational teams are the primary coordinators of services between the school, home, and community programs.

Audiologist

The audiologist is trained to identify types and degrees of hearing loss or dysfunction and to provide guidelines to the team on equipment, such as hearing aids, as well as procedures such as environmental adaptation that help students compensate for their hearing impairment. Depending on the amount and type of hearing loss, the audiologist may also help students with aural rehabilitation to facilitate their use of residual hearing. The school audiologist—who may be working with young children or with students with multiple cognitive, physical, and sensory impairments—must have training in and experience with a variety of alternative, nontraditional assessment procedures to effectively function on the educational team.

■ **FIGURE 1-8** A school nurse looking up information about a student's medication

Nurse

The nurse can be an invaluable information source for the educational team concerning students' physical or medical conditions and their effects on the students' educational program. (See Figure 1-8.) The nurse can also perform specialized medical procedures such as tube feeding, catheterizing, suctioning, or administering medicines, or a nurse can train other team members to perform these procedures. Training parents or professionals in emergency first aid procedures is also part of the nursing role, as is acting as a liaison between the educational team and the medical community.

Nutritionist/Dietitian

Although nutritionists and dietitians are not commonly included on educational teams, they can offer the team valuable information concerning nutrition and its effects on students' physical and instructional needs. Nutritionists and dietitians can help increase or decrease students' caloric intake to affect body weight. They can maximize the effectiveness and minimize the side effects of various medications, and they can design special diets for students with specific health care needs or certain food allergies.

Optometrist

The optometrist is a highly trained professional who is licensed to measure visual functioning and prescribe corrective lenses (such as glasses or contact lenses). Some optometrists have also received specialized training in low-vision devices (such as magnifiers and telescopes) and assess and prescribe low-vision devices for students with visual impairments. When an eye disease is suspected, the optometrist will refer the student to an ophthalmologist, who has a medical degree in the diagnosis and treatment of eye diseases.

Physicians

Physicians may be included on the educational team, according to students' needs. Most common to the team are pediatricians, orthopedists (bone and muscle), and neurologists (nervous system). However, the team may also include ophthalmologists (eye), otorhinolaryn-

gologists (ear, nose, and throat), urologists (urinary system), gastroenterologists (digestive system), pulmonologists (lung), cardiologists (heart), and physiatrists (rehabilitation), among others.

Other Medical and Nonmedical Specialists

School personnel and parents are likely to need the services of other specialists during the course of a student's educational program. These may include such professionals as dentists, respiratory therapists, **orthotists** (braces, splints, and casts), psychiatrists, rehabilitation engineers, computer scientists, and others. Students' needs should dictate which disciplines are called upon to be part of the educational team and the duration and frequency of their participation.

SUMMARY

Teachers may have students with physical, sensory, or health impairments in their classrooms. Students may have neuromotor impairments (seizure disorders, cerebral palsy), degenerative diseases (muscular dystrophy), orthopedic and musculoskeletal disorders (scoliosis, osteogenesis imperfecta), sensory impairments (deafness), major health impairments (asthma), or infectious diseases (AIDS). Some students may have a combination of impairments. In order to meet students' needs, teachers should be familiar with such impairments and with the educational implications of those impairments.

Often a team of individuals is needed to help provide an appropriate education for a student with a physical, sensory, or health impairment. Several team members may provide services to the student with the impairment and work together to design instructional programming. Some of these team members include: special education teacher, orientation and mobility instructor, student, family member, teaching assistant, regular classroom teacher, adapted physical education teacher, physical therapist, occupational therapist, speech and language pathologist, community service provider, psychologist, social worker, audiologist, nurse, nutritionist/dietitian, physician, and a nonmedical specialist. Understanding these professionals' roles and their areas of expertise will help the team work together smoothly.

CHAPTER 2

Typical and Atypical Motor Development

Before the motor development of atypical children with disabilities can be discussed, the principles behind typical motor development must be clear. Typical motor development occurs as an orderly process of skill acquisition; early motor skills form the basis for later, more advanced skills. Knowing about this process is critical to understanding motor delays or the atypical motor development often seen in children with disabilities.

Current theory describing and explaining motor development is based on a compilation of a number of developmental theories derived from a variety of fields of study, including psychology, education, neuroscience, and health science. These developmental theories can generally be summarized as follows: (1) Development is a collection of processes; (2) development occurs in stages; and (3) development is a transactional process between genetic or neurological makeup and environment (Anastasiow, 1986; Bly, 1983; Fisher, Murray, & Bundy, 1991; Gallahue, 1982).

Development may be described as a collection of overlapping processes that includes the cognitive, psychosocial, and sensorimotor domains. Each follows a relatively predictable pattern and has its own milestones or markers. Usually, early milestones must be achieved before higher-level skills can be learned because skills are built in sequence. For example, a child must learn to sit before learning to walk. Additionally, achieving milestones in one domain may be necessary before those in another can occur. For example, until a baby girl begins to move herself through space by creeping or walking, she would probably not learn to perceive distance.

Although developmental processes do follow a somewhat predictable pattern, there are always variations among individuals. Milestones may occur at different ages and still be within normal limits. Children may also exhibit differences in the pattern and rate of development within the various domains and be developing normally.

Development also occurs in stages. In stage theory, it is assumed that an individual must pass through a certain period of development—or stage—and learn all of the adaptive behaviors within that stage before moving onto other stages successfully. Piaget's theory of cognitive development is an example of a stage theory. Current developmental theory takes a more flexible view and considers stage theory to be a frame of reference for development while recognizing that development is a dynamic process that continues throughout life.

Finally, development is influenced by two major factors—**genetics,** or neurological makeup, and environment. The state of the **central nervous system (CNS)** in the newborn, as well as the functioning of the motor and sensory systems and the early development of these systems, are programmed genetically. (This will be described in more depth when primitive reflexes are explained, later in the chapter.) Development of the motor and sensory systems, however, can only occur normally when appropriate environmental stimuli are present and interactions can occur. Normal development can take place when there is transaction between a normal CNS and normal environmental stimuli. If either of these critical elements is missing, development will probably not proceed in a normal fashion.

CONCEPTS OF DEVELOPMENTAL MATURATION

In contrast to growth, which refers to an increase in physical size, *developmental maturation* refers to the acquisition and refinement of skills in several different but interconnected categories. The developmental process is typically subdivided as follows: gross motor skills, fine motor skills, speech and language abilities, cognitive abilities, social skills, and self-help skills. Because these components of the developmental process are so interrelated, progress in one skill or ability often depends on, or is affected by, progress in another area. For example, development of a fine pincer grasp is necessary before a child can finger-feed. However, a child's speech skills usually decrease when walking begins.

We will explore the topic of motor development for the rest of this chapter. In doing so, however, it is important to keep in mind the interrelatedness of maturational processes when assessing a child's development.

TYPICAL MOTOR DEVELOPMENT

A child's ability to exercise control over body movement develops in an orderly fashion and is guided by certain general developmental principles. Motor development tends to proceed as follows:

1. *In a cephalo-caudal (head-to-tail) direction.* Control of head movement occurs first, and subsequent motor control proceeds downward toward the feet. Therefore, children first learn to lift their heads, then to control movement of the upper trunk, arms, and hands, and last, to control their lower trunk and leg and foot movements.

2. *In a proximal-to-distal (central-to-peripheral) direction.* Control of movement occurs first at the center of the body and progresses outward to the extremities. Young children initially gain control over the muscles of the trunk, which provides the stability they need to move their arms and legs against gravity.

3. *From gross-to-fine movements.* Control of movement is at first more generalized and proceeds to the refinement of skilled movement. For example, infants respond very early with widely fluctuating, flailing movements of the arms when presented with a toy. These movements later become refined into a precise, accurate, visually directed reach toward the toy when it is presented.

4. *From physiological flexion (general bending at the joints) to development of antigravity control.* The newborn infant is predominantly flexed at all joints of the body, with arms and legs bent and hands fisted. As development proceeds, the infant—in our example, a boy—gains more and more control over extending or lifting his body against gravity while lying on his stomach (prone) in a cephalo-caudal direction. These controlled movements, along with the effects of gravity,

help to decrease the earlier physiological flexion by causing the muscles to lengthen. By 3 months of age, the infant begins to control the flexion of his body parts against gravity while lying on his back (supine), again in a cephalo-caudal direction. This development of a balance between control over flexor and extensor muscles is important; the child learns to use these muscle groups together, which allows for stable control over his posture and movement, the ability to shift his body weight, and the ability to make the rotational movements necessary to eventually move into space and into the upright position. (Alexander, Boehme, & Cupps, 1993; Bly, 1983)

5. *From stability to mobility to skilled movement.* Development of antigravity control over body movements allows the child to proceed from being able to assume and hold a developmental position (for example, on hands and knees), to moving within that position (for example, rocking on hands and knees), to performing a skilled action while in the position (for example, creeping).

Table 2-1 depicts the sequence of gross and fine motor development in the first 2 years of life (Molnar, 1992), which directly relates to the developmental principles just described. Box 2-1 clarifies motor terminology.

Joint Structure and Muscle Tone

Before examining the role of primitive reflexes in motor development, we should consider several other key points about movement. First, body movement requires the force of muscles acting on the jointed structure of the skeleton. Normal joint movement occurs within a range that is specific to each joint. The types of movements made at each joint depend on that joint's construction.

Three major types of **joints** are found in the body. (1) *Hinge joints* allow the movements of flexion (bending) and extension (straightening); these are found in the fingers and toes, for example. (2) *Pivot joints* permit rotational movements. The elbow joint is an example of a pivot joint. (3) *Ball-and-socket joints* are found at the shoulders and hips, for example; these allow body parts to move in flexion and extension (bending and straightening), **abduction** and **adduction** (moving laterally away from and toward the midline of the body), internal and external rotation (turning a limb inward—toward the body midline—and outward—away from the body midline), and circumduction—a combination of all the movements just described.

It is important to know what constitutes normal direction and range of joint movement when assessing the movements of young children. Freedom from joint

TABLE 2-1

Gross and Fine Motor Developmental Milestones (Newborn to Age 2)

Age	Gross motor	Fine motor
Newborn to 1 month	• Flexor tone predominates (arms and legs are under body in prone). • Baby turns head to side in prone. • Baby turns head in supine due to ATNR. • Baby "walks" automatically (reflex walking) when suspended. • Baby's spine is rounded when held sitting.	• Hands are fisted. • Baby grasps reflexively. • Baby has state-dependent ability to fix and follow bright object.
2 to 3 months	*In prone:* • Baby can lift head against gravity due to labyrinthine righting reflex. • Head-raised position elicits neck righting reflex, stimulating upper part of the trunk to raise up. • Baby's arms and hands move in front of the shoulders. *In supine:* • The head begins to come to midline. • Baby tries to lift head when pulled to sitting.	• Eyes begin to converge. • Arms begin to come together at midline.
4 to 5 months	• The head is midline. • Baby holds head in midline when pulled to sitting. • Baby lifts head to 90° and lifts chest slightly in prone. • Baby turns from supine to side-lying. • In supine, baby can reach hands to knees. • In prone, baby "swims" in air.	• Hands are mostly open. • Midline hand play begins. • Crude palmar grasp appears. • Baby begins reaching.
5 to 6 months	• Strong optical righting develops and facilitates head lifting. • Baby can bear weight on extended arms with hip extension in prone. • The equilibrium reaction in prone allows for control of flexion and extension against gravity. • Rolls from back to stomach.	• In supine, body can bear weight with one arm and reach with the other.
7 to 8 months	*In prone:* • Baby can lift the stomach off the supporting surface. • Baby can shift weight between arms and legs in the quadruped position (hands and knees) and push back into a seated position. • Creeping may begin. • Baby begins to belly-crawl, with the arms doing most of the work. • Baby's arms are free in sitting to move and reach without loss of balance. *In supine:* • When pulled to sitting, baby flexes chin and pulls up. • Baby maintains sitting; may lean on arms. • Baby moves from sitting to prone. • Baby rolls to prone. • Baby bears all weight; bounces when held erect. • Baby may begin to cruise. • Baby may assume kneeling.	• In prone, baby can bear weight with one arm and reach with the other. • Intermediate grasp appears. • Baby transfers cube from hand to hand. • Baby bangs objects.

TABLE 2-1 *(Continued)*		
Gross and Fine Motor Developmental Milestones (Newborn to Age 2)		
Age	Gross motor	Fine motor
9 to 10 months	• Baby can push back into sitting with rotation from prone. • The presence of the righting reflex allows baby to get onto the knees from prone. • Baby may use half-kneeling to pull to stand. • Baby cruises forward.	• Pincer grasp, mature thumb-to-index grasp appears. • Baby bangs two cubes held in hands.
12 to 14 months	• Baby walks alone, arms in high guard or mid-guard. • Wide base, excessive knee and hip flexion. • Foot contact on entire sole.	• Baby piles two cubes. • Baby scribbles spontaneously. • Baby holds crayon, full length in palm. • Baby casts objects.
18 months	• Arms are at low guard. • Mature supporting base and heel strike appear. • Baby seats self in chair. • Baby walks backwards.	• Hand dominance emerges. • Crude release appears. • Baby holds crayon, butt end in palm. • Baby dumps raisins from bottle spontaneously.
2 years	• Baby begins running. • Baby walks up and down stairs alone. • Baby jumps on both feet, in place.	• Hand dominance is usual. • Baby builds eight-cube tower.

SOURCE: Based on *Pediatric Rehabilitation*, by G. E. Molnar. Copyright ©1992 Williams & Wilkins. Used with permission.

restriction is critical to the development of normal movement. A physical or occupational therapist can perform this assessment and help plan programs for atypical children to ensure that normal joint movement is maintained.

Although the skeleton provides the foundation for movement, the muscles acting on the skeleton provide the force to create body movements. Every muscle in the body is made up of a muscle belly (containing thousands of muscle fibers) and muscle tendons. Muscle fibers are connected to muscle tendons, which are attached to bones. Movement occurs when the brain sends electrical signals through the **spinal cord** and the nerves to the muscle fibers, causing the fibers to shorten. The force of the shortening muscle fibers acting on the bones to which they are attached causes the body part to move.

The spinal cord exerts continuous stimulation on all muscles of the body in order to maintain a certain level of tension. This state of tension is called muscle tone. Muscles are thus ready for movement at any time. The physiological state of the body can modify muscle tone. For example, the stimulation to the muscles decreases during sleep, allowing relaxation, while during times of anxiety, fear, or excitement, stimulation to the muscles increases, preparing the body for "fight or flight."

This normal tension in the muscles is sometimes called *postural tone* and provides the background for normal movement. When there is a breakdown in communication between the brain and the muscles in the developing child due to damage in the communication pathway (in the brain, spinal cord, nerves, or muscles), muscle tone and body movement will be atypical and, as a result, motor development will be affected.

Reflexes and Reactions

At birth, the typical infant's movements are dominated by primitive **reflexes** or involuntary movements stimulated by various kinds of external stimuli. These reflexes are genetically programmed. Some function to protect the baby; others form the beginnings of motor skills. For example, a baby's initial reflex grasp of an object placed in its hand is important in the eventual development of voluntary grasp.

As the central nervous system (CNS) matures, usually by about 6 months of age, these primitive reflex patterns of movement gradually fade and are replaced by higher-level, automatic **postural reactions** that continue for life. These automatic reactions allow the individual to function upright in space against gravity. For example, if an individual is standing on a bus, automatic postural reactions allow the person to maintain an upright position, even though the bus is moving and making starts and stops. The individual does not need to think about standing; muscles adjust as necessary to hold the position.

BOX 2-1

Motor Terminology

Abduction: the lateral movement of a body part away from the midline of the body

Adduction: the lateral movement of a body part toward the midline of the body

Asymmetrical: one side of the body assumes a different posture than the other. For example, one arm bends while the other straightens.

Bilateral: pertaining to or affecting both sides of the body

Distal: point farthest from the central part of the body, the trunk. For example, the hand is distal to the shoulder.

Extension: straightening a body part

External rotation: turning a limb outward, away from the midline of the body

Flexion: bending a body part

Internal rotation: turning a limb in toward the midline of the body

Lateral: pertaining to or relating to the side

Medial: pertaining to or relating to the middle

Obligatory: having to occur as seen in atypical motor development when primitive reflexes cannot be overcome

Prone: lying on the stomach

Proximal: point closest to the center of the trunk. For example, the shoulder is proximal to the hand.

Reaction (or postural reaction): subconscious movement that uses visual, vestibular, tactile, and proprioceptive information to establish the normal relationship of the body in space

Reflex: movement performed involuntarily in response to a stimulus

Supine: lying on the back

Symmetrical: correspondence in shape, size, and position of body parts on both sides of the body

Trunk rotation: process of turning or twisting the body. Movement takes place between the shoulders and hips.

Primitive Reflexes

In the typically developing child, primitive reflexes are never totally obligatory; that is, they do not have to occur. Although automatic responses can be elicited with the appropriate stimulus, the child with normal CNS function can always supersede the expected response by responding to other environmental stimuli instead of the one intended to evoke a primitive reflex. For example, a 4-month-old child, turning the head to one side, would normally assume what is called a "fencer's position" (straight limbs on the face side of the body and bent limbs on the skull side) due to the asymmetrical tonic neck reflex (ATNR). (The position resembles a fencer's stance.) However, in the typical child, this reflexive posturing can be interrupted if a strong environmental stimulus is introduced. If the mother were to offer a toy to the child, for example, the child's reaching toward the toy would interrupt and take the place of the fencer's position.

The child with CNS damage is often unable to interrupt this response; it occurs every time the stimulus is presented. Frequently, the response persists beyond its expected age range. When this happens, rather than facilitating the development of normal movement patterns, the persistent primitive reflex interferes with the progression of motor development.

Some primitive reflexes are closely associated with obtaining nourishment and protecting the infant. An explanation of several of these reflexes follows. For a more in-depth listing of the primitive reflexes, including their normal age ranges, stimulus and response parameters, and clinical significance, see Table 2-2 (Molnar, 1992).

1. *Rooting reflex.* A baby's rooting reflex is stimulated by stroking the corner of the baby's mouth, upper lip, or lower lip. The typical response is a moving of the tongue, mouth, and head toward the stimulus in an attempt to seek out the nipple. An atypical response is either a diminished orientation toward the source of nourishment or an obligatory response, with orientation occurring every time the mouth or lips are touched. This response is normally suppressed by about 4 months of age.

2. *Moro and startle reflexes.* In these reflexes, the stimulus is different but the components of the responses are similar. These reflexes are often confused. In the Moro reflex, the stimulus is a sudden neck extension, such as when the baby's head is allowed to suddenly drop back for a short distance. The response is a sudden extension and abduction of the arms and spreading of the fingers (see Figure 2-1). The legs and toes may perform the same action but less vigorously. The limbs then return to a normal flexed position against the body. This reflex is thought to be protective. The response is suppressed by about 4 to 6 months of age and is considered to be abnormal if it persists beyond this period.

In the startle reflex, the stimulus is a loud noise and the response is a strong flexion of the limbs toward the body. Again, this reflex is thought to be protective in

TABLE 2-2

Infantile Reflex Development

Reflex	Stimulus	Response	Suppression	Clinical significance
Primitive Reflexes: Present at Birth, Suppressed with Maturation				
Asymmetric tonic neck	Head turning or tilting to the side	Extension of the extremities on the chin side, flexion on the occiput side	Suppressed by 6–7 months	Obligatory abnormal at any age
				Persistent suspicious of CNS pathology
Symmetric tonic neck	Neck flexion	Arm flexion, leg extension	Suppressed by 6–7 months	Obligatory abnormal at any age
	Neck extension	Arm extension, leg flexion		Persistent suspicious of CNS pathology
Moro	Sudden neck extension	Arm extension abduction followed by flexion-adduction	Suppressed 4–6 months	Abnormal if persists
Tonic labyrinthine	Head position in space, strongest at 45° angle to horizontal		Suppressed 4–6 months	Abnormal at any age if hyperactive or if persistent
	Supine	Predominant extensor tone		
	Prone	Predominant flexor tone		
Positive supporting	Tactile contact and weight-bearing on the sole	Leg extension for supporting partial body weight	Suppressed by 3–7 months and replaced by volitional standing	Abnormal at any age if obligatory or hyperactive; suggests spasticity of the legs
Rooting	Stroking the corner of mouth, upper or lower lip	Moving the tongue, mouth, and head toward the site of stimulus	Suppressed by 4 months	Searching for nipple Diminished in CNS depression; obligatory persistence may be immature CNS development
Palmar grasp	Pressure or touch on the palm, stretch of finger flexors	Flexion of fingers	Suppressed by 5–6 months	Diminished in CNS depression; absent in lower motor neuron paralysis; persistence suggests spasticity, i.e., cerebral palsy
Plantar grasp	Pressure on sole just distal to metatarsal heads	Flexion of toes	Suppressed by 12–18 months	Absent in lower motor neuron paralysis; persists and hyperactive in spasticity, i.e., cerebral palsy
Automatic neonatal walking	Contact of sole in vertical position tilting the body forward and from side to side	Automatic alternating steps	Suppressed by 3–4 months	Variable activity in normal infants; absent in lower motor neuron paralysis of the legs
Placing	Tactile contact on dorsum of foot or hand	Flexion to place the leg or arm over the obstacle	Suppressed before end of first year	Absent in lower motor neuron paralysis or extensor spasticity of the legs
Postural Responses: Emerge with Maturation, Present Throughout Life, Modulated by Volition				
Head righting	Visual and vestibular	Align face vertical, mouth horizontal	Emerge at	Delayed or absent in CNS immaturity or damage or motor unit disease
		Prone	2 months	
		Supine	3–4 months	
Body, head righting	Tactile proprioceptive vestibular	Align body parts	Emerge from 4–6 months	Delayed or absent in CNS immaturity or damage or motor neuron disease
Protective extension or propping	Displacement of center of gravity outside of supporting surface	Extension-abduction of the extremity toward the side of displacement to prevent falling	Emerge between 5 and 12 months	Delayed or absent in CNS immaturity or damage, or motor unit disease
Equilibrium or tilting	Displacement of center of gravity	Adjustment of tone and trunk posture to maintain balance	Emerge between 6 and 14 months	Delayed or absent in CNS immaturity or damage, or motor unit disease

Source: Based on *Pediatric Rehabilitation*, by G. E. Molnar. Copyright ©1992 Williams & Wilkins. Used with permission.

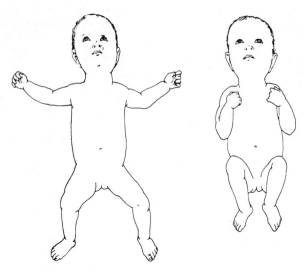

■ **FIGURE 2-1** Moro reflex
SOURCE: From *Understanding Motor Development in Children*, by D. L. Gallahue, pp. 143–165. Copyright ©1982. All rights reserved. Reprinted with permission of Allyn & Bacon.

■ **FIGURE 2-2** Palmar grasp reflex
SOURCE: Reprinted with permission from Alexander, Boehme, and Cupps, *Normal Development of Functional Motor Skills: The First Year of Life*, pp. 46–199, illustrations by John Boehme, ©1993.

nature. It may persist normally up to 1 year of age and is thought to be abnormal if it persists beyond this time.

Another class of primitive reflexes provides the basis for early voluntary movement. A few examples follow. (See Table 2-2 for a more extensive listing.)

1. *Palmar grasp reflex.* In this reflex, the stimulus is pressure or a touch on the palm of the hand or a stretch of the finger flexors. The response is flexion of the fingers around the presenting object (see Figure 2-2). This reflex facilitates eventual voluntary hand function. It is suppressed, or begins to disappear because higher-level skills take over, by the time the baby is about 5 to 6 months old. An abnormal response would be absent, significantly weak or strong, or significantly persistent finger flexion beyond 6 months of age, as well as an obligatory response.

2. *Plantar grasp reflex.* In this reflex, the stimulus is

pressure on the sole of the foot just below the toes. The response is flexion of the toes (see Figure 2-3). The reflex facilitates eventual voluntary control over the foot musculature, which is necessary for standing and walking. It is suppressed by 12 to 18 months of age. Absence, hyperactivity, or persistence of the response would all be abnormal responses.

3. *Asymmetrical tonic neck reflex (ATNR).* In this reflex, the stimulus is turning the head to one side. The response is extension (straightening) of the extremities on the face side and flexion (bending) of the extremities on the skull side (see Figure 2-4). This reflex facilitates visually directed reaching and rolling from back to side. It is usually suppressed by 6 to 7 months. An obligatory response at any age or persistence beyond the expected 6 to 7 months is pathological.

4. *Symmetrical tonic neck reflex (STNR).* In this reflex, the stimulus is either neck flexion (chin to chest) or neck extension (chin away from chest). The response is flexion of both arms with leg extension following neck flexion or extension of both arms with leg flexion

■ **FIGURE 2-3** Plantar grasp reflex
SOURCE: From *Understanding Motor Development in Children*, by D. L. Gallahue, pp. 143–165. Copyright ©1982. All rights reserved. Reprinted with permission of Allyn & Bacon.

■ **FIGURE 2-4** Asymmetrical tonic neck reflex
SOURCE: Reprinted with permission from Alexander, Boehme, and Cupps, *Normal Development of Functional Motor Skills: The First Year of Life*, pp. 46–199, illustrations by John Boehme, ©1993.

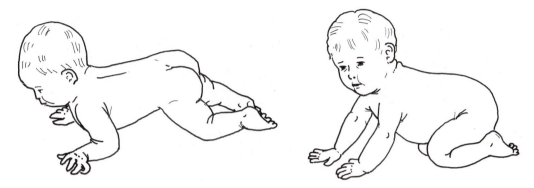

■ **FIGURE 2-5** Symmetrical tonic neck reflex

following neck extension (see Figure 2-5). The reflex facilitates movements necessary for assuming the hands-and-knees position and creeping. It usually disappears by 6 to 9 months of age. An obligatory response at any age or persistence beyond the expected age range indicates pathology.

Postural Reactions

As the CNS matures, higher-level reactions take over from the early primitive reflexes to help regulate postural control against gravity. The postural reactions established at this time are the *righting, protective,* and *equilibrium reactions.*

Righting Reactions
These reactions use visual information (optical righting), vestibular information from the inner ear (labyrinthine righting), and information from tactile and proprioceptive or position receptors in the skin and joints (neck-on-body, body-on-head, and body-on-body righting) to interact with each other and thus establish normal head and body relationships in space. They en-

able the child to learn to roll, get onto hands and knees, and sit up and stand. They also permit the restoration of the normal head position in space when displacement occurs, and they maintain the normal postural relationship of the head, trunk, and limbs during all activities (Illingworth, 1987; Orelove & Sobsey, 1991).

Those reactions using visual and vestibular information (optical and labyrinthine) emerge at about 2 to 4 months of age. Their response is to align the face vertically to the horizon through the contraction of appropriate muscle groups in response to what is seen or to the pull of gravity (see Figure 2-6). They are present throughout life, but with CNS immaturity or damage, their response is either absent or delayed.

Those reactions using tactile and proprioceptive information occur at two different times. An early reaction is the *neck-righting reaction,* which is present at birth, is strongest at age 3 months, and remains present throughout life. The stimulus is turning the head to one side, which activates joint receptors in the neck and results in the contraction of limb and body muscles to align the body with the head. The response is that the entire body follows the head (see Figure 2-7). Absence

■ **FIGURE 2-6** Labyrinthine righting reaction
Source: From *Understanding Motor Development in Children,* by D. L. Gallahue, pp. 143–165.
Copyright ©1982. All rights reserved. Reprinted with permission of Allyn & Bacon.

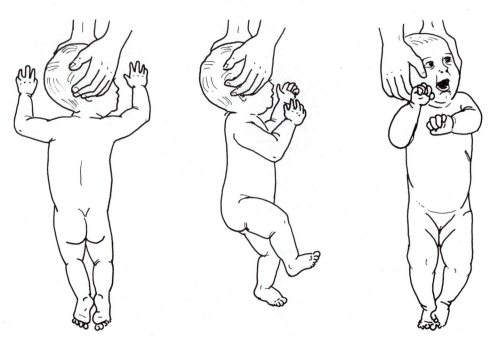

■ FIGURE 2-7 Neck-righting reaction

or delay of response indicates CNS pathology or immaturity.

The *body-righting-on-head* and the *body-righting-on-body reactions* emerge later, at about 4 to 6 months. These reactions use asymmetrical stimulation of skin receptors in contact with their supporting surface to activate trunk and limb muscles. This results in a raising of the head and body, respectively, into an upright position and aligning body parts (see Figure 2-8). The latter reactions play an important part in the child's early attempts to sit and stand. They are present

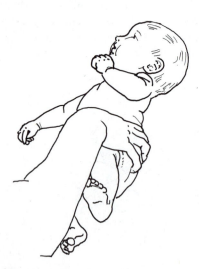

■ FIGURE 2-8 Body-righting-on-head reaction

throughout life; absence or delay of response indicates pathology or CNS immaturity (see Table 2-2).

Protective Reactions

These reactions protect the child from a loss of balance and are seen in the extremities (arms and legs). Their stimulus is a rapid displacement of the center of gravity outside the supporting surface, which occurs when the child is pushed or begins to fall off balance. Their response is straightening and an outward movement of the extremity toward the side of displacement to prevent falling (see Figure 2-9). In the arms, these reactions first develop forward, then sideways, and finally backward. Protective reactions of the arms normally emerge between 5 and 12 months, when the child is first learning to sit. Protective reactions of the legs normally emerge between 15 and 18 months, when the child is first learning to walk. In either case, their absence or delay may indicate CNS damage or immaturity (see Table 2-2).

Equilibrium Reactions

These reactions develop after the child can maintain a developmental position, such as supporting himself on his stomach or on hands and knees, or when sitting or standing. Equilibrium reactions emerge, depending on the position, between 5 and 18 months of age. Equilibrium reactions are elicited when the child's body is displaced off its center of gravity, either when the supporting surface or the body itself moves. They differ in stimulus from protective reactions in that the displacement is neither rapid nor outside the child's area of

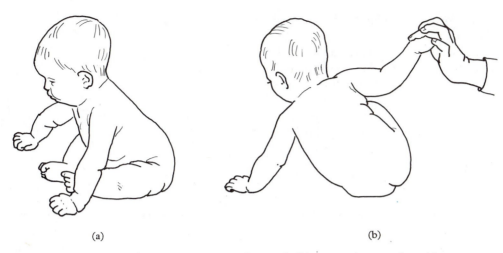

(a)   (b)

■ **FIGURE 2-9** (a) Protective reaction forward; (b) protective reaction sideways

support but instead is a gradual or subtle movement. The response is generated through the vestibular system (with probable assistance from the tactile and proprioceptive systems) and occurs through contraction of muscles of the whole body in order to adjust muscle tone and the resultant head, trunk, and extremity posture to maintain balance. Delay or absence may indicate CNS immaturity or damage (see Table 2-2).

Early Motor Milestones

During the first year or two of life, the young child takes in large amounts of data from the environment and, in response to that information, develops in all ways at an amazing rate. Specific skills are intradependent, as well as interdependent, on each other.

In this section, we will outline the typical developmental sequence of motor skills in this early period to provide context in which to explain atypical motor development. Although age ranges will be used as a frame of reference, both the rate and sequence of development may vary.

The very young infant reacts to environmental stimuli with a motor response because of the various reflexive movement patterns described earlier. With maturation, the primitive reflex patterns are more and more integrated; postural reactions replace these more primitive patterns, and the young child's response to environmental stimuli becomes more individualized, more controlled, and more sophisticated. Generally, children follow a sequence of development of motor skills illustrated in the following example of a baby girl (Alexander, Boehme, & Cupps, 1993; Bleck & Nagel, 1982; Bly, 1983; Molnar, 1992):

1. *Birth to 2 months.* During this period, the full-term baby demonstrates physiological flexion, or bend-

ing at all joints of the body, while lying on her back or stomach (see Figure 2-10). Although the body weight is shifted onto the face, the baby can still lift her head and turn it to the side due to reflex activity and the early influence of the righting reactions. The baby's movements occur at random and are generalized and jerky in appearance.

2. *Two months.* By 2 months of age, the baby is much less flexed because of gravity's pull on the body, and she performs active movements in an attempt to lift her body off the supporting surface while lying on her stomach. Muscles surrounding joints have lengthened (see Figure 2-11). Because the hips are less bent, the

■ **FIGURE 2-10** 0–2 weeks of age; pelvis high, knees drawn up under abdomen

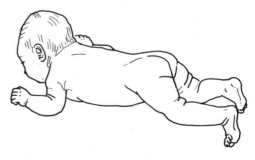

■ **FIGURE 2-11** 6 to 8 weeks; pelvis flat, hips extended

baby's weight is less forward, making head-lifting and turning easier. Because the shoulders are less bent, the upper chest and arms and hands can also accept some weight when the baby raises her head (see Figure 2-12).

Lying on her back, the baby can turn her head further to the side, increasing the influence of the ATNR, and can now begin to orient vision toward her hand for early hand regard and gross swiping at toys. Some random, accidental rolling to the side may be seen due to the influence of the early righting reactions.

3. *Three months.* A 3-month-old's posture is much more symmetrical, and the ATNR is less influential. A baby lying on her stomach is able to lift her head and

■ **FIGURE 2-12** 8 weeks; chin held off surface intermittently, plane of face at a 45° angle to surface

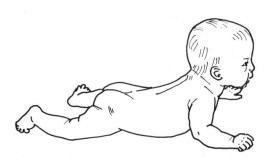

■ **FIGURE 2-13** 10–12 weeks; weight on forearms, plane of face almost reaches angle of 90° to surface

■ **FIGURE 2-14** "Swimming" in extension
SOURCE: Reprinted with permission from Alexander, Boehme, and Cupps, *Normal Development of Functional Motor Skills: The First Year of Life*, pp. 46–199, illustrations by John Boehme, ©1993.

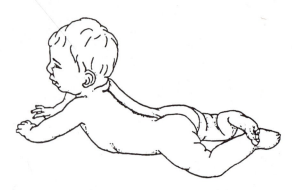

■ **FIGURE 2-15** Weight bearing on extended arms
SOURCE: Reprinted with permission from Alexander, Boehme, and Cupps, *Normal Development of Functional Motor Skills: The First Year of Life*, pp. 46–199, illustrations by John Boehme, ©1993.

■ **FIGURE 2-16** Shifting weight onto one arm and reaching with the other
SOURCE: Reprinted with permission from Alexander, Boehme, and Cupps, *Normal Development of Functional Motor Skills: The First Year of Life*, pp. 46–199, illustrations by John Boehme, ©1993.

upper trunk off a surface, bear weight on her forearms, and turn her head (see Figure 2-13). While lying on her back, the baby's head is held in the midline, her hands come together on the body, and the baby begins to tuck her chin to her chest, although she still cannot lift her head off the surface in this position. The baby's feet come together in play during this time, an important step in making the feet less sensitive so future standing may be accomplished.

4. *Four months.* The 4-month-old has developed excellent control over the extensor muscles while lying on her stomach and spends a good deal of time making swimming motions in the air (see Figure 2-14). The flexor muscles are also better developed, enabling the baby to show excellent head control while bearing weight, now on extended arms, with her chest lifted off the supporting surface (see Figure 2-15). Accidental rolling to the side is even more likely now, as the baby falls out of the forearm weight-bearing position. Although not yet under the baby's direct control, these experiences in movement are important for the motor learning that is taking place.

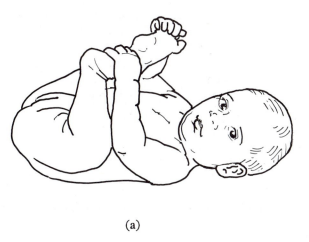

(a)

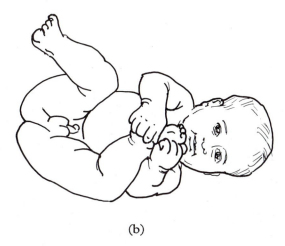

(b)

■ FIGURE 2-17 (a) Playing with feet; (b) putting feet in mouth

While lying on her back, the 4-month-old infant can bring her hands together in space above her body and reach toward her knees, an important beginning of body awareness, as well as the development of abdominal strength. This position frequently leads to rolling onto the side due to the righting reactions. Because there is now balanced muscle activity around her neck, the baby can also lift her head off a surface while lying on her side.

5. *Five months.* During the fifth month, the body-righting reactions are beginning, as are early equilibrium reactions in the prone position. Besides being able to bear weight easily on straight arms, the baby can now shift her weight onto one elbow and reach while lying on her stomach (see Figure 2-16). All of these new reactions and skills work together to allow the 5-month-old to finally achieve the milestone of rolling from stomach to back, although true volitional rolling will not come until months later.

On her back, a 5-month-old baby has enough control over her flexor muscles that she can lift her legs and bring her feet to her hands or mouth (see Figure 2-17). This is another important step toward body awareness. Reaching in this position is also better controlled, and the baby can now roll well from back to side and can prop-sit on extended arms, once placed, for short periods (see Figure 2-18).

6. *Six months.* The 6-month-old infant has developed good head control in all planes of movement and can now shift weight onto a straight arm and reach with the other arm while lying on her stomach. The developing equilibrium reactions in this prone position allow the baby to reach without losing balance.

Control of movement while lying on the back is also improved for the 6-month-old. The baby can now lift her head off the supporting surface, can reach out with straight arms, and can transfer an object from one hand to another. Controlled rolling from back to stomach is also possible now. When in a sitting position, the baby's back is straight, and her arms are free for reaching, for manipulating toys, or for protective extension forward when the baby is displaced (see Figure 2-19). Finally, the 6-month-old can bear weight well on her legs when someone supports her and can bounce up and down in this position—important prerequisites for future walking (see Figure 2-20).

7. *Seven months.* The 7-month-old prefers to be on her stomach because she can perform many functional movements in this position. She can crawl on her stomach or pivot around in a circle (see Figure 2-21). The body movements used in these activities are precursors to the movements used later in creeping on hands and knees. From a prone position, the 7-month-old can also roll onto her side and can prop on one arm and play in

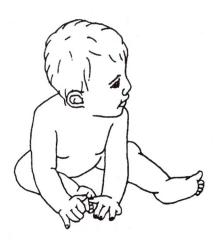

■ FIGURE 2-18 Sitting with hands forward for support
SOURCE: Reprinted with permission from Alexander, Boehme, and Cupps, *Normal Development of Functional Motor Skills: The First Year of Life,* pp. 46–199, illustrations by John Boehme, ©1993.

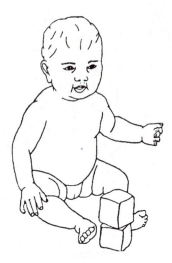

■ FIGURE 2-19 Sitting with arms free
SOURCE: Reprinted with permission from Alexander, Boehme, and Cupps, *Normal Development of Functional Motor Skills: The First Year of Life*, pp. 46–199, illustrations by John Boehme, ©1993.

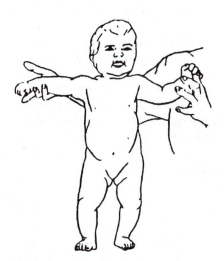

■ FIGURE 2-20 Bearing weight on legs, with support
SOURCE: Reprinted with permission from Alexander, Boehme, and Cupps, *Normal Development of Functional Motor Skills: The First Year of Life*, pp. 46–199, illustrations by John Boehme, ©1993.

this position (see Figure 2-22). The baby can also push back into a hands-and-knees position and rock by shifting her weight (see Figure 2-23). From hands and knees, the 7-month-old can also push back into a sitting position. In sitting, the righting, equilibrium, and protective reactions continue to be perfected (see Figure 2-24).

From a hands-and-knees position, the 7-month-old is also beginning to pull up to standing, and then bouncing in place. At this stage, the baby usually cannot shift her weight laterally well enough to take steps to the side (cruise).

8. *Eight months.* Because the 8-month-old has developed good equilibrium reactions in sitting and protective reactions to the side, sitting becomes the favored position. The baby can now rotate and, while sitting, can shift weight laterally without falling, which makes play and functional activity easy in this position (see

■ FIGURE 2-21 Crawling
SOURCE: From *Understanding Motor Development in Children*, by D. L. Gallahue, pp. 143–165. Copyright ©1982. All rights reserved. Reprinted with permission of Allyn & Bacon.

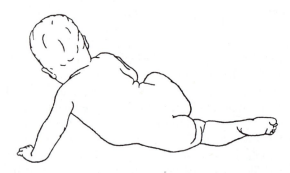

■ FIGURE 2-22 Propping on one arm to play
SOURCE: Reprinted with permission from Alexander, Boehme, and Cupps, *Normal Development of Functional Motor Skills: The First Year of Life*, pp. 46–199, illustrations by John Boehme, ©1993.

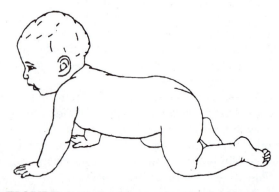

■ FIGURE 2-23 Rocking on hands and knees
SOURCE: Reprinted with permission from Alexander, Boehme, and Cupps, *Normal Development of Functional Motor Skills: The First Year of Life*, pp. 46–199, illustrations by John Boehme, ©1993.

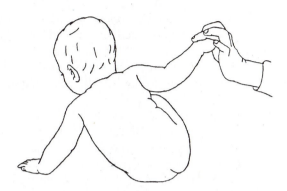

■ **FIGURE 2-24** Showing balance reactions in sitting

Source: Reprinted with permission from Alexander, Boehme, and Cupps, *Normal Development of Functional Motor Skills: The First Year of Life*, pp. 46–199, illustrations by John Boehme, ©1993.

lower herself from standing and, therefore, falls into sitting to get down.

9. *Nine months.* The 9-month-old uses a variety of sitting positions: long-sitting—with legs straight in front; tailor-sitting—in a cross-legged fashion; side-sitting—with both knees positioned to the same side; and W-sitting—with buttocks in between the heels. The baby constantly changes from one position to another. These changes in position further enhance the development of trunk control and control over the legs while improving postural reactions in sitting.

Transitions between different developmental positions are also becoming easier for the 9-month-old. She can quickly move between sitting and the hands-and-knees position. From kneeling, the 9-month-old can

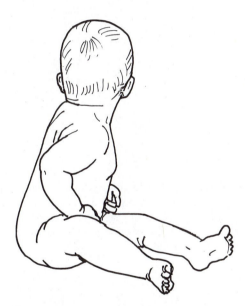

■ **FIGURE 2-25** Pivoting—turning around to pick up a toy without overbalancing

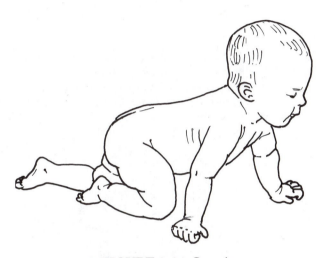

■ **FIGURE 2-26** Creeping

Figure 2-25). From sitting, the 8-month-old can also assume the hands-and-knees position and, because her control has improved in this position, creeping begins as a primary way of moving around (see Figure 2-26).

From hands and knees, the 8-month-old may begin to assume a kneeling position without support (see Figure 2-27). Support of the arms is still required to pull up from kneeling to standing, however. Once standing, the 8-month-old can free one hand to reach into space, which promotes trunk rotation, balance, and equilibrium in the standing position (see Figure 2-28). The baby now also begins to cruise sideways around furniture by shifting her weight and stepping to the side and can walk forward if both hands are held (see Figure 2-29). The 8-month-old does not yet have the control to

■ **FIGURE 2-27** Assuming kneeling position

Source: Reprinted with permission from Alexander, Boehme, and Cupps, *Normal Development of Functional Motor Skills: The First Year of Life*, pp. 46–199, illustrations by John Boehme, ©1993.

10. *Ten months.* During the tenth month, the baby cruises. Only one hand is needed for support; her body faces in the direction in which she is going. Because her leg muscles have gained increased control, the 10-month-old can now lower herself from standing (see Figure 2-32).

11. *Eleven months.* The 11-month-old has well-developed equilibrium reactions in sitting and can therefore move from sitting into all other positions. Rising from the floor to standing requires only minimal hand support, and the baby begins to use squatting as a position to make the transition into and out of standing

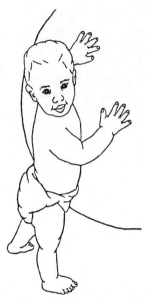

■ **FIGURE 2-28** Standing with rotation
SOURCE: Reprinted with permission from Alexander, Boehme, and Cupps, *Normal Development of Functional Motor Skills: The First Year of Life*, pp. 46–199, illustrations by John Boehme, ©1993.

■ **FIGURE 2-30** Half-kneeling to standing
SOURCE: Reprinted with permission from Alexander, Boehme, and Cupps, *Normal Development of Functional Motor Skills: The First Year of Life*, pp. 46–199, illustrations by John Boehme, ©1993.

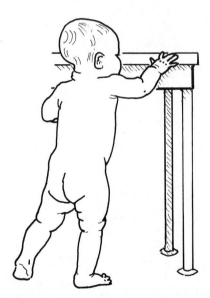

■ **FIGURE 2-29** Cruising (standing and walking while holding on to a stationary object for support)

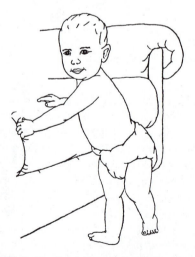

■ **FIGURE 2-31** Cruising while facing forward
SOURCE: Reprinted with permission from Alexander, Boehme, and Cupps, *Normal Development of Functional Motor Skills: The First Year of Life*, pp. 46–199, illustrations by John Boehme, ©1993.

place one foot on the floor and use a half-kneeling position to make the transition to standing (see Figure 2-30). This allows her legs to do more of the work of coming to standing, and the baby relies less on pulling up with her arms. The 9-month-old is also starting to face forward while cruising, an important step toward the development of movements necessary for later independent walking (see Figure 2-31).

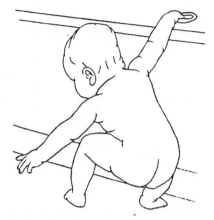

■ **FIGURE 2-32** Lowering self from a standing position
SOURCE: Reprinted with permission from Alexander, Boehme, and Cupps, *Normal Development of Functional Motor Skills: The First Year of Life*, pp. 46–199, illustrations by John Boehme, ©1993.

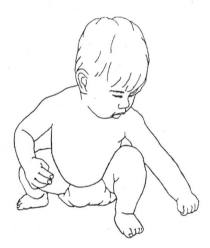

■ **FIGURE 2-33** Squatting in play
SOURCE: Reprinted with permission from Alexander, Boehme, and Cupps, *Normal Development of Functional Motor Skills: The First Year of Life*, pp. 46–199, illustrations by John Boehme, ©1993.

(see Figure 2-33). The 11-month-old's increased control in standing allows her to cruise between pieces of furniture without constant arm support. Standing alone without support soon follows.

12. *Twelve months.* The 12-month-old's righting reactions are well-developed during most movements, and the equilibrium reactions are present in all positions except standing. No support is needed to come to standing. Some 12-month-olds may even attempt to take their first steps, although balance and control are usually not yet developed sufficiently for walking to be used as a main mode of mobility.

Over the next few months, between 12 and 18 months of age, the baby perfects her equilibrium and protective reactions in standing and gains progressively more control in walking. Initially when walking, the hands are held up and away from the body in a high guard position, and the feet are held wide apart to give a larger base of support (see Figure 2-34). First steps are exaggerated high-steps; they are flat-footed, and the trunk does not rotate. As postural reactions in standing develop through experience and practice, the baby's arms lower, her legs move closer together, and her steps take on a more mature pattern, with heel strike and rotational movement in the trunk occurring during walking.

Gross motor development in the first 2 years of life is based on initial reflex control, which is modified over time by other, more mature, postural reactions and by the baby's movement experiences.

The need to move and explore the environment is an inherent drive in the newborn and continues throughout life. Increased control over movement, with refinement of balance and coordination, continues to occur throughout childhood and beyond.

ATYPICAL MOTOR DEVELOPMENT

Typically, children acquire sensorimotor skills by experimenting with sensory information from the envi-

■ **FIGURE 2-34** Early walking, with hands in high guard
SOURCE: Reprinted with permission from Alexander, Boehme, and Cupps, *Normal Development of Functional Motor Skills: The First Year of Life*, pp. 46–199, illustrations by John Boehme, ©1993.

ronment through movement and its consequences. Development of cognitive concepts is also intimately tied to motor development. The continual experimentation of young children eventually results in their learning to play, socialize, communicate, feed and dress themselves, and handle their personal hygiene—all functional life tasks.

This development presupposes a normal CNS and normal sensorimotor systems. When there is damage to the CNS or disruption of the sensorimotor systems, due to disease, **trauma**, or genetic abnormalities, the normal experimentation process does not occur. Normal patterns of movement do not develop, and the child has difficulty developing the abilities necessary to perform functional life tasks.

The atypical child learns to move in some fashion and at some level, depending on the degree of physical impairment, but movements may or may not be functional for skill development. Some atypical children may experience delays in motor skill acquisition but eventually do develop along a more or less typical sequence. Others may never develop certain motor skills.

Although each atypical child has an individual pattern of motor strengths and weaknesses, the following physical characteristics (or combination of characteristics) that can interfere with the acquisition of motor skills may be observed; (Geralis, 1991; Orelove & Sobsey, 1991).

Abnormal Muscle Tone

A disturbance of the underlying tension of muscles may occur with damage to the CNS. Tone may be lower than expected, resulting in decreased power to move body parts against gravity and an interference with postural alignment. Joints may be overly flexible. Tone may also be higher than expected, resulting in labored movement that often occurs in abnormal patterns and within a limited range of motion. Interference with postural alignment and inflexible joints may be present. Muscle tone may also fluctuate in some children, making movement imprecise and uncontrolled. Atypical children may also display combinations of muscle tone problems. Disorders of muscle tone may be observed on a continuum from mild involvement that only minimally affects a child's movement and function to severe involvement that makes independent movement and function very difficult.

In all cases, since muscle tone is the basis of the capacity of muscles to act, abnormal muscle tone interferes with a child's ability to respond to sensory stimulation in the environment through movement. Therefore, abnormal muscle tone may interfere with progression through the various developmental motor milestones and performance of functional tasks.

Intervention

Intervention with children with atypical muscle tone can take several different forms:

1. *Physical and occupational therapy.* Pediatric therapists employ various handling and positioning techniques to decrease the effects of abnormal muscle tone and increase the normal actions of muscles for postural stability and functional movement at a developmentally appropriate level for each child. Many of these techniques can be taught to parents and teachers for carryover throughout the child's day.

2. *Splints, casts, and orthoses.* These are all custom-made devices that physicians (usually orthopedists) sometimes prescribe in order to hold a body part (usually an extremity) in a position that makes movement easier for the child. These devices can decrease muscle tone or stretch tight soft tissue and thereby improve mobility and function. Due to children's rapid growth and the close fit of these devices, they must be monitored carefully and changed frequently.

Splints are normally made of molded, rigid plastic and are used to position arms and hands. Occupational therapists usually construct custom splints for a child. The splints are removable and may be worn only at night or for part of the day for certain activities.

Casts are normally prescribed for legs and feet, and sometimes for elbows or wrists, in order to decrease abnormally high muscle tone or stretch out joint contractures caused by shortened muscles. Casts are often used for children with more severe impairments to achieve a functional position so that orthoses or splints can then be prescribed. Most casting is done either by an orthotist—a professional skilled in custom making such devices—or by a therapist trained and experienced in doing so. Casts may be made in one piece or may be bi-valved (cut in half) so they can be easily taken off and put on. They may be worn for weeks or months. Casts are usually made serially; that is, they are changed every few weeks as muscle tone decreases or contractures are stretched.

About 85% of children with abnormal muscle tone use an orthotic device at some time (Geralis, 1991). Orthoses are made of molded, rigid plastic and are used to reduce tone and to position or stabilize the leg or foot. Ankle/foot orthoses (AFOs) control the position of the ankle and foot. Knee/ankle/foot orthoses (KAFOs) control the position of the knee, as well as the ankle and foot. Orthoses are normally prescribed when the child begins weight-bearing activities. They may be constructed by an orthotist or by a trained physical therapist. Wearing time gradually increases, usually to include most of the child's waking hours. Parents and professionals must work closely together to ensure proper fit of orthoses and to gradually increase the child's wearing time in order to prevent pressure injuries to the child's skin. Frequent adjustments and refitting are necessary.

3. *Medication.* Medication can be used in intervention. However, although some medications do reduce muscle tone, they are not usually used for that reason in children because of their adverse side effects (sedation) and their potential toxic effects (Bleck & Nagel, 1982; Geralis, 1991).

4. *Nerve blocks.* Nerve blocks, or injections of medications such as anesthetics, alcohol, or phenol into a nerve, can impair the transmission of the electrical impulse along the nerve. This weakens or paralyzes the muscle supplied by that nerve; results can be temporary or permanent, depending on the type of medication used and the dosage. Although muscle tone can be decreased using nerve blocks, the procedure can be painful and is difficult to regulate. Total muscle function can be lost using this procedure.

5. *Surgery.* Surgical intervention is usually not considered until every attempt has been made to maintain or improve a child's mobility through a therapy program. Various types of surgeries involving the body's soft tissues can be used on the nerves, muscles, or tendons in order to reduce tone and improve joint range and general motor function. *Neurectomy* involves cutting, or otherwise destroying, a nerve or part of a nerve supplying a particular muscle group in order to reduce muscle tone. Tendons that attach muscle to bone can also be cut (tenotomy) and lengthened or transferred to another attachment site in an attempt to improve function when there is abnormal muscle tone. Muscles can also be cut (myotomy) and reattached in order to achieve more length and mobility. As with nerve blocks, however, these procedures can be difficult to regulate, and undercorrection or overcorrection can occur. Since the initial problem of abnormal muscle tone due to damaged central regulatory processes would still be present after surgery, muscles may also shorten again over time.

The traditional surgical procedures described in this section are orthopedic in nature, but in recent years, a neurosurgical approach to treating abnormally increased muscle tone has been gaining favor. This procedure, known as *selective dorsal rhizotomy*, involves selectively cutting some of the dorsal nerve roots at the level of the spinal cord; selection is based on the measured output of these nerves to the muscles they supply. Success in reducing muscle tone has been reported with this technique (Geralis, 1991), but long-term study has not yet been possible. Careful selection of candidates for this surgery, including consideration of age, cognitive functioning, and type of distribution of abnormal tone is currently a part of the procedure (Geralis, 1991). Primary candidates for rhizotomy are children between 4 and 7 years of age, with at least average intelligence and with increased muscle tone that primarily affects the legs. Long-term commitment to a rigorous rehabilitation program of therapy after surgery is needed.

Persistence of Primitive Reflexes

As noted earlier, in normal development, primitive reflexes are automatic, involuntary movements the young baby makes in response to various kinds of external environmental stimuli. They normally occur in the first few months of life; they protect the baby and form the basis for early motor skill development, facilitating interaction with the environment.

The persistence of these primitive, reflexive patterns of movement beyond their developmentally normal occurrence is also a possible characteristic of atypical motor development. Rather than promoting motor development, persistent primitive reflexes interrupt a child's ability to gain control over body movement. Attempts at functional motor performance are interrupted by an obligatory motor response from a primitive reflex pattern. For example, if a young girl with a persistent ATNR is attempting to feed herself with her right hand, then turns her head to the right to look at a sibling who is calling from across the room, she will have difficulty getting the food to her mouth. The change in head position will cause an increase in extensor tone in her right arm, making it difficult to bend and limiting her ability to get her hand to her mouth.

A physical or occupational therapist can assist the child's parent or teacher in positioning and handling her and in setting up activities so that the influence of these persistent primitive reflexes is minimized. The therapist can also work with the child to establish more mature movement patterns and help to integrate these reflexes.

Abnormal Postural Control and Movement

Children with abnormal tone or persistent primitive reflexes are unable to make graded movement adaptations to environmental stimuli. They may become fixed in certain positions, held there by the force of gravity or by their own muscle tone. The quality of their movement is also limited by these tone and reflex factors; the result is a decreased efficiency of movement. Since postural control and movement both support children's ability to interact with people and objects, learning and cognitive development may be affected by their inability to explore and interact with the environment (Orelove & Sobsey, 1991).

To facilitate development of both motor and cognitive skills, early therapeutic and educational intervention that is directed toward improving postural control, movement skills, and environmental exploration is critical for children with atypical motor development.

Relation of Atypical Tone and Reflex Development to Gastrointestinal and Respiratory Problems

The child with abnormal muscle tone and primitive reflex residuals may also display these characteristics in the oral-motor areas (Geralis, 1991). (See Table 2-2.) That is, the child may find sucking, chewing, and swallowing difficult. Either low or high muscle tone in the face and tongue, a persistent bite reflex (a touch on the gums or teeth causes a strong, lengthy clenching of the teeth), a hyperactive or hypoactive gag reflex (stimulation of the palate or tongue causes gagging or choking), or a strong tongue thrust (food on the tongue causes a forceful protrusion of the tongue out of the oral cavity) can cause difficulty.

The child may have trouble eating enough food to maintain health and growth, or food in the stomach may be ejected into the esophagus, a condition known as *gastroesophageal reflux*. This occurs when the esophageal sphincter muscle does not close normally, and stomach contents escape, either irritating the esophagus, causing pain and bleeding, or resulting in frequent vomiting. Feeding problems can also make mealtime extremely frustrating, time-consuming, and frightening for the parent, teacher, and child, which creates behavioral and socialization problems.

Physical, occupational, or speech therapists can help parents and teachers use proper (possibly adapted) positioning of the child in conjunction with specific techniques to normalize oral sensitivity, decrease the influence of primitive oral reflexes, and help the child learn how to suck, bite, chew, and swallow more efficiently.

Upright or semi-upright positioning for an hour or so after meals and the feeding of smaller portions or thicker textures of food can sometimes help refluxing, as can certain medications. When more conservative measures do not work, surgery to tighten the esophageal sphincter may be performed.

If feeding problems prevent a child from growing and gaining weight, or if frequent aspiration pneumonias caused by food or drink ending up in the lungs occur, surgery to implant a gastrostomy tube may be recommended (Bleck & Nagel, 1982; Geralis, 1991). During this surgery, a tube is inserted into either the stomach or the small intestine and brought through the abdominal wall. Liquid nutrients may then be introduced directly into the stomach or intestine, bypassing the oral cavity.

Children who have had gastrostomies should still experience non-nutritive oral stimulation, such as tooth brushing and the oral exploration of toys, to maintain or facilitate normal oral sensitivity and responses. Supplemental oral feedings may also be given to children with a gastrostomy tube if that is deemed safe by their physician. Children with a gastrostomy tube should receive ongoing medical evaluation to determine whether the gastrostomy tube is still necessary or whether oral feedings can be resumed.

Appropriate medical personnel, such as nurses, can safely teach parents and teachers to perform gastrostomy feedings. In addition, older children with gastrostomy tubes should be taught to assist with or to independently perform the tube feedings if they are physically and intellectually able to do so.

Atypical children with abnormal muscle tone may not be able to keep saliva and food from being aspirated (inhaled) into their lungs. Poor muscle control may make it difficult for these children to cough and thereby to clear aspirated material. When this occurs, chronic congestion can result, which can lead to pneumonia if the lungs become infected. Abnormal muscle tone may also make it difficult for atypical children to breathe deeply enough to take in adequate oxygen. Not only can this lead to fatigue and health problems, but rib-cage formation may be affected. The lack of coordination between breathing, sucking, and swallowing may further complicate feeding, and the breath support and control necessary for speech may be inadequate (Alexander, Boehme, & Cupps, 1993).

Speech, physical, and occupational therapists can work with teachers and parents on finding ways to use positioning and facilitation techniques that decrease aspiration and encourage better respiration in atypical children. Physical therapists can also teach parents and teachers postural drainage when appropriate; that is, positioning the child in various postures, in conjunction with percussion and vibration of the chest wall, in order to loosen congestion and drain the various lobes of the lungs. This helps the child clear the congestion.

Constipation is also a frequent problem for atypical children. Low or high muscle tone, lack of activity, lack of upright positioning, poor sensation, and the lack of enough abdominal strength to produce the pressure required for elimination can all contribute to problems with elimination. Changing positions and activity levels, using abdominal massage, increasing fiber in the diet, and using lubricants and stool softeners can help this problem. Parents, teachers, and professionals (PTs, OTs, physicians, and nutritionists) should work closely together to generate solutions (Bleck & Nagel, 1982; Orelove & Sobsey, 1991).

Abnormal muscle control and disturbed sensation can also lead to problems with bladder control in atypical children. Bladder control problems, compounded by hygiene difficulties, can lead to urinary tract infections. A hygiene program, antibiotics, and increased fluid intake can help decrease the number of infections. Control over the bladder and bowel can be significantly delayed in atypical children. Parents, teachers, physicians, and therapists should work together to determine a child's readiness for control over these functions and to establish a physical and behavioral program for training that is appropriate for the developmental level and physical needs of each child.

Secondary Orthopedic Changes

Abnormal muscle tone, persistent primitive reflexes, and limitations in positions and movements that the child can use independently can also lead to secondary changes in joints, muscles, and bones. Because the atypical child is not moving his or her joints through their normal full range of motion, muscles can shorten and connective tissue can tighten around joints, which physically limits the child's ability to move or be moved. If intervention to prevent or correct these secondary changes does not occur, abnormal muscle tone and the resultant abnormal body positions and movement patterns can cause changes in bone formation and growth, which requires major orthopedic surgery to correct. For example, if the legs of a child with increased muscle tone are allowed to remain in a classic scissored position—with the legs straight, turned in, and crossed over each other (extended, internally rotated, and adducted), abnormal forces are exerted on the hip joints, and they may not form normally. Instead, the end (or head) of the long thigh bone (the femur) may be straighter than normal; the acetabulum (pelvic cup into which the femur fits) may be shallower than normal. As a result, the child will be much more prone to dislocation or partial dislocation (subluxation) of the hips.

Early therapeutic intervention, with therapists, parents, and teachers all working together to properly position and handle the atypical child, can help prevent these secondary orthopedic changes. However, once they occur, serial casting of the soft tissue, surgical procedures on tendons, or muscle lengthening may be required to correct soft-tissue limitations. In the case of bony changes, surgical procedures on the bones themselves are necessary, and these procedures require long-term casting until the bones are healed. The surgery is usually performed on older children so as not to interfere with bone growth.

Two commonly performed bony procedures are *osteotomy* and *arthrodesis*. Osteotomies are often performed to correct chronic hip dislocations, for example. The procedure is used to realign a joint by removing a part of a bone and repositioning it at a more normal angle. Arthrodesis is used to fuse bones to one another in order to lend more stability to a joint. Arthrodesis is often used on the foot or ankle when there is severe deformity (Geralis, 1991).

Difficulty with Development of Functional Skills

When children have atypical postural control and movement patterns, they often cannot make the postural adaptations needed to independently perform the functional tasks of eating, dressing, washing, and toileting at an age-appropriate level. Additionally, once the child reaches school age, functional tasks necessary for classroom performance, such as writing, may be impaired. Physical and occupational therapists can assist children, families, and teachers with activities, adapted positions, and adapted equipment that can help the child function independently.

For example, training parents and teachers in the therapeutic preparation of the oral cavity before eating, or in therapeutic measures to use during eating (using touch and pressure techniques to either stimulate oral muscles, decrease persistent oral reflexes, or decrease or increase oral sensitivity) can improve feeding. A spoon with a curved bowl and a built-up handle may help the child eat independently. Allowing the child to use the support of a chair, a wall, or a small bench, and adapting clothing with velcro fasteners may improve dressing skills. A wash mitt, a hand-held shower nozzle, or a special bath chair may increase the child's independence with regard to personal hygiene. Special supports or seats on the toilet, or individual training in transferring out of a wheelchair onto a toilet, may also facilitate more independence. Specially adapted writing equipment or the use of a computer to type responses may help the child write more easily (Molnar, 1992).

Increasing functional skills can not only improve the child's motor performance but is important to developing cognitive, social, and communication skills.

Motor Problems Associated with Hearing Loss

The child who acquires a sensorineural hearing loss (see Chapter 17) as a result of a disease such as **meningitis** may also lose motor control and the sense of balance. The disease process destroys the sensory hair cell receptors in both the organ of Corti (the organ of hearing) and in the sensory hair cells in the vestibular mechanism of the inner ear (utricle, saccule, and the semicircular canals). The latter mechanism interacts, through the CNS, with the visual system, the muscles of the body, and the skin and joint receptors to produce a coordinated muscle response. This keeps the body upright against gravity when balance is upset.

Frequently, children recovering from meningitis will revert to a level of motor development lower than they exhibited before contracting the disease. Children who were walking may revert to crawling or may even be unable to sit without support. Postural reactions that depend on an intact vestibular system and that were well-established before the disease occurred (for example, equilibrium reactions in various developmental positions) no longer operate. The amount of vestibular damage and, to some extent, the age of the child determine the level of regression.

The child with a hearing impairment and motor problems due to vestibular damage has a good prognosis for developing normally with therapeutic intervention geared toward balance and equilibrium activities and facilitation of movement patterns aimed at moving the child along the normal developmental sequence. If no brain damage resulted from the disease, the visual, tactile, and proprioceptive systems gradually accommodate to the loss of vestibular information and work together to restore balance and equilibrium. The child's motor skills may be delayed for a period of time, but these will eventually catch up. Balance and equilibrium, however, may continue to be impaired when vision is removed—for example, in the dark or with eyes closed (Connolly & Montgomery, 1987; Fisher, Murray, & Bundy, 1991).

Motor Problems Associated with Vision Loss

Early head control occurs because the baby practices moving his head when he looks toward objects in the environment. Early grasp occurs because the baby is stimulated to reach out and grasp for objects in his line of sight. Young children are motivated to first move toward people and objects simply because they see them. Vision plays a central role in enabling children to monitor what is in the environment, to make comparisons, to anticipate events, to understand cause and effect, and to gain the stimulation from the environment that is necessary for developmental progress.

Children with visual impairment often exhibit developmental delays in many areas, such as language, socialization, self-help skills, and motor development (Best, 1992). Motor development includes both the elements of movement and orientation. Young children with visual impairment cannot easily monitor their own movements, nor can they easily copy other people as models of movement. Awareness of their own bodies and their position in space, as well as the relation of other objects in space, can be delayed. Without clear vision, children

may experience orientation problems caused by difficulties with creating a mental map of the surroundings. For example, a girl with visual impairment may be unable to find her way around obstacles that are in the way of reaching a goal. A lack of confidence, or even fear, may stem from uncertainties about her surroundings and from unsuccessful or painful past experiences with her attempts to move. Poor vision may also remove an important source of motivation for her to move into and interact with the environment. Reaching or moving toward sound sources, which is possible for children with vision impairment, is a more complex task than visually directed reaching. It usually occurs later in motor development (at about 9–12 months), which further delays the motor skills progression of a child with a visual impairment (Best, 1992).

Table 2-3 compares the developmental motor milestones of a child with normal sight with those of a child with a visual impairment, one with little or no usable vision. Early in development, the young baby with a visual impairment lacks the visual reference to motivate him to lift his head and assume a more erect posture. Positional preferences occur due to the vision loss. The baby with a visual impairment much prefers being on his back because lying on his stomach is not a functional position. The baby also prefers lying on his back to being upright in space, because he feels more secure in this position.

Because the baby with a visual impairment practices general movements less often than the baby with normal

---

TABLE 2-3

Milestone Comparison Chart

Skill	Sighted child (months)	Blind child (months)
Head lifted in prone	1	4
Elevates self on elbows in prone	4	8.75
Prone: forearm reaching for an object	3–5	9–12
Supine: rolls to prone	3–5	5–9
Sits alone steadily	6–8	6–9
Raises from floor to sitting	8	11
Stands holding furniture	6–8	10–16
Achieves four-point crawling	9–11	13
Stands alone	11	13
Walks with one hand held	9–11	16
Walks alone	12–15	19

Source: From transparency to accompany section on "Motor Development of the Child Who Is Blind," in E. Morgan (Ed.), *The INSITE Model: Trainer's Manual*, Vol. II. Copyright ©1989 Hope, Inc. Reprinted with permission.

sight, postural reactions (righting, protective, and equilibrium reactions) are slower to develop in all positions, which results in delayed balance. The "stability milestones" (such as sitting and standing) are less delayed than the "mobility milestones" (such as crawling and walking) because the child with a visual impairment is prevented by fear and lack of motivation from moving out into the environment. The child with a visual impairment will cruise for longer periods in order to maintain physical contact with an environmental reference and will probably walk later than peers with normal sight, not usually until about 18–20 months, often later (Best, 1992).

When a girl with a visual impairment first walks, she may exhibit some abnormalities of gait. Her stance may be wide-based in order to give her more support and stability. She may also have a shuffling gait, sliding her feet along the floor in order to maintain contact and provide additional cues about the walking surface; she holds her arms up (for protection) in a high guard position. There is little trunk rotation, and her gait appears stiff.

The child's fine motor skills may also be delayed. As we noted earlier, reaching to sound does not occur until about 9–12 months, so reaching skills appear later than do those of the child with normal sight. Her interpretation of tactile stimulation may also be disordered, which creates tactile defensiveness or a reluctance to touch or be touched. The child may have fewer ways to manipulate objects, so she may need hands-on help, as well as more time to explore objects with her hands (Fisher, Murray, & Bundy, 1991).

Tactile defensiveness may also be seen in the self-care area, with the child with a visual impairment being defensive to certain food textures and developing strong food preferences. Mealtimes can be messy because the child cannot see the food.

Learning to dress herself can be difficult because the child lacks visual references and has poor body awareness. Dressing skills take extra time, hands-on help, and patience. Tactile cues may be added to the older child's clothing to help differentiate top from bottom and one color from another. Toileting skills will also come later due to the lack of body awareness and to delayed motor skills.

In perceptual-motor development, the child with a visual impairment can be slower to develop the concepts of time and space, object permanence, and problem-solving strategies (Best, 1992). The child with a visual impairment also tends to be egocentric longer than usual and may, as a result, develop self-stimulatory behaviors. These mannerisms (blindisms) give the child some degree of sensory stimulation and may manifest themselves in a number of ways. The most common behaviors are flipping the hands in front of the face and

■ VIGNETTE 1 ■

Emily was born with CHARGE syndrome (a genetic syndrome that results in multiple organ involvement). She has a mild hearing loss and moderate vision loss in one eye. Due to cardiac, respiratory, feeding, and health problems early in her life, along with her sensory impairments, Emily was significantly delayed in her motor skills at the age of 1 year. She was fearful of movement and preferred to lie on her back. Scooting along the floor on her back was her main mode of locomotion. Emily was enrolled in an early intervention program at about this time and received weekly home intervention services from a special educator and a physical therapist. Her parents were instructed in activities that encouraged a variety of movement and sensory experiences and were assisted in positioning and handling Emily in order to encourage normal movement patterns. Emily's parents borrowed several pieces of adaptive equipment to use at home in order to encourage Emily's motor development (for example, special seating equipment and a walker).

At 3 years of age, Emily is ready for preschool. She is sitting independently, creeping, cruising along furniture, beginning to stand on her own for brief periods, and has taken a few steps on her own. Although still delayed in her motor skills, Emily has followed a normal developmental progression and is continuing to improve her motor skills. She has also shown significant cognitive potential, because she has been able to explore her world using her newly acquired motor skills.

---

poking the eyes. These behaviors can also serve as a way for the child with a visual impairment to release tension and anxiety. However, they are socially inappropriate and can be injurious, so the child should be helped to develop different coping strategies and should be discouraged from self-stimulatory behaviors by substituting appropriate opportunities for environmental exploration.

EDUCATIONAL IMPLICATIONS

The teacher must understand typical motor development in children in order to understand how the atypical child functions, what concomitant problems may occur, and what secondary problems should be prevented. This will help the teacher meet the student's needs, determine appropriate educational goals and interventions, and make appropriate environmental adaptations and necessary referrals to support personnel such as physical, occupational, or speech therapists, and nutritionists.

■ VIGNETTE 2 ■

Donna is a 13-year-old girl with a diagnosis of severe spastic quadriplegic cerebral palsy and normal intellectual functioning. Donna receives specialized instruction in math from a teacher certified in orthopedic impairments, but the rest of the time she attends regular junior high classes. She works with a team of specialists who meet regularly to help with the necessary classroom adaptations. The team includes a physical therapist, an occupational therapist, a speech and language pathologist, the regular education teachers, a teacher certified in orthopedic impairments, an adapted PE teacher, Donna's family, and Donna herself.

Donna uses an electric wheelchair to get around, special equipment for feeding, an augmentative communication device, and a computer for most of her school-work. Classroom materials have to be adapted for her computer. Donna is now independent in feeding (using special utensils), but she still requires assistance in many of her daily living activities. All members of the team have become familiar with her adaptations and lifting and handling techniques. Donna's parents credit the collaboration and cooperation of her team with her success at school.

The child with atypical motor development will require ongoing assistance from a team of professionals if his or her physical and sensory needs are to be met and motor development is to reach its maximum potential. Physical and occupational therapists should instruct teachers on proper positioning and handling techniques to encourage the student's optimal motor performance and allow for maximum functional independence. Additionally, the teacher should be instructed in the use of any adaptive equipment (such as special seating and feeding equipment) or adaptive devices (such as braces and splints) that can facilitate a student's functional motor performance.

Depending on the nature of the student's diagnosis, that is, whether the impairment is progressive or nonprogressive, the student's motor performance may either improve and goals will be reached, or motor performance may decline. Even in the case of a nonprogressive diagnosis such as cerebral palsy, the student's motor skills may regress if motor activities and adaptations are not continually assessed and necessary changes made in order to keep that from happening. In any case, ongoing assistance from the professional team will be important in making necessary changes in the motor program. Likewise, motor program changes are often needed following surgical interventions.

Other members of the team might instruct teachers in special procedures related to a child's motor problems. The speech therapist and nutritionist, in conjunction with the child's physical and occupational therapists, could periodically review the student's feeding program with the teacher. The speech therapist may also need to help develop a communication system for the student with atypical motor development. Adaptations that promote as much independence as possible in daily living, such as dressing, hygiene, and toileting, should be discussed. Orientation and mobility specialists can help with the mobility needs of the student with a visual impairmemt. Adaptive physical education instructors can help plan for the social and recreational needs of students with atypical motor development.

The teacher may need to adapt the presentation of classroom material and the expectation of a student's response. These adaptations should take into account the student's motor strengths and weaknesses and allow for either a response mode that does not require movement or one that allows for the use of alternative movement that the student can accomplish—switches, eye gazes, and so on. Whatever adaptations are chosen, they should be used across all settings.

SUMMARY

In this chapter, we discussed typical and atypical motor development. Our theoretical framework for discussing development included the following assumptions: (1) Development is a collection of processes; (2) Development occurs in stages; and (3) Development is a transactional process between genetic makeup and environment. An understanding of normal motor and reflex development is critical to understanding atypical motor development; therefore, normal reflex and motor development was covered extensively. General motor development was described as proceeding from (1) head to tail, (2) proximal to distal, (3) gross to fine, (4) flexion to extension, and (5) stability to mobility to skilled movement. Joint structure and muscle tone were also discussed. Reflex and motor development in the first year of life were described in detail. Some of the common problems with atypical motor development and their interventions were discussed, including therapy, splints, casts, orthoses, medications, and surgeries. Motor development as it relates to sensory impairmemt (visual or hearing loss) was also discussed. The importance of a team approach in the educational evaluation and planning for students with atypical motor development was stressed.

CHAPTER 3

Learning and Behavioral Characteristics of Students with Physical, Sensory, and Health Impairments

Physical, sensory, and health impairments may affect learning and behavior, and in turn scholastic performance. In some instances, this may be the direct result of the impairment; in other instances it may be attributed to environmental variables (such as frequent hospitalizations) or to psychological factors (such as poor self-concept) that are associated with the impairment. The impact of an impairment in conjunction with environmental variables and psychological factors may result in underachievement. For example, children with osteogenesis imperfecta (brittle bone disease) have normal intelligence but often do not perform as well academically as their unimpaired peers. This poorer academic performance is often misinterpreted or overlooked as a behavioral or motivational problem; often no connection is made to the effects of an impairment or to other possible causes (Cole, 1993; Smith, Francis, & Houghton, 1983).

As teachers educate students with physical, sensory, and health impairments, it is important that they know the educational implications of impairments. The teacher may need to provide adaptations, such as arranging for extra experiences, using different ways to make up missed work, implementing specific teaching strategies, locating books about individuals with similar disabilities, or listening to the student's concerns.

In this chapter, we will discuss some broad concepts regarding the impact of physical, sensory, and health impairments on learning and behavior. Specific recommendations for meeting learning needs as well as behavioral and social needs are provided.

MODEL FOR STUDENTS WITH PHYSICAL, SENSORY, AND HEALTH IMPAIRMENTS

Three major areas can affect how well a student with an impairment learns: (1) characteristics of the impairment, (2) environmental variables, and (3) psychological factors. As seen in Figure 3-1, each of these variables interacts with the others. Student performance may vary as a result of the type and severity of the impairment, but students with the same type of impairment may perform differently because of differences in environmental variables. Even when the environmental variables are the same, psychological factors vary, and this creates a unique learning situation for each student.

TYPES OF IMPAIRMENTS

Several types of impairments can affect the student's functioning. Although there are a number of ways to classify diseases and conditions, an adapted version of Gearheart, Mullen, and Gearheart's (1993) classification system will be used here. In this system, impairments are divided into three major categories: (1) physical impairments, (2) sensory impairments, and (3) other health impairments (see Box 3-1).

Physical impairments can be defined as "those that involve primarily the joints, skeleton, and muscles and that interfere with an individual's mobility, motor coordination, general muscular ability, ability to maintain posture and balance, or communication skills to the

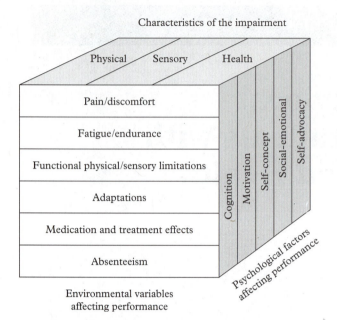

■ FIGURE 3-1 Impact of environmental variables and psychological factors on performance for students with physical, sensory, and health impairments

extent that they inhibit learning or social development" (Gearheart, Mullen, & Gearheart, 1993, pp. 309–310). This definition includes neuromotor, degenerative, and orthopedic impairments. Box 3-1 lists some of the major disorders that are considered to be neuromotor, degenerative, and orthopedic. Each of these physical impairments has varying characteristics among the different types and within each particular disorder. Each physical impairment may have additional characteristics that can also affect the student's performance. For example, students with severe cerebral palsy often speak unintelligibly and use communication systems that might not allow them to fully express their intent.

Although sensory impairments could be categorized as physical impairments, we consider them separately here because of their unique effect on learning. Sensory impairments pertain to disorders that affect the senses enough to inhibit learning or social development. Several senses—including vision, hearing, touch, smell, and taste—may be affected by a variety of diseases. However, visual impairments, hearing impairments, and deaf-blindness are the types of sensory impairments most often considered together. Since most of what people learn is through the visual and auditory senses, when these are impaired, learning can be severely affected, requiring adaptations to accommodate for the sensory loss.

The third category is health impairments, or "conditions that disrupt and interfere with normal daily functioning—and thus possibly with the learning process—unless special interventions are implemented" (Gearheart, Mullen, & Gearheart, 1993, p. 310). This category includes major health impairments, such as diabetes, and infectious diseases, such as AIDS. (See Box 3-1.) Typically, students with health impairments require monitoring for special health care needs. Educators may need to administer or monitor the effects of medication, watch for signs and symptoms of distress, know what to do in an emergency, administer special health care procedures, and know how to modify physical activities.

Disorders in each category can interfere with efficient learning. Physical disorders tend to negatively affect physical functioning; the use of arms or legs can be affected in many cases. In conditions such as cerebral palsy, spinal cord injury, spina bifida, and, in some cases, traumatic brain injury, the individual may have

---

BOX 3-1

Categories of Impairments

I. Physical Impairments
    A. Neuromotor impairments
        Traumatic brain injury
        Seizure disorders
        Cerebral palsy
        Spinal cord disorders
    B. Degenerative diseases
        Muscular dystrophy
        Spinal muscular atrophy
    C. Orthopedic and musculoskeletal disorders
        Curvature of the spine
        Hip conditions
        Limb deficiencies
        Juvenile arthritis
        Musculoskeletal disorders
II. Sensory Impairments
    A. Visual impairments
    B. Hearing impairments
    C. Deaf-blindness
III. Health Impairments
    A. Major health impairments
        Heart disorders
        Blood disorders
        Asthma
        Cystic fibrosis
        Juvenile diabetes
        Chronic renal failure
        Childhood cancer
    B. Infectious Diseases
        Hepatitis B
        Human immunodeficiency virus and AIDS

partial or complete loss of motor function in some parts of the body for life. This can affect participation in activities requiring physical movement. In the case of **seizure disorders,** some seizures result in a temporary loss of motor function often lasting only minutes or seconds. However, this can disrupt a student's concentration on the lesson being taught. Degenerative diseases result in a progressive loss of motor movement, which can have a progressively detrimental impact on activities requiring physical participation.

Sensory impairments can affect learning because they interfere with the reception of visual or auditory information. Health impairments may interfere with learning when procedures must interrupt lessons. The extent of the impact of physical, sensory, or health impairment depends not only on the severity of the impairment but also on the environmental variables that occur along with the impairment.

ENVIRONMENTAL VARIABLES

At least six environmental variables may affect students' learning: (1) pain and discomfort, (2) fatigue and endurance, (3) functional physical and sensory limitations, (4) adaptations, (5) medication and treatment effects, and (6) absenteeism. Each of these variables is partially or completely controlled by environmental causes and can influence a student's performance (see Box 3-2).

Pain and Discomfort

The first variable is pain and discomfort. In some instances, students may experience pain or discomfort from their impairment, such as when a student has very severe curvature of the spine. Or a student with cerebral palsy may have leg cramps. Sometimes, pain occurs in conjunction with an activity the student is performing. For example, a student with juvenile arthritis might have pain upon moving a joint after remaining in one position for a long time. A student feeling pain or discomfort will be unable to fully attend to the lesson being taught in class. According to Maslow (1954), physiological well-being, including lack of pain or discomfort, is the most basic need that must be met if an individual is to reach his or her full potential. (The other needs are for safety, belongingness, esteem, and self-actualization.)

Whether pain is recognized in a student and dealt with will influence the student's performance. For example, an astute teacher may recognize that a student is in pain—younger children do not necessarily talk about pain—and address the issue. This may be done through modifying the activity that is causing the pain; for example, by decreasing the amount a student needs

---

BOX 3-2

Environmental Variables

1. Pain and discomfort
   Characteristics of condition
   Environmental activity
2. Fatigue and endurance
   Temporary
   Steadily increasing
   Constant
3. Functional physical and sensory limitation
   Activity has physical involvement
   Activity has sensory involvement
4. Adaptations
   Provide access to the task
   Change instruction of the task
   Change part or all of the task
5. Medication and treatment effects
   Effective use of medications and treatments
   Side effects
6. Absenteeism
   Procedures
   Doctors' appointments
   Hospitalizations

---

to walk or by allowing the student to change positions. Other remedies include giving medication for the pain, letting the student take a short break, having the student go to the nurse, or other similar interventions. In some instances, an older student may prefer to be left alone to cope with the pain. The teacher may later provide a review of any material that was missed due to the distraction of experiencing pain.

Fatigue and Endurance

The second variable is fatigue and limited endurance. Some students with physical, sensory, or health impairments may exhibit fatigue and limited stamina, which affects their ability to concentrate (Sirvis, 1989). An example of such a physical impairment is the student with severe spastic cerebral palsy who must expend a great deal of effort to move and therefore tires by early afternoon and is not mentally alert. Students with health impairments such as sickle cell anemia and cancer may feel tired and have limited stamina and endurance as a result of their condition and the amount of work they are doing. Fatigue may be constant or temporary. For example, students with poor vision may be fatigued after reading for a protracted period, and may need to rest their eyes. This fatigue is more temporary than that of a child with sickle cell anemia who may have chronic fatigue. Some teachers who have tired students in their classrooms may not realize that a lack of endurance is causing a lack of participation in the classroom. More obvious conditions such as muscular dystrophy will typically have gradually increasing fatigue and loss of endurance, for which the teacher will need to adjust.

When fatigue and endurance problems are recognized and addressed, the student's performance can be positively affected. Some problems may be addressed by programming more difficult subjects and material for times when the student is most alert. Often this is in the morning. In some cases, the student may need a break or a rest time as is often true for students with advanced muscular dystrophy. In extreme cases, the student may need a shortened school day.

Functional Physical and Sensory Limitations

The third variable is the student's functional physical or sensory limitations, which present themselves in the activities requiring physical or sensory responses. Students with severe spastic cerebral palsy or blindness, for example, will not be able to fully participate in the dissection of frogs in biology class. Performance and learning can be adversely affected if no modifications are made in activities such as this. The teacher's selection of an appropriate activity and the use of necessary modifications will determine how well the student learns and performs (see Figure 3-2.) Also, functional limitations due to physical or sensory impairment may have limited some students' experiences, and they may lack common information. For example, an 18-year-old girl who was blind was walking in the snow with her friend, who said, "The bottom of your cane looks just

■ **FIGURE 3-2** Kindergarten teacher modifies spelling activity to allow student with cerebral palsy to participate with the class in his standing frame

like applesauce from the dirty snow." The girl who was blind replied, "How did the snow turn red?" She had been told that apples were red, but no one had thought to explain to her that only the outside is red and that the inside is white. Teachers should be sure to provide complete information on the topic at hand and not assume that something is common knowledge.

Adaptations

The fourth variable is the use of adaptations to compensate for physical, sensory, or health impairments. As will be discussed in Chapter 28, adaptations can range from providing access to a task (modifying the classroom environment, using assistive devices, changing modes of response), to changing instruction in a task, to changing part or all of a task. For example, more concrete items might be used for students who are blind. Whether adaptations are provided in the instructional environment and whether they are effective with the student will influence the student's performance.

Medication and Treatment Effects

The fifth variable is the effect of medication or treatment on the student with physical, sensory, or health impairments. Medication can be used to manage many conditions effectively. If the student with diabetes routinely takes medication, it is more likely that diabetic emergencies can be avoided. When medication is not taken routinely, a diabetic emergency such as diabetic ketoacidosis can occur. Also, side effects of medication can affect student performance. For example, fatigue is a common side effect of many antiepileptic medications taken by students who have seizures (Pellock, 1989; *Physicians' Desk Reference*, 1995). Treatments such as radiation, taken by students with some forms of cancer, can also result in fatigue and malaise (generalized achy feelings) (Crooks et al., 1991).

Medication must be properly administered, and side effects and the effectiveness of medication must be tracked. In this way, student performance can be enhanced and medication can be changed as needed. (For more information on tracking medications, see Chapter 27.) Also, various treatments may improve performance, such as the effective use of physical therapy, occupational therapy, and speech therapy.

Absenteeism

The last environmental variable is absenteeism, which may range from a student with spina bifida missing 10 minutes of class to perform a catheterization procedure, to a student with cystic fibrosis missing many days of school due to frequent hospitalizations. Missing part or all of a school day can result in missing crucial information that is needed for adequate school performance. Some theorists have suggested that lower academic achievement in children with diabetes as compared to their peers is due to frequent school absences (Lloyd & Orchard, 1993). How the teacher compensates for this missed work can make a difference in how the student performs.

PSYCHOLOGICAL FACTORS

The effect of a physical, sensory, or health impairment will only partially be determined by the characteristics of the impairment and environmental variables. The psychological effect of the impairment and its limiting factors also affects the student. At least five major psychological factors affect how the student will learn and will deal with an impairment: (1) cognition, (2) motivation, (3) self-concept, (4) social and emotional factors, and (5) self-advocacy (see Box 3-3).

Cognition

The first psychological factor affecting performance is cognition, which can be categorized as follows: (1) intellectual capacity, (2) developmental level, and (3) concept development. Students with physical and sensory impairments vary as to their intellectual abilities. Some students may be intellectually gifted; others may have normal intelligence or mental retardation. In some conditions, such as cerebral palsy, there is a higher incidence of mental retardation. Other conditions, such as cerebral palsy and spina bifida, are associated with learning disabilities that may affect performance (Bleck & Nagel, 1982; Keele, 1983; Rowley-Kelly & Reigel, 1993; Umbreit, 1983). The intellectual ability of the student will affect performance and the need for enrichment, remediation, or the use of specialized learning strategies.

Developmental milestones may be reached differently or more slowly in students with physical, sensory, and health impairments, possibly because restricted movement or the lack of sensory input may limit experiences. Students with physical impairments often have delays in reaching cognitive milestones such as concrete and formal operations (as delineated by Piaget) because they have fewer opportunities to interact with the environment and fewer confrontational interactions with peers (Yoos, 1987). Infants who are blind often have different rates of achieving developmental milestones due to their impairment.

BOX 3-3

Psychological Factors

1. Cognition
   Intellectual ability
   Developmental level
   Concept development
2. Motivation
   Learned helplessness
   Despair/priorities
3. Self-concept
   Self
   How others feel about me
   How I feel about me because of my environment
4. Social and emotional factors
   Social interactions
   Behavioral problems
5. Self-advocacy

Some children may exhibit delays, deterioration, or stagnation in development as a result of the disease itself. For example, children born with AIDS may exhibit mild developmental delays due to the loss of motor, social, and language skills that results from the neurological course of the disease (Johnson, 1993).

Students with physical, sensory, or health impairments may have incomplete concept development due to their restricted movement or lack of sensory input. A lack of meaningful experiences may limit a student's knowledge, and thus, their concepts may be incomplete or inaccurate. For example, children with physical impairments who have never held an orange may think that an orange is hard. Students with visual impairments may lack certain concepts such as positioning the body in space (top, bottom), environmental awareness (back yard), object characteristics (short, long), time (begin, end), spatial awareness (parallel), actions (throw), quantity (more, less), or certain symbols—for example, that red means stop (Hall, 1982). Certain concepts may need to be taught to students who lack this knowledge because of impairments.

Motivation

The second factor has to do with motivation. How motivated a student is to learn will influence his or her performance. In addition to typical individual differences in motivation, students with impairments may have additional factors that contribute to their motivational level. In some instances, students with impairments may react negatively, which in turn affects motivation. For example, some students with degenerative diseases such as Duchenne's muscular dystrophy may become depressed and display a lack of motivation because of despair over their condition. In some cases, counseling and antidepressant therapy have been found to improve motivation (Brumback, Staton, & Wilson, 1987).

In other instances, a lack of motivation may stem from others' reactions to the student. Parents and school personnel may be overly protective; they may do things for the student that he or she could do without help. Learned helplessness—the lack of persistence at tasks that could be mastered—may result. Also, individuals' reactions to the student may contribute to an external locus of control in which the student attributes success or failure to external factors rather than to his or her own accomplishments or errors. Both learned helplessness and an external locus of control negatively affect school performance and the motivation to succeed (Lefcourt, 1976; Rotter, 1966; Tomlison, 1987). Educational personnel should let the student be as self-sufficient as possible. Also, pointing out accomplishments and attributing good results to the student may be of help in improving motivation.

Self-Concept

The term *self-concept* includes: (1) how the student with an impairment feels about himself or herself, (2) how the student thinks others feel about him or her, and (3) how the environment affects the student's feelings.

Students with physical, sensory, or health impairments vary as to how they feel about themselves in light of their disability. As early as preschool, children with physical impairments begin to recognize that they are different from others. At ages 3 and 4 years, many children can associate the name of their disability with at least one of its effects (Dunn, McCartan, & Fuqua, 1988). Children who have a visual impairment know there is something wrong with their vision as early as age 2. (This is a difficult concept. The child must understand that others use a method—sight—that the child does not possess in order to understand the world around them [Erin & Corn, 1994]). A child's self-perception will be partially determined by what he or she knows, does not know, or misunderstands. Lack of information or misinformation about an impairment may adversely affect a child's self-concept and create feelings of inferiority and isolation.

Some studies have reported feelings of lower self-esteem in children with cerebral palsy (Teplin, Howard, & O'Connor, 1981); others have found similar self-esteem scores between children with cerebral palsy and their unimpaired age-matched peers (Ostring & Nieminen, 1982). One study found that adolescent girls with cerebral palsy scored lower on self-esteem measures as adolescents but had scores similar to those without disabilities as adults (Magill-Evans & Restall, 1991). Esteem needs are a major area in Maslow's hierarchy of needs; these may have to be addressed in individuals with disabilities.

Children's self-concept does not necessarily depend on the severity of their impairment. Students with less severe eye conditions or milder forms of osteogenesis imperfecta may have a more negative concept about themselves than those with more severe impairments. Some children may develop a self-image as a "sick patient with end-stage renal disease" (Cole, 1991) and react in a manner reflecting this self-concept. Some students with seizure disorders may feel stress, anxiety, and embarrassment about having such an unpredictable condition, which may interfere with developing a good self-concept and impede progress in school (Frank, 1985). One boy with Duchenne's muscular dystrophy—a degenerative disease resulting in death in the teens—expressed his feelings toward himself and his condition by saying, "I am a snowflake melting in your hand." In some cases, counseling may help a child understand his or her own problems and achieve some sense of control (Marshak & Seligman, 1993).

Self-concept is also tied to how individuals with impairments think others react to them and their impairment. The childhood memories of adults with disabilities often include ridicule, exclusion, and physical abuse by other children, as well as more subtle but equally distressing situations such as having one's ability underestimated by adults (Marshak & Seligman, 1993). Children with AIDS (or the HIV virus) often have to cope with stigma and rejection (Johnson, 1993), which can contribute to a negative self-concept.

Other beliefs, superstitions, folklore, and mythology regarding individuals with impairments can also affect a person's self-concept. Blindness, for example, is surrounded by several negative and positive beliefs. Blindness has been viewed as a punishment from God, as worse than being dead, or as the mark of an evil person. Unrealistic positive beliefs are equally damaging. One example of such beliefs is the notion that individuals who are blind have "second sight," magical abilities, or a keener sense of the other senses (Wagner-Lampl & Oliver, 1994). The influence of such folklore is often expressed in attitudes toward individuals who have impairments.

The third aspect of self-concept is how the individual feels about his or her environment. The student may view the school, community, or home environment as supportive or as lacking support. According to Maslow (1954), major needs include the need to feel safe and to belong, which may or may not be furnished by the person's environment. Family stress at home that is caused by having a family member with a disability may be significant (Nixon, 1994); strangers who stare in the mall may cause a child to feel like an outsider. A lack of effective accommodations or adaptations at school may make the student feel unsafe or promote a sense of not belonging. Environments that include the student as a valued member of the group can help with developing a positive self-concept.

Social and Emotional Factors

The fourth set of major psychological factors that may affect performance are social and emotional factors. In some instances, social functioning may be delayed or maladaptive, as with some children who have a history of end-stage renal disease or seizure disorder (Brownbridge & Fielding, 1991; Frank, 1985; Reynolds, Morton, Garralda, Postlethwaite, & Goh, 1993). In other types of impairments, such as blindness, social interaction may be impeded due to the inability to incidentally observe and model nonverbal interactions (eye contact, body position). Instruction in social interaction is often needed (Heubner, 1986).

Social and emotional factors also include emotional responses to having a disability. These emotional factors vary among individuals and can interfere with learning. Some individuals have no atypical emotional responses and are quite well-adjusted. Others display such behaviors as denial that a disability exists, anger, depression, hopelessness, manipulation, or viewing others as unjust (Bigge, 1991; Jourard, 1958; Marshak & Seligman, 1993). (See Chapter 9 for reactions in students who have such terminal, degenerative diseases as muscular dystrophy.) In extreme cases, some individuals with impairments will have severe emotional and behavioral problems (Knights et al., 1991; Thompson et al., 1992; Utens et al., 1993). Counseling may be indicated in some instances.

Self-Advocacy

The fifth psychological factor is self-advocacy. In the context of the model used here, self-advocacy refers to the student's willingness to inform others of his or her needs in order to effect change. Often, students with physical, sensory, or health impairments have special needs that must be met if students are to succeed at a task. Teachers may quickly identify the modifications needed for the student in biology lab with limited hand use. However, other needs may be more subtle and go unrecognized. Students must then serve as their own advocate and state their needs. For example, a student with a physical impairment may need to have material repositioned. Similarly, a student with a hearing impairment may need the teacher to stop turning away while lecturing. Unless the student says something, performance can be affected. A student with diabetes may recognize that it is time for a snack, but the teacher may not realize this. If the student does not speak up, a medical emergency could result.

Even more difficult for some children is to disagree with an adult. The substitute physical education instructor may tell a boy with a heart disorder to run faster, when he has been doing modified walking in the past. The student may have difficulty explaining the situation and then refusing to do what he is told. It is important not only for educational performance but for the child's well-being that educators and family members promote self-advocacy skills in children with impairments.

INTERACTION BETWEEN IMPAIRMENT, ENVIRONMENTAL VARIABLES, AND PSYCHOLOGICAL FACTORS

The combination of the characteristics of the impairment, environmental variables, and psychological factors creates a student's unique response to his or her situation and shapes performance in an academic setting. Although students can have the same type of impairment, differing environmental variables and psychological factors will create different learning and behavioral responses. For example, two students may have severe spastic quadriplegia cerebral palsy in addition to the same type of visual impairment but may perform very differently in school. The first student may have had scheduling to decrease fatigue, modifications and adaptations to allow participation despite physical and sensory limitations, medication adjusted to minimize the side effects, and the scheduling of appointments after school when possible to decrease absenteeism. The second student may have had none of this. Even if these environmental variables were identical, the differences in psychological factors would create individual differences. Psychological factors can range from having normal intelligence and a wide range of meaningful experiences, high motivation, good self-concept, and social and emotional factors, and strong self-advocacy skills, to having difficulty in each of these areas.

Although there is no way to control the characteristics of a student's impairment, environmental variables, and to some extent, psychological factors, can be manipulated. For example, educators should take each of the variables into account when planning instruction. Providing useful adaptations is of particular importance in helping the student succeed. (See Chapter 28 for a discussion of adaptations.) With regard to psychological factors, educators should try to create a positive, caring atmosphere in which to improve students' self-concept, address a lack of experiences and social and emotional needs, and teach self-advocacy. Educators and other members of the educational team should avoid promoting learned helplessness by having students with impairments do things for themselves whenever feasible.

SUMMARY

In this chapter, we have provided a broad overview of the impact that physical, sensory, and health impairments can have on learning and behavior, and, hence, on scholastic performance. A model was proposed that illustrated the interrelatedness of the impairment, envi-

ronmental variables, and psychological factors on performance. Impairments were divided into the three categories: (1) physical (including neuromotor, degenerative, and orthopedic impairments), (2) sensory (including vision impairments, hearing impairments, and deaf-blindness), and (3) health impairments (including major health impairments and AIDS). Environmental variables included pain and discomfort, fatigue and endurance, functional physical and sensory limitations, adaptations, medication and treatment effects, and absenteeism. Psychological factors included cognition, motivation, self-concept, social and emotional factors, and self-advocacy.

Individuals differ in their learning and behavioral performance according to the interaction of the three areas. Even students with similar diseases will differ in their responses. Since the impairment cannot be changed, educators and the educational team should manipulate environmental variables and psychological factors when possible in order to promote a positive atmosphere for growth.

PART II

Neuromotor Impairments

CHAPTER 4

Neuroanatomy

The nervous system is one of the most complex and fascinating systems of the human body. It has reached a level of complexity that separates humans from all other animals on the earth. The nervous system provides us with the ability to do such things as think, move, feel, and breathe. A basic understanding of the components of the nervous system (neuroanatomy) and how the nervous system works (neurophysiology) will provide a better understanding of disorders that adversely affect it. This will especially apply to disorders such as traumatic brain injury, seizure disorders, cerebral palsy, spina bifida, and spinal cord injury.

The nervous system can be divided into three parts: (1) the central nervous system (CNS), which consists of the brain and spinal cord; (2) the peripheral nervous system (PNS), which consists of the nerves that connect the spinal cord and other parts of the body; and (3) the autonomic nervous system (ANS), which regulates the functioning of internal organs as well as the internal environment (for example, blood pressure).

The following are the major functions of the nervous system:

1. To receive sensory information from the environment and the body and transmit that information to the brain. This is called an afferent system.
2. To send information down the spinal cord and out the peripheral nerves to the various organs and muscles to create a motor response. This is called an efferent system.
3. To integrate the information (DeLisa & Stolov, 1981).

For these three functions to occur there must be adequate functioning of the nerve cells, or neurons.

THE NEURON

The nervous system is composed of approximately 100 billion **neurons** that transmit information between the different parts of the brain as well as between the brain and other parts of the body. Neurons may be considered the basic communicators of the nervous system. Neurons are surrounded by glial cells, which function as supporting structures of the nervous system. Glial cells play a role in transporting nutrients and other material to neurons by forming myelin (a fatty substance that covers part of the neuron and aids in transmitting information) and by maintaining the electrically charged environment of the neurons.

Neurons vary in size and shape (see Figure 4-1). However, most neurons are composed of several basic parts (see Figure 4-2). The neuron typically consists of several radiating branches known as *dendrites,* a *cell body* (soma), and one long fiber known as the *axon.* Dendrites receive information from other neurons and transport the information to the cell body. From the cell body, information is transported down the long axon. The axon may be as short as a few microns (approximately .00004 of an inch) or several feet in length. The axon terminates in twiglike branches and may also have side branches (collaterals) radiating from it. To speed transmission, some axons are encased in myelin, which serves as a conductor. When several axons are bound together, they form what is known as a *nerve fiber.*

Since no single neuron is long enough to send messages from the brain to the rest of the body (or from the body to the brain), a chain of neurons is needed to transmit the information through the nervous system. For example, if a boy wants to move his leg to kick a ball, a chain of neurons is needed to send that information and cause the movement (see Figure 4-3). Neurons

Neuron from
olfactory area
of brain

Neuron from
cortex of brain

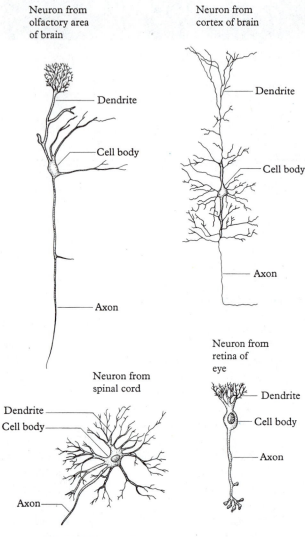

■ **FIGURE 4-1** Different types of neurons

body down the axon. As the electrical impulse travels down the axon, transmission is speeded if the axon is wrapped in myelin. Along the myelinated axon, there are gaps in the myelin called *nodes of Ranvier,* as seen in Figure 4-2. In these axons, the electrical impulse jumps along the axon from node to node. When the axon is not myelinated, transmission is slower and the electrical impulse moves like a burning fuse.

The electrical impulse stops at the end of the axon, or the *axon terminal.* Between the axon terminal and

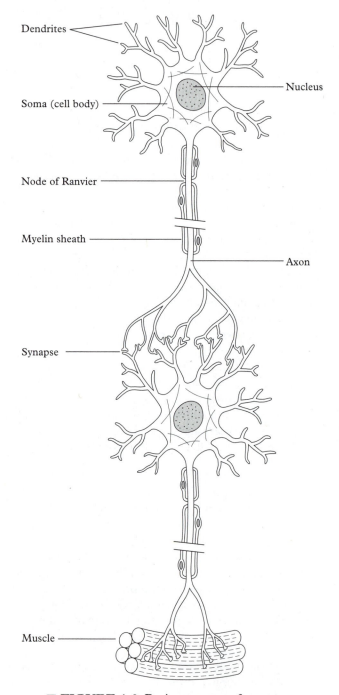

■ **FIGURE 4-2** Basic anatomy of a neuron

that send information to the muscles are called *motor neurons.* The upper motor neurons are located in the brain; axons descend down the spinal cord. At the spinal cord, another group of neurons known as the *lower motor neurons* receive the information and send it down long axons to the leg muscles to make the muscle move. In order for the brain to know the ball has been kicked, another chain of neurons known as *sensory neurons* will transmit information from the leg back to the brain, informing the brain of the leg movement and the sensation of hitting the ball.

A message is transmitted by the neurons through an electrical-chemical response. First, an electrical impulse arises in the dendrites and cell bodies. This occurs by an alteration in the permeability of the cell membrane to sodium and potassium ions, resulting in a brief electrical phenomenon known as an *action potential.* This electrical impulse rapidly travels from the dendrites and cell

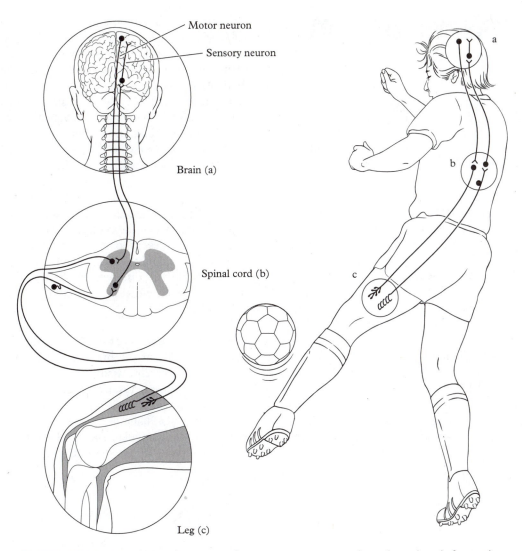

Motor neuron

Sensory neuron

Brain (a)

Spinal cord (b)

a

b

c

Leg (c)

■ **FIGURE 4-3** A chain of motor and sensory neurons sends and receives information

the next neuron is a space about a millionth of an inch wide, known as a *synapse* or *synaptic cleft* (see Figure 4-2). When the electrical impulse reaches the synapse, it stimulates the release of *neurotransmitters*—chemicals that travel across the synapse to the next neuron. Over 40 neurotransmitters have been found, including dopamine, epinephrine, and acetylcholine (Guyton, 1991). Some of these neurotransmitters will cause a sequence of events resulting in an electrical impulse in the next neuron, which will continue to transmit the message. Other neurotransmitters will inhibit the next neuron from firing. Thousands of axon terminals synapse with the dendrites and cell bodies of each neuron, and the collective action of the neurotransmitters will determine whether the next neuron fires an electrical impulse.

Too much or too little of a neurotransmitter can affect a person's thinking, mood, or even muscle

strength. Certain diseases, such as Alzheimer's and Parkinson's, have been attributed to a lack of certain neurotransmitters (Berkow, 1992). Several medications, such as Ritalin and the antipsychotic medication Clozaril, work through inhibiting or facilitating neurotransmitters.

THE CENTRAL NERVOUS SYSTEM (CNS)

The central nervous system consists of the brain and spinal cord (see Table 4-1). Both are protected by bone, membrane, and fluid. The brain is contained in and protected by the skull, while the spinal cord is protected by the bones of the vertebral column. At the base of the brain, a hole known as the *foramen magnum* connects the cranial cavity and the vertebrae.

TABLE 4-1

Parts of the Nervous System

System	Components of the System
Central nervous system	Brain
	Spinal cord
Peripheral nervous system	Peripheral nerves
Autonomic nervous system	Parasympathetic system
	Sympathetic system

Both the brain and the spinal cord are also surrounded by three layers of membranes: the *dura mater,* the *arachnoid,* and the *pia mater* (see Figure 4-4). Together, these three membranes are known as **meninges.** They provide further protection for the brain and spinal cord. (The infection known as *meningitis* is the inflammation of these meninges.)

The brain and spinal cord are further protected by a continuous flow of clear fluid—cerebral spinal fluid (CSF). The CSF originates from certain cells lining the ventricles (cavities) of the brain. The CSF circulates through the ventricles to the space between the arachnoid and pia mater (subarachnoid space). It circulates from the brain, down the spinal column in the subarachnoid space, and back around the brain where it is then reabsorbed into the *arachnoid villa*—the fingerlike

projections of the arachnoid membrane of the brain. The CSF has a special quality of being buoyant, and the brain floats in it. This buoyancy helps to decrease the brain's momentum when, for example, the brain is suddenly displaced by a person's head hitting a dashboard in a car wreck. The amount of damage is thus reduced. In addition to the CSF's protective quality, it assists with exchanging nutrients and wastes. CSF is withdrawn for testing to determine whether a person has certain diseases, such as meningitis.

The Brain

The brain is part of the central nervous system. It can be divided into several parts: the **cerebral hemispheres,** the **cerebellum,** and the **brain stem.** Each of these parts is responsible for different functions that work together to give an individual the ability to think, move, feel, and live.

Cerebral Hemispheres of the Brain

The largest part of the brain is the **cerebrum,** which consists of two cerebral hemispheres, or two sides of the brain. The hemispheres are almost identical; each has numerous convolutions. The humps of the convolutions are known as *gyri* (singular, *gyrus*), and the furrows are known as *sulci* (singular, *sulcus*). Each cerebral hemisphere appears gray on the outside and white on the

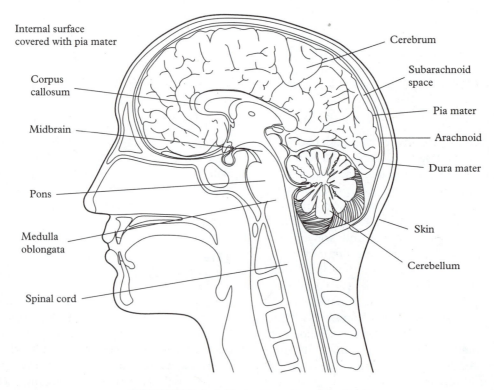

■ **FIGURE 4-4** Basic anatomy of the brain

inside. The gray matter (cerebral cortex) is made up of the cell bodies (soma) of the neurons, while the white matter is primarily composed of axons and their myelin. The two cerebral hemispheres are joined in the middle by a band of nerve fibers known as the *corpus callosum,* which provides for the transfer of information from one hemisphere to another.

The cerebral hemispheres are divided into four lobes: the *frontal, parietal, temporal,* and *occipital lobes* (see Figure 4-5). Each lobe has a specific location and is associated with certain functions of the brain.

Frontal lobe. The frontal lobe is located at the front of the brain and ends at a long, vertical sulcus known as the *central sulcus.* This lobe also starts at the top of the brain and goes down to a long, horizontal sulcus known as the *lateral sulcus.* Functions such as reasoning, judgment, behavior, and personality are attributed to the frontal lobes. This area can be viewed as a behavior regulator. Persons with frontal lobe damage often have a lack of tact and restraint; they use coarse language and behave aggressively. The other behavioral extreme has also been found: apathy, indifference, lack of initiative, and little emotion. The frontal lobe has also been found to play a role in learning associations and in the temporal ordering of events. This has been demonstrated by persons with frontal lobe damage who have difficulty learning new tasks involving associations, as well as difficulty organizing everyday activities.

The frontal lobe also has a role in voluntary motor movement. In the back of the frontal lobe, there is a gyrus just before the central sulcus known as the *motor strip,* which controls voluntary movement of the body. The neurons in the motor strip are the upper motor neurons. They are arranged on the strip like an upside-down person (a homunculus), with the neurons on the top of the motor strip controlling the feet and legs. Those in the middle control the trunk and arms, and those at the bottom control the face and tongue. Figure 4-6 shows which areas of the body the motor strip controls. (Notice that areas such as that for the hand, which makes many fine movements, take up more of the motor strip than areas for the back.)

The axons from the motor strip descend through the brain; most cross to the opposite side at the lower portion of the brain. From there, most axons continue down the spinal cord and synapse onto the next neuron—the lower motor neuron—and from there leave the spinal cord and branch out into the body. This pathway, composed of upper motor neurons descending from the brain and converging on lower motor neurons in the spinal cord, is known as the *pyramidal tract.* Because most of the axons cross over,

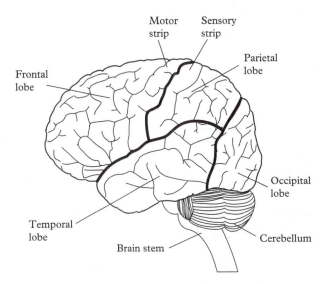

■ FIGURE 4-5 The lobes of the cerebral hemispheres

the left side of the brain controls the right side of the body, and the right side of the brain controls the left side.

In the frontal lobe, there is an area found only in one hemisphere, known as *Broca's area* (see Figure 4-7). For almost all right-handed individuals and approximately 70% of left-handed individuals, Broca's area is found in the left cerebral hemisphere. For the remaining population, it is in the right cerebral hemisphere (Rasmussen & Milner, 1977). This area is associated with the motor movements needed for speech.

Parietal lobe. The lobe posterior to the central sulcus is the parietal lobe (see Figure 4-5), located above the lateral sulcus and extending to near the back of the brain. The parietal lobe detects and interprets sensory information such as pain, pressure, temperature, form, shape, texture, and position. The gyrus that is directly behind the central sulcus in this lobe is the *sensory strip,* which receives information about simple bodily sensations. Like the motor strip, the sensory strip can be viewed as an upside-down person with sensations occurring in the feet and legs traveling to the top of the strip, while sensations on the face travel to the lower part of the strip (see Figure 4-6). As the sensory input moves from the sensory receptors in the skin and other parts of the body to the spinal cord and up to the brain, most cross to the opposite side of the body. Some cross over at the level of the spinal cord, while others cross over in the brain. This results in the right side of the body sending impulses to the left side of the brain and the left side of the body sending impulses to the right side of the brain.

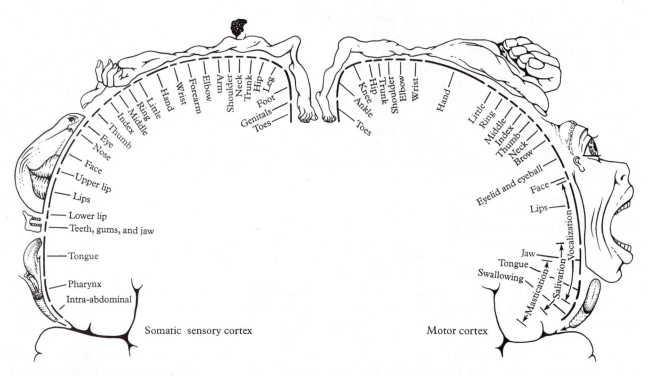

■ **FIGURE 4-6** The motor and sensory strips of the brain are associated with different parts of the body.

Other parts of the parietal lobe provide a higher level of interpretation and integration of sensory information. For example, damage to the part of the parietal lobe behind the sensory strip may result in a loss of the spatial perception needed for locating different parts of the body. For example, a man with parietal lobe damage may not be able to tell you where his hand is unless he is looking at it. The parietal lobe is also associated with some short-term memory functions.

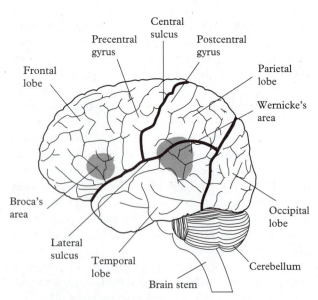

■ **FIGURE 4-7** Broca's area and Wernicke's area

Temporal lobe. The temporal lobe is located below the lateral sulcus (see Figure 4-5). The primary receptor area for auditory information is in the temporal lobe. Several other functions have been partially attributed to the temporal lobe, including long-term memory, categorization of material, and certain personality characteristics. Damage to this area in both hemispheres may result in almost complete deafness (see Chapter 5).

Primarily located in the temporal lobe is an area known as *Wernicke's area* (see Figure 4-7). Like Broca's area, Wernicke's area is located in only one of the cerebral hemispheres, usually the left hemisphere. Language comprehension is attributed to Wernicke's area.

Note that although language production and comprehension typically occur in the left hemisphere, the right hemisphere has been credited with understanding the prosody of language, or the melodic quality that informs a person if someone's verbal message is sarcastic, angry, or sincere. Other differentiations between the right and left hemispheres exist but are beyond the scope of this chapter.

Occipital lobe. The occipital lobe is located at the very back portion of each cerebral hemisphere (see Figure 4-5). It is the primary receptor area for visual information and the associated functions of vision. Damage to the occipital lobe in both hemispheres can cause blindness (see Chapter 5). Although the visual area (cortex) in the occipital lobe may detect visual images, the interpretation of a visual image requires the rest of the occipital lobe as well as other areas of the brain. The adjacent regions of the temporal and parietal lobes can provide additional information about how to assign meaning to the visual image.

For the complete interpretation of information and response, the lobes of the cerebral hemisphere work together, not only for visual interpretation but for other functions as well. Functions such as reading, writing, and calculating are not localized; they require the use of several different lobes. Neurons connecting to other neurons between the lobes provide a network of cognitive functions and processes to allow the person to function adequately.

Basal ganglia. Several internal structures of the cerebral hemispheres are important for proper functioning. Aggregates of somas, which resemble gray islands, are found among the white axons (see Figure 4-8). These islands are known as *basal ganglia* and are part of the extrapyramidal system, which means they are outside the pyramidal system. They work in conjunction with the motor strip. The basal ganglia play a role in controlling complex patterns of motor activity such as writing the letters of the alphabet. When the basal ganglia are damaged, the person can no longer provide the patterns; writing becomes very crude, as if one were just learning them (Guyton, 1992). The basal ganglia are also associated with inhibiting muscle tone throughout the body. Because of these different functions, damage to the basal ganglia can result in abnormal patterns of movement or very rigid muscle contractions. Damage to the basal ganglia is responsible for **athetoid** cerebral palsy.

Limbic system. The limbic system is made up of several different structures that are located near the middle of the brain (see Figure 4-9). Some of these are the *hippocampus, amygdala, olfactory bulbs, septum,* and *fornix.* The sense of smell was originally attributed to the limbic system. However, several additional functions of these structures have also been proposed. Some of these include species-specific behaviors (such as emotions and instincts), memory, and learning.

Thalamus. The thalamus is an egg-shaped mass of gray matter. Its primary function is to serve as a relay center of sensory impulses from the body and parts of the brain to the cerebral cortex.

Hypothalamus. The hypothalamus is located below the thalamus and is considered by some authorities

to be part of the limbic system. It activates, integrates, and controls several critical functions. The hypothalamus secretes hormones that influence the pituitary gland (the "master gland") that is responsible for the functioning of other glands. The hypothalamus also regulates water balance, body temperature, fluid intake, and sleep. It is also thought to play a part in the development of secondary sex characteristics such as facial hair. Additionally, the hypothalamus controls the ANS.

The Cerebellum

The cerebellum is an oval-shaped structure located below the occipital lobes of each hemisphere. Like the cerebral hemispheres, it has gray matter on the outer surface with many sulci and gyri, as well as white matter, on the inside (see Figure 4-4). The cerebellum has three main functions: (1) to regulate muscle tone, (2) to maintain balance and equilibrium of the trunk and limbs, and (3) to coordinate movements, including programming rapid movements and correcting the

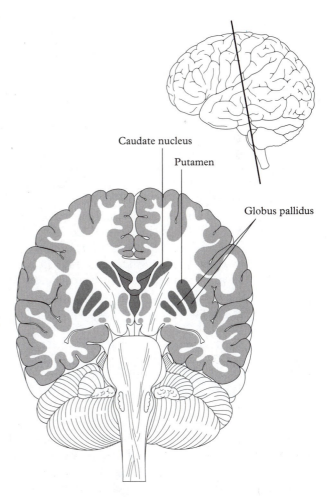

Caudate nucleus

Putamen

Globus pallidus

■ **FIGURE 4-8** The basal ganglia

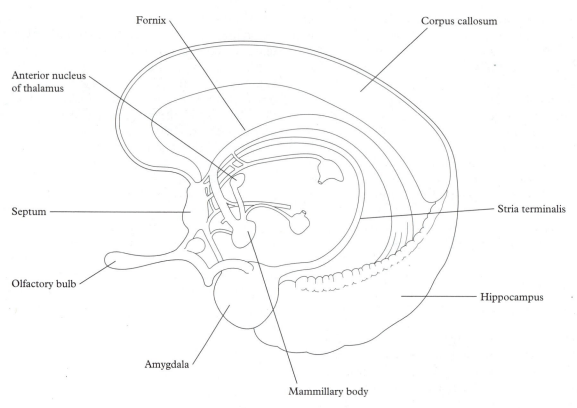

Fornix

Corpus callosum

Anterior nucleus
of thalamus

Septum

Stria terminalis

Olfactory bulb

Hippocampus

Amygdala

Mammillary body

■ **FIGURE 4-9** The limbic system

course of the movements. Damage to the cerebellum results in a form of cerebral palsy known as **ataxia**.

The Brain Stem

The brain stem is located below the cerebral hemispheres in front of the cerebellum (see Figure 4-4). The brain stem is composed of three areas: the *midbrain,* the *pons,* and the *medulla oblongata.* The brain stem is responsible for vital functions, such as the regulation of heartbeat, breathing, and blood pressure, as well as reflexes such as coughing, vomiting, and eye-pupil reflexes. Scattered throughout the brain stem are cell masses known as the *reticular formation,* which maintains states of sleep and wakefulness. The brain stem also functions as a relay center for motor and sensory activity taking place between the cerebral hemisphere and the spinal cord.

Radiating from the brain stem are 10 of the 12 cranial nerves. The two not included are the olfactory and optic nerves, which enter the brain at different sites. Cranial nerves are responsible for such functions as eye movement, sensation in some facial skin, chewing, movement of muscles of facial expression, hearing, swallowing,

neck movement, and tongue movements. Unlike the information flow to and from the cerebral hemispheres, the cranial nerves on the left side of the brain stem control the left side of the body, and the nerves on the right control the right side of the body.

The Spinal Cord

The spinal cord makes up the other part of the central nervous system. It is less than one-half an inch wide and approximately 18 inches long in the adult male. Unlike the brain, it is gray on the inside and white on the outside. The gray matter consists of the cell bodies and is arranged in the shape of an H (see Figure 4-10). The front part of the H is known as the *anterior horn* and carries the motor information. The back portion is known as the *posterior horn* and carries sensory information. The white matter surrounding the gray matter consists of axons; information is carried to and from the brain by bundles of axons known as *tracts.* The pyramidal tract, for example, carries impulses from the motor strip down the spinal cord where it synapses with lower motor neurons. To continue to transmit the impulses to the muscles, the peripheral nervous system is required.

THE PERIPHERAL NERVOUS SYSTEM (PNS)

The peripheral nervous system consists of the *spinal nerves* (nerves that directly exit and enter the spinal cord) and the nerves found throughout the body. The peripheral nervous system is responsible for sending and receiving information between the spinal cord and the body. These nerves serve all of the body except the head, which is served by the cranial nerves.

Spinal Nerves

Each spinal nerve consists of two roots: (1) an *anterior (front) root* that transmits impulses to cause motor movement (via motor neurons), and (2) a *posterior (back) root* that receives sensory information by way of sensory neurons. These two roots combine to make up a nerve that connects with the skin, muscles, and joints (see Figure 4-10).

The spinal nerves exit the spinal column through the bony vertebrae that surround and protect the spinal cord. There are 7 cervical vertebrae (bones of the neck), 12 thoracic vertebrae (bones of the back and chest), 5 lumbar vertebrae (bones of lower back), and 5 sacral and 4 coccygeal vertebrae (bones of the tailbone that are fused). These approximately correspond to the 8 cervical spinal nerves, 12 thoracic, 5 lumbar, 5 sacral, and 1 coccygeal nerve (see Figure 4-11). Each of the spinal nerves is numbered to correspond with

the vertebrae from which it exits. So, for example, the fourth thoracic spinal nerve exits by the fourth thoracic vertebrae.

Spinal nerves in the upper spinal cord send and receive information from the upper body. For example, some cervical and high thoracic nerves (C5 to T1) control arm movement and receive sensory information from the arms. The nerves that exit from the lower part of the spinal cord send and receive impulses from lower areas of the body. For example, some leg movement and sensation in the legs are transmitted by spinal nerves L1–S2. (For more extensive information, see Chapter 8.)

The spinal cord is shorter than the column of vertebrae; it ends at about the second lumbar (L2) vertebra. Several nerves extend beyond the spinal cord to their corresponding vertebrae. These spinal nerves are known as the *cauda equina* (horse's tail), which they resemble.

Reflex Arc

Several reflexes occur at the level of the spinal cord without brain involvement by what is known as a *reflex arc*. The most common example of a reflex arc is the knee-jerk reflex (see Figure 4-10). When a person's knee is tapped with a rubber hammer, the leg jerks forward because first, the sensory receptors in the quadricep muscle tendon pick up stretch pressure that is applied by the hammer. Then the sensory impulse travels through the peripheral nerve to the posterior horn of the spinal cord. The impulse then travels to the motor cell body in the anterior horn, which sends a motor impulse through

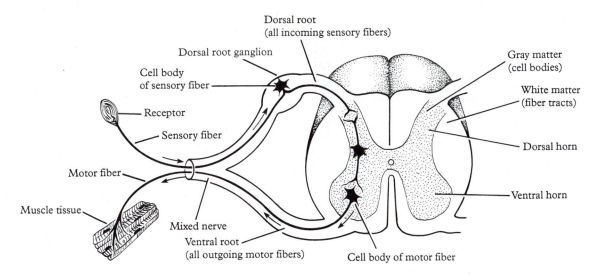

■ **FIGURE 4-10** A section of the spinal cord showing the reflex arc

the nerve and down the leg, and makes the leg muscle contract and kick forward. Impulses travel up the spinal cord to the brain for interpretation.

THE AUTONOMIC NERVOUS SYSTEM (ANS)

The autonomic nervous system controls the body's involuntary internal structures. It regulates such inter-nal structures as the heart, the smooth muscles around the arteries (blood vessels), the stomach, the intestines, the pupil of the eye, the sweat glands, and the tubes of the lungs (bronchi) and the bladder. The internal struc-tures are controlled by two subsystems of the autonomic nervous system, known as the *sympathetic* and the *parasympathetic* nervous systems.

The sympathetic and parasympathetic nervous sys-tems are located in different areas. The sympathetic

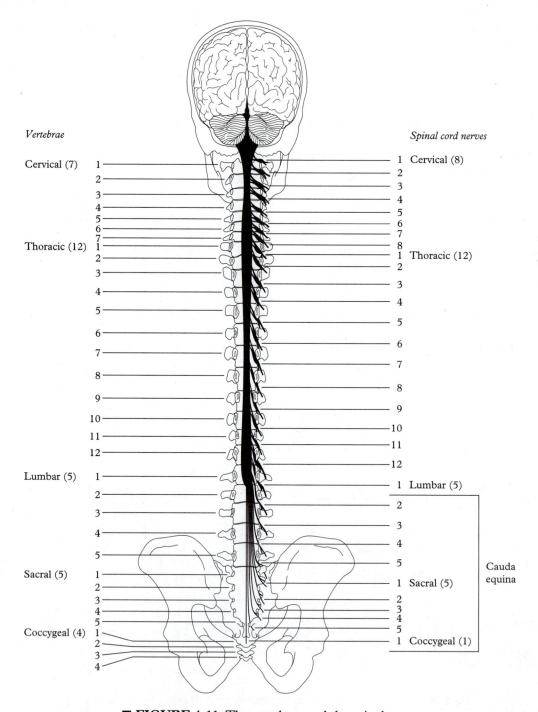

■ FIGURE 4-11 The vertebrae and the spinal nerves

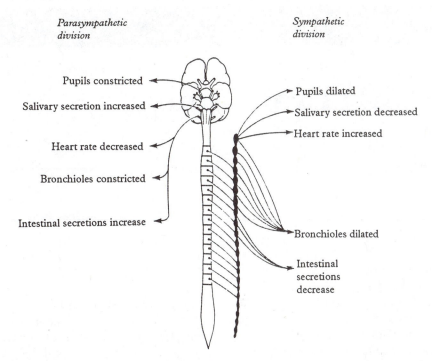

Parasympathetic division

Pupils constricted

Salivary secretion increased

Heart rate decreased

Bronchioles constricted

Intestinal secretions increase

Sympathetic division

Pupils dilated

Salivary secretion decreased

Heart rate increased

Bronchioles dilated

Intestinal secretions decrease

■ **FIGURE 4-12** The sympathetic and parasympathetic systems that compose the autonomic nervous system

nervous system is located beside the spinal cord as small clusters of neurons (see Figure 4-12). Impulses leave the spinal nerve through sympathetic nerve fibers that branch off the spinal nerves. These synapse with the small clusters of neurons. The impulse then goes directly to blood vessels or organs, or it reenters the spinal nerve. The parasympathetic nervous system leaves the central nervous system through the cranial and sacral spinal nerves. The clusters of neurons are located close to the organs they affect.

The sympathetic and parasympathetic systems have opposite roles. The sympathetic nervous system is responsible for such activities as increasing the heart rate, increasing blood pressure, dilating (enlarging) the bronchi (tubes) of the lungs, decreasing digestion, increasing sweat, and dilating pupils. The body's response to the influences from the sympathetic nervous system is to prepare for fight or flight. If a person is surprised by finding a burglar in the bedroom, for example, or by some other traumatic event, the sympathetic nervous system would dominate. The parasympathetic nervous system, on the other hand, does the opposite by decreasing the heart rate and increasing digestion. Together, the two systems work to maintain the balance of the internal environment.

SUMMARY

This chapter has presented an overview of basic neuroanatomy and neurophysiology. The neuron's structure and function were initially described to provide a foundation for understanding the nervous system, which was divided into the central nervous system, peripheral nervous system, and autonomic nervous system. The central nervous system consists of the brain and spinal cord; parts of the brain and spinal cord were explained. The peripheral nervous system consists of the nerves that transmit and receive information between the spinal cord and the body. The autonomic nervous system was discussed in terms of its two components, the sympathetic and parasympathetic nervous systems. All three of these systems work together to promote normal functioning. When there is injury, disease, or dysfunction in one or more of the components of the nervous system, disorders such as traumatic brain injury, seizure disorders, cerebral palsy, traumatic spinal cord injury, and spina bifida can occur. These will be discussed in the following chapters.

CHAPTER 5

Traumatic Brain Injury

A significant number of traumatic brain injuries (TBIs) occur in children and adolescents. In the United States, approximately 1 million children a year have some form of head injury; 165,000 require a hospital visit. About one in ten of these children has moderate to severe injury that interferes with their lives for months, years, or even permanently (Hutchison, 1992). Many of these children will have cognitive, language, physical, and behavioral problems when they return to school. Teachers are faced with the challenge of recognizing these students' deficits and providing appropriate interventions. In this chapter, we will present an overview of pediatric head injuries, including descriptions, etiologies, neuropathologies, characteristics, courses of recovery, means of detection, treatments, and educational implications.

DESCRIPTION OF TRAUMATIC BRAIN INJURY

A variety of terms may be used to describe injury to the brain. The two terms used most frequently are *head injury* and *traumatic brain injury*. Head injury includes *closed head injury,* which encompasses injuries that have not caused a skull fracture (break in the skull), and *open head injuries,* in which the skull has been penetrated. Since some studies have classified children with only lacerations (cuts) on the head as head-injured when there has been no brain injury (Goldstein & Levin, 1987), the term *traumatic brain injury* has been viewed as a more specific term. It includes injuries that have, as well as those that have not, resulted in a skull fracture.

Usually, one or more of the following symptoms will be present in traumatic brain injury: (1) changes in the level of consciousness, (2) posttraumatic amnesia of 5 minutes or more, and (3) physiological evidence found through physical examination or diagnostic testing (Bigler, 1987). Although brain injury can occur from near-drowning accidents, status epilepticus (a series of epileptic seizures occurring without interruption), cardiac arrests, abnormalities in fetal development, and other factors, traumatic brain injury usually refers to acquired causes in which the brain is damaged by some type of trauma (injury).

ETIOLOGY OF TRAUMATIC BRAIN INJURY

A number of etiologies underlie pediatric traumatic brain injury. When it occurs in a child less than 2 years old, traumatic brain injury may be a result of child abuse (Dykes, 1986). Infants can sustain severe developmental and neurological damage, even death, when shaken. This syndrome, known as the Whiplash Shaken Infant syndrome (or shaken infant syndrome), presents itself with no external signs of trauma to the head or neck but with signs of intracranial injury such as increased head circumference (swelling), increased **intracranial** pressure (pressure in the head from swelling), lethargy, irritability, retinal hemorrhage, and bulging anterior fontanel (Dykes, 1986).

TBI can also occur accidentally. In young children, accidental falls are one of the most frequent causes of TBI (Bagamato & Feldman, 1989). In adolescents, motor vehicle accidents are the most common cause. However, infants and young children are at risk in car accidents because the head often becomes the point of impact; infants' heads are heavy, and their neck muscles are weak. Other frequent etiologies include sports accidents (such as trampoline accidents) and unsuccessful suicide attempts (such as a leap from a building or a self-inflicted gunshot wound that results in brain injury) (Parmelee, Kowatch, Sellman, & Davidow, 1989).

DYNAMICS OF TRAUMATIC BRAIN INJURY

Depending on the cause of the traumatic brain injury, different effects on the brain may be present. The type of effects depends on whether the injury results from penetration, such as from a gunshot, or from acceleration, such as might occur in a car accident. The difference in the amount of injury inflicted by a penetration wound and an acceleration wound can be quite dramatic. A blow of moderate intensity to a movable head can produce devastating brain damage, but a blow 20 times that intensity to a rigidly fixed head may produce very little damage. In fact, a car has been reported to have fallen on the supported head of an auto mechanic and resulted in crushing the face bones and skull but leaving the neurological system without injury (Pang, 1985). If the mechanic's head had hit the car's dashboard in an auto accident with the same force, the results would have been quite different.

A penetration injury often produces very specific (focal) effects. For example, a bullet that goes through the motor strip in the left hemisphere will typically result in impairments or paralysis on the right side of the body. Several complications may result from this type of injury, such as hemorrhage or the embedding of bone fragments in parts of the brain. Although certain types of penetrating injuries can cause diffuse effects, the primary brain damage in penetrating injuries occurs at the site of injury, with secondary effects in other areas due to complications.

The vast majority of traumatic brain injuries occur as the result of an impact such as in a car accident. This is known as an acceleration injury, and it causes nonspecific and diffuse brain damage. In an acceleration injury, damage results from the brain moving against the skull. The brain is suspended in cerebrospinal fluid, so when there is a blow to the head, the brain is thrown against the skull—this is called the coup—and then the brain is thrown back and hits the opposite side of the skull (contracoup) (see Figure 5-1). Usually, the brain continues to move back and forth, hitting the inside of the skull several times; this results in further injury (Bagamato & Feldman, 1989). At the sites of impact on the cerebral cortex (coup and contracoup), a contusion (bruise) or hemorrhage (bleeding) results. (Note that in the example, the auto mechanic's brain could not move back and forth and strike against the inner walls of the skull.)

Further damage is caused by an acceleration injury because of the several sharp, bony protrusions of the skull at the base of the brain. As the brain oscillates back and forth, it rubs against or strikes these protrusions, and the brain is usually contused (bruised) on the

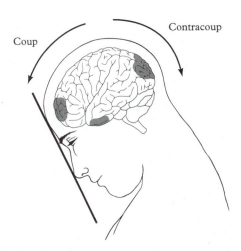

■ **FIGURE 5-1** Traumatic brain injury showing coup and contracoup damage

undersurface of the temporal and frontal lobes, regardless of the location of the impact (Ghajar & Hariri, 1992; Hutchison, 1992) (see Figure 5-2).

In an acceleration injury, damage can also occur due to a shearing (breaking) effect on the neurons, which results in more diffuse and nonspecific damage. This brain damage results as the brain tissue twists from the rapid acceleration of being thrown back and forth. The neuronal fibers (axons) that connect different brain regions are stretched by the acceleration, which results in a shearing and tearing of the connections. This is known as a *diffuse axonal injury* (DAI). It may occur throughout the brain, but more frequently occurs in the deep, white area of the brain and brain stem (Bigler, 1987).

In infants less than 5 months of age, an unusual type of brain injury may be present in which gross and extensive tears occur in the subcortical white matter of the temporal, orbital, and frontal lobes. This may be due to the soft consistency of the infant's unmyelinated brain (Bagamato & Feldman, 1989).

When traumatic brain injury occurs, secondary injuries may also occur. One common secondary injury is a *subdural hematoma*—a compact mass of blood located below the dura mater (one of the membranes surrounding the brain). It is caused by a laceration (tear) of the cerebral veins. The blood slowly accumulates between the cerebral cortex and dura covering. A particularly high prevalence (79%) of subdural hematoma has been found in infants with brain injuries. This may be because the connective tissue is not as tough or supportive of the thin-walled veins in infants as it is in adults (Bigler, 1987). Hematomas, such as epidural hematomas, can occur in other areas of the brain; these are more associated with the breaking of a cerebral artery due to a fractured skull than with shearing forces.

In this type of hematoma, bleeding may be quick, resulting in rapid neurological changes. Depending on the type and location, the hematoma can cause decreasing levels of consciousness, hemiparesis, **nystagmus**, ataxia, seizures, and death. Fortunately, medical intervention can usually minimize the hematoma's effects.

Another significant secondary injury is cerebral edema (swelling of the brain). Edema is an excessive accumulation of fluid in the cells or tissue spaces—fluid that comes from inside the cells and from the blood vessels (Gerring & Carney, 1992). As the brain swells, it becomes restricted by the skull, which impedes blood flow to the brain. The neurons of the brain are particularly sensitive to a decrease or lack of oxygen resulting from impeded blood flow. Because of this, the nerve cells die, causing more damage. The edema can also lead to structural compression of the brain tissue, which leads to cell loss. Since the brain has nowhere to go in an enclosed skull, herniation of the brain tissue can result. Herniation is the pressing of the brain through the opening (foramen) in the skull where the spinal cord exits, as shown in Figure 5-3. As the brain herniates, it displaces the brain stem, which is responsible for such vital functions as breathing. This can lead to death. In an infant with an open suture (soft spot on the top of the head), the brain can expand outward. However, the skull is usually unable to expand quickly enough, and cerebral blood flow is impeded (Bagamato & Feldman, 1989). Often, these secondary injuries can be more neurologically damaging than the primary ones.

A loss of consciousness may occur in traumatic brain injury. A transient loss of consciousness lasting less than 24 hours is considered a *concussion*. A loss of consciousness that can last for hours, days, or months is known as a *coma*. A child in a coma cannot be aroused by the usual verbal, sensory, or physical means of stimulation.

TBI has been classified by measures such as the Glasgow Coma Rating Scale (see Table 5-1). Typically, eye opening, verbalizing, and the ability to make motor movements are assessed. A mild TBI is rated on this scale as an initial score of 13 to 15, moderate TBI as a score of 9 to 12, and severe TBI as a score of 8 or less (Jaffe et al., 1992). Children who have a rating of 7 or below are considered to be in a coma. Adaptations of this scale have been made for infants and toddlers.

As the child progresses from a coma with no responses to a more alert state, he or she will go through a number of stages. As presented in Table 5-2, a child may go through the early stages of a generalized response, followed by a localized response to stimulation. The middle stages usually consist of different levels of confusion. The late stages are associated with automatic-appropriate activity, followed by purposeful-appropriate activity (National Task Force, 1988; Ylvisaker, 1986).

Several studies in the early literature reported that the duration of a coma is correlated with the expected outcome. However, there is now a general consensus that a better indicator is the duration of the amnesia that follows an injury—also known as posttraumatic amnesia (PTA). PTA has been defined as the period of time after the trauma when the child is not storing continuous memories (Gerring & Carney, 1992). It may occur without any loss of consciousness preceding or following a concussion or coma. PTA may range from a few minutes to several months (Ewing-Cobbs, Fletcher, & Levin, 1986). Unfortunately, PTA cannot be directly

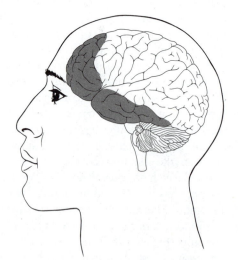
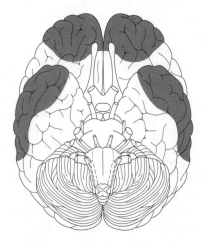

■ **FIGURE 5-2** Areas of the brain that are commonly damaged in traumatic brain injury

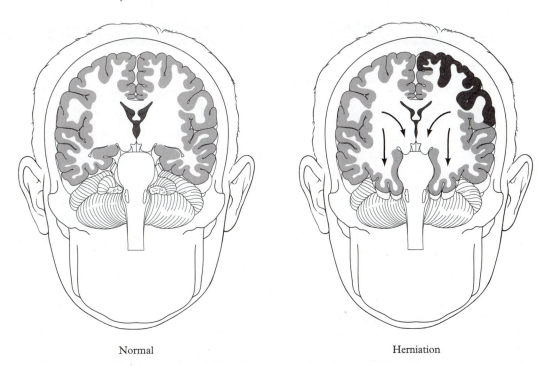

Normal

Herniation

■ **FIGURE 5-3** Herniation of the brain

TABLE 5-1

Measurements of the Severity of Coma

Area score	Glasgow Coma Scale (GCS) (Teasdale & Jenner, 1974)	Modified for Infants and Young Children	
		James, 1986; Modification of GCS	Ewing-Cobbs et al., 1988; Modification of GCS
Eye opening			
4	Spontaneous	★	★
3	To verbal stimuli	★	★
2	To pain	★	★
1	None	★	★
Verbal			
5	Oriented	Coos, babbles	Babbles, attempts communication, gestures
4	Confused	Irritable cries	Cries to indicate need
3	Inappropriate sounds	Cries to pain	★
2	Nonspecific sounds	Moans to pain	★
1	None	None	★
Motor			
6	Follows commands	Normal spontaneous movement	Goal-directed movement (for example, reaching)
5	Localizes pain	Withdraws to touch	★
4	Withdraws to pain	Withdraws to pain	★
3	Flexion response to pain	Abnormal flexion	★
2	Extension response to pain	Abnormal extension	★
1	None	None	

*No change from GCS

SOURCE: Based on "The Glasgow Coma Scale," by G. Teasdale and B. Jeanett, 1974, *The Lancet*, 2(81). Copyright ©1974 The Lancet Ltd. Used with permission.

TABLE 5-2

Rancho Los Amigos Hospital Scale

Level I	*No response*—Patient is unresponsive to stimuli.
Level II	*Generalized response*—Patient reacts inconsistently and nonpurposefully to stimuli. Responses are limited and often delayed.
Level III	*Localized response*—Patient reacts specifically but inconsistently to stimuli. Responses are related to type of stimuli presented, such as focusing on an object visually or responding to sounds.
Level IV	*Confused, agitated*—Patient is extremely agitated and in a high state of confusion. Shows non-purposeful and aggressive behavior. Unable to fully cooperate with his/her treatments due to short attention span. Maximal assistance with self-care skills is needed.
Level V	*Confused, inappropriate, nonagitated*—Patient is alert and can respond to simple commands on a more consistent basis. Highly distractible and needs constant cueing to attend to an activity. Memory is impaired with confusion regarding past and present. The patient can perform self-care activities with assistance. May wander and needs to be watched carefully.
Level VI	*Confused, appropriate*—Patient shows goal-directed behavior but still needs direction. Follows simple tasks consistently and shows carryover for relearned tasks. The patient is more fully aware of his/her deficits and has increased awareness of self, family, and basic needs.
Level VII	*Automatic, appropriate*—Patient appears oriented in home or hospital and goes through daily routine automatically. Shows carryover for new learning but still requires structure and supervision to ensure safety and good judgment. Able to initiate tasks in which he/she has an interest.
Level VIII	*Purposeful, appropriate*—Patient is totally alert, oriented, and shows good recall of past and recent events. Independent in the home and community. Shows a decreased ability in certain areas but has learned to compensate.

SOURCE: Reprinted from *An Educator's Manual: What Educators Need to Know about Students with Traumatic Brain Injury*, edited by Ronald C. Savage, Ed.D., and Gary F. Wolcott, M.Ed., pp. 21–22, for the National Head Injury Foundation. Reprinted by permission of the National Head Injury Foundation. Copyright ©1988.

evaluated in nonverbal infants and toddlers, but cognitive functioning can be described (Bagamato & Feldman, 1989).

Frequently, traumatic brain injury has been divided into categories based on length of posttraumatic amnesia. A very severe injury typically has PTA for more than 7 days, a severe injury from 1 to 7 days, a moderate injury from 1 to 24 hours, a mild injury from 5 minutes to an hour, and a very mild injury has PTA of less than 5 minutes (Bigler, 1987). At one time, little attention was given to individuals with mild (and very mild) traumatic brain injury, even though 75% of TBI cases may be categorized as mild. This is partly because in a mild injury, there are no skull fractures and no abnormalities appear on neurological exams (Novack, Roth, & Boll, 1988). Often, children with mild injuries have cognitive impairments that go undetected until difficulties occur in classroom activities. More efforts are being made to explore the effects of mild injury.

CHARACTERISTICS OF TRAUMATIC BRAIN INJURY

Traumatic brain injury may adversely affect a child's thinking, language processing, speaking, seeing, hearing, movement, and behavior. The extent to which the child is adversely affected depends on the severity of injury. The greater the degree of brain injury, the greater the magnitude of the deficits (Jaffe et al., 1992).

Following a mild traumatic brain injury, there are often a variety of vague and subjective problems that fall under the category of *postconcussive syndrome* (PCS). These problems include dizziness, headache, irritability, anxiety, blurred vision, insomnia, fatigue, distractibility, and memory problems. There can also be deficits in manual dexterity and social comprehension, as well as perceptual motor slowing (Slater, 1989). These symptoms can persist for months or years. Although many symptoms will dissipate over time, some researchers have demonstrated residual cognitive deficits (Mahon & Elger, 1989).

Children with moderate and severe traumatic brain injury will have more dramatic cognitive, language, motor, sensory, and behavioral deficits. These may persist for months or years, or they may be permanent. The length of time will depend on the severity of the injury. A discussion of each of the major problems found in these domains follows. A good understanding of these difficulties will help the teacher be alert for possible problems in the school environment.

Cognitive Effects

Several cognitive deficits may be present, including problems with retrieving information stored in memory, organizing information, sequencing, and generalizing. Also, perceptual and attention deficits, poor judgment, decreased abstraction, decreased learning abilities, deficits in processing information, rigidity, and inflexibility may occur (Kreutzer, Devany, Myers, & Marwitz, 1991; National Task Force, 1988).

The most common impairment following pediatric brain injury is memory loss (Jaffe et al., 1992). Some researchers have found that the ability to remember and retrieve information differs according to the severity of the injury. For example, severely injured children would do worse than those with mild injuries (Ewing-Cobbs et al., 1986). After the injury, a child might not remember what happened before the accident (retrograde amnesia) or what happened after the accident (anterograde amnesia). However, memory functions in general may be affected for some time after the injury. Memory defects have included short-term memory loss that interferes with new learning, long-term memory loss that involves forgetting what was previously learned, difficulty returning to old tasks after interruption, and inconsistent memory function that causes misinterpretation and confusion (National Task Force, 1988).

The child may be easily distracted and concentrate poorly, which may lead to difficulty following instructions and an inability to shift attention. Difficulty organizing information may include problems with summarizing, sequencing, outlining, and differentiating more relevant from less relevant information. Impaired problem-solving may take the form of being inflexible in the selection and use of learning strategies, a limited ability to use divergent or convergent thinking, and an inability to anticipate the consequences of actions.

Deficits in cognitive abilities have a negative impact on academic learning. A decline in all academic areas, including reading comprehension, spelling, math, and language and vocabulary has been found to occur. Reading comprehension is one of the most impaired abilities for many students having from one to several years' delay (Shaffer, Bijur, & Rutter, 1980).

Speech and Language Effects

Speech and language impairments can take the form of motor-speech disorders or expressive and receptive language deficits. One motor-speech disorder known as *posttraumatic mutism* has been found in about 3% of 350 children and young adults with moderate-to-severe head injury. In this condition, the individual cannot speak at all but can communicate nonverbally. In some cases, this form of mutism has been found to continue 12 months after the injury (Ylvisaker, 1986). Another motor-speech disorder is *dysarthria,* which includes articular imprecision, phonatory weakness, hypernasality, and a slow rate of speech (Ylvisaker, 1986).

The most frequently cited language impairments are naming, retrieving words, and organizing ideas expressively (Jordan, Ozanne, & Murdoch, 1988). Although there may be impairments of the auditory comprehension of language, this has been less commonly identified. Defects in this ability, however, probably occur because the general processing of information is defective. In studies of the rate of comprehending speech or written information, children with traumatic brain injury were found to respond in a delayed manner and to need extra time. Also, difficulties in understanding verbal abstraction (metaphor, synonym) and high-level verbally mediated items (main idea) have been reported (Ylvisaker, 1986). A study by Braun, Baribeau, Ethier, Daigneault, & Proulx (1989) showed that individuals with severe TBI had difficulty processing facial affects, which may cause some difficulty in understanding.

Motor and Sensory Effects

When a child has TBI, there may be other physical involvement, including reduced motor speed, muscle weakness, reduced eye-hand coordination, and spatial disorientation (National Task Force, 1988). Two of the most common motor system disorders in children are spasticity and involuntary movement from the basal ganglia and other extrapyramidal structures. *Spasticity* is a state of increased muscle tone that can interfere with fine and gross motor movements such as ambulation and self-feeding. It can continue over time and result in contractures.

Several manifestations may occur as a result of damage to the basal ganglia or extrapyramidal system. The child may exhibit rigidity (sustained and rigid contractions of the muscles), dyskinesia (involuntary movements such as chorea, which consists of jerking, rapid movements of limbs), athetosis (slow, purposeless movements), akinesia (lack of movement of the affected part of the body in natural activities, such as crossing legs or making facial expressions), or resting tremor (fine shaking of extremities) (Pang, 1985).

Sensory impairment may also occur as a result of traumatic brain injury. The most frequent sensory impairment involves hearing loss that results from damage to the structures of the ear, auditory nerve, and portions of the brain that regulate hearing. Many symptoms of a sensorineural hearing loss may continue permanently, especially when the organ of Corti (organ in the inner ear) has been injured (Healy, 1982). Vision problems may also occur when the structures of the eye, eye tracts (optic nerve and optical pathways), or portions of the brain that process visual information are damaged. When vision loss occurs from traumatic brain injury, the extent and type of loss varies. In some instances, parts of the child's field of vision may be absent, or total blindness can occur on rare occasions (Gerring & Carney, 1992).

Another physical manifestation of TBI is seizures.

Seizures are common in children after brain injury, but only a small portion of children will go on to develop seizure disorders (epilepsy) (Kennedy & Freeman, 1986). Several types of seizures may occur. Although some may be convulsive, the majority are nonconvulsive and are often simple-partial or complex-partial seizures (see Chapter 6). Seizures may begin the first week following the trauma or not occur until years after the injury. About 90% of seizures occurring from traumatic brain injury will develop within the first 2 years after the injury (Bruce, 1990).

Behavioral Effects

Behavioral problems are likely to occur in children with traumatic brain injury. Due to the brain injury, there is often a release of activity from the limbic system; behaviors may emerge that are contrary to social norms (Pang, 1985). Damage to the frontal lobes causes a release of inhibition and, consequently, the injured person may behave inappropriately. The person with traumatic brain injury may be overreactive, restless, destructive, aggressive, prone to crying and having tantrums, impulsive, lacking in goal-directed behavior, apathetic, sexually aggressive, and socially uninhibited (McGuire & Rothenberg, 1986). But opposite types of behaviors may occur; the person may be apathetic, withdrawn, and poorly motivated.

Injury of the temporal lobe may result in other behaviors. Such injuries are common because the skull is rough at that point. With temporal lobe injuries, agitation and combative behaviors are often present, and behavior problems that were present before the accident (sometimes causing the accident) are exacerbated afterward (Ewing-Cobbs et al., 1986).

Other difficulties caused by a person's reaction to an injury include anxiety and depression. With severe brain injury, the reaction commonly is a "catastrophic reaction" in which the injured person is very depressed and withdrawn. Suicidal tendencies can appear (National Task Force, 1988).

Psychiatric disorders may occur in about one-half of those suffering from severe TBI. In one study, the rate of behavioral disturbances after severe TBI was 3 times higher than that of a control group 2 years after the injury (Ewing-Cobbs et al., 1986).

DETECTION OF TRAUMATIC BRAIN INJURY

Several diagnostic procedures are used to detect traumatic brain injury as well as to determine the long-term effects of the injury. Initial diagnostics include a full neurological evaluation to determine the extent of damage. A physical examination will be given, as well as blood tests, X-rays, and various brain imagery techniques will be used. During the physical examination, the neurologist will assess abnormalities and give the Glasgow Coma Scale if indicated. Brain imagery techniques will help determine the location of structural damage as well as the presence of a hematoma or edema. Commonly used neuroimaging techniques include the *computed tomography scan* (CT or CAT scan) and the *magnetic resonance imagery* (MRI) scanner. The CT scan uses a series of X-rays in different locations of the brain (see Figure 5-4), while the MRI uses the magnetic properties of the molecules to produce an image. Figure 5-5 shows an image of the brain using an MRI. Other tests—electroencephalogram (EEG), brain stem–evoked response (BSER), visual-evoked re-

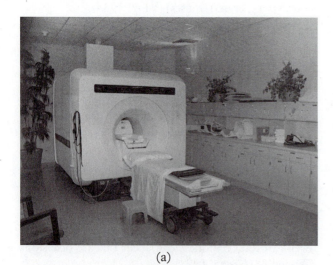

(a)

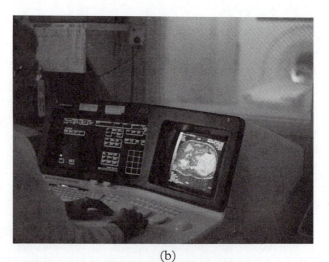

(b)

■ **FIGURE 5-4** CT scanner (a) and picture from a CT scanner (b)

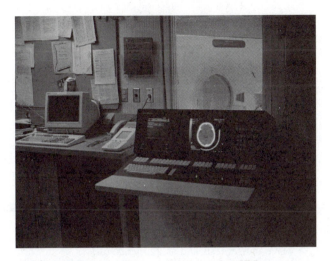

■ FIGURE 5-5 Picture of MRI with MRI scanner in the background

sponse (VER), audiological analysis—may be performed as well.

Assessment for residual problems resulting from the traumatic brain injury is also performed. Unfortunately, no simple test battery can assess all the possible impairments. Usually, a series of neuropsychological tests will be given to detect deficits, typically including tests of intelligence, adaptive behavior, problem-solving, memory, academics, motor performance, and psychomotor performance.

Children who do not receive a full battery of tests may be misdiagnosed as having no significant impairment. Many children with traumatic brain injury are severely debilitated by the effects of their injuries but may score within the normal range on simple standardized tests. This can occur in the school setting where simple reading, word recognition, and computation skills are assessed (Hutchison, 1992). Intelligence tests may also be misleading. IQ scores that fall into the normal range only reflect the child's retention of information that was stored before the injury (Mira & Tyler, 1991). A child can have a normal IQ but be unable to learn or process new information.

Because rapid changes occur during recovery, assessment of long-term effects must be an ongoing process. What a child cannot accomplish one day, he or she may be able to accomplish the next day, week, or month.

TREATMENT OF TRAUMATIC BRAIN INJURY

Treatment immediately following traumatic brain injury requires careful assessment and treatment of all injuries sustained in the accident. Equipment used to support vital functions (for example, ventilators) may

be needed for extensive injuries. Cerebral edema, which can cause death, will usually be controlled by medications. The surgical management of traumatic brain injury may include the repair of depressed skull fractures with removal of bony fragments and evacuation of intracerebral hematomas (Avery & First, 1994). Careful monitoring for complications and for the resolution of the injuries will be needed.

Treatment of the long-term effects of TBI requires coordinated team approach. Severely injured children will need inpatient rehabilitation, which may begin even while the child is comatose. In addition to the neurologist and other physicians, specialists will be involved in providing care. A physical therapist (PT) will be concerned with muscle tone, positioning, and ambulation. An occupational therapist (OT) may assist with the rehabilitation of fine motor control. A feeding team may be needed to determine how to achieve maximum nutrition and by which route feeding should be given. When speech and language difficulties occur, a speech and language pathologist will be needed to determine the appropriate treatment of language problems. A social worker will help provide family support; a nurse will provide care and training and be a liaison between the team members and the family; and a psychologist may help with the management of behavior problems (Hutchison, 1992).

After receiving hospital-based acute rehabilitation, the child may continue to receive rehabilitation on an outpatient basis. Some children will benefit from a postacute rehabilitation program. Some children with traumatic brain injury who are not quite ready for re-entry into the regular school system may have to be placed in a transition program that provides an educational setting with assistance from specialists before returning to school.

COURSE OF TRAUMATIC BRAIN INJURY

Children with traumatic brain injury may have minor to devastating deficits from the injury. Typically, recovery occurs rapidly during the first few months. Motor functions usually recover first; communication skills also tend to recover rapidly. However, more complex language skills, such as comprehending complex instructions and word finding, may continue to be difficult (Ylvisaker, 1986).

Recovery of the higher cognitive functions related to attention, memory, and behavior tends to occur more slowly. Typically, after rapid progress in the first few months, significant improvements continue over the first year; change will be slower after that. A gradual recovery of deficits usually occurs up to 5 years after the injury (Behrman, 1992).

At one time, the prognosis was considered to be age-related; that is, the younger the child, the less damage would occur from traumatic brain injury. Now it is clear that injuries in young children may have greater effects than those in adults (Thomsen, 1989). Because there are no longer clear correlations with age, misconceptions about the effects of age still persist (Hart & Faust, 1988) and may result in minimizing treatment for the child with TBI.

Intervention will be aimed at trying to restore normal function by providing training. Compensatory strategies will also be introduced; these may be needed permanently or may be discontinued when functioning improves.

EDUCATIONAL IMPLICATIONS OF TRAUMATIC BRAIN INJURY

Before a student with traumatic brain injury returns to school, all teachers and staff members who will be working with the child should receive information about TBI in general, as well as about the child's specific deficits. The staff should learn and then employ assessment and educational strategies in the classroom that help the student function optimally. This help can mean the difference between a student's experiencing success or failure in the program.

Training and simple explanations of traumatic brain injury should also be given to the student's peers. Classmates may be under the false impression that the student with traumatic brain injury will be unchanged; accurate information will dispel fears and allow smoother social interactions.

Meeting Physical and Sensory Needs

Physical disorders resulting from TBI can vary widely. Typically, a physical therapist and an occupational therapist will be involved in promoting motor and sensory function. Adapted equipment, such as adapted cups, spoons, prone standers, sidelyers, and microswitches, may be used. At times, various medications may be prescribed to treat seizures and spasticity. Surgical procedures have also been used to decrease spasticity and release contractures.

Students with traumatic brain injury often tire easily and have decreased endurance (see Box 5-1). Rest breaks will help with this problem. Some students may need a modified schedule that allows full periods as breaks; others may need a shortened day. In some instances, students may need more time to complete tests because their motor reactions are slower. For the same reason, getting from room to room may require more time or assistance. An informed staff is needed to

---

BOX 5-1

Compensatory Strategies for Physical Problems in a Classroom Setting

Problem: Fatigue and lack of endurance

STRATEGIES
- Schedule rest breaks. (T/S)*
- Have shortened day if needed. (T)
- Have scheduled period for rest. (T)
- Have more difficult subjects scheduled earlier in the day when students are more alert. (T)
- Have two sets of books: one at home and one at school so students don't have to carry them home. (T)
- Have shorter tests and assignments. (T)
- Allow students to sit rather than stand when possible.

Problem: Physical and sensory impairments

STRATEGIES
- Use adapted equipment. (T)
- Provide adaption to materials and activities to allow for student participation. (T/S)

---

*Strategies followed by the letter *T* in parentheses are to be implemented by the teacher. Strategies followed by *T/S* in parentheses can be used by either the teacher or the student. In the latter case, the teacher may initiate the use of the strategy and later require that the student use it independently.

SOURCE: From *Head Injury Rehabilitation: Children and Adolescents*, by M. Ylvisaker (Ed.). Copyright ©1985 Butterworth-Heinemann. Reprinted with permission.

---

work with students who have a seizure disorder due to the brain injury (see Chapter 6).

Some retraining may be needed to help the student compensate for sensory deficits. For example, one boy learned a simple, self-instructional procedure to remediate his visual neglect, which resulted in an increased scanning of items on his left side (Robertson, Gray, & McKenzie, 1988). Adaptive equipment as well as adaptations to the classroom, to instructional materials, and to instructional techniques may be needed. (See Chapter 29.)

Meeting Communication Needs

Language difficulties are one of the most destructive deficits in terms of academic functioning (see Box 5-2). When a student with an impairment has trouble finding a word, strategies such as guessing the category or subcategory, drawing or writing the word, saying the opposite word, or talking about it may be helpful

(Cohen et al., 1985). Other strategies include simplifying language, elaborating on messages to ensure effective transmission, repeating what is said to assist with processing, and using nonverbal means to communicate (Penn & Cleary, 1988). In some instances, augmentative communication systems may be used in addition to other forms of communication or as the main mode of communication (DeRuyter & Donoghue, 1989).

Sometimes students with disabilities, such as traumatic brain injury, will be asked by other children what happened to them. Depending on the age of the child and the severity of the injury, the teacher, parents, counselor, and child can formulate a simple explanation to convey the information. Explanations, such as "I hit my head in a car wreck, and it made me forget some things," may be helpful.

Meeting Learning Needs

Assessment

A student returning to school with TBI may or may not have undergone a battery of tests to assess cognitive functions. In one case, a girl fell out of a window and was taken to the emergency room; she had no apparent damage but failed the school year. The teacher was the one who noticed that some impairment had begun after the accident, which seemed to have caused cognitive deficits.

Even when a student with more severe TBI has been tested, she may not have undergone a full battery of neuropsychological tests but may have been given a single intelligence test (for example, WISC-III) to assess the deficits. Also, since there is some return of function for up to approximately 5 years, defects can improve after an assessment, so the teacher must keep in mind that the student's condition is not static. Studies have shown that the cognitive, physical, and behavioral effects of a brain injury do not remain fixed after the acute phase of the injury is over (Harrington & Levandowski, 1987).

Educational assessments of students with traumatic brain injury must be interpreted differently from the scores of other students. They cannot be used to predict future performance, only to mean that the student with traumatic brain injury could not perform the specific test items at the time of the testing (Cohen et al., 1985). To get a broad view of how the student is functioning, the teacher may, for example, want to observe the boy with a traumatic brain injury playing a board game. Can he organize by setting up the game? How well does he attend and process directions? Does he remember the steps involved and the content of the game? How well does he interact with peers (Cohen et al., 1985)? Additionally, observing the student during the daily routine will help the teacher target some possible deficits in functioning.

BOX 5-2

Compensatory Strategies for Language Problems in a Classroom Setting

Problem: Language comprehension (following directions). Students have difficulty understanding language that is spoken rapidly, is complex, or is lengthy.

STRATEGIES
- Limit amount of information presented—perhaps to one to two sentences. (T/S)*
- Use more concrete language. (T)
- Teach students to ask for clarification or repetitions or for information to be given at a slower rate. (T/S)
- Use pictures or written words to cue students: Use a picture of a chair and the written word *sit* if you want the students to exhibit that behavior. (T)
- Pair manual signs, gestures, or pictures with verbal information. (T/S)
- Act out directions: If the student is to collect papers and put them in a designated spot, demonstrate how this should be done. (T)
- Use cognitive mapping (Gold, 1984): Diagram ideas in order of importance or sequence to clarify content

graphically. This also helps students to see part-whole relationships. (T/S)

Problem: Difficulty understanding student

STRATEGIES
- Have student point to alphabet chart. (S)
- Have student use communication device.
- Have student point to pictures to communicate.

---

*Strategies followed by the letter *T* in parentheses are to be implemented by the teacher. Strategies followed by *T/S* can be used by either the teacher or the student. In the latter case, the teacher may initiate the use of the strategy and later require that the student use it independently.

SOURCE: From *Head Injury Rehabilitation: Children and Adolescents*, by M. Ylvisaker, (Ed.). Copyright ©1985 Butterworth-Heinemann. Reprinted with permission.

Learning Problems

Because of the cognitive problems a student with TBI may encounter, modifications may be needed in the educational program. Initially, the emphasis should often be on teaching the student the *process* of learning rather than on teaching specific content. This means having the student focus on attending to each task, following simple directions, and learning to shift from one task to another. For example, when a girl with traumatic brain injury first enters a group, she may only be able to listen to a story, watch activities, look at pictures, and listen to the staff talk. In a written activity, she may only be able to listen to the directions and complete the first step of the direction. It would not be uncommon for her to forget the directions shortly after they have been given; the teacher must be sure that she understands directions. The teacher should never take silence or an impulsive or incorrect answer at face value; the student may have a processing problem and should be taught to ask for assistance when needed. To determine whether there is a problem, the teacher should verify the student's understanding of the directions. Also, it is helpful if the material and assignments follow a logical progression from simple assignments to more complex ones. The teacher must be careful not to require too much at one time, because the student can be easily overloaded (National Task Force, 1988). When the student is doing well with the process of learning, content can be reintroduced.

Many strategies may be used to help the student with traumatic brain injury to clarify, organize, remember, and express his or her thoughts (see Box 5-3). Typically, these strategies assist in structuring parts of the learning process; they structure the environment or behavior, such as blocking out everything but the sentence the student is to read. Next, the teacher will cue the student to use compensatory strategies in a particular situation—in a sentence diagram, in problem-solving guides, and on cue cards. Typically, the teacher will spend a great deal of time teaching the student how and when to use these strategies and why they are to be used; then the student can use strategies independently.

Many types of strategies are available for use with cognitive problems. These include decreasing unnecessary distractions and verbalizations (limiting material), providing visual cues (sign on desk, diagrams using pictures or words, written or illustrated list of steps needed in tasks), and using a tape recorder. Often the student is taught to use cognitive behavior modification (cues, verbal rehearsal, and self-questions). The ability to self-monitor by using cues, symbols, or signs to assist storage and the ability to organize a task by using a checklist or visual cues, or by setting up the environment in a particular way are often crucial for student learning (Cohen et al., 1985). Other successful strategies include using a microcomputer to remediate attentional difficulties (Gray & Robertson, 1989) and using electronic memory aids such as a hand-held microcomputer (Giles & Shore, 1988) that not only shows time and does calculations but has a diary, alarm, and memo pad. These strategies can easily be implemented in the classroom. Whatever the strategy, care must be taken to see that it will generalize to a number of environments and that ample opportunities are available for the student to use the strategies in real-life situations in school, at home, and in the community.

School Placement

Depending on the severity of a child's impairment following hospitalization, the child may return to his or her original classroom or receive special services. If the child is to return to the same classroom as before the injury, certain modifications may be needed, including a reduced course load, special scheduling, rest breaks, a student aide, an extra set of books to avoid having to carry them between school and home, more time to complete tests, counseling, and other modifications (Mira & Tyler, 1991).

Many students with more serious traumatic brain injury will need a special education program. With the passage of the Individuals with Disabilities Education Act Amendments (IDEA), traumatic brain injury became a specific category of disability in special education. Placement of students with TBI varies according to needs, and when placement is being determined during the individual educational program (IEP) meeting, how best to meet the student's needs should be the primary consideration. Some students should be placed in a special transition class for students with traumatic brain injury. Others may do best in a self-contained or resource class of students with LD (learning disability), MR (mental retardation), OI (orthopedic impairment), or BD (behavior disorders). Other options include receiving special assistance or consultation from a special education teacher while in a regular class. A child with TBI presents unique problems and characteristics that do not typically fit into any single category. Because the nature of a child's deficits can change during recovery, placement changes may occur frequently.

Meeting Daily Living Needs

Because of possible cognitive, behavioral, and physical disabilities resulting from traumatic brain injury, the student may find daily living skills difficult to perform. In this case, a functional curriculum that includes instruction in daily living skills should be included in the

---

BOX 5-3

Compensatory Strategies for Cognitive Problems in a Classroom Setting

---

Problem: Attending. Students are unable to attend to auditory and visual information. They may do such things as talk out of turn or change the topic, be distracted by noise in the hall, fidget, or poke others. It is important to note that students may maintain eye contact and appear to be listening and actually not be attending.

STRATEGIES

- Remove unnecessary distractions, such as pencils and books. Limit background noise at first and gradually increase it to more normal levels. (T)*
- Provide visual cues to attend (e.g., have a sign on student's desk with the word or pictured symbol for behaviors, such as *Look* or *Listen.* Point to the sign when students are off task). (T)
- Limit the amount of information on a page. (T/S)
- Adjust assignments to the length of students' attention span so that they can complete tasks successfully. (T)
- Focus students' attention on specific information: "I'm going to read a story and ask *who* is in the story." (T)

Many of the strategies listed under memory and attending can also be used to improve language comprehension.

Problem: Memory. Students are unable to retain information they have heard or read. They may not remember where to go or what materials to use.

STRATEGIES

- Include pictures or visual cues with oral information, since this multisensory input strengthens the information and provides various ways to recall it. (T/S)
- Use visual imagery. Have students form a mental picture of information that is presented orally. Retrieval of the visual images may trigger the recall of oral information (Clark et al., 1984; Rose, Cundick, & Higbee, 1983). (T/S)
- Use verbal rehearsal. After the visual or auditory information is presented, have the students "practice" it (repeat it) and *listen to themselves* before they act on it (Dawson, Hallahan, Reeve, & Ball, 1980; Rose et al., 1983). (T/S)
- Limit the amount of information presented so that students can retain and retrieve it. (T/S)
- Provide a matrix for students to refer to if they have difficulty recalling information (Number Fact Chart). (T/S)
- Have students take notes or record information on tape. (T/S)

- Underline key words in a passage for emphasis. (T/S)
- Provide a log book to record assignments or daily events. (T/S)
- Provide a printed or pictured schedule of daily activities, locations, and materials needed. (T/S)
- Role-play or pantomime stories or procedures to strengthen the information to be remembered. (T/S)
- Write down key information to be remembered, such as who, what, where, when. (T/S)

Problem: Retrieving information that has been stored in memory

STRATEGIES

- Have students gesture or role-play. They may be able to act out a situation that has occurred but not have adequate verbal language to describe it. (T/S)
- Provide visual or auditory cues: "Is it __or __?" or give the beginning sound of a word. (T)
- Include written multiple-choice cues or pictures in worksheets. (T)
- Teach students to compensate for word-finding problems by describing the function, size, or other attributes of items to be recalled. (T/S)

Problem: Sequencing. Students have difficulty understanding, recognizing, displaying, or describing a sequence of events presented orally or visually.

STRATEGIES

- Limit the number of steps in a task. (T/S)
- Present part of a sequence and have students finish it. (T)
- Show or discuss one step of the sequence (lesson) at a time. (T)
- Give general cues with each step: "What should you do first? Second?" (T)
- Have students repeat multistep directions and listen to themselves before attempting a task. (T/S)
- Provide pictures or a written sequence of steps to remember: Tape a cue card to the desk with words or pictures of materials needed for a lesson, then expand original written directions. For example, if the direction was "Underline the words in each sentence in which *ou* or *ow* stands for the vowel sound. Then write the two words that have the same vowel sound," change it to "(1) Read the sentence; (2) underline *ou* and *ow* words; (3) read the underlined words; (4) find the two words that have the same vowel sounds; (5) write these two words on the lines below the sentence." (T)

Continued

BOX 5-3 *Continued*

Compensatory Strategies for Cognitive Problems in a Classroom Setting

- Tell students how many steps are in a task: "I'm going to tell you *three* things to do." (Hold up three fingers.) (T)
- Act out a seqence of events to clarify information. (T/S)
- Provide sample items describing how to proceed through parts of a worksheet. (T)
- Number the steps in a written direction and have the students cross off each step as it is completed. (T/S)
- Teach students to refer to directions if they are unsure of the task. (T/S)

Problem: Thought organization. Students have difficulty organizing thoughts in oral or written language. Students may not have adequate labels or vocabulary to convey a clear message; they may tend to ramble without getting to the point.

STRATEGIES
- Attempt to limit impulsive responses by encouraging the students to take "thinking time" before they answer. (T/S)
- Have students organize information by using categories, such as who, what, when, where. This strategy can be used in an expanded form to write a story. (T/S)
- Teach students a sequence of steps to aid in verbal organization: have the students use cue cards with written, pictured steps when formulating an answer. (T/S)
- Focus on one type of information at a time (e.g., main idea). (T/S)
- Decrease rambling by having students express a thought "in one sentence." (T/S)

Problem: Generalization. Students learn a skill or concept but have difficulty applying it to other situations (e.g., they may count a group of coins in a structured mathematics lesson but not be able to count their money for lunch).

STRATEGIES
- Teach the structure or format of task (e.g., how to complete a worksheet or mathematics problem). (T)
- Maintain a known format and change the content of a task to help students see a relationship: Two pictures are presented and students must say if they are in the same category or have the same initial sound; a worksheet format requires filling in blanks with words or numbers. (T)
- Change the format of the task: Have students solve mathematics facts on a worksheet as well as on flash cards. (T)
- Have completed sample worksheets in a notebook serve as models indicating how to proceed. (T/S)
- Demonstrate how skills can be used throughout the day: Discuss how students rely on the clock or a schedule to get up in the morning, begin school, or catch a bus. (T)
- Role-play in situations that simulate those students may encounter, emphasizing the generalization of specific skills taught: completing school assignments and going to the store may involve the same strategies (making a list or asking for help). (T)

---

*Strategies followed by the letter *T* are to be implemented by the teacher. Strategies followed by *T/S* can be used by either the teacher or the student. In the latter case, the teacher may initiate the use of the strategy and later require that the student use it independently.

SOURCE: From *Head Injury Rehabilitation: Children and Adolescents*, by M. Ylvisaker (Ed.), p. 390. Copyright ©1985 Butterworth-Heinemann. Reprinted with permission.

---

student's program. The skills to be taught will be determined by the student's team.

Meeting Behavioral and Social Needs

The classroom teacher should be able to provide appropriate intervention for students who manifest behavioral or social problems after they are injured. When the student demonstrates inappropriate behavior, several strategies may help control the behavior (see Box 5-4), including (1) setting up an organized, uncluttered environment to assist with disorientation or confusion; (2) using verbal and visual cues to help the student orient to a task; and (3) using printed or picture schedules as well as verbal cues to indicate a change of activity for students experiencing transition problems.

When inappropriate behaviors, such as hitting or talking-out, occur, behavior modification techniques have been used with varying success. For example, using a token system and awarding contracts have been successful in increasing compliant behavior in students with traumatic brain injury (Hegel, 1988). However, the use of extinction (ignoring the behavior) is often unsuccessful, probably because the method is too subtle. A direct approach is often needed, one that specifically informs the student about what to do or what not to do. Such directness helps the student with traumatic brain injury because understanding what is

BOX 5-4

Compensatory Strategies for Behavioral and Social Problems in Classroom Settings

Problem: Disorientation or confusion

STRATEGIES

- Provide an uncluttered, quiet environment. (T)★
- Provide printed or pictorial charts, schedules, or classroom maps that describe routines and rules of expected behaviors. Review these before each session and as needed throughout the day. (T)
- Maintain consistent staff, room arrangement, and materials. (T)
- Label significant objects and areas; provide name tags for staff. (T)
- Redirect undesirable behavior by focusing students' attention on tasks that are sufficiently interesting to break the pattern of disruptive or perseverative responses. (Note: Do not use this technique if the student's behavior is attention-seeking. Consultation with a behavior psychologist may be indicated.) (T)
- Teach students to look for permanent landmarks and name the landmarks when they come to them. (T/S)
- Have students verbalize how to go to a specific place before starting or while moving. (T/S)
- Use a buddy system. (T/S)

Problem: Transitions. Changing activities (e.g., moving from a reading group to a mathematics lesson or from a "free" period to a learning session).

STRATEGIES

- Provide verbal cues: "In five minutes it will be time for math"; "After our reading lesson, we will go to lunch." (T)
- "Walk through" transitions with the students: Return to reading at your desk, take out the math book, and move to the appropriate area for the math lesson. (T)
- Encourage students to refer to printed or pictorial schedules with changes of activities, materials, or lesson locations. (T/S)
- Have students observe peers for cues for what to do next. (T/S)

Problem: Beginning an activity. Students may not remember what to do, know what to expect, or know if they possess the skills needed to perform accurately.

STRATEGIES

- Explain the purpose of the lesson; relate following directions to functional, everyday situations, such as assembling a model car or reading a recipe. (T)
- Review printed or pictorial descriptions of how to do a task to relieve tensions that result from the student's not knowing what is expected. (T/S)

- Talk through several examples to help individuals get started. (T)
- Review pictorial or printed rules of behavior before each lesson: "Look, listen, raise your hand." (T/S)
- Praise students once they have begun a task, and remind them that they are capable of completing the activity. (T)
- Role-play or tell students what to say when they are initiating social contacts with peers. (T)

Problem: Ending an activity

STRATEGIES

- Emphasize closure of activities by giving students jobs such as collecting papers, cleaning up materials, or writing in their log books. (T/S)
- Encourage students to observe the behavior of others as tasks end. (T/S)
- List steps to the task and check them off when completed; emphasize where they are in relation to the final step. (T/S)
- List end-of-session behaviors: "Put papers in blue box, return to desk." (T/S)

Problem: Impulsive responses. Students with head injuries often call out answers during lessons, grab materials, begin activities before directions are provided, have difficulty taking turns, and may even leave the room or lesson without warning.

STRATEGIES

- Place unnecessary materials out of sight or out of reach. (T)
- Discuss rules and their importance at the beginning of the lesson. (T)
- Explain how students' impulsive acts (e.g., calling out) disturb others. (T)
- Role-play appropriate responses (e.g., raising hand). Place a sign on the student's desk with a picture of a hand and point to this when the student interrupts. (T)
- Employ "stop-action" technique: Immediately stop individuals from disrupting an activity, encourage them to verbalize an alternative behavior, and have them follow through appropriately. (T)
- Provide time at the end of a session for students to tell personal stories or jokes. (T)

Problem: Recognizing the need for help or asking for help

STRATEGIES

- Make students aware of what they can and cannot do: Expand tasks that are done successfully by adding one step that will be "harder." (T)

Continued

BOX 5-4 *Continued*

Compensatory Strategies for Behavioral and Social Problems in Classroom Settings

- Make asking for help a student goal and reinforce this heavily. (T)
- Attach cue cards to desk: "Raise your hand for help." (T/S)
- Decrease daydreaming that results from an inability to proceed by asking direct questions or by providing cue cards: "Are you stuck?" "Is it clear?" (T/S)
- Model desired behavior; role-play situations. (T)

Problem: Working independently. Individuals with head injuries may be hesitant to perform, even when they are able to do the task.

STRATEGIES
- Review directions or sample items. (T)
- Provide a written sequence to follow and thus circumvent memory problems and anxiety. (T/S)
- Assure them that they can complete the task. (T)
- Select only a portion of the task or short assignments to be completed independently. (T/S)
- Point to a sign ("Return to Work") when students stop working. (T)
- Use a timer intermittently, and reward students who are working when it rings. (T)
- Provide additional time for students who work slowly to complete tasks. (T)

Problem: Self-criticism or perseveration. Students may erase excessively, tear up papers, redo activities in an

effort to perform with pretraumatic efficiency, or refuse to participate in structured lessons.

STRATEGIES
- Emphasize what the individuals can do and point out progress that they have made: Compare recent past and present work. (T)
- Chart achievement of goals to build self-confidence. (T/S)
- Limit perseverative behavior by using verbal directions ("Erase only once") or by focusing attention on less threatening tasks. (T)

Problem: Aggression

STRATEGIES
- Redirect students. (T)
- Use key words in phrases. (T/S)
- Allow students to work it off. (S)

---

*Strategies followed by the letter *T* in parentheses are to be implemented by the teacher. Strategies followed by *T/S* can be used by either the teacher or the student. In the latter case, the teacher may initiate the strategy and later require that the student use it independently.

SOURCE: From *Head Injury Rehabilitation: Children and Adolescents,* by M. Ylvisaker (Ed.), p. 398. Copyright ©1985 Butterworth-Heinemann. Reprinted with permission.

---

appropriate in a particular context is often difficult. For example, telling a boy who talks too much in class to stop talking to his neighbor, or using a token system, would probably be more effective than planned ignoring (extinction).

Some students may be apathetic or depressed; some teachers may feel sorry for them and make excuses for bad behavior. The teacher must be firm and expect the student to do all work. Providing choices often helps. Another strategy is to attempt to get a peer group involved with the student.

If the student exhibits aggressive behavior, it is important for the teacher to understand that this behavior is not purposeful but is a reflexive action. Some ways to help deal with aggression include redirecting the student or offering an alternative action. When the student is restless or irritable, letting the student talk or do something physical may be calming and thus may avoid a confrontation. Sometimes having a key word or

phrase for the student to say when angry feelings begin will help the student decrease impulsive behavior (National Task Force, 1988).

Often students with TBI are unaware of their own behavior and lack the internal feedback to self-correct. Social skills training may be of help if it is adjusted to the processing and memory problems of the student (McGuire & Sylvester, 1987). Having simple interaction rules, such as "Don't stand too close" and "Ask the person if he is done with it," can help students interact with others more successfully.

When there is a lack of structure or appropriate goal-setting, frustration and undesirable behavior may result. Structure can be arranged by having a daily schedule, assigning tasks, setting limits, explaining changes in advance, and building in support systems. Appropriate goal-setting should occur with the student; it should be realistic and measurable and should include short- and long-term goals.

Leroy sustained a very severe head injury during a car accident when he was 8 years old. He was in a coma for 2 months and experienced extensive hospitalization and rehabilitation. His cognitive, language, physical, and behavioral functions were all severely impaired. Four years after this injury, Leroy is receiving special education services in a self-contained class, with some inclusion with regular students. He continues to have difficulty with long-term and short-term memory, distractibility, and inattention. Leroy is primarily nonverbal but uses an augmentative communication board to communicate. He has hemiparesis and no sensory impairments. Leroy often gets angry and yells out, waving his fist. Although Leroy has serious deficits, he has splinter skills, one in which he identifies any numeral. However, he cannot do simple addition. Although it has been 4 years since his injury, little assessment has been done regarding his progress. In accordance with his IEP, the teacher was working on picture identification, assuming that was the best he could do. It was not until he laughed at a misspelling on the bulletin board that the teacher discovered he could read. Although slow, return of functioning can continue for several years past the time of injury. Frequent assessment and reevaluation are necessary to determine changes.

A lack of inhibition is a very common type of behavior in pediatric brain injury. These behaviors consist of saying or doing things that would ordinarily be inhibited. Since these behaviors can lead to reaction by peers and teachers, the teacher must understand this as involuntary and educate peers as well (Deaton, 1987).

A lack of support may also add to the feelings of depression and withdrawal that are common in people with severe brain injuries. Since suicide is a possible reaction, the teacher must be alert for any mention of,

Marvlyn sustained a mild-to-moderate head injury when she fell out of a window at age 7 years. She had some problems with organization, short-term memory, impulsivity, and distractibility. It has been 6 months since her injury, and she is receiving her education in a regular education classroom in consultation with the special education teacher. To compensate for her impairment, the teacher has positioned Marvlyn where there are a minimal number of distractions. She has cue cards on her desk to remind her to "stop, think, then ask" to decrease her impulse responses. A token system is also used to target in-seat behavior. The teacher is very careful to be sure that Marvlyn understands all directions and often makes picture cues to assist with her memory impairment. A notebook organizational system and a checklist were provided to improve her organizational skills. With these modifications, Marvlyn can function and succeed in the classroom.

joke about, or threat of suicide. Professional help is needed in these circumstances.

SUMMARY

Traumatic brain injury is a diverse condition that may result in cognitive, language, physical, sensory, and behavioral impairments. The brain may be injured from such causes as child abuse or bicycle, car, or trampoline accidents. Primary damage to the brain may also be accompanied by such secondary damage as hematoma and edema. The effects of the traumatic brain injury may be transient or permanent. Students with traumatic brain injury may come to the classroom with a wide variety of difficulties that can adversely affect educational performance. Cognitive, language, physical, and behavioral problems should be identified and addressed. Teachers can use a number of strategies targeting these problems to help provide support to the student.

CHAPTER 6

Seizure Disorders

Seizures are one of the most common disorders of the nervous system in children. Seizures may occur as a symptom of a disorder or disease or as a chronic condition of the nervous system. The chronic condition is known as *seizure disorder* or **epilepsy.**

Seizures occur in approximately 5 children out of 1,000 (Epilepsy Foundation of America, 1994; Hauser & Hesdorffer, 1990), and the majority of those who develop seizure disorders will do so before age 20 (Holmes, 1992). Seizure disorders are found approximately 20 times more frequently in individuals with disabilities than in those without. Most people think of a person having a seizure as someone stiff and shaking uncontrollably on the ground, but there are many types of seizures with many different characteristics, prognoses, treatments, and educational implications.

Throughout history, misconceptions and prejudices about people with seizure disorders have been common. Often these people were considered to be possessed by evil spirits or by a divine presence. In primitive history, seizures were often attributed to evil spirits, and holes were cut through the brain to presumably let the evil spirits escape. Hippocrates wrote about seizure disorders 2,000 years ago in a work titled "The Sacred Disease." During the Middle Ages, individuals who had seizures were burned at the stake as witches or were thought to be possessed (Temkin, 1971); before the 20th century, they were frequently locked away in insane asylums or jails because they were considered insane. Because seizure disorders were thought to be inherited, mandatory sterilization of individuals with seizure disorders was required by law, which remained in effect in several states until 1971.

Even today, many misconceptions and social prejudices regarding individuals with seizure disorders persist. Classmates and adults who are not taught about the condition may fear being around a child with a seizure disorder. Teachers who lack understanding may not recognize certain behaviors as seizures or may not know what to do when a child has a convulsive seizure (a violent, involuntary contraction of the voluntary muscles). As the child with seizure disorders grows older, he or she may be denied access to certain extra-curricular activities. Later, employment opportunities may be missed. It is clearly important that the teacher understand the **etiology,** characteristics, detection, treatment, course, and educational implications of seizure disorders.

DESCRIPTION OF SEIZURE DISORDERS

Seizures

A *seizure* can be defined as a sudden, involuntary, time-limited disruption in the normal functions of the central nervous system, which may be characterized by altered consciousness, motor activity, sensory phenomena, or inappropriate behavior (Berkow, 1992; Holmes, 1992). Seizures may exhibit only one of these characteristics or different combinations, depending on the type.

Seizure Disorder/Epilepsy

Seizure disorder, also known as epilepsy, refers to a chronic condition in which the person has recurring seizures. A seizure that occurs as a result of a short-term condition, such as meningitis or a fever, is not considered symptomatic of a seizure disorder. At least two seizures that are unrelated to a short-term underlying cause must have occurred to be considered a seizure disorder.

ETIOLOGY OF SEIZURE DISORDERS

Seizures

Since a seizure may occur and not be part of a seizure disorder, it is important to know which conditions may cause a seizure. The ingestion of poisons, an overdose of drugs, head trauma, heat exhaustion, heat stroke, drug withdrawal, metabolic disorders (such as low blood sugar), and infections (such as meningitis or encephalitis) can all cause seizures. The most common cause of convulsive seizures in childhood is a high temperature. These are known as **febrile** seizures and can occur with temperatures above 102°F (39°C). They are typically found in children younger than 5 years of age (Hirtz, 1989). Box 6-1 is a summary of the various etiologies of seizures.

When seizures occur as a symptom of a short-term condition, the person will no longer have seizures once the condition is gone unless the condition results in damaged—scarred—nervous tissues. Because nervous tissue cannot regenerate, a scar may form when glial cells divide and fill up a neural space. Electrical activity causing seizures has been found to occur at these scarred areas (Schmidt, 1985). When the condition has caused a permanent lesion in the brain, seizures may continue to occur. The person would then be considered to have a seizure disorder.

Seizure Disorders

Seizure disorders are considered either **idiopathic** or *symptomatic*. Seizures that are called idiopathic occur for unknown reasons. Some theorists believe that some idiopathic seizure disorders may result when brain tissue is scarred by trauma or insult. Autopsies have shown that the brains of many individuals with seizure disorders considered to be idiopathic were scarred or contained lesions. However, others have hypothesized that inherited **metabolic** abnormalities may be the cause of most seizure disorders that are classified as idiopathic (Berkow, 1992). It should be noted that most theorists do not think seizures are hereditary, although there is family predisposition to certain types of seizures. Others, such as absence seizures, are considered to have a genetic basis, although the mechanism of inheritance is unknown.

Seizure disorders may also be classified as symptomatic; that is, there is a known, underlying cause, usually a chronic condition involving abnormalities of the brain. Tumors, **aneurysms,** abnormalities in the blood system, and congenital abnormalities of brain structures are only a few of the possible brain abnormalities that can result in seizure disorders. Such abnormalities may occur during fetal development or later in life.

A seizure disorder may occur as a single impairment or in conjunction with other impairments. Most individuals with seizure disorders have no other disability, but children with conditions such as cerebral palsy; traumatic brain injury; autism; moderate, severe, and profound mental retardation; and congenital infections have an increased incidence of seizures along with their other impairments.

DYNAMICS OF SEIZURE DISORDERS

We said earlier that neurons transport signals between the various areas of the brain as well as between the brain and the rest of the body by electrochemical means. During a seizure, there is abnormal, sudden, excessive, and disorderly electrical firing of neurons in the brain. Some people like to visualize this as an electrical storm. For a seizure to occur, the electrical activity must reach a certain threshold of excitation—often referred to as a *seizure threshold.* Everyone has a threshold of excitation that will result in a seizure under certain circumstances.

There are many different types of seizures; the type depends on which part of the brain is affected. Electrical stimulation of certain parts of the brain can result in the movement of body parts (including such complex movements as running), tingling sensations, visual images, and certain smells. Anything the brain can do, a seizure may also do.

In most instances, the cause of a seizure is unknown. Seizures may occur in response to certain stimuli originating inside or outside the body. For individuals who have a seizure disorder, internal stimuli (such as excess fatigue, lack of sleep, illness, fever, excessive alcohol

---

BOX 6-1
Causes of Seizures

1. Drugs and poisons
2. Traumatic brain injury
3. Low oxygenation levels
4. Metabolic disorders (for example, hypoglycemia)
5. Infections
6. Congenital abnormalities (for example, aneurysms)
7. High fever
8. Chemical imbalances (for example, electrolyte imbalances)
9. Seizure disorder
10. Tumors

consumption, or withdrawal from an antiepileptic medication) may precipitate a seizure. Some seizures may be triggered by such external stimuli as flashing lights (for example, strobe lights), visual patterns (for example, reflecting geometric designs), or certain sounds (for example, a fire alarm) (Dreifuss, 1983).

Anyone can have a seizure, even when there is no abnormality in the brain. Under certain circumstances, such as a lack of oxygen or low blood sugar, the brain can have an abnormal electrical discharge that results in a seizure.

CHARACTERISTICS OF SEIZURE DISORDERS

Different types of seizures have different characteristics, treatments, and prognoses. One of the most commonly used classification systems is *The International Classification of Epileptic Seizures,* in which seizures are placed into three main categories: partial seizures, generalized seizures, and unclassified seizures. *Partial seizures* are those that occur in one area of the brain in one cerebral hemisphere. *Generalized seizures* occur in both cerebral hemispheres. In some instances, a seizure may begin in one area of the brain and then move to both cerebral hemispheres. This is known as a *partial seizure with secondary generalization.* Box 6-2 shows an outline of the major types of seizures, and Figure 6-1 illustrates some possible brain locations of seizures.

Partial Seizures

Partial seizures are divided into *simple partial seizures, complex partial seizures,* and *complex partial seizures evolving to secondary generalized seizures.* Partial seizures account for a large percentage of seizures in children, approximately 40% (Behrman, 1992).

Simple Partial Seizure (SPS)

In simple partial seizures, there is one focal (localized) area of electrical discharge that can cause motor, sensory (somatosensory), autonomic, or psychic responses, depending on the location of the seizure activity. Unlike other forms of partial seizures, simple partial seizures result in no impairment of consciousness (Wyllie, Rothner, & Luders, 1989). The person is awake and alert as the seizure occurs. These seizures are usually brief, lasting about 10 to 30 seconds. For those unfamiliar with seizures, simple partial seizures may be dismissed as nothing important or missed altogether.

The most common type of simple partial seizure produces motor symptoms. In this type, the abnormal bursts of electrical impulses occur in the neurons on the motor strip. Depending on the location of this electrical

---

BOX 6-2

Types of Seizures (Based on the International Classification System)

   I. Partial Seizures
      A. Simple partial
         1. Motor
         2. Sensory
         3. Autonomic
         4. Psychic
      B. Complex partial
      C. Partial seizures with secondary generalization
  II. Generalized Seizures
      A. Absence
         1. Typical
         2. Atypical
      B. Generalized tonic-clonic
      C. Tonic
      D. Clonic
      E. Myoclonic
         1. Typical myoclonic of early childhood
         2. Complex myoclonic of early childhood
         3. Juvenile
         4. Infantile spasms
      F. Atonic
 III. Unclassified

---

activity on the motor strip, any part of the body may be involved (see Chapter 4). If the electrical activity occurs on the part of the motor strip that moves the arm, the arm will make a jerking motion during the seizure. If it occurs near the top of the motor strip where the foot is controlled, the foot will move. Even very small muscles, such as those controlling the movement of a finger or facial muscle, can be affected. Simple partial seizures of the motor area may involve one select area (such as the foot) or may spread to other motor areas along the motor strip. When this occurs, the foot may move, then the lower leg, then the upper leg; this may continue down the motor strip. This sequential involvement of body parts is referred to as a "Jacksonian march" (Holmes, 1992; Wyllie, Rothner, & Luders, 1989).

Simple partial seizures with somatosensory involvement result from abnormal electrical discharge occurring along the sensory strip or other sensory centers in the brain. Any kind of sensation may occur. This type of seizure may result in a feeling of numbness or tingling in any body part. When the electrical activity occurs on the sensory strip, the resulting seizure may remain in one location or travel to adjacent areas. Other seizures may be caused by an abnormal burst of electrical impulses in special sensory areas. This may cause the individual to smell a certain odor or have a particular taste in the mouth. Visual hallucinations (for example, lights or bright color) and a feeling of falling or floating can be present as well.

Simple partial seizures may produce autonomic symptoms if they involve the autonomic nervous system. Symptoms may include a fast heart rate, dilation of the pupils of the eye, or "goose bumps" (piloerection). Complaints of abdominal pain have been reported, although this is rarely a seizure.

Simple partial seizures may occur with psychic symptoms when higher cortical functions are involved. The individual may feel certain emotions, have hallucinations, or experience other disturbances in cognitive functioning. Although psychic symptoms can occur as a simple partial seizure, they are more often associated with more complex seizures.

All of the described simple partial seizures may occur as an *aura*—a simple partial seizure that precedes a more complex seizure. Auras are often present before a complex partial seizure or a tonic-clonic seizure. The aura can serve as a warning that a more complex seizure is about to occur.

Complex Partial Seizure (CPS)

In a complex partial seizure, consciousness is impaired. This type of seizure often originates in the temporal lobe and has been referred to as a *temporal lobe seizure* or a *psychomotor seizure*. Since the temporal lobe is associated with some memory and personality characteristics, complex partial seizures are often multisymptomatic and usually involve certain motor behaviors and psychic symptoms. These seizures typically last from 30 seconds to several minutes.

Automatisms (involuntary motor movements) are a common occurrence in complex partial seizures. These automatisms may be simple motor behaviors such as chewing, blank staring, scratching, laughing, gesturing, or repeating a phrase. The person may appear dazed and engage in random, purposeless activity such as walking in a circle, picking up objects, or picking at his or her clothes. Automatisms can also be quite complex and appear more purposeful, such as drawing or playing music (Holmes, 1992). Whatever form of automatism the person exhibits, the same pattern will typically be repeated with each seizure.

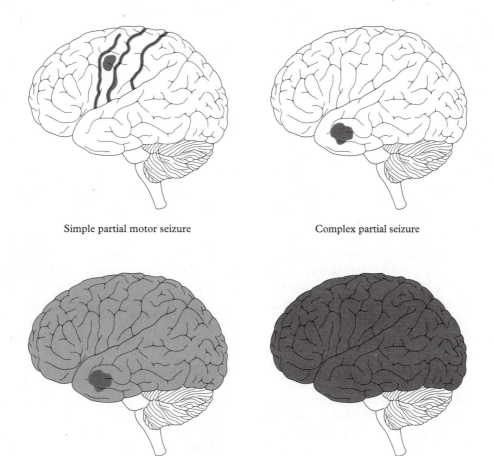

Simple partial motor seizure

Complex partial seizure

■ **FIGURE 6-1** Locations in the brain of different types of seizures

Psychic symptoms may be present in complex partial seizures. These may occur as an aura just before a seizure begins. Certain emotions, such as fear, joy, or embarrassment, may be expressed; illusions and hallucinations are also possible. Distortions of memory may occur, along with flashbacks to earlier events or feelings of déjà vu (the sensation that the experience has occurred before).

When the seizure is over, the person may feel confused about what has occurred. This is known as a *postictal phase* in which certain effects are felt for a period of time directly after the seizure activity is over. During this time, the child may either be tired or actually sleep.

Complex Partial Seizures to Generalized Seizure

In this category, the seizure begins with a complex partial seizure and then spreads to the other parts of the cerebral cortex across both hemispheres. This results in a generalized seizure.

Generalized Seizures

Generalized seizures involve both cerebral hemispheres. There are many different types of generalized seizures, ranging from the subtle absence seizure to dramatic convulsive seizures.

Absence Seizures

Absence seizures, formerly known as *petit mal seizures,* may occur in typical or atypical forms. In the typical absence seizure, the child will suddenly lose consciousness, stop what he or she is doing, and either stare straight ahead or roll the eyes upward. There is usually no movement or change in posture except for some possible automatisms. Automatisms such as eye-blinking or mouth-twitching are typically present, although more complex automatisms can occur. These seizures usually last a few seconds and rarely continue for more than 30 seconds. At the completion of the seizure, the child resumes his or her previous activity as if nothing occurred. If the seizure occurs in midsentence, the child will complete the sentence when the seizure ends. Absence seizures can occur from dozens to hundreds of times a day (Browne et al., 1983). The frequency may vary from day to day and may be associated with stress and fatigue.

The onset of these seizures occurs with no warning because an aura is not associated with absence seizures. There is no postictal confusion or drowsiness, so the child can continue with the activity he or she was performing. However, the child may be confused as to

what is occurring in class. Frequent absence seizures can make classroom activities incomprehensible, frustrating, or dull. A student who is experiencing several absence seizures during a reading lesson might hear the lesson this way:

> Today, class, we are going t...
> ....
> .... begins with a
> boy who wanted to h ....
> ....
> ....
> .... Margaret cried out, I.......................

Because seizures are subtle, they are frequently missed. The student may be reprimanded for daydreaming and for not paying attention. Unlike with daydreaming, however, the child cannot be brought out of a seizure by being touched or being spoken to in a loud voice. If these seizures are frequent, school performance may be affected and psychological testing will produce inaccurate results (Lockman, 1989). Careful observation is needed to detect these seizures in children.

In some instances, the suspension of consciousness may be less than complete. In these cases, the child having a seizure may continue simple behavior with mild confusion and not lose contact. These seizures may not be detectable by observation. A neurological examination with an electroencephalographic (EEG) analysis would be needed (Holmes, 1992).

Atypical Absence

In atypical absence seizures, the onset and cessation of the seizure is not as abrupt as in a typical absence seizure. This type of seizure is also associated with changes in muscle tone. Certain syndromes, such as the Lennox-Gastaut syndrome, are considered when atypical absence seizures are present.

Generalized Tonic-Clonic Seizure (GTC)

Generalized tonic-clonic seizures, previously known as *grand mal seizures*, are the dramatic seizures that people usually think of when they learn someone has a seizure disorder. It is a convulsive seizure disorder that is not difficult to detect or diagnose. In a generalized tonic-clonic seizure, there is a sudden discharge of neuronal impulses that spreads throughout the cortex in both hemispheres. The spread of the electrochemical impulses depends on age-related factors such as threshold of excitation, neuronal excitability, and the ability to inhibit the spread of the discharge.

Seizures in newborns are often fragmented. When the inhibitory-excitatory mechanisms are more balanced in older children, tonic-clonic seizures are more common.

In adults, more inhibitory channel mechanisms may result in less likelihood that tonic-clonic seizures will occur (Hirtz, 1989). In the primary generalized tonic-clonic seizure, the abnormal burst of electrical activity occurs in both hemispheres at the onset, whereas in secondary generalized tonic-clonic seizures, the electrical activity begins in one part of the brain and then travels to both hemispheres, becoming generalized. Children with generalized tonic clonic seizures are sometimes aware that a seizure is about to occur; an aura may begin minutes or seconds before the onset of the seizure. Because an aura indicates that the seizure began in one area of the brain and became generalized, it aids in classifying the seizure as a secondary tonic-clonic seizure.

Children may also be aware that a seizure is going to occur when certain prodromal symptoms are present, such as headaches, mood changes, irritability, difficulty sleeping, or a change in appetite (Holmes, 1992). Unlike auras, these can occur hours or days before a seizure. Although both auras and prodromal symptoms can warn the person of an impending seizure, many children have neither, and seizure onset is sudden.

When a generalized tonic-clonic seizure occurs, the person loses consciousness suddenly. A brief cry or scream may occur as the chest and abdominal muscles contract, causing air to be forced out of the lungs. The seizure will progress through a tonic and then a clonic phase. In the tonic (rigid) phase, the muscles are rigid and the arms and legs are extended; often the back is arched. A child who is standing will fall and possibly sustain injury from the impact. During this phase, the eyes may roll upward, and cyanosis (blueness of lips, nailbeds, and skin) may occur from a lack of oxygen that accompanies irregular or shallow respiration. The tonic phase usually lasts for less than a minute (Hirtz, 1989). Following this phase, the clonic (jerking) phase begins with rhythmic, jerking motions of the body that gradually decrease in frequency. Following the last jerk, urinary **incontinence** (loss of bladder control) or bowel incontinence may occur. Throughout the seizure, saliva may pool in the mouth and bubble at the lips. Inefficient swallowing and the accumulation of saliva may result in noisy breathing. Breathing may also become shallow and irregular, resulting in cyanosis. Aspiration of saliva, as well as biting the tongue and vomiting, may occur. The entire seizure usually lasts 2 to 5 minutes.

After the seizure, the child will be exhausted and will typically sleep for 30 minutes to 2 hours. (It is as if the child has just run a 10-mile race!) The child may wake up confused and lethargic and may have sore muscles and a headache.

All generalized tonic-clonic seizures are not alike. Younger children may have a short clonic stage with a few brief jerks (Hirtz, 1989). Those with other medical conditions involving contractures may not have the same extension responses.

Tonic Seizures

Seizures may also have just a tonic phase. These are known as tonic seizures.

Clonic Seizures

Some individuals may have only a clonic phase. These are referred to as clonic seizures.

Myoclonic Seizures

Myoclonic seizure disorder is another type of generalized seizure characterized by sudden, brief muscle jerks that may involve part or all of the body. Severity varies; some myoclonic seizures are very subtle and difficult to recognize, and others are severe enough that the child falls. Sometimes the seizures are mistaken for clumsiness. Although injury can result if the child falls forward into a desk or other object, the child usually does not lose consciousness.

There are several types of myoclonic seizures. Some are grouped with the typical myoclonic epilepsy of early childhood, complex myoclonic epilepsy, and juvenile myoclonic epilepsy. In typical myoclonic epilepsy of early childhood, children develop the seizure disorder between 6 months and 11 years of age (Behrman, 1992). Seizures may occur several times a day or not occur for several weeks.

In complex myoclonic epilepsy, partial or tonic-clonic seizures often predate the onset of myoclonic seizures. Individuals with complex myoclonic epilepsy often have several accompanying disorders, such as microcephaly. Delays in reaching developmental milestones may occur.

In juvenile myoclonic epilepsy, seizures begin in adolescence. Typically, the seizures are mild and involve the hands and arms; the adolescent may spill or drop objects. Myoclonic jerks may begin occurring after awakening, causing the adolescent to drop a toothbrush, for example. These seizures may be ignored, but the adolescent may go on to develop generalized tonic-clonic seizures.

Another form of myoclonic seizures is known as *infantile spasms* (also known as salaam seizures, jackknife seizures, flexion spasms, massive spasms, and infantile myoclonic seizures). This type of seizure disorder typically begins when the child is between 4 and 6 months of age, with 90% of the infantile spasms occurring before 1 year of age (Holmes, 1992). Although symptoms vary, the infant may suddenly flex his or her arms in a hugging motion combined with flexion of the neck and legs. For some infants, instead of flexion, extension of the arms and legs can occur. There can also be a combination of flexion occurring for some seizures and extension occurring for others (mixed infantile spasms). These seizures may take place during sleep, but most commonly occur after awakening or when the person is drowsy. Seizures often occur in clusters, sometimes as many as 60 clusters a day.

Infantile spasms have been associated with several disorders. Many children with infantile spasms have mental retardation with neurological impairments. Other types of seizures, such as generalized tonic-clonic or other forms of myoclonic seizures, may develop. The Lennox-Gastaut syndrome, to be discussed later, may occur as well.

Many myoclonic movements are not seizures. Some of these may be normal "sleep starts," other movement disorders, or symptoms of infection. A physician can differentiate these from an actual myoclonic seizure.

Atonic Seizures

Atonic seizures, formerly known as *akinetic* or *drop attacks,* consist of a sudden loss of muscle tone—almost the opposite of myoclonic seizures in which there is a high degree of muscle tone. In an atonic seizure, the child suddenly falls to the ground and then gets back up. Injury can result from the fall.

Other Seizures

There are many other types of seizures, some of which are highly unusual. In a *gelastic seizure,* the child stares blankly and then starts to laugh. In a *cursive seizure,* the child runs (Nealis, 1983). Other unusual forms may require neurological testing to determine whether or not they are seizures. Many seizures are not classified.

Mixed Types of Seizures

Children may have one type of seizure disorder, or they may have two or more types. Children with multiple disabilities and neurological impairments are more likely to have several types, sometimes taking the form of a syndrome.

One of the most difficult syndromes to control is the Lennox-Gastaut syndrome. The intractable nature of the seizures often makes them difficult to treat. The child with this condition often has mental retardation and has several types of seizures. The most frequently occurring ones include tonic-clonic, atypical absence, tonic, atonic, and myoclonic seizures. Seizures are usually frequent and may range from approximately 9 to 70 seizures daily. In one study, most seizures occurred while the children were awake and inactive (Papini,

Pasquinelli, Armellini, & Orlandi, 1984). A significantly smaller number occurred when the children were awake and active. A stimulating environment may help reduce the number of daily seizures.

Status Epilepticus

Although seizures usually stop within a few minutes without intervention, in a dangerous condition known as *status epilepticus,* seizures are continuous and last for 30 minutes or more. If the individual has recurrent seizures without regaining consciousness, the term *status epilepticus* also applies (Shields, 1989). This should be treated as an emergency situation that requires immediate medical intervention. When intervention is not provided, permanent brain damage or death can result.

Status epilepticus may result from symptomatic or idiopathic causes. For children, the most frequent symptomatic causes are central nervous system infections, nonspecific illnesses with fever, and certain degenerative diseases of the brain. In adolescents and adults, tumors and brain injury are more commonly the cause (Holmes, 1992).

Status epilepticus can occur for both generalized and partial forms of seizures. The most serious is the generalized tonic-clonic form. The tonic-clonic seizure begins in the same way but continues. During this seizure, high body temperature, low blood sugar, low blood pressure, and low concentrations of oxygen can occur, which can increase the possibility of brain damage.

In a classic study by Aicardi & Chevrie (1970), the effects of status epilepticus (tonic-clonic or clonic type) were examined in 239 children. Eighty-eight children in this study had permanent neurological disorders after the initial episode, including **hemiplegia, diplegia,** and other movement abnormalities. About half of these children were normal before the status, so the status is presumed to be the cause of the neurological problem. The other half may have had these conditions previously. After the status, mental retardation was present in 114 children, 78 of whom were documented as developing normally before their first status. The gravity of status epilepticus is reaffirmed in this study, because 13 children's deaths were attributed to the seizures. Fortunately, status epilepticus will usually respond to intravenous medication that stops the status.

Although nonconvulsive status epilepticus is not as serious because body functions (such as respiration) are unaffected, negative consequences may still occur. Prolonged simple partial status epilepticus, for example, can result in neurological damage, such as hemiparesis (Shields, 1989).

DETECTION OF SEIZURE DISORDERS

The diagnosis of a seizure disorder consists of ruling out other, mimicking conditions, determining what type of seizures the child has had, and discovering their underlying cause. Several conditions may be mistaken for seizures, including breath-holding spells, fainting, migraine headaches, temper tantrums, nightmares, movement disorders, newborn trembling, abnormal posturing, shuddering spells, excessive sleepiness, daydreaming, and narcolepsy (sleeping attacks) (Barron, 1991; Keele, 1983). A careful history, a neurological examination, and medical testing will determine whether a diagnosis of a seizure disorder will be made.

One of the best ways to diagnose a seizure is for the neurologist to observe it in progress. Unfortunately, a seizure is unlikely to occur during a physical examination. A careful description by those observing the incident will assist in the diagnosis. Information regarding any precipitating factors, subjective experiences prior to onset (aura or prodromal symptoms), duration, time of day, and precise behavior should be given accurately. This will help rule out other conditions and determine the type of seizure. Even subtle observations, such as whether a seizure began on one part or side of the body (focally) and then became generalized or began in a generalized manner, can help determine diagnosis and treatment.

A neurological examination will be performed to evaluate any abnormal physical findings. The neurologist will look for anomalies such as abnormal head size, differences in reflexes between the right and left side of the body, balance problems, and ability to detect sensory information. Throughout the examination, the neurologist will look for signs of underlying disorders that mimic or cause seizures.

Blood tests are routinely performed to determine whether there are any chemical imbalances, such as an electrolytic imbalance in the body. Other tests, such as a spinal tap, may be performed if the child is suspected of having meningitis. In a spinal tap, a needle is inserted into the spinal column to remove spinal fluid, which would then be examined for infection.

An electroencephalogram (EEG) can provide critical information as to whether a seizure disorder exists and what type it is. An EEG consists of placing several electrodes (small round disks) on the scalp, or infrequently on the surface of the brain or within the brain. Wires from the electrodes are connected to the EEG machine, which records the electrical activity of the brain on a graph (see Figure 6-2). Abnormalities in the EEG are often present when a seizure disorder exists, even if a seizure is not occurring at the time of the test. Approximately 60 to 80% of individuals with seizure disorders will have an abnormal EEG (Holmes, 1992; Keele, 1983). The EEG can also determine the location of the seizure activity in the brain.

However, a normal EEG does not eliminate the possibility of a seizure disorder. If the abnormal electrical activity is occurring in an unusual place in the brain, the standard positioning of the electrodes may not detect it. In other instances, there may be no abnormal electrical activity occurring between seizures, and a normal EEG results. Conversely, some individuals with abnormal EEGs are healthy and have no abnormal symptoms.

Conditions that are known to precipitate a seizure will often be simulated during an EEG. For example,

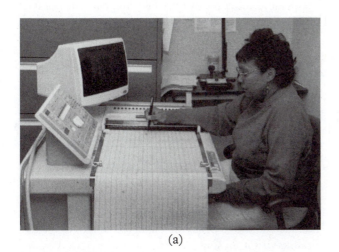

(a)

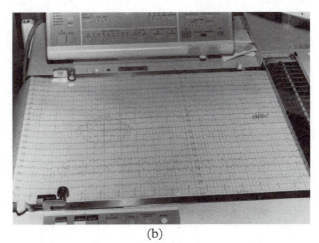

(b)

■ **FIGURE 6-2** EEG machine with technician monitoring the readout (a) and EEG showing the electrical activity of the brain (b)

children will be encouraged to hyperventilate, which often brings on an absence seizure in children who have this form of seizure disorder. Sleep may be induced by medication or, conversely, testing may be conducted after a child has been deprived of sleep. Parents might need to keep the child awake all night before the testing. Photic stimulation, which involves the presentation of blinking, strobing lights, may be used as well.

When the type of seizure is difficult to diagnose, an ambulatory EEG monitoring system or a prolonged EEG monitoring with simultaneous closed-circuit video recording may be used. In an ambulatory monitoring system, electrodes are hidden under the child's hair, wires are placed under the clothes, and a recorder is usually worn on a belt. This provides a longer time to record possible seizure activity (Gadow, 1986). A prolonged EEG monitoring system with simultaneous closed-circuit video allows the electrical recording of seizures, levels of consciousness, and precise behaviors. This type of testing, known as *telemetry,* aids in precise diagnosis.

Brain imagery techniques may be used to determine the presence of underlying brain pathology, such as tumors, **atrophy,** calcification, aneurysms, and other abnormalities. There are several types of imagery techniques. The *computerized tomography scan* (CT scan or CAT scan) takes a series of X-rays in different parts of the brain; a dye may be injected into the bloodstream to enhance visualization of the blood vessels. Another technique is *magnetic resonance imagery* (MRI). Instead of using X-rays, MRI visualizes different parts of the brain by making use of the magnetic qualities of the molecules to detect finer details of the cranial structures. Less frequently used techniques include *positron emission tomography* (PET) and *single photon emission computerized tomography* (SPECT). These tests require the injection of a small amount of radioactive material, and the scanners can then detect metabolic activity of the brain as well as cerebral blood flow. Abnormalities in the amount of glucose being metabolized by a particular part of the brain can help pinpoint the location of the seizures.

TREATMENT OF SEIZURE DISORDERS

Treatment for seizures may involve medication, surgery, or possibly both. A special diet may be used in rare cases. The goal of treatment is to control the seizures and prevent complications from them, so if seizures are symptomatic, control of the underlying condition will be targeted as well. General treatment precautions may include managing the seizures medically, using a Medic Alert bracelet that indicates the child has a seizure disorder and lists antiepileptic medications, using a

protective helmet for frequently occurring seizures that result in falls, avoiding certain external stimuli that elicit seizures, and providing information about seizure management.

Antiepileptic Drugs (AEDs)

After a child has his or her first seizure, an antiepileptic medication is usually not prescribed if there is a normal physical examination, normal EEG, negative family history, and a compliant family. A recurrence is unlikely in the majority of these cases. The child is at risk for a seizure to recur when there is an abnormal EEG and a neurological abnormality is found during the neurological exam. Possible risk factors are family history, type of seizure, the occurrence of nocturnal seizures, and prior febrile seizures. If the child is at definite risk, medication will usually be prescribed.

If the seizure recurs, an antiepileptic medication is prescribed, and the child may be retested. The choice of medication depends on the seizure type. The goal is to use one drug with the fewest number of side effects, but multiple medications may be prescribed in difficult-to-control seizures or when multiple seizures are involved.

The first drug of choice for the specific type of seizure disorder will be tried first, usually in a small dose that is gradually increased. Blood will be drawn at various times to determine the blood concentrations of the medication. This will help determine whether the child is getting the correct amount. If seizures continue, the amount of medication will be increased until seizures are controlled; the child is observed for undesirable side effects. This is so that serious, toxic concentrations of the drug can be avoided. If the seizures continue, another medication may be added or substituted. Antiepileptic medication may be successful in eliminating the person's seizures or only in reducing their number. Once seizures are controlled as well as possible through medication, the dosage may need to be changed as the child grows and matures. Effective treatment of some seizures requires the careful monitoring and reporting of seizure activity to a physician.

Unfortunately, no single drug can control all the different types of seizure disorders. There are several kinds of antiepileptic medications, some of which are more effective for certain types of seizures than others. The most common antiepileptic medications used in treating the various types of seizure disorders are listed in Table 6-1. Unfortunately, all medications have potential side effects. Common side effects of AEDs include sedation, behavior changes, tremors, vertigo, double vision, nystagmus, ataxia, and gastrointestinal problems (Pellock, 1989; *Physicians' Desk Reference,* 1995; Schmidt, 1982). If the side effects become too

TABLE 6-1

Antiepileptic Medications

Trade Name	Generic Name	Seizure Typology	Side Effects
Depakene	valproic acid	Absence Myoclonic Generalized	Tremor, hair loss, nausea, liver disease
Depakote	divalproate	Simple and complex Absence	Nausea, vomiting, drowsiness
Dilantin Caps/Pb Dilantin Infatabs Dilantin Kapseals	phenytoin	Tonic-clonic Psychomotor Partial	Nausea, excitement, eye symptoms, hyperplastic gums
Mesantoin	mephenytoin	Tonic-clonic Psychomotor Partial	Sedation
Milontin Kapseals	phensuximide	Absence	Nausea, vomiting, anorexia
Mysoline	primidone	Tonic-clonic Psychomotor Partial	Headache, skin rash, edema, nausea, vomiting, painful gums
Paradione	paramethadione	Absence (used when refractory to other drugs)	Nausea, vomiting, anorexia, depressed bone marrow, kidney damage
Peganone	ethotoin	Tonic-clonic Psychomotor	Sedation, nausea, vomiting, headache, visual disturbance, depression, dizziness
Luminal	phenobarbital	Tonic-clonic Psychomotor Partial	Hyperactivity, sedation, irritability
Phenurone	phenacemide	Tonic-clonic Absence Psychomotor	Anorexia, nausea, and vomiting may herald serious toxicity
Tegretol	carbamazepine	Grand mal Partial Psychomotor	Vomiting, headache, drowsiness, ataxia, blood dyscrasia

severe, such as incapacitating drowsiness, the dosage of the medication or the medication itself may be changed.

Ketogenic Diet

A ketogenic diet may be used in certain circumstances to control seizure activity. This controversial and infrequently used method restricts the amount of carbohydrates and proteins in the child's diet. Most calories are provided by fatty foods, and for some individuals this diet has reduced seizure activity. Although the exact mechanism is unknown, the diet seems to increase the amount of the inhibitory neurotransmitter GABA (Schwartz et al., 1989). However, most children over the age of 2 or 3 will not tolerate this diet and compliance is difficult to control.

Surgical Treatment

In certain circumstances, surgery may be used to control seizures, although it is infrequently used. Surgery is considered a last resort and is performed when medication is ineffective and the seizures are significantly interfering with the child's life.

Surgical interventions used to control seizure disorders are *focal excision, hemispherectomy,* or *cutting the corpus callosum*. In a focal excision, a small portion of the brain where the seizure originates is removed. Part of a lobe or the entire lobe (lobectomy) may be removed. This procedure can only be used when the seizure's point of origin is well-defined. The results of this surgery have typically been highly successful; 50 to 90% of the children having it are seizure-free or nearly so after the surgery. Behavior and social status also improved after surgery. Possible complications include visual field defects and transient dysphasia—a speech impairment with a lack of motor coordination. Only 5% of individuals having this type of surgery have been documented as having more permanent impairments, such as hemiparesis (weakness or partial paralysis on one side of the body) (Duchowny, 1989).

Another type of surgery is *hemispherectomy*, in which one entire cerebral hemisphere is removed. (In an alternative form of hemispherectomy, the end parts of the frontal and occipital lobes are left but are disconnected from each other.) This treatment has been effective for children with intractable partial seizures who have additional symptoms of hemiparesis and visual deficits. Most children (80 to 90%) having this surgery are seizure-free or have a significant reduction in seizure activity. Some children's behavior and cognitive functioning improve after surgery. However, many have additional problems, such as cerebral palsy and mental retardation, and continue with considerable disability. Complications such as **hydrocephalus** have occurred, as have cognitive deficits when the surgery is performed later in life (Duchowny, 1989).

Cutting the corpus callosum is another surgical option. This means severing the corpus callosum or other structures, such as the anterior commissure, that connect the two cerebral hemispheres to prevent the spread of abnormal electrical impulses (Sass et al., 1988). This type of surgery has been successful primarily with children having atonic seizure disorder; approximately 75% of these children have a decrease or absence of seizures. The improvement eliminates the likelihood of self-injury when the child falls. There has been 5 to 75% improvement reported in the group with generalized tonic or clonic seizures, or partial seizures with secondary generalization. However, partial seizures may increase or activate with this type of surgery (Duchowny, 1989). Children with Lennox-Gastaut syndrome may also benefit from this surgery.

Besides the potential complication of partial seizure activation, long-term neurological consequences may occur that are now poorly understood. Although most of these consequences do not significantly affect the person's daily functioning, deficits in manual dexterity and language functioning have occurred (Sass et al., 1988).

What to Do When a Seizure Occurs

Any time a seizure occurs, close observation is warranted so an accurate report can be made. If the child has no history of seizures but seems to be having one, the occurrence should be immediately reported to the parent, who should contact the family doctor or pediatrician. The physician will determine whether neurological workup is needed.

Depending on the type of seizure disorder, the observer may need to assist the child who is having a seizure. The observer should stay with the child while the seizure is occurring and note any postictal confusion after the seizure is complete. Additional measures may be needed, especially for convulsive seizures. See Table 6-2 for an overview of seizure management for the different types of seizures.

Partial Seizures

When a child has a simple partial seizure, first aid is not usually needed. However, a child having a complex partial seizure may walk around and could be injured. The observer should gently guide the child away from any obvious hazards and should talk calmly to the child but not expect any verbal instructions to be obeyed. The child should not be restrained. After the seizure is over, the child may be confused and have no memory of what happened during the seizure; reorientation to the environment, reassurance, and support may be necessary.

Generalized Tonic-Clonic Seizures

When a generalized tonic-clonic seizure occurs, there are several things an observer can do to help the child:

1. Stay calm and note the time of onset of a seizure to determine its duration.
2. Put the child into a lying position; move furniture out of the way so the child will not be injured. Do not be afraid of arm and leg movements.
3. Loosen shirt collars and put something soft such as a jacket or a hand under the student's head.
4. Do *not* restrain the child's movement or put anything in the child's mouth because this may result in injury or may compromise respiration.
5. Turn the child on his or her side to allow saliva to drain from the mouth and prevent aspiration. If vomiting occurs, turning the child to the side will also help to prevent the child from accidentally inhaling the vomit.
6. If the seizure continues for more than 5 minutes or there are multiple seizures occurring immediately after each other, call an ambulance (Epilepsy Foundation of America, 1994). This is because the child may go into status epilepticus and need emergency help immediately.
7. If the seizure stops but the child is not breathing, give mouth-to-mouth resuscitation. This happens rarely.
8. After the seizure is over, the child often does not remember what has occurred and will be confused. Reassure the child and inform him or her about what has happened. Do not give liquids during this time because the child may aspirate the fluid.
9. Assess the child for injuries if he or she fell. Give first aid as needed. If a hard blow to the head occurred when the child fell, medical attention is warranted.
10. The child will be exhausted after the seizure and should be allowed to rest. If the seizure occurred in

TABLE 6-2

Seizure Recognition and First Aid

Seizure Type	What It Looks Like	What It Is Not	What to Do	What Not to Do
Generalized tonic-clonic	Sudden cry, fall, rigidity, followed by muscle jerks, shallow breathing or temporarily suspended breathing, bluish skin, possible loss of bladder or bowel control, usually lasts a couple of minutes. Normal breathing then starts again. There may be some confusion and/or fatigue, followed by return to full consciousness.	Heart attack; stroke.	Look for medical identification. Protect from nearby hazards. Loosen ties or shirt collars. Protect head from injury. Turn on side to keep airway clear. Reassure when consciousness returns. If single seizure lasted less than 5 minutes, ask if hospital evaluation wanted. If multiple seizures or if one seizure lasts longer than 5 minutes, call an ambulance. If person is pregnant, injured, or diabetic, call for aid at once.	Don't put any hard implement in the mouth. Don't try to hold tongue. It can't be swallowed. Don't try to give liquids during or just after seizure. Don't use artificial respiration unless breathing is absent after muscle jerks subside or unless water has been inhaled. Don't restrain.
Absence	A blank stare, beginning and ending abruptly, lasting only a few seconds, most common in children. May be accompanied by rapid blinking, some chewing movements of the mouth. Child or adult is unaware of what's going on during the seizure but quickly returns to full awareness once it has stopped. May result in learning difficulties if not recognized and treated.	Daydreaming; lack of attention; deliberate ignoring of adult instructions.	No first aid necessary, but if this is the first observation of the seizure(s), medical evaluation should be recommended.	
Simple partial	Jerking may begin in one area of body, arm, leg, or face. Can't be stopped, but patient stays awake and aware. Jerking may proceed from one area of the body to another and sometimes spreads to become a convulsive seizure.	Acting out; bizarre behavior.	No first aid necessary unless seizure becomes convulsive, then give first aid as above.	

Continued

TABLE 6-2 *Continued*

Seizure Recognition and First Aid

Seizure Type	What It Looks Like	What It Is Not	What to Do	What Not to Do
	Partial sensory seizures may not be obvious to an onlooker. Patient experiences a distorted environment. May see or hear things that aren't there, may feel unexplained fear, sadness, anger, or joy. May have nausea, experience odd smells, and have a generally "funny" feeling in the stomach.	Hysteria. Mental illness. Psychosomatic illness. Parapsychological or mystical experience.	No immediate action needed other than reassurance and emotional support. Medical evaluation should be recommended.	
Complex partial	Usually starts with blank stare, followed by chewing, followed by random activity. Person appears unaware of surroundings, may seem dazed and mumble. Unresponsive. Actions clumsy, not directed. May pick at clothing, pick up objects, try to take clothes off. May run, appear afraid. May struggle or flail at restraint. Once pattern established, same set of actions usually occurs with each seizure. Lasts a few minutes, but postseizure confusion can last substantially longer. No memory of what happened during seizure period.	Drunkenness. Intoxication on drugs. Mental illness. Disorderly conduct.	Speak calmly and reassuringly to patient and others. Guide person gently away from obvious hazards. Stay with person until he or she is completely aware of environment. Offer to help person get home.	Don't grab hold unless sudden danger (such as a cliff edge or an approaching car) threatens. Don't try to restrain. Don't shout. Don't expect verbal instructions to be obeyed.
Atonic	A child or adult suddenly collapses and falls. After 10 seconds to a minute he or she recovers, regains consciousness, and can stand and walk again.	Clumsiness. Normal childhood "stage." In a child, lack of good walking skills. In an adult, drunkenness, acute illness.	No first aid needed unless child is hurt in a fall, but the child should be given a thorough medical evaluation.	

TABLE 6-2 *Continued*

Seizure Recognition and First Aid

Seizure Type	What It Looks Like	What It Is Not	What to Do	What Not to Do
Myoclonic	Sudden brief, massive muscle jerks that may involve the whole body or parts of the body. May cause person to spill what they were holding or fall off a chair.	Clumsiness. Poor coordination.	No first aid needed but a thorough medical evaluation is needed.	
Infantile spasms	These are clusters of quick, sudden movements that start between 3 months and 2 years of age. If a child is sitting up, the head will fall forward, and the arms will flex forward. If lying down, the knees will be drawn up, with arms and head flexed forward as if the baby is reaching for support.	Normal movements of the baby. Colic.	No first aid but doctor should be consulted.	

SOURCE: Copyright ©Epilepsy Foundation of America, 1994.

the water, have a physician check to see whether or not water was aspirated (Epilepsy Foundation of America, 1994).

11. Help protect the student's dignity during and after the seizure. If the student's clothes are soiled, for example, make arrangements for the clothes to be changed.

Generalized, Nonconvulsive Seizures

Children who have generalized seizures that are not convulsive do not usually need first aid. They should be assessed for any injury that might have occurred from a fall (such as atonic seizure). Any unusual seizures, such as a running seizure, will require the observer to guide the child away from injury. Reassurance, support, and orientation should be given.

COURSE OF SEIZURE DISORDERS

The prognosis for seizure disorders depends on the cause of the seizures; those resulting from brain abnormalities are typically more difficult to control.

Medication can control some types of seizure disorders better than others. For example, medication can control generalized tonic-clonic seizures for 50% of those who have them, while reducing the frequency of seizures in another 35%. Absence seizures are controlled in about 40% of cases; significant reduction occurs in another 35%. For complex partial seizures, only about 35% of the individuals are made seizure-free by drug therapy; another 50% have their seizures reduced (Berkow, 1992).

As the child matures, some seizure disorders may stop. When the individual has been seizure-free for 2 or more years, the medication may be decreased and then eliminated. The relapse rate has been found to be approximately 25 to 28% for some children after withdrawal from antiepileptic medication (Shinnar et al., 1985; Thurston, Thurston, Hixon, & Keller, 1982). Factors associated with the increased risk of relapse are neurological dysfunction, a long period of time before seizures are controlled, and certain types of seizures (simple partial motor with sequential involvement and mixed types) (Thurston et al., 1982).

Most children who have a seizure disorder that is controlled by medication and who do not have additional impairments lead normal lives. No intellectual deterioration has been reported in children with seizure disorders except for those with status epilepticus (Ellenberg, Hirtz, & Nelson, 1986). Typically, no physical limitations are placed on the child. Special precautions are unnecessary, although the child may be monitored for seizure activity by the teacher. Excessive physical activity is not known to elicit a seizure. Adolescents can usually drive automobiles in most states when they have been seizure-free for a year. The child may need emotional support from time to time, as well as education regarding the condition.

■ **VIGNETTE 1** ■

Nina is a 12-year-old girl with generalized tonic-clonic seizures who was enrolled in a summer school program. Unfortunately, the baseline information regarding her seizures was not shared with the student teacher. Upon returning from lunch, the student teacher flipped on the lights, causing a generalized tonic-clonic seizure to occur. After 30 seconds, the tonic-clonic seizure was over and Nina rested. Baseline information obtained from the parent indicated that turning on lights would usually cause a seizure. If the instructor had shared this information with the student teacher, the seizure could have been avoided.

SEIZURE DISORDER INFORMATION SHEET

STUDENT _____ DATE _____

PARENTS _____ PHONE _____

EMERGENCY PHONE NUMBER AND NAME _____

PHYSICIAN _____ PHONE _____

1. Describe your child's seizures:

2. Is there anything that causes the seizure to occur? (Please describe.)

3. Does the child know when he or she is about to have a seizure (i.e., aura)? Does the child do anything to indicate a seizure is about to occur?

4. How long does the seizure usually last?

5. What is your child like right after a seizure has occurred?

6. What would you like the teacher to do when a seizure occurs?

7. What medication or additional treatment is the child currently receiving?

8. Please list any limitations.

9. Comments:

■ **FIGURE 6-3** Sample seizure disorder information sheet

EDUCATIONAL IMPLICATIONS OF SEIZURE DISORDERS

It is important that the school staff be acquainted with the different types of seizures. Sometimes a teacher is the first person to notice that a student is having a seizure, especially with the more subtle seizures, such as absence seizures. The teacher may also be the first on hand to assist a student who is having a seizure. If a student has a generalized tonic-clonic seizure, for example, the teacher and staff need to know what to do and be ready to act. Information regarding seizure management should be provided to the school staff. Inservice workshops and literature are often available through national or local organizations such as the Epilepsy Foundation of America.

Meeting Physical and Sensory Needs

When a child with a seizure disorder enters school, the teacher should obtain some baseline information, including the type of seizure and a description of what it looks like, any known factors that will elicit a seizure, the occurrence of any auras or prodromal symptoms, the typical duration of the seizure, and the child's behavior after a seizure. Treatment should be specified, including the names of medications and their possible side effects. If the child has any limitations, these should be recorded as well. This information will assist the teacher in better management. The Seizure Disorder Information Sheet will help the teacher obtain the desired information. Figure 6-3 is a sample form (Heller et al., 1991).

Teachers, paraprofessionals, staff members, and others should receive training in what to do when a seizure occurs. Anytime a seizure occurs, the teacher should also document its occurrence along with vital information about it. A postseizure report like the one in Figure 6-4 should be completed (Heller et al., 1991). A description of the seizure, its time and duration, the occurrence of injuries, first aid given, and notification information should be included. After a postseizure report is filled out, one should be sent home and a copy should be retained for the student's records. If the student typically has dozens of seizures a day, the teacher should record how many occurred that day and any other pertinent information regarding daily seizure activity.

Meeting Communication Needs

Typically, students with seizure disorders will have no problems communicating unless there is a secondary disability. In that case, the teacher and speech therapist

■ **VIGNETTE 2** ■

Hiroshi is a 3-year-old boy with multiple disabilities. He was diagnosed as having a seizure disorder consisting of infrequent, short, generalized tonic-clonic seizures. He typically turned blue during the seizures due to shallow breathing. His physician had requested that he receive oxygen during seizures occurring over several minutes and when he turned bluish in color. The school nurse was out one morning when Hiroshi went into a generalized tonic-clonic seizure. After 2 minutes, Hiroshi turned cyanotic around the lips and nailbed (which is the first place someone will turn blue, indicating a lack of oxygen). None of the teachers knew how to turn on the oxygen tank. When they finally figured it out, the oxygen mask was the wrong size for the small child. After the seizure had continued for 5 minutes, the parents and an ambulance were called at the suggestion of a visiting instructor. After 12 minutes, the seizure stopped, just as the emergency team arrived. The emergency team assessed Hiroshi and said that the call was made in good faith and did not charge for it. The father arrived 10 minutes later to take the child home and call the neurologist. The father was glad the teachers had responded so well. He didn't know they were unprepared. In this situation, the teachers should have been more prepared for the seizure and should not have relied on the presence of a school nurse.

will collaboratively implement intervention strategies to help the student communicate more effectively.

Often children may ask a student with a seizure disorder what is wrong, and it helps to have a simple explanation ready. Classmates can then better understand the condition. One possible explanation a young child could give is, "Your brain tells your body how to move. Sometimes my brain gets the message wrong and my arms, legs, and body shake. When that happens, I'll be OK in a couple of minutes. You can't catch it. Most of the time the medicine I take makes it not happen" (Morrow, 1985).

Meeting Learning Needs

Seizures do not typically affect intellectual ability. Students with seizure disorders may be gifted, have normal intelligence, or have mental retardation. However, individuals with disabilities like mental retardation have a higher prevalence of seizure disorders that result in a need to adapt academic content to compensate for accompanying disabilities.

SEIZURE REPORT

After a student has a seizure the teacher/designated person should complete the following form and follow county policy.

NAME _____ DATE _____

1. Significant behavior or aura preceding seizure (if any):

2. Describe the seizure:

3. Time of the seizure: _____

4. Length of the seizure: _____

5. Who observed the seizure? _____

6. Did the student fall?   NO ☐   YES ☐

7. Were there any injuries?   NO ☐   YES ☐

8. What first aid was given (and by whom)?

9. Was 911 and ambulance called?   NO ☐   YES ☐

10. How was the student after first aid was administered after the seizure?

11. Were the parents notified?   NO ☐   YES ☐

■ **FIGURE 6-4** Sample postseizure report form

Students' learning may be affected directly or indirectly by both minor and major seizures. The student may miss academic content while seizures are occurring and afterward as well if there is disorientation or fatigue. Teachers will need to bring the student up to date on missed information. In the case of frequent absence seizures, the student can be assigned a buddy who helps reorient him or her after a seizure. Buddies are especially useful in a reading group to help the student find his or her place on the page after the seizure is over.

Learning may also be affected by the medication students take for seizures. For example, high therapeutic doses of barbiturates may have a negative effect on short-term memory (Gadow, 1986). Attention may also be impaired due to drowsiness or hyperactivity caused by an antiepileptic medication. The teacher needs to be aware of these effects and be sure the parents and physician are informed about them.

Meeting Daily Living Needs

Typically, the educator will not need to provide instruction in daily living skills unless the student has disabilities other than a seizure disorder. The adolescent may feel a loss of independence if driving is contraindicated. Alternate forms of transportation will need to be learned.

Meeting Behavioral and Social Needs

Students with seizure disorders may have difficulty adjusting socially because of their disability (Frank, 1985). It is the teacher's responsibility to maintain a positive attitude toward the student and help promote social interaction. Students with seizures often feel stress from this chronic condition, which may interfere with their interactions with others. The unpredictability of when a seizure may occur, the need to take medication regularly, and social prejudice can all have negative psychosocial effects. Feelings of dependency and loss of control may result in a decreased sense of self-worth or other negative feelings and behaviors. A warm, supporting atmosphere is helpful. At times, counseling may be indicated (Frank, 1985). (See Chapter 3.)

If a seizure occurs at school, the teacher needs to react in a calm, nonchalant manner because the teacher's tone influences the reaction of the class. The class should be educated about seizures, perhaps by including information during a health class or by discussing famous people who have seizures. Some students may think they can catch seizures from another student. Students have

thought that a child in their class having a convulsive seizure was dying and then was dead when he or she slept afterward. There is much fear and misconception regarding seizures. Nonconvulsive seizures may not seem involuntary. It is important that the teacher be alert to misconceptions and social prejudices and try to properly educate students as well as staff members.

Students with seizure disorders are often overprotected and denied access to activities they can perform. The educator should not restrict the student unnecessarily and should find out what limitations, if any, have been ordered by a physician.

SUMMARY

A seizure is a sudden, involuntary, time-limited disruption of the normal functions of the central nervous system. There are many types of seizures and seizure disorders that can be characterized by altered consciousness, motor activity, sensory phenomena, or inappropriate behavior. Seizures are usually classified as partial seizures, generalized seizures, and unclassified seizures. Partial seizures refer to seizures that occur in one area of the brain; generalized seizures refer to seizures occurring in both hemispheres of the brain.

There are many types of seizures under each category; each type has its own characteristics, prognosis, and treatment. Seizures usually last a few seconds to a few minutes and end spontaneously. However, if status epilepticus occurs, medical treatment is needed. The teacher plays an important role in identifying children who have seizures and taking the necessary steps to ensure the child's safety and dignity should a seizure occur in the classroom. Treatment is often with antiepileptic medications, and the teacher should be alert for side effects and for the effectiveness of treatment. Modifications may be needed in the classroom when the student misses material due to seizures or feels fatigued from medication.

CHAPTER 7

Cerebral Palsy

Cerebral palsy means *brain* (cerebral) *paralysis* (palsy). It is a loosely descriptive term that refers to a variety of disorders of voluntary movement and posture. Dr. George Little first used the term almost 150 years ago to describe a form of cerebral palsy that he thought resulted from a lack of oxygen at birth.

It is estimated that 5,000 babies are born each year with cerebral palsy, with an additional 1,200 to 1,500 preschool children acquiring it annually (United Cerebral Palsy Association, 1993). As more low-birth-weight infants have survived premature birth, the prevalence of cerebral palsy has risen, often resulting in additional, associated conditions (Nicholson & Alberman, 1992).

Children with cerebral palsy present a wide diversity of characteristics. Some children's cerebral palsy will be barely noticeable; others will have such severe motor impairment that they need assistance or adaptations to perform even simple physical tasks. The diversity among children with cerebral palsy requires a close examination of each student and of the severity of the disability in order to provide optimal treatment and educational support.

In this chapter, we review the types of cerebral palsy in terms of etiology, dynamics, and characteristics. This will provide a foundation for the second half of the chapter in which we explain treatment and educational considerations.

DESCRIPTION OF CEREBRAL PALSY

Cerebral palsy (CP) can be defined as a nonprogressive disorder of voluntary movement or posture that is caused by a malfunctioning of or damage to the brain occurring before birth, during birth, or within the first few years of life (Bleck & Nagel, 1982; Russman, 1992). Even though the disease itself does not progress, with-

out appropriate therapeutic intervention, the symptoms of this disorder may get worse. For example, movement may become more inhibited over time. These changes are caused by the muscles and tendons shortening (contractures) and not from any additional damage to the brain. Since cerebral palsy occurs in infants and young children, it influences the way children develop and therefore is considered a developmental disability.

The definition refers to cerebral palsy as a disorder of voluntary movement or posture. This encompasses different types of cerebral palsy, each having distinctly different kinds of abnormal movement. These types may be classified as *spastic* (hypertonic, high muscle tone), *dyskinetic* or *athetoid* (fluctuating muscle tone), *ataxia* (decreased balance and coordination), and *mixed*. Each is described in detail later in this chapter.

The last part of the definition concerns the cause of cerebral palsy. Cerebral palsy results from malfunctioning or damage to the motor areas of the brain; the type depends on which motor system is affected.

ETIOLOGY OF CEREBRAL PALSY

When Little originally described a form of cerebral palsy, he thought it resulted from complications of labor and delivery. As a result, a commonly held assumption was that perinatal problems that resulted in a lack of oxygen to the baby at birth (birth **asphyxia**) were the primary cause of cerebral palsy. This belief persisted until the Collaborative Perinatal Project was formed to determine how to improve obstetric management and thus prevent cerebral palsy. Quite unexpectedly, the data indicated that birth asphyxia was an *un*common cause of cerebral palsy (Russman, 1992). Problems of labor and delivery may occur due to pre-existing problems and brain injury incurred in utero. It is now clear that prenatal factors and, to a lesser extent, perinatal

---

BOX 7-1

Causes and Risk Factors Associated with Cerebral Palsy

Causes	*Risk Factors*
PRENATAL	Toxemia
Brain malformation	Maternal bleeding
Genetic syndrome	Placental insufficiency
Prenatal infection	Maternal infection
Severe anoxia	Multiple births
PERINATAL	Maternal bleeding
Asphyxia	Maternal mental retar-
CNS infection	dation
POSTNATAL	
CNS infection	
Traumatic brain injury	
Poison	
Anoxia	

and postnatal factors can cause cerebral palsy (Nelson & Ellenberg, 1986).

A number of commonly associated conditions may cause cerebral palsy or place a child at-risk for developing the disorder (see Box 7-1). Prenatal infections such as rubella, cytomegalovirus (CMV), and toxoplasmosis are known causes of cerebral palsy. Several rare genetic diseases such as Lesch-Nyhan disease, phenylketonuria, hereditary microcephaly, familial spastic paraplegia, ataxia-telangiectasia, and Behr's Syndrome are associated with cerebral palsy (Russman, 1992). In addition to these causes, there are several risk factors for the development of cerebral palsy prenatally, including maternal mental retardation, toxemia of pregnancy, maternal bleeding, multiple births, placental insufficiency, and maternal chronic infection (Hagberg & Hagberg, 1984; Nelson & Ellenberg, 1986).

The extent to which perinatal factors are actual causes or are contributing risk factors is controversial. However, asphyxia occurring during labor and delivery has been associated with cerebral palsy. Hyperbilirubinemia (high concentrations of bilirubin in the blood) may also result in cerebral palsy, especially the athetoid type. Infants who were born small for gestational age or with a small head circumference are also at-risk (Nelson & Ellenberg, 1986).

Several postnatal causes have been identified. Infections such as meningitis and encephalitis or the injestion of certain toxins or poisons such as lead have been shown to result in cerebral palsy. Anoxia, as in a near-drowning or strangulation, can also result in cerebral

palsy. Strokes that result in cerebral palsy are rare, although a premature infant who suffers an intracranial bleed may do so (Russman, 1992). Unless the cause is a postnatal factor, determining the precise etiology of cerebral palsy in some children is often difficult. In many circumstances, it cannot be determined.

DYNAMICS OF CEREBRAL PALSY

Several classification systems are used to describe cerebral palsy. Two systems are based on anatomy. One of these is a neuroanatomical system, while the other is a topographical system.

Neuroanatomical Classification System of Cerebral Palsy

The neuroanatomical system categorizes the type of cerebral palsy based on location of damage in the brain. In this system, cerebral palsy is described as damage to (1) the pyramidal system, (2) extrapyramidal system (basal ganglia), (3) extrapyramidal system (cerebellum), and (4) mixed (see Figure 7-1).

We discussed earlier the three motor systems in the central nervous system. First, the pyramidal system, which consists of the motor strip and descending pathways (see drawing in Figure 7-1), controls voluntary motor movement and is especially crucial in fine motor control. Second, the basal ganglia are part of the extrapyramidal system—those portions of the brain and brain stem that are outside the pyramidal system and involve motor function. The basal ganglia appear as gray islands in the brain; they work in conjunction with the motor cortex in providing movement, and they serve as a relay center through which the pathways to and from the motor strip pass. Third, the cerebellum assists with balance and equilibrium and regulates muscle tone. The type of cerebral palsy a child has will depend on which motor system is damaged.

Pyramidal System
Damage to the pyramidal system results in spastic (hypertonic) cerebral palsy; increased muscle tone (spasticity) interferes with voluntary movement. Fine motor movement, such as movement of the hand or fingers, is often involved. The part of the body affected and the level of motor involvement depend on the location and extent of damage to the brain.

Extrapyramidal System: Basal Ganglia
Damage to the basal ganglia results in athetoid cerebral palsy. Damage to the basal ganglia can interfere with its functions as a relay center that works with the cerebral

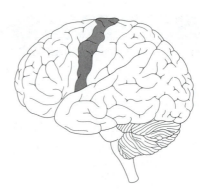

1. Pyramidal system damage:
   Spastic cerebral palsy

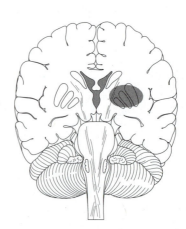

2. Extrapyramidal system damage: Basal ganglia
   Athetoid cerebral palsy (basal ganglia)

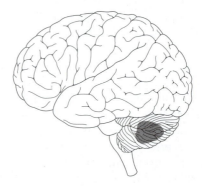

3. Extrapyramidal system damage: Cerebellum
   Ataxia

4. Pyramidal/extrapyramidal system damage:
   Mixed

■ **FIGURE 7-1** Neuroanatomical classification system of cerebral palsy

cortex. In these instances, there is an interruption of the normal feedback circuits that are thought to allow for finely progressive movements. When these circuits are blocked due to brain damage, the impulses take alternate, deviant routes through the basal ganglia and motor cortex. This results in a succession of abnormal, involuntary movements that may be slow and writhing or quick and jerky. If the part of the basal ganglia that inhibits muscle tone is affected, extremely high muscle tone (rigidity) can occur as well as abnormal posturing.

Cerebellum

Damage to the cerebellum may result in ataxia. In this form of cerebral palsy, there is difficulty in the coordination of voluntary movement and problems with balance. Some students will have difficulty maintaining their posture and equilibrium.

Mixed Cerebral Palsy

It is common for children with cerebral palsy to have damage in more than one motor system. When this occurs, the child will have a combination of the cerebral palsies; for example, the spastic and athetoid types. This combination of different types is known as mixed cerebral palsy.

Classification of Cerebral Palsy by Topography

The part of the body that is affected by cerebral palsy is determined by the location of brain damage. When the part of the brain that controls the legs is damaged (the upper motor strip) only the legs will be affected. When only the right side of the brain is affected (the motor strip on the right), there will only be symptoms on the left. A topographical classification system that describes which part of the body is affected was developed in 1956 by Minear (see Box 7-2). The most common types are *hemiplegia* (involvement on one side of the body), *diplegia* (involvement more in the legs than arms), and *quadriplegia* (involvement of all four limbs).

CHARACTERISTICS OF CEREBRAL PALSY

Cerebral palsy may affect a child's motor ability, communication, cognition, and daily living skills. An in-depth look at these areas will provide a better understanding of the characteristics and implications of cerebral palsy.

Effects of Cerebral Palsy on Motor Patterns

Different types of cerebral palsy have different motor responses and motor patterns. In Box 7-3, a classification of cerebral palsy by motor patterns is presented.

BOX 7-2

Topographical Classification System

A. *Monoplegia:* one limb
B. *Paraplegia:* legs only
C. *Hemiplegia:* one-half of body
D. *Triplegia:* three limbs (usually two legs and one arm)
E. *Quadriplegia:* all four limbs
F. *Diplegia:* more affected in the legs than the arms
G. *Double Hemiplegia:* arms more involved than the legs

BOX 7-3

Classification System by Motor Symptoms (Physiological)

A. Spastic
B. Athetoid
   1. Tension
   2. Nontension
   3. Dystonic
   4. Tremor
C. Rigidity
D. Ataxia
E. Tremor
F. Atonic (rare)
G. Mixed
H. Unclassified

Spastic (or Hypertonic) Cerebral Palsy

Students with spastic cerebral palsy have muscles that are **spastic,** other muscles that are weak, and others that are unaffected. Spastic muscles have increased tone; they usually contract strongly with sudden movement. The movement has often been called a *clasp-knife response,* which refers to the similarity of movement between opening a pocket-knife blade and the movement pattern of a child with spastic cerebral palsy. As an arm or leg is moved, there is initial resistance followed by a sudden release of resistance (Keele, 1983). This motor response interferes with voluntary movement, resulting in slower movement with abnormal movement patterns or postures.

Certain muscles are more likely to be affected than others. As muscles work together to cause movement, one set causes bending (flexion) of a body part and another set causes straightening (extension). In spastic cerebral palsy, certain muscles tend to have excessive muscle tone, while the opposite muscles will tend to have reduced tone. In spastic cerebral palsy, the excess muscle tone tends to result in flexion (bending) of the fingers, wrists, and elbows. The hips are usually internally rotated, which results in the knees being brought together and the legs often crossing (scissoring). There may also be plantar flexion, which causes the child to be on tiptoe (see Figure 7-2). Not all children with cerebral palsy have all of these motor abnormalities. The extent of involvement depends on which brain parts are affected.

The topographical classification system described previously is commonly used in the diagnosis of the location of cerebral palsy (for example, spastic quadriplegia and spastic hemiplegia). The most common types are diplegia, hemiplegia, double hemiplegia, and quadriplegia (see Figure 7-3).

Diplegia. In diplegic spastic cerebral palsy, the legs are primarily affected and there is some arm involvement. Depending on severity, the knees may tend to come tightly together, the legs may cross over each other (scissoring), and the child may walk awkwardly and on tiptoe. Spastic diplegia is caused by damage to the motor cortex and motor tract to the legs. In premature infants, the blood vessels are fragile, particularly in the area of the brain near the lateral ventricles. The motor tracts that go to the legs pass through this area. A bleed will often result in damage to the tracts and cortex, resulting in this type of cerebral palsy (Pidcock, et al., 1990).

Hemiplegia. In hemiplegic spastic cerebral palsy, only one side of the body is affected. The arm and the leg on the affected side have increased muscle tone; the arm is typically more affected than the leg (Uvebrant, 1988). The leg muscles are tight; the child is often on tiptoe; the arm may be drawn into a bent position at the elbow. As discussed earlier, the motor tracts cross at the brain stem. Therefore, when there is spasticity on the left side of the body, brain damage occurs on the right side (and vice versa).

Double hemiplegia. In this type, all four limbs are involved, but there is more involvement of the arms than the legs. Also, one side of the body is usually affected more than the other. Like quadriplegia, both sides of the motor cortex are affected but usually one side more than the other, and the arms are more affected than the legs.

Quadriplegia. In spastic quadriplegia (also known as tetraplegia), all four limbs are involved—the legs usually more severely than the arms. The trunk and the face may be involved as well. All of the conditions described earlier pertaining to the arms, legs, and hips are usually found. For this type of spastic cerebral palsy to occur, there must have been extensive damage to the motor strip and motor tracts on both sides of the brain.

Athetoid Cerebral Palsy

Children with athetoid (dyskinetic) cerebral palsy have abnormal motor movements that are usually most observable when the child initiates a movement. In athetoid cerebral palsy, the child will have a succession of abnormal, purposeless movements. These are movements in which the initiation of a movement of one muscle group leads to the movement of others (known as motor overflow) (Russman, 1992). This appears as abnormal writhing movements in which the limb rotates back and forth, extends and flexes, and slowly makes its way to the intended destination (see Figure 7-4). Involuntary, jerking, and irregular movements are also present.

Athetoid cerebral palsy may also be classified as *dystonic athetoid cerebral palsy* or *tremor*. A child with this condition has abnormal shifts of muscle tone in which he or she assumes and retains abnormal and distorted postures (Russman, 1992). Tremor refers to an irregular and uneven type of involuntary contraction and relaxation that results in rapid shaking movements (Minear, 1956).

Rigidity

Rigidity is a term used to describe constant (lead-pipe type) or intermittent (cogwheel type) resistance to passive motor movement. Unlike a clasp-knife response, there is no release of tension near the end of the movement. Also, there is usually greater resistance to slow movement than to rapid movement. This is the opposite of spastic cerebral palsy in which there is more resistance to rapid movement. Rigidity may be present

■ **FIGURE 7-2** Typical posture of a student with spastic cerebral palsy

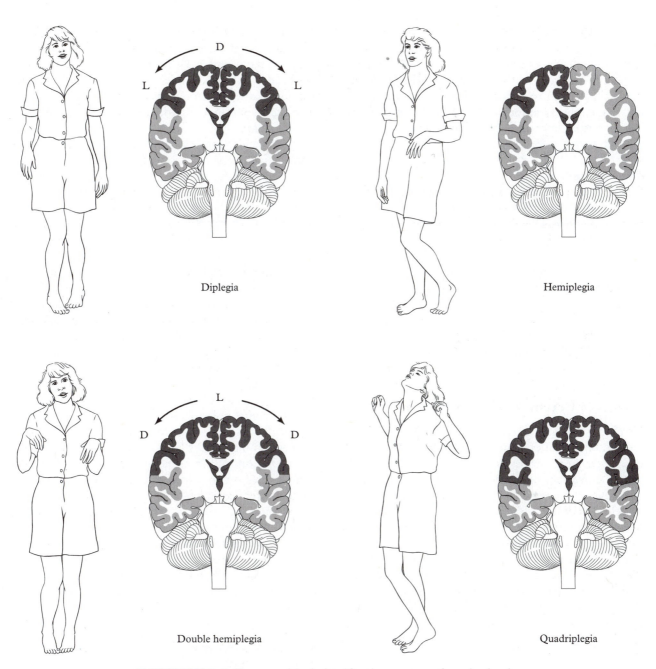

Diplegia

Hemiplegia

Double hemiplegia

Quadriplegia

■ FIGURE 7-3 Topographical classification system of cerebral palsy

in spastic or athetoid cerebral palsy or may occur alone in a classification by itself.

Ataxia

Children with ataxia have uncoordinated voluntary muscle movement with poor balance and equilibrium. Children often walk with a wide gait, feet wide apart, trunk weaving back and forth, and arms held out. They often appear to walk as if they were walking on a rolling ship in the ocean (Bleck & Nagel, 1982) or as if they were drunk. This type of cerebral palsy rarely occurs alone but is often seen with other types.

Tremor

Tremor refers to regular, rhythmic oscillations of the limbs or trunk that are uncontrollable and involuntary. Typically, no other neurological problem is present with this condition.

Atonic (Hypotonic)

Atonia refers to a lack of tone, or low tone. Children with atonia have been described as "floppy" children, like rag dolls. Usually, atonia does not refer to a type of cerebral palsy but to a symptom. It is often one of the first presenting symptoms of an infant with cerebral palsy who may later develop spastic, athetoid, or mixed cerebral palsy.

Mixed Cerebral Palsy

Cerebral palsy often will appear in combinations. It is not unusual for a child to have both spastic cerebral palsy and athetoid cerebral palsy. Any combination is possible. Mixed cerebral palsy usually indicates more extensive damage of the motor cortex and motor pathway. Often additional problems such as developmental delays and mental retardation occur in mixed types.

Unclassified

Other types of cerebral palsy that do not fall in the existing classification system are placed in this category.

Effects of Cerebral Palsy on Movement

No matter which type of cerebral palsy a child has, there will be abnormalities of movement because normal motor movement requires a coordination of the muscles. A simple movement like bending the arm at the elbow requires using one set of muscles to relax (extensor muscles) and the opposing set to contract (flexor muscles). In a child or adult without disabilities, motor movement also depends on groups of muscles working together in patterns. No single muscle is responsible for the movement. One illustration of how muscles work together is the way a girl moves from a lying position on the floor (with her back against the floor) to a sitting position. As she lifts her head off the floor to sit up, her shoulders assist with the lifting, her arms move forward,

■ FIGURE 7-4 Typical movement found in students with athetoid cerebral palsy

her back rounds, and there is bending at the hips. This coordination of movement allows the easy execution of the desired movement. On the other hand, if she pushed her head back, her shoulder would go back, her spine would hollow, and her hips would straighten. This type of muscle coordination would make it almost impossible to sit up.

In the child with cerebral palsy, movements also occur in muscle patterns, but, due to the damage of the motor areas of the brain, the movements are uncoordinated and abnormal (Finnie, 1974). These abnormal movements may be very mild and only noticeable when the child engages in a particular motor activity such as running, or so severe that the child can move very little independently.

In addition to abnormal motor movements, the child with cerebral palsy will have continued primitive reflexes. As we discussed in Chapter 2, primitive reflexes are reflexes that are normally present in the first few months of life. Most are integrated into voluntary motor patterns within the first year. Children with cerebral palsy typically have a continuation of these primitive reflexes, which can interfere with maintaining or moving into various positions and with achieving developmental milestones such as sitting and walking. Abnormalities of the postural reactions also contribute to these problems. (See Chapter 2.)

Further difficulties in movement are present when contractures occur. Contractures are permanent muscular shortenings in which the muscle length is reduced or there is a fixed resistance to movement. This reduces the child's range of motion and ability to move the limb fully. Contractures result when the child remains in abnormal postures and is unable to move his or her joints through their full range of motion. Contractures can be very debilitating and can result in minimal use of limbs.

Effects of Cerebral Palsy on Communication

The lack of coordinated muscle movement and the persistence of abnormal reflexes found in cerebral palsy may also affect the oropharyngeal muscles—those controlling the mouth and throat. Speech may be slurred and poorly articulated (dysarthria), which makes it difficult to understand. In some cases, expressive language cannot develop because the child cannot carry out purposeful oral movements (verbal apraxia) (Alexander & Bauer, 1988).

Cerebral palsy may also affect nonverbal forms of communication. Facial expressions may be strained, and difficulty with head control may impede making eye contact. This may be mistaken for a lack of interest. A student with severe spastic cerebral palsy may want an item and reach for it but knock it away due to abnormal motor movements. This could be mistaken for the student's not wanting the item.

Effects of Cerebral Palsy on Cognition

Children with cerebral palsy may be gifted, have normal intelligence, or be mentally retarded. Overall, there is a significant incidence of mental retardation in children with cerebral palsy. Specific learning disabilities, such as those involving visual perception, as well as attention deficit disorders are also present more frequently than would be expected in the general population (Alexander & Bauer, 1988). However, it is often difficult to obtain an accurate assessment of intelligence and learning when there is severe motor and verbal involvement. This is especially true when the child has no reliable means of responding to questions; that is, has not learned an augmentative or alternative form of communication well enough that it is dependable.

Certain types of cerebral palsy have been associated with an increased incidence of mental retardation. Persons with spastic diplegia and athetoid cerebral palsy may have no intellectual deficiencies. There is approximately a 25% incidence of persons with spastic hemiplegia having mental retardation or learning disorders. However, children with spastic quadriplegia, spastic double hemiplegia, and ataxia have a higher association of mental retardation or learning disabilities (Behrman, 1992).

Effects of Cerebral Palsy on Daily Living

Cerebral palsy has also been defined by the functional effect of the disorder on daily living skills. This classification system divides cerebral palsy into mild, moderate, and severe or uses a numbered system. Box 7-4 shows the two systems of describing the severity of cerebral palsy. Mild cerebral palsy indicates very little impairment of motor movement; often, the fine motor movements are only slightly affected. Students who appear to have only a minor motor impairment while writing, for example, would fall into this classification. Students with moderate cerebral palsy can still perform the usual activities of daily living, although the motor impairment is quite visible and may result in a longer period of time needed for completion of the activities.

Severe cerebral palsy refers to motor involvement so severe that the usual activities of daily living cannot be carried out without extensive adaptations. Note that this classification system does not reflect the presence or absence of mental retardation. Children with severe cerebral palsy may have normal intelligence, just as a

---

> **BOX 7-4**
>
> **Functional Classification of Cerebral Palsy**
>
> ---
>
> *Mild cerebral palsy:* Minimal impairment with very little limitation of activity or incoordination.
>
> *Moderate cerebral palsy:* Impairments in gross and fine motor movements; affects ambulation and speech; independent functioning limited without use of assistive devices.
>
> *Severe cerebral palsy:* Impairments almost completely incapacitating; inability to perform the usual activities of daily living without extensive adaptations.
>
> or
>
> *Class I:* No limitation of activity.
>
> *Class II:* Slight-to-moderate limitation of activity.
>
> *Class III:* Moderate-to-great limitation of activity.
>
> *Class IV:* Individuals are unable to carry on any useful physical activity (without assistive technology).
>
> ---
>
> SOURCES: Bigge (1991); Kopriva & Taylor (1992); Umbreit (1983).

---

student with mild cerebral palsy may have mental retardation or learning problems.

Depending on the severity of motor involvement, some children will have difficulty with various daily living skills, including feeding, dressing, toileting, personal hygiene, and carrying out normal activities of daily living. The lack of coordination in oral movement, combined with the persistence of primitive reflexes (for example, asymmetrical tonic neck reflex and bite reflex), may result in severe feeding difficulties and drooling. The child may have a tongue thrust, and food will be pushed back out of the mouth. A bite reflex may be present, which results in the child's biting the spoon. Children with arm involvement may be unable to bring the spoon to their mouths. In some children, the involvement of the oropharyngeal area may not affect feeding but result in excessive drooling. This is a major cosmetic problem that can interfere with social interaction and result in chapped skin.

Toileting difficulties may be present for a child with severe cerebral palsy. The child may have difficulty sitting on a toilet even with adaptations, and there may be a concomitant lack of balance and fear of falling. The child must be able to detect sensory stimulation from the bladder or rectum and then relax enough to allow for elimination. Bladder and bowel training may be difficult. Constipation is common due to the lack of movement and to dietary deficiencies, which further compounds toileting problems.

Other activities of daily living may be difficult. Dressing, brushing teeth, making a bed, or shopping in the community may pose serious physical challenges. The combination of poor motor coordination, lack of range of motion, unsteadiness in certain positions, and lack of fine motor control adversely affect the child's independence. As discussed earlier, adaptations may help the student perform these activities successfully.

Additional Impairments

There is an increased incidence of other types of disabilities occurring in children with cerebral palsy. Seizures are often present. Tonic-clonic seizures occur in about 25% of individuals with cerebral palsy, most often with the hemiplegic spastic type (Berkow, 1992). Sensory impairments also commonly occur. In athetosis, hearing impairment (of the sensorineural type) is often present. Any one of several types of visual impairments may be present, the most common of which are motility defects (defects in moving the eye as in such conditions as **strabismus**), nystagmus, refractory errors, and optic atrophy (Harley & Altmeyer, 1982).

Additional disorders may be the result of the cerebral palsy itself. These conditions usually result from abnormal motor movement and unequal muscle pull. One example is hip dislocation in which the hip bone is displaced from the socket. This is most commonly present in spastic cerebral palsy. Another example is curvature of the spine (scoliosis, **kyphosis,** or **lordosis**) due to the tight, abnormal pull of the muscle.

DETECTION OF CEREBRAL PALSY

It is difficult to detect cerebral palsy in the newborn. The baby will not display the typical motor characteristics of a child with cerebral palsy. After a few months, very subtle changes can be mistaken for any number of conditions or may even be considered normal. The child may have an excessive or a feeble cry. There may be some asymmetry in motion or contour. The infant may appear listless or irritable. There may be some difficulty feeding, sucking, or swallowing. The child may have low muscle tone or abnormal muscle tone.

Near the end of the first year and into the second, the infant may display persistent primitive reflexes, lagging motor development (with failure to reach motor milestones when normally indicated), and altered muscle tone. Hand preference may also be present, which is abnormal before 12 to 15 months of age. A particular type of cerebral palsy often cannot be distinguished until the second year of life when the specific motor symptoms develop (Berkow, 1992). However, early detection and treatment of at-risk children may pro-

mote development and independence and prevent secondary problems.

TREATMENT OF CEREBRAL PALSY

The goal of treating cerebral palsy is to develop maximum independence. This typically involves the collaborative effort of several individuals, including the pediatrician, physical therapist, occupational therapist, speech and language pathologist, special education teacher, parents, and the student. The earlier the child receives treatment, the more likely it is that he or she can develop more typical movement patterns. Early therapy makes it less likely that the child will develop secondary problems like contractures. Treatment may include managing the motor impairment, the communication problems, and daily living skills.

Management of Motor Impairment

The child with cerebral palsy may have physical therapy and occupational therapy, positioning devices, orthotic devices, medications, and sometimes surgery to improve motor function.

Physical and Occupational Therapies

Physical and occupational therapies provide treatment to children with cerebral palsy. Most therapy is based on the principles of neurodevelopmental treatment (NDT) and sensory integrative (SI) therapy. NDT attempts to reduce the number of abnormal movement patterns and encourage normal, purposeful movement in an active and functional manner (Bobath, 1967; Mayo, 1991). SI therapy helps the child take in, sort out, and connect information from the environment. Common to both types of therapies is the emphasis on proper positioning, therapeutic handling, use of automatic reactions, and equilibrium responses. Both emphasize active involvement and the integration of therapeutic techniques into activities of daily living.

Positioning Devices

The child with cerebral palsy may need to be positioned in several different types of adaptive equipment. The purpose of this equipment is to promote good body alignment, prevent contractures and deformities, promote movement and comfort, lessen effects of abnormal muscle tone and reflexes, improve circulation and other ANS functions, decrease risk of pressure sores (decubitus ulcers), decrease fatigue, and promote bone growth (when standing) (Bergen, Presperin, & Tallman, 1990; McEwen, 1992). Positioning also provides access to the environment and facilitates the performance of certain activities. There is a correspondence between activities

■ **FIGURE 7-5** Student with cerebral palsy using his wheelchair for mobility while playing ball

and specific positions. For example, a boy with cerebral palsy positioned in a sidelyer may have better use of his left arm, which allows him to participate in a group activity by using a switch.

Specific equipment is prescribed according to the type of motor problem, the child's size and weight, and the nature of the activity. Equipment (such as sidelyers, wedges, special seating devices, and prone standers) is commonly used (see Chapter 27). Such equipment needs to be adjusted for an individual child by a qualified professional (physical therapist or occupational therapist). There is typically a prescribed period of time the child should spend in the equipment to avoid injury or fatigue; the therapist determines the length of time.

Other equipment, such as scooters, bikes, walkers, and wheelchairs, may assist with mobility (see Figure 7-5). Often, modifications are made to these mobility devices to allow for proper positioning. Wheelchairs, for example, may have special inserts to keep the knees apart (abductor pad) or the body aligned (lateral supports). Head support may be necessary as well. Some wheelchairs are motorized to allow independent movement for children with upper-arm involvement. Again, a physical therapist or an occupational therapist should help prescribe or modify this mobility equipment, which should help the student be as independent as possible. Since much of this equipment is custom fitted, it is not interchangeable among students.

Orthotics

The child with cerebral palsy may also need to use various braces or splints (orthotics). By applying an orthotic splint or brace, the muscle group is placed in a more lengthened position. This helps to maintain proper alignment, improve range of motion, and decrease the development of contractures.

There are many different types of orthotics (see Figure 7-6). To prevent toe-walking and the shortening of the Achilles tendon, a short leg splint may be worn. This is known as an ankle/foot orthosis (AFO). To help improve hand function, a resting hand splint or hand cone may be used. Since most of these are made specifically for the child, they must be carefully monitored by the therapists for correct fit as the child grows. Staff members should look for and report any reddening of the area or skin breakdown. Also, close adherence to the times the orthotic is supposed to be worn is important if treatment is to be effective.

Medication

Several medications may be taken to control excess muscle tone and promote relaxation of the muscles. Two of the most commonly prescribed medications are Valium and Dantrium. Side effects of these medications include drowsiness and drooling. These oral medica-

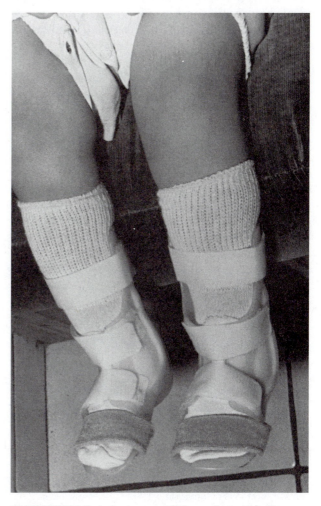

■ **FIGURE 7-6** A young child wearing ankle/foot orthoses (AFOs)

tions often have limited effectiveness and are ineffective in reducing spasticity in many cases (Park & Owen, 1992). Careful monitoring of the side effects, adverse effects, and effectiveness is necessary to make any needed adjustments in dosage or to try new treatments.

Surgery

Cerebral palsy may be so severe because of the shortening of muscles that it interferes with normal functioning. The child may be unable to sit, stand, or experience any functional arm or leg use. Surgery may be needed to allow the child to reach his or her optimal functioning level, decrease discomfort, or prevent deformity. This typically involves releasing muscles, lengthening muscles, or transferring muscles.

Several different surgical procedures are designed to treat the child with cerebral palsy. The most common is surgical correction of the deformity of the ankle that results in the child being on tiptoe. The Achilles tendon (heel cord) is lengthened. As seen in Figure 7-7, there are different types of surgical cuts that result in allowing the foot to be placed flat on the ground. Because this surgery will allow the child to stand with feet flat, it may assist in walking.

Other surgical procedures improve the range of motion in the arms and legs. The surgical goal of treating children with spasticity in the arms is to release the spastic deformity and reposition the arm to improve its functional use (Sprague, 1992). The hamstring muscles in the legs may be released to help with sitting and walking. Surgery to release the tendons and muscle that result in hip deformities may be needed. These surgeries are aimed at preventing hip dislocation and allowing the child to assume a sitting position.

Neurosurgical procedures have also been used to treat cerebral palsy. These procedures involve surgery on the central nervous system. One such procedure, known as selective posterior rhizotomy, involves cutting the spinal nerve roots that cause severe spasticity of the legs (Berman, Vaughan, & Peacock, 1990). This procedure has resulted in reduced spasticity and improvement in sitting, standing, and moving.

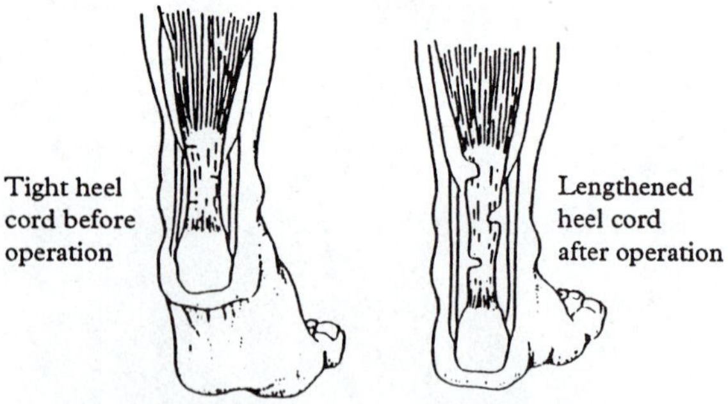

Management of Communication Problems

Children with cerebral palsy have a range of communication skills, from no speech impairments to no understandable speech. The speech and language pathologist, parent, teacher, and child should work closely together to promote effective forms of communication, which may include speech, augmentative communication, or both.

Students with cerebral palsy may benefit from nonelectronic or electronic communication devices. Depending on the extent of the cerebral palsy, the student may have a combined system of gestures, signs, or a communication board, as well as nonsymbolic forms of communication (facial expressions, body movements). In using a communication board, the student may access the board by pointing with his or her finger, mouth stick, head wand, eye gaze, or computer interface. The child may also access a communication board by pressing or pulling a switch to indicate a response (see Figure 7-8). (See also Chapter 28.)

Promoting Daily Living Skills

The extent of motor involvement will affect the child's success in participating in various daily living skills. Often to promote success, adaptations and adapted devices may be used in home, school, and community environments.

Some devices used for feeding may include a scooper dish, adapted utensil with a built-up handle, a nonslip pad on which to place the dish and sandwich holders, among others. Drinking cups may be adapted with cutout areas to facilitate drinking or may have special handles (see Figure 7-9). Certain feeding techniques, such as those that provide jaw control, may be needed. To allow the student to be as independent as possible while feeding, the combined efforts of an occupational therapist, physical therapist, speech and language pathologist, teacher, and parent are often needed.

Adaptations may be made in the bathroom to allow the student to be as independent as possible. This may include installing railings and wider stalls for wheelchair access. Modifications may be made to the toilet to allow supportive sitting, or an adapted toilet may be used. It is important that the student be taught proper

■ **FIGURE 7-7** Achilles tendon lengthening
SOURCE: From *Children with Disabilities: A Medical Primer,* Third Edition, by M. L. Batshaw and Y. M. Perret, pp. 343, 460, 477. Copyright ©1992 Paul H. Brookes Publishing Co. Reprinted with permission of Dr. Mark L. Batshaw.

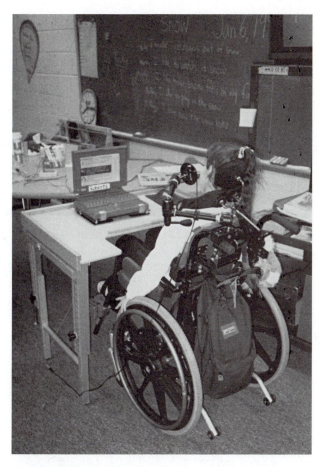

■ **FIGURE 7-8** Student using communication device at her cutout table, which she controls with a switch positioned at the left side of her head

transferring techniques and that personnel be trained in correct lifting and handling techniques.

Activities of daily living may require adaptations that allow the child to participate to the maximum extent possible. Toothbrush and toothpaste holders may be used to assist with toothbrushing. A dressing rack and adapted clothing fasteners may help the student dress; push-pull sticks may help with putting on socks. Environmental control devices that allow the child to activate items with a switch (turn on lights, turn on the TV) may be useful. Switches may also be used for turning on any number of devices, such as electric blenders. (See Chapters 27 and 28 for more adaptations.)

COURSE OF CEREBRAL PALSY

Cerebral palsy is a chronic condition that will continue throughout the person's life. It is not considered a progressive condition because no further brain damage occurs. However, as the child matures, further impair-

ments (such as contractures, curvatures of the spine, and hip dislocation) may result from continued abnormal flexion and extension.

EDUCATIONAL IMPLICATIONS OF CEREBRAL PALSY

It is important that the teacher have a good understanding of cerebral palsy and each student's specific motor involvement and concomitant problems so the student's educational needs can be met.

Meeting Physical and Sensory Needs

The teacher must learn proper positioning and handling techniques in order to be of most help to the student and to effectively integrate these techniques throughout the day. (See also Chapter 27.) Proper positioning is needed so the student can participate in activities. To avoid injury to both the teacher and the student, the teacher should be trained in proper body mechanics when positioning a student (for example, lifting with the legs and not with the back). The teacher must also know the use of adaptive positioning devices and be able to verify that the student is positioned in them correctly. The student's physical therapist and occupational therapist can help with positioning and handling techniques.

■ **FIGURE 7-9** Adapted spoons, cup, and glass

Teachers should be familiar with any additional treatment the student is receiving and with their own role in providing carryover. The teacher should know the types, dosage, and side effects of medication the student is taking at school. When splints or braces are used, the teacher should be alert for any redness or skin breakdown, as well as for poor fit. For the benefit of students in wheelchairs, the teacher should be familiar with minor wheelchair repairs. When the child returns to school after surgery, the teacher should understand any restrictions placed upon him or her.

Because students with cerebral palsy may have other problems, such as seizures, learning or cognitive problems, or sensory impairments, the teacher needs a good understanding of what modifications need to be made for each case. It is also important that the teacher educate others about the child's disability. Often when a child has severe cerebral palsy, others assume that the child has mental retardation, which may not be the case. Sensitivity and support should be given, as well as encouragement in being as independent as possible.

Meeting Communication Needs

Augmentative communication devices may be used by the student to communicate with others when his or her speech is not understandable. The teacher, as part of the educational team, needs to help the student to use the device and to add vocabulary as the child becomes more proficient. The teacher must keep in mind that when the student is still learning a system of communication, assessments of the student's ability and intelligence may be inaccurate.

Sometimes the student with cerebral palsy may need to explain to a classmate about having cerebral palsy. One possible explanation is, "My muscles don't get the right messages to make them move how I want them to move. These plastic things are braces. I wear them to help my legs, like kids who wear braces to help their teeth" (Morrow, 1985).

Meeting Learning Needs

Academic instruction for a child with cerebral palsy should be based on the student's cognitive level, not motor disability level. Depending on the severity of the cerebral palsy, special equipment and adaptations may be needed to allow the student to function optimally in the school setting. Some students with very mild cerebral palsy may be slower in writing an assignment and need more time, while students with more severe cerebral palsy may need to use a computer with a switch to complete an assignment.

■ VIGNETTE 1 ■

Sally is a 10-year-old student with a rare combination of severe spastic quadriplegic cerebral palsy and spina bifida. She also is legally blind in her right eye (and has no light perception in her left eye); she has seizures and severe scoliosis. She can only move her jaw, tongue, and, to some extent, her face. She had been placed in a self-contained class for students with severe intellectual disabilities since she entered school. Using a team approach, modifications were used to assist with Sally's instruction and included enlarged print, a multiple-choice format, the use of a scanning device, modified yes and no response, and adapted seating and positioning. As modifications were put in place and Sally learned a consistent means of response using her residual vision and limited motoric responses, she began to learn basic math skills and spelling words very rapidly. As her communication system was developed by the team, she was accurately tested and found to have near-normal intelligence. The IEP team met and placed her in a resource room serving students with orthopedic impairments in a different school. However, the new teacher had never worked with a student with such severe physical and sensory impairments, and the school had never had a student this physically disabled. A few teachers at the new school doubted that Sally could possibly have near-normal intelligence. Sally overheard their comments and refused to work at the new school, further reinforcing to the teachers that Sally could not do the work. Many of the students picked up on the teachers' attitudes and did not associate with Sally. The teachers and students were not adequately prepared to interact with Sally, and inservicing and support from Sally's earlier school was lacking. The teachers demonstrated prejudice, which spread to the other students and adversely affected Sally's performance and her ability to succeed.

Adapted devices, such as pencil grips (either commercially available or made of clay or sponge) and page turners, may be needed. For students unable to hold paper on the desk, the paper may be taped to the desk, or a clipboard may be used. Cutout desks may be used to allow the wheelchair to fit under the table and provide additional arm support. Other tables may be lowered for best fit. Chalkboards may also be lowered to allow the student access. The need for equipment should not preclude students from going into the community and to various classes in school. Failure to provide these adaptations when the child is in the

■ **VIGNETTE 2** ■

Chantell is an 8-year-old student in second grade who loves school. She has severe spastic cerebral palsy that has caused her to be nonambulatory and nonvocal. She receives instruction in an inclusive second-grade class with support from the teacher of students with orthopedic impairments. Chantell is very popular among the second graders. Although she is learning an electronic communication board with vocal output, she presently uses a multiple-page eye-gaze board that allows her to have conversations on such things as last night's TV programs or what is going on in school. Academically, she is about one grade level behind her peers in reading, but her regular education teacher and the teacher of students with orthopedic impairments are assisting her in this subject. Her math skills are appropriate for her age. Due to Chantell's disability, the regular education teacher and the teacher of students with orthopedic impairments must work closely together coordinating lessons and adapting material and activities. Materials are adapted so they can be selected by eye-gaze or placed on a scanner that Chantell controls with a switch. Chantell also does her work on a computer, which she controls with a switch and adaptive firmware card or with a head pointer. The school's willingness to make the necessary adaptations and work collaboratively has enabled Chantell to succeed at school.

regular classroom is as much a problem as not integrating the child because equipment is required.

For students who have severe communication problems, the teacher may need to adapt the presentation of material. Material may be presented in a multiple-choice format (with numbers for each possible selection) to allow the student to choose the answer, or students may indicate their response by eye-gazing the answer presented in a multiple-choice format or by using a scanning device. Computers with adaptations such as switches, touch windows, and powerpads often facilitate academic work. These adaptations can require only minimal movement to activate the device or allow for activation using alternative movement. The adaptations should be used across all settings.

Meeting Daily Living Needs

Students with cerebral palsy will typically need to incorporate daily living skills into their curriculum.

Teachers should be aware of possible adaptations and devices. Students must also learn how to become self-advocates so they can direct their own care if they are physically unable to care for themselves.

Meeting Behavioral and Social Needs

The teacher should be alert for any difficulty the student may have with social interactions. Students with visible physical impairments, such as cerebral palsy, may become socially isolated because of their appearance and, often, because of poor social skills. The teacher may need to provide social skills training as well as specific strategies to use in maintaining interactions when communication is slow.

Students with cerebral palsy may also exhibit frustration and have behavioral outbursts when they cannot communicate effectively or are unable to accomplish a task due to their unintentional motor movements. Teachers need to be sensitive to the student's needs, provide augmented forms of communication, and provide alternate ways of accomplishing tasks.

SUMMARY

Cerebral palsy refers to several different disorders of posture and movement. Cerebral palsy occurs because of malfunction or damage to the motor areas of the brain, which can result from prenatal, perinatal, or postnatal causes. There are several types of cerebral palsy; the most common are spastic, athetoid, and ataxia. Often a mixed form of cerebral palsy is present in which there is a combination of these types.

Cerebral palsy can range from mild to severe involvement. In mild cases, a mild limp may be detected only when the student runs. In severe cases, the student has limited movement of arms and legs, nonunderstandable verbal communication, and accompanying sensory impairments. Treatment may include medication to control excess muscle tone, physical and occupational therapy, positioning and handling techniques, use of orthotics, and possibly surgery. The teacher may need to make adaptations to accommodate for physical, sensory, communication, learning, and behavioral and social needs to allow the student to take an active part in the learning process. A team approach is crucial for best results.

CHAPTER 8

Spinal Cord Disorders: Spinal Cord Injury and Spina Bifida

When a spinal cord is severely injured or is defective in its development, muscle paralysis and sensory loss to parts of the body below the level of injury often result. Two types of spinal cord disorders that can result in paralysis and sensory loss are *spinal cord injury* and *spina bifida*. These disorders can affect every aspect of a person's life.

Each year, approximately 25 to 35 spinal cord injuries occur for every 1 million people (Hu & Cressy, 1992). Although spinal cord injuries occur at all ages, they are most frequent in adolescents. When these injured young people return to school, they often face problems adjusting to their disability and to the use of adaptations. This provides special challenges to the educator who must help the student adjust to the physical, psychological, and social impact of an injury.

Spina bifida, on the other hand, is one of the most serious congenital disorders affecting the nervous system. Spina bifida is a defect in the spinal column that affects the spinal cord, often resulting in paralysis and sensory loss. The incidence of spina bifida has been estimated to be about 1 per 1,000 live births (Hobbins, 1991). Due to the characteristics of this disorder, there may be additional problems in learning and social interaction. Children with spina bifida often need adaptations and training in such areas as mobility, self-help, social competence, and learning strategies.

In this chapter, we will describe the various forms of spinal cord injury and spina bifida, as well as the characteristics and complications that may occur. Although many similarities can be seen between a child with spina bifida and a child with a spinal cord injury, some problems are unique to each impairment.

DESCRIPTION OF SPINAL CORD INJURY

The term *spinal cord injury* refers to damage to the spinal cord that can be caused by a wide range of disorders and traumatic events. Depending on the location and severity of the injury, the child may have symptoms ranging from weakness of a limb to paralysis of all parts of the body below the neck with ventilator-assisted breathing. Typically, the term implies motor paralysis and loss of sensation for certain parts of the body.

ETIOLOGY OF SPINAL CORD INJURY

Spinal cord injury may be caused by any number of disorders or traumatic events, the most frequent of which are accidents. Car accidents are usually ranked first among many possible causes of spinal cord injury in children. This includes both children as passengers and adolescents who are driving. The second most common cause is falling; other accidents are sports accidents, such as diving and trampoline accidents. Gunshot wounds that penetrate the spinal cord are also responsible for spinal cord injuries (Hu & Cressy, 1992).

Spinal cord injury may also result from medical conditions such as spinal cord tumors that disrupt functioning of the spinal cord. Tumors may grow from within the substance of the cord (intramedullary tumors) or next to the dura (the outer membrane) surrounding the cord (extramedullary). Certain medical syndromes may also result in spinal cord injury. *Transverse myelitis*, for example, is a syndrome in which there is an acute transection of the spinal cord in the thoracic (chest) area. The cause is unknown, although nonspecific viral infections have been found to occur before the onset of the syndrome. Some prenatal conditions may not cause symptoms until later in life. An example of this is a tethered cord. In this condition, thick, ropelike tissue anchors the spinal cord below the level of the vertebrae where the cord normally ends. The resulting abnormal tension on the cord can cause neurological damage, especially during growth spurts (Behrman, 1992).

Spinal cord damage can also occur during birth if a child is born in a breech position—feet first. As the child passes out of the birth canal, the neck can become hyperextended, which stretches the spinal cord to the point of injury. This can cause paralysis and sensory loss below the neck (Umbreit, 1983).

Spinal cord injuries also can occur from child abuse. Extensive shaking of a child or infant may result in spinal cord damage. Since this results in cervical injuries at the neck, the child will often be quadriplegic, with muscle paralysis below the neck.

Certain congenital syndromes may predispose children to spinal cord injuries. Children with Down syndrome, for example, are susceptible to dislocation of the area between the first and second cervical vertebrae (atlantoaxial joint) because of lax ligaments. If dislocation occurs, weakness of the arms and legs may also occur, or in extreme cases, some paralysis. Children with this problem are advised not to engage in activities that cause extensive flexion and extension of the neck, such as diving and tumbling (Shapiro, 1992).

DYNAMICS OF SPINAL CORD INJURY

The spinal cord is approximately one-half inch wide and 18 inches long in the adult male. It is surrounded by membranes (meninges) that assist in protecting the spinal cord. Both the spinal cord and the meninges are enclosed in the spinal vertebrae, which provide further protection. The spinal cord is actually shorter than the vertebral column; the end of the spinal cord terminates at about the level of the first lumbar vertebra (see Figure 8-1).

The spinal cord itself is part of the central nervous system and is composed of billions of neurons (nerve cells). Unlike the brain, the spinal cord contains gray matter on the inside and white matter on the outside. The gray matter consists of cell bodies arranged in an H pattern (see Figure 8-2). The front section of the H, called the *anterior horn*, carries motor information. The back part of the H, called the *posterior horn*, carries sensory information. The white matter that surrounds the gray matter is made up of *axons*; bundles of axons are known as *tracts*. Information is carried to and from the brain along these tracts.

The function of the spinal cord is to carry impulses (messages) from the brain through the nerves exiting the spinal cord to various parts of the body. In addition, the spinal cord receives messages from the body through the nerves entering the spinal cord and sends these messages to the brain. This transfer of information occurs through a complex system of electrical and chemical impulses traveling along the tracts.

Information exits or enters the spinal cord on its way to or from the brain through the *spinal nerves*. These spinal nerves are named and numbered according to which vertebra they exit near. Just as there are cervical, thoracic, lumbar, sacral, and coccygeal vertebrae, so are there cervical, thoracic lumbar, sacral, and coccygeal nerves. There are 8 cervical nerves (referred to as C1, C2, C3, . . ., C8), 12 thoracic nerves (referred to as T1, T2, . . ., T12), 5 lumbar nerves (referred to as L1, L2, . . ., L5), 5 sacral nerves (referred to as S1, S2, . . ., S5), and 1 coccygeal nerve. The T1 spinal nerve, for example, exits from the T1 vertebra. Since the spinal column is longer than the spinal cord, several spinal nerves extend lower than the cord in order to exit by their corresponding vertebrae. The spinal nerves extending below the spinal cord are referred to as the *cauda equina*, or horse's tail (see Figures 8-1 and 11-3).

Each of the spinal nerves exits the spinal cord, branches out into peripheral nerves, and connects with various muscles in the body. These motor nerves exiting the spinal cord control movement. The sensory nerves that go from the skin and other tissue to the spinal cord carry sensory information about pain, temperature, pressure, and proprioception. Each motor and sensory nerve corresponds to certain parts of the body. As seen in Figure 8-2, specific sensory and motor information is sent to and from the spinal cord via certain spinal nerves. Sensory information from the chest and back, for example, is primarily received by thoracic sensory nerves. Movement of the chest and back result from thoracic motor nerve impulses.

In addition to being a relay between the brain and the body, the spinal cord is also responsible for eliciting certain reflexes. As we discussed in Chapter 4, these reflexes occur by a reflex arc. When a knee is tapped with a rubber hammer, for example, a sensory impulse is sent to the posterior horn of the spinal cord. The impulse then travels to the motor cell body in the anterior horn of the spinal cord. The impulse then exits the spinal cord via the motor nerve and travels to the leg muscles to cause a kicking motion. All of this happens at the level of the spinal cord without brain involvement. In an intact central nervous system, a signal is sent from the spinal cord to let the brain know what has happened.

Spinal Cord Injury from Trauma

During an accident, the bones or ligaments (or both) of the **vertebral column** are disrupted. The vertebral bones may break (fracture) or the vertebral column may become dislocated from damage to the supporting ligaments that are located between each vertebra. When this occurs, the normal configuration of one vertebra on top of another is disrupted. The spinal cord, which lies within the vertebral column, then becomes bruised, compressed, crushed, or torn.

After an initial spinal cord injury from trauma, the damage may worsen in three different ways. First, the spinal column may be unstable from the injury, and movement of the area may cause further damage. It is important that the area of damage be immobilized before the person is moved. Second, further damage can occur from edema (swelling) at the site of injury. As in

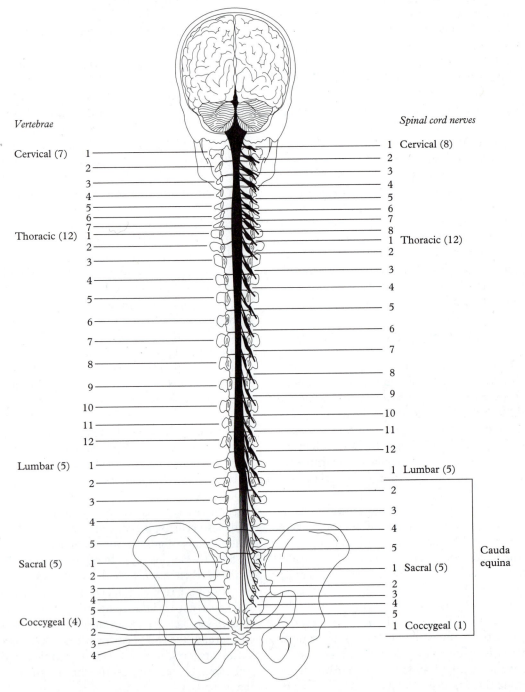

Vertebrae

Cervical (7)

Thoracic (12)

Lumbar (5)

Sacral (5)

Coccygeal (4)

Spinal cord nerves

Cervical (8)

Thoracic (12)

Lumbar (5)

Sacral (5)

Coccygeal (1)

Cauda equina

■ **FIGURE 8-1** The spinal cord is shorter than the vertebral column.

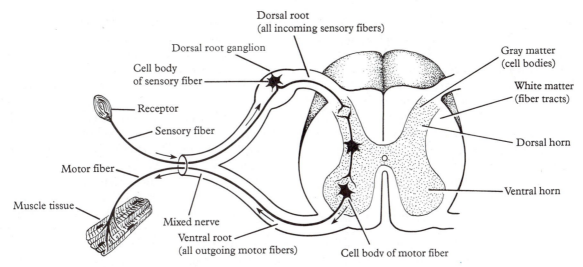

■ FIGURE 8-2 Cross section of the spinal cord, showing an "H" pattern

traumatic brain injury, the swelling at the site may cause pressure on adjacent areas, which can cause damage at that site. Treatment will be aimed at reducing the edema to prevent further paralysis. Third, a person may go into spinal shock; that is, may lose reflexes below the level of injury. This is usually temporary, lasting days or weeks, unless the injury occurs to the cauda equina, in which case the loss of reflexes is permanent (Behrman, 1992).

When a person has a spinal cord injury, impulses sent to and from the brain are interrupted. Motor messages traveling from the brain cannot complete their transmission when they come to the area of the spinal cord damage. Because communication is interrupted, the brain is unable to control voluntary muscle movement at and below the point of injury. In the same manner, sensory information traveling from the skin cannot reach the brain when encountering a cut, compression, or interruption at the area of the spinal cord injury. Loss of sensation will then occur at and below the level of the injury. Spinal cord damage is very similar to having a bridge collapse across a major highway. Cars who exit before the accident are unaffected and can travel from the highway (spinal cord) to various locations unimpeded. However, the accident prevents cars from continuing down the highway to other locations. Unlike this bridge accident, when the spinal cord is damaged, it cannot be fixed and does not regenerate.

Spinal Cord Injury from Nontraumatic Causes

Spinal cord injuries may also be caused by diseases and medical disorders. These diseases (for example, multiple sclerosis and amyotrophic lateral sclerosis) and disorders (such as tumors) adversely affect the spinal cord by exerting pressure on it or through degeneration of the spinal cord. This disrupts and often permanently damages the spinal cord, causing a loss of motor and sensory function.

Some diseases and disorders may result in the spinal cord being affected all the way across, while others may affect only some of the spinal tracts that travel up and down the spinal cord. For example, the tracts on the right may be compressed from a tumor or congenital cyst and cease to function, while the tracts on the left are unaffected. This is similar to when a bridge collapses across part of a major highway. If the bridge only collapses across certain lanes, some cars can continue on their journey, while others cannot. This disorder is known as an incomplete lesion.

CHARACTERISTICS OF SPINAL CORD INJURY

The effects of a spinal cord injury will depend on two factors: (1) the level of the spinal cord at which the injury occurred, and (2) the type of injury. In spinal cord injury, this is determined by whether the trauma, syndrome, or congenital disorder cuts across or affects the entire cord or whether there is an incomplete lesion that allows transmission of some of the impulses past the point of injury.

Muscle Paralysis

The level of injury will determine which muscles are paralyzed. The spinal cord can be affected anywhere from top to bottom, although many instances of spinal cord injury occur in the cervical area.

When the injury is above the C5 level, the arms and legs are completely paralyzed and unable to move. The person is considered quadriplegic. However, if the injury occurs between the C5 and T1 level, there will be some arm control because the arms are controlled by the C5–T1 nerves. For example, a C5 injury may allow some movement of the upper arm. Injury at C6 or C7 may allow wrist and lower-arm movement. A C8 injury may allow some uncoordinated finger movement (Jubala & Brenes, 1988).

Spinal cord injury below the T1 level results in paraplegia, which is paralysis of the trunk and legs. When damage occurs above the L1 level, there is complete paralysis in the legs. If the injury occurs between L1 and S1, the person will have some voluntary leg movement because the leg is controlled by those nerves. Walking is possible when the injury occurs at T12 or below, although braces and training will be needed due to the loss of some muscle control and the lack of sensation in certain areas of the leg.

When the spinal cord injury occurs above the T12–L1 vertebra level (where the spinal cord ends), reflexes are still present below the area of injury. Damage occurring above the T12–L1 area is referred to as upper motor neuron damage or lesion. As we discussed previously, a reflex arc occurs from a sensory stimulus (such as a soft hammer on the knee) that travels to the spinal cord via the sensory nerves and then synapses to the motor nerves and travels back to the muscle, causing a movement. Because no stimulation is needed from the brain for these to occur, reflexes are still present below the area of injury when they occur along the spinal cord. These reflexes are involuntary, and the person may be unaware of them because communication with the brain is absent. Because reflexes persist, they tend to become exaggerated, and the affected muscles become spastic. Muscle contractures, in which there is an actual shortening of the muscles, may develop.

When the injury or myelomeningocele occurs around or below the T12–L1 vertebrae (where the spinal cord ends), the lowest part of the spinal cord—the cauda equina—is destroyed. This is known as *lower motor neuron damage* or *lesion*. In this case, the anterior horn cells or their axons that lead to the muscles are destroyed. No reflex activity is possible because the pathway from the lower motor neuron in the spinal cord to the muscles has been interrupted. When there is lower motor neuron damage, there is no spasticity as seen in upper motor neuron damage. Instead, the affected muscles will be limp and flaccid.

Loss of Sensation

As is true of injury resulting in muscle paralysis, the level of spinal cord injury will determine which areas are affected— which have a loss of sensation. When there is complete spinal damage across the cord, there will be a loss of sensation at that level and all areas below it. A loss of sensation would include a loss of touch, pressure, pain, temperature, and proprioception.

A loss of sensation is very serious because sensation provides information about whether a body part is hurt and in need of attention. Individuals with spinal cord injury cannot feel below the level of injury and will be unable to determine whether a body part is hurt or damaged.

Due to the paralysis and lack of movement, individuals with spinal cord injury can develop pressure sores (decubitus ulcers) and skin breakdown (Curry & Casady, 1992). Because sensation is absent, the person will be unable to feel the pressure that indicates a need to move, so movement must be based on a timed schedule instead of sensation.

Respiratory Complications

When the spinal cord is affected in the cervical and thoracic regions, respiratory problems can result. When the injury is above the C3 level, the person will not be able to breathe independently. A mechanical ventilator will be needed continuously if the person is to survive (Mathewson, Finley, & Reeves, 1994). The individual with an injury above C3 often dies at the time of injury because he or she cannot breathe and assistance may be slow in coming. When the injury is below C3, the person can breathe, although respiration may be impaired. This is because the diaphragm muscle that controls breathing is supplied by the spinal cord nerves C3, C4, and C5, and there will be partial control of the diaphragm if the injury occurs below C3.

When the spinal cord disorder occurs in the high thoracic area, the diaphragm will function, but other respiratory muscles (such as the intercostals and abdominal muscles) that assist breathing will not function well. Breathing can be compromised as much as 50%, which would increase susceptibility to respiratory infections and decrease oxygenation. When the spinal cord injury occurs above the T8 level, the person cannot usually cough well enough to clear the lungs of respiratory secretions. The lack of an effective cough will also increase the possibility of respiratory infections such as pneumonia.

Bowel and Bladder Problems

The muscles controlling the bowel and bladder are supplied by the sacral nerves. When an injury occurs at or above this point, the person cannot have a sensation of fullness to indicate a need to void or defecate. Also, in a complete lesion, the muscles allowing the emptying of urine and feces cannot be controlled. If there is an incomplete lesion, some control of the bowel and bladder may be retained.

Effects on Sexual Function and Daily Living Skills

Individuals with spinal cord injury often may have sexual dysfunction. The extent of dysfunction depends on the sex of the individual, the level of injury, and whether the lesion is complete or incomplete. For males, achieving an erection may be difficult, although several methods to stimulate a reflex erection can result in successful intercourse. Achieving ejaculation is more difficult and rare. In females, intercourse is possible, although the loss of sensation precludes physiological orgasm (Umbreit, 1983). Fertility is usually unimpaired.

Figure 8-3 shows the effects of paralysis and loss of sensation on daily living skills. Individuals who are

quadriplegic will need some type of personal or mechanical assistance, or adaptation to allow for execution of the tasks; those who are paraplegic will be able to perform most tasks with minimal to no adaptations.

Incomplete Spinal Cord Injury

In an incomplete spinal cord injury, some of the nerves at the site of injury are not damaged. The person may then have some function in certain areas at and below the injury because some nerves in certain spinal tracts are unharmed. Because of the variability of nerve damage, individuals with the same level of spinal cord damage may look very different. An anatomical classification system of incomplete spinal cord injuries is shown in Figure 8-4. Incomplete lesions have been classified as *central cord syndrome, Brown-Sequard syndrome, anterior cord syndrome,* and *posterior cord syndrome* (American Spinal Injury Association, 1990).

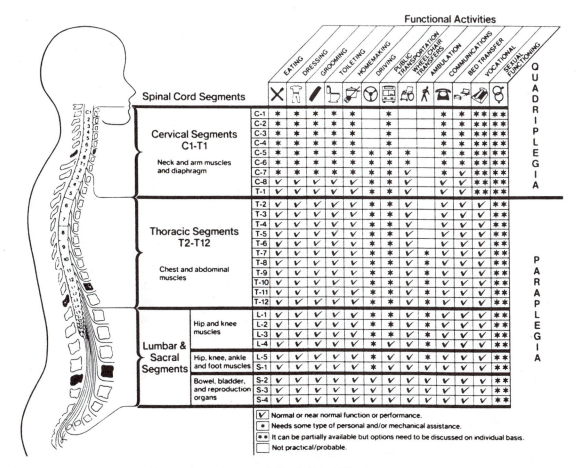

■ **FIGURE 8-3** The effects of paralysis on daily living skills
SOURCE: From *Handbook of Developmental and Physical Disabilities*, by V. B. Van Hasselt, P. S. Strain, and M. Hersen (Eds.). Copyright ©1992. Reprinted by permission of Allyn & Bacon.

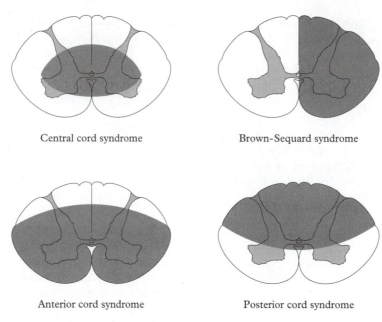

Central cord syndrome   Brown-Sequard syndrome

Anterior cord syndrome   Posterior cord syndrome

■ **FIGURE 8-4** Classification of incomplete spinal cord injury

In central cord syndrome, a lesion damages the central part of the spinal cord, including the gray matter and parts of the white matter. This lesion is usually found only in the cervical region. Typically, there is greater weakness in the arms than in the legs. Sensation usually remains in the sacral area (American Spinal Injury Association, 1990).

The Brown-Sequard syndrome refers to spinal cord damage occurring to one side of the spinal cord. If there was damage on the right side of the spinal cord, for example, there would be paralysis on the right side of the body but not on the left. In terms of sensation, there would be loss of proprioception and pressure on the right side of the body; the left side of the body would be unaffected. However, because the sensory nerves for pain and temperature cross to the opposite side of the body at the level of the spinal cord they innervate, sensations of pain and temperature would be lost on the left side of the body. In this instance, at and below the level of the lesion, the right side of the body would have paralysis and loss of proprioception and pressure, but the right side would still have pain and temperature sensation. The left side of the body would have normal movement, proprioception, and sensations of pressure but would not feel pain or temperature at and below the level of the lesion (American Spinal Injury Association, 1990).

An anterior cord syndrome usually involves a lesion affecting the anterior two-thirds portion of the cord. This produces paralysis and loss of pain and temperature sensation. However, proprioception and pressure are unaffected (American Spinal Injury Association, 1990).

A posterior cord syndrome is very rare; it results in a loss of proprioception. Motor and other sensory functions remain intact (American Spinal Injury Association, 1990).

Specific Problems in Spinal Cord Injury

Psychological and Adjustment Problems

Most individuals are aware of paralysis immediately upon injury. Those who are not aware are often in a state of shock. The initial and subsequent psychological adjustment to a spinal cord injury can produce any number of behaviors and emotions. Even with low spinal cord injuries, changes in body image combined with difficulty in performing routine tasks may have profound emotional effects. Denial, anger, depression, impulsiveness, frustration, egocentricity, and many other reactions may occur. The severity of the injury does not necessarily align with the person's reaction and psychological adjustment to the impairment (Hu & Cressy, 1992).

General Complications in Spinal Cord Injury

Individuals with spinal cord injury may have several possible complications. Pain may be present in those with incomplete lesions. Individuals with high-level spinal cord injuries may have problems with body temperature regulation. When this occurs, the person will be unable to adjust to changes in the temperature of the external environment. Care must to taken to be sure the individual is appropriately clothed and protected from extreme temperatures. Spinal deformities may develop because of the paralysis. Other possible complications include urinary tract infections and respiratory infections (Suddarth, 1991).

Autonomic Dysreflexia

One of the most serious complications is a pathological reflex known as *autonomic dysreflexia*. This reflex occurs in people with spinal cord injury of T6 or higher (Mathewson, Finley, & Reeves, 1994). This pathological reflex is caused by any noxious stimuli that occur below the area of injury, including such problems as a distended bladder (from not urinating), distended rectum (from constipation), or a pressure sore. Autonomic dysreflexia causes a dangerous, rapid elevation of blood pressure. Symptoms include headache, flushing, goose bumps, nasal stuffiness, anxiety, sweating, chills, and a generally miserable feeling (Mathewson, Finley, & Reeves, 1994; Suddarth, 1991). If treatment is not given immediately, bleeding in the brain (cerebral hemorrhage) could result and the person could die.

DETECTION OF SPINAL CORD INJURY

Spinal cord injury is diagnosed in several ways. The physical symptoms of paralysis and loss of sensation will help the physician make a diagnosis. Spinal X-rays will show fractures in the spinal column, collapse of the spinal column, or severe bony changes. However, it is possible to have a normal-looking X-ray and a damaged spinal column in infants and young children because their columns have not yet formed into solid bone. The spinal column can thus be stretched several inches without damage, while the spinal cord can be stretched only a fraction of an inch. When the vertebral column is stretched beyond a fraction of an inch, the spinal cord will be severely damaged, leaving the spinal column without injury. Tumors or lesions of the spinal cord may also be missed by X-ray. Other imaging techniques, such as a CT scan with contrast or an MRI, will more fully define the lesion or damage (Berkow, 1992).

TREATMENT OF SPINAL CORD INJURY

Emergency treatment of a spinal cord injury depends on its cause. If the damage is the result of trauma, the spinal cord must be stabilized immediately by splinting, bracing, or using orthoses. If a high cervical lesion has occurred, a ventilator will be needed to maintain breathing. Medication will be needed to reduce the swelling (edema). Surgical intervention may be used to stabilize the spinal cord by fusing the vertebrae where the fracture has occurred or by using stabilizing devices inside the vertebrae.

When the spinal cord damage results from nontraumatic means, this is still an emergency situation, but treatment will be aimed at the specific cause. Medications will typically be given to reduce swelling. For cancerous tumors, radiation therapy may be started. Surgery will be aimed at reducing the pressure on the spinal cord and removing the tumor.

After the emergency phase, a team effort will be needed to help the person achieve the fullest recovery and adapt to the paralysis. Team members often include the physical therapist, occupational therapist, speech therapist, nurse, physician, nutritionist, parent (or parents), child, respiratory therapists, social workers, counselors, and psychologists.

Treatment for Muscle Paralysis

Since the muscle paralysis in spinal cord injury is irreversible, the aim of medical care will be to determine which muscles are functioning and to strengthen them. Physical and occupational therapists will provide therapy to teach functional skills using these muscles. If some muscle control remains in the legs, the therapists will often institute a program aimed at teaching the person to walk with braces using unaffected muscles. If control of only the arm muscles remains, therapy will be designed to strengthen these muscles to help with mobility.

Therapy will also include the management and prevention of contractures and spinal deformity. Contractures can interfere with achieving functional use of a muscle group. People who could otherwise walk with braces cannot do so with contractures at the knees. Severe contractures may result in hygienic problems because the difficulty in extending or moving a limb with a contracture makes some parts of the body inaccessible. Assuming different positions such as sitting or lying may be difficult or uncomfortable as well, and spinal deformities may result from the lack of muscular support of the vertebral column. Interventions for both contractures and spinal deformities will include range-of-motion exercises, splints, braces, and orthotic devices. A brace, for example, is commonly used to prevent severe curvature of the spine. In some instances, surgery may be necessary to release contractures or to manage spinal deformities. When muscle spasms are present, medications such as Liorsal or Dantrim may prevent the spasms.

Treatment for Sensory Loss

The loss of sensation from a spinal cord injury can result in further injury. Individuals with sensory loss will be unable to detect burns or frostbite because the affected areas have no sensation. For example, if their foot falls off a wheelchair foot support and is dragged along the pavement, they will be unaware of the injury unless they see it and will not be able to stop the problem immediately. The person with the injury and the individuals assisting him or her must be attentive to such possible problems.

Another frequent problem is pressure sores (decubitus ulcers). Individuals with unaffected spinal cords typically move around a lot and shift their weight as they sit. They do this because the pressure exerted on the skin as a result of being in one position for a while causes a sensation of discomfort that, in turn, stimulates movement. A person with a sensory loss will not feel discomfort below the level of injury. If he or she does not change positions or relieve the pressure, circulation will be cut off, causing tissue death (**necrosis**) in the area. This area of tissue death is called a pressure sore (decubitus ulcer) and can occur in as little as 2 hours. A reddened area on the skin is often the initial symptom. The person must be kept off the area completely until the skin returns to a normal color. If this does not happen, the pressure sore will continue to develop and cause an opening in the skin. Often, what appears as a small open area on the surface of the skin obscures a much larger area of damage beneath the skin. Individuals are often readmitted to the hospital because of severe pressure sores, which can become infected as well.

Pressure sores are completely preventable if the individual changes positions often and does not stay in one place for extended periods of time. Since sitting causes substantial pressure on the buttocks, it is important that the person not sit for longer than 1 to 2 hours (for some individuals, even less time) without an assisted position change or a chair lift. A chair lift can be performed by the person who has arm movement; it consists of lifting the buttocks off the chair by pushing down on the armrests with the arms, like a vertical push-up. If the person has enough motor function, he or she should be taught to do lifts, and they should be performed about every hour. Pressure relief devices (such as foam or gel pads for sitting) are also used to decrease the chance of a decubitus ulcer.

Pressure sores can also develop from the pressure of braces and splints, so the person should be taught to inspect for pressure sores each day. Mirrors can be used to examine areas that are difficult to see. If the child in school has a high cervical injury and is unable to do a daily skin check, the teacher, parent, or caretaker should assist the child.

In spinal cord injuries, the higher and more complete the injury to the spinal cord, the greater the loss of temperature regulation. Below the level of the injury, there may be no heat production or sweating (Mathewson, Finley, & Reeves, 1994). It becomes important for the teacher to be sure that the student is not exposed to extremes in temperatures and that proper clothing is worn. Also, fluid intake should be adequate for physical activity.

Treatment for Respiratory Problems

Students with a high cervical involvement will need a ventilator in order to breathe. A ventilator is a machine that pushes air mixed with oxygen into the lungs. There are many types of ventilators. Some are large machines that stand on the floor; others are very compact and portable and are about the size of a suitcase. The small ones can easily attach to the back of a wheelchair. There are several dials on the ventilator that control such functions as the amount of oxygen, the amount of air pressure pushed into the lungs (inspiratory pressure), the volume of air delivered (tidal volume), and the speed with which air is delivered. The tidal volume, the rate, and the amount of oxygen all help to control the student's concentrations of carbon dioxide and oxygen. Ventilators have alarms that should be on continually to inform people if the ventilator becomes accidentally disconnected or malfunctions. Some ventilators also have high-pressure alarms that buzz or beep if there is an obstruction, such as a kink in the tubing (Heller et al., 1991).

Although the child using a ventilator may appear frightening at first, when people know the student and understand the function of the ventilator, fear should dissipate. Often students feel isolated because of teachers' and students' fears about the ventilator. The student's overall needs should not be overlooked amidst all the machinery. Having someone familiarize teachers and peers with the ventilator will make it less frightening.

Students on ventilators often have a tracheostomy—an artificial, external opening into the windpipe (trachea) through which a tube is passed. The hole is often called a *stoma,* and the tube may be called a *tracheostomy tube, trach tube,* or *trach.* The tube from the ventilator attaches to the tracheostomy. The ventilator attachment may be momentarily disconnected if the child receives suctioning (placing a tube into the tracheostomy to remove thick respiratory secretions). Unless the child has a special type of tracheostomy tube, normal speech will not be possible. For some children, the tracheostomy tube can be covered momentarily with a clean finger or trach cap to allow proper speech production. (This should never be done without the physician's approval.) Others may use augmentative communication such as electronic boards or sign language to communicate (Adamson & Dunbar, 1991; Vanderheiden & Smith, 1989).

If a child has a tracheostomy only for suctioning and it is not connected to a ventilator, objects should not be allowed to enter or obstruct the tracheostomy. The child should not play in sandboxes or boxes filled with small pellets of rice; plastic bibs or fuzzy blankets should be avoided because they can obstruct the tracheostomy. The child should always avoid going under water because water can get into the lungs through the tracheostomy.

Respiratory infections are more frequent in children with cervical and thoracic injuries, so infection control procedures should be carefully adhered to. This includes washing hands thoroughly, disinfecting objects, and sending students home who are sick (see Chapter 26). If the child with a spinal cord injury acquires a respiratory infection, antibiotics and other forms of treatment will be prescribed.

Treatment for Bowel and Bladder Control

Students with spinal cord injury frequently have no bowel or bladder control unless their lesion is incomplete. Bowel programs are set up in which the child uses suppositories and other bowel-evacuating medications (such as Therevac, Dulcolax, or Metamucil) or procedures that allow emptying of the bowel at home at certain times. Impaction and constipation can thus be avoided.

Many students with spinal cord injury and myelomeningocele will have a neurogenic bladder; that is, a bladder whose muscle does not function properly. In this situation, the bladder may not empty completely or may not empty at all. Urine can back up from the bladder to the kidneys, causing infection and serious kidney problems. To empty the bladder, a clean intermittent catheterization (CIC) procedure will often be used. In this procedure, a catheter (a long, thin tube) is placed through the urinary opening into the bladder long enough to allow urine to be released from the bladder; then the catheter is removed. This is a clean (not sterile) procedure that is quick and easy to do and is effective in bladder control. The child can learn to do this if hand function is adequate. Medication, such as Ditropan or Tofranil, may be given if bladder spasms are present. Medication can relax the spasm, which relieves the urgency to urinate and helps prevent leakage.

If the child has no bladder control and the bladder empties on its own, the child may need to wear urine-collecting devices. For boys, an external urinary catheter may be used. These external urinary catheters consist of a condomlike device that goes over the penis and a tube that is attached to a bag which is usually attached to the child's leg. The bag must be emptied at different times of the day when it is nearly full. External urinary devices made for girls do not usually stay on well. Padded underwear may be helpful.

Treatment for Improving Function

With a spinal cord injury, the child may have difficulty accomplishing several of the daily activities routinely performed before the injury. Part of the treatment process will include training on how to accomplish tasks in spite of the existing paralysis and sensory loss. Use of other functioning muscles will be stressed, as will the use of adaptations and devices.

Psychological Adjustment and Sexual Function

Part of the treatment will be to provide the child and his or her family with emotional support and accurate information. Some children may benefit from counseling. All children will need someone to talk with and to help them cope with the change in their life that the disability has caused. Knowing other children with spinal cord injury and attending support groups may be helpful.

Adolescents will need accurate information about sexual function. As we discussed earlier, sexual intercourse may still be possible. Someone who can provide the adolescent with accurate, specific information should be made available. This may be a physician, counselor, nurse, or a teacher from a spinal clinic.

COURSE OF SPINAL CORD INJURIES

With today's advanced technology, the chance of survival for a child with a spinal cord injury is good. Usually, if the child has survived the first 3 months following injury, which is considered the acute period, **prognosis** for continued survival is good (Umbreit, 1983).

Life expectancy for children with spinal cord injury depends on the level of the injury, whether the injury was complete or incomplete, and the age of the child. The lower the injury, the longer the life expectancy. Incomplete lesions have a more positive prognosis than complete lesions; children usually have a better chance of surviving than older individuals. It is common for individuals to survive between 30 and 60 years after the injury. Life expectancy is determined by the development of complications, such as severe respiratory problems, kidney failure, and infection. Careful management will help minimize the development of complications and will prolong life.

DESCRIPTION OF SPINA BIFIDA

Spina bifida is a defective closure of the bony vertebral column. There are three types: *spina bifida occulta*, *meningocele (spina bifida cystica)*, and *myelomeningocele* (see Figure 8-5).

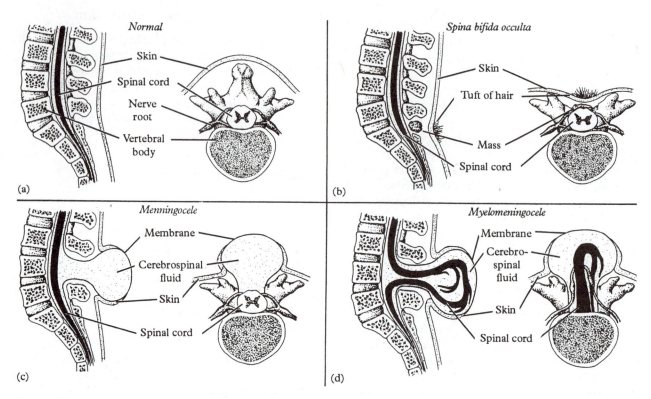

■ **FIGURE 8-5** Three types of spina bifida
SOURCE: From *Physical Disabilities and Health Impairments: An Introduction*, by J. Umbreit,
Ed., pp. 118, 123, 251. Copyright ©1983 Merrill Publishing Co. Reprinted with
permission.

Spina Bifida Occulta

A common type of spina bifida is spina bifida occulta—a failure of fusion of the backarches of vertebrae, which results in malformation of a few vertebrae. In this condition, there is usually no damage to the spinal cord or spinal nerves, so the child will have no paralysis or sensory loss.

Meningocele

The least common type of spina bifida is meningocele, which refers to the outpouching of the meninges (membranes covering the spinal cord) through the malformed vertebrae. The child is born with a saclike protrusion on the back at the level of malformation. The sac contains only meninges and cerebrospinal fluid (CSF). Since the spinal cord and the spinal nerves are unaffected in this condition, there is usually no paralysis or sensory loss.

Myelomeningocele

Myelomeningocele refers to the outpouching of the meninges and the spinal cord (part or all of it) through

the malformed vertebrae. The child is born with a saclike protrusion on the back at the level of malformation. Since the sac contains the poorly developed spinal cord or spinal nerves, paralysis and sensory loss will be present. When people refer to a child as having spina bifida, they are usually referring to the myelo-meningocele type. In this chapter, we will discuss the myelomeningocele form of spina bifida because of its impact on function.

ETIOLOGY OF SPINA BIFIDA

Spina bifida is classified as a neural tube defect (NTD). Within the first 28 days of gestation, a neural tube is formed from which the brain and spinal cord develop. As seen in Figure 8-6, the normal development of the neural tube involves a complete closing of the tube surrounding the spinal cord by the meninges and encasement of the cord and meninges by the protective vertebrae. In spina bifida, myelomeningocele type, closure of the neural tube is incomplete, and because the tube fails to close, the vertebrae also fail to enclose the back portion of the spine in the area of the neural tube defect. In the myelomeningocele type, an outpouching of the meninges and spinal cord appears on the child's back at the level of the defect.

The exact mechanism that prevents neural tube closure is uncertain. Several possible environmental causes have been proposed, including nutrition, medication, and exposure to high temperatures. The role of folic acid, calcium, vitamin C, and zinc intake has been investigated (Laurence, James, Miller, & Campbell, 1980; Sandford, Kissling, & Joubert, 1992; Smithells et al., 1983). Studies have demonstrated that the use of vitamins, especially folic acid, may decrease the risk of spina bifida (*Morbidity and Mortality Weekly Report*, 1992). Maternal hyperthermia (elevated temperature) from the use of hot tubs or from febrile illnesses incurred during the early stages of pregnancy have also been suggested as possible causes (Sandford, Kissling, & Joubert, 1992). Maternal illness and the use of medications (such as some antiepileptic medications) have also been suggested as possible causes of spina bifida (Rosa, 1991).

Although spina bifida has not currently been shown to be inherited, there is some evidence of genetic predisposition to the disorder. If a couple has had one child with spina bifida, the possibility of having another child with spina bifida is about 50 times greater than in the general population (Noetzel, 1989).

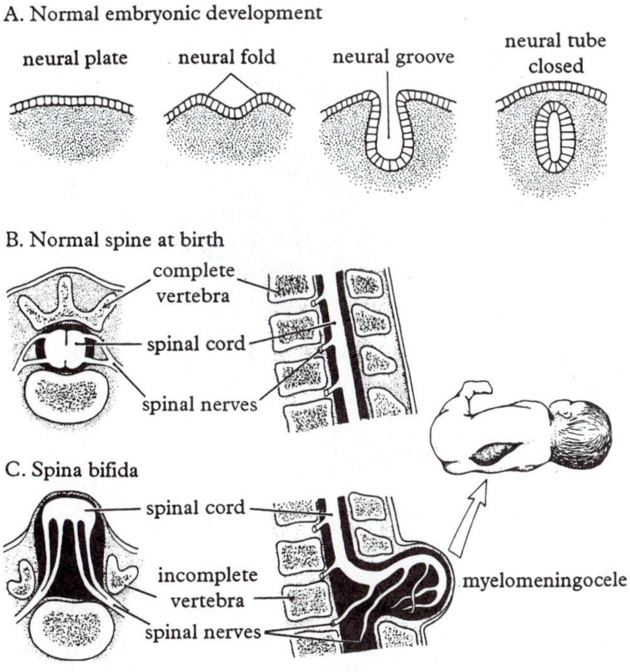

■ FIGURE 8-6 Normal development of the neural tube, normal spine at birth, and spina bifida

DYNAMICS OF SPINA BIFIDA

The location of the neural tube defect will determine the type of disorder and extent of impairment. If the tube fails to close at the top, several conditions may result: *cranial meningocele, cranial encephalocele,* or *anencephaly.* Cranial meningocele is a sac filled with meninges and cerebrospinal fluid. Children with this disorder usually have a good prognosis. Cranial encephalocele is the protrusion of nervous tissue (portions of the cerebral cortex, cerebellum, or brain stem) and meninges through a defect in the skull. Prognosis varies with this disorder, depending on the type and quantity of nervous tissue involvement. Anencephaly is the absence of the cerebral hemispheres of the brain. Typically, these infants will not survive.

When the neural tube defect occurs on its **distal** end, spina bifida occulta, meningocele, or myelomeningocele may occur. Children with spina bifida occulta or meningocele typically have no impairment of function because the spinal cord is unaffected by the malformation. However, the myelomeningocele form of spina bifida results in an outpouching of the spinal cord, which damages the cord and results in a lack of formation of nerves below that point. The myelomeningocele can occur anywhere along the spinal cord. The most common areas are the lower thoracic, lumbar, and sacral regions (Berkow, 1992). A child with a myelomeningocele will have good motor and sensory function above the level of the damaged spinal nerves. However, the area of spinal cord impairment will have damaged spinal nerves, and the nerves below that area cannot communicate with the brain and often do not even develop. This results in paralysis and sensory loss in those areas where the spinal nerves would have innervated (made connections).

CHARACTERISTICS OF SPINA BIFIDA

The type of spina bifida and the level at which it occurs in the spinal cord will determine the effects of the disorder. As we said, spina bifida occulta and meningocele typically have no impairments. Myelomeningocele results in motor and sensory impairments below the area of the spinal cord damage. In most instances, myelomeningoceles occur in the thoracic, low lumbar, or sacral areas, which usually results in leg paralysis and loss of sensation in the legs. Students often use braces, wheelchairs, or both for mobility (see Figure 8-7). Bowel and bladder problems typically occur, often resulting in the need for clean intermittent catheterization and a bowel program. Sexual dysfunction is usually present as well. In addition to these impair-

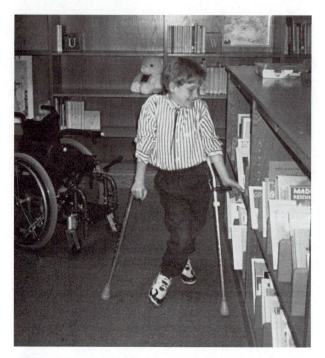

■ FIGURE 8-7 Student with spina bifida uses his crutches when traveling and his wheelchair (*in background*) for long distances

ments, other problems may occur with a myelomeningocele.

Specific Problems in Spina Bifida

Arnold-Chiari Malformation

Children with myelomeningocele are often born with an additional congenital malformation known as Arnold-Chiari Type II malformation (ACM). This malformation involves the displacement of part of the brain stem (medulla) and the cerebellum down into the neck region, through the foramen magnum (a hole at the base of the skull)(Griebel, Oakes, & Worley, 1991). Typically, there is no impairment of function with this abnormality unless the top of the spinal cord is compressed or the flow of CSF is blocked.

A compression to the top of the spinal cord may result from trauma. For children with Arnold-Chiari malformation, it is an emergency situation in which the child will have some of the following symptoms: severe headache, vomiting, noisy breathing (stridor), paralysis, back and neck pain, weakness and loss of sensation, and loss of tongue movement. This emergency situation requires immediate medical attention.

A common complication of Arnold-Chiari malformation is the obstruction of the flow of cerebrospinal fluid, which is produced by a special group of blood vessels known as the *choroid plexus*. The choroid

plexus secretes CSF into the four ventricles (spaces) of the brain and especially into the two larger ventricles known as the *lateral ventricles* (see Figure 8-8). As cerebrospinal fluid is formed and is secreted into the lateral ventricles, the cerebrospinal fluid flows from the lateral ventricles to the third and fourth ventricles. The cerebrospinal fluid leaves the fourth ventricle through three small openings into a large fluid-filled space beneath the cerebellum. The CSF flows through the subarachnoid space of the brain and spinal cord. CSF is then reabsorbed as it flows back across the brain surface (Guyton, 1991). With the Arnold-Chiari malformation, the normal flow of CSF may be blocked. A blockage disrupts the normal balance of production and reabsorption, causing the accumulation of excess CSF. This causes a condition known as *hydrocephalus* (water on the brain).

Hydrocephalus

Hydrocephalus is the enlargement of the ventricles of the brain due to the accumulation of CSF. About 60 to 95% of children with myelomeningocele develop hydrocephalus (Griebel et al., 1991) either because of

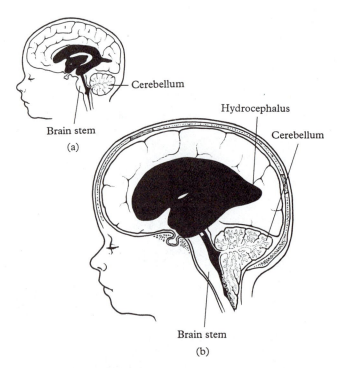

■ FIGURE 8-8 Flow of cerebrospinal fluid through ventricles: (a) the normal brain; (b) hydrocephalus
SOURCE: From *Children with Disabilities: A Medical Primer*, Third Edition, by M. L. Batshaw and Y. M. Perret, pp. 343, 460, 477. Copyright ©1992 Paul H. Brookes Publishing Co. Reprinted with permission of Dr. Mark L. Batshaw.

Arnold-Chiari malformation or some other abnormality. In the infant who still has a soft spot on the head (that is, the sutures of the skull have not closed), the head may expand because of excess cerebrospinal fluid. Some infants' heads may get quite large without intervention. The excess CSF exerts pressure on the brain, which causes compression and subsequent damage to the brain structures. Without intervention, the head may get large enough to exert pressure on the brain stem and result in death. Other untreated children may eventually reach a level of equilibrium with only mild-to-moderate head enlargement. This is called *compensated* or *arrested hydrocephalus*.

Musculoskeletal Abnormalities

Students with spina bifida typically have several types of musculoskeletal abnormalities due to the paralysis. Ankle and foot deformities such as club foot may be present. Hip deformities such as hip dislocation may occur as well. Curvatures of the spine, such as scoliosis (a lateral curve), kyphosis (a humpback), or lordosis (swayback), are often present (Rowley-Kelly & Reigel, 1993; Swnak & Dias, 1992). Curvatures of the spine can progress to interfere with sitting or walking. (See Chapter 11.)

Seizures

Approximately 15 to 30% of individuals with myelomeningocele develop seizures (Noetzel, 1989; Shurtleff & Dunne, 1986). Seizures are sudden, involuntary, time-limited disruptions in the normal function of the central nervous system that may be characterized by altered consciousness, motor activity, sensory phenomena, or inappropriate behavior (Berkow, 1992; Holmes, 1992). Children with spina bifida may exhibit any of the various types of seizures as well as combinations. (See Chapter 6.)

Eye Abnormalities

Children with myelomeningocele have been documented as having a higher incidence of strabismus than the general population (Rowley-Kelly & Reigel, 1993). Strabismus is a deviation in the alignment of the eye. The eye may deviate inward (esotropia, cross-eye) or outward (exotropia, walleye). This occurs due to an imbalance of the muscles of the eyeball. If strabismus is untreated, it may result in **amblyopia** (lazy eye), which can lead to blindness. (See Chapter 16.)

Cognitive Impairments

Children with myelomeningocele have varying levels of cognitive ability. Approximately two-thirds have normal intelligence; about one-third have mental retardation, usually in the mild range (Batshaw & Perret,

1992). Even when mental retardation is not present, there may be learning problems due to deficits in visual-perceptual skills, organizational abilities, attention, memory, and hand function (Rowley-Kelly & Reigel, 1993; Wills, Holmbeck, Dillon, & McLone, 1990). These problems can negatively affect the child's academic performance.

Language Abnormalities

Children with myelomeningocele may also have language abnormalities that give a false impression of their intelligence and lead to problems in social interactions. For example, many children with hydrocephalus have a disorder known as *cocktail party language* or *cocktail party syndrome,* which refers to verbose, well-articulated speech that is excessive and is riddled with jargon and clichés (Hurley, Dorman, Laatsch, Bell, & D'Avignon, 1990). Children exhibiting this type of language may appear highly intelligent to the casual observer, but they actually may have cognitive and learning deficits. Unrealistic demands and expectations may be placed on the child as a result of this misjudgment. The astute listener can tell that the conversation lacks relevance or depth. Difficulties in social interactions may occur due to this type of speech, which may be compounded by deficits in social perception or abstract conceptualization and delays in developing good socialization skills (Rowley-Kelly & Reigel, 1993).

DETECTION OF SPINA BIFIDA

Myelomeningocele is easily detected at birth because of the sac on the infant's back. Further medical testing is often performed—X-rays and scans (CT or MRI), blood analysis, and urinary tract evaluation—to provide further information about the myelomeningocele and any associated congenital malformation.

Myelomeningocele can be detected prior to birth. A maternal blood test that checks for alphafetoprotein (AFP) is commonly performed as a screening measure. When myelomeningocele is present, AFP leaks from the open spine into the amniotic fluid, after which it enters the mother's bloodstream. It can be detected by this simple blood test. Further testing is done to confirm the diagnosis. One commonly performed test is an ultrasound that visualizes the fetus (or structures of the body) by recording the reflections of sound waves directed toward the fetus (see Figure 8-9). Amniocentesis may be performed between the 14th and 17th weeks of gestation. In amniocentesis, a small amount of amniotic fluid is extracted from the amniotic sac with a needle and then is examined for concentrations of AFP. Other types of analysis can be done to detect

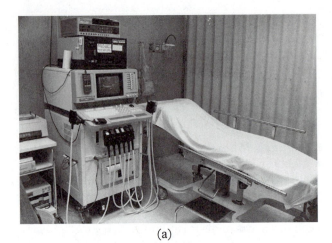

(a)

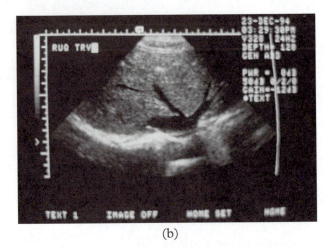

(b)

■ **FIGURE 8-9** An ultrasound machine (a) and an ultrasound picture (b)

chromosomal or biochemical disorders (see Figure 8-10). Chorionic villus sampling, a procedure in which placental (chronic) tissue is extracted by suction at 8 to 10 weeks of gestation, is not appropriate for detection of spina bifida. This procedure can be performed earlier than the others and can detect chromosomal and biochemical conditions, but because it does not involve the amniotic fluid, it cannot help with the diagnosis of spina bifida.

TREATMENT OF SPINA BIFIDA

When an infant is born with meningocele or myelomeningocele, the sac containing the meninges and or spinal cord may be open or closed. Sacs that are open have a high risk of introducing infection, which can result in meningitis. Sacs that are closed can easily rupture when there is a thin layer of skin covering the sac. Whether the sac is open or closed, surgical intervention will be needed in the first few days of life. Surgery involves closing the defect by tucking in the meninges and spinal cord. Skin graphs may be necessary to close the site if the sac is large. After surgical intervention, there will no longer be a sac on the child's back, but the surgery does not improve function. The damage has been done to the spinal cord and cannot be repaired or improved by surgery with current knowledge and skill.

As with spinal cord injury, treatments are available for muscle paralysis, sensory loss, bowel and bladder control, functional improvement, psychological adjustment, and sexual function. There are also specific treatments for spina bifida.

Treatment of Problems Specific to Spina Bifida

Arnold-Chiari Type II Malformation and Hydrocephalus

Children will be assessed for Arnold-Chiari Type II malformation and hydrocephalus after birth. When the child has Arnold-Chiari Type II malformation, surgical intervention may be needed if there is crowding of the brain stem and/or repeated bleeding infarcts (death of tissue from the bleeding) due to distortions of the blood supply. Surgical correction has been performed by enlarging the foramen magnum (a hole in the base of the skull) (Haller, 1992).

If hydrocephalus is present, a **shunt** will be implanted surgically. A shunt is a long, thin tube. One end is placed in the enlarged ventricle in the brain and typically is attached to another catheter that is placed in the skin behind the child's ear. This tube runs under the skin of the neck and chest to the peritoneal (abdominal) cavity (Charney, 1992) (see Figure 8-11). This is called a ventriculo-peritoneal (V-P) shunt. An alternative placement is to put the end of the shunt in the large vein that enters the heart; this was more commonly done in previous years. The V-P shunt allows the excess CSF to exit the brain and travel down the tube to the peritoneal cavity where it is reabsorbed into the body. This prevents a build-up of CSF in the brain and prevents any pressure caused by the excess fluid. Valves are also used to prevent the backflow of CSF to the brain. Shunts, however, can become infected and blocked. If the blockage occurs in an infant, the head will enlarge because the skull bones have not fused. If a blockage occurs after the bones have fused (usually by 18 months), the shunt blockage may result in some of the following symptoms: headache, fainting, nausea, vomiting, fever, irritability, drowsiness, or uneven dilation of the pupils. This requires immediate medical attention.

Treatment of Additional Problems

Other problems that may be present in a child with myelomeningocele may be addressed through bracing, surgery, or medication. Musculoskeletal abnormalities may be corrected or improved through bracing or surgery. Seizures will typically be treated with antiepileptic medication. Strabismus may be surgically managed; cognitive impairments and learning deficiencies can be addressed educationally.

COURSE OF SPINA BIFIDA

Myelomeningocele is not a progressive disease. With advanced medical treatment and the development of the shunting procedure, the outlook for living well into adulthood is good. The lower the myelomeningocele, the fewer complications typically occur.

One possible complication of myelomeningocele is a tethered cord. A tethered spinal cord results in a stretching of the spinal cord caused by the adherence of the end of the spinal cord to surrounding tissue. As the person grows, the spinal cord is stretched by these adhesions. This may result in no symptoms, in a deterioration of muscle strength, or in a lessening of

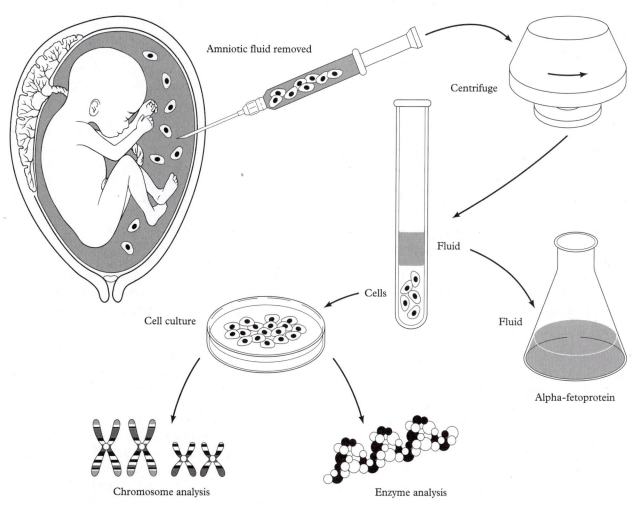

Amniotic fluid removed

Centrifuge

Fluid

Cells

Fluid

Cell culture

Alpha-fetoprotein

Chromosome analysis

Enzyme analysis

■ **FIGURE 8-10** Amniocentesis can be used to detect fetal abnormalities.

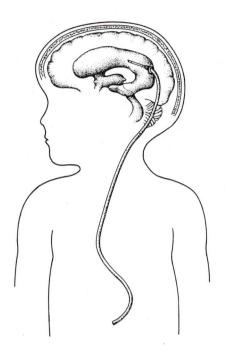

■ FIGURE 8-11 A ventricular-peritoneal shunt used for hydrocephalus

SOURCE: From *Physical Disabilities and Health Impairments: An Introduction*, by J. Umbreit, Ed., pp. 118, 123, 251. Copyright ©1983 Merrill Publishing Co. Reprinted with permission.

sensation as well as other possible problems (McEnery, Borzyskowski, Cox, & Neville, 1992; Petersen, 1992). Surgery may be performed to release the spinal cord from its connection to the surrounding tissue.

EDUCATIONAL IMPLICATIONS OF SPINAL CORD INJURY AND SPINA BIFIDA

To help a child with a spinal cord injury or myelomeningocele most effectively, teachers and staff members should know about the medical condition in general and the student specifically. A child with a high spinal cord injury or high myelomeningocele will have different needs from those of a child with a low spinal cord injury or low myelomeningocele. The challenge for the educational team is to work together to determine how to best meet students' unique needs. A physical therapist, an occupational therapist, a nurse, a teacher, a speech therapist, and others will be involved in helping the student to reach maximum potential. Providing information on the implications of spinal cord injury and spina bifida to all professionals working with the student will aid in achieving his or her goals.

Meeting Physical and Sensory Needs

The teacher should understand the effects of muscle paralysis and the loss of sensation. For example, movement in the legs (if the legs are affected) that results from involuntary reflexes does not mean that the student's voluntary muscle control is returning. Often the teacher must educate others about this. Since the student has sensory loss, the teacher must monitor the student for temperature control and for any accidents that may occur to the paralyzed areas. Also, the teacher will need to be alert for the appearance of any reddened areas on the skin indicating the development of pressure sores. Skin should be checked for breakdown when splints, braces, or other orthoses are removed or applied. Students should not sit in one position for extended lengths of time; a change of position or chair

■ VIGNETTE 1 ■

Hieu was a 16-year-old boy in tenth grade. After getting his driver's license, he drove too fast on a wet road, which resulted in a serious accident. The accident caused him to have a C5 spinal cord injury that left him quadriplegic. After many months in rehabilitation, Hieu returned to his home school. Before his arrival, his teachers received inservice training regarding the effects of spinal cord injury. The students also worked on a unit on spinal cord injury in their health sequence. Although Hieu was going to be staffed into special education due to a lack of stamina and the need for extra educational support, it was determined that the majority of his time would be in regular classes. When Hieu arrived at school, the educational team (OT, PT, special education teacher, regular education teacher, nurse, adapted PE instructor, counselor, and parents) was ready to assist Hieu and provide appropriate programming. Individuals from the rehabilitation center also came to the school to answer questions and provide information. Several adaptations (such as computers adapted with switches) were used to allow Hieu access to material and a means of written response. Adaptations were made in PE to allow him to participate as much as possible. (He often kept score or participated in adapted sports.) Hieu received occupational and physical therapy three times a week. Hieu was able to get around with an electric wheelchair that he maneuvered with a sip-and-puff switch. Some of Hieu's friends continued to be friends, and Hieu also made some new friends. Although his anger and frustration made adjustment difficult, the educational team was able to assist Hieu in making the transition.

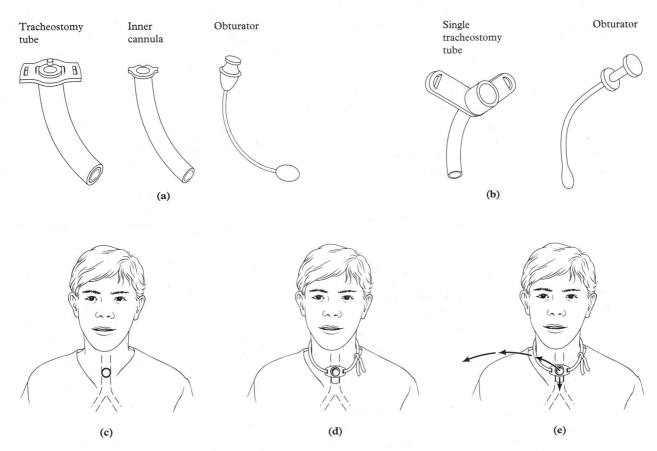

■ **FIGURE 8-12** (a) Tracheostomy tube with inner cannula and obturator; (b) single tracheostomy tube with obturator; (c) stoma; (d) tracheostomy; (e) placement of obturator

lifts should be implemented hourly. Consultation with a physical therapist will be needed to determine proper positioning and the correct application and removal of splints, braces, or other orthoses.

Students with some muscle paralysis in the legs may use braces, crutches, or other devices to walk. The teacher should keep in mind that some students may tire from a lot of walking, and some may be very slow changing classes. Giving them extra time may be helpful. Depending on the extent of paralysis and the student's vitality, some students may be able to walk only short distances and use a wheelchair for longer distances. Many peers and adults do not understand why a child who is able to walk needs a wheelchair. Education of others will help clear up misunderstandings and prevent teasing. As a child matures, he or she may tend to become overweight, which may result in more frequent wheelchair use. Sensitivity to this, as well as to the importance of diet and exercise, cannot be stressed enough.

The student's physical needs with regard to using a ventilator, bladder and bowel control, and prevention of

complications will need to be addressed in the school setting. If the student is on a ventilator, the teacher and others who help the student will need to become familiar and comfortable with the ventilator; instruction in using the equipment should be provided by a nurse or other medical personnel; familiarity will help dispel fears. Peers should also be given basic information about ventilators.

A plan should be in place for any emergencies that could occur. If the ventilator stops working, the teacher should know what to do. This may involve giving artificial respiration through the tracheostomy or using an ambu bag that attaches to the tracheostomy to give artificial respiration. Who responds to this type of emergency and who calls the paramedics should be decided before the emergency happens.

Another possible emergency would be that the tracheostomy tube comes out when the ties around the tracheostomy become loose. When this happens, the opening into the student's windpipe could close. The tracheostomy tube should then be reinserted so the student can breathe. Usually, an obturator that fits into the tracheostomy tube is used to aid in reinsertion (see Figure 8-12). While the obturator is in the tracheostomy tube, the student cannot breathe, so the obturator must be removed immediately after reinsertion of the tracheostomy. The ties that hold the tracheostomy in place must then be retied. One finger should fit comfortably under the ties if they are fitted properly. A plan describing what to do if the tracheostomy accidently comes out should be in place before the child comes to school.

Students who use clean intermittent catheterization (CIC) for bladder control will need to have this procedure performed at school at specified times. In some school districts, the teacher does this; in others, a nurse performs the procedure, but the teacher knows about it and about any complications that can arise. If the teacher is to perform the procedure, he or she should have received thorough training from a person in the medical field and receive training updates. Permission forms should specify who is responsible for performing the procedure (Heller et al., 1991). Whoever is responsible should perform it with dignity and in private.

As we discussed earlier, a serious complication is autonomic dysreflexia. Teachers should be aware of the possible triggers of this condition, such as a distended bladder and constipation with distended abdomen. These should be prevented when possible by closely observing the times the bladder is emptied by clean intermittent catheterization and by knowing the student's bowel regime and protocol for constipation. The teacher must be aware of the signs and symptoms of this pathological reflex (headache, sweating, chills) and call an ambulance immediately if this is suspected. If a nurse is available, she or he will closely monitor the child and take appropriate action.

Teachers should also be alert for any additional problems or complications the student with myelomeningocele may develop, such as seizures or visual problems. Each teacher, paraprofessional, and staff member should be aware of the signs and symptoms of shunt obstruction. If this is suspected, it can be an emergency and the child may need to see a physician immediately.

Meeting Communication Needs

Students with a high spinal cord injury or those who are on a ventilator may be unable to speak. In these circumstances, an augmentative communication device may be used to allow the student to communicate effectively. The communication device can be accessed any number of ways, including by eye-gazes and switches (see Chapter 27).

Students with myelomeningocele may have difficulty with conversational skills when cocktail party syndrome speech is present. These students do not use

■ VIGNETTE 2 ■

Stacy was a 12-year-old girl with myelomeningocele. She had normal intelligence but some learning disabilities. She was in a resource room to assist with reading and math instruction for two periods of the day but was mainstreamed into the regular class for the remainder of the day. Stacy was well-liked by her peers. She could ambulate with crutches for short distances (across a room) but otherwise used a wheelchair for mobility. Stacy performed the CIC procedure six times a day and was independent in doing it at school. Visitors to the school who were unfamiliar with Stacy were very impressed by her speech and often felt that she must be gifted. Her teacher often had to explain to school personnel who were unfamiliar with Stacy about her cocktail party syndrome so that they would have a realistic view of Stacy's abilities and would encourage her to stay on relevant topics. Some children were uncomfortable talking with Stacy due to her speech. As a part of Stacy's IEP, the teacher included the goal of maintaining relevant conversations and appropriate conversational interactions.

conversation for the communication of ideas but as a means of social contact (Swisher & Pinsker, 1971). However, because this type of conversation is often irrelevant and disorganized, it may result in unsuccessful interactions with others. Some students with myelomeningocele may not have cocktail party speech but have difficulty initiating and maintaining conversation. The teacher can promote social interaction and conversational speech skills. Depending on which type of problem the student has, the teacher may (1) foster independent communication skills by encouraging students to speak for themselves; (2) encourage students to listen carefully to the thoughts of others, acknowledge thoughts, and respond on the same topic; (3) use role-playing of different social interactions; and (4) pair students on projects and presentations. These are just a few suggestions that may assist with improving conversational skills and social interactions.

Occasionally, students with spina bifida and spinal cord injury may need to explain their disability to other children. One simple explanation for spina bifida is, "I was born with part of my back open and the doctors closed it. Because of that, I have trouble walking and have to use special crutches (or a wheelchair). I like to do the same things you do, but I can't run" (Morrow, 1985). A child who had a spinal cord injury could say something like, "I was in a car wreck and it messed up my back, so I can't move my legs."

25.		25	25	25	25	25	25	25	25	25	25	25	25	25	25	25	25	25	25	25	25
24.		24	24	24	24	24	24	24	24	24	24	24	24	24	24	24	24	24	24	24	24
23.		23	23	23	23	23	23	23	23	23	23	23	23	23	23	23	23	23	23	23	23
22.	Wash hands	22	22	22	22	22	22	22	22	22	22	22	22	22	22	22	22	22	22	22	22
21.	Wash cup	21	21	21	21	21	21	21	21	21	21	21	21	21	21	21	21	21	21	21	21
20.	Wash cath	20	20	20	20	20	20	20	20	20	20	20	20	20	20	20	20	20	20	20	20
19.	Empty urine into toilet	19	19	19	19	19	19	19	19	19	19	19	19	19	19	19	19	19	19	19	19
18.	Fasten belt	18	18	18	18	18	18	18	18	18	18	18	18	18	18	18	18	18	18	18	18
17.	Snap pants	17	17	17	17	17	17	17	17	17	17	17	17	17	17	17	17	17	17	17	17
16.	Zip pants	16	16	16	16	16	16	16	16	16	16	16	16	16	16	16	16	16	16	16	16
15.	Pull up pants	15	15	15	15	15	15	15	15	15	15	15	15	15	15	15	15	15	15	15	15
14.	Pull up briefs	14	14	14	14	14	14	14	14	14	14	14	14	14	14	14	14	14	14	14	14
13.	Pull out cath	13	13	13	13	13	13	13	13	13	13	13	13	13	13	13	13	13	13	13	13
12.	Insert cath	12	12	12	12	12	12	12	12	12	12	12	12	12	12	12	12	12	12	12	12
11.	Place cath (urethra, penis)	11	11	11	11	11	11	11	11	11	11	11	11	11	11	11	11	11	11	11	11
10.	Put cath in K/Y Jelly	10	10	10	10	10	10	10	10	10	10	10	10	10	10	10	10	10	10	10	10
9.	Clean area with Turgex	9	9	9	9	9	9	9	9	9	9	9	9	9	9	9	9	9	9	9	9
8.	Unscrew cap of K/Y Jelly	8	8	8	8	8	8	8	8	8	8	8	8	8	8	8	8	8	8	8	8
7.	Pull down briefs	7	7	7	7	7	7	7	7	7	7	7	7	7	7	7	7	7	7	7	7
6.	Pull down pants	6	6	6	6	6	6	6	6	6	6	6	6	6	6	6	6	6	6	6	6
5.	Unzip pants	5	5	5	5	5	5	5	5	5	5	5	5	5	5	5	5	5	5	5	5
4.	Unsnap pants	4	4	4	4	4	4	4	4	4	4	4	4	4	4	4	4	4	4	4	4
3.	Undo belt	3	3	3	3	3	3	3	3	3	3	3	3	3	3	3	3	3	3	3	3
2.	Lay out cath equipment	2	2	2	2	2	2	2	2	2	2	2	2	2	2	2	2	2	2	2	2
1.	Wash hands	1	1	1	1	1	1	1	1	1	1	1	1	1	1	1	1	1	1	1	1

■ **FIGURE 8-13** Task analysis of clean intermittent catheterization. A slash (/) is written through the number if the step is correct; the number is circled if the step is incorrect.

Meeting Daily Living Needs

Because of the paralysis and sensory loss resulting from spinal cord disorders, students will need instruction in daily living skills. Difficulties may arise in mobility, bathing, transferring to a chair or bed, and other areas as well. If the injury or defect is located high on the spinal cord, the use of many adapted devices may assist the student in everyday tasks. Special feeding devices may be used. Adaptations on toothbrushes and hairbrushes may be needed. Putting on clothing may require a push-pull stick or other device. Physical and occupational therapists will typically work with the teacher to instruct the student in these skills (see Chapters 27 and 28).

Other forms of daily living skills may include such physical health care procedures as clean intermittent catheterization. Helping the student learn the procedure is imperative. Often such procedures are included on the student's IEP as an educational goal so that instruction on how to do the procedure is targeted. A task analysis may be used, which breaks down the steps of the procedure (see Figure 8-13).

Meeting Learning Needs

The student with a spinal cord injury or myelomeningocele may need adaptations in the educational setting to promote learning. Depending on the level of paralysis, the student may be unable to physically respond to

■ **FIGURE 8-14** Student using a head-pointer to type on the computer

questions, do written homework, or study in the same way as his or her peers. The development of various adaptations may be needed to allow the student to fully participate in class (see Figure 8-14).

Students may participate in classroom discussions in any number of ways. The student may participate verbally, use an augmentative communication device, eye-gaze a response, or respond to a choice that is presented sequentially, either verbally or visually. Depending on the extent of paralysis, students may use adaptations and devices to allow for independent responding. For students who are quadriplegic, a mouth stick can be used to type out answers, draw, paint, access

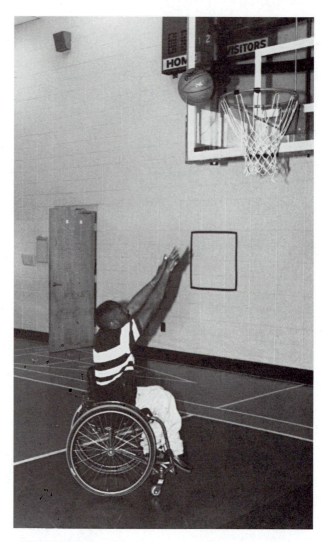

■ **FIGURE 8-16** Student with spinal cord injury playing basketball

a communication device, dial a phone, or complete any number of actions.

Several different types of switches may also be used so that students who are quadriplegic can activate computers, toys, or items in the environment (see Figure 8-15). Some switches can be activated by head movement. This may be a pressure switch that requires the student to move his or her head against it. Another type requires the contraction of a muscle, such as an eyeblink, head wrinkle, or similar motion. Some students with high cervical injuries use sip-and-puff switches that are controlled by the child sipping or puffing into a switch that resembles a straw. Some switches use the person's eye-gaze to activate a device, while others can be voice-activated.

Switches can be used to activate and type out assignments on a computer. Several programs and

■ **FIGURE 8-15** Teacher of students with orthopedic impairments setting up a computer with a switch (*round switch on table*) and removing a touch window screen

computer peripherals can provide scanning of the letters of the alphabet or the selection of an answer to a problem. Even if the student cannot access the keyboard, he or she can provide an answer with a switch by activating the switch when the correct answer is scanned or by spelling out the answer by activating the switch when each desired letter is scanned. Many software programs are available that can teach various concepts. The student can use the computer to practice and refine his or her skills is in addition to following the teacher's instruction.

Other devices may be necessary. A page turner will allow the student to turn the pages of a book; a tape recorder may be used to record lectures. Peers may take notes for the student using carbon paper.

Teachers may also need to present information differently for the student with a high spinal cord injury or a high myelomeningocele. Young children with cervical injuries lose the ability to explore and feel things around them. The teacher needs to take extra care and allow the student to experience things in an adapted manner. For example, the student may need to feel the item with his or her cheek to receive needed information.

Although students with spinal cord injury usually have the same level of cognitive functioning as before the accident, students with myelomeningocele may be born with learning deficits. Students may be placed in the regular academic curriculum, or an alternate curriculum may be needed. When there are perceptual-motor deficits, teachers will need to use specific strategies to compensate for or remedy these deficits. For example, if a student has difficulty with abstract concepts, the teacher could provide concrete examples.

Meeting Behavioral and Social Needs

Students with spinal cord injury and myelomeningocele will vary as to their behavioral and social needs. Students with spinal cord injury may have special difficulty adjusting to an acquired disability. Unfortunately, former friends and teachers may draw away or avoid the student because of the pain of knowing the student before the injury and seeing his or her present condition. Teachers and peers need information about spinal cord injury and the difficulties in adjustment that sometimes accompany it. Information about spina bifida is also crucial because of its impact on physical capacity, communication, and learning and because adjustment problems may arise. Teachers should be aware of their attitudes and actions toward students with spinal cord disorders. The attitude of the teacher can set the tone for the rest of the class. Encouraging student involvement in clubs or adapted sports activities can be helpful (see Figure 8-16). A warm, understanding environment will help students emotionally, as well as help them achieve their potential. Counseling and support groups may be beneficial.

SUMMARY

In this chapter, we discussed the etiology and mechanism of spinal cord injury and spina bifida. Spinal cord injury refers to damage to the spinal cord from traumatic or medical causes. In spinal cord injury, the extent of muscle paralysis and sensory loss depends on the level of the injury and whether the injury is complete or incomplete. Spina bifida is a congenital disorder in which there is a defective closure of the bony vertebral column. There are three types of spina bifida: spina bifida occulta, meningocele, and myelomeningocele.

In spina bifida, the extent of impairment depends on the type of spina bifida and the level of damage. In both spinal cord injury and spina bifida, there is muscle paralysis and sensory loss below the area of damage to the spinal cord. Additional problems may include bowel and bladder control, emotional responses, sexual functioning, and respiration. Other problems may include Arnold-Chiari malformation, hydrocephalus, musculoskeletal abnormalities, seizures, eye abnormalities, language impairment, and cognitive impairment. Both types of disorders are detected through observation and tests, such as a CT scan. Treatment for both requires a team approach to address the multiple impairments occurring from the damage to the spinal cord. Adaptations must be made in the school setting to allow the student to reach his or her potential.

PART III

Degenerative Diseases

CHAPTER 9

Muscular Dystrophy

Muscular dystrophy (MD) refers to a group of congenital degenerative diseases that result in progressive muscle weakness and a wasting away of the affected muscles. Duchenne muscular dystrophy (DMD), which is the most common form of muscular dystrophy, is the second most common lethal human genetic disease; it affects approximately 1 in 3,300 live male births (Emery, 1991). In Duchenne muscular dystrophy, marked physical degeneration occurs during the school-age years, so teachers will need to provide adaptations and a supportive school environment to help students with the disorder.

DESCRIPTION OF MUSCULAR DYSTROPHY (MD)

Muscular dystrophy can be broadly defined as a group of inherited diseases characterized by progressive muscle weakness due to the primary degeneration of muscle fibers (Sher, 1990). For a disease to be classified as muscular dystrophy, four main criteria must be met: (1) the disease must be a primary myopathy (a disease of the muscle); (2) the disease must be genetically based; (3) there must be a progressive course; and (4) degeneration and death of the muscle fibers must occur at some stage in the disease process (Behrman, 1992). This definition does not include such diseases as spinal muscular atrophy or cerebral palsy, which primarily affect the nervous system and, in turn, the muscles are affected.

ETIOLOGY OF MUSCULAR DYSTROPHY

In 1879, William Gowers identified and described what is known as Duchenne muscular dystrophy. Although it was thought to be genetically based, little

was known about the exact gene responsible. Not until a century after Gowers's description were the defective gene and the accompanying defective protein products identified through a unique process of reversed genetics (Dubowitz, 1992). In the early 1990s, genes responsible for other forms of muscular dystrophies were analyzed and identified as well (Bushby, 1992).

The breakthrough in determining the genetic origins of the various forms of muscular dystrophy has resulted in updating Appel and Rose's 1978 genetic classification system (Bushby, 1992; Sher, 1990). As seen in Box 9-1, there are X-linked muscular dystrophies, autosomal-dominant muscular dystrophies, and autosomal-recessive muscular dystrophies.

A genetic error or defect may result in several differing types of diseases; muscular dystrophy is one type. The type of genetic error will determine how the disease is transmitted from parent to child. In X-linked diseases such as Duchenne and Becker, the defective gene is carried by the mother and may be passed on to her sons. Hence, it is rare that females have this form of muscular dystrophy. However, daughters may be carriers of the defective gene. In autosomal-dominant diseases such as facioscapularhumeral muscular dystrophy, either the mother or the father carries the defective gene, which can be transmitted to a son or daughter. In autosomal-recessive diseases such as some forms of **limb-girdle muscular dystrophy,** both the mother and father must carry the gene in order for the disease to develop in their offspring.

DYNAMICS OF MUSCULAR DYSTROPHY

The various forms of muscular dystrophy affect different muscle groups, progress in different patterns and at different rates, and vary greatly as to their prognosis and

---

BOX 9-1

Select Types of Muscular Dystrophy

I. X-linked muscular dystrophy
  A. Xp21 myopathies
    1. Duchenne type
    2. Becker type
  B. Xq28 myopathies (Emery-Dreifuss dystrophy)
II. Autosomal-dominant muscular dystrophy
  A. Facioscapulohumeral (4q chromosome)
  B. Distal
  C. Ocular and oculopharyngeal
  D. Myotonic
III. Autosomal-recessive muscular dystrophy
  A. Limb-girdle (one form identified on the 15q chromosome; another form has been identified as autosomal-dominant on 5q chromosome)
  B. Congenital

---

severity. Knowledge of muscle types and function will be helpful in understanding the form and progression of muscular dystrophy.

Approximately 50% of the body is composed of muscles (Guyton, 1991), which can be classified into three major types: *skeletal, cardiac,* and *smooth.* Skeletal muscles are all muscles that can be moved voluntarily. An example is the biceps muscle in the arm, which a person can voluntarily contract to make the arm move. The second type of muscle is the cardiac (heart) muscle, which is involuntary. Both skeletal and cardiac muscles are striated, which refers to the transverse striations in the muscle that can be seen under a microscope. The third type are the smooth muscles; these include all involuntary muscles except the heart. Examples of smooth muscles include the muscle layers of the blood vessels and intestines. Smooth muscles do not have transverse striations and are classified as unstriated muscles.

Although all types of muscles can contract (shorten), there are some structural differences between the three types of muscles. The striated skeletal and cardiac muscles are composed of muscle fibers made up of cylindrical cells with transverse striations. Unstriated smooth muscles are composed of elongated, spindle-shaped cells and have no transverse striations.

Muscular dystrophy is a primary myopathy—a disease that develops in the muscles first. In most forms of muscular dystrophy, only the striated muscles are affected, and there is no associated abnormality of the central or peripheral nervous system (Dubowitz, 1992). When a person has muscular dystrophy, the genetic abnormality is thought to affect the chemical makeup

of the muscle cell. In Duchenne and Becker muscular dystrophies, for example, there is a lack of the protein dystrophin. The muscle fiber begins to die (necrose); regeneration occurs but becomes ineffective because muscle structure is distorted by the development of fat tissue in and between the muscle. Over time, fat cells replace muscle cells and both muscle structure and function are lost (Partridge, Cross, & Westminster Medical School, 1992).

CHARACTERISTICS AND COURSE OF MUSCULAR DYSTROPHY

There are several types of muscular dystrophy. Duchenne, Becker, and myotonic muscular dystrophies are more commonly found in the school-age population, because these diseases have a childhood onset. Although several of the less-common forms occur in adulthood, these have been found to occur in childhood and adolescence in rare cases. When this does happen, the characteristics and prognosis may be different from the typical pattern.

Duchenne Muscular Dystrophy (DMD)

The most common form of muscular dystrophy is Duchenne muscular dystrophy, and it is also one of the most severe forms. Muscle weakness appears early; often death occurs in the late teens or early twenties. Because of the early age at which muscle deterioration begins, Duchenne muscular dystrophy is the type most frequently seen in schools.

As compared to the other forms of muscular dystrophy, Duchenne muscular dystrophy typically has a rapid downward progression. Although the rate of progression varies, a typical progression can be described. For many children, muscular dystrophy is recognized by the time they are 3 years of age, when leg weakness is observed as difficulty in walking, running, or climbing stairs (Swash & Schwartz, 1988). By age 5, walking may appear abnormal, with a hip-waddling gait known as a Trendelenburg gait. The child will also have calf enlargement (pseudohypertrophy), which appears to be a muscular leg but is actually the result of the infiltration of fat cells. The child will typically present with **Gowers's sign** at this time. Gowers's sign is present when the child can only push up into a standing position by walking the hands up the thighs (Figure 9-1). At this age, there is usually no hand or arm weakness. Between ages 5 and 10 years, there is further weakening of the legs accompanied by arm weakness. Other muscles may appear to be enlarged. Scoliosis (lateral curvature of the spine) often appears due to the weakening of the muscles in the back. Contractures (permanent shortening of muscles) may occur, especially of the Achilles tendon (at the back of the ankle). Since the child has entered school by this time, learning disabilities or mild mental retardation may be diagnosed, although many children with muscular dystrophy have no cognitive problems and can in fact be gifted.

Around 10 to 12 years of age, the child often can no longer walk and will need a wheelchair. At first, a manual chair is used, but as weakness continues, an electric wheelchair will be needed (see Figure 9-2). Throughout the teenage years, contractures develop that result in limitations of movement; the painless progression of muscle weakness continues until it is difficult for the adolescent to hold his or her head upright. The voice may take on a breathy, nasal quality; the eye muscles usually retain their strength. The muscles of the fingers ordinarily retain enough strength to allow the person to continue to use a spoon and a pencil or keyboard (Sher, 1990). Because the cardiac (heart) muscle is a striated muscle, changes occur within the heart muscle's tissue. However, only 10% of individuals with Duchenne muscular dystrophy will have symptoms resulting from the tissue changes in the heart

(Iannaccone, 1992). Because of the weakness of the muscles used for breathing and the diminished ability to cough, the adolescent is more prone to respiratory infections. Most adolescents with Duchenne's muscular dystrophy will die at around 20 years of age from a respiratory infection or, in some instances, heart complications.

Becker Muscular Dystrophy (BMD)

Another type of muscular dystrophy is Becker's muscular dystrophy. This type follows the same progression as Duchenne muscular dystrophy, but the onset and course are slower. In light of new methods of genetic identification, new procedures are emerging to identify the genetic type of muscular dystrophy and study its clinical characteristics. The validity of studies done before muscular dystrophy forms could be determined unequivocally has been questioned.

In one landmark study by Bushby and Gardner-Medwin (1993), 67 individuals genetically determined to have Becker muscular dystrophy were studied for their clinical characteristics. In this study, a mean age at

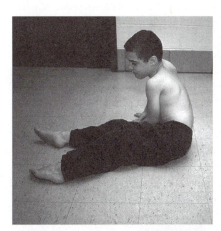

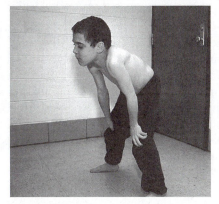
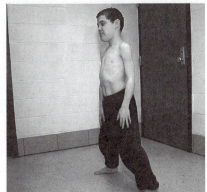

■ **FIGURE 9-1** Gowers's sign

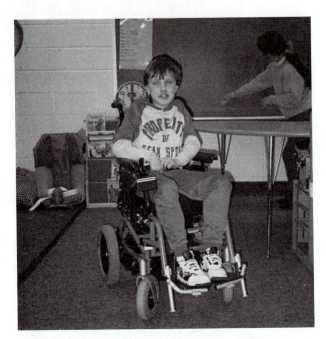

■ FIGURE 9-2 Student who has muscular dystrophy shows his electric wheelchair. Adapted positioning equipment is in the background.

muscles of the gastrointestinal tract result in slow emptying of the stomach, which results in constipation. Lack of bowel control may be present as well. Associated conditions such as cataracts, diabetes, and intellectual impairments are common. Life expectancy can be normal in certain cases.

Emery-Dreifuss Dystrophy

This is a rare form of muscular dystrophy that has no hypertrophy (enlargement) of the affected muscles. Symptoms begin with weakness and muscle deterioration in the arms, then progress to the legs, accompanied by early contractures. Symptoms begin in early childhood, but progression is very slow; some individuals have no further muscle weakness progression past the age of 20 years. Unlike people with Duchenne muscular dystrophy, most individuals retain the ability to walk, but there is a tendency toward more heart involvement (Sher, 1990). Individuals may live until late adulthood.

Facioscapulohumeral (FSH) Muscular Dystrophy

Facioscapulohumeral muscular dystrophy encompasses a rare group of diseases that vary in severity. Muscle weakness begins in the face, shoulder, and upper arms, usually in the second to third decade of life, although symptoms have occurred as early as 5 years and as late as the 50s (Soueidan, 1992). The individual may be unable to whistle, drink from a straw, lift arms up, or close his or her eyes. The disease usually progresses to the pelvis and legs. Heart involvement does not typically occur. Most forms of facioscapulohumeral muscular dystrophy are slowly progressive, with the first signs occurring in the first or second decade of life. Usually, death occurs at a normal age in late adulthood (Sher, 1990; Swash & Schwartz, 1988).

which muscle problems were noticed was 11 years (with a range of 10 months to 38 years) and the mean age of diagnosis of a muscle disease was 17 years. Weakness of the arms was typically first noticed at a mean age of 31 years, with a loss of the ability to walk at 37 years (range 11 to 78). Mean age of death from Becker muscular dystrophy was 47 years (range 23 to 89). This study suggests that most individuals had a typical, mild form of Becker muscular dystrophy, as characterized by late onset and slow progression. However, a small number of these individuals had a more severe form of Becker muscular dystrophy that is similar to Duchenne muscular dystrophy.

Myotonic Muscular Dystrophy (Steinert's Disease)

Myotonic muscular dystrophy is the second most common type of muscular dystrophy. Infants may be born with an inverted-V-shaped upper lip, thin cheeks, and facial weakness, or they may develop some of these symptoms later. Weakness is initially present in the lower part of the arms and legs. Gradually, weakness spreads, and shoulder and neck muscles become involved. Gowers's sign is usually present. Most individuals with myotonic muscular dystrophy do not lose the ability to walk. Unlike in other forms, smooth muscles (involuntary muscles) are affected as well as striated muscles (voluntary muscles and the heart). Smooth

Distal Muscular Dystrophy (Welander Type)

This type of muscular dystrophy is slowly progressive, with the initial onset usually occurring between 20 and 77 years of age. Weakness begins in the hands and feet with some progression to the arms and legs. There is usually no trunk involvement (Sher, 1990; Swash & Schwartz, 1988).

Ocular and Oculopharyngeal Muscular Dystrophy

This is a rare form of muscular dystrophy that involves the muscles of the eyes, the pharynx, or both. Usually, the upper eyelid droops (ptosis) and there is some paralysis of the eye muscles. In oculopharyngeal muscular dystrophy, swallowing is difficult. Other muscle weakness is often involved. This type of muscular dystrophy does not usually occur until the fourth decade of life (Sher, 1990; Swash & Schwartz, 1988).

Limb-Girdle Muscular Dystrophy

Limb-girdle muscular dystrophy usually occurs in the second or third decade of life. Muscle weakness usually begins in the hip and/or shoulder and after 5 to 10 years, spreads to other muscles. Individuals may lose the ability to walk after the disease has progressed for 10 to 20 years. Life expectancy may be slightly decreased because of possible respiratory complications (Sher, 1990).

Congenital Muscular Dystrophy

Although all forms of muscular dystrophy are congenital, the term *congenital muscular dystrophy* refers to a group of diseases with a specific set of symptoms that are present at birth. The child with congenital muscular dystrophy has muscle weakness of the limbs, trunk, and face, as well as low muscle tone (**hypotonia**). Arthrogryposis (multiple contractures) is common in this type of muscular dystrophy. (See Chapter 15.) Intelligence is usually normal. Unlike the other forms of muscular dystrophy, this form is usually nonprogressive after birth. However, in one variety of congenital muscular dystrophy that occurs primarily in Japan, there is accompanying malformation of the brain, mental retardation, seizures, and early death (Sher, 1990; Swash & Schwartz, 1988).

DETECTION OF MUSCULAR DYSTROPHY

The symptoms of muscular dystrophy may initially be dismissed as clumsiness or lack of coordination. However, as the symptoms progress, a diagnosis will be made based on the person's history, family history, clinical findings, and laboratory tests—one of which is to test for enzymes (such as the CK enzyme) that are released when muscles are damaged, as they are in muscular dystrophy. Studies to test the electrical properties of skeletal muscles—electromyographic (EMG) studies—are often performed, along with muscle biopsies. A muscle biopsy allows direct analysis of the muscle tissue. Further analysis may include molecular genetics tests and protein-based testing; these tests can be used in the further diagnosis of such forms as Duchenne, Becker, and myotonic dystrophy (Anderson & Kunkel, 1992; Shelbourne et al., 1993).

For parents who are known carriers of the disease or who have the disease, a prenatal diagnosis is possible. Conventional methods to determine the fetal sex (by amniocentesis) and examine family history may be used. Fetal tests to determine enzyme abnormality or genetic abnormalities may also be used. This may be done by amniocentesis, chorionic villus sampling (Monni et al., 1993), and fetal blood sampling (Suzumori, 1992).

TREATMENT OF MUSCULAR DYSTROPHY

There is no specific medical treatment and no cure for muscular dystrophy at this time, although some new treatments (such as gene therapy) appear promising. All are still in the experimental stages. The goal of treatment now is to help individuals with muscular dystrophy to live as normally as possible. Treatment efforts are typically carried out by a team, and they address the complications and symptoms of muscular dystrophy.

Orthopedic complications appear early. Often a physical therapist will play an important role in motivating, designing, and teaching an exercise plan and will train the student in the use of orthotics and adaptive equipment. Exercise is an important element of the individual's program because inactivity can be detrimental and can accelerate decline. Exercise programs will help maintain strength and prevent contractures for as long as possible. Swimming is an excellent form of exercise because a person with muscular dystrophy is more buoyant in the pool due to the decrease in muscle cells and the increase in fat cells. However, care should be taken to avoid overactivity and fatigue. Independent mobility should be encouraged for as long as possible; manual and electric wheelchairs should be prescribed as needed.

Braces and orthotics may be prescribed either to help with walking or for positioning to prevent contractures. Short leg braces, such as ankle/foot orthoses, are common. Other devices may be implemented by the physical therapist or occupational therapist to assist with mobility and daily living skills.

An orthopedic surgeon may perform surgery to prevent early deformity or to release contractures that inhibit walking. However, release of some contractures may not be desirable if the student has more functional use of the contracted limb. Scoliosis is also a problem in many cases of muscular dystrophy. Bracing may be used and, in some cases, spinal fusion may be performed to prevent progression of spinal deformity (Miller, Moseley, & Doreska, 1992).

A dietitian may be needed to help provide a balanced diet. People with muscular dystrophy tend to become obese, but obesity should be controlled because it may decrease the amount of time a person with muscular dystrophy will be able to walk. Obesity may also increase the person's chances of developing scoliosis.

Medication will be prescribed to combat infections and other problems. Because respiratory infections are more frequent in most types of muscular dystrophy, antibiotics are commonly used to combat bacterial infections; respiratory treatments and interventions may be needed. Proper infection control should be implemented to decrease the risk of infection. Depending on the type of heart condition that may develop, medication such as digoxin may be prescribed to decrease abnormal heartbeats (arrhythmia) or to increase the number of effective heart contractions.

EDUCATIONAL IMPLICATIONS OF MUSCULAR DYSTROPHY

Students with degenerative diseases such as muscular dystrophy have unique needs in the educational environment. As the student's physical abilities decrease, the educator must make increasing modifications to allow for physical participation in all activities related to school and community life. The teacher must also be ready to provide emotional support to a student with muscular dystrophy and to cope emotionally with having a student with a degenerative disease.

The teacher must also deal with other people's attitudes. For example, some people think that having a child with a terminal disease go to school, do homework, and expend energy on academic work is unkind when the child may not have long to live. These same people may even insist that a child should not have to be in school. The teacher may have to explain that school is a great normalizing factor for all children. One of the major points of treatment is to normalize life and prolong living. To have a child quit school may give the impression that all is lost (Simons, 1994). A caring attitude and collaborative effort will help the teacher make a positive school experience for the student.

Meeting Physical and Sensory Needs

The teacher must understand the type of muscular dystrophy a student has and its typical progression. Duchenne muscular dystrophy usually progresses fairly rapidly compared with Becker muscular dystrophy. Knowing about this difference will help the teacher work with the parents or guardians to set realistic goals and ascertain the future physical needs of the student.

To adequately meet the physical needs of a student with muscular dystrophy, the teacher must carefully monitor the student's physical ability and be alert for changes in ability and stamina that occur as the disease progresses. Use of a form that provides information about the student's physical status will be helpful. The form should be completed with the parent before the student comes to school. Information from observation, other teachers, and related service staff (physical and occupational therapists) should be compiled as well. The form in Figure 9-3 can be used to obtain this information. The information obtained on the checklist can be used as baseline information to monitor physical change. Sometimes parts of the form are used before the beginning of each school year to see whether adaptations are needed. Ongoing assessment of the student's physical status is necessary to detect subtle changes that may require adaptations. The checklist in Figure 9-4 can be used by teachers and educational team members to communicate with each other about problems the student might be having.

In some types of muscular dystrophy (Duchenne), the first noticeable muscle degeneration typically begins in the legs. As weakness progresses, the student will begin to fall. The student should be encouraged to get up without help unless help is requested. This will help maintain independence and self-esteem. The physical therapist can help with training to make falls as safe as possible and to teach ways of making the transition back into a standing position. The teacher should be alert to any injury that can occur from the fall and seek appropriate medical treatment if needed. Students should use the handrails on stairs to prevent serious injury if a fall should occur in that location. Ramps may be selected rather than stairs.

Maintaining physical activity is important because inactivity causes faster progression of the disease. Students should participate in physical education as much as possible, using a modified program if necessary. Not only does this help with the physical aspects of the disease but it also promotes socialization. Unfortunately, one study by Crosley and Vella (1987) showed that physical education directors were misinformed about muscular dystrophy. Some had the misconception that physical activity was contraindicated for students with muscular dystrophy. Only in the advanced stages of the disease should the student participate through more sedentary activities such as scorekeeping.

In Duchenne muscular dystrophy, the disease will progress to the point that a wheelchair will be necessary. The teacher should be alert to that need. Introducing a wheelchair often requires making a difficult decision. The teacher, physical therapist, occupational therapist, nurse, parents, physician, and the student should be involved in that decision. When a move to a wheelchair occurs, the teacher will need to learn proper handling and transferring techniques from the physical therapist.

NAME: _____   BIRTHDATE: _____

PARENTS: _____   HOME PHONE: _____

ADDRESS: _____   EMERGENCY #: _____

_____   _____
                                               (Relationship and Name)

Physician Name and Phone Number: _____

_____

CHECK APPROPRIATE NEED

WALKING ABILITY:

_____ Independent
_____ Uses furniture for support
_____ Wears braces
_____ Needs assistance
_____ Requires extra time
_____ Needs "buddy" system

Additional Information: _____

_____

_____

STEPS:

Going Up:
_____ Independent
_____ Uses railing
_____ Needs assistance
_____ Needs elevator

Coming Down:
_____ Independent
_____ Needs railing
_____ Requires assistance
_____ Needs elevator

Additional Information: _____

_____

_____

■ **FIGURE 9-3** Data base for the student with muscular dystrophy

SOURCE: Reprinted from *Understanding the Child with a Chronic Illness in the Classroom*, edited by Janet Fithian, pp. 209–212. Copyright ©1984. Used with permission from The Oryx Press, 4041 N. Central Avenue, Suite 700, Phoenix, AZ 85012, (800) 279-6799.

(Continued)

CHAIR:

Sitting Down:
_____ Independent
_____ Needs assistance

Getting Up:
_____ Independent
_____ Needs assistance

Additional Information: _____

_____

_____

WHEELCHAIR:
_____ Independent
_____ Needs assistance (explain: help on and off ramps, "buddy" system in halls, locking chair to make it immo-
         bile, etc.)

_____

_____

_____

_____

CAFETERIA:
_____ Independent
_____ Needs assistance (explain: needs help in carrying tray, cutting food, have special eating utensils)

_____

_____

_____

_____

TOILETING:
_____ Independent
_____ Needs assistance (explain)

_____

_____

_____

_____

■ **FIGURE 9-3** *(Continued)*

OUTER CLOTHING (Putting on and taking off):
_____ Independent
_____ Needs assistance (explain: needs extra time or help with buttons, etc.)

_____

_____

_____

_____

ANCILLARY HELP needed:
_____ Physical therapy
_____ Occupational therapy
_____ Speech therapy
_____ Explain frequency and type needed:

_____

_____

_____

_____

_____ ADDITIONAL INFORMATION (i.e. prescription sent to school, receiving therapy at home, etc.)

_____

_____

_____

_____

PERTINENT INFORMATION
_____ Information concerning the student (i.e. needs encouragement to participate, do NOT offer help unless requested, etc.)

_____

_____

_____

_____

_____

_____

■ **FIGURE 9-3** *(Continued)*

NAME: _____ DATE: _____

TEACHER: _____

Please give progress report. Stress difficulties as well as assets.

_____ Getting about and being mobile (in the classroom, halls, stairs, cafeteria, restroom, etc.)

_____

_____

_____

_____ Ease with using special equipment (braces, writing devices, eating utensils)

_____

_____

_____

_____ Classroom skills (writing skills, energy level, participation, need for adaptive equipment)

_____

_____

_____

_____ Academic skills (in comparison with expectations, need for special evaluations or ancillary help, such as physical therapy, occupational therapy, speech therapy, psychological testing)

_____

_____

_____

_____ Special notations: (include whether or not a conference is indicated)

_____

_____

_____

■ **FIGURE 9-4** Anecdotal record

Source: Reprinted from *Understanding the Child with a Chronic Illness in the Classroom*, edited by Janet Fithian, pp. 209–212. Copyright ©1984. Used with permission from The Oryx Press, 4041 N. Central Avenue, Suite 700, Phoenix, AZ 85012, (800) 279-6799.

Training in proper care and management of the wheelchair will be needed as well.

The location of a student who has a wheelchair in the classroom is crucial. He or she should be located so that interaction with the teacher and fellow students is possible and instructional materials are visible. Maps, displays, the chalkboard, and other items used for demonstration should be in clear view. As the disease progresses, the student will lose the ability to reposition in the chair, so seeing these materials may be difficult when something blocks the way.

Depending on the type of muscular dystrophy and how the student is affected by it, there may be some deterioration in hand function. The teacher needs to be alert for this and provide modifications as necessary. The student may need an adaptation that provides arm support. A typewriter or computer may be easier to use than writing by hand. A note taker may be assigned to assist the student, or a fellow student may use carbon paper to make a duplicate set of notes. Taping the lecture is another possibility.

Fatigue may present a problem for students with muscular dystrophy (especially Duchenne). The teacher should be aware of this and be ready to make accommodations for it. Shorter tests and homework assignments may be needed. Several alternative positions out of the wheelchair as discussed with the physical therapist may ease fatigue and decrease the risk of decubitus ulcers (pressure sores). As the disease progresses, students often need to take rest breaks and lie down. It is not unusual for special educators to have a cot or special table in their room for this purpose. At times, a student may need a shortened school day.

Students with muscular dystrophy often die from respiratory infections, so it is imperative that the teacher and students use good infection control in the classroom. (See Chapter 26.) Students with minor respiratory infections should be careful not to spread their infection and should avoid direct contact with the student with advanced muscular dystrophy. Students with flu symptoms should be sent home. Any wheezing, coughing, or sniffling by the student with muscular dystrophy should be immediately reported to the parents or school nurse. Breathing difficulties require immediate emergency procedures.

Meeting Communication Needs

Much communication takes place through body language and other nonvocal forms, so students with advanced muscular dystrophy may be misunderstood. Their facial muscles may become dysfunctional and show a flat affect that can be interpreted as a lack of interest or awareness. Teachers and others should be aware that a lack of expression does not necessarily mean the student is not interested.

Students with muscular dystrophy may be occasionally asked what is wrong with them. Young students may respond by saying something like, "My muscles are very weak, so I can't move very well." Further explanation may be given based on the student's age and how he or she wants to handle inquiries from others.

Meeting Learning Needs

To effectively meet the learning needs of students with muscular dystrophy, the teacher should know how the disease progresses and how it affects student performance and attitude. Several studies have shown the lack of information teachers have on diseases, including muscular dystrophy, and their resulting unrealistic attitudes and expectations (Porter & Hall, 1987). Students may fail to perform tasks not because they are unable to do so but because they need adaptations. In these cases, a negative school experience can result. Providing information to teachers about muscular dystrophy and possible classroom adaptations has been shown to improve the school experience (Porter & Hall, 1987). Inservices and information from staff members from such organizations as the Muscular Dystrophy Association can be extremely beneficial.

The educator should remember that no mental deterioration is inherent in this disease. Students may be have normal intelligence or mental retardation; they may be gifted or have a learning disability. Teaching techniques that address students with cognitive impairments or giftedness should be continued as needed. Adaptations discussed in the physical management section should be implemented as necessary. Activities that require a high degree of manual dexterity should be adapted or deemphasized.

Even when there is no change in cognitive status, the increase in fatigue associated with efforts to move and speak may cause the student to begin to fall behind in school. Absences due to respiratory infections such as pneumonia may also cause the student to fall behind; homebound instruction may be required at times. When a student is not feeling well, learning will be more difficult. Students may be less motivated academically when the effort to live from day to day becomes more critical. Proper support and modifications should be available to the student.

Meeting Daily Living Needs

When the student's muscular dystrophy causes significant muscular deterioration, adaptations will allow maximum independence in such skills as eating, dressing, and toileting. Eating may become difficult, and the student may have to use his or her elbows for support or use adapted arm supports. The teacher should note whether food needs to be cut or a straw needs to be used in a drink. The student may need help carrying the lunch tray.

As for dressing, parents may choose clothes that are easy to put on and take off. Adaptive clothing that uses Velcro closings may be used; adaptive devices that easily button shirts may be used as well. The teacher should serve as a resource for the parent about these options. Useful information may also be obtained from the Muscular Dystrophy Association.

Most students with muscular dystrophy do not have incontinence (loss of bowel or bladder control). However, as muscles weaken, the student may need help getting from the wheelchair to the toilet. Using a urinal can be a feasible alternative. The need for assistance or modification can be embarrassing and result in a student's not asking for help. The student will then be uncomfortable throughout the day and may develop constipation. The student may also drink little fluid to avoid the need to urinate, which may result in discomfort and dehydration. The teacher needs to be sensitive to the student's situation and work out an arrangement so that someone with whom the student is comfortable can help with toileting needs in a dignified, private, and supportive manner.

Meeting Behavioral and Social Needs

There are several stages of disability for an individual with muscular dystrophy, especially the Duchenne type. These are the early and late walking phases, wheelchair use, and dying (Hsu & Lewis, 1981). The needs and concerns of the student, and those of the rest of the educational team, change in each phase. In the early and late walking phase, there may be a great deal of concern about falls and subsequent injuries. The timing of the student's move to a wheelchair can become a sensitive matter in which the student plays an active role in decision-making along with the team. When the student begins using a wheelchair, the other students, family, and educational staff may be relieved that there will be no more falls or feel despair that the student is declining. Practical and emotional concerns about how the student will carry out daily living skills and the rigors of academics will emerge as weakness continues. Ways of fostering independence by using adaptations become important. Finally, as the student is rapidly declining, questions about death and about how to prepare for dying come to the forefront (Gossler, 1987).

Emotional support will be needed for the family, student, friends, teacher, and staff. Some denial is common in any type of physical impairment; that is, the impairment may be treated as if it did not exist (Gossler, 1987). Denial can be healthy in that it prevents incapacitating anxiety and depression, but it can be detrimental if it keeps people from acting on something that needs immediate attention. Family, student, friends, teachers, and staff may deny some aspects of the disease, and this should be perceived as a beneficial reaction unless it negatively interferes with the student's functioning or creates negative responses to those interacting with the student. Counseling is recommended when this occurs.

Discrepancies may occur between the family's attitude and perception of the disease and the student's. At times, family members may be concentrating on the second phase of the disease (wheelchair use and adaptations), while the student is coping with the possibility of dying. Other times, family members may be in complete denial while the student accepts the situation. Another possibility is that the family knows the student is dying but thinks the student does not know. Therefore, discussions with the student are impossible. Very rarely is the outcome of the disease successfully hidden from the student. Excessive denial on the part of the family or hiding this fact from the student only serves to isolate the student and is not beneficial. The consensus in the literature is toward openness and frankness in communication (Lansdown, 1994).

Although the parents and individuals around the student may be open about the disease, the student's ideas about his or her own illness may vary. As seen in Box 9-2, a student may go through five stages. In the first stage, the student feels ill but does not think the illness is terminal. Not until the fifth stage does the student have the view that he or she is going to die (Lansdown, 1994). The student may react to the knowledge that he or she is dying by going through five stages: denial, anger, bargaining, depression, and acceptance (Kübler-Ross, 1969) or through a broad range of responses (Corr, Nabe, & Corr, 1994).

A student with muscular dystrophy may seek out another person—possibly a teacher—to talk to because of parental denial, because he does not want to upset his

---

BOX 9-2

Perception of the Terminal Illness

Stage 1: I am ill.
Stage 2: I have an illness that can kill people.
Stage 3: I have an illness that can kill children.
Stage 4: I am never going to get better.
Stage 5: I am going to die.

■ VIGNETTE ■

Bob is a 16-year-old boy with Duchenne muscular dystrophy. He has lost most mobility in his legs and is in an electric wheelchair. The muscles in his torso and arms are weak. He needs to take a rest break during the day due to fatigue. Other adaptations include shorter lessons, use of a computer instead of handwriting his assignments, and a modified exercise program. A peer takes notes for Bob and helps him get his lunch tray. He is involved in a chess club after school and has several supportive and understanding friends. Bob is well-informed about his disease. He had an older brother with Duchenne muscular dystrophy who died of respiratory complications 5 years ago. However, Bob did become very depressed in biology class when he learned that the heart was a muscle. He turned to his English teacher for support because he did not want to burden his parents. Overall, Bob is keeping a positive outlook and is looking forward to beating his next opponent in chess.

parents or because he does not want to let them know that he is fully aware of the consequences of the disease. (Teachers should let students know that they are available to talk.) If this boy, for example, selects a teacher as his confidant, it is important that the teacher be supportive of this because the teacher may be the only person the student feels comfortable talking to about his disease and about dying. It is helpful if the teacher knows what has been said at home and by physicians.

Information like this should have been obtained before the start of each year. If it is not available, the teacher must rely on what the student says. Reflective listening and questioning techniques, in which the teacher summarizes what the student is saying and asks him what he thinks about it, are helpful. It is not the teacher's responsibility to tell the student he is dying, however; he probably knows this. He may be denying it or may want to discuss it in detail. The teacher need not have answers for the questions the student is asking; being a supportive listener is usually sufficient. If there is a question the teacher cannot answer, he or she can simply acknowledge that fact and ask what the student thinks about it. In any discussion about death, it is important that the teacher not bring religion into it. Students' religious beliefs may be very different from teachers'. The teacher should support whatever coping mechanism the student is using.

Teachers should also realize that death can be perceived differently at different ages. The teacher may have a very different perspective on death from that of the student. A student's age and prior experience with those who were dying may influence how they perceive death. Table 9-1 shows how death is perceived at different ages. As can be seen in the table, young children do not see the finality of death, and older children do not readily perceive it as occurring to them, although having a terminal illness can change this (Fredlund, 1984). If the teacher is in a position to explain about death, simple explanations of the life cycle are best. Examples of planting a flower or having a classroom aquarium and then watching the flower or fish live and then die naturally help explain this natural process.

The student with muscular dystrophy may also have a lack of self-esteem. He may view himself as a burden and unable to accomplish things. The teacher needs to find ways to help him feel useful and valued. Giving him tasks that he can accomplish that are valued by others can enhance a feeling of self-worth. These tasks should be rotated to all students so their purpose is not obvious (Morrow, 1985). Development of skills or expertise in certain areas may also enhance the student's feeling of self-worth. Books about others with muscular dystrophy can be helpful.

The teacher needs to maintain a supportive atmosphere in the classroom. Some teachers may say, "What difference does it make whether this student learns geometry in my class?" Others may make special exceptions for the student if he exhibits inappropriate behavior. These attitudes foster hopelessness and despair; they send the message, "You're dying, so it doesn't matter." This can be tremendously upsetting to the student. Maintaining the same expectations for success and for appropriate behavior in school, as well as maintaining the normal routine of going to school, provides hope,

TABLE 9-1

Children's Concept of Death

Stage	Perception
Stage 1 (<3 years)	Little understanding; experience grief due to separation
Stage 2 (3–5 years)	Death is a departure; death is temporary, reversible; death does not happen to oneself; think they can wish someone dead
Stage 3 (6–9 years)	Death is final and irreversible; death happens to old people (early in stage, belief one never grows old); death may be viewed as a person
Stage 4 (10 years and older)	Death happens to anybody at any age; death is inevitable, universal, final, and irreversible; anxiety about death; adolescent may engage in dangerous activities, feeling invincible

socialization, and a feeling of accomplishment that every child and adolescent needs. Hope for one child may be looking forward to a cure. Another child may hope to graduate from high school, or hope to maintain a friendship. Another student with muscular dystrophy may hope to master calculus, and yet another student may hope that the deterioration slows down. This type of hope sustains life and is very positive (Gossler, 1987). It should be encouraged.

As the student's status changes over time, teachers and fellow students may begin to feel uncomfortable around the student and may avoid him or her. Students and teachers should receive the proper information about muscular dystrophy and specific information about helping students with the condition. Information can be obtained from the Muscular Dystrophy Association, from the library, and from individuals in the medical profession. Young students with muscular dystrophy are often helped to tell other students about their disease. Often a simple explanation, such as, "Some of my muscles are different and become weak," will help peers understand the disease. Teachers should dispel misconceptions by being sure that peers do not think this is a contagious disease. Teachers can also foster positive interactions between the student with muscular dystrophy and his or her peers. Group activities and cooperative learning strategies in which students help each other with assignments may be helpful. Teachers should find things the student with muscular dystrophy does well and emphasize those to boost self-esteem. Interested peers can be designated helpers with carrying books or getting the lunch tray. Participation in clubs should be fostered if the student is interested.

Even with proper information, the emotional effect of being around a student with a degenerative disease may be difficult for some students, teachers, and even family members. It is not unusual for close friends and teachers to begin to avoid the student as the disease becomes severe. Some peers and teachers will go through "anticipatory grief." This is when the individual grieves for the loss of the ill person before they have died. The problem with this is that the ill person often becomes isolated because friends are grieving and often avoiding contact. Support for the student's friends may be needed. Information and the availability of a counselor, or just someone to talk with, may help students maintain contact with the student with muscular dystrophy.

Teachers also need support when they have a student with a terminal illness. One study by Smith, Alberto, Briggs, and Heller (1991) showed that teachers lacked support from the school system in working with students who were dying. It was suggested that a school psychologist or counselor be trained and made available to provide support. The teacher must also find support through other teachers who have had a student who was terminally ill, as well as build or rely on an external support network—friends, family, or clergy.

When the student dies, support should be given to the student's classmates. The facts surrounding the death should be conveyed to the class in an open and honest manner. The teacher should share his or her reactions with the class. The students should be given an opportunity to discuss their feelings and concerns as a group. Often, allowing students to talk, write, or illustrate their feelings in drawings is helpful. A regular day should not be forced on the students, and the availability of a trained counselor is considered ideal. It is important to remember that grief responses vary widely; individuals may act as if nothing has happened, crack jokes, or be depressed. No response is inappropriate because people deal with death in different ways. When a classmate dies, it is always important to inform the parents of the other students in the class that a death has occurred.

SUMMARY

Muscular dystrophy is a group of inherited diseases that are characterized by progressive muscle weakness. There are several different types of muscular dystrophy; Duchenne muscular dystrophy is the most common and severe. In Duchenne muscular dystrophy, there is muscle weakness beginning in the lower extremities (legs). Muscle weakness progresses to the point that the student will need a wheelchair to get around. As the disease progresses, upper arms will be affected and the student may have difficulty holding his or her head up. Tests (such as those for enzyme concentrations and muscle biopsies), family history, and clinical findings are used for diagnosis. There is no specific medical treatment for muscular dystrophy at this time. Medical efforts are aimed at promoting useful function for as long as possible. The educator needs to be knowledgeable about the disease in order to effectively meet the student's needs and make appropriate adaptations. Providing emotional support is crucial.

CHAPTER 10

Spinal Muscular Atrophy

More than 100 years ago, Werdnig and Hoffmann described a condition characterized by pelvic weakness, progressive muscle weakness, muscular atrophy (wasting away of the muscles), and death by age 7 (Wessel, 1989). This condition is now known as *spinal muscular atrophy* (SMA), and since the time of Werdnig and Hoffmann, several different types of spinal muscular atrophies have been identified. The various forms have similar characteristics and courses but differ in age of onset, pattern of inheritance, and prognosis (Ionasescu & Zellweger, 1983).

SMAs occur in approximately 1 in 25,000 births (Russman et al., 1992). They are the second most common autosomal-recessive diseases in children (after cystic fibrosis) and the second most common of the neuromuscular diseases, following Duchenne's muscular dystrophy (Brzustowicz et al., 1990; Sheth et al., 1991). In some forms of spinal muscular atrophy, physical deterioration begins during the school-age years. As with other types of degenerative conditions, the teacher will need to provide adaptations and a supportive environment.

DESCRIPTION OF SPINAL MUSCULAR ATROPHY (SMA)

Spinal muscular atrophy refers to a group of degenerative diseases that are characterized by progressive weakening and atrophy of the skeletal muscles due to the degeneration of motor (anterior horn) cells in the spinal cord. For a disease to be classified as one of the spinal muscular atrophies, (1) it must be degenerative, (2) it must be a primary neuropathy (that is, affecting the nerves first), and (3) it must specifically target the motor cells of the spinal cord. When these motor cells are involved, the muscles that they control are affected.

There are several different forms of spinal muscular atrophy (see Table 10-1). The most prevalent forms are the *proximal* spinal muscular atrophies—those in which the muscles closest to the center of the body atrophy. Other forms are so rare in comparison that the term *spinal muscular atrophies* usually refers only to the proximal forms of the disease. Due to the prevalence of proximal spinal muscular atrophies and their initial presence in children, this chapter will only describe that type.

ETIOLOGY OF SPINAL MUSCULAR ATROPHIES

In most cases, spinal muscular atrophies are genetic and are predominantly caused by autosomal-recessive inheritance (Brzustowicz et al., 1990; Daniels, Thomas, et al., 1992; Sheth et al., 1991). Autosomal inheritance implies that the gene is not sex-linked, and hence it can be passed down from either the mother or father to either a son or daughter. When genetic transmission is autosomal-recessive, both parents must be carriers of the disease, and the child must inherit the affected gene from each parent if the disease is to be expressed. Only rarely are any of the types caused by autosomal-dominant inheritance (Brzustowicz, Wilhelmsen, & Gillian, 1991). When this does occur, only one parent would have to carry the affected gene for any offspring to be at-risk, and that parent would be affected by spinal muscular atrophies.

DYNAMICS OF SPINAL MUSCULAR ATROPHY

Spinal muscular atrophies affect the anterior horn cells of the spinal cord. As we discussed in Chapter 4, the anterior horn cells are the part of the spinal cord that carry motor information to the muscles. Motor information travels from the brain down the spinal cord. When the impulses reach the anterior horn

TABLE 10-1

Spinal Muscular Atrophies

Type	Characteristics	Inheritance
Juvenile progressive bulbar palsy	Progressive weakness of facial muscles Progressive paralysis of extraocular muscles Onset birth to 10 years	Autosomal-recessive with rare cases of autosomal-dominant
Scapuloperoneal syndromes	Several conditions with scapuloperoneal distribution of muscle weakness	Autosomal-dominant
Facioscapulohumeral muscular atrophy	Muscle weakness similar to facioscapulohumeral muscular dystrophy	Autosomal-dominant
Distal spinal muscular atrophy	Slow, progressive weakness and atrophy of distal muscles Affects twice as many males as females Onset before age 20	Autosomal-dominant more frequent than recessive
Juvenile type of distal muscular of the upper extremities	Weakness and atrophy of hands and forearm muscles Rarely affects proximal muscles	Unknown
Proximal spinal muscular atrophies	Most common forms of SMA Proximal muscle weakness greater than distal Onset from birth to adulthood, depending on type	Autosomal-recessive with rare cases of autosomal-dominant

SOURCE: Based on data from Ionasescu & Zellweger, 1983.

cells, they leave the spinal cord along the spinal nerves and travel through the peripheral nervous system. When the impulses reach the muscle via the peripheral nerve, the muscle contracts. Sensory information, on the other hand, travels in the reverse direction along the sensory nerves of the peripheral nervous system until the impulses reach the spinal cord where they enter the posterior horn cells. From that point, sensory information travels up the spinal cord to the brain.

As a primary neuropathy affecting the motor cells of the spinal cord, spinal muscular atrophy negatively impedes the function of the spinal cord. Because part of the function of the spinal cord is to carry messages to various parts of the body, including the muscles, the degeneration of the anterior horn cells blocks motor information from reaching the muscles. The individual is unable to move the corresponding muscles voluntarily, and the muscles weaken, have low muscle tone (hypotonia), and waste away (atrophy) (Sheth et al., 1991; Wessel, 1989). Unlike muscular dystrophy, which is a primary myopathy in which the muscle cells are affected, the muscles of an individual with spinal muscular atrophy cannot react because the messages from the brain are no longer being transmitted to them through the nerves. The muscle tissue does not change, except that it wastes away from disuse (atrophy).

Spinal muscular atrophy affects only the anterior horn cells, which carry motor information, and not the posterior horn cells, which carry sensory information, so spinal muscular atrophy does not cause sensory loss. Even though children with spinal muscular atrophy experience progressive loss of muscle use, they retain full sensation in the affected areas. In addition, the affected muscles are flaccid (have decreased muscle tone) (Brzustowicz et al., 1991) and deep tendon reflexes (such as the knee-jerk reaction) are diminished or absent (Ionasescu & Zellweger, 1983; Phillips, Roye, Farcy, Leet, & Shelton, 1990).

CHARACTERISTICS AND COURSE OF SPINAL MUSCULAR ATROPHY

The proximal spinal muscular atrophies represent several forms of the disease that are characterized by the weakening of the proximal muscles of the body—those closest to the center. In spinal muscular atrophy, the muscle weakness typically begins with the pelvic girdle—the pelvic bones and surrounding muscles. Since this area is crucial for maintaining stability in sitting, standing, and walking, these functions are adversely affected.

Once a diagnosis of spinal muscular atrophy has been made, the course and prognosis may vary considerably depending on the type of spinal muscular atrophy. The age of onset, while not an absolute predictor of course, plays a role in the rate of progression, severity of symptoms, and life expectancy. A younger age of onset generally indicates a more rapid progression and more severe symptoms.

Symptoms that are common to all types of SMA include muscle weakness and atrophy, with motor function losses. Skeletal deformities are also common, with scoliosis (a lateral curve of the spine) being the most common type of skeletal deformity. Scoliosis may further inhibit functioning. (See Chapter 11.) Individuals with spinal muscular atrophy may have respiratory problems, although there is no heart involvement. Intelligence is normal in individuals with spinal muscular atrophy, and, as with other types of physical impairments, students with spinal muscular atrophy may appear brighter than their peers because they hear adult speech more than most children, and they often exert extra effort in academics to compensate for physical limitations.

Type I: Acute Infantile Spinal Muscular Atrophy

Acute infantile spinal muscular atrophy, also known as Werdnig-Hoffmann disease, is characterized by hypotonicity (low muscle tone), a distinctive frog-leg position seen with low muscle tone, severe weakness, and a rapid progression of symptoms (see Figure 10-1). The symptoms of Type I spinal muscular atrophy are generally present at birth or appear within the first few months of life. While some cases of acute infantile spinal muscular atrophy begin prenatally, almost all show evidence of muscle weakness between 3 and 6 months of age (Ionasescu & Zellweger, 1983; Soueidan, 1992). (See Table 10-2.)

Infants with Type I spinal muscular atrophy generally have a weak cry and exhibit excessive drooling due to swallowing difficulties, which in turn causes feeding difficulties (Ionasescu & Zellweger, 1983;

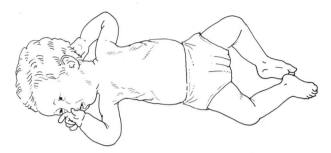

■ **FIGURE 10-1** Typical frog-leg position of child with spinal muscular atrophy

Soueidan, 1992; Wessel, 1989). The muscles of these infants tend to be thin and poorly developed and feel flabby when touched. Movement of the extremities is generally limited to the hands and feet. Deep tendon reflexes are absent (Wessel, 1989). These infants usually do not achieve independent head control or the ability to maintain a sitting position without support (Merlini et al., 1989). Because the facial muscles are spared, they generally appear alert and have a full scope of facial expressions (Adams & Victor, 1989; Ionasescu & Zellweger, 1983; Soueidan, 1992; Wessel, 1989).

These children do not have a long life expectancy because of the severity of symptoms and rate of progression of Type I spinal muscular atrophy. Rapidly weakening muscles eventually lead to the impairment of respiratory function, and death usually occurs before or during the second year of life due to respiratory complications such as frequently recurring infections (Brzustowicz et al., 1991; Harriman, 1984; Soueidan, 1992; Wessel, 1989). Some die early in infancy, which is why this form of spinal muscular atrophy is the leading cause of infant death from inherited conditions (Brzustowicz et al., 1990; Sheth et al., 1991).

TABLE 10-2			
Proximal Spinal Muscular Atrophies			
Type	Age of Onset	Characteristics	Prognosis
Type I Acute Infantile Werdnig-Hoffmann disease	Birth–6 months	Low muscle tone; severe weakness; absent reflexes	2 years of life
Type II Intermediate	6–12 months	Legs more affected than arms; reflexes present but later lost	Difficult to predict: some reach adulthood
Type III Juvenile Kugelberg-Welander disease	2–15 years	Delayed motor milestones; slow progression; can remain ambulatory until mid-30s	Long-term prognosis generally good

Type II: Intermediate Spinal Muscular Atrophy

Intermediate spinal muscular atrophy, also referred to as chronic infantile spinal muscular atrophy or Type II SMA, progresses more slowly than Type I SMA. Onset of Type II spinal muscular atrophy is generally between 6 and 12 months of age. Because of the slightly later onset, infants with Type II spinal muscular atrophy may develop the ability to sit and stand, and some may even take a few steps before the deterioration severely affects their motor ability (Soueidan, 1992; Wessel, 1989).

Children with Type II spinal muscular atrophy exhibit a more generalized weakness than the primarily proximal weakness of Type I, although proximal weakness is still greater than distal weakness (Harriman, 1984; Soueidan, 1992; Wessel, 1989). An example of proximal weakness would be a child who has good hand and muscle control and can hold a spoon, but weakness in the shoulder muscles prevents lifting the spoon to the mouth. In this type of spinal muscular atrophy, the legs are generally more affected than the hands (Merlini et al., 1989; Wessel, 1989), although a fine tremor of the hands is common. Deep tendon reflexes are initially present but are eventually lost (Wessel, 1989). Children with Type II spinal muscular atrophy can achieve head control and independent sitting but cannot walk unaided (Merlini et al., 1989).

Because of the progressive loss of motor function and the continued growth of the skeleton, children with Type II spinal muscular atrophy generally develop skeletal deformities and contractures over time. Two types of such deformities are scoliosis and kyphosis—a forward curvature of the upper part of the spine, or a humpback. These skeletal deformities further impair general functioning (such as in achieving balance for sitting) and respiratory function; physical appearance is also affected (Granata, Merlini, Magni, Marini, & Stagni, 1989).

The outlook for infants diagnosed with intermediate spinal muscular atrophy is variable and difficult to predict. The progression of the disease may be slow and steady over a period of years, or the child may experience long periods of stability. Either of these courses may be interrupted by periods of rapid deterioration. Prognosis depends largely on the degree of respiratory involvement. Weakened respiratory muscles increase susceptibility to respiratory infection. It is possible for some children, even those severely affected, to reach adulthood (Brzustowicz et al., 1991; Daniels, Suthers, et al., 1992; Daniels, Thomas, et al., 1992; Merlini et al., 1989; Wessel, 1989). Life expectancy can range from a few months to 30 years after diagnosis (Harriman, 1984).

Type III: Juvenile Spinal Muscular Atrophy

Type III spinal muscular atrophy, also known as Kugelberg-Welander disease, is the mildest form of spinal muscular atrophy affecting children initially (Brzustowicz et al., 1991; Daniels, Suthers, et al., 1992; Daniels, Thomas, et al., 1992). Children with Type III spinal muscular atrophy generally exhibit delayed motor milestones, clumsiness, and the inability to run as well as their peers. The onset of these symptoms generally occurs between 2 and 15 years of age (Wessel, 1989).

This type of spinal muscular atrophy is commonly mistaken for muscular dystrophy, particularly in boys, and sometimes leads to a misdiagnosis of Duchenne or Becker muscular dystrophy. This is due to the later age of onset, much slower progression, and initial problems with walking (Harriman, 1984; Soueidan, 1992; Wessel, 1989). Because of the disease's slow progression, individuals usually remain able to walk until their mid-30s, at which time they generally require the use of a wheelchair (Merlini et al., 1989; Soueidan, 1992). While mild cases of scoliosis are common in individuals still able to walk, once an individual loses the ability to walk, scoliosis can become a severe problem because it can compromise respiratory function. The long-term prognosis is generally good, although it is affected by the individual's degree of muscle weakness and respiratory involvement (Daniels, Thomas, et al., 1992).

DETECTION OF SPINAL MUSCULAR ATROPHY

Spinal muscular atrophy may escape detection for some time or may be misdiagnosed because of the range in age of onset and severity of symptoms associated with the different types of the disease. The more severe the spinal muscular atrophy (Type I), the earlier the diagnosis is typically made. It is important to note that age of onset alone is not an adequate criterion for determining the type of spinal muscular atrophy affecting the child (Wessel, 1989). In many cases of Type I spinal muscular atrophy, infants have severe hypotonia and generalized weakness at birth, with about one-third of mothers noticing a change in the strength of fetal movements during the third trimester (Wessel, 1989). Children affected with Types II and III spinal muscular atrophy are usually suspected of having some kind of problem because they fail to reach major motor milestones (Harriman, 1984; Wessel, 1989).

Spinal muscular atrophy is diagnosed through the child's history, physical examination, and clinical tests. Several tests are conducted to differentiate spinal muscular atrophy from primary muscle diseases such as muscular dystrophy. These include nerve conduction tests, CK (enzyme) concentrations, electromyography (EMG), and muscle biopsies. Conventional methods, such as amniocentesis, can be used to test for spinal muscular atrophy when the parents are known to be carriers or are themselves affected by some form of spinal muscular atrophy.

TREATMENT OF SPINAL MUSCULAR ATROPHY

At this time, there is no cure for spinal muscular atrophy. Treatment is centered on minimizing the symptoms of the disease in an attempt to maintain quality of life for affected individuals.

Treatment for the infant with Type I spinal muscular atrophy is supportive in nature and will have no effect on the eventual outcome (Wessel, 1989). Maintaining nutrition for these infants can become difficult because of rapidly deteriorating motor function, and tube feeding may become necessary. In tube feeding, a tube is passed into the stomach through the esophagus or through the abdominal wall, and liquified food or enrichment is supplied in that way. An adaptive seating device with a tray can be used to facilitate sitting while encouraging age-appropriate activities. Frequent respiratory infections are treated with antibiotics and postural drainage; that is, placing the child in specific positions to allow for drainage of respiratory secretions. To further alleviate respiratory congestion, chest physiotherapy is commonly used in addition to postural drainage (Wessel, 1989). Chest physiotherapy uses such specialized techniques as percussion (tapping a cupped hand over the lung area) or vibration to loosen secretions.

Because the onset of Type II spinal muscular atrophy is in late infancy or early childhood, deterioration occurs before crucial, early motor milestones (such as sitting, standing, and walking) have been achieved. Therefore, the initial emphasis of a treatment program is on maintaining normal range of motion and preventing contractures. Adapted chairs and equipment are often used to help the child sit so that activities to ensure cognitive development can be encouraged.

As the child with Type II spinal muscular atrophy enters the second year of life, a standing frame and scooter board may be used to promote functional gains. Some children are able to walk with the aid of lightweight braces and a walker. For most, the use of a wheelchair becomes a necessity, and the use of a motorized model can provide independent mobility at an early age (Wessel, 1989).

Respiratory involvement with Type II spinal muscular atrophy can be quite severe. Some children require the use of a ventilator to extend the length and improve the quality of life. Respiratory compromise can be treated by providing assisted ventilation at night or, for those with more severe respiratory problems, by using a portable, battery-operated model that is attached to the wheelchair.

Treatments for children with juvenile spinal muscular atrophy (Type III) are essentially the same as those prescribed for Type II; the difference is in the age at which treatment is necessary. Type III spinal muscular atrophy progresses at a much slower rate than Type II, therefore it may be many years before the need for braces and wheelchairs becomes apparent.

As we discussed previously, severe scoliosis is a problem for children with Types II and III spinal muscular atrophy. While adaptive seating and spinal orthoses aid in sitting and allow for functional activity, they do not slow the progress of scoliosis. Surgical intervention, such as spinal fusion or the insertion of rods, may become necessary (Granata et al., 1989; Merlini et al., 1989). While some reports indicate improved sitting ability, comfort, and endurance after surgery (Granata et al., 1989), some studies have shown that patients may experience a loss of motor function after spinal fusion (Brown, Zeller, Swank, Furumasu, & Warath, 1989; Furumasu et al., 1989), becoming dependent in areas, such as self-care skills, where they were once independent.

EDUCATIONAL IMPLICATIONS OF SPINAL MUSCULAR ATROPHY

A child with spinal muscular atrophy declines physically. Because of this, it is important that the teacher pay particular attention to areas beyond the student's academic needs. It is important for the teacher to have a good understanding of spinal muscular atrophy in order to provide the student with the appropriate learning environment. As the student's condition deteriorates, adaptations will be needed so the student may continue to participate in as many activities as possible.

Modifications should be made collaboratively with all members of the educational team. Information from the student's doctor, physical therapist, occupational therapist, school nurse, parents, teachers, and the student should be sought and taken into consideration when making these modifications. Many of the educational needs of students with spinal muscular atrophy are similar to those of students with muscular dystrophy (See Chapter 9.)

Meeting Physical and Sensory Needs

In order to best meet the physical needs of the student with spinal muscular atrophy, the teacher must understand the characteristics and course of the disease. Knowing the type of spinal muscular atrophy in question and its rate of progression will help the teacher make appropriate adaptations and set realistic goals. Students with Type II spinal muscular atrophy deteriorate physically at a much more rapid rate and will therefore require more adaptations sooner than a student with Type III spinal muscular atrophy.

The student should be encouraged to participate in physical activity for as long as possible, modifying activities as necessary. Because individuals with Type III spinal muscular atrophy generally do not lose the ability to walk until adulthood, these students will still be able to walk when they reach school age, and fewer adaptations will be needed for participation in physical activities. However, since weakness will be greater in the legs than in the arms, activities involving the strenuous use of the legs will be the first to need modification, possibly placing the student in a less physically active role.

Students who have lost the ability to walk and must rely on the use of a wheelchair require modifications to a classroom program that allow participation despite the student's physical limitations. Full participation in all aspects of the classroom program can be accomplished by assigning the student to the less physically demanding aspects of an activity. During physical education activities, for example, the student with spinal muscular atrophy could participate in modified sports activities or, in some cases, participate as a coach assistant or scorekeeper. In addition, students who rely on the use of a wheelchair can participate in wheelchair sports.

The student's location in the classroom should also be considered. Because the student's wheelchair may be cumbersome and need ample room for mobility, the student should be located where he or she has an adequate view of the teacher, other students, and all sources of visual instruction, such as chalkboard, maps, and so on. Because the student will lose endurance and the ability to reposition himself or herself as the disease progresses, location is an important consideration if the student is to have adequate access to classroom activities.

Meeting Communication Needs

Communication is usually not severely affected in spinal muscular atrophy. However, if the individual is placed on a ventilator to provide respiratory support, alternative forms of communication must be available. Writing messages is often physically taxing. A functional communication board will often be helpful.

Sometimes a fellow student may ask students with spinal muscular atrophy what is wrong with them. For a young child, a simple explanation is useful. For example, a child could say, "I have weak muscles that won't let me run, but I do like to play a lot of things you do. You can't catch it."

Meeting Learning Needs

Students with spinal muscular atrophy are generally of average or above-average intelligence (Ionasescu & Zellweger, 1983; Russman et al., 1992). Because of the progressive nature of the disease, some teachers may expect a decrease in cognitive ability along with the decrease in motor function. Consequently, they lower their expectations of the student's academic ability. This should not happen. Teachers should understand the disease process so that unrealistic expectations, either too high or too low, can be avoided. While some physical adaptations, such as using a computer, may be necessary, academic requirements should not be changed unless the student becomes overly tired.

Inappropriately high expectations must also be avoided. Some physical adaptations may be necessary for the student to keep up with his or her classwork. Because of progressive muscle weakness, the student may be unable to complete an assignment as quickly as other students and may be unable to take notes during a lecture. Additional time can be given for assignments, or perhaps the student can complete assignments in a different way, such as orally instead of in writing. Videotapes or audiotapes of lessons could be made; the student could review these at a later time and take notes at his or her own pace. Instead of requiring copying from the board or overhead projector, the teacher could provide a copy of the information. Assigning a peer buddy may also be helpful. The buddy could be responsible for making copies of class notes or for transcribing dictated assignments. Many possible adaptations can be made, but a good understanding of the student's abilities is required.

Meeting Daily Living Needs

As the student's muscle weakness progresses and functioning deteriorates, assistance with feeding, dressing, and toileting may become necessary. The teacher should monitor these aspects of the student's day carefully so as to intervene when necessary, while still allowing the student as much independence as possible. Daily living goals may be targeted in the student's individualized education program (IEP) as the disease worsens. For example, goals relating to tube feeding or to using an adapted device may be targeted in addition to regular academic content.

Parents should be encouraged to inform the teacher of any changes that affect the difficulty of activities. The flow of information among parents, teacher, and stu-

■ VIGNETTE ■

Jeff is a 10-year-old student who is currently in the fifth grade. When he was about 7 months old, his parents began to notice that he was not reaching the developmental milestones at the same age as his siblings. In fact, they felt he was quite significantly delayed. After seeing several physicians, a diagnosis of chronic infantile spinal muscular atrophy (Type II) was reached. Jeff is a bright student who has little trouble keeping up with his assignments. Jeff gets around with the aid of leg braces (for short distances) and a wheelchair. Because of his progressive muscle weakness, his teacher has made some adaptations for Jeff that have enabled him to fully participate in all of the classroom activities. Jeff's desk is situated so that he has plenty of room to maneuver in his braces or wheelchair and is able to see and hear what is going on throughout the room. Because of his progressive muscle weakness, he cannot complete all of his assignments as rapidly as the other students and sometimes needs the opportunity to use nontraditional methods. Some of the adaptations the teacher has made for Jeff include allowing him more time to complete assignments, allowing him to dictate instead of writing some assignments, providing him with copies of assignments that are to be copied from the board, and providing him with a buddy who shares notes and assists Jeff in making sure that he has all of the materials he may need. Jeff's teacher collaborated with the occupational and physical therapists to determine what types of adaptive equipment would be appropriate. Some of the adaptive equipment that is being used include a computer, a book rest and page turner, a larger desktop, and a tape recorder. Jeff is also using a special spoon, plate, and cup at lunchtime so he can eat independently. The adaptations made by Jeff's teacher and her willingness to collaborate with other professionals are making Jeff's school experiences positive and successful.

---

dent is imperative to ensure accurate information and proper adaptations. If the student is having difficulty removing or putting on clothing, for example, he or she may have trouble using the bathroom and may be reluctant to ask for assistance. If family members are providing assistance at home, or if the student can make accommodations at home that are not feasible at school, school personnel and the family may not be aware that there is a problem. Providing the student with roomy clothing with easily manageable fasteners is one option; help with toileting is another. The loss of motor function may result in the inability to transfer from wheelchair to toilet, and the student may avoid going to the restroom altogether. Restroom use must be carefully monitored for health reasons, and if the student stops using the restroom, the family should be informed. Toileting is a particularly sensitive issue, and the teacher should do everything possible to maintain the student's privacy and dignity.

At mealtimes, the teacher should be aware of any modifications that may become necessary, such as support for elbows or arms or the need for food to be cut up. The need for adaptive equipment (such as adaptive plates, utensils, or cups) should also be monitored. An occupational or physical therapist—or both—can help evaluate needs and suggest adaptations.

Meeting Behavioral and Social Needs

The teacher should also be aware of the student's emotional needs. Because spinal muscular atrophy does not affect intelligence, the child will be fully aware of what is happening to his or her body. The student's feelings and reactions to the disease process can vary; depression, anger, and a lack of motivation are possible. The teacher should encourage a positive classroom environment, show a positive attitude toward the student, and be ready to provide emotional support. A school counselor can help with this issue. (See Chapter 9.) Because the student with spinal muscular atrophy has many of the same or similar needs as the student with muscular dystrophy, the information in Chapter 9 will be relevant when planning for the student with spinal muscular atrophy.

SUMMARY

Spinal muscular atrophy refers to a group of inherited, progressive neuromuscular diseases that are characterized by progressive weakening and atrophy of the muscles. These diseases lead to a loss of ambulation and in many cases, death. The most common form of spinal muscular atrophy is proximal spinal muscular atrophy, in which muscle weakness is present in the proximal muscles of the body. As the disease progresses, muscle function is lost while sensory function remains intact. There are primarily three types of proximal spinal muscular atrophy: acute infantile, intemediate, and juvenile. Each has a different rate of progression and range in severity. Medical treatment is supportive in nature. Nutrition and respiratory therapy are stressed, as well as use of adapted equipment and occupational and physical therapies. Teachers who have students with spinal muscular atrophy will need to have a good understanding of the type of spinal muscular atrophy, its progression, and the individual needs of the student. This knowledge will help the teacher better meet the student's needs.

PART IV

Orthopedic and Musculoskeletal Disorders

CHAPTER 11

Curvatures of the Spine

Several conditions can affect the skeletal system. Curvatures of the spine are among the most common of these conditions. Such curvatures may be caused by neuromotor impairments and degenerative diseases as well as other conditions and can also occur independently; that is, without other impairments. Curvatures of the spine vary in severity and in the extent to which they interfere with daily functioning and classroom learning. With severe curvatures, motor impairment may be great enough that sitting or walking becomes difficult. Body organs, such as the heart and lungs, may also be affected. To effectively meet the needs of children in the classroom who have spinal curvatures, the educator must know about proper positioning, therapy, treatment, and adaptations.

DESCRIPTION OF CURVATURES OF THE SPINE

There are three main types of abnormal curvatures of the spine: *scoliosis, kyphosis,* and *lordosis.* These conditions may occur singly or in combination. The most common curvature is *scoliosis*—a **lateral** (sideways) curve of the spine. When a person with scoliosis is viewed from the back, the spine appears to curve out to one side or the other instead of appearing straight (see Figure 11-1).

Kyphosis refers to an abnormal posterior (convex) curve of the spine. When a person with kyphosis is viewed from the side, the affected section of the spine appears to curve outward more than usual. This usually occurs in the thoracic (upper trunk) section of the spine, and a person with this condition is sometimes said to have a "hunchback" or "humpback."

Lordosis is an abnormal anterior (concave) curve of the spine, usually in the low back. When a person with lordosis is viewed from the side, the small of the back (lumbar and sacral vertebrae) appears to curve further inward than usual. Nonclinical terms for lordosis are "swayback," "hollow back," or "saddle back."

ETIOLOGY OF CURVATURES OF THE SPINE

While curvatures of the spine have several different etiologies, they can usually be divided into two primary categories: *nonstructural* and *structural* curvatures (see Box 11-1). Nonstructural curvatures (also known as functional curves) are due to secondary causes that usually do not produce permanent changes in the spine. For example, a child whose legs are different lengths or an individual with a herniated disk may acquire a nonstructural curvature of the spine. This type of curvature is usually corrected when the underlying cause is corrected. For example, when an insert is added to the shoe to correct the discrepancy in leg length, or the herniated disk is repaired, the curvature of the spine no longer exists. Curvatures like this are usually mild and are not permanent (Bleck & Nagel, 1982).

Other curvatures of the spine are structural. These curves are permanent and need to be treated directly for correction. There are several different causes of structural curvatures, including idiopathic, congenital, neuropathic, myopathic, osteopathic, irritative phenomena, trauma, and other causes. Curvatures of the spine are often idiopathic, meaning they have unknown causes, or they are self-originating. A genetic predisposition has been found for abnormal proprioception and vibratory perception, collagen abnormalities, and abnormal growth of the vertebral column in families with idiopathic scoliosis (Carr, Jefferson, & Turner-Smith, 1993). Idiopathic scoliosis may be further classified according to the area of the spine involved or the age at

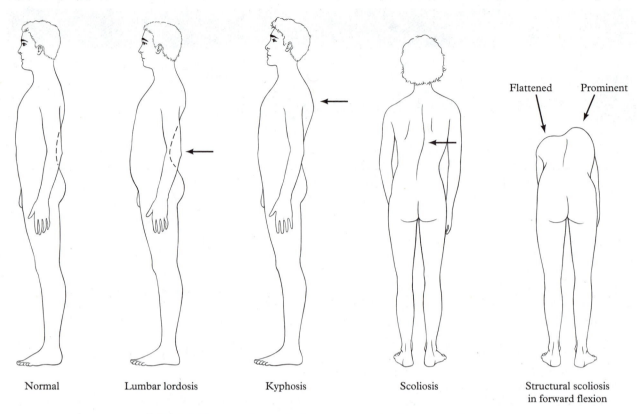

| Normal | Lumbar lordosis | Kyphosis | Scoliosis | Structural scoliosis in forward flexion |

■ FIGURE 11-1 Normal spine, scoliosis, kyphosis, and lordosis

BOX 11-1

Etiologies of Curvatures of the Spine

I. Nonstructural
II. Structural
  A. Idiopathic
    1. Idiopathic infantile scoliosis
    2. Idiopathic juvenile scoliosis
    3. Idiopathic adolescent
        or
    1. Thoracic
    2. Lumbar
    3. Thoracolumbar
  B. Congenital
  C. Neuropathic
  D. Myopathic
  E. Osteopathic
  F. Irritative phenomena
  G. Trauma
  H. Other

which the curvature appears, which is often during adolescence.

Another type of structural curvature is congenital; that is, it is present at birth and often the result of malformed vertebrae (see Figure 11-2). This type may be part of a congenital syndrome.

Other structural curvatures are caused by secondary conditions and result in permanent, abnormal curves of the spine. These are frequently present in diseases of the central nervous system (neuropathic) and muscles (myopathic) and may be referred to as neuromuscular curves. Neuromuscular scoliosis is one example. Conditions resulting in curvatures of the spine under these two etiologies include cerebral palsy, spina bifida, spinal cord injury, poliomyelitis, muscular dystrophy, and spinal muscular atrophy (Loder, 1992; Suzuki et al., 1993; Westcott, Dynes, Remer, Donaldson, & Dias, 1992).

Osteopathic causes of curvatures include certain bone diseases and arthritis. Irritative causes include tumors, such as a tumor of the kidney (for example, Wilm's tumor) or vertebral and spinal cord tumors (Cosentino et al., 1993). (See Chapter 24.) Abnormal curvatures may also result from trauma, such as when

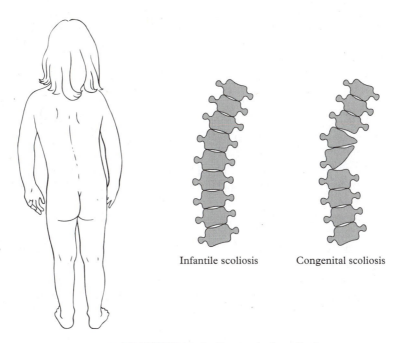

Infantile scoliosis   Congenital scoliosis

■ **FIGURE 11-2** Congenital scoliosis

the spine is **fractured** (broken). Other causes, such as nutrition and endocrine factors, may also contribute to conditions that result in spinal curvatures (Suddarth, 1991). Most major curvatures are thoracic and convex to the right.

DYNAMICS OF CURVATURES OF THE SPINE

The spine, also known as the *spinal column* or *vertebral column,* is composed of 33 bony units known as vertebrae. Each vertebra is positioned on top of another with pads of fibrocartilage and intervertebral disks between each one. The spinal column runs vertically through the body with the top of the spinal column located at the base of the skull and the bottom attached to the **pelvis** (see Figure 11-3).

The vertebrae are named according to their location. For example, the cervical vertebrae are primarily in the neck, the thoracic vertebrae are in the chest, the lumbar vertebrae are in the lower back, and the sacral vertebrae are in the pelvic area. In each group of vertebrae, the individual vertebrae are numbered. The 7 cervical vertebrae are numbered C1 through C7; the 12 thoracic vertebrae, T1 through T12; and the 5 lumbar vertebrae, L1 through L5. The 5 sacral vertebrae fuse to form the sacrum, and the 4 coccygeal vertebrae fuse to form the coccyx—the tailbone.

The spinal column serves several functions. As we discussed in Chapter 8, the vertebral column protects

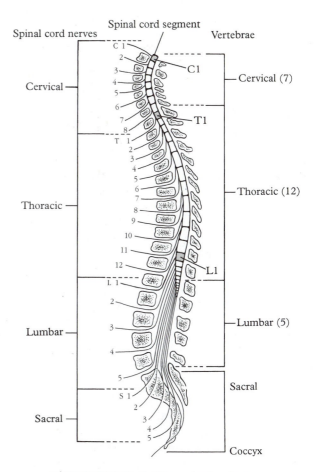

■ **FIGURE 11-3** The spinal column

the spinal cord, which runs through the middle of the vertebrae. Exiting between the vertebrae are spinal nerves that carry impulses to and from the spinal cord. The vertebrae also have a number of muscles attached to them that either move the spinal column or parts of the body in relation to the column.

Another major function of the spinal column is to provide support for the body and posture for the trunk through the spine's own normally curved structure. When viewed from the side, the normal spinal column can be seen to curve forward in the cervical area. This is called a *normal cervical lordosis* (see Figure 11-3). The spine then curves backward in the thoracic area, which is called a *normal thoracic kyphosis*. In the lumbar area, the spine curves forward again at what is commonly called the hollow of the back. This last curvature is referred to as a *normal lumbar lordosis*.

These normal curvatures of the spine occur within a typical range. When curvatures exceed their normal ranges, larger, abnormal curves are present that are pathological and may cause problems. These larger curves are called *lordosis* and *kyphosis*. No sideways curve is normal; this is referred to as *scoliosis*. When scoliosis is present, it is usually not a simple lateral curve of the spine but is almost always accompanied by a spinal rotation—a secondary compensatory curve that results from the body's attempt to realign itself in space—and is often a kyphosis or lordosis (Suzuki et al., 1993). Occasionally, a child may have two scoliotic curves—a double C or S curve.

The exact mechanism causing an abnormal curvature of the spine depends on the etiology of the abnormality. Spinal curvatures resulting from neuropathic and myopathic etiologies are often attributed to unequal muscle support or lack of muscle support. In severe spastic cerebral palsy, scoliosis is often found to be the primary type of spinal deformity. Although the exact mechanism is not fully known, there is often asymmetrical spasticity present that results in an uneven pull on the spinal cord. This is thought to play a role in causing the scoliosis. Additionally, gravity may also be a factor because gravitational forces are exerted on the spinal column. Many individuals with cerebral palsy have difficulty maintaining balance in an upright sitting position and gravity pulls them either to the side or to the front, possibly contributing to or causing scoliosis or kyphosis (Suzuki et al., 1993).

In spinal cord injuries, a curvature of the spine can result from the accompanying paralysis that reduces the amount of muscle support. Without muscle support for the spinal column, it becomes unstable and may curve abnormally. Scoliosis, for example, is present in approximatley 95% of individuals with thoracic or upper lumbar paralysis (Lovell & Winter, 1986; Westcott et al., 1992).

In spina bifida, scoliosis and other curvatures may result from the paralysis, as well as from unequal skeletal growth due to the bone malformation associated with this disorder. Neurological abnormalities found in spina bifida, such as tethered cord, may also contribute to scoliosis (Westcott et al., 1992). Lordosis is one of the most common curvatures found in spina bifida and is thought to occur because the spinal column compensates for pelvic or hip abnormalities (such as pelvic obliquity, dislocated hip, or hip flexion contracture). In muscular dystrophy, curvatures of the spine are thought to result from weakness of the trunk muscles. Lumbar kyphosis is often present in muscular dystrophy because the muscles lose their tone and cannot pull the lumbar vertebrae forward (Suzuki et al., 1993).

Other curvatures may result from the spinal column being pushed out of alignment by the growth of a tumor, or trauma affecting the spinal column (such as a fracture), or a bone disease. If the vertebral column is incorrectly formed, as in congenital forms of curvatures, a curve results directly from the malformation.

CHARACTERISTICS OF CURVATURES OF THE SPINE

Characteristics of curvatures of the spine depend on the type of curvature, the severity of the curve, and its etiology. In scoliosis, the severity of the curve is measured by degrees. A mild curve is usually less than 30°, a moderate curve is 30°–50°, and a severe curve is more than 50° (Bleck & Nagel, 1982).

Individuals with mild scoliosis usually have very subtle symptoms. One shoulder blade, hip, or breast may appear more prominent or higher than another; hemlines may be uneven. In mild idiopathic scoliosis, there is usually no physical discomfort or effect on the person's functioning. However, when the scoliosis is severe, its effects may be severe. Incapacitating back pain or an inability to sit straight are possible effects. An individual with a severe curvature may have to achieve sitting by partially sitting on his or her side, which requires arm support to hold the body up (see Figure 11-4). This increases the risk of pressure sores (decubitus ulcers) and does not allow the use of both hands unless special support is provided (Suzuki et al., 1993). A severe curve, especially one over 60°, often distorts the rib cage and may compromise heart and lung functioning by decreasing the lung volume and placing pressure on the heart. This can lead to an increase in **respiratory** insufficiency (lack of oxygen), respiratory infections, heart complications (such as heart enlargement), and a shortened life span. Also, severe cases can affect the hip joints and pelvis.

As with scoliosis, mild kyphosis may have only slight symptoms but when the curvature is severe, it can

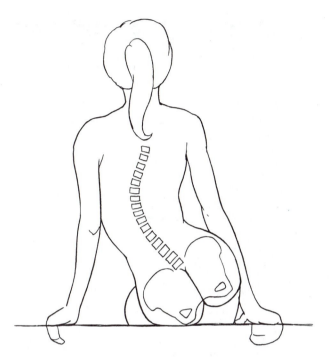

■ **FIGURE 11-4** A severe curve causes a student to need to use her hands for holding up her body while sitting.

SOURCE: From Eugene E. Bleck, Donald A. Nagel, *Physically Handicapped Children: A Medical Atlas for Teachers,* Second Edition, pp. 437–442. Copyright ©1982. All rights reserved. Reprinted by permission of Allyn & Bacon.

compromise the person's functioning. Individuals with mild kyphosis may appear to have poor posture. Severe kyphosis, however, often appears as a large humpback and can actually reduce a person's height. Sitting may be affected if the kyphosis is located in certain areas. It may be difficult to sit back, for example, when the kyphosis is located in the upper spinal area. When the kyphosis is located in the lower spinal area, the kyphosis becomes a part of the sitting area, which increases the risk of skin breakdown (decubitus ulcers). Severe kyphosis can also decrease lung capacity. In very severe cases, the kyphosis can produce arching of the spinal cord, which subsequently causes compression of the spinal cord and paralysis (Behrman, 1992).

In mild lordosis, very few symptoms may be noticeable. Sometimes the buttocks appear more prominent. Pants may not fit closely against the small of the back but gather outward. When the lordosis is severe, the individual may be unable to lie down flat on his or her back.

The onset of spinal curvatures depends on their etiology. In idiopathic scoliosis, for example, the curvature may occur during infancy, childhood, or adolescence. Periods of accelerated growth, such as adolescence, are frequently associated with the development of spinal curvatures (Goldberg, Dowling, & Fogarty, 1993).

Some curvatures stabilize (stop progressing), while others continue to progress. Several risk factors are associated with the occurrence of spinal curve progression. In idiopathic scoliosis, these risk factors include occurrence of a younger age of diagnosis, higher-level thoracic curves, double thoracic curves, premenarchal appearance of a curve, and increased rotation of the curve. Being female is also a risk factor in idiopathic scoliosis; it is eight times more prevalent in girls than boys (Godley & Monks, 1984). There is also an increased likelihood that curves greater than 30° before the child reaches skeletal maturity—about 15 years of age in females and 17 years of age in boys—will continue to progress (Behrman, 1992). Usually, curves do not progress when they are less than 20° to 25° at the time skeletal maturity is reached. It is not uncommon for curves to progress as much as 20° to 30° after skeletal maturity is reached, especially if the initial curve is greater than 50° (Bleck & Nagel, 1982). Curve progression also varies as to the rate of progression and severity of the curve. In degenerative conditions such as muscular dystrophy, scoliosis can progress rapidly (Suzuki et al., 1993).

DETECTION OF CURVATURES OF THE SPINE

In idiopathic curvatures of the spine, early detection may occur through informal observation of such subtle signs as uneven hip or shoulder height. However, curvatures may go undetected until they are more significant unless the child is screened for a curvature.

Screening procedures, which are primarily conducted for scoliosis, are commonly performed in the schools by trained personnel, as well as during routine medical examinations. These screenings have allowed for earlier diagnosis of scoliosis. Before the inception of school-based screening, the incidence of 45° curvatures was eight times greater than after the screening programs were implemented. Screening has also decreased the need for surgery because of earlier diagnosis and treatment (Montgomery & Willner, 1993).

Screening for scoliosis consists of having the child remove his or her shirt and stand facing away from the inspector—possibly a nurse or gym teacher—with arms at his or her side. The back should be closely inspected for any uneven shoulder or hip height. The back should appear straight, with the spine straight from the neck to the buttocks. The child should then bend over with arms hanging down until the back is parallel to the floor. No bulges should be apparent on the shoulders or sides. Bulges can indicate the spinal rotation sometimes associated with scoliosis (see Figure 11-5). A checklist found in Box 11-2 provides a guide to the procedure. If any of these abnormalities are present, the student should be referred to a physician for further evaluation (Godley & Monks, 1984). Note that evaluating the child bending over is important. Scoliosis may not be observable when the child is standing, but bending over throws the spine into relief, making it more visible. Also, what may appear to be a minor curvature on observation may actually be much more serious. Because the vertebrae rotate in scoliosis, the curvature always appears less than the actual curve that will be revealed by X-ray (Bleck & Nagel, 1982) (see Figure 11-6).

Screening procedures are similar for kyphosis and lordosis. When assessing for kyphosis, the child bends over in the same manner as in scoliosis screening. This

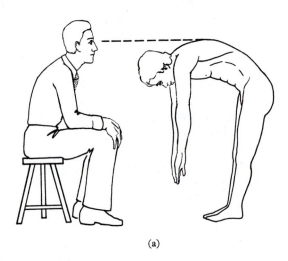

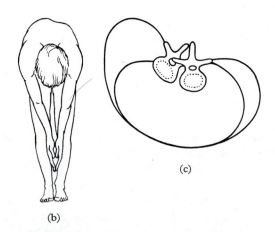

■ **FIGURE 11-5** Scoliosis is detected with the student bending over (a). A bulge indicates spinal rotation, which is present in scoliosis (b).
Source: From Eugene E. Bleck, Donald A. Nagel, *Physically Handicapped Children: A Medical Atlas for Teachers,* Second Edition, pp. 437–442. Copyright ©1982. All rights reserved. Reprinted by permission of Allyn & Bacon.

BOX 11-2
Scoliosis Checklist

Have the child face away from you with his or her shirt off, and answer questions 1 through 6. For question 7, have the child bend over parallel to the floor, with arms hanging down.

	Yes	No
1. Is the body straight in appearance?		
2. Are the shoulders level? Does the neck appear more full on one side?		
3. Are the shoulder blades at the same height?		
4. Is the waistline at the same height with the space between the truck and arms even at both sides?		
5. Does the spine appear straight from the neck to the buttocks?		
6. Are the hips the same height?		
7. When the child bends over, do both sides of the back look identical, with no bulges on the shoulder or side areas?		

If the answer to these questions is "no," the child should be referred to a physician for further follow-up.

---

time the child is viewed from the side. A break in the normal contour of the back may indicate kyphosis. In lordosis, the child may also be viewed from the side for any unusual curvature in that direction.

When a child has a neuropathic, myopathic, orthopedic, or other primary disease that is associated with scoliosis, or has kyphosis and/or lordosis, the child should be routinely evaluated for a curvature. For children with a history of spinal curvature in the family, closer monitoring for the development of curvatures should be performed.

When an abnormal curvature is suspected, the child is referred for further testing. A specialist in orthopedics is often the physician who makes the diagnosis. X-rays are taken of the spine to confirm an abnormal curve and to determine the location and number of curves, as well as any other associated vertebral bony abnormalities (see Figure 11-7). The degree of severity of the curvature is calculated, often by a formula such as the Cobb angle formula, to determine the curve's severity. Further tests

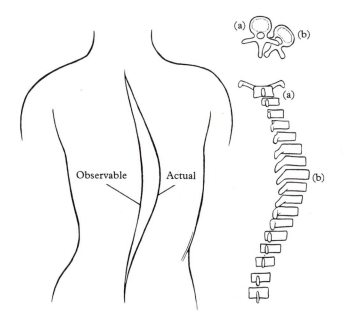

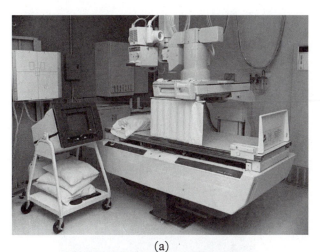

■ **FIGURE 11-6** The spinal curve that is seen during observation appears less severe than when seen in an X-ray.

Source: From Eugene E. Bleck, Donald A. Nagel, *Physically Handicapped Children: A Medical Atlas for Teachers,* Second Edition, pp. 437–442. Copyright ©1982. All rights reserved. Reprinted by permission of Allyn & Bacon.

will be performed to determine whether or not there are underlying causes, such as myopathies or tumors.

TREATMENT OF CURVATURES OF THE SPINE

Early detection and treatment of curvatures of the spine is aimed at preventing the curve from worsening. The exact treatment will depend on the severity of the curve. Very mild curves may only require close observation and X-rays to monitor progression. For curves that progress to 20°, bracing and special exercises may be prescribed. More severe curves—more than 60°—often require surgery (Godley & Monks, 1984).

The use of orthoses (bracing) to prevent further worsening of an abnormal curvature has been widely accepted as an effective nonsurgical treatment, especially for scoliosis. However, a recent study has questioned whether bracing is effective in late-onset, idiopathic scoliosis (Goldberg, Dowling, Hall, & Emans, 1993). Additional research is needed to verify the effectiveness of bracing in certain types of scoliosis. Overall, it is commonly accepted that brace management has been most effective for thoracic and lumbar curves between 20° and 30° or 40°.

Brace programs usually last for 4 to 6 years, depending on when the child reaches skeletal maturity. The child may need to wear the brace full-time, which is 23 hours a day, or part-time, which is usually about 16 hours a day. In order for the treatment to be effective, strict compliance to a brace-wearing schedule is imperative (Suddarth, 1991).

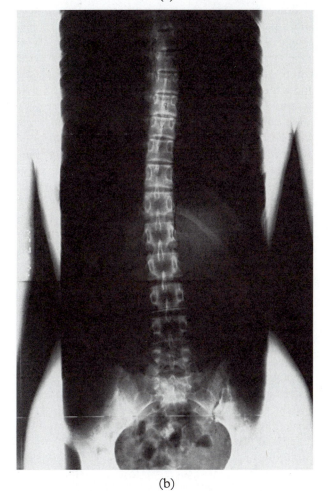

(a)

(b)

■ **FIGURE 11-7** X-ray machine (a) and chest X-ray showing scoliosis (b)

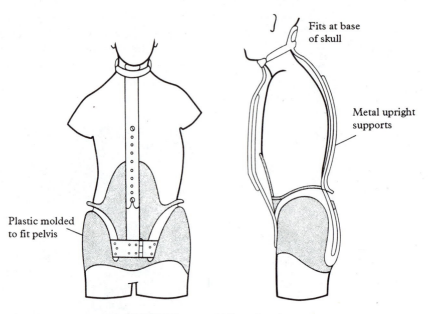

Fits at base of skull

Metal upright supports

Plastic molded to fit pelvis

■ **FIGURE 11-8** Milwaukee brace

Braces for spinal curvatures differ in their structure and function. The Milwaukee brace, for example, provides support from the cervical area to the sacral area but is primarily used for upper thoracic curves (see Figure 11-8). It has a molded pelvic portion of plastic and a metal upright portion extending from the pelvic area to a ring that fits around the neck. Pressure pads often connect to the metal upright portion to assist with correct positioning. In order for the brace to be comfortable, the child must stand as straight as possible in the brace. Orthoses such as the thoracolumbar-sacral curve orthoses (TLSO), also known as the Boston brace, may be used to provide support to low thoracic lumbar curves. The TLSO consists of a molded plastic jacket that holds the spine straighter (see Figure 11-9).

Exercises may be paired with the use of a brace. The aim of an exercise program is to maintain flexibility of the spine while preventing any muscle atrophy that could occur because of the bracing (Suddarth, 1991). However, the effects of exercises are controversial.

Surgery is often recommended when the curve has progressed to an angle of greater than 50° or when bracing has been either ineffective or not feasible. Determination of surgical correction is based on several variables, including the child's age, etiology of the curve, previous treatment, effect of the curvature on functional living skills and activities, effect of the curvature on sitting, and the child's general physical condition. The goal of surgery is to achieve stabilization of the spine, which should correct the curvature as much as possible and prevent further abnormal curving and subsequent heart or lung involvement.

Several surgical techniques and pieces of support equipment may be used to treat the abnormal curve. All techniques aim at achieving a vertical trunk balanced over a level pelvis. One technique uses a rod, known as

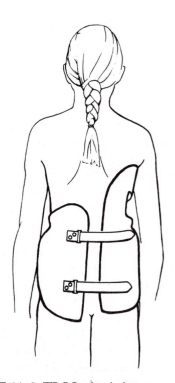

■ **FIGURE 11-9** TLSO plastic brace
Source: From Eugene E. Bleck, Donald A. Nagel, *Physically Handicapped Children: A Medical Atlas for Teachers,* Second Edition, pp. 437–442. Copyright ©1982. All rights reserved. Reprinted by permission of Allyn & Bacon.

■ FIGURE 11-10 Harrington rod
Source: From Eugene E. Bleck, Donald A. Nagel, *Physically Handicapped Children: A Medical Atlas for Teachers,* Second Edition, pp. 437–442. Copyright ©1982. All rights reserved. Reprinted by permission of Allyn & Bacon.

a Harrington rod, which is attached along the posterior aspect of the spine (see Figure 11-10). The spine is often fused with a bone graft to further stabilize the site. A body cast is often worn after the surgery to maintain stability.

Another type of surgery uses Luque rods—two metal rods that are placed on either side of the spine. Wires are then woven under each vertebra and tightened over the rod. A cast is not necessary after this type of surgery because this surgery stabilizes both sides of the spine. Newer surgeries have successfully placed bone screws into the lateral surface of the vertebrae and connected them to a solid, contoured rod. After partial placement, the rod is rotated to produce the correct lumbar lordosis; this partially corrects the scoliosis. Each disk space is then packed with a bone graft (Turi, Johnston, & Richards, 1993). Other techniques, such as Zielke instrumentation, often use a combination of metal instrumentation (rods) and anterior, posterior, or anterior and posterior spinal fusion (Lowe & Peters, 1993).

COURSE OF CURVATURES OF THE SPINE

The clinical course of abnormal curvatures varies according to the treatment and its effectiveness. Without treatment, the abnormal curve may progress or may not, depending on its etiology and other factors. For example, the scoliosis found in muscular dystrophy usually progresses rapidly if the child uses a wheelchair. Conservative management is often difficult because the sitting position promotes kyphosis as well, which in turn elevates the lower internal organs and presses on the diaphragm. This increases pressure on the lungs or heart. Additional lordosis also occurs, further reducing lung space. Some individuals may be unable to sit with their hands free, and decubitus ulcers may complicate the condition (Suzuki et al., 1993). In most circumstances, when the curvature is allowed to progress, function will be impaired and the life span shortened because of adverse effects on the heart and lungs.

For children and adolescents who receive treatment in the form of bracing or surgery, most curves are either kept from progressing further or corrected to some extent. However, in some complicated cases, bracing and surgery may not produce the desired effect. Muller, Nordwall, and von Wendt (1992) found that surgical treatment of scoliosis in children with spina bifida was successful in its corrective effect on the scoliosis but did not have the desired effect on ambulation and motor skills for some children. Although there was no significant difference between the children's ability to manage daily living skills before and after surgery, 57% of the children lost some of their ability to ambulate. Several had an increase in hip flexion contractures. The precise reason for this is unclear, but using a wheelchair and failing to use assistive standing devices (contraindicated for a few months after surgery) may contribute to the problem. The need for early detection and treatment and for postoperative physical therapy is clear.

EDUCATIONAL IMPLICATIONS OF CURVATURES OF THE SPINE

Teachers need to be informed about various abnormal curvatures of the spine and their educational implications. Knowledge in detection of these curvatures will aid in early prevention, and knowledge of their possible impact will assist the teacher in providing adequate adaptations.

Meeting Physical and Sensory Needs

Teachers should be alert to signs of a possible abnormal curvature of the spine in all children. Clothes that hang unevenly or jeans that gather in the back may indicate an abnormal curvature of the spine. Any suspicion of an abnormal curve should be reported to the school nurse for subsequent screening. Screening procedures can take place in school and should be carried out by someone trained to look for subtle signs of an early curve. The screening procedure should be a regular part of school services, in the same way that vision screening is conducted routinely.

If a student has a curvature, the teacher should be alert for any needed adaptations. For students with severe curvatures, adapted seating equipment may be needed to allow the student to sit independently and comfortably and to facilitate hand movement. The physical therapist should work with the teacher to determine appropriate positioning and any equipment needed to achieve the best position.

Students who wear an orthosis may need support or encouragement to wear the device, especially if it is uncomfortable. However, complaints of discomfort should not go unheeded. Orthoses that fit improperly may result in skin abrasion. Students should be checked or check themselves for any signs of skin breakdown. This is especially important for students who have such conditions as spina bifida and would not feel pain due to the loss of sensation in affected areas. Any type of abrasion or redness on the skin should be reported to the nurse, physical therapist, or parent. The orthosis may need to be reevaluated for proper fit; the schedule for wearing the brace may need adjustment, or the device may need to be refitted or adjusted.

Students who have had surgery may require modifications in activities afterward. For example, the student may not be allowed to use the standing equipment he or she had used previously for a few months. Clarification from the physician must be obtained before the student returns to the classroom; any restrictions on the student, and their duration, should be noted.

Meeting Communication Needs

Students with abnormal curvatures of the spine do not have language impairments unless they have an underlying condition such as cerebral palsy. However, students with abnormal curvatures of the spine may need to explain their condition to their peers. Simple explanations are useful, such as, "My spine curves too much, which makes it hard to sit. I wear this brace to straighten my spine, just like braces straighten teeth."

Meeting Learning Needs

No learning deficits are associated with curvatures of the spine unless the curvatures are part of a condition with an increased incidence of mental retardation. Cerebral palsy is one such condition. Students being treated for scoliosis, lordosis, or kyphosis will need to learn how to wear an orthosis or to assist with their own care after surgery. Students who have uncorrected severe scoliosis or other abnormal curves may need to learn to modify their activities; those who have spinal

■ **VIGNETTE** ■

Dushal is a 15-year-old girl who is in tenth grade. She has spina bifida and a severe scoliosis. Although she spends most of her time in regular classes, for literature she does attend the resource room for students with orthopedic impairments because she requires additional tutoring. She wore a brace for several years, but it was ineffective in preventing the progression of scoliosis. Although surgery was recommended, her parents declined this option, fearing complications. Dushal presently has some compromised lung and heart functioning, with increased respiratory infections. When Dushal sits, her spinal curve is so severe that her spine almost touches the floor. Her classmates tease her by saying she is fat, when it is actually the scoliosis that gives her this appearance. Dushal's teachers are trying to educate her peers and to teach Dushal to be an advocate for herself.

surgery will miss school and must be helped to catch up with missed material.

Meeting Daily Living Needs

Mild curvatures of the spine rarely have any significant impact on the performance of daily living skills. However, students with severe curvatures and deformity due to the curve may have difficulty performing certain activities such as dressing. Clothing should be easy to put on and large enough to fit over a brace. The teacher or occupational therapist may need to teach the student to use various types of adaptations that can allow maximum independence. A device that assists in putting on socks is one example. Which adaptations are used depends on the student's underlying condition as well as the type and severity of the curve.

Meeting Behavioral and Social Needs

Students who have curvatures of the spine may need emotional support from the teacher and from those in the school setting. Deviations in body appearance have been found to be responsible for psychological distress (Theologis, Jefferson, Simpson, Turner-Smith, & Fairbank, 1993). Along with the obvious effects of curvatures on a person's appearance and self-esteem, such images in literature and television as that of "the ugly, evil humpback" do not help the student with a kyphosis form a positive self-image. Clothes that do not fit well may also create a negative self-image, especially when the spinal deformity is present during adolescence. Teachers should make themselves available to listen if the student needs someone to talk with. Also, discussing scoliosis, lordosis, and kyphosis as part of the screening process may dispel curiosity and false fears. For those who have cerebral palsy or some other underlying condition, discussions of scoliosis or other curves may be a part of the discussions of the other conditions. (See Chapter 7.)

The teacher should provide support and stress compliance with wearing an orthosis when one is prescribed. The Milwaukee brace will be quite noticeable because the brace extends outside the shirt and around the neck. Other, smaller types of braces are less noticeable and can fit under clothing. Regardless of the type of brace, lack of compliance with wearing an orthosis will undermine the effectiveness of the treatment.

SUMMARY

The spinal column normally has several convex and concave curves. However, when these curves exceed the normal angles or when curves excessively present to one side, an abnormal curvature of the spine is present. The main types of curvatures are scoliosis, a lateral (sideways) curve; kyphosis (posterior curve); and lordosis (anterior curve). Curvatures of the spine may occur idiopathically or may be caused by any number of underlying conditions. Treatment is aimed at preventing the curve from progressing or correcting it as much as possible. The use of an orthosis and surgery are two main treatment modalities. The teacher can help by noting the signs of an abnormal curve and by being an empathetic listener for students who are diagnosed with an abnormal curvature of the spine.

CHAPTER 12

Hip Conditions

A number of hip conditions that can affect children and adolescents may cause pain, decreased range of motion, gait abnormalities, or a combination of these symptoms. Without prompt diagnosis and early treatment, several of these conditions may also result in considerable disability throughout the individual's life.

Of the many types of hip conditions, the three most common ones found in children are *congenital dislocation of the hip, Legg-Calvé-Perthes disease,* and *slipped capital femoral epiphysis.* These conditions differ as to their characteristics and treatment; we will describe them separately in this chapter.

DESCRIPTION OF HIP CONDITIONS

Hip condition can refer to any number of processes that affect the ball-and-socket **joint** of the hip. The ball is the rounded head (femoral head) of the thigh bone (femur) (see Figure 12-1). In certain hip conditions, the head may be malformed or damaged. The socket is the rounded-out portion of the pelvis known as the *acetabulum* in which the ball's femoral head fits. In some hip conditions, the acetabulum may have structural abnormalities that affect the function of the hip.

Other hip conditions involve no structural abnormalities of the hip but reflect problems in the fit of the ball in the socket or the placement of the ball in relation to the socket. In these situations, the cartilage, ligaments, and surrounding hip muscles that hold the ball in the socket may be affected.

Several terms are used to describe hip conditions. Some of these are *dysplasia, hip dislocation,* and *subluxation. Dysplasia* is the most commonly used (and abused) term describing **neonatal** hip disease. The term sometimes refers to the predisposing factors found in early hip disease, such as ligament laxity (ligaments are loose) or a shallow acetabulum (the socket is not deep enough). More typically, it is used to describe the results of an abnormal relationship of the femur with the acetabulum, such as an abnormal shape of the acetabulum or femur. An example of this would be a small, flat femoral head.

Dislocation of the hip is present when the femoral head lies outside the acetabulum. Subluxation of the hip is present when the femoral head is not completely covered by the acetabulum but remains in the joint space. Subluxation can be thought of as the ball being partially displaced from the socket. The term *subluxation* is also sometimes used to describe the clinical finding that the femoral head can be partially displaced on examination (Dvonch, Bunch, & Scoles, 1988; Scoles, 1988). Figure 12-2 illustrates a comparison of these conditions with the normal hip.

DYNAMICS OF HIP CONDITIONS

The hip joint differentiates during the first 3 months of gestation. By the 8th week, the general shape of the head of the femur bone of the thigh is identifiable; by the 11th week, the pelvic cavity (the acetabulum) has appeared. Joint cartilage, the joint capsule, and ligaments—which together act to stabilize the hip joint—are all present by the end of the first trimester, as are the ossification centers—the centers where bone growth occurs in the main bones making up the hip joint. The hip joint's rich blood supply is also established by this time. During the second and third trimesters, the hip joint enlarges and matures (Benson, Fixsen, & Macnicol, 1994; Scoles, 1988). Although the hip joint is well formed at birth, much of its structure is still made up of cartilage. During normal growth and development, some remolding of the hip structures occurs as the cartilage ossifies into bone.

The hip is one of the major weight-bearing joints of

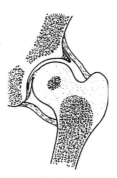

■ **FIGURE 12-1** Anatomy of the hip joint
SOURCE: From *Children's Orthopaedics and Fractures*, by M. K. D. Benson, J. A. Fixsen, and M. F. Macnicol (Eds.), p. 419. Copyright ©1994 Churchill Livingstone, Inc. Reprinted with permission.

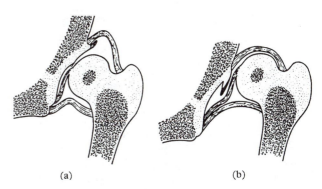

(a)   (b)

■ **FIGURE 12-2** Hip subluxation (a) and dislocation (b)
SOURCE: From *Children's Orthopaedics and Fractures*, by M. K. D. Benson, J. A. Fixsen, and M. F. Macnicol (Eds.), p. 419. Copyright ©1994 Churchill Livingstone, Inc. Reprinted with permission.

the body. When movement across the hip joint occurs, such as in sitting and walking, forces much greater than the body's weight are generated by the hip muscles (Scoles, 1988). The femur must fit and move smoothly in the acetabulum (socket) if the hip joint is to grow and develop normally. If the joint is not aligned properly, abnormal weight-bearing forces can act on the growing skeleton, which changes the shape of the bones around the hip and causes permanent joint deformity. Initially, this deformity may not interfere with the child's functioning, but with time, if left untreated, the abnormal wear will result in joint degeneration, pain, and loss of function.

DESCRIPTION AND ETIOLOGY OF CONGENITAL DISLOCATION OF THE HIP (CDH)

Congenital dislocation of the hip (CDH) may also be called *congenital dysplasia* of the hip, *congenital displacement* of the hip, *developmental dislocation* of the hip (DDH), or *developmental dysplasia* of the hip. One of the most significant advances in the study of congenital dislocation of the hip has been the recognition that it is a spectrum of diseases with different etiologies, varying pathologies, and differing natural histories that require different treatments (Bennett & MacEwen, 1989).

Between 1 and 10% of infants are born with subluxable, dislocatable, or dislocated hips (Churgay & Caruthers, 1992). In the United States, the incidence of CDH is approximately 10 cases per 1,000 live births. The dislocation rate among second children born to parents of a child with congenital dislocation of the hip approximates 22 to 50 cases per 1,000 live births (Bennett & MacEwen, 1989).

The etiology of congenital hip dislocation is multifactorial. Mechanical, physiological, ethnic, genetic,

and teratogenic factors associated with malformation can produce the hip dislocation. The congenital dislocation usually occurs just before or just after delivery in an infant who is otherwise normal. A combination of mechanical and physiological factors accounts for most cases of congenital dislocation of the hip. The most common risk factors are listed in Box 12-1.

The mechanical factors in CDH occur primarily during the third trimester and result from limited space for the **fetus** in utero. About 60% of infants with the disorder are firstborn. It is postulated that the tight and unstretched uterine and abdominal musculature of a woman in her first pregnancy prevents the fetus from

---

BOX 12-1

Risk Factors for Congenital Dislocation of the Hip

First child
Decreased amniotic fluid
Breech
Congenital knee dislocation
Female sex
Genetic predisposition
Swaddling or use of cradleboard
Presence of infection
Maternal illness or toxins

SOURCE: From "Diagnosis and Treatment of Congenital Dislocation of the Hip," by C. A. Churgay, M.D., and B. S. Caruthers, M.D., M.S., 1992, *American Family Physician, 45,* No. 3, p. 1217. Copyright ©1992 American Academy of Family Physician. Reprinted with permission.

assuming the normal flexed position of the hip and knee, a position that best seats the femoral head in the acetabulum (Churgay & Caruthers, 1992).

Pregnancies complicated by decreased amniotic fluid (oligohyramnios) and breech presentation are also associated with a higher incidence of congenital dislocation of the hip. Pregnancies with decreased amniotic fluid result in restricted fetal movement, which can affect proper hip development. Breech presentation also appears to be significant in the etiology of congenital dislocation of the hip, regardless of whether the baby is delivered vaginally or by cesarean section. Approximately 30 to 50% of children with the disorder are delivered in the breech position. (Churgay & Caruthers, 1992).

If the infant in the breech position has extended knees, knee dislocations are also possible. The incidence of congenital dislocation of the hip on the left is 67%, on the right is 6%, and involving both hips is 25%. It is thought that the left hip is more often involved because most fetuses in the breech position lie with the left thigh against the mother's sacrum. This position pushes the left hip into adduction (leg toward the midline of the body) and flexion (leg bent up toward the body), which moves the femoral head away from the acetabulum.

Physiological factors may also be responsible for hip dislocation. The maternal estrogens that increase pelvic relaxation prior to delivery may lead to temporarily lax ligaments surrounding the ball-and-socket hip joints in the newborn, predisposing the infant to dislocation.

The incidence of congenital dislocation of the hip is six times higher in females than in males (Bennett & MacEwen, 1989; Churgay & Caruthers, 1992; Dvonch, Bunch, & Scoles, 1988). This higher incidence in females is thought to be due to increased female susceptibility to maternal estrogen effects and the fact that twice as many females as males are born in the breech position.

Genetic factors may also be associated with hip dislocation. In some instances, there have been familial occurrences of hip dislocation, which may be attributed to a family's predisposition for having lax ligaments or for abnormal development of the acetabulum.

Ethnic factors may also play a role in hip dislocation. The incidence of congenital dislocation of the hip is as high as 25 to 50 cases per 1,000 live births in Native Americans, Lapps, Japanese, and some central and southern European groups. In these societies, mothers either swaddle their babies or use cradleboards. The infants' hips are thus maintained in extension, which predisposes them to possible dislocation. Congenital dislocation of the hip appears to occur less frequently in Chinese, Korean, and black populations (Churgay & Caruthers, 1992; Dvonch, Bunch, & Scoles, 1988).

Teratogenic factors are conditions such as infection, maternal disease during pregnancy, or the presence of toxins that can cause physical defects in the developing fetus. Teratogenic dislocations occur in approximately 2% of congenital dislocation of the hip cases and are due to malformation of the acetabulum and/or the femoral head. These types of dislocations are commonly associated with arthrogryposis (see Chapter 15), myelomeningocele (see Chapter 8), and various chromosomal abnormalities. Shaw and Beals (1992) studied the hips of 114 individuals with Down syndrome and found a higher incidence than normal of dislocation and dysplasia without dislocation. Congenital dislocation of the hip also occurs in such conditions as congenital scoliosis and cerebral palsy.

CHARACTERISTICS OF CONGENITAL DISLOCATION OF THE HIP

Usually due to a combination of the etiologic factors, in congenital dislocation of the hip, the femoral head dislocates from the acetabulum either before, during, or shortly after birth. Often, the dislocation is not noticeable to the child's care-givers. Routine physical examination easily determines whether hip dislocation is present. If the condition is recognized right after birth, the integrity of the soft tissue surrounding the hip can be maintained, and the femoral head can easily be put back into proper alignment. A stable hip with a good long-term prognosis will develop if proper hip joint alignment is maintained until the period of lax ligaments in the neonate has passed—by 2 to 3 months of age.

Persistent dislocation causes the soft tissue and bone of the hip joint to change, making alignment more difficult and increasing the chance of long-term sequelae and the necessity for surgical correction. The sequelae of prolonged congenital hip dislocation are listed in Box 12-2. Several characteristics may be noticed by the

---

BOX 12-2

Sequelae of Prolonged Congenital Dislocation of the Hip

Migration of the femoral head along the pelvis
Contraction of the hip adductor, iliopsoas, and hamstring muscles
Flattened acetabulum
Femoral head trapped behind the acetabulum
Flattened femoral head
Development of a false acetabulum

SOURCE: From "Diagnosis and Treatment of Congenital Dislocation of the Hip," by C. A. Churgay, M.D., and B. S. Caruthers, M.D., M.S., 1992, *American Family Physician, 45,* No. 3, p. 1217. Copyright ©1992 American Academy of Family Physician. Reprinted with permission.

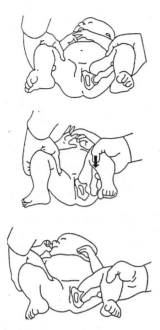

■ FIGURE 12-3 Ortolani test

Source: From *Fundamentals of Pediatric Orthopedics*, by
L. T. Staheli. Copyright ©1992 Staheli, Inc. Reprinted
with permission.

family and school personnel. Most noticeable are abnormalities in walking. Often, there is a prominent limp
caused by the shortening of the leg and the telescoping
of the femoral head. The limp seen in congenital
dislocation of the hip is increased in severity by fatigue
or vigorous activity. The child may compensate for the
shortened limb by walking on the toes of the affected
side. Other, less noticeable characteristics are tightened
muscles, shortening of the thigh because the femoral
head is outside the acetabulum, extra folds of skin on
the affected thigh due to shortening, and telescoping or
pistoning of the involved femur—that is, when the
femur can be moved up and down freely because the
femoral head is outside the acetabulum. Lordosis (swayback) may also be present.

DETECTION OF CONGENITAL DISLOCATION OF THE HIP

A hip dislocation may be detected by physical examination, X-rays, ultrasound, arthrography, computed
tomography (CT) scan, and magnetic resonance imaging (MRI). Physical examination in the newborn consists of several routine tests that are typically conducted
and are considered the most reliable means of diagnos-
ing congenital dislocation of the hip. The *Ortolani test*
(see Figure 12-3) is performed on a relaxed, contented
infant. The infant is placed on his or her back with hips
and knees flexed. Each hip is evaluated separately. The

examiner grasps the infant's thigh and lifts it upward,
then moves it outward away from the body while the
examiner's other hand stabilizes the pelvis. If an au-
dible, palpable "click" or "clunk" occurs, a positive
Ortolani test is noted. It is assumed that the "clunk"
occurs because the head of the dislocated femur is
passing over the rim of the acetabulum and sinking back
into normal position in the hip socket.

The *Barlow examination* (see Figure 12-4) is a test of
hip dislocatability as the femoral head "falls" or is
pushed posteriorly out of the acetabulum. The relaxed
infant is placed on his or her back with hips and knees
bent. The examiner's hands are placed in the same
position as for the Ortolani test. Pressure is applied in
the reverse direction, that is, so the hip is adducted (in
toward the body), and the thigh is pressed downward.
An unstable hip can be dislocated with the Barlow test
and then realigned with the Ortolani test. Although
careful and repeated newborn screening using these two
tests can help diagnose congenital dislocation of the hip,
they are not infallible, and some infants with congenital
dislocation of the hip may not be diagnosed.

The physical examination for an older child will
involve examining for signs of hip dislocation such as
a limp or muscle tightness. The examiner will also look
for the *Galeazzi sign,* in which the involved knee is
lower when the individual is on his or her back and
the knees and hips are flexed. The *Trendelenburg test*

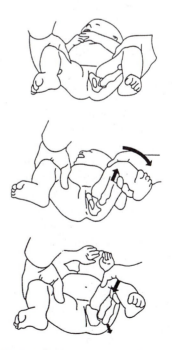

■ FIGURE 12-4 Barlow examination

Source: From *Fundamentals of Pediatric Orthopedics*, by L.
T. Staheli. Copyright ©1992 Staheli, Inc. Reprinted with
permission.

is often performed, in which the child is asked to stand on one leg. The child with a normal hip can keep the pelvis level while standing on one leg by using the hip abductor muscles on that side for stabilization. Because the child with congenital dislocation of the hip has weak abductor muscles on the affected side, the pelvis sags toward the opposite side when the child stands on the affected leg.

Radiographs, or X-rays, are not reliable in evaluating newborns for congenital dislocation of the hip because a large part of the infant's hip joint is still cartilaginous and will not show up on X-ray. After about 3 to 6 months of age, the growth plates are observable on radiographs, and comparisons of both hips can be made, which helps diagnose unilateral congenital dislocation of the hip. During conservative treatment of the young child using external positioning devices, monitoring of hip position and blood supply to the hip may be assisted with periodic radiographic evaluation.

Many authorities consider ultrasound examination to be the ideal modality for monitoring infants with congenital dislocation of the hip up to 6 months of age, before ossification of the femoral head occurs. The infant need not be sedated, radiation is absent, and the casted infant may also be examined (Churgay & Caruthers, 1992).

Arthrography of the hip, in which dye is injected into the hip, can be useful in congenital dislocation of the hip if significant joint abnormality is suspected or if the diagnosis has been delayed. Arthrography provides the most accurate image of the hip joint, but its use is limited by possible infection, possible damage to the vascular supply, and the need for anesthesia for this invasive technique. It is rarely used.

Computed tomography scanning offers the best means of visualizing the hip joint if the child is casted but cannot be used before 3 to 6 months of age because of lack of ossification of the femoral head.

Magnetic resonance imaging in the evaluation of congenital dislocation of the hip has not been studied extensively. MRI has some disadvantages; its effects on infants are not known, scanning times are long and require sedation, and MRI is expensive and not widely available. Yet it is an excellent diagnostic tool (Churgay & Caruthers, 1992).

TREATMENT AND COURSE OF CONGENITAL DISLOCATION OF THE HIP

A variety of treatment modalities for congenital dislocation of the hip are available. All have the common goal of returning the femoral head to the acetabulum and maintaining good hip alignment while maintaining pain-free function until the hip becomes stable and pathological changes have been reversed.

Positioning Devices

In newborns and in infants up to about 6 months of age, the *Ortolani maneuver* is used to partially or completely realign the hip, which is then kept in place with a simple positioning device. Positioning of the realigned hip is very important. The femoral head must be prevented from dislocating again without applying excessive stress on the joint. If the hip is held in excessive abduction (frog position), blood supply to the hip may be blocked, creating cell death (avascular necrosis) of the femoral head and potentially severe hip joint deformity (Benson, Fixsen, & Macnicol, 1994; Churgay & Caruthers, 1992; Dvonch, Bunch, & Scoles, 1988).

Newborns with congenital dislocation of the hip can be managed with a secure restraint that holds the hip in the position of flexion and abduction described earlier. A variety of braces and splints are used, including plastic-covered metal splints, abduction pillows, and cloth harnesses. For treatment to be successful, the appliance must fit comfortably, hold the hip in alignment, and not interfere with diapering or bathing. Abduction-flexion braces are usually worn continuously for 2 to 4 months. Night splinting is sometimes prescribed for an additional 2 to 6 months after continuous bracing is complete to ensure proper remodeling of the hip.

The *Pavlik harness* is one of the most commonly used positioning devices in the management of congenital dislocation of the hip. The Pavlik device is a shoulder harness with hook and loop straps and foot cuffs that maintain the hip in the proper position (see Figure 12-5). The harness has a posterior strap that controls the degree of hip abduction and that can be adjusted to avoid the frog position and the resultant avascular

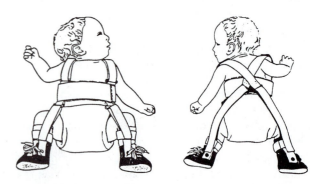

■ **FIGURE 12-5** Pavlik harness
SOURCE: From *Fundamentals of Pediatric Orthopedics*, by L. T. Staheli. Copyright ©1992 Staheli, Inc. Reprinted with permission.

necrosis of the femoral head. The Pavlik harness is inexpensive and can be adjusted easily for growth. It also allows the hip to move so that hip and knee muscles are not affected by inactivity. Fewer problems are noted with this device than with other restraining devices.

Traction

After 6 months of age, the child with congenital dislocation of the hip usually presents with a hip that cannot be realigned by manipulation. Realignment is prevented by bony changes and contractures of the soft tissue around the joint, hence traction may be used. Traction is the use of various devices to exert a pulling force along the longitudinal plane of a structure such as a bone. In children under 1 year of age, skin traction—traction on a body surface—can be used to stretch the soft tissue around the hip. Skeletal traction, or traction exerted directly to the long bones by pins or wires, may be required in older and larger children. Traction is maintained for a minimum of 2 to 3 weeks, with the knee in moderate flexion and the hip in some flexion and abduction. Once radiographs or ultrasonograms indicate that the femoral head is back in position, traction is completed. The child is then placed under anesthesia, and the femur is realigned with the acetabulum. The hip is then usually immobilized by placing the child in a spica cast that extends from hips to ankles; a hole is cut in the cast's perineal area to allow for diapering. Most children wear casts for 2 to 6 months, with cast changes every 2 months to allow for growth.

Surgery

Surgical reduction is performed when the more conservative (nonsurgical) procedures described earlier fail or when the child with congenital dislocation of the hip is older than 2½ years of age. Significant acetabular and femoral deformities are usually present, and remodeling cannot be expected to occur even with prolonged immobilization. A combination of muscle release, skeletal traction, open reduction, and pelvic or femoral osteotomy—surgery on the femoral head or the pelvic socket to restructure these bony elements—may be required to obtain a stable hip. After the spica cast is removed, an abduction brace is usually worn for a time and physical therapy is begun.

Unilateral hip dislocations can be surgically reduced until the child is approximately 8 years of age. Bilateral hip dislocations are surgically reduced until the child is approximately 5 years of age. Surgical reduction of a dislocated hip in children beyond these times is associated with a high incidence of stiffness and painful redislocation. Because the child first diagnosed with congenital dislocation of the hip after the fourth or

fifth year usually has relatively good function and no pain, unless a near-perfect surgical result is obtained, the child may have significantly more disability after surgery than before. Therefore, surgery on these children is usually postponed; they are closely monitored for loss of function and for increase in pain around the hip. In an adolescent or young adult, the complications of surgery are great and the results are so poor that surgery is indicated only if the individual is in constant pain (Churgay & Caruthers, 1992; Dvonch, Bunch, & Scoles, 1988; Heinrich, Missinne, & MacEwen, 1992).

DESCRIPTION AND ETIOLOGY OF LEGG-CALVÉ-PERTHES DISEASE (LCPD)

In 1910, Arthur Legg in Boston, Jacques Calvé in France, and Georg Perthes in Germany each independently described this condition as a form of arthritis of the hip in children with severe symptoms of short duration that led to permanent alterations in the shape of the femoral head. This condition was hence named **Legg-Calvé-Perthes disease** (LCPD) or Legg-Perthes disease. It has been studied extensively since its original description and although the condition is now better understood, a great deal of controversy remains about its etiology, natural history, and treatment.

Normal development of the head of the femur is the result of coordinated growth at the growth plates (epiphyses). These sites are supplied by a rich network of blood vessels. If the femoral head is deprived of blood flow for a sufficient period of time, the cells within the head die. When circulation is reestablished, healing occurs through a gradual process of substitution of new bone for old. In Legg-Calvé-Perthes disease, most probably a combination of predisposing factors and events deprive the femoral head of blood supply for a period of time, leading to death of the bony tissue (avascular necrosis) and deformation of the femoral head.

The incidence of Legg-Calvé-Perthes disease is approximately 1 per 9,000 children; 80% of the cases are between the ages of 4 and 9 years. The disease is more prevalent in boys, with an incidence of 1 in 8,000 boys versus 1 in 30,000 girls (Catterall, 1994); 10% of cases are bilateral with an interval between the onset of each side (Staheli, 1992). Although Legg-Calvé-Perthes disease is typically found in white children, Filipino, Eskimo, Chinese, Korean, and rarely, African American children have also been diagnosed with the disease (Chung, 1986).

Although the exact cause of this disease is unknown, the literature cites several potential predisposing factors and events that may contribute to the development of Legg-Calvé-Perthes disease. Birth weight, trauma, and hormonal influences have been suggested as possible contributors to this disease. Children with a low birth weight (less than 5.5 pounds) are five times more likely to develop Legg-Calvé-Perthes disease than children who weighed more than 8.5 pounds (Chung, 1986).

Trauma to the affected hip has also been proposed as a potential etiological factor. Since avascular necrosis (death of tissue due to lack of blood supply) of the femoral head occurs in Legg-Calvé-Perthes disease, trauma may cause damage to the blood vessels supplying the hip, according to some theorists. Equally possible as a contributing factor is an alteration in the coagulability of the blood. Blockages in the blood vessels may also cut off blood supply to the femoral head (Catterall, 1994; Scoles, 1988; Staheli, 1992).

Hormonal influences have also been suggested as influencing the development of Legg-Calvé-Perthes disease. One study of thyroid function in children with Legg-Calvé-Perthes disease and a group of control subjects indicated a moderate alteration of thyroid function in the children with Legg-Calvé-Perthes disease (Neidel et al., 1993).

CHARACTERISTICS OF LEGG-CALVÉ-PERTHES DISEASE

It is postulated that the initial episode of blood loss to the femoral head is asymptomatic (Scoles, 1988). As the disease progresses in its early stages, children may complain of hip pain or leg pain and may refuse to walk. Tenderness may also be present over the front part of the groin area. This pain and the loss of motion described earlier are due to the inflammation in the joint cavity (acute synovitis). Later in the disease process, vague thigh and knee pain may also be present; pain can be aggravated with activity.

A limp and the restriction of voluntary motion are often present. Staheli (1992) cites loss of hip medial rotation (rotating the leg in toward the body) as an early sign. Later, general loss of mobility occurs, with loss of abduction (moving the leg to the side away from the body) as the major problem.

In children with long-standing disease and significant damage to the femoral head, movement may be markedly restricted. The legs may be of unequal length (shorter on the affected side) secondary to damage to the growth plate.

The child with Legg-Calvé-Perthes disease is often of short stature with delayed bone growth. This short stature is disproportionate; the shortening involves the distal (farthest away from the body) limb segments but not the spine and pelvis (Catterall, 1994).

Legg-Calvé-Perthes disease can be classified by the extent of femoral head involvement: grades 1–4, with 1 being the least involved. The stage of the disease provides another classification. The disease can be divided into four stages: (1) synovitis, (2) necrosis, (3) fragmentation, and (4) reconstitution (Staheli, 1992). In the synovitis stage, there is joint inflammation that is of short duration (weeks). Synovitis produces stiffness and pain. X-rays may show joint space widening, and bone scans show decreased blood supply. In the necrosis stage, cells die in the femoral head, resulting in its collapse. Radiographs show a reduction in size and an increased density of the head. This stage lasts for 6–12 months. The fragmentation stage is a healing stage. Bone is reabsorbed, which produces the patchy areas of deossification visible on radiograph. Deformation (change in shape and flattening) of the femoral head often occurs during this stage, which lasts from 1 to 2 years. In the last stage of reconstitution, new bone is formed. Overgrowth often produces a larger-than-normal, flat femoral head and a widened femoral neck called *coxa magna*.

DETECTION OF LEGG-CALVÉ-PERTHES DISEASE

Legg-Calvé-Perthes disease is often diagnosed by physical examination and imaging studies. During the physical exam, the physician will look for signs and symptoms. A positive Trendelenburg sign reflecting weakness of the hip abductor muscles may be observed and indicate Legg-Calvé-Perthes disease. Clinical findings in Legg-Calvé-Perthes disease are quite variable and often correlate poorly with what is seen on X-ray.

Early in the course of the disease, X-rays may be normal, show a slight widening of the cartilage space, or show a cleft or fracture line in the femoral head, usually between the area of necrotic tissue and the healthy bone. In the vast majority of cases, the conventional radiograph is sufficient to diagnose Legg-Calvé-Perthes disease, although bone scan (particularly early in the disease) and MRI may also be used.

A number of diseases produce symptoms, signs, and laboratory findings similar to those of acute Legg-Calvé-Perthes disease. If characteristic radiological signs of Legg-Calvé-Perthes disease are present, the diagnosis can be made easily, but this is often not the case. Simple fracture and slipped capital femoral epiphysis must be ruled out on X-ray. Withdrawing fluid from the joint and laboratory examination of the fluid may be necessary to rule out infection; blood tests may rule out possible hematological disorders. Systematic examination and attention to ruling out other diseases that cause avascular necrosis of the femoral head may be necessary in order to diagnose Legg-Calvé-Perthes disease. Such a diagnosis would allow the early treatment that can prevent hip problems later in life.

TREATMENT AND COURSE OF LEGG-CALVÉ-PERTHES DISEASE

The objective of management of Legg-Calvé-Perthes disease is to preserve the shape of the femoral head in order to reduce the risk of stiffness and degenerative arthritis. The first step in treatment is to reduce the synovitis (inflammation of the membrane surrounding the joint) and improve range of motion. This usually entails hospitalization for bed rest and skin traction for 1 to 4 weeks to relieve tenderness and spasm around the hip joint. Once the initial synovitis has subsided, the child is evaluated. Whether or not extended treatment is needed depends on such factors as level of involvement of the femoral head, age at onset, and level of containment of the femoral head in the acetabulum.

Both surgical and nonsurgical techniques are employed to achieve containment of the femoral head in the acetabulum. In this way, the roundness of the femoral head is preserved during the healing stage of Legg-Calvé-Perthes disease. Essentially, the acetabulum is used as a mold for the healing femoral head. Containment is only effective while the femoral head is still plastic or moldable. This plastic phase continues throughout most of the fragmentation stage.

Braces

A variety of braces have been designed to hold the hip in abduction during the weight-bearing phase of walking (see Figure 12-6). Although excellent results can be obtained with bracing, 12–18 months of bracing may be necessary. Additionally, although children are independent in most braces, the braces can be awkward and inconvenient, and compliance and correct usage can be difficult to monitor.

Surgery

Common surgery for Legg-Calvé-Perthes disease includes a varus osteotomy on the femoral head (cutting of the femoral head) or a pelvic osteotomy (cutting of the pelvic bone), or both, in order to position the acetabulum to completely cover the femoral head. Pins and other internal devices may be used to hold the femoral head in correct position. Surgical treatment is usually indicated for the older child with severe involvement (a grade 3 or 4) or for those who are not good candidates for brace treatment. The disadvantages of surgery include the magnitude of the procedure itself, the need for a second surgery to remove the internal fixation devices, and the general risks of anesthesia.

In a study by Fulford, Lunn, and Macnicol (1993) of 85 children with Legg-Calvé-Perthes disease, 38 of whom were treated nonsurgically and 47 of whom were treated surgically, outcomes were similar. Prognosis appeared to depend more on the age and spherity (rounded shape) of the femoral head at onset of treatment than on the type of treatment given.

There are relatively few long-term reports of the consequences of Legg-Calvé-Perthes disease. However, several conclusions can be drawn from existing studies (Benson, Fixsen, & Macnicol, 1994). About 86% of children with Legg-Calvé-Perthes disease will develop osteoarthritis by the age of 65 but in the majority, symptoms will not become a problem until the fifth or sixth decade of life. About 9% of children with Legg-Calvé-Perthes disease will require reconstructive surgery by age 35, and 45% of these will require a hip replacement by age 45.

The children most likely to develop long-term problems are those with late onset of the disease (usually over the age of 9 years) or those who were not treated until significant involvement of the femoral head had oc-

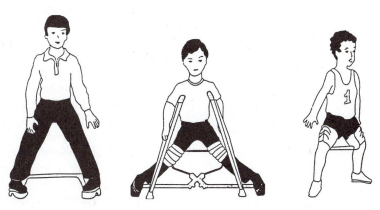

■ **FIGURE 12-6** Braces used to hold hip in abduction
SOURCE: From *Fundamentals of Pediatric Orthopedics*, by L. T. Staheli. Copyright ©1992 Staheli, Inc. Reprinted with permission.

curred (grade 3 or 4). Early diagnosis and treatment of Legg-Calvé-Perthes disease can improve the long-term prognosis.

DESCRIPTION AND ETIOLOGY OF SLIPPED CAPITAL FEMORAL EPIPHYSIS (SCFE)

Slipped capital femoral epiphysis (SCFE) is the most common cause of hip discomfort in adolescence. Essentially, the disease results in a slippage of the femoral head (ball) off the thigh bone (femur). This slippage occurs through the growth plate (epiphysis). Slipped capital femoral epiphysis is sometimes also referred to as *epiphysiolysis* or simply *slipped epiphysis.*

In most children with slipped capital femoral epiphysis, the femoral head displaces posteriorly (back) and inferiorly (down) with respect to the femoral head (see Figure 12-7). The slip occurs at the growth plate (or epiphysis), which shows disorganization of cell structure. Acute trauma to this area or the chronic stresses of heavy weight-bearing may initiate the slippage. Once slippage has begun, it will continue unless the growth plate is stabilized by either natural or surgical closure.

Deformity develops slowly in children with chronic slippage. As the slip progresses, bone is absorbed at the upper portion of the femoral neck and deposited at the lower portion. If growth ceases or if the slip is stabilized before significant displacement occurs, minimal deformity and restriction of movement will occur. However, if slippage continues, upper femoral deformity may develop, which would limit motion and lead to early degenerative arthritis.

The differences between slipped capital femoral epiphysis and an acute fracture to this area (due to trauma) are that the growth plate area is previously abnormal in slipped capital femoral epiphysis but normal in an acute fracture, and the severity of the traumatic episode is usually much less in slipped capital femoral epiphysis than in acute fracture (Scoles, 1988).

Between 2 and 3 children per 100,000 are diagnosed with slipped capital femoral epiphysis. Most studies indicate that boys are affected three times more frequently than girls. Slipped capital femoral epiphysis usually occurs in boys between 10 and 17 years of age, with a peak incidence at age 13–14 years. Girls are at-risk between the ages of 8 and 15 years, with a peak incidence at about 11 years. Girls who are postmenstrual are almost immune to slipped capital femoral epiphysis (Benson, Fixsen, & Macnicol, 1994; Scoles, 1988).

The left hip is more frequently involved, but in at least 30% of cases, the opposite hip will slip also. There may be subtle changes, such as pre-slipping in the opposite hip, in as many as 70% of unilateral cases. While both epiphyses may slip simultaneously, bilateral slips may be separated both in time and severity.

The adolescents at greatest risk appear to be those who are skeletally immature and obese. Obesity is reported in as many as 75% of individuals presenting the condition (Scoles, 1988). Chronic stress from the increased body weight on the growth plate is thought to be the mechanism. Another distinct group presenting with slipped capital femoral epiphysis are tall, slender, adolescent boys with delayed maturity (Benson, Fixsen, & Macnicol, 1994).

Slipped capital femoral epiphysis is also associated with other genetic, racial, and geographical factors. It is very rare in southern Asia and in the black population of Africa. It is at least two to three times more common in African Americans and Puerto Ricans than in the general population. The disorder also appears to have an autosomal-dominance because there is about a 7% risk of a second family member being affected (Benson, Fixsen, & Macnicol, 1994).

The interplay of factors that contribute to slipped capital femoral epiphysis is complex. Mechanical stress, trauma, and endocrine and immunological abnormalities have been considered separately and together as etiologically important.

Growth plate failure occurs when mechanical stresses exceed the strength of the plate. The hip joint is anatomically vulnerable to growth plate failure because of the biomechanics of the joint. Considerable weight is placed across the hip joint in such normal movement as walking, which is about four times body weight. Five to six times the body weight may be delivered as a shear force to the hip during an activity such as running. During puberty, the epiphyseal plate widens with the adolescent growth spurt, making it more susceptible to the shear forces, particularly when overloading, such as in obesity, occurs.

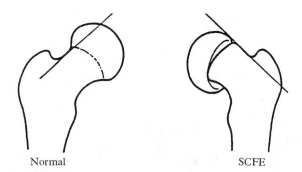

Normal   SCFE

■ **FIGURE 12-7** Normal hip (a) and hip with slipped capital femoral epiphysis (b)
SOURCE: From *Children's Orthopaedics and Fractures,* by M. K. D. Benson, J. A. Fixsen, and M. F. Macnicol (Eds.), p. 461. Copyright ©1994 Churchill Livingstone, Inc. Reprinted with permission.

Because epiphyseal slipping in slipped capital femoral epiphysis occurs at a time of maximum growth and because a significant number of affected adolescents are either overweight or lean, the contribution of endocrine factors has been studied. Sex hormones have been found to increase the strength of the epiphyseal plate, whereas growth hormones decrease it. When children with decreased growth due to hypopituitarism are treated with growth hormone, there is a significant risk of slipped capital femoral epiphysis, especially if sex hormones are not given at the same time. A deficiency of sex hormones also delays epiphyseal closure and increases the time span in which slippage may occur. In addition, a deficiency of sex hormones is associated with obesity, adding a mechanical factor to the problem (Benson, Fixsen, & Macnicol, 1994; Wells, King, Roe, & Kaufman, 1993).

Other endocrine-related problems have been described in association with slipped capital femoral epiphysis (Benson, Fixsen, & Macnicol, 1994; Wells et al., 1993). Hypothyroidism has a clear association, as does primary hyperparathyroidism and the secondary type that is a complication of renal failure. The majority of children with slipped capital femoral epiphysis do not have a recognizable endocrine abnormality, but those whose physique suggests that such an abnormality may be present should be tested for endocrine factors.

Trauma appears to be a factor in the initiation or continuance of displacement of the epiphysis in one-fourth to one-half of adolescents with slipped capital femoral epiphysis. This is logical, considering the sports activities in which many adolescents are engaged and the high incidence of increased body weight among individuals with slipped capital femoral epiphysis.

Studies have revealed a group of individuals with slipped capital femoral epiphysis who have an increased concentration of immunoglobulins, especially IgA. This suggests that the SCFE might be a local manifestation of a generalized inflammatory disorder (Benson, Fixsen, & Macnicol, 1994).

CHARACTERISTICS AND DETECTION OF SLIPPED CAPITAL FEMORAL EPIPHYSIS

Approximately 30% of cases of slipped capital femoral epiphysis are described as chronic (slow displacement), 20% are described as acute (sudden displacement), and 50% are described as acute on chronic (sudden major displacement occurring in an already chronically displaced hip (Benson, Fixsen, & Macnicol, 1994). Symptoms in children with slipped capital femoral epiphysis are variable and may depend on whether the displacement is **acute** or chronic. Those with chronic, slowly progressing slips often, but not always, complain of leg

TABLE 12-1

Grading of SCFE by Degree of Displacement

Measure	Grade
Displacement	
0–25%	Grade 1
25–50%	Grade 2
50–75%	Grade 3
75–100%	Grade 4
Degree angle	
0–30 degrees	Mild
30–60 degrees	Moderate
60+ degrees	Severe

SOURCE: From *Fundamentals of Pediatric Orthopedics*, by L. T. Staheli. Copyright ©1992 Staheli, Inc. Reprinted with permission.

pain. The pain may be vague and difficult to localize. Many children have hip pain, but some also experience thigh and knee pain. In some instances, "silent slips" occur in which there is no pain. Some researchers estimate that the incidence of silent or pain-free slips may be as high as 20% (Scoles, 1988). For children with acute traumatic slippage, hip pain is most commonly present.

The nonspecific nature of complaints with slipped capital femoral epiphysis often leads to prolonged delay in diagnosis. Frequently, children with early slipped capital femoral epiphysis are assumed to have muscle strains, ligament sprains, or growing pains. Limitation of active and passive motion often begins and is a constant finding in slipped capital femoral epiphysis. Medial rotation (rolling the leg toward the center of the body) is restricted and, when at rest, the leg is usually held in an externally rotated position (with the leg rolled out away from the body). Full flexion (bending), **extension** (straightening), and abduction (lateral movement way from midline) of the affected leg are usually impossible. Most children with slipped capital femoral epiphysis have a limp and a positive Trendelenburg test. Leg-length inequality of 1 to 3 cm (shorter on the affected side) may also be present (Benson, Fixsen, & Macnicol, 1994; Scoles, 1988).

Because the condition is progressive and may produce chronic disability, adolescents who complain of hip or knee pain should be examined and given a radiographical evaluation of both hips. Both front-to-back and lateral X-ray views are necessary for proper evaluation of the hip, although the lateral view gives a more precise indication of the extent of slip. A number of methods have been devised to grade the degree of slip. In Table 12-1, the grading of slipped capital femoral epiphysis by the degree of displacement of the femoral head or by the change in the angle of the femoral head with respect to the femoral neck is described (Staheli,

1992). The most common measure appears to be of the degree of slip (Benson, Fixsen, & Macnicol, 1994; Scoles, 1988). Less than 30° is regarded as mild, 30°–60° is moderate, and greater than 60° is severe.

Diagnosis of slipped capital femoral epiphysis should be made early in the disease process if significant hip deformity and a resultant disability are to be avoided. Careful attention to clinical symptoms reported by adolescents, particularly those in high-risk categories, along with appropriate radiological follow-up, is critical to early diagnosis.

TREATMENT AND COURSE OF SLIPPED CAPITAL FEMORAL EPIPHYSIS

Once a slip of the femoral head on the femoral neck has begun, it will continue until the growth plate is stabilized either by skeletal maturation or by surgical intervention. Treatment should be started immediately after diagnosis to prevent further slippage. Adolescents with minimal slips have a much better long-term prognosis than those with severe slips, the latter being predisposed to early degenerative arthritis.

Prevention of further slip is the goal of treatment. Nonsurgical techniques such as bed rest, crutch-walking, or immobilization in a spica cast do not achieve this goal reliably. Surgical stabilization is the treatment of choice for young people with slipped capital femoral epiphysis.

Several surgical procedures have been used to stabilize the growth plate in mild cases of slipped capital femoral epiphysis. Pins or screws are often inserted through the skin using a fluoroscope to track placement and thereby avoiding a major surgical incision. Several studies have reported a high incidence of complications, such as protrusion of the pins through the bone, in stabilization using the necessary multiple pinning approach (Aronson, Peterson, & Miller, 1992; Benson, Fixsen, & Macnicol, 1994). Using screws for fixation seems to give a better result (see Figure 12-8).

With slips of greater than 30°, pinning or screwing procedures endanger the blood supply to the growth plate, and realignment of the femoral head, while necessary, is not possible. Therefore, osteotomies (surgeries on the femoral bone itself) are often required. Because corrective surgery at the site of the slippage frequently leads to death of bone (avascular necrosis), this is not usually performed. Instead, the realignment procedure is more frequently done below the site of the deformity. Once better alignment is achieved, slippage is usually halted. Full weight-bearing is not allowed for about 2 months after surgery.

In few other orthopedic conditions are complications

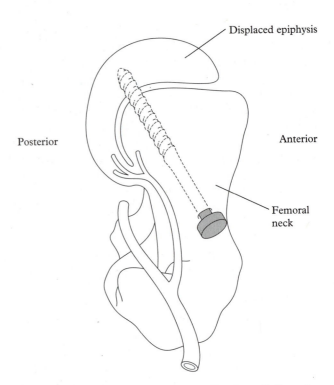

■ **FIGURE 12-8** Anterior screw fixation of slipped capital femoral epiphysis
SOURCE: From *Children's Orthopaedics and Fractures*, by M. K. D. Benson, J. A. Fixsen, and M. F. Macnicol (Eds.), p. 464. Copyright ©1994 Churchill Livingstone, Inc. Reprinted with permission.

more frequently seen than after an operation for slipped capital femoral epiphysis (Benson, Fixsen, & Macnicol, 1994). Avascular necrosis has already been mentioned as a possible complication. Other potential problems include the penetration of pins into the joint, which is characterized by pain, limitation of motion, progressive loss of joint cartilage, and binding down of the joint by fibrous tissue—a process called ankylosis. The breakage of pins, migration of pins, fracture at the site of pin insertion, infection, nerve and blood vessel injury, and scarring are other possible complications.

EDUCATIONAL IMPLICATIONS OF HIP CONDITIONS

Meeting Physical and Sensory Needs

Teachers educating students with congenital dislocation of the hip, Legg-Calvé-Perthes disease, and slipped capital femoral epiphysis may play a part in detecting the impairment, as well as in providing modifications for pain management and adaptations for brace management and assisting in making up missed work due to surgeries.

Because early treatment is so important to a good long-term prognosis, the classroom teacher can also be important in the early diagnosis of these hip conditions. Any hip pain (thigh or knee pain) reported by the student or any limping should be discussed with the student's family at the earliest opportunity so that medical follow-up can be pursued.

The physical education teacher may be one of the best observers of these signs and symptoms. The school nurse or the school physical therapist may also help to make appropriate contact with the student and family.

Even after a diagnosis has been made, discomfort may become an issue for the untreated child. The teacher should be aware that decreased stamina accompanied by pain can have an effect on the student's performance. Schedule adjustments and rest times may be needed. Communication with the student, his or her family, and the physician will be important if pain management becomes an issue.

Students with hip conditions may undergo surgeries to correct the impairment. Most children with congenital dislocation of the hip are diagnosed and treated within the first year of life. However, some children are not diagnosed until they are preschool or early school age. For these children, as well as those with Legg-Calvé-Perthes disease and slipped capital femoral epiphysis, prolonged hospital stays to undergo a period of traction and recuperate from major hip surgery may be necessary.

The teacher may need to help prepare the student and the student's classmates for an upcoming hospitalization through discussions appropriate for the child's age. Working with the child's parents and physician would be critical at this stage.

As with any potentially long-term condition and the possible need for surgical intervention, a teacher's monitoring of the student's condition would be indicated. It would also be important for the teacher to be familiar with any limitations to a student's activity and to support the student in adhering to these limitations.

In some instances, students will return from surgery with casts or will be braced instead of undergoing surgery. In both instances, teachers should be prepared to make necessary adaptations, such as to accommodate the use of crutches or braces, and should have a plan for managing the student's physical needs. After surgery, the student may return to school in a spica cast in a wheelchair, which would necessitate classroom accommodations. For example, the student might need a different location in the class, special desk adaptations, a long-handled reacher to retrieve dropped items, and so on. If post-surgical bracing is needed, the teacher will also need to understand brace management and any restrictions placed on the child.

■ VIGNETTE ■

Jerrod was 6 years old when his teacher noticed that he was limping. She talked to the physical education teacher, who confirmed this and added that he had also seen Jerrod having trouble with certain hip movements during physical education activities for over a month. Jerrod's teacher called his parents in for a conference and, together with Jerrod, talked about her concerns. Jerrod's parents took him to their physician, and, based on Jerrod's symptoms and X-ray studies, a diagnosis of Legg-Calvé-Perthes disease was made. Jerrod and his teacher learned more about the disease from the physician and were able to explain to Jerrod's classmates about the disease and that he was going to be in the hospital for a few weeks to rest his hip and would return to school in a special brace.

Jerrod returned to school several weeks later in an abduction brace. Surgery was not needed due to the early diagnosis. Jerrod showed his classmates his new brace. He was able to handle all classroom activities without difficulty and was only restricted from hard, jumping activities in physical education. Jerrod's teacher sees to it that he is using his brace correctly at school. The doctor predicts a good eventual result, partly because of the early diagnosis made by Jerrod's observant teacher.

The child with a hip condition who is treated with bracing (for example, as in Legg-Calvé-Perthes disease) is usually independent in the brace with minor restrictions on activity, with the exception of jumping sports. Little direct effect on the student's educational programming should occur. However, compliance with brace use and enforcement of the correct use of the brace may be issues for the classroom teacher. He or she may have to monitor brace use and discuss it with the student, the family, and the rest of the educational team. This monitoring requires that the teacher have knowledge of the disease, as well as of the particular child's brace and its correct usage.

For the student with congenital dislocation of the hip who has not yet received surgical treatment or who may not be a candidate for surgical intervention, the teacher will need to be aware of the student's diagnosis and how the hip condition may affect the child's mobility. The characteristic leg-shortening and limp on the affected side found in such conditions as congenital dislocation of the hip may affect the student's stamina and mean that some restrictions on vigorous physical activities should be imposed. Allowing the student more time to move from place to place may be necessary.

Meeting Communication Needs

Students with a hip condition do not have any impairments in communication unless there is an associated condition such as cerebral palsy. However, students with hip conditions may need to to explain to their peers about their condition. A simple explanation can be used to explain brace use such as, "I wear this brace to make my leg and hip go in the right position, just like other kids wear braces to straighten their teeth."

Meeting Learning Needs

Unless there is an associated condition, learning problems do not typically occur in children with hip conditions. With bracing or casting, the student may need to learn modifications, such as to use a long-handled reacher to pick up items. Because the student may miss school due to surgeries, assistance in making up missed work will be needed.

Meeting Daily Living Needs

Typically, daily living skills may be affected by a hip condition or by treatment for the condition. As we discussed, mobility problems may affect a student's independence. The use of casts and splints may result in the need for additional adult assistance to manage bathroom trips. Depending on the type of splint or cast, the student may need assistance in dressing, especially putting on shoes.

Meeting Behavioral and Social Needs

The teacher also should be aware of self-esteem issues related to hip conditions. The student with an obvious gait abnormality may be self-conscious about it or be teased by fellow classmates. An open, honest discussion with the class, in which the student helps to explain his or her condition and answer questions, can help to alleviate some of the negative social issues.

Because of the long-term nature of bracing, the psychological effect on the student must also be considered by the teacher and the educational team. Counseling should also be available to the student if needed.

SUMMARY

Many types of hip conditions affect the structure or the placement of the ball (top part of the thigh bone known as the femoral head) in its socket (part of the pelvic bone known as the acetabulum). Three common hip conditions are congenital hip dislocation, Legg-Calvé-Perthes disease, and slipped capital femoral epiphysis. Congenital hip dislocation is usually detected during infancy but

may not be found until the child is older. Legg-Calvé-Perthes disease affects children primarily between the ages of 4 and 9, with boys being affected about four times more than girls. Slipped capital femoral epiphysis primarily affects adolescents at the growth spurt, with a peak incidence for boys at ages 13–14 and for girls at age 11. Boys are affected three times more often than girls.

In congenital dislocation of the hip, the ball (femoral head) is not in its socket (acetabulum). If diagnosed early, congenital dislocation of the hip can be easily treated using conservative methods with good results and with few, if any, long-term problems. If left undiagnosed beyond the first 2 years of life, major structural changes occur in the developing hip. Surgical intervention is then necessary, and the potential for future hip problems is much increased. If intervention does not occur by early school-age, permanent, life-long disability is almost certain.

In Legg-Calvé-Perthes disease, there is an interruption of blood supply to the femoral head with a resulting death of bone tissue. Treatment is centered on preserving the rounded shape of the femoral head in order to reduce the risk of degenerative arthritis and to prevent hip problems later in life. Nonsurgical and surgical treatment techniques are employed to keep the femoral head well-seated in the acetabulum and thereby maintain its round shape. Nonsurgical treatment entails long-term bracing in devices that hold the leg in abduction. Surgical treatment includes surgery on the femoral head, the acetabulum, or both. Early diagnosis and treatment of Legg-Calvé-Perthes disease can improve the child's prognosis and decrease the likelihood of hip disability later in life.

In slipped capital femoral epiphysis, the growth plate is unable to accept either a traumatic insult or the chronic stress from increased body weight. The failed growth plate allows displacement of the femoral head on its neck. Due to the importance of early detection and treatment to a good long-term prognosis, any complaint of pain or limitations in range of motion in a high-risk adolescent should be quickly followed up medically, including radiographic evaluation. Stabilization of the slippage is the goal of treatment and requires immediate surgical intervention. Prognosis is good for early treatment of mild cases, but premature degenerative arthritis later in life may occur in many students with moderate-to-severe slips.

All three conditions require that the teacher be alert for signs and symptoms of a hip condition. Modifications may be needed in the classroom to accommodate for brace or wheelchair use. Teachers should provide a supportive environment and address self-esteem and emotional concerns.

CHAPTER 13

Limb Deficiency

The term **limb deficiencies** refers to any number of skeletal problems in which the limbs (arms or legs) are missing or malformed. A limb deficiency may occur in one limb or in multiple limbs; it may be the only impairment or part of a syndrome that includes other problems. The management of these deficiencies in children is distinctly different from the management of them in adults.

The two major categories of limb deficiencies are *congenital* and *acquired deficiencies*. Congenital limb deficiencies are those present at birth. They make up 70% of the pediatric limb deficiency population (Gillespie, 1981). Upper-extremity (arm) involvement is the most common congenital limb deficiency (approximately 60%), and multiple limbs are involved in one-fourth of these cases (Challenor, 1992). Congenital limb deficiencies are fairly common, occurring in 1 in every 2,000 births (Scott, 1989). The remaining 30% of children with limb deficiencies have acquired limb deficiencies—those occurring after birth due to injury (trauma) or disease. Such deficiencies may involve surgical removal of all or part of a limb.

In this chapter, we will describe the characteristics of various types of limb deficiencies and discuss their etiology and associated problems. Long-term medical management and interventions as well as developmental and educational considerations will also be addressed.

DESCRIPTION OF LIMB DEFICIENCIES

Limb deficiencies make up a very diverse category, encompassing a wide range of skeletal problems in which an individual's limb or limbs are shortened, absent, and/or malformed. The use of the term *limb deficiency* encompasses both congenital and acquired forms. Often the term **amputation** is used to refer to a limb deficiency.

Because limb deficiencies are so diverse, five different classification systems have been used to describe them. Use of a well-defined classification system is very important for reporting accurate information about incidence and etiology. Also, a well-defined classification system helps facilitate communication about the extent of the deficiency and aids in planning a course of treatment.

The Franz-O'Rahilly classification developed in 1961 has been the most widely used system. It describes two major categories of limb deficiencies: *terminal* and *intercalary* deficiencies.

Terminal Limb Deficiency

A terminal limb deficiency refers to a limb that has correctly developed near the top but at some point down the limb, correct development stops and part or all of the rest of the limb is missing (see Figure 13-1). When all of the end of the limb is missing, it is referred to as a *terminal transverse limb deficiency;* that is, it extends across the entire width of a limb. (See Figure 13-2.) For example, a terminal transverse limb deficiency can refer to a limb that is unaffected from the top of the arm to right below the elbow, but the rest of the limb is missing. As shown in Box 13-1, several additional terms may be used to describe the exact type of terminal transverse limb deficiency based on location. Often, these additional terms are used to describe the exact type of terminal limb deficiency more completely. For example, a child with an arm missing from above the elbow would have a *terminal transverse above-elbow limb deficiency.*

Terminal limb deficiency may also mean that only some bones are missing. This is called a *terminal longitudinal (or paraxial) limb deficiency*. For example, a terminal longitudinal limb deficiency could mean that certain bones from the elbow to the end of the arm are missing.

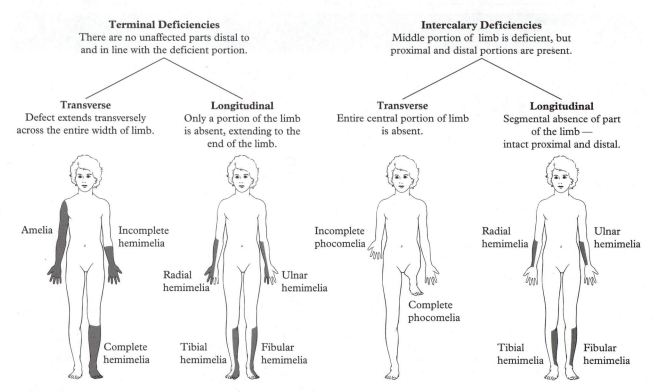

Terminal Deficiencies
There are no unaffected parts distal to and in line with the deficient portion.

Transverse
Defect extends transversely across the entire width of limb.

Longitudinal
Only a portion of the limb is absent, extending to the end of the limb.

Intercalary Deficiencies
Middle portion of limb is deficient, but proximal and distal portions are present.

Transverse
Entire central portion of limb is absent.

Longitudinal
Segmental absence of part of the limb — intact proximal and distal.

Amelia

Incomplete hemimelia

Radial hemimelia

Ulnar hemimelia

Complete hemimelia

Tibial hemimelia

Fibular hemimelia

Incomplete phocomelia

Complete phocomelia

Radial hemimelia

Ulnar hemimelia

Tibial hemimelia

Fibular hemimelia

■ **FIGURE 13-1** Types of limb deficiencies
SOURCE: From "Congenital Skeletal Limb Deficiencies," by C. H. Frantz and R. O'Rahilly, 1961, *Journal of Bone and Joint Surgery, 43*(A), p. 1202. Copyright © 1961 Journal of Bone and Joint Surgery. Reprinted with permission.

■ **FIGURE 13-2** Student with right-arm transverse terminal limb deficiency working in class

Intercalary Limb Deficiency

The second major category in the Frantz-O'Rahilly classification system is *intercalary limb deficiency*. In this deficiency, all or part of the middle section of the limb is missing. When all of the middle section of a limb is missing and the rest is present, an *intercalary transverse limb deficiency* has occurred. For example, the hand may be connected to the elbow, and the entire forearm is missing. When some skeletal elements are missing in the middle portion of a limb and the other parts are unaffected, an *intercalary longitudinal limb deficiency* is present. An example is when one of the bones from the forearm is missing (see Figure 13-1). (Gillespie, 1981; Scottish Rite Children's Medical Center, 1993; Setoguchi & Rosenfelder, 1982).

Some additional terms used in the Frantz-O'Rahilly classification system to describe limb deficiencies are *amelia, hemimelia,* and *phocomelia.* **Amelia** is a complete absence of a limb. **Hemimelia** is any limb in which a part is missing. **Phocomelia** refers to a condition in which the hands or feet appear to be directly attached to the trunk.

In 1989, the International Society of Prosthetics and Orthotics (ISPO) developed a new classification system for limb deficiencies. This method also divides the

---

BOX 13-1

Classification of Limb Deficiencies

I. Terminal Limb Deficiency—deficiency in which the end portion of an arm or leg is missing
  A. Transverse—all of the end portion of the limb is missing
    1. Arms
      a. Forequarter amputation (entire shoulder girdle and limb)
      b. Shoulder disarticulation (amputation through the joint)
      c. Above-elbow
      d. Elbow disarticulation
      e. Below-elbow
      f. Wrist disarticulation
      g. Digits
    2. Legs
      a. Hindquarter amputation (entire side of pelvis and limb)
      b. Hip disarticulation
      c. Above-knee
      d. Knee disarticulation
      e. Below-knee
      f. Ankle disarticulation
      g. Foot ablation
      h. Toes
  B. Longitudinal (paraxial)—one of the bones in the end part of an arm or leg is missing
II. Intercalary Limb Deficiency—the middle section of an arm or leg is missing
  A. Transverse—the entire middle section of an arm or leg is missing
  B. Longitudinal (paraxial)—one of the bones in the middle section of an arm or leg is missing

---

deficiencies into two major categories: *transverse* and *longitudinal*. However, the ISPO classification uses the anatomical names of the bones (and additional subcategories) to describe a deficiency. For example, in this classification system, a *longitudinal deficiency of the femur* refers to a short or missing long bone in the thigh (femur) in which the lower leg and foot are present. This new system is gaining in popularity and use because it is logical and descriptive. However, it is very cumbersome to use and most of the literature still uses the Frantz-O'Rahilly system or a combination of descriptors (Gillespie, 1981; Peregrine, 1992).

ETIOLOGY OF LIMB DEFICIENCIES

Acquired limb deficiency in the pediatric population is most commonly the result of trauma. About 70–75% of pediatric amputations are the result of some form of trauma (Peregrine, 1992). The remaining 25–30% of juvenile amputations are due to cancer (for example, osteogenic sarcoma), vascular problems, burns, infection, and surgery to remove part of a limb due to injury or disease. Cancer, which is the second most frequent cause of **acquired amputations,** usually occurs in children 10 years of age or older, and the lower extremity (leg) is most frequently affected (Setoguchi & Rosenfelder, 1982).

Approximately 60–70% of congenital limb deficiencies have no known etiology; the remainder are believed to have environmental or genetic origins (Peregrine, 1992). (See Box 13-2.) Environmental factors include intrauterine infection (for example, syphilis), drugs (for example, thalidomide), irradiation, maternal health factors (for example, diabetes), and mechanical factors (for example, intrauterine cramping). Risk factors also include pollutants and the father's condition (for example, diabetes or environmental exposure).

The most well-known cause of congenital limb deficiencies is the use of thalidomide. Thalidomide was a drug popular in Europe for its sedative qualities with few side effects; it was also found to alleviate morning sickness. Thalidomide was used from about 1958 to 1961 until its use was linked with a significant increase in severe, multiple-limb deficiencies. The classic appearance of babies born to mothers who took thalidomide is the child with "flipper" arms—hands that were attached directly to the trunk. The drug was being considered for approval for use in the United States when its consequences were discovered (Gillespie, 1981).

Congenital limb deficiencies may also be the result of genetic abnormalities. About 5% of limb deficiencies have been attributed to chromosomal origin, and approximately 15% are the result of a single-gene mutation (Dixon, 1989; Peregrine, 1992). Chromosomal abnormalities associated with limb deficiencies include Trisomy 13 and Trisomy 18. Several single-gene syndromes have been associated with congenital limb deficiencies. Other genetic syndromes, congenital anomalies, and isolated limb deficiencies have also been attributed to genetic causes.

DYNAMICS OF LIMB DEFICIENCIES

Congenital limb deficiencies may originate at various times during gestation; usually, the earlier the problem occurs the more severe the consequence (Scott, 1989). Because the limb buds develop early, most congenital limb deficiencies are caused by problems occurring in the first 2 months of gestation. This early critical period is when external agents or insults have the most disruptive effect on limb development.

BOX 13-2

Etiology of Limb Deficiencies

I. Acquired
 A. Trauma
 B. Malignancy
 C. Other surgical
II. Congenital
 A. Environmental
  1. Intrauterine infection
   a. Syphilis
  2. Drugs
   a. Proven: thalidomide
   b. Possible: (no convincing evidence) oral contraceptives; synthetic female hormones; antidepressants; antiemetics (Bendectin); antimetabolies (Aminopterin); anticoagulants (Warfarin); anticonvulsants (Dilantin); quinine; alcohol; and so on
  3. Irradiation
  4. Maternal health factors
   a. Diabetes mellitus
  5. Mechanical factors
   a. Intrauterine cramping
   b. Amniotic band syndrome (Streeter)
  6. Other possible risk factors (no good evidence)
   a. Occupational exposure (hydrocarbons)
   b. Pesticide (agent orange)
   c. Pollutants
  7. Paternal risk factors (no evidence)
   a. Age
   b. Diabetes mellitus
   c. Environmental exposure

 B. Genetic
  1. Chromosomal
   a. Trisomy 13
   b. Trisomy 18
  2. Single gene
   a. Autosomal-dominant: Holt Oram; ECC (ectrodactyly, ectoderma dysplasia, cleft palate); Fibula agenesis—complex brachydactyly
   b. Autosomal-recessive: TAR (thrombocytopenia absent radius); Coney syndrome; Fanconi syndrome; Baller-Gerold syndrome; Hanhart syndrome; Robert's pseudothalidomide; and so on
 C. Unknown
  1. Syndromes
   a. Aglossia-adactylia
   b. Cornelia deLange
   c. Amniotic band syndrome (Streeter)
  2. Multiple congenital anomalies (no specific syndrome)
  3. Isolated limb deficiency
   a. Single limb
   b. Multiple limb
   c. PFFD
   d. Fibula agenesis
   e. Tibia agenesis

SOURCE: From "The Pediatric Amputee: An Epidemiologic Survey," by M. J. Goldberg, 1981, *Orthopedic Review, 10*, p. 50. Copyright © 1981 Excerpta Medica, Inc. Reprinted with permission of Orthopaedic Review.

Congenital limb deficiencies can be classified by how they occur, that is, whether they are *malformations* or *deformations*. Malformations occur when the tissue does not initially form correctly. Deformations are the result of normal tissue undergoing abnormal forces. The plan of treatment and prognosis may be different, depending on whether the deficit is the result of a malformation or a deformation (Scottish Rite Children's Medical Center, 1993). The type of malformation depends on the timing and the process occurring in **intrauterine** development. Some parts may fail to form. This could completely arrest development of a limb, resulting in a terminal transverse limb deficiency. If the arrest is temporary and development continues, then the result is more likely to have an intercalary limb deficiency—the middle part of a limb would be missing. Other problems that may occur during development and result in malformations are failure of tissue differentiations, duplications (extra digits), hypoplasia (undergrowth), or overgrowth. The type of causative agent and the timing of the insult will determine the effect.

CHARACTERISTICS OF CONGENITAL LIMB DEFICIENCIES

Although numerous types and variations of limb deficiencies can occur, several have been well-defined and can be characterized. A more detailed study of these will assist in understanding the broad scope of this diagnosis.

In general, a congenital limb deficiency can occur at any limb level, and one or more limbs may be affected. A terminal transverse limb deficiency—one that extends across the entire limb—of only one limb is usually not associated with other abnormalities. However, deficits involving both legs often occur with other physical and organic anomalies. Children with severe lower-extremity deficiencies are likely to have upper-extremity deficits also. In the lower extremity, intercalary limb deficiencies (middle portion of limb is missing) occur more frequently than terminal deficits (Gillespie, 1981). Absence defects are more common in the upper extremity than the lower extremity (Scott, 1989). The characteristics of congenital deficiencies described next are the most common terminal and intercalary limb deficiencies of the arms and legs. Special types of limb deficiencies—sacral agenesis, amelia, and phocomelia—are described as well.

Terminal Transverse Limb Deficiency of the Arm

This type of limb deficiency can occur as a congenital above-elbow or below-elbow limb deficiency. This deficiency may occur at any level, and there are no structures except possibly nubbins (small fingerlike projections) below the site of the deficit (Setoguchi & Rosenfelder, 1982). The above-elbow limb deficiency occurs rather infrequently, whereas the below-elbow limb deficiency is the most prevalent type of congenital deficiency. It commonly occurs unilaterally (on one side). The child with the congenital below-elbow limb deficiency is usually an excellent candidate for a myoelectric prosthesis—a type of artificial arm (Gillespie, 1981).

Intercalary Limb Deficiency of the Forearm

In this condition, one or both of the two forearm bones (the ulnar and radial) are absent or short, but the hand is present. The child with this type of limb deficiency also tends to have hand deformities, but hand use is usually quite functional (Gillespie, 1981).

Terminal Transverse Limb Deficiency of the Leg

This deficiency, as in the upper extremity, can occur either above or below the knee. Children with this limb deficiency are managed just the way a child with an acquired amputation is managed (Setoguchi & Rosenfelder, 1982).

Intercalary Deficiency of the Thigh Bone (Femur)

There are three main types of intercalary deficiencies of the femur (thigh bone): *congenital short femur,*

congenital hypoplasia of the femur, and *proximal femoral focal deficiency.* The child with the congenital short femur has a slightly shortened thigh bone; other structures are normal.

Congenital hypoplasia of the thigh bone denotes a much more severe shortening of the thigh bone along with other structural problems in the affected lower extremity. The knee may also be unstable (Eilert, 1989; Gillespie 1981).

Proximal femoral focal deficiency (PFFD) is a deficiency of the thigh bone, including the point at which the thigh bone connects with the hip joint (iliofemoral joint) (Peregrine, 1992). This condition can occur on one or both sides and ranges in severity. Only about 15% of all cases are bilateral, and these tend to be the ones with the major deficits. Proximal femoral focal deficiency has a very marked appearance. The thigh bone is extremely short; there is hip flexion (bending at the hip), abduction and external rotation (leg turning outward), and knee flexion contracture (see Figure 13-3). The foot on the affected side—if only one side is affected—is often even with the knee on the other side. There is varying involvement of the hip and knee joints,

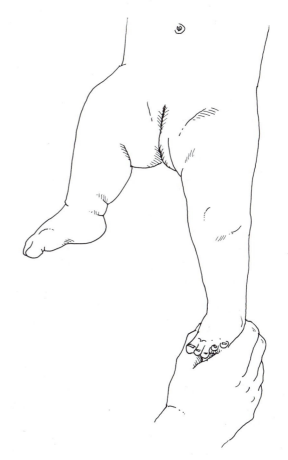

■ FIGURE 13-3 Proximal femoral focal deficiency

each of which may be unstable. As many as 50% of proximal femoral focal deficiency cases have other anomalies, including a short or absent fibula and foot deformities. Proximal femoral focal deficiency is also characterized by delayed ossification. Treatment priorities for a child with proximal femoral focal deficiency are to provide a stable hip and a functional method for independent ambulation. Cosmesis may also be a significant factor (Krajbich, 1989).

Intercalary Limb Deficiency of the Bones in the Calf

Shortening of the bone in the calf (the fibula) is more common than the complete absence of this bone. It is one of the more common lower-extremity limb deficiencies. This type of deficiency produces a shortened limb, and the other bone (tibia) is usually bowed. Other problems often seen in conjunction with this are a femoral shortening, knee instability, foot deformities, and upper-extremity anomalies. Leg-length and foot deformities are the major considerations for management of this condition. It can also be associated with cardiac and renal problems (Kalamchi, 1989).

In some instances, there may be shortening of the other bone in the calf area, the tibia. This is very rare. When it does occur, it is characterized by a very much shortened and bowed leg with an unstable knee. In two-thirds of the cases with limb deficiency affecting the tibia, there are other congenital problems such as defects of the hands, feet, femur, and gonads (Gillespie, 1981; Kalamchi, 1989).

Sacral Agenesis

In this condition, the sacrum (the end of the spine) is absent, as is some of the lumbar spine. Neurological deficits are usually associated, including lower-extremity paralysis. The major concerns regarding a child with sacral agenesis are for an unstable spine and for urinary and intestinal problems. The lower extremities may also have contractures, webbing, or other deformities (Setoguchi & Rosenfelder, 1982; Scottish Rite Children's Medical Center, 1993).

Amelia

Amelia is defined as a congenital limb deficiency with a total absence of one or more limbs. When a leg is missing, it is also called congenital hip disarticulation and is very rare (Setoguchi & Rosenfelder, 1982). When an arm is missing, there may be nubbins at the disarticulation site; nubbins are frequently present at the end of the stump (Setoguchi, 1989). Either nubbins or some

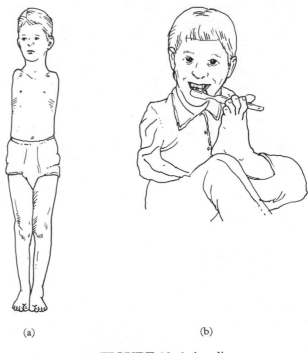

(a)   (b)

■ **FIGURE 13-4** Amelia

shoulder area gives the child a way to control an electric prosthesis (Gillespie, 1981). Other anomalies are often observed in these children.

A major problem for children with upper- or lower-extremity amelia is significantly decreased body surface, which decreases their ability to lose body heat. Children can become overheated very easily and should be dressed lightly. They also must drink enough fluids to avoid dehydration (Patton, 1989). Additionally, because of decreased body size and possibly a decrease in activity level, weight control becomes very important in keeping these children as functional as possible (Setoguchi & Rosenfelder, 1982). (See Figure 13-4.)

Phocomelia

In phocomelia, the hand or foot is attached directly to the trunk; one or more extremities can be affected. A small portion of the extremity may be present; the hand or foot may have deformities also. This was the classic outcome known as a "thalidomide baby." These children may have joint deformities and are prone to many of the same problems as children with amelia (Setoguchi & Rosenfelder, 1982). (See Figure 13-5.)

Acheiria and Apodia

Acheiria refers to a complete absence of the hands, and *apodia* refers to missing feet. Hands are absent more frequently than feet (Scott, 1989). When only one hand is absent, or especially if any portion of the hand is present, no prosthesis is required. The child will be more functional without a prosthesis than with one. For those who require a prosthesis, an electric hand is often the best choice (Gillespie, 1981).

Other Congenital Deficiencies

Other examples of conditions that can occur in the upper or lower limbs are *adactylia* (absence of the fingers or toes), *split-hand* or *split-foot,* and *syndactyly* (webbing of the fingers or toes). Management of these conditions depends on the presence of other anomalies and the function available in the deficient hands or feet (Setoguchi & Rosenfelder, 1982).

General Problems in Congenital Limb Deficiencies

Several problems may be associated with these congenital limb deficiencies. One of the most common problems in children with severe upper-extremity (arm) deficiencies is scoliosis. Other congenital problems frequently observed in children with limb anomalies are dislocated hips, webbing at the knee or elbow, abnormal musculature, and fingernail and toenail abnormalities (Peregrine, 1992; Setoguchi & Rosenfelder, 1982). It is important to note that children with a limb deficiency usually have normal intelligence. The anticipated outcome for the child with a limb deficiency is directly related to the presence of associated anomalies (Scott, 1989).

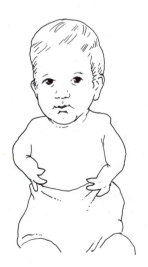

■ **FIGURE 13-5** Phocomelia

DETECTION OF CONGENITAL LIMB DEFICIENCIES

A congenital limb deficiency is typically apparent at birth. Some anomalies can be diagnosed in utero by ultrasonography, which allows for prebirth treatment planning and gives the family valuable adjustment time. A deficiency may entail missing or altered muscles, nerves, and blood vessels, as well as bony structures. Radiographs or magnetic resonance imaging (MRIs) are often needed to determine the severity of the defect, such as the condition of the hip or knee joint, partial presence of a bone, and so on. It is important to determine the condition of the rest of the extremity (Scott, 1989). A correct diagnosis and assessment is critical to determining the possibility of associated problems and to planning for optimal management and functional outcomes. Genetic counseling is indicated if a syndrome or genetic origin is suspected.

A mild congenital limb deficiency may sometimes not be diagnosed at birth and may begin to be noticeable as the child grows and starts to walk. Acquired shortenings are generally the result of trauma and will also be more noticeable with growth.

CHARACTERISTICS OF ACQUIRED LIMB DEFICIENCIES

As with congenital deficiencies, acquired amputations may occur at any level and in multiple limbs. The reason for the amputation will be the primary determinant of the course of treatment. A major difference between a congenital and an acquired limb deficiency is the state of health of the child. The child with an acquired amputation has most likely undergone a major trauma or a serious medical problem. The child may be debilitated and may have other medical problems that slow the rehabilitation process (Setoguchi, 1989). Complications that may develop after an amputation are hematoma, infection, tissue death, contracture, tumor, and phantom pain (Peregrine, 1992).

A longitudinal study by the Ontario Crippled Children's Center in Toronto followed 94 children with acquired limb deficiencies from 1963 to 1979. They found that nearly 60% had amputations caused by trauma—primarily motor vehicle accidents, and train, farm machinery, and lawn-mower accidents. Bicycles, motorcycles, electrical burns, thermal burns, and explosives were also responsible for some of the traumatic amputations. About 56% of the amputations were lower-extremity losses. Below the knee was the most common lower-extremity amputation level and below the elbow was the most common upper-extremity level.

The male-to-female ratio for these patients was 12 males to 1 female. Almost 40% of the patients required surgical revision during the period of the study, and some had multiple revisions (Galway, Hubbard, & Mowbray, 1981).

TREATMENT AND COURSE OF LIMB DEFICIENCIES

The long-term management and treatment planning for a child with a limb deficiency is most comprehensive when a team approach is used. The team should include a pediatrician, orthopedic surgeon, physical therapist, occupational therapist, prosthetist, psychologist, social worker, and nutritionist (Dixon, 1989; Peregrine, 1992). The child with a limb deficiency, whether congenital or acquired, should begin treatment early, shortly after birth or at the time of the amputation— even before birth in some instances—and will require ongoing comprehensive management, at least until growth is finished.

The major goal of treatment for the child with a limb deficiency is to maximize independent functioning. Issues that must be considered in planning long-term treatment include projection of the ultimate deficiency, growth, cosmesis, development of skills, psychological effects, family dynamics, and the disruption to the child's life for surgeries, hospitalizations, rehabilitation, and so forth. The treatment plan must also address any associated problems such as scoliosis (Dixon, 1989; Peregrine, 1992).

Treatment for the child with a limb deficiency will actually be a progression that allows and plans for normal development. Critical periods of physical and psychosocial development should be taken into account, such as the time a child learns to walk, enters school, and begins to wrestle with the teenage issues of sexuality, independence, driving, and employment (Dixon, 1989).

In general, children with congenital skeletal deficiencies have problems not only with the limb-length discrepancy but also with joint instability, malrotation, and abnormal or inadequate musculature. Stability, alignment, and strength become critical issues in treatment. The treatment plan must either correct these problems or give the child a method of compensation (Kritter, 1989). In addition, the treatment plan must allow and facilitate muscular and motor skill development, and should prevent additional deformities. Children with acquired amputations usually have normal joint structure and musculature until the amputation—in contrast to the child with a congenital limb deficiency—so that expectations for strength and ability may be quite different for them (Peregrine, 1992).

Surgeries

Some reasons for surgery for the child with a limb deficiency include leg-length discrepancy, joint instability, severe contractures, severe webbing, poor weight-bearing surfaces, polydactyly, malrotation, bony overgrowth, cosmesis, and an inability to attain a functional prosthetic fit. The team, including the child and family, should consider the child's current and potential abilities before surgery and note what the child is presently doing so that surgery does not take valuable functions away (Peregrine, 1992).

Sometimes, congenital anomalies require amputation to improve function. In such cases, surgery within the first year is recommended so that the child learns motor skills wearing a prosthesis from the beginning; adjustment is easier that way.

An important surgical principle when dealing with these children is that, if possible, the amputation should be done through the joint (joint disarticulation) rather than through a long bone. This is important for three reasons. First, the growth plate of the bone is preserved so that growth can continue, thus preventing an extremely short residual limb. Second, this type of amputation provides excellent end-bearing stumps that can aid in prosthetic management (Gillespie, 1981). Third, it prevents bony overgrowth, which occurs when the bone grows faster than the soft tissue and forms a spike on the end of the stump. The skin becomes red and shiny, and the child may cease weight-bearing activities or complain of pain at the end of the stump. The bony protrusion must be surgically removed to keep it from piercing the skin (Gillespie, 1981; Peregrine, 1992).

Amputation through the joint may not be possible when a child has an acquired amputation. The surgeon will attempt to preserve the knee joint if at all feasible because a below-knee prosthesis is much easier to control than one above the knee.

When a child undergoes a surgical amputation due to cancer, the level of the amputation will depend on the site of the tumor. Osteogenic sarcoma (bone cancer) is most frequently found in the leg bones. With the success of **chemotherapy**, the surgery does not have to be quite as radical as previously. These children will most likely have an above-knee amputation, but it could be as severe as a hindquarter amputation. An immediate postoperative prosthetic fit—a temporary prosthesis is placed on the stump via a cast at the time of the surgery—may help speed the rehabilitation process. The child may have skin problems and become debilitated during the chemotherapy treatment. The cancer does not usually recur in the stump, but the prognosis depends on whether it has already spread prior to treatment (Gillespie, 1981).

For the child with a shortened limb, the severity of the deficit is one of the primary determinants as to the treatment progression. For the child with a lower-extremity deficit of 0 to 2.5 cm, a shoe lift is the only treatment that is required. For 2.5 to 4 cm leg-length discrepancy, the usual treatment is the fusing of the growth plate so that the longer leg ceases to grow and the shorter leg is allowed to catch up and equalize the length. This is known as an epiphysiodesis (Raney, Brashear, & Shands, 1971).

If there is a more severe discrepancy, one or more lengthening procedures may be selected. Lengthenings are considered a good option for deficiencies of between 4 and 18 cm. Lengthenings may be performed in the upper extremity or the lower extremity. With a deficit of 18 cm or more, the discrepancy is too severe for lengthening, and the choice becomes prosthetic management with or without amputation (Scottish Rite Children's Medical Center, 1993).

Several limb-lengthening procedures are in use; procedures using the Wagner and Ilizarov devices are two of the most common. The decision to undergo a lengthening procedure is a serious commitment for both the child and the family. The procedures are complex and time-consuming and can have many complications. In any of the procedures, the bone is surgically cut and a device used to separate the bone is inserted. The Wagner device is a bar attached on one side of the leg with pins. It is less bulky than the Ilizarov. The Ilizarov is a cage-like device that encircles the leg; wires are inserted into the bone. One of its major benefits is that rotation can be controlled and corrected at the same time as the lengthening.

Children have these devices for about 8 months at a time and may have to undergo a succession of lengthening procedures; an increase of about 6 to 7 cm can be expected from one procedure. During and after treatment, intensive physical therapy is required. Problems that can develop during a lengthening procedure include muscle shortening, joint dislocation, kneecap dislocation, pin-site infection, pain due to nerve stretching, depression, and possible nonunion. The procedure is not usually begun until about the age of 8 years, and it requires several years to complete (Bowen & Choi, 1989).

Prosthetics

The reason for using a prosthesis is to provide optimum function, improve the child's looks, and increase comfort. Growth must always be considered, and a child's prosthesis may only last a year or less due to growth. By the teenage years, it may last only 1 to 2 years, so cost can become an issue. One of the main considerations for the child's prosthesis is that it must be durable (Galway, 1981; Peregrine, 1992). Prosthetic choice depends on the age of the child, the amount of residual limb, cosmesis, the child's ability to manage the prosthesis, and the functions the child needs to be able to perform. There are many different types of prostheses and components. Choices must be made as to the type of socket, joint, terminal device, and suspension system.

Children often require a strap suspension for lower-extremity prosthetics, especially for sports or for toddlers' activities such as climbing. A liner may be used with a prosthesis initially and then may be removed to allow room as the child grows. Cosmesis may be a problem in fitting the child with an unusual residual limb. If fit is compromised too much, amputation or surgical revision may be needed to improve function. Children who have had burns or skin grafts may have problems with skin breakdown underneath the prosthesis (Bochmann, 1981).

The stump changes as the child grows, matures, and loses or gains weight. The prosthesis will need to be revised to accommodate these changes, as well as changes in functional demands. When the length of the child's prothesis no longer matches the rest of his or her body or that of his or her peers, a change will be needed. A child's bilateral lower-extremity prosthesis must "grow" to maintain body proportions and age-appropriate height (Peregrine, 1992).

If a prosthesis is useful to the child, it will be worn, assuming that it fits and functions appropriately and that the child has had adequate prosthetic training. Wearing patterns do change as the child matures. A younger child who feels slowed down by a prosthesis may choose to wear it as cosmesis becomes more important. In general, a lower-extremity prosthesis is accepted much more readily than an upper-extremity one. The technology of lower-extremity prosthetics has made significant progress in the last few years, and they have become very functional and acceptable in appearance. Children with lower-extremity limb deficiency run, ski, and play competitive sports. Upper-extremity prosthetics also have made tremendous technological advances but still have a more restricted function because they do not provide for sensation, fine motor control, or strength—all of which are vital functions of the hand. For the child with a residual hand, whether deficient or not, a prosthesis is not used. Any kind of a hand is better than a prosthetic hand (Gillespie, 1981).

With regard to prosthetics for the arm, the choices are between passive and externally powered and body-powered types, with a variety of terminal device options (see Figure 13-6). Body-powered (conventional) prostheses use shoulder and/or arm movements with a harness system to control the terminal device or elbow. An externally powered prosthesis uses a motor with

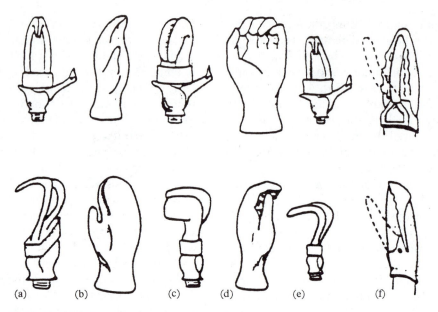

■ **FIGURE 13-6** Types of prosthetic devices
SOURCE: From "Limb Deficiencies in Children," by Y. Challenor. In G. E. Molnar (Ed.),
Pediatric Rehabilitation, 2nd Ed., pp. 400–424. Copyright © 1992 Williams & Wilkins.
Reprinted with permission.

batteries and is operated by a myoelectric (EMG) signal or control switches.

The myoelectric prosthesis is activated by an EMG signal from a contracting muscle in the residual limb. This electrical signal is picked up by surface electrodes inside the prosthetic socket. A controller switch interprets the signal from the electrodes and controls the flow of current to an electric motor, which powers the terminal device using a rechargeable battery. Prosthetic functions that can be controlled by myoelectric devices are hand-opening/closing, elbow flexion/extension, and wrist supination/pronation (turning palm up and down). Several options for control are available, depending on the availability of control sites and the strength of contractions. The easiest is the one-site myoelectric device. This prosthesis requires that one muscle site open the hand. When the muscle is not contracting, the hand closes automatically. Other control options are one-site or two-site devices, with proportional or speed control (Hubbard, Bush, Kurtz, & Naumann, 1991; Scott, 1989). (See Figure 13-7.)

Myoelectrics were initially used only with teenagers and adults, but recently they have been gaining popularity for use with young children. Most progressive clinics are routinely fitting children with myoelectrics by about the age of 2½, and the trend is to start even sooner; some centers use myoelectrics for children as young as 12 to 18 months. Beginning to use the device at such a young age means that children do not have to unlearn patterns later (Hubbard et al., 1991).

There is still some argument as to when and if myoelectrics should be used rather than the body-powered prosthesis. The myoelectric prosthesis is usually less cumbersome and more comfortable because there is no harness. However, the myoelectric is heavier because of the battery. The myoelectric hand has much better ability to grip and pinch than a hook, which increases its functional appeal. Unfortunately, it still is difficult to control more than one movement at a time, even with a myoelectric.

A major attraction for the myoelectric prosthesis is that the wearer's appearance is much more cosmetically acceptable. This has been a big issue both for children and their parents. On the negative side, the myoelectric requires much more maintenance and more down-time due to repairs. It also costs significantly more than a conventional prosthesis.

Lower-Extremity Prosthesis

In general, for the child with a limb deficiency in both legs or with deficiencies at a high level, walking with a prosthesis becomes very energy-consuming, slow, and less functional. Therefore, other methods might work better. For the child with a unilateral high limb deficiency, a better choice may be to use crutches without a prosthetic leg. A wheelchair is the usual option for the child with a bilateral high limb deficiency (Peregrine, 1992; Thompson & Leimkuehler, 1989).

The child with lower levels of limb loss, even both legs, will most likely be independent in ambulation with their prostheses and will be able to participate in numerous physical activities with minimal-to-no adaptations (Peregrine, 1992; Scottish Rite Children's Medical Center, 1993; Thompson & Leimkuehler, 1989).

The child with a limb deficiency can participate in a wide variety of sports activities, sometimes even without the prosthesis. Either the prosthesis or a prosthesis designed especially for the sport may be used. Children should be encouraged to find some sport in which to participate because they will benefit from increased self-esteem and improved strength and endurance. Sports such as track, cross-country running, cycling, aerobics, tennis, horseback riding, soccer, skiing, wrestling, and swimming are all possible for some children with limb deficiencies. Football and hockey are not usually good options. Several sports associations, such as National Handicapped Sports and the National Wheelchair Athletic Association, can provide information for the child with a limb deficiency (Dodds, 1992; Peoples, 1989).

Therapy

The child with a limb deficiency will require physical and/or occupational therapy periodically throughout their growing years. The primary concern for the therapist is to help the child be functional and develop as normally as possible.

The infant with a limb deficiency should be seen by a physical therapist or an occupational therapist shortly after birth. Parents can begin learning ways to help the baby compensate for limb absences. Extremity losses affect the early motor development of trunk control, balance, protective reactions, and mobility skills. The therapist will help the child gain motor skills by facilitating movement, using adapted equipment, using prosthetics, or doing all three.

A baby with an upper-extremity loss will usually be fitted with a passive hand at least by 3 months of age. It is extremely important to start early because motor skills (such as prone propping, bilateral hand play, eye-hand coordination, and the development of symmetry and midline play) begin early.

The baby with a lower-extremity absence should also be fitted early with a prosthesis. If the loss is very high-level, the child may require a prosthesis for sitting balance or to provide a symmetrical base for sitting. Thus, it is usually beneficial to have a lower-extremity prosthesis by the time a child is sitting independently. The child must at least have a prosthesis once he or she is ready to pull to standing. Early prosthetic fit helps to promote continued prosthetic use and helps children incorporate the prosthesis into their body image.

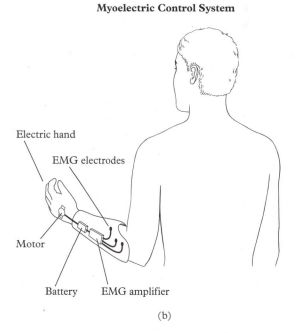

■ **FIGURE 13-7** Types of control options for prosthetic devices

Source: From *Clinical Prosthetics & Orthotics, 10* (2), 57–65. Copyright © 1986 Journal of Prosthetics & Orthotics. Reprinted with permission.

The child is encouraged to use the residual limb as much as possible. Therapy may also focus on gaining motion and strength to increase function. As the child grows and develops, age-appropriate skills are addressed. Additional components of the prosthesis are added as the child has the cognitive and motor abilities to control them. Between the ages of 1 and 2 years, the young child with an upper-extremity limb deficiency should be able to learn to control a terminal device. If the limb deficiency is above the elbow, the child must also learn to control an elbow joint, probably by about the age of 3 years.

The child with an above-knee prosthesis who is just learning to stand and walk will not initially have a knee joint. This will be added as the child gains balance and the ability to control the knees. The therapist and prosthetists working together can move the child through stages of greater independence and more normalized functioning.

The therapists should help parents find or adapt equipment, such as tricycles. Therapy will include practice in daily living activities, with special emphasis on eating, dressing, and toileting for the child with an upper-extremity limb deficiency. Putting on, taking off, and caring for the prosthesis, as well as monitoring skin status, must be learned.

Psychological Concerns

Both child and family will have feelings of loss with a limb deficiency. The parents of a child with a congenital limb deficiency are faced with feelings of guilt and sadness over not having the perfect baby. The child will notice that he or she is different and may have to endure teasing at school. The child with an acquired limb deficiency has the additional adjustment of losing what they once had. The biggest problem that the child with a limb deficiency may have is the attitudes of others.

Support groups are excellent for helping both the child and the family adjust to the deficiency. Regular attendance at a multidisciplinary clinic also provides the family and child with access to a team of professionals who are knowledgeable about limb deficiencies, available resources, and the problems the child is facing (Friedmann, 1978; Galway, 1981).

EDUCATIONAL IMPLICATIONS OF LIMB DEFICIENCIES

It is imperative that the teacher be knowledgeable about the student's condition and abilities in order for the child to successfully function in school. Because many of the children with limb deficiencies will use adaptive equipment, prosthetics, and alternative methods for performing skills, the teacher should have ongoing communication with a key person on the comprehensive medical team. The teacher should be aware of planned surgeries or prosthetic changes so that educational plans can be made.

Meeting Physical and Sensory Needs

The student who has adequate medical management should have devices or prostheses that help him or her function independently. As the child is learning to master the use of a device, some accommodations may be needed in the classroom, such as reducing the amount of written work or allowing additional time for self-care activities. The teacher should know the correct use of a child's device and also what assistance is needed. Again, communication with the team is vital. The teacher also has valuable information to send back to the team about how successfully a device is being used and about which functions the child still cannot perform independently. The team, although knowledgeable about the child and the treatment, sees the child in an isolated environment. The teacher can provide a more complete picture of the child's functioning.

The teacher should be aware of how the prosthetic device works and fits. He or she may be the first to note a change in gait or to see patterns that might signal a problem with the prosthesis. The child's physical therapist or occupational therapist is a good resource to help solve problems in the classroom.

If the prosthesis is removed sometime during the day, the teacher should help the child check for reddened areas that may signal skin irritation and may be indicators of skin breakdown. In general, any red mark that does not go away in 20 to 30 minutes is cause for concern.

The child's mobility may be different, depending on location and distance. Extra time may be required for changing classes. A backpack is usually adequate for carrying books, but some children may need to have one set of their books in each class and another set at home. Some children with lower-extremity limb deficiencies may always walk; others may use a wheelchair for covering distances. Sometimes, children may only need a wheelchair for community outings. The teacher should be aware of this and make sure that the wheelchair is available when needed. The physical therapist or parent should be contacted if there is a problem with the wheelchair; a seat belt should always be used.

The child may require adaptations for playground use and for physical education. The physical therapist, occupational therapist, or adaptive physical education teacher should be able to find appropriate ways for the child to participate in these activities. Safety is an issue for a child with bilateral upper-extremity limb deficiency, and protective head gear may be needed at times.

Children with amelia or phocomelia will need to be watched to make sure they do not get overheated. They should dress lightly and drink plenty of fluids. The child with significant involvement may require a special desk and chair for best positioning. Assistance with transfers may be needed for changing positions or moving from one seat to another. The teacher should have instruction in how to perform the transfer as well as in appropriate body mechanics and techniques.

If it appears that the child is not receiving adequate comprehensive management, the teacher should be aware of the local resources available and should inform and encourage the parents to seek out services. If funding is an issue, the school's counselor or clinic's social worker should be contacted for assistance.

Meeting Communication Needs

The child with a limb deficiency does not usually have problems with communication unless there are additional neurological or other problems. The child with a limb deficiency usually has normal intelligence. However, in some circumstances the child may need to explain his or her limb deficiency or the prothesis. The child could say, "My prosthesis helps me do things with two arms like you do, but I can also do things without my prosthesis. Sometimes I can work better with it, and sometimes I can work better without it."

Meeting Learning Needs

The curriculum material should be based on the cognitive, not the physical, abilities of the student with a limb

■ **FIGURE 13-9** Individual with limb deficiencies using her feet to type on the computer

deficiency, but performance expectations may have to be altered due to ability and speed.

For children with only lower-extremity deficiencies, the problems will be primarily with mobility and physical activities. However, it is very likely that they will undergo several surgical procedures that interrupt the educational process. The teacher should be aware of significant time lost in previous years as well as current and future plans. Hospital or home-bound instruction may be necessary.

The child with an upper-extremity limb deficiency will have prosthetics, adaptive equipment, or both. The occupational therapist should be very involved with the child in the classroom and should help find ways for the child to compensate independently. For very mild limb deficiencies, such as a few fingers missing, the child may need to adapt how she holds a pencil or picks up items (see Figure 13-8). For individuals with more severe limb deficiencies, writing may or may not be feasible, and a computer or tape recorder may be needed. Children with short arms may need a very high desk; extensions or holders may be useful for pencils, crayons, paint brushes, and so forth. Many adaptive devices can provide a boost to independence. Switches, dycem, clipboards, page turners, and Velcro are but a few.

Some children with upper-extremity limb deficiencies will use mouthsticks or their feet for fine motor skills (see Figure 13-9). If this is the method of choice by the child and team it should be allowed in the classroom. This may present a challenge to the teacher with regard to seating, table or desk work space, and social acceptability. A discussion of why the child is using this alternate method and a time for classmates to try it may help. It is important for the child's educational outcome

■ **FIGURE 13-8** Student who has missing fingers adapts how to pick up puzzle pieces

and self-esteem that everything possible be tried so that the child can participate in as many classroom activities as possible.

The adolescent with a limb deficiency will need help in vocational and career planning. Talking with adults with limb deficiencies in the work force may be beneficial.

Meeting Daily Living Needs

Toileting, dressing, and eating may be real challenges for the child with a limb deficiency. Clothing should be loose and easy to put on. Velcro, button aids, and zipper assists may be needed. An adapted toilet and a method for transferring to it may be needed by the severely affected child. Sometimes, these children will simply need someone else to assist them physically. Adapted utensils and seating are often necessary for eating. The occupational and physical therapists will be involved in finding ways to help these students perform daily living skills as independently as possible.

■ FIGURE 13-10 Student repairing his leg prosthesis

■ VIGNETTE 1 ■

Jenny is a 5-year-old girl with bilateral upper-extremity phocomelia who just started kindergarten. She is in a regular classroom and receives additional instruction from a teacher certified in orthopedic impairments. Jenny did not attend preschool and has been very protected and sheltered by her family. Jenny is actually quite functional with her right residual arm. The other arm is very short, and a lengthening procedure has been discussed to make it more functional. Jenny can do many things with her right arm with adaptations. She must have her desk very high, and she frequently uses her mouth as an assist. Because of this, Jenny looks very different, and the other children have not accepted her well. As Jenny has had little social experience, she also does not know how to interact with them. To help address this problem, the educational team decided to have a person come to the classroom to do a special presentation on disabilities. Jenny also received social skills training and was encouraged to bring in some special games for playtime that the other children enjoyed. The teacher also began pairing students to do projects together, and Jenny enrolled in the after-school soccer program. These strategies assisted Jenny in making friends and fostered appropriate social interactions between Jenny and the other children.

A part of the student's daily life will be to manage and care for the stump and prosthesis. Minor repairs may be needed, and these should be checked by the physical therapist (see Figure 13-10).

Meeting Behavioral and Social Needs

By school age, the child with a limb deficiency is very aware of the fact that he or she is different. Friedmann (1978) states that "the disability entailed by amputation . . . is far more the result of individual and social attitudes than it is with loss of function" (p. 17). The child will be influenced by the family's attitudes toward his or her residual limb and the prosthesis. It may improve peer acceptance to have a time in class for the child with a limb deficiency to show his or her stump and the prosthesis and explain how it works (Peregrine, 1992), if the child is willing and able to do so. Support groups are invaluable for helping children accept and adjust to a limb loss.

The family may have greatly overprotected and coddled the child with a limb deficiency. This may create

■ VIGNETTE 2 ■

Tani is a 10-year-old boy who acquired a double amputation after falling on a live high-voltage power line when he was 5. The current entered and exited through his hands. Tani has two myoelectric prostheses but cannot put them on himself. Tani can actually do many things with his toes but is reluctant to do this at school. He can feed himself but has problems with cutting. He is also slow with eating. He is nearly totally dependent with dressing. His occupational therapist is working with him on this. Tani uses a tape recorder and adapted computer with switch access for most of his class work. Tani had been a very withdrawn child until this year, frequently daydreaming in class. He was often frustrated with school work because of the effort it took him and his slow speed. His teacher this year began asking what Tani was thinking about when he was not doing his work. She found out that he created elaborate stories in his head. She began giving Tani some alternate assignments, letting him dictate his stories into a voice-activated tape player. Depending on the lesson of the day, he is asked to use certain vocabulary words, geographical or historical information, or grammatical usage in the stories. Students in the secretarial vocational program at the local high school transcribe the stories. The teacher asked a few high school art students to illustrate some of the stories. The stories are now available for Tani's classmates to read, and they have enjoyed them. Tani has been very proud of his work and their acceptance, and he has become more social. Because of this teacher's creativity and willingness to try a different way, Tani is now succeeding in school and learning to like himself, too.

behavioral problems, especially in the early years of school. A coordinated plan worked out with the family and team can help.

The child should be encouraged to participate in a variety of activities, including art, music, sports, and social functions. Sports are an excellent activity to boost a child's self-esteem and promote physical development. The child should be encouraged to choose an interesting activity and pursue it.

SUMMARY

In this chapter, we have discussed the variety of conditions included in the category of limb deficiency. There is tremendous variability in the abilities of children with limb deficiencies; most are more limited by attitudes and ignorance of resources and technology than by the actual limb deficiency. The child with a limb deficiency should be seen regularly by a comprehensive team of professionals who specialize in this diagnosis. The teacher must communicate regularly with the team members if the child is to be optimally successful in school. Surgeries, prosthetics, therapy, and adaptive equipment are treatment options. Creative problem solving and persistence are keys to helping the child with a limb deficiency be as independent as possible.

CHAPTER 14

Juvenile Rheumatoid Arthritis

Juvenile rheumatoid arthritis (JRA) is a chronic arthritic condition that is present in a child or adolescent before the age of 16 years. Although arthritis is typically considered to be a disease of older adults, it is a major source of disability in children and adolescents. Approximately 250,000 children are afflicted with this disease (Behrman, 1992). Juvenile rheumatoid arthritis can cause significant musculoskeletal changes, deformities, and pain, all of which can negatively affect a child's classroom performance. Additional disabilities affecting the visual and auditory systems may also be present. Because this disease is often not readily apparent, the severity and the impact of the disease may be misunderstood. If this occurs, the resulting lack of adaptations and modifications may adversely affect the student's school performance.

Although the term *juvenile rheumatoid arthritis* may give the impression that it is one disease with one set of characteristics, it actually consists of several different subtypes with different characteristics, treatments, and prognoses. Controversy exists, as it has for almost 100 years in the study of arthritis and other rheumatoid disorders, over the exact nomenclature to use and classification system to adopt (Laxer, 1993). Terms that may be encountered include *juvenile arthritis* (JA), *juvenile chronic arthritis* (JCA), and *juvenile chronic polyarthritis* (JCP). Each of these refers to chronic rheumatoid arthritis in children but can differ as to the inclusion of various subtypes.

Although we will not discuss the arguments about nomenclature and categorization in this chapter, we will provide a framework for understanding the major subtypes, and we will also provide information about the characteristics, treatment, and educational implications of juvenile rheumatoid arthritis.

DESCRIPTION OF JUVENILE RHEUMATOID ARTHRITIS (JRA)

The term *arthritis* is taken from the root *arthro*, meaning "joint," and *itis*, meaning "inflammation." Juvenile arthritis refers to chronic joint **inflammation** beginning before the age of 16 years, which may be associated with additional inflammatory manifestation affecting other areas as well (Behrman, 1992). The term *juvenile rheumatoid arthritis* has been used primarily in the United States and includes the major subtypes of *polyarticular, pauciarticular,* and *systemic* arthritis (see Box 14-1). *Polyarthritis* refers to juvenile rheumatoid arthritis that involves five or more joints. *Pauciarticular juvenile rheumatoid arthritis* refers to arthritis in less than five joints. *Systemic juvenile rheumatoid arthritis* refers to a generalized body (systemic) response involving multiple joints.

Other terminology may include additional subtypes. *Juvenile chronic arthritis* is a European term that includes the same subtypes as juvenile rheumatoid arthritis but also includes arthritis of inflammatory bowel disease, psoriasis (a chronic skin disorder), and ankylosing spondylitis (an arthritislike condition involving the spine and peripheral joints) in the classification scheme (Laxer, 1993). An even more inclusive term is *juvenile arthritis,* which is beginning to gain popularity in this country because the term *rheumatoid* in *juvenile rheumatoid arthritis* is inaccurate, since not all forms of juvenile arthritis are associated with a rheumatoid factor in the blood. The term *juvenile arthritis* also includes other subtypes such as *septic arthritis.* Proponents of this term believe it is the best inclusive descriptor for all types of chronic arthritis in children. However, others view it as overly inclusive and think it fosters ambiguity by including subtypes that do not belong (Laxer, 1993; Siegel &

BOX 14-1

Major Types of Juvenile Rheumatoid Arthritis

Systemic (generalized body response)
Polyarthritis (involves five or more joints)
Pauciarticular (involves fewer than five joints)

Baum, 1993). Regardless of the terminology and subtype debate, this book will treat juvenile rheumatoid arthritis as including the three major subtypes because this terminology now predominates in this county.

ETIOLOGY OF JUVENILE RHEUMATOID ARTHRITIS

The precise etiology of juvenile rheumatoid arthritis is unknown, but there are several hypotheses about this; one hypothesis suggests that there may be an immunological basis for the disease (Yoshino, 1993). In this hypothesis, the body reacts to an unknown stimulus, and **antibodies** whose function is to destroy bacteria and viruses begin to attack normal cells. This is called an *autoimmune* response. Support for this hypothesis was provided by the discovery of rheumatoid factors—a certain type of antibodies—in some individuals with juvenile rheumatoid arthritis. The rheumatoid factors may play a part in the inflammatory process involved in juvenile rheumatoid arthritis; these factors are considered to be immunologically based. However, the exact role and etiology of the factors are not clear, and they are not always present in individuals with juvenile rheumatoid arthritis (Moore & Dorner, 1993). (Because the rheumatoid factor is only present in some children with JRA, the use of the term *rheumatoid* in *juvenile rheumatoid arthritis* is considered to be inaccurate by some researchers.)

Another hypothesis is that the disease is caused by an unidentified microorganism. Support for this hypothesis is provided by the fact that some types of the disease are caused by infectious agents like the one causing Lyme disease. Also, infection by other microorganisms can result in inflammation of the joints (Behrman, 1992).

Individuals with juvenile rheumatoid arthritis are thought to have a genetic predisposition to the disease; often there is a family history of it. Genetic markers have been found in individuals with juvenile rheumatoid arthritis, although not in all cases. This finding has provided information and has stimulated discussions regarding etiology and the construction of a new classification system (Scholz & Albert, 1993).

DYNAMICS OF JUVENILE RHEUMATOID ARTHRITIS

The human body is composed of more than 500 joints. A joint is the area in which two or more bones of the skeleton come together. Some of these joints may normally have limited or no range of movement, such as those between the bones of the skull or between the vertebrae. Other joints may be freely movable, such as those in the knees and elbows. These are known as *synovial* or *diarthrodial joints*. They have two bone ends that come together with a space between them known as a *joint space* (see Figure 14-1). The ends of the bones have cartilage on them (known as **articular** cartilage) and have joint fluid in between. This type of joint is surrounded by a *synovial lining* (synovium) that secretes joint fluid and contains it within the joint. Surrounding the synovial lining is connective tissue containing blood vessels. This whole, encased joint is known as the *joint capsule*. The synovial joints are affected in juvenile rheumatoid arthritis.

A joint is moved by the contraction of the surrounding muscles. When a muscle contracts, it causes the bone to move. The cartilage layer on the end of the bone glides smoothly over the cartilage surface of the opposing bone. The joint fluid that nourishes the cartilage also serves as a lubricant that facilitates smooth joint motion.

When the joint is injured, an inflammation process begins as part of the body's defense mechanism, and as part of the healing process (Umbreit, 1983). The

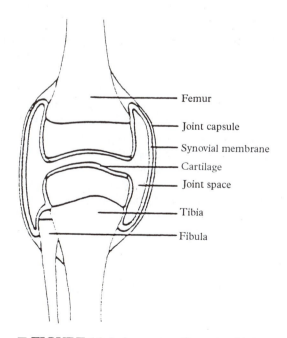

■ **FIGURE 14-1** Anatomy of a normal joint

Femur
Joint capsule
Synovial membrane
Cartilage
Joint space
Tibia
Fibula

inflammation process consists of several subprocesses: (1) dilation of the blood vessels with excess local blood flow, (2) movement of large quantities of fluid to the spaces between the cells, (3) clotting of the fluid in the spaces between the cells, (4) movement of specialized cells into the area, including those that devour destroyed tissues, and (5) swelling (Guyton, 1991). This process is accompanied by pain and stiffness. The individual usually restricts his or her own movement of the joint in a protective manner. As the inflammation process subsides, the specialized cells that devour destroyed tissues may at times further injure the still-living tissue cells.

In arthritis, the inflammation process does not occur because of injury or infection; the causes are unidentified. The inflammation process occurs in the usual manner, with swelling of the joint and infusion of blood cells and plasma. However, the frequency and duration of the inflammation process occurring in the joint means that the inflammation process does not serve a beneficial purpose. Initially, the inflammatory process results in chronic inflammation of the synovium. Over time, projections of thickened synovial membrane form protrusions into the joint space, and synovium may begin to adhere to the articular cartilage. Late in the disease, with continued inflammation and proliferation of the synovium, the articular cartilage and other structures may begin to erode and become damaged (Behrman, 1992). If this occurs, the cartilage on one end of a bone no longer glides smoothly over the cartilage surface of the opposing bone. Joint deformity and impaired movement may occur. This process takes a long time in children, and permanent joint damage only occurs in some of the cases.

Joint abnormalities may also develop because of the child's natural tendency to minimize pain. When a joint is inflamed, moving the joint is painful, so children with a joint abnormality may not fully extend their arms or legs. Contractures may develop that further limit the joint's range of motion and may result in difficulty walking (Alvarez, Espada, Maldonado-Cocco, & Gagliardi, 1992) or reaching. Also, the child may hold an arm or leg in a pain-relieving position, which may result in a change of the position of the joint. The pain-relieving position, initially harmless in appearance, may develop over time into a fixed joint deviation (Truckenbrodt, 1993).

CHARACTERISTICS OF JUVENILE RHEUMATOID ARTHRITIS

Regardless of the type of juvenile rheumatoid arthritis, there are some overall characteristics of the disease. Juvenile rheumatoid arthritis has a pattern of occurring at certain ages, such as between 1 and 3 years of age or between 8 and 12 years of age. It occurs almost twice as frequently in girls as in boys in most subgroups (Cassidy, 1990; Vandvik & Hoyeraal, 1993). When juvenile rheumatoid arthritis is present, four symptoms can occur: (1) stiffness after immobility, (2) pain with joint movement, (3) limitations in joint motion, and (4) in some children, fever. One of the main symptoms of the disease is stiffness. After the child's joint has been inactive for a period of time, such as after sleeping or sitting for a period of time (that is, half an hour to several hours), the joint may become stiff and difficult or painful to move. When the child begins moving the joint, it may loosen up within a few minutes or may take hours to do so.

Pain accompanies the inflammatory process, as it does when inflammation occurs after joint injury. However, in some cases, pain in juvenile rheumatoid arthritis may be underestimated or even missed. How well the child tells about pain depends on the child's developmental level, experience with pain, and individual disposition. The child may not acknowledge the pain verbally at all. Often, nonverbal expressions of pain predominate. The only signs may be an alteration in joint position or abnormal movement patterns upon walking or grasping. The child with juvenile rheumatoid arthritis may express pain by having difficulty sleeping and by crying during the night. The child may be hesitant to walk due to the pain; this has been misinterpreted as laziness (Truckenbrodt, 1993).

Limitations in joint mobility and fever may also occur. Mobility may initially be limited because of muscle spasms, fluid in the joint, and synovial proliferation. Later, joint destruction or muscle contractures may limit mobility (Behrman, 1992). Low-grade or spiking fever may occur as part of the disease and not as a result of a contagious infection.

There are three primary types of juvenile rheumatoid arthritis: (1) *systemic-onset*, (2) *polyarticular*, and (3) *pauciarticular juvenile rheumatoid arthritis*. *Systemic-onset juvenile rheumatoid arthritis* is the most severe and dramatic form of the disease; several symptoms occur throughout the body (and outside the joints). This form occurs in approximately 20% of children with juvenile rheumatoid arthritis and is also known as *Still's disease*. It was named after the physician who first described it (Avery & First, 1994).

Systemic-onset juvenile rheumatoid arthritis often begins before the child is 10 years of age and frequently starts as early as 2 years of age. It starts with a fever that can be as high as 102° to 105° F. Usually, this fever spikes once or twice a day and then returns to normal. During the day when the fever occurs, the child may seem very ill; later in the day when the fever is absent, the child may seem very healthy. This pattern can continue for months, stop for a period of time, then begin again. This may continue for years. Although the fever can be quite high, febrile seizures rarely occur. However, a pink rash may appear on the chest, arms, legs, and occasionally the face; the liver and spleen may be enlarged. Weight loss and decreased appetite may occur. Although rare, heart (pericarditis) and lung (pleuritis) involvement may occur, requiring rigorous intervention. Joint involvement may be present from the very beginning, or it may take several months to develop. Occasionally, this may result in misdiagnosis. Once diagnosed, the involvement of bodily systems may overshadow the joint involvement. Eventually, children with systemic-onset JRA will have characteristics similar to those with polyarticular disease (Siegel & Baum, 1993). Rheumatic factor is not usually present in systemic-onset juvenile rheumatoid arthritis (Berkow, 1992).

Polyarticular juvenile rheumatoid arthritis is characterized by the involvement of five or more joints. Approximately 30% of children have this form of the disease (Avery & First, 1994). It consists of two main subgroups: *rheumatoid factor-negative polyarthritis* and *rheumatoid-positive polyarthritis*. The presence or absence of the rheumatoid factor determines the type. Children with rheumatoid factor-negative disease could have onset of the disease at any time during childhood. The disease is usually mild. Those who are diagnosed with rheumatoid-positive polyarthritis usually have onset late in childhood with more severe symptoms (Behrman, 1992).

In polyarticular juvenile rheumatoid arthritis, any joint in the body may be affected. Affected joints may slowly or suddenly develop swelling, stiffness, and loss of motion. Often, this type of the disease begins around age 2 years or older. Small joints of the hand, as well as larger joints of the knee and hip, may be involved. Hip involvement occurs in about one-half of the children with polyarthritis. When the hip is involved, walking may be painful or difficult. Involvement of the hand may result in difficulty grasping. Occasionally, a claw hand deformity occurs in which the fingers are stiffened (Siegel & Baum, 1993). The cervical vertebrae (especially C2 and C3) may also be involved, presenting with restricted neck movement. Although not as severe as in systemic-onset JRA, there may be involvement outside the joint, such as a mild fever, an aching feeling all over the body (**malaise**), an enlarged liver and spleen, and some growth retardation (Behrman, 1992).

In pauciarticular arthritis, fewer than five joints are involved. This is the most common type of juvenile rheumatoid arthritis; approximately 40–55% of children have this form of the disease (Avery & First, 1994).

Pauciarticular arthritis has been categorized as having two or three different subtypes. Those category systems with three subtypes include *females with antinuclear antibody (ANA) position, males with HLA-B27 position,* and *early-onset pauciarticular rheumatoid arthritis.* Those with a two-category system include early onset within the other two divisions.

The most common subtype is the female with ANA, which occurs in girls usually younger than 4 years of age (Siegel & Baum, 1993). In this subtype, the most frequently involved joints are the knees, ankles, and elbows, although single toes or fingers, wrist, neck, or jaw may occasionally be affected. Usually, there is no hip involvement. Boys with HLA-B27 subtype often have onset after 8 years of age. In this subtype, large joints are also primarily affected, but those of the legs are usually affected most, including the hip and girdle area (Behrman, 1992). Those cases falling under the early-onset subtype have symptoms early and have similar types of joint involvement but are not associated with ANA or HLA-B27. The course of pauciarticular arthritis, especially the early-onset type, has been found to vary. Disease may occur with an intermittent pattern of symptoms, or a continuous pattern may be present (Cate, de Vries-van-der Vlugt, vanSuijlekom-Smit, & Cats, 1992).

Children with pauciarticular arthritis are especially at-risk for additional complications affecting sensory systems. One of these is *iridocyclitis,* which occurs in the female with ANA subtype at a rate of about 10%. Iridocyclitis is an inflammation of the iris and choroid of the eye. When iridocyclitis occurs, initial symptoms may be pain, sensitivity to light, or decreased visual acuity. Complications such as cataracts (Fox, Flynn, Davis, & Culbertson, 1992), glaucoma, and degeneration of the globe of the eye can occur. In very severe cases, permanent blindness may result. Eye examinations are indicated 3 to 4 times a year for the first 5 years of the disease in children with pauciarticular JRA. Although this happens rarely, sensorineural hearing loss has been reported in an adolescent with pauciarticular JRA (Dekker & Isdale, 1992).

Other complications of pauciarticular arthritis may occur, especially in boys with HLA-B27 subtype. This includes *spondyloarthropathy,* which is a disease of the joints of the spine. Measurements of back flexion should be monitored for this complication (Behrman, 1992).

The severity of JRA varies greatly across individuals, depending on the type of JRA, which joints are involved, and whether or not there has been joint destruction. The functional status of the child should be assessed in order to determine severity. One instrument, known as the Child Health Assessment Questionnaire (Child HAQ), provides information as to the type of juvenile rheumatoid arthritis, the status of the disease (active or stable), and the functional class. The functional classification system is based on Steinbrocker's work and provides a useful classification system for determining the effect of the disease. This functional classification system includes dressing, getting up, eating, walking, washing, reaching, gripping, and other activities. The ratings of these functions are factored into determining the four functional classes. In Class I, children have complete functional capacity. In Class II, functional capability is adequate for normal activities, although discomfort and limited joint mobility are present. In Class III, functional capability is limited; only a few daily activities or self-care procedures can be performed. In Class IV, the person often needs a wheelchair for mobility or is confined to bed (Gare, Fasth, & Wiklund, 1993). A student's classification can be determined through such assessment instruments as presented in Figure 14-2.

DETECTION OF JUVENILE RHEUMATOID ARTHRITIS

There are no specific diagnostic tests for juvenile rheumatoid arthritis. Diagnosis usually depends on (1) a child being under 16 years of age, (2) persistence of symptoms for a specified length of time, such as 3 consecutive months, and (3) ruling out other diseases (Behrman, 1992). If the child is over 16 years of age, other diseases will be investigated. Since part of the diagnosis depends on the continuation of symptoms over a period of time, waiting may be part of the diagnostic process. It may appear that nothing is being done, so the importance of waiting should be stressed to parents, who may think that medical personnel are unresponsive to their concerns.

Several other diseases may have symptoms similar to those in juvenile rheumatoid arthritis, especially the systemic type. These include such diseases as systemic lupus, Lyme disease, rheumatic fever, trauma, Legg-Calve-Perthes disease, **sickle-cell anemia,** and acute **leukemia** (Siegel & Baum, 1993). Part of the diagnosis of juvenile rheumatoid arthritis will be to rule out these and other diseases. The child's medical history, physical examination, and laboratory tests will aid in the diagnosis. Possible laboratory tests include white blood cell counts, hemoglobin and platelet levels, the presence of rheumatoid factor, the presence of ANA, and a complete blood count. Other tests such as X-rays or a biopsy of the synovial lining and fluid may be done to give further information. Additional tests, specific to the other suspected diseases, should be performed to arrive at an accurate diagnosis. Diagnosis of a particular type of juvenile rheumatoid arthritis will also include a history, physical examination, and diagnostic tests. Once the

diagnosis is made, other tests to determine systemic involvement will be performed. Ultrasound, CAT scans, or MRI scans may be used.

TREATMENT OF JUVENILE RHEUMATOID ARTHRITIS

Although juvenile rheumatoid arthritis may resolve itself over time, there is currently no cure for the disease. Treatment goals include (1) reducing and suppressing chronic inflammation that can cause destruction of the joint cartilage, (2) relieving pain, (3) controlling the systemic effects of inflammation (for example, growth retardation and eye complications), and (4) preventing contractures and deformities (Rose & Doughty, 1992). There are several medications that may be prescribed to reduce inflammation and relieve pain. The most common are anti-inflammatory drugs such as aspirin. Although aspirin is commonly used to alleviate arthritic and systemic manifestations, it should be carefully monitored for adverse reactions. Stomach inflammation (which results in poor eating habits, abdominal pain, diarrhea, or gastrointestinal bleeding) or Reye's syndrome (which results in neurological symptoms), are possible reactions (Rose & Doughty, 1992). Several other medications have been prescribed (such as corticosteroids, methotrexate, gold salts, sulfasalazine, penicillamine, immunosuppressants, and gammaglobulin) with varying results (Rooney, 1992; Rose & Doughty, 1992). Also, heat treatment programs may be used on the joints.

Pain may be controlled with medication, but additional treatments may also be used. Cognitive behavior therapy techniques may be used as an adjunct to medication to assist with pain management. One primary type of cognitive-behavioral treatment for chronic pain in juvenile rheumatoid arthritis is the modification of pain perception through self-regulatory techniques such as muscle relaxation, meditative breathing, and guided imagery. The other primary type is pain behavior modification, which modifies socioenvironmental factors that may influence pain (Varni, 1992).

Controlling the systemic effects of juvenile rheumatoid arthritis involves screening and monitoring for additional effects such as eye involvement. Ophthalmological screening should be performed as soon as possible after a diagnosis of arthritis because the child is at-risk for iridocyclitis. If that condition is detected, appropriate and prompt treatment should be implemented. Systemic, topical, or injectable steroids are often used. If iridocyclitis is not detected, screening should continue every 3 to 4 months for those at high risk, such as children with pauciarticular arthritis

Activities	Date Examined					
Dressing: Fastening buttons Putting on pullover Putting on shirt with buttons Putting on/taking off pants Pulling on/taking off socks Putting on/taking off shoes						
Personal hygiene: Washing hands Washing face Wringing a towel Trimming nails Combing hair Taking a bath Washing body Shampooing hair Toileting						
General hand activities: Using chopsticks Using a spoon Using cup with one hand Filling kettle Handwriting						
Mobility: Getting into/out of bed Getting into/out of chair Walking Walking up/down stairs Standing on tiptoes Sitting with thrown-out legs Sitting straight Standing up from sitting position Stooping down to pick up Running						

Please give points to each activity as follows:

3 points: you can do it by yourself perfectly.

2 points: you can do it by yourself but not perfectly.

1 point: you need help to do the activity.

0 points: you cannot do it at all.

■ **FIGURE 14-2** Self-assessment of activities of daily life

SOURCE: From "Quality of Life and Daily Management of Children with Rheumatic Disease," by S. Takei and M. Hokonohara, 1993, *Acta Paediatrica Japonica, 35,* 454–463. Copyright © 1993 Blackwell Scientific Publications. Reprinted with permission.

or children with polyarticular arthritis under 7 years of age and positive ANA titers. Those at low risk, such as children with systemic juvenile rheumatoid arthritis, should be evaluated once a year for the first 4 to 5 years after the onset of arthritis (Rheumatology and Ophthalmology Executive Committee, 1993; Southwood & Ryder, 1992).

To decrease the risk of contractures, physical therapy and occupational therapy may be prescribed. These therapies will help maintain the child's ability to perform certain activities and functions (Schaller, 1993). Physical therapy, in particular, is a priority for all types of juvenile rheumatoid arthritis because it improves the range of motion of the joints, increases muscle power, reduces pain, and restores and maintains functional capabilities (Siegel & Baum, 1993). If there is hip involvement, additional treatments may be indicated, such as supportive aids for walking, traction during the evening, or hydrotherapy—therapy implemented in the water (Jacobsen, Crawford, & Broste, 1992). Depending on the severity of involvement and complications of the joints, surgery (such as joint replacement) may be indicated to correct joint deformities.

COURSE OF JUVENILE RHEUMATOID ARTHRITIS

Over time, juvenile rheumatoid arthritis may progress, stabilize, or go into remission. In 1983 in Moscow, a committee on pediatric rheumatology provided the following guidelines for determining the activity of the disease. Juvenile rheumatoid arthritis is *active* if an increasing number of joints become affected while the child is receiving drug therapy. Juvenile rheumatoid arthritis is *stable* if there is no increase in the number of joints involved, but drug therapy is required. Juvenile rheumatoid arthritis is classified as *inactive* if there is no active inflammation of the synovium or other structures without drugs for less than 2 years. Juvenile rheumatoid arthritis is considered to be in **remission** if there is no evidence of joint inflammation or other symptoms outside the joint without drug treatment for more than 2 years (Gare, Fasth, & Wiklund, 1993).

Approximately 75% of individuals with juvenile rheumatoid arthritis have been found to eventually go into long-term remission without significant deformity or loss of function (Avery & First, 1994). However, in some cases, juvenile rheumatoid arthritis can relapse in adult life or may continue to progress without going into remission. Despite treatment, some individuals may have permanent joint damage. If hip joints are affected, for example, this could negatively affect functioning (Jacobsen, Crawford, & Broste, 1992). Other complications, such as those affecting the eye, may result in loss of vision.

EDUCATIONAL IMPLICATIONS OF JUVENILE RHEUMATOID ARTHRITIS

Students with juvenile rheumatoid arthritis often appear very healthy, but this appearance can be misleading and result in misunderstandings. Pain, stiffness, and joint immobility can affect these students' educational performance. Teachers must have an understanding of the disease and of the adaptations the student may need in order for him or her to succeed in school.

Meeting Physical and Sensory Needs

Students with juvenile rheumatoid arthritis may be confronted by several problems in school that should be identified and remediated by the teacher. Some physical issues include dealing with stiffness and/or pain, medication schedules, and lack of stamina (Taylor, Passo, & Champion, 1987). The longer a student sits, the more likely he or she is to experience stiffness and pain with movement. After a few minutes of movement, the stiffness and pain usually decrease or dissipate, and movement is much more free. Misunderstanding can occur when a teacher sees a student moving slowly and painfully, and then later sees the student running around as if nothing had happened. Teachers should understand how stiffness and pain may only be present after periods of immobility. A good understanding of juvenile rheumatoid arthritis will prevent unnecessary misunderstandings. To help decrease the effects of prolonged sitting, the teacher may allow the student to stand for 15 or 20 minutes in the middle of the class period and work at a desklike surface (Umbreit, 1983). Allowing for frequent movement during class may also be beneficial; this prevents "gelling" or stiffness of the joints. Changing classes may take longer because the initial stiffness and pain can result in slower movements. Once again, it is important to inform all the student's teachers about the effects of juvenile rheumatoid arthritis. For example, a teacher may not understand why it takes a boy so long to get to class when, by the time he arrives, he looks fine and is moving well. In severe cases, the student may need a modified school day. Some students may have such severe early morning stiffness that they need to attend school later in the morning.

Students with juvenile rheumatoid arthritis may take several medications during the day. Teachers need to be aware that certain medication (such as nonsteroidal anti-inflammatory medication) should be taken after meals to avoid adverse effects on the gastrointestinal tract. Other medications should be taken with small snacks (Takei & Hokonohara, 1993). In one study (Taylor, Passo, & Champion, 1987), teachers found it more difficult to schedule medication for those students with milder JRA than for those with more severe forms.

This finding suggests that teachers had more difficulty making concessions when the disease was not readily apparent. Education of school personnel is needed in these situations. Another lack of understanding of the disease occurs when students with juvenile rheumatoid arthritis are sent home when they have a fever. Fever is a symptom of juvenile rheumatoid arthritis and does not indicate an infectious disease. Children with juvenile rheumatoid arthritis should not usually be sent home because of a fever unless there are other symptoms indicating an infection.

Students with juvenile rheumatoid arthritis may lack stamina and may tire easily, making it difficult for the student to perform a task or concentrate on difficult subject material. More difficult subjects may need to be scheduled earlier in the day when the student is freshest. juvenile rheumatoid arthritis may be exacerbated by increased physical and emotional fatigue. Some students may need to take a nap or rest in the nurse's office during the day (Takei & Hokonohara, 1993).

The teacher should be alert for any indications of a visual problem. If a visual impairment is suspected, the teacher should notify the parents. If a visual impairment is diagnosed, the teacher should work closely with the teacher who specializes in educating students with visual impairments to determine appropriate modifications, additional instruction, or both, for the student.

Other considerations include the need for the student to have well-balanced and high-calorie meals because of their increased metabolic needs and pain. Occasionally, nutritional supplements may be prescribed to ensure adequate caloric intake (Takei & Hokonohara, 1993). The teacher should be alert as to how well the student is eating and report any change in appetite.

Certain adaptations may be needed to accommodate the student with juvenile rheumatoid arthritis. Because of joint damage or joint pain, modified physical education that limits strenuous games in which extended pressure is placed on the joints or limits the amount of running may be needed. A modified physical education program would take a student's tolerance for exercise into account, as well as his or her use of upper and lower extremities. Table 14-1 contains a classification of physical education exercises for children with juvenile rheumatoid arthritis.

Meeting Communication Needs

Although children with juvenile rheumatoid arthritis have no difficulties in verbalization, they may have difficulty expressing whether or not they are in pain. Pain occurs physiologically in children the same way it does in adults, but the perception of pain is a subjective, emotional, and an individual sensation. Children's development, emotional experiences, and former pain experiences all play a role in how children understand and interpret pain. The presence of pain may not be expressed verbally, and pain perception may vary (Truckenbrodt, 1993). The teacher should be alert for nonverbal signs of pain, such as a lack of movement of a limb, holding a limb in a certain position, or hesitancy in moving about.

Students with juvenile rheumatoid arthritis may have difficulty explaining to peers about the disease, especially when they do not appear to have anything physically wrong with them. Children with juvenile rheumatoid arthritis may say, "I have children's arthritis. That means my joints hurt me sometimes. I sometimes have to move slowly when I haven't moved around much."

Meeting Learning Needs

Students' learning may be adversely affected by juvenile rheumatoid arthritis. Students with juvenile rheumatoid arthritis may be in pain, which interferes with concentration and productivity at school. Also, fatigue and lack of stamina may affect the students' performance. This is sometimes compounded by a lack of sleep brought about by the pain and discomfort of the disease.

Teachers should understand this disease process and realize that the student's academic performance may vary on a daily basis, depending on how he or she is feeling that day. Although no cognitive deficits are associated with this disease, as is true with other chronic illnesses, students' performance may still be adversely affected. As we discussed earlier, scheduling more difficult subjects early in the day may be easier for the student; breaks may be needed as well.

Meeting Daily Living Needs

Students should be encouraged to perform daily living skills independently as much as possible. Students who are mildly affected with juvenile rheumatoid arthritis may require no modifications or may require a longer period of time to complete some tasks. However, for some students who are severely affected, adaptations may be needed. These may include using adaptive tools that help compensate for limited range of motion of the joint. Examples of adapted tools include such items as long-handled reachers to retrieve items out of reach, adapted pencils, adapted spoons, long shoe horns, and sock aids (see Figure 14-3). Door handles and faucets with levers on them are easier for students to manage when their arms and fingers are affected. An adapted toilet with a raised seat and a grab bar may be needed for students with hip involvement. When possible, some students may need to have their classes or rooms on the

TABLE 14-1

Classification of Physical Education Exercises for Children with Juvenile Rheumatoid Arthritis

		Upper limbs		
		Light exercise	Moderate exercise	Heavy exercise
Lower limbs	Light exercise	Gymnastic exercise (upper body) Jungle gym Swedish bars Slide Seesaw Balance beam Rhythmic walking	Grabbing sticks Rolling a ball	Monkey bars Push-ups
	Moderate exercise	Gymnastic exercise (lower body) Swing Tag Elastic rope jumping Kick ball Exercise using rings Walking in water pool	Various kinds of walking, running, and jumping Rope skipping Hurdle Track relay Picking up stones in water Dodgeball	Horizontal bar Mat exercise Horse
	Heavy exercise	Tag hopping on one leg Light jogging Soccer Jumping rope Rhythmic running or jumping	Fast running Distance race Track relay Water tag Portball	Complete body exercise Varied: rope skipping, horizontal bar, swimming, and horse Pole climbing Sprinting Hurdle Softball Tennis Marathon Soccer Basketball Baseball Sumo

SOURCE: From "Quality of Life and Daily Management of Children with Rheumatic Disease," by S. Takei and M. Hokonohara, 1993, *Acta Paediatrica Japonica, 35,* 454–463. Copyright © 1993 Blackwell Scientific Publications. Reprinted with permission.

first floor if an elevator is not available. Distances between classes should be minimized to decrease the amount of walking. When out in the community, students may need to pace themselves if they are walking long distances.

Meeting Behavioral and Social Needs

Juvenile rheumatoid arthritis may impair a student's mobility and limit his or her ability to join in activities that peers enjoy. Participation in activities that are appropriate to the child's age, and even the joy of movement, may become restricted. Some students with juvenile rheumatoid arthritis are at risk for developing behavioral or psychosocial problems because of the frustrations, limitations, and pain of the disease (Cate et al., 1992; Truckenbrodt, 1993). Additional problems

may arise for the student because of concern over altered body image and impaired peer interaction (Taylor, Passo, & Champion, 1987).

It is important that the teacher be alert for the development of any social or behavioral difficulties and discuss these with the educational team. Modifying activities so the student can participate in them is important. With proper peer education and modifications, the student should be able to participate in and enjoy most activities. If some activities cannot be modified enough, partial participation can usually be achieved, such as by batting the ball while someone else runs. It is always important to emphasize to the student what he or she can, rather than cannot, do. This approach helps improve self-esteem (White & Shear, 1992). The teacher should also promote social interactions between students. This requires using activities

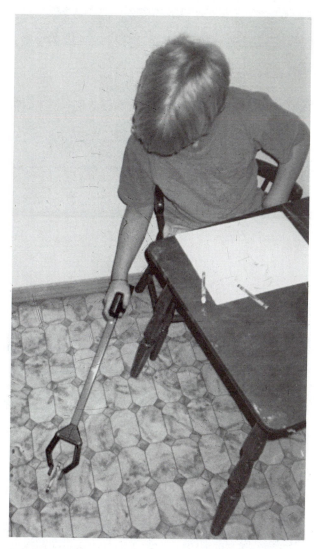

■ **FIGURE 14-3** Student using a long-handled device to pick up a crayon

that require group participation as well as peer education. Exposure to other students with juvenile rheumatoid arthritis is also important. The student then can talk to someone who understands the common frustrations the disease causes. Camps for students with juvenile rheumatoid arthritis can be valuable in this regard. Books with main characters who have physical disabilities can also be beneficial. In some instances,

■ **VIGNETTE** ■

Jake was diagnosed with polyarticular juvenile rheumatoid arthritis when he was 4 years old. He has had severe involvement in several joints, which has caused him pain and stiffness, fatigue, and fever. He is presently 7 years old and in the second grade. He is a very bright student but has difficulty moving about after sitting for extended periods of time. He also feels bad about his inability to play kickball with the other students. To help Jake during the day, he stands to do some of his work during each hour-long class period. He also is given a longer period of time between classes to allow enough time to move as comfortably as possible. Because he becomes fatigued during the late morning, he has a rest break in which he goes to the nurse's office to relax. His teachers have modified games and activities to encourage his participation. Jake, however, has very low self-esteem and appears withdrawn at times. He is presently receiving counseling.

students with juvenile rheumatoid arthritis, as with any other chronic illness, may need counseling to help them with their feelings.

SUMMARY

Juvenile rheumatoid arthritis is a chronic form of arthritis found in children. There are three main types: pauciarticular, polyarticular, and systemic arthritis. Each of these may result in very mild symptoms or in severe physical impairment. One of the main characteristics of juvenile rheumatoid arthritis is joint inflammation that results in painful and stiff joints. A combination of medication, physical therapy, occupational therapy, pain management techniques, surgery, and adaptive devices may be used to treat the disease. Teachers need to have a good understanding of the disease and modify the school environment with such adaptations as extending time limits for completing activities, minimizing periods of immobility, providing rest as needed, and using adapted devices in order to optimize the student's functioning during the school day.

CHAPTER 15

Musculoskeletal Disorders

Several types of musculoskeletal disorders can affect student performance in school, home, and community settings. Two of these are *osteogenesis imperfecta* and *arthrogryposis multiplex congenita*. *Osteogenesis imperfecta* is a disorder in which the bones are brittle and break easily. *Arthrogryposis multiplex congenita* is a disorder in which the child is born with multiple contractures. Although both diseases affect the musculoskeletal system, the diseases do not have similar etiologies, characteristics, treatment, or educational implications.

The teacher will need to have a clear understanding of both conditions and their implications and prognoses in order to be of most help to students with osteogenesis imperfecta or arthrogryposis in the school setting. Because the two conditions are different, we will discuss the etiology, dynamics, characteristics, detection, treatment, and course for osteogenesis imperfecta and arthrogryposis separately.

DESCRIPTION OF OSTEOGENESIS IMPERFECTA (OI)

The term *osteogenesis imperfecta* refers to several inherited conditions that are characterized by excessive bone fragility and deformity. Osteogenesis imperfecta may be accompanied by additional abnormalities of collagen-containing tissues such as the ligaments, tendons, and sclera (white part of the eye). Typically, the sclera appears blue-tinged in color, although there is no visual impairment. In many cases, a conductive hearing loss may be present when the bones in the middle ear are affected (Marion & Hinojosa, 1993).

Several different genetic mutations can occur on select genes and be diagnosed as osteogenesis imperfecta. Because the mutations are different, there is a large variability in the severity of osteogenesis imper-

fecta. For example, when osteogenesis imperfecta occurs in its severest form, death usually occurs in the perinatal period. When it occurs in a milder form, a normal life span usually occurs with a minimal increase in fractures. Fortunately, osteogenesis is a fairly rare condition that occurs in approximately 1 out of every 5,000 to 10,000 individuals (Byers & Steiner, 1992).

ETIOLOGY OF OSTEOGENESIS IMPERFECTA

Osteogenesis imperfecta is inherited and is caused by mutations in either of the two genes (COL1A1 and COL1A2) on chromosomes 17 and 7 (Ross, Laszig, Bornemann, & Ulrich, 1993). The mutation may occur in several places on the two chromosomes, resulting in differing characteristics. This has led to difficulty in classification, because any classification system imposes arbitrary boundaries in a continuum of mutational events (Byers & Steiner, 1992).

In most cases, osteogenesis imperfecta is autosomal-dominant, especially in the mildest forms. The more severe forms of osteogenesis imperfecta are still primarily autosomal-dominant, although an autosomal-recessive trait has been found. As with other conditions, cases have occurred without any clear history, probably due to a spontaneous mutation of the gene.

DYNAMICS OF OSTEOGENESIS IMPERFECTA

Although the exact mechanism is still under investigation, the mutation of either of the two genes resulting in osteogenesis imperfecta has been found to result in defective collagen production or to alter the structure of the collagen molecule (Byers & Steiner, 1992; Willing, Pruchno, Atkinson, & Byers, 1992). Collagen is found throughout the body and is essential to bone formation and bone strength.

Bone is a tough, organic matrix that is primarily composed of collagen fibers. Adhering to the collagen fibers are the bone salts, calcium and phosphate. Collagen fibers and organic salts work together to give strength to the bone, in much the same way that concrete is reinforced. The steel in reinforced concrete provides tensile strength; collagen fibers do this for bone. In reinforced concrete, the cement, rock, and sand provide compressional strength; bone salts do this for bone (Guyton, 1991).

Unlike reinforced concrete, however, bone is not static but is composed of living cells that are constantly changing. New bone is constantly being deposited, while old bone is constantly being reabsorbed. This constant deposition and absorption of bone serves many functions. First, as old bone becomes weak and brittle, new collagen fibers are needed to replace the old matrix as it degenerates. Second, this process allows bones to change their shape and strength in proportion to the amount of stress exerted on them. Bones may actually thicken when exposed to heavy loads or thin out when there is little weight bearing on them.

In osteogenesis imperfecta, the collagen fibers are defective. In addition, there are fewer bone salts (with a lower calcium to phosphate ratio) present in the bone (Cassella & Ali, 1992). This decrease in bone salts is not thought to be due to a defect in their production but in their ability to adhere to the defective collagen fibers. These defects result in the bone being more brittle and subject to breakage.

When a bone breaks, it is often placed in a cast and immobilized. The lack of stress on the bone results in the bone becoming thinner due to the process described earlier. When the cast is removed and the bone is no longer immobilized, the bone is more brittle than before the break. For a child with osteogenesis imperfecta, a vicious cycle may result in which the bone breaks, becomes thinner and weaker while it is healing, and breaks again.

CHARACTERISTICS OF OSTEOGENESIS IMPERFECTA

The primary characteristics of osteogenesis imperfecta are the fragility of the bones and the effect of that fragility on bone structures. A child may have such a severe case of osteogenesis imperfecta that picking him or her up can break a bone. In other instances, the osteogenesis imperfecta may be so mild that it is not diagnosed. Some children will have additional skeletal abnormalities, such as scoliosis, kyphosis, and bowing of the long bones. The effect of osteogenesis imperfecta

on bone structure may result in variable degrees of shortness in stature. Many children with osteogenesis imperfecta will not be able to walk independently and will need wheelchairs to achieve independence.

Collagen defects and decreased mineral salts commonly result in additional abnormalities, often affecting the sclera, middle ear, teeth, joints, and ligaments. The sclera, which is the white part of the eye, is composed of collagen fibers. In some types of osteogenesis imperfecta, a thinning of collagen fibers results in the sclera being more translucent. In these instances, the choroid layer of the eye shows through the sclera, giving it a bluish color (Vetter, Pontz, Zauner, Brenner, & Spranger, 1992). If the bones of the middle ear are affected, a hearing loss may occur, sometimes later in life. Teeth may also develop improperly due to the low mineral content. The teeth tend to be discolored and transparent, ranging in color from a dusky blue to yellow-brown. The teeth often wear down quickly, leaving short brown stumps, or they may break easily (dentinogenesis imperfecta) (Dorland, 1988). Joints and ligaments may be lax. In some instances, there may be associated neurological abnormalities, such as hydrocephalus, macrocephaly, and cerebral atrophy (Charnas & Marini, 1993).

Because of its varying characteristics and prognoses, osteogenesis imperfecta has been divided into several types. Initially, osteogenesis imperfecta was divided into two main categories: *OI congenita* and *OI tarda*. In OI congenita, the child is born with evidence of the disease and is so severely affected that death often occurs shortly after birth. *OI tarda* refers to the appearance of the condition later in childhood and includes a range of severity (Brodin & Millde, 1990). However, some theorists have thought that this classification system is not differentiated enough. One alternative system divides OI by radiographic characteristics (Hanscom et al., 1992). In 1979, Sillence, Senn, and Danks developed another system that divides OI according to clinical characteristics. At present, the latter system is the one most commonly used; it is presented in Table 15-1.

The order of severity of the different types of osteogenesis imperfecta is: Type I, Type IV, Type III, and Type II. Type I is the mildest, and Type II is the most severe (Charnas & Marini, 1993). Osteogenesis imperfecta Type I is the most common form; there is mild bone fragility and little or no bone deformity. Only about 10% of infants with this type have fractures at birth. Although fractures may occur from minimal trauma, not all accidents will produce fractures. When deformities do occur, they are often a result of fractures, although bowing of the legs can occur without a history of fracture. Children often have very lax ligaments, especially in the hands, feet, and knees, although this

TABLE 15-1

Types of Osteogenesis Imperfecta

Type	Bone abnormality	Stature	Teeth abnormality	Blue sclera	Hearing loss	Inheritance
I	Little-to-no deformity	Normal	Rare	Yes	50%	Autosomal-dominant
II	Lethal in perinatal period; severe deformity	—	—	—	—	Autosomal-dominant; autosomal-recessive (rare)
III	Progressively deforming bones; moderate deformity at birth	Very short	Common	Blue at birth; may become white with age	Not reported	Autosomal-dominant; autosomal-recessive (uncommon)
IV	Mild-to-moderate bone deformity	Variable	Common	White	Some	Autosomal-dominant

laxity diminishes in adulthood. Other types of deformities include flat feet, knock knees (genu valgam), and kyphosis or kyphoscoliosis (curvature of the spine), which usually occurs in adulthood (Behrman, 1992). Hearing loss often begins after the second to third decade of life and rarely occurs before 10 years of age (Byers & Steiner, 1992). Individuals are usually of normal height or of slightly short stature. Motor development may be delayed in Type I, but by the age of 4 years, the majority of children are able to walk independently. This condition may improve, with less fracturing reported, after puberty.

Osteogenesis imperfecta Type IV has mild-to-moderate bone deformity; age of onset varies from birth to adulthood. In some cases, bowing of the legs at birth is the only symptom of this condition. Deformity of the long bones and the spine may occur without fractures (Behrman, 1992) but in many individuals, fractures do occur with mild trauma. Most children will have short stature and some will have tooth deformity. The sclera of the eye is usually white. However, as with osteogenesis imperfecta Type I, improvement may accompany the onset of puberty; fewer fractures may occur. Hearing impairment is less common. Motor performance may be delayed or impaired with only about one-third of the individuals able to walk on crutches by age 4 years. Some will be able to walk without crutches, but many can become independent only with the use of a wheelchair (Vetter et al., 1992).

Osteogenesis imperfecta Type III has moderate-to-severe bone fragility. The newborn or young infant often has multiple fractures, which lead to progressively more deformed bones. Fractures occur frequently throughout childhood, and most children have very short stature. Kyphoscoliosis (curvature of the spine) is usually present in childhood and progresses to adolescence. Skull deformity often results in a triangular appearance to the head (Behrman, 1992). Tooth deformity is common. By age 10 years, the majority of children with osteogenesis imperfecta Type III may sit without assistance, but only a few can walk short distances on crutches; most use wheelchairs (Vetter et al., 1992). Many individuals with osteogenesis imperfecta Type III do not live to adulthood; most die from heart and lung complications.

The most severe type of osteogenesis imperfecta is Type II. The infant usually dies at birth or shortly afterward. Infants are born with a crumpled (accordion-like) appearance of the long bones with multiple fractures of the ribs. Limbs are usually very short, bent, and deformed; the skull is soft (Behrman, 1992). The nose is often beaked. In this lethal form of osteogenesis imperfecta, approximately one-half of the infants are stillborn. The rest usually die shortly after birth because of the breathing difficulty that is secondary to a defective rib cage.

DETECTION OF OSTEOGENESIS IMPERFECTA

Osteogenesis imperfecta may be diagnosed through clinical observation, radiological examination, and biochemical and molecular genetic studies. At birth, multiple fractures usually indicate the more severe forms of osteogenesis imperfecta. A family history of osteogenesis imperfecta, dental abnormalities, and blue scleras all provide additional evidence of this disease. In osteogenesis imperfecta, radiological examination will usually reveal the characteristic decreased bone mass (osteopenia). Shortened and bowed bones can also be examined with X-rays to determine whether or not osteogenesis imperfecta is present.

Skeletal deformities may occur in other conditions, such as certain generalized skeletal disorders (for example, Marfan syndrome), metabolic bone diseases (such as renal osteodystrophy), and neurological conditions (such as neurofibromatosis). The clinical, radiological, and laboratory findings will help differentiate these from osteogenesis imperfecta (Umbreit, 1983).

Prenatally, only the more severe forms of osteogenesis imperfecta are usually detected by ultrasound (D'Ottavio, Tamaro, & Mandruzzato, 1993). Ultrasound will reveal fractures and bowing, as well as decrease in bone mass. Recent advances in prenatal diagnosis also include a biochemical analysis of collagen and protein obtained from an amniocentesis or chorionic villus sampling (Byers & Steiner, 1992; Carlson & Harlass, 1993).

In most cases, diagnosis of osteogenesis imperfecta is very straightforward, but when the osteogenesis imperfecta is mild, an initial diagnosis of child abuse may be made incorrectly. One factor that contributes to the misdiagnosis is the failure to recognize that osteogenesis imperfecta can occur without a family history, without blue scleras, without reduced bone mass, without bowed limbs, or without multiple severe fractures (Paterson, Burns, & McAllion, 1993). Many symptoms may appear the same in child abuse and in osteogenesis imperfecta. One characteristic of child abuse is a lack of history of significant trauma in a person with fractures, but this also describes osteogenesis imperfecta. Bruising occurs in both osteogenesis imperfecta and child abuse. One clinical finding is that fractures in children with osteogenesis imperfecta may be accompanied by less superficial evidence of injury than would have been expected if the bones had been normal (Paterson, Burns, & McAllion, 1993). A very careful examination for osteogenesis imperfecta is needed because a misdiagnosis of child abuse can be extremely damaging to the family. In some mistaken cases of child abuse, the child has been taken away from the family and criminal charges have been pressed before osteogenesis imperfecta was diagnosed.

TREATMENT OF OSTEOGENESIS IMPERFECTA

There is currently no cure for osteogenesis imperfecta. Although administration of vitamins (for example, vitamin C), minerals (for example, calcium), dietary supplements, and medications (such as calcitonin) has been used as treatment, none of the results have been conclusive. Treatment of osteogenesis imperfecta has been aimed at prompt treatment of fractures to prevent deformity and to maximize mobility. Standard means of treating fractures are used—splinting and casting.

However, the period of immobilization is kept as short as possible to reduce bone loss. Lightweight, short casts are used whenever possible, thereby immobilizing only one joint and encouraging the use of the limb.

Several surgical procedures may be used to treat osteogenesis imperfecta. Surgery may be performed to correct bowing of the bones, minimize scoliosis, treat the hearing loss, or correct fractures. *Intramedullary rodding* is a surgical procedure that has been used as a form of orthopedic management (Cole, 1993). Rodding consists of placing metal rods in the shaft of bones (intramedullary) in order to provide support and reduce the possibility of fractures. Several types of rodding procedures are used. The Sofield and Millar procedure is a combination of cutting bone, realigning bones, and inserting rod fixations, typically in the legs. Different types of rods are also available, such as rods that extend with bone growth. Rodding is often indicated when there are recurrent fractures in a single bone, difficulty in performing activities of daily living, or problems using crutches or performing transfers. An alternative to rodding is to use external plates and screws, but their use has declined in favor of rodding (Byers & Steiner, 1992).

Other forms of orthopedic management may include the use of external support after surgery or in certain other circumstances, instead of surgery. Plastic splints may be used to stabilize limbs. Inflatable braces or inflatable trouser splints that become rigid when inflated with air may be used. Another option is vacuum pants—lightweight trousers containing Styrofoam beads that become rigid when air is removed (Byers & Steiner, 1992). An important part of orthopedic management also includes the use of occupational and physical therapy to assist with maximizing the child's physical functioning (Binder, Conway, & Gerber, 1993; Binder et al., 1993).

COURSE OF OSTEOGENESIS IMPERFECTA

The course of osteogenesis imperfecta depends on its type. The milder forms such as Type I usually do not affect the life span, while the more severe Types II & III usually result in an early death. However, it must be remembered that varying degrees of involvement and deformity occur in all types of osteogenesis imperfecta. Also, improvement in the condition is often present after puberty in Types I and IV.

DESCRIPTION OF ARTHROGRYPOSIS

Arthrogryposis, also known as *arthrogryposis multiplex congenita* (AMC), is a term used to refer to multiple congenital contractures and stiffness in joints. It is not a disease but a term used to refer to several different conditions in which multiple congenital contractures occur. The term originated from two Greek words: *arthro*, which means "joints," and *gryposis*, which means "curved." The first written account of arthrogryposis was made in 1841, but AMC is still not fully understood (Umbreit, 1983).

ETIOLOGY OF ARTHROGRYPOSIS

The exact etiology of arthrogryposis is unknown, but it is usually not inherited. The multiple contractures could be due to a lack of movement during fetal development caused by neurogenic or myogenic disorders (Fedrizzi et al., 1993). Neurogenic disorders are those directly affecting the nervous system, while myogenic disorders are those directly affecting the muscles. Many reports have indicated that neurogenic disorders may cause arthrogryposis more often than myogenic ones (Fedrizzi et al., 1993).

The term *arthrogryposis* is often loosely—and some authorities argue incorrectly (Berkow, 1992)—applied to well-defined disorders that have multiple congenital contractures as part of their symptomatology. Some of those that are neurogenic are infantile spinal muscular atrophy, Pena-Shokeir Syndrome, and Marden-Walker Syndrome. Some conditions that are myogenic and are associated with multiple congenital contractures are myotonic muscular dystrophy, congenital myopathies, and intrauterine viral myositis (Behrman, 1992).

Despite these different neuropathies and myopathies, classic arthrogryposis often refers to multiple congenital contractures that do not appear to be evidence of a specific, well-defined disease entity, such as spinal muscular atrophy or muscular dystrophy. Differentiating arthrogryposis from a well-known disease with multiple contractures becomes important because of the differences in characteristics and prognosis. Here, we will continue to discuss arthrogryposis as it is described when a precise, underlying disease entity is unknown.

DYNAMICS OF ARTHROGRYPOSIS

Movement of a joint depends on an intact nervous system and an intact muscular system. As we discussed in Chapter 4, the brain sends electrical impulses down the spinal cord. From the spinal cord, they travel through the peripheral nervous system. When the impulses reach muscle, via the peripheral nerves, they cause the muscle to contract. The ends of the skeletal muscles are attached to bones by tendons and ligaments that are located on opposite sides or within a joint.

When the electrical impulse causes the muscle to contract, one muscle group shortens and another muscle group relaxes, causing a pull on the bone across the joint and making the bone move.

In arthrogryposis, a defect in either the nerves or the muscles results in an inability to move a joint properly. This occurs during prenatal development when the fetus would normally be moving. Without the normal amount of physical movement, certain joints may remain in a fixed position or move minimally. When this occurs, contractures and muscle atrophy (wasting away of the muscle) result. Often, a decrease in muscle mass is accompanied by replacement of muscle by connective and adipose (fatty) tissue (Gullino, Abrate, Zerbino, Bricchi, & Rattazzi, 1993). This may occur either because of an abnormality of the muscles (myopathy) or from abnormality of the nervous system affecting the muscles (**neuropathy**).

There is also evidence to show that in some instances, arthrogryposis can be due to an intrauterine vascular accident in which blood flow has been interrupted in certain arteries during fetal development, resulting in reduced fetal movement (Robertson, Glinski, Kirkpatrick, & Pauli, 1992). Also, mechanical restriction from such occurrences as a decrease in amniotic fluid may also be a cause of arthrogryposis.

CHARACTERISTICS OF ARTHROGRYPOSIS

When infants are born with arthrogryposis, they have either flexion (bent) or extension (straight) contractures. In classic (typical) arthrogryposis, the joints of all limbs are fixed with a characteristic spindle-shaped deformity. The elbows and knees are usually in extension. The shoulders are turned inward. The spinal column may be involved and abnormally flexed; the wrists and fingers are usually flexed. The hips are usually slightly flexed, and the hips may be dislocated; the feet are usually turned in and downward (Behrman, 1992; Bleck & Nagel, 1982). Despite these classic characteristics, infants may be born with the joints extended where they are typically flexed, and flexed where they are typically extended.

The degree of severity of arthrogryposis can vary greatly. Some children may have mild involvement that results in a few mild contractures, while others may have severe contractures of all limbs, as is often found in classic arthrogryposis. Depending on the severity and on the limbs involved, some children are unable to walk, but many can do so after treatment (see Figure 15-1). As the child matures, many contractures often remain, or they may recur after treatment. Due to the presence of

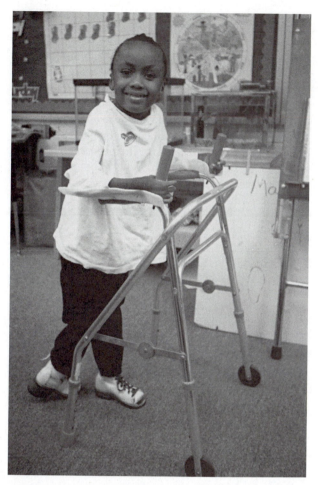

■ FIGURE 15-1 Student who has arthrogryposis using a walker for mobility

usually be performed to confirm the diagnosis and to gain a better understanding of the extent of involvement. X-rays are used to determine the extent of the contractures and to detect any bowing, fractures, or abnormal alignment of the bones of the spinal column. A muscle biopsy, in which a few muscle cells are examined microscopically, may be performed to determine whether the muscle cells appear healthy or whether they have been replaced by fat or scar tissue. An electromyography is usually performed to further test the muscle and to determine whether the electrical activity (action potential) of the muscle is within normal limits. Muscle ultrasonography and MRI may also be done to determine the extent of the involvement (Fedrizzi et al., 1993; Sodergard, Jaaskelainen, & Ryoppy, 1993).

Part of the diagnostic process will be to determine whether or not a well-defined disease has resulted in multiple congenital contractures. Differential diagnosis may be used, for example, to rule out muscular dystrophy (see Chapter 9) or spinal muscular atrophy (see Chapter 10), which may have similar symptoms. There are also similar bone deformities found in arthrogryposis and osteogenesis imperfecta, but in osteogenesis imperfecta, joint motion is not impaired as it is in arthrogryposis; in osteogenesis imperfecta, the deformities affect the bones.

Prenatal diagnosis has occurred for fetuses with arthrogryposis. Often, the mother detects minimal-to-no movement of the fetus, which results in testing by the obstetrician. Usually, a sonogram is performed. Sonograms have successfully revealed the unnatural position of limbs with absence of active fetal movement, which will often lead to a diagnosis of arthrogryposis. Further testing is often done at that point to try to determine etiology.

TREATMENT OF ARTHROGRYPOSIS

Treatment is aimed at improving the individual's functional ability. Because extensive physical involvement usually occurs in arthrogryposis, only those deformities that interfere with the ability to perform activities of daily living are usually targeted. Traditional orthopedic measures (such as surgery, casting, splinting, bracing, and physical and occupational therapy) are typically used to improve mobility.

Contractures of the elbows are serious because movement of these joints is necessary if independence in most activities of daily living is to be achieved. Flexion contractures of the wrist also interfere with needed hand use and with finger movement. Surgery on the wrist and elbow to release the contractures has been successful in

contractures, hand and arm usage may be functional but limited, even after treatment. Although severe physical involvement may be present, intelligence is usually normal, with only about 10% of children having mental retardation (Avery & First, 1994).

Several conditions may be associated with arthrogryposis. These include cleft palate, cardiac defect, club foot, dwarfism, urinary tract impairment, scoliosis, hip dislocation, respiratory problems, and various myopathies. In some rare instances, there may be central nervous system involvement. In an atypical form of arthrogryposis, there are no associated conditions or muscle wasting and only limited joint involvement (Berkow, 1992).

DETECTION OF ARTHROGRYPOSIS

Diagnosis is usually made at birth based on the presence of multiple contractures. However, several tests will

improving movement and appearance, especially when performed between 3 and 6 months of age. The amount of mobility varies, and total range of motion is usually not achieved (Mennen, 1993). In some instances, splinting of the wrist may be used instead of surgery if the joint is not fully contracted. Surgery is not usually necessary on the fingers unless the thumb is contracted against the palm and would interfere with grasping. Despite stiff finger joints, most children can develop good use of their hands by using alternate movements (Umbreit, 1983). (See Figure 15-2.) Surgery is not usually performed to correct shoulder deformities because they do not interfere with activities of daily living.

Contractures of the hip and knees may interfere with standing or walking, so surgery may be performed to release the contractures in order to allow a stable base and satisfactory gait. If there is hip dislocation, this should be corrected at an early age (see Chapter 12). Foot deformities typically require surgery to allow the child to stand. Other abnormalities, such as scoliosis, may require surgery or bracing (see Chapter 11).

■ **FIGURE 15-2** Student with arthrogryposis does her schoolwork using an adapted hand position to hold her pencil.

The following describes a young boy with a mild form of osteogenesis imperfecta. His mother relates: "We have had a few problems since moving . . . to a new school—one being that he was put into a soccer team and played goalie! I just could not believe it when he told me, especially as everything had been explained in detail to the principal. [The principal] seems to think that I have exaggerated his condition and is reluctant to . . . make allowances for him even when he has had a fracture" (quoted by Shea-Landry, 1985).

COURSE OF ARTHROGRYPOSIS

The course of arthrogryposis depends on its etiology. If the term is loosely applied to other well-defined conditions such as spinal muscular atrophy, the course will be dependent upon the known condition. However, when the term is used in its strictest sense to refer to classical arthrogryposis, which occurs without evidence of a well-defined condition, it is a nonprogressive disorder. Arthrogryposis is at its worst at birth and improves after treatment. For individuals who have severe involvement affecting both legs, surgical and orthopedic treatments will usually result in improvement of mobility, which may allow limited but independent functioning.

EDUCATIONAL IMPLICATIONS OF OSTEOGENESIS IMPERFECTA AND ARTHROGRYPOSIS

When a student has a musculoskeletal condition, it is imperative that the educator have a good understanding of the type of condition, its characteristics, treatment, and prognosis. This will assist in planning for the student appropriately. In the case of osteogenesis imperfecta and arthrogryposis, some of the planning will be similar; some will be quite diverse.

Meeting Physical and Sensory Needs

In both osteogenesis imperfecta and arthrogryposis, the student may be independently **ambulatory,** ambulatory with mechanical or physical assistance, or nonambulatory. It is important that the educator, in conjunction with the physical therapist, learn proper lifting and handling techniques. For the child with osteogenesis imperfecta, this is important in order to minimize the chances of breaking a bone. For the child with arthrogryposis, the importance lies in placing minimal stress on joint contractures. Proper lifting and handling is also necessary to prevent pulling the teacher's own back muscles (see Chapter 27).

Adapted physical education will usually be needed for students with osteogenesis imperfecta and arthrogryposis. Physical fitness and activity is important in maintaining health, although modifications are usually needed. Physical activity that places stress on the bones is contraindicated in osteogenesis imperfecta. Activities may need to be modified to protect the student from being hit. The student also should not hit or kick an object, especially when the student has a more severe type of osteogenesis imperfecta. More sedentary activities, such as board or card games, and creative outlets, such as playing musical instruments or fine arts, may be stressed. In arthrogryposis, joint deformity usually requires adaptations to allow the student to participate in games. Rules of games may be modified, balls may be lightweight, or adapted equipment such as that in adapted bowling may be used.

In both conditions, it is important that the educator not be too restrictive. Often, upon hearing that a child has brittle bone disease or multiple contractures, undue limitations may be placed on the child. If the child has a very mild form of OI (Type I), this may be unnecessary and hinder social relations and physical health. However, if the condition is severe, extra care and precautions are usually necessary. Close communication between the parent and medical personnel regarding any restrictions is necessary in order to gain the right balance between the student's capabilities and the limitations of the condition.

There is usually no sensory impairment in arthrogryposis. However, in osteogenesis imperfecta, there is a risk of a hearing impairment. The educator should be alert to any symptoms of a possible hearing impairment and refer the student for testing should one be suspected.

Meeting Communication Needs

In both arthrogryposis and osteogenesis imperfecta, there is usually no speech impediment. Students with these conditions can be clearly understood. The challenge in communication for these students is not speech but in properly communicating about the disorder to others. It is imperative that classmates and school personnel gain an accurate understanding of the conditions. This is especially crucial in osteogenesis imperfecta; a playful shove in the hall may result in a broken bone (Cole, 1993).

Often, it is helpful for young students to have some ideas of how to respond to the inquiries of others. Depending on the severity of the osteogenesis imper-

■ **VIGNETTE 2** ■

Anthony is a 7-year-old in second grade who is diagnosed with arthrogryposis Type III. He is very bright for his age, but has numerous bone deformities due to multiple breaks. He is in a wheelchair and has some use of his arms. Teachers have been shown proper lifting and handling techniques by the physical therapist. Anthony has on occasion broken a bone at school due to the extreme fragility of the bone. Anthony has a few friends who have been taught how to play with him without injuring him. However, injury has occurred when a friend inadvertently knocked into him when they were putting up a board game and playing around. Anthony and his parents are glad for his friends, even when a fracture occurs.

fecta, young students may say, "My bones break easily, like glass. I can play with you; I just have to be careful and people have to be careful not to run into me." Young students with arthrogryposis may say to peers, "When I was born, my arms and legs would not bend right, and they still don't bend the same as yours." As with other noninfectious conditions, it is important to explain that these conditions cannot be transmitted.

Meeting Learning Needs

Students with osteogenesis imperfecta and arthrogryposis usually have normal intelligence. Often it is important to stress academics because of the student's physical limitations. However, these children often underachieve and perform worse academically than their nondisabled peers (Cole, 1993). Physical disability and chronic illness often create special problems that may hinder performance at school. Fatigue, absences, low self-esteem, and lack of experiences may all have a negative impact on performance. These and similar issues need to be closely assessed and addressed in the educational setting to promote a successful experience.

Meeting Daily Living Needs

The need for modifications in performing daily living skills will vary according to the severity of the condition. In some instances, no intervention may be necessary, while in others, assistance from the teacher may be needed. The student with osteogenesis imperfecta or arthrogryposis may use adapted devices to meet daily living needs. For students with osteogenesis imperfecta, adapted devices are used to minimize stress on the bone

■ VIGNETTE 3 ■

April is a 12-year-old girl in seventh grade, and she has arthrogryposis. Although she has had numerous surgeries to correct her contractures, she still has limited range of motion of her arms. She can ambulate fairly well. Despite her limitations, she and her teachers, therapists, and parents have worked closely together to come up with many adaptations that assist her in performing her academic tasks as well as daily living activities. Some of the adaptations are unconventional, requiring use of her mouth stick, but she has been able to accomplish most tasks because of her own ingenuity and determination and that of people around her.

structure as well as to compensate for any contractures or weakness. For students with arthrogryposis, adapted devices can compensate for limited range of motion from contractures as well as for muscle weakness. For example, a student with either condition may use a long-handled device to pick up items from the floor or table. In eating, students with osteogenesis imperfecta or arthrogryposis may be unable to reach their mouths with a standard utensil due to bone or joint deformity. Adapted utensils that are long-handled and lightweight may be of assistance. The exact type of adapted device will be individually selected and assessed using a team approach. It is important in both types of cases that the teacher foster as much physical independence as possible and not be overly protective or restrictive.

Meeting Behavioral and Social Needs

It is especially important that the educator be aware of the behavioral and social needs of students with osteogenesis imperfecta or arthrogryposis. Students may feel frustrated, depressed, and angry over their condition and need counseling to help them cope with it. Social isolation can occur due to the obvious physical deformity inherent in both conditions. Students, especially those with OI, may have few friends or playmates because everyone worries that playing with others may result in fractures (Brodin, 1990). Students and others need to learn about capacities and limitations and be supportive of the student.

SUMMARY

Osteogenesis imperfecta and arthrogryposis are two conditions affecting the musculoskeletal system. In osteogenesis imperfecta there is excessive bone fragility, which often results in multiple fractures. In arthrogryposis, the child is born with multiple contractures.

In both conditions, there is a range of severity. Osteogenesis imperfecta has been classified into four types (Types I, II, III, and IV) based on severity and clinical features. In the most severe form (Type II), death often occurs in infancy due to the multiple fractures. In the most mild form (Type I), fractures are minimal and a normal life span is anticipated. In arthrogryposis, contractures may be severe and affect all functional movement of the arms or legs, or may be more mild with minimal impact on functioning. In both conditions, intelligence is usually normal.

The treatment of osteogenesis imperfecta and arthrogryposis is aimed at relieving the symptoms. Depending on the severity of the condition, treatment may include the use of surgical and nonsurgical intervention. Despite treatment efforts, the symptoms of these conditions usually persist; students with osteogenesis imperfecta continue to have bone fragility, and students with arthrogryposis often have some contractures remaining. The teacher will need to provide modifications in many instances to decrease the incidence of fractures in students with osteogenesis imperfecta and to increase functioning with the use of adaptations for students with arthrogryposis.

PART V

Sensory Impairments

CHAPTER 16

Visual Impairments

A wide range of visual impairments can adversely affect a student's functioning in school. Certain visual impairments will affect the clarity with which a student sees, while others can affect how much a student can see at one time. Understanding how the eye works, knowing the common conditions causing visual impairments, and taking account of their implications in the classroom will help the educator know how to best meet the needs of students with visual impairments.

In this chapter, we will describe the major anatomical features of the eye, explain how the eye functions, define terms used in the field, describe common visual impairments, and discuss the educational implications of visual impairments.

DESCRIPTION OF VISUAL IMPAIRMENTS

Several terms are used to describe visual impairments; one that is commonly used is *legal blindness*.

Legal blindness is defined as "central visual acuity of 20/200 or less in the better eye with best correction, or widest diameter of visual field subtending an angle of no greater than 20 degrees" (Vaughn, Asbury, & Riordan-Eva, 1992, p. 404). The term *visual acuity* refers to the measurement of the acuteness of vision, or the finest of detail that the eye can distinguish (Vaughn, Asbury, & Riordan-Eva, 1992). In this definition, the expression *20/200* means that the person with the visual impairment can see an object or symbol at 20 feet that a person with unimpaired vision can see at 200 feet. *Field of vision* refers to the ability to see objects in the periphery of one's vision when looking straight ahead. Individuals with unimpaired vision can see objects within a 180° arc when looking straight ahead.

Educators have developed other definitions that are more functional and meaningful for programming. Many of the following definitions have been adopted and incorporated into state and federal definitions.

1. *Visual impairment.* This term encompasses a wide range of vision loss that can include deficits in acuity, visual field, ocular motility, or color perception. The visual impairment may be permanent or temporary. The term *visual disability* is often used synonymously with the term *visual impairment* to refer to a vision loss that, even with correction, adversely affects a child's educational performance.

2. *Blind.* Individuals who are totally without vision or who have light perception only are said to be blind. In education, this term refers to children who use other senses such as hearing and touch as primary channels for learning or receiving information.

3. *Light perception only.* Individuals who are without vision but who can perceive the absence or presence of light are said to have light perception only.

4. *Low vision.* This is a broad term that is used to refer to individuals who have significant visual impairments even with best correction but who still have usable vision. Vision is used as the primary channel for learning or receiving information. Visual functioning may increase with the use of optical devices, environmental modifications, training, or a combination of these (Corn, 1983; Scholl, 1986).

5. *Visual functioning.* This term refers to how a person uses the vision he or she has. Visual functioning is considered a learned behavior that is not necessarily reflected by visual acuity. It is possible for a student to have poor visual acuity and good visual functioning, or vice versa (Gothelf, Rikhye, & Silberman, 1988). Individuals who fail to use their vision in an efficient or meaningful way have poor visual functioning, despite the level of acuity.

DYNAMICS OF VISUAL IMPAIRMENTS

The visual system may be divided into four areas: (1) the supporting structures of the eye, (2) the eye, (3) the visual pathways to the brain, and (4) the visual cortex (the part of the brain that processes visual information). The supporting structures of the eye assist the eye in proper functioning. The eye receives and converts light energy into electrochemical impulses. The visual pathways transmit these impulses to the visual cortex, which interprets the impulses and relays them to other, higher cerebral centers (Biglan, Van Hasselt, & Simon, 1988).

The Supporting Structures of the Eye

Several supporting structures of the eye assist the eye in proper functioning, including the extraocular muscles, the eyelids, and the lacrimal apparatus. Eye movement (known as motility) is controlled by six extraocular muscles that surround the eyeball (see Figure 16-1). These muscles can move the eye up, down, diagonally, and sideways. The eye muscles, in combination with specific cognitive functions, provide the means by which a person can shift attention (look from one object to another), track objects (use the eyes to follow a moving object), scan for objects (use the head and eyes to search for objects in the environment), and follow approaching objects (convergence). The extraocular muscles allow the eyes to move together in a coordinated manner and give proper alignment of the eyes so that a single, instead of a double, image may be seen when two images are fused by the brain (Asbury & Burke, 1992).

The eyelids are folds of skin that close over the eye. Eyelids protect the eye from foreign objects and irritation, limit the amount of light entering the eye, and distribute tears over the anterior outer surface of the eye-

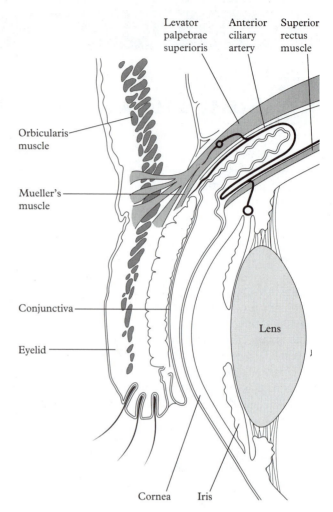

■ **FIGURE 16-2** The conjunctiva

ball to assist with hydration. The inner surface of the eyelid has a thin, transparent membrane known as the conjunctiva, which wraps from the eyelid onto the anterior surface of the eye (Newell, 1992) (see Figure 16-2). This makes it impossible for a contact lens to go behind the eye—it cannot move past the conjunctiva. The conjunctiva also contains small blood vessels. When someone has bloodshot eyes, the blood vessels in the conjunctiva have enlarged (dilated).

Another supporting structure is the *lacrimal apparatus,* which is made up of the lacrimal gland and secretory ducts. The lacrimal gland assists in making tears, which have several functions: keeping the eye moist, providing nutrients, and providing oxygen. Tears also remove cellular debris as they wash over the outer surface of the eye, and they contain an enzyme that fights the growth of bacteria on the eye. The ducts, located at the nasal corners of each eye, collect the excess tears and channel them into the nasal cavities.

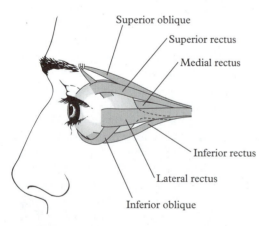

■ **FIGURE 16-1** Muscles of the eye

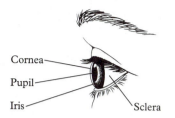

■ **FIGURE 16-3** The anatomy of the eye as seen from the front

The Eye

The outer surface of the eye consists of the **sclera** and the **cornea** (see Figure 16-3). The sclera is the white portion of the eye that covers five-sixths of the eyeball, wrapping over the entire eye except in the front where the cornea is located. The sclera consists of tough, dense, connective tissues that help to protect the inner contents of the eye (Jose, 1983). The cornea is the transparent portion of the outer surface of the eye that covers the remaining one-sixth of the eyeball. It is the most sensitive tissue of the entire body; that is, it has the most nerve fibers in an area of its size. The cornea is often called "the window of the eye" because light first passes through the cornea as it travels to the inner structures of the eye. As the light passes through the curved shape of the cornea, it refracts (or bends). This refraction helps to direct the light rays to the back structures of the eye.

As light passes through the cornea, it travels through the anterior chamber of the eye, which extends from the cornea to the colored part of the eye, known as the *iris* (see Figure 16-4). The iris is a colored, circular muscle with a hole in the center, called the *pupil*. The pupil appears to be black because the inside of the eye is dark. (In a photograph taken with a flash, a person may appear to have red eyes because light illuminates the back of the eye through the pupil.) The iris controls the amount of light entering the eye by regulating the size of the pupil, similar to the way a camera lens regulates light entering a camera. In dim light, certain muscles of the iris will contract, causing the pupil to become larger (dilate). With the pupil dilated, more light can enter the eye. In bright light, other muscles in the iris contract, causing the pupil to become smaller. This allows less light into the eye.

As light continues through the anterior chamber of the eye, it passes through the pupil and into the posterior chamber of the eye. This chamber extends from the pupil to the ciliary body (see Figure 16-4). The ciliary body is continuous with the iris and produces a fluid known as the *aqueous humor*, which is present in both the posterior and anterior chambers. The aqueous humor flows from the ciliary body, through the posterior chamber, through the pupil, and into the anterior chamber (see Figure 16-5). From the anterior chamber, the fluid flows through the drainage area (trabecular meshwork) and into the canal of Schlemm. The aqueous humor carries nutrients to these parts of the eye and removes waste products.

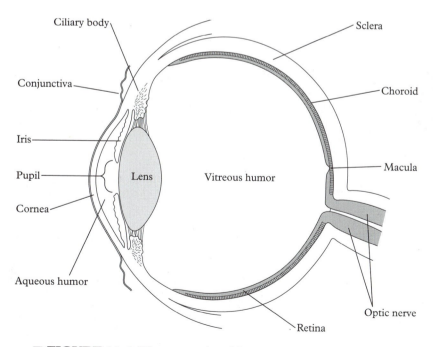

■ **FIGURE 16-4** The external and internal structures of the eye

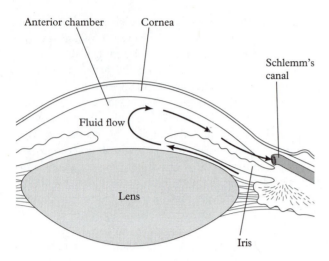

Anterior chamber   Cornea

Schlemm's canal

Fluid flow

Lens

Iris

■ **FIGURE 16-5** The normal flow of aqueous humor

At the end of the posterior chamber and behind the pupil is the lens of the eye. The lens is a transparent structure that is curved on either side (biconvex). It is suspended by fibers that are connected to the ciliary body. As light travels through the lens, it further refracts (bends) the light rays to focus them properly. In order for the lens to focus on near objects, the lens must actually change shape. When an object is within 6 m of the eye, the muscles of the ciliary body contract, and the lens is squeezed into a greater degree of curvature. This permits focusing of the near object (see Figure 16-6).

This changing of the curvature and thickness of the lens is known as *accommodation*.

After light passes through the lens, it passes into a large cavity filled with a gelatinlike substance known as *vitreous humor* or *vitreous body*. Vitreous humor is a clear substance that aids in keeping the shape of the eyeball. It is self-contained and does not flow out of the eye as does the aqueous humor. Light rays pass through the vitreous humor to the innermost lining of this cavity, known as the *retina*.

The lining of the cavity occupied by the vitreous humor consists of three layers. The outermost layer is the tough, white sclera, which surrounds most of the eye. The middle layer is the choroid, which contains many blood vessels and provides nutrients to the retina. The inner layer is the retina, upon which the light rays are focused.

The retina is a light-sensitive, multilayered membrane that converts light rays to electrical impulses. Contained within the retina are approximately 125 million photoreceptors, known as *rods* and *cones*. The rods and cones are responsible for the conversion of light rays to electrochemical impulses (Ward, 1986). The rods are sensitive to low-intensity illumination (dim light) and can detect gross form and movement. Rods are primarily responsible for peripheral vision and night vision. The cones are sensitive to high-intensity illumination (daylight) and can detect fine detail and colors. On the retina, there is a small central area in which most of the cones are located. This area is known as the

■ **FIGURE 16-6** Accommodation

macula. In the center of the macula is the *fovea*—the area for most distinct vision. The fovea and the macula together are responsible for central vision.

Several structures are responsible for focusing the light onto the retina and producing a clear image. First, light rays pass through the cornea, which produces the greatest amount of refraction of light rays. The light rays then pass through the aqueous humor, which refracts the light slightly. The light passes through the pupil to the lens. The lens provides the second-greatest amount of refraction to further focus the light. As the light rays pass through the vitreous humor, they are still further refracted. The cornea, aqueous humor, lens, and vitreous humor each refract the light to different degrees. The calculated amount that light is refracted by a given structure is known as the *index of refraction.* When working properly, each of these structures re-

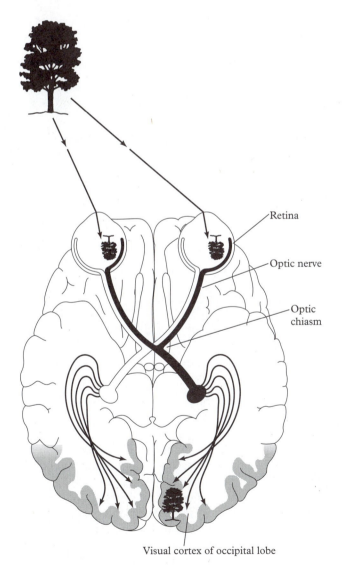

Retina

Optic nerve

Optic chiasm

Visual cortex of occipital lobe

■ **FIGURE 16-7** The optic tracts

fracts light to focus the image on the retina. The retina then converts the light rays to electrochemical impulses that travel from the retina, exit via the optic nerve, and continue along the optic pathways to the brain.

The Visual Pathways

After the image has been converted into electrochemical impulses by the retina, the impulses travel to the optic disk (the only visible portion of the optic nerve) and then exit the eye through the optic nerves located behind each eyeball. Some of the fibers of each optic nerve cross each other at a junction known as the *optic chiasm.* This occurs in such a way that the visual field on the right side of the body is transmitted to the left side of the brain, and the visual field on the left side of the body is transmitted to the right side of the brain. This means that the images on the right side of the person's vision are transmitted to the left side of the brain, and images on the left side of the person's vision are transmitted to the right side of the brain. The impulses continue through the rest of the optic tracts and optic radiations and on to the visual cortex, which is located in the occipital lobe (the posterior part of the brain) (see Figure 16-7).

The Visual Cortex

The visual cortex permits recognition of the transmitted impulses. From the visual cortex, the impulses are transmitted to higher cerebral centers; in these centers, visual information is integrated with other sensory information to allow a person to interpret or remember perceived images.

Effect of Visual Impairments on Visual Abilities

Visual disorders may negatively affect one or more visual abilities. Problems affecting vision include (1) poor visual acuity, (2) visual-field deficits, (3) ocular motility abnormalities, (4) light and color reception impairments, and (5) abnormalities of the visual cortex and brain function (Corn, 1983).

Poor Visual Acuity

Visual acuity refers to the acuteness of images—how clear or sharp an image is with regard to forms or patterns (Vaughn, Asbury, & Riordan-Eva, 1992). It is described in terms of near and far vision. Near vision is the ability to perceive objects clearly at about 14 inches from the eye (Ward, 1986). When individuals cannot see near objects clearly due to a refractive error, this is known as **hyperopia** (farsightedness). When

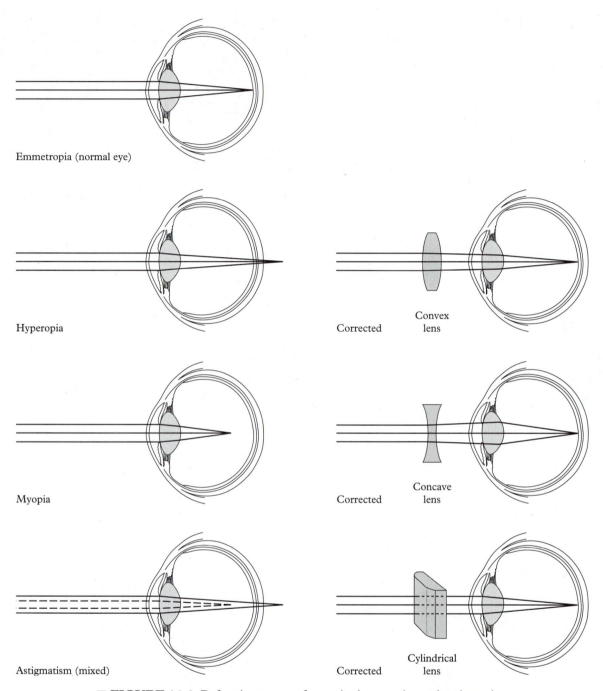

Emmetropia (normal eye)

Hyperopia   Corrected   Convex
                                              lens

Myopia   Corrected   Concave
                                              lens

Astigmatism (mixed)   Corrected   Cylindrical
                                              lens

■ **FIGURE 16-8** Refractive errors of myopia, hyperopia, and astigmatism

hyperopia exists, the eye is either smaller than normal or its refractive power is weaker than in a normal system due to a decreased curve of the cornea or lens or to a low index of refraction of the cornea, aqueous humor, lens, or vitreous humor (Jose, 1983). When light rays enter the eye, they do not focus properly on the retina. The light rays fall behind the retina (theoretically), resulting in the ability to see far objects clearly, while near objects appear unfocused (see Figure 16-8). A convex lens (in glasses or contacts) is used to focus the light rays on the retina to allow for clear near vision.

Farsightedness also occurs as a person ages because the eyes lose the ability to accommodate. The lens of the eye creates new cells, but unlike in other parts of the body, the older cells are not discarded. They are compressed into the center of the lens. As the person ages, this process causes the lens to become less pliable and thus less able to focus clearly on near objects. For example, an 8-year-old can accommodate for an object located as close as 8 cm from the eye, while a 40-year-old person can accommodate for an object around 18 to 20 cm but not closer (American Optical, 1982).

Far vision describes how well someone sees objects or symbols at a distance. As we discussed earlier, it is typically reported in ratios such as 20/20, 20/80, 20/100, and so forth. Normal visual acuity is 20/20. The first number refers to how many feet the letters or symbols on a chart are from the person. The second number refers to the size of the letters or symbols that represent the distance from which a person with normal vision could read them. For example, a person with 20/80 vision sees at a distance of 20 feet what a person with unimpaired vision sees at a distance of 80 feet. Individuals with a refractive error affecting distance vision have **myopia** (nearsightedness). That is, they can see better at nearer ranges. Although there is no single cause of myopia, it may be caused by a hereditary disposition and/or abnormalities in the structures and functioning of the eye. In myopia, the eyeball is either longer than normal or the eye has greater than normal refractory power because of an abnormally strong curve of the cornea or lens or a high index of refraction of the cornea, aqueous humor, lens, or vitreous humor (see Figure 16-8). In either case, the light rays focus in front of the retina, causing difficulty in seeing objects that are far away. A concave lens (in glasses or contacts) is used to focus the light rays on the retina.

Another condition that may affect visual acuity is **astigmatism,** in which there is typically an unequal curvature of the cornea. In this condition, light does not come to a clear point of focus on the retina. Astigmatism results in blurred or distorted images and may occur in combination with farsightedness or nearsightedness. Cylindrical lenses are prescribed to correct astigmatism.

Visual Field Deficits

A person's field of vision refers to the entire area that can be seen without shifting one's gaze. Certain visual conditions may result in a loss of vision in certain areas of a person's field of vision. Defects in visual fields may occur in a person's central field of vision, peripheral field of vision, or both (see Figure 16-9).

Central vision refers to the direct line of vision, which is essential for discerning details. Certain conditions that damage the macular portion of the retina (for example, macular degeneration or atypical retinitis pigmentosa) result in a central field loss. A person with a central vision loss may be unable to read print, discern facial features, or perceive objects when looking straight

at them (Vaughn, Asbury, & Riordan-Eva, 1992). Important information may be missed easily. Often the person will use peripheral vision by directing his or her gaze off to the side to see a desired item or person. This is known as *eccentric viewing;* the individual appears not to be looking at the targeted item or person but is actually using peripheral vision to see them.

Peripheral vision refers to the ability to perceive the presence of objects outside the direct line of vision and is necessary for the awareness of objects and hazards in the periphery (Vaughn, Asbury, & Riordan-Eva, 1992). When a peripheral field loss exists, the person is unable to see objects in part or all of his or her peripheral vision. One of the common types of peripheral vision losses involves loss of vision in a ring shape along the periphery, which results in a narrower visual field. This is like looking through a cylinder. Another name for this is *tunnel vision;* a person can see only a limited amount at one time across a viewed area. This occurs in such conditions as retinitis pigmentosa and **glaucoma.** Because the rods are primarily located in the periphery and they permit seeing in dim light, a deficit in this area may be accompanied by loss of night vision. A person with a peripheral loss will find it difficult to see in dim light or to travel independently at night.

Blind spots, also known as *scotomas,* may occur in the peripheral or in the central visual fields. These may be present in such conditions as end-stage glaucoma and other peripheral retinal diseases. Scotomas may result in missed information—how much depends on their size, their location in the eyes, and how well the person compensates for them.

Other visual-field deficits include types in which sections of the field of vision are missing. In **hemianopsia,** one-half of the visual field is missing (see Figure 16-10). A quadrant loss can occur in which approximately one-fourth of the visual field is missing. These deficits often occur from traumatic brain injury or a tumor along the visual pathways. Individuals with large field losses in both eyes may miss visual information that is presented where the field loss occurs.

Impairment in Motility

Ocular motility refers to the movement of the eye when controlled by any of the six extraocular muscles surrounding each eye. Difficulties in ocular motility may occur in individuals with facial paralysis, eye muscle imbalances, or cranial nerve damage. Impairments in ocular motility may result in difficulties with tracking, shifting gaze, and scanning.

Impairments in eye muscle movement can result in **strabismus,** which occurs when one or both eyes deviate from correct alignment. Types of strabismus are esotro-

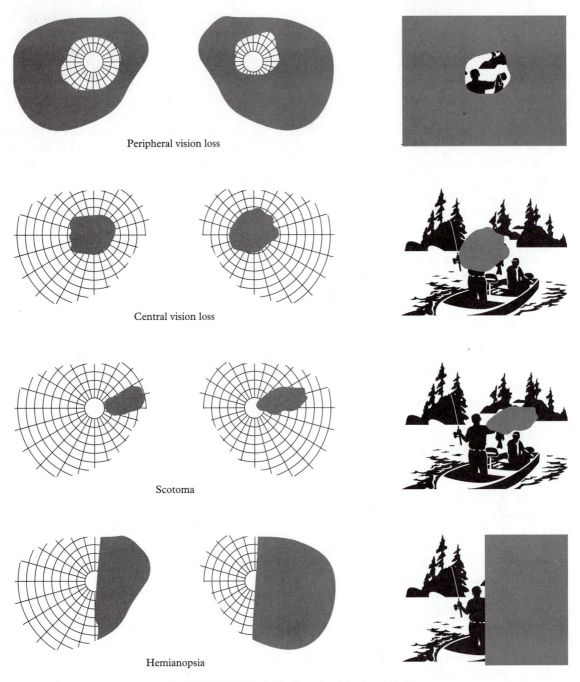

Peripheral vision loss

Central vision loss

Scotoma

Hemianopsia

■ **FIGURE 16-9** Defects in the visual field

pia (one or both eyes turn in toward nose), **exotropia** (one or both eyes turn out, away from nose), and **hypertropia** (the eye deviates upward) (see Figure 16-11). When one eye deviates, **diplopia** (double vision) can occur. Often the brain will suppress one image so that only one visual image will be seen instead of a double image.

The suppression of one image by the brain in individuals with strabismus is the leading cause of **amblyo-**

pia. Amblyopia is a reduction of visual acuity in the absence of any detectable anatomical defect in the eye or visual pathways. It can occur when one eye sees an image different from the image the other eye sees, such as in strabismus, unequal refraction errors, or visual deprivation of one eye during the time the eyes are developing—from birth to 6 years (Friendly, 1987; Newell, 1992; Vaughn, Asbury, & Riordan-Eva, 1992). The suppression of images transmitted by one eye can lead to eventual blindness in the unused eye (Rosenthal, 1982). Blindness can usually be avoided with appropriate intervention; that is, by patching the good eye, correcting the refraction error, or making surgical muscle adjustments at an early age.

Another abnormal ocular movement is **nystagmus,** which consists of involuntary, rhythmic eye movements. These eye movements occur primarily in the horizontal

Esotropia (cross-eyed)   Exotropia (wall-eyed)

■ **FIGURE 16-11** Types of strabismus

plane, but movement can be vertical, diagonal, or rotary and can be fast or slow. Drifting eye movements may appear as slow, searching movements with no evidence of fixation. The etiology of primary nystagmus is unknown. However, it may occur secondary to another condition, such as visual pathway disease, systemic disorders (for example, hypothyroidism), genetic disorders (for example, Down syndrome), profound malnutrition, or other conditions (for example, hydrocephalus) (Taylor, 1990). The child with nystagmus may have poor visual acuity in the affected eye, although binocular vision also may be impaired. Individuals with nystagmus will usually perceive objects as stationary because the brain adjusts perceptually for the movement.

Impairment in Light and Color Reception

The primary impairment in color reception is *color blindness*. Individuals who are color blind usually cannot see certain colors due to missing or damaged cones (color receptors) in the eye. This is typically a sex-linked genetic abnormality and results from an absence of color genes on the X chromosome. The most commonly occurring congenital color defect is a red-green color defect in which red and green appear to be the same color. Acquired color defects are more commonly blue-yellow color defects (Hardy, 1992).

Some children may be sensitive to light (photophobia). Photophobia is an unusual sensitivity to light that makes a person uncomfortable in normal lighting conditions (Day, 1990). This may be caused by a wide range of conditions, one of which is albinism—a lack of pigmentation in the skin, the skin and eyes, or the eyes alone. This condition is often accompanied by photophobia and a lack of clear vision (Day, 1990). Many other conditions may also include photophobia. Congenital glaucoma, **aniridia,** inflammation of the iris, **cataracts,** retinal dystrophies, and certain systemic diseases can include photophobia.

Impairment in Brain Function

Impairment of brain function may adversely affect visual functioning. Impairment of the occipital lobe or other areas of the brain may affect visual fixation, fusion, awareness of motion, and changes in the shape

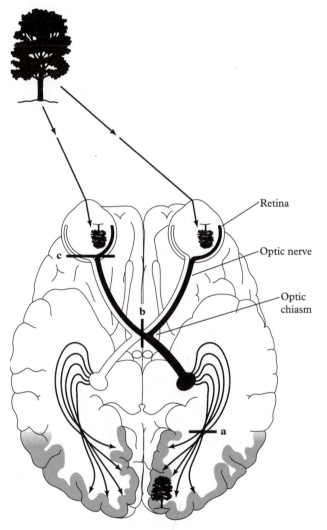

Retina

Optic nerve

Optic chiasm

Visual cortex of occipital lobe

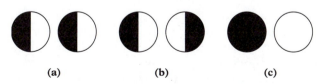

(a)   (b)   (c)

■ **FIGURE 16-10** Damage to the optic tracts can result in a loss of vision in one eye, hemianopsia, or other field losses.

of the intraocular lens (Corn, 1983). In some conditions, objects may not be perceived.

DETECTION OF VISUAL IMPAIRMENTS

Visual impairments may be noticed by the person having difficulty seeing, or individuals around the person may notice that the person does not appear to be seeing well. The person's signs and symptoms, and an ophthalmological examination that includes several different types of procedures, will allow the ophthalmologist to make a diagnosis.

ETIOLOGY, CHARACTERISTICS, COURSE, AND TREATMENT OF COMMON VISUAL DISORDERS

A number of common visual disorders may result in visual impairments or blindness. These disorders may result in the previously described impairments of visual functioning, such as poor acuity, field loss, abnormal color and light reception, or impaired brain function affecting visual abilities. We will discuss these common visual disorders in the order in which they are related to the structures that light first encounters in the eye. Then we will progress through the structures of the eye to the visual pathways and then to the visual cortex.

Disorders of the Cornea

Diseases and disorders of the cornea can result in serious visual impairment ranging from blurring of vision to total blindness. Perforation of the cornea from an ulceration or an object may result in a range of impairments; prompt medical treatment is needed to minimize damage. Because the cornea refracts light rays, a lesion on the cornea from a disease or scarring from a perforation may result in blurred vision. One example of a disease of the cornea that results in blurred vision is keratoconus.

Keratoconus

Keratoconus is a rare progressive disorder in which there is thinning of both corneas, which have become cone-shaped. This results in a distortion of the entire visual field.

Etiology. The etiology of this condition is unknown, although it is occasionally familial; that is, it runs in families. It occurs with greater frequency in rare syndromes such as Marfan syndrome, as well as in eye conditions such as retinal dystrophies (deterioration of the retina) and aniridia (malformed or absent iris) (Good & Hoyt, 1990). Keratoconus has also been found to occur in individuals with congenital rubella and Down syndrome (Lucas, 1989).

Characteristics. Keratoconus usually begins during adolescence and is slowly progressive. Initially, a mild vision loss with myopia (nearsightedness) and astigmatism occurs. Bilateral thinning, scarring, and stretching of the center of the cornea occurs, and visual acuity then worsens (Apple & Rabb, 1991). Frequent changes of glasses or contact lenses are needed as the visual acuity worsens. If left untreated, this condition may slowly progress to the point that the cornea ruptures, resulting in blindness.

Treatment. Most cases can be managed with the use of hard contact lenses. Severe cases will require a corneal transplant. If a corneal transplant is performed before the cornea thins, 80 to 95% of individuals will retain enough vision for reading (Bishop, 1986).

Disorders Related to the Aqueous Humor

Glaucoma. Glaucoma is an abnormal increase in intraocular pressure in one or both eyes that can damage the eye. The increase in intraocular pressure is due to an imbalance between production and outflow of aqueous humor. There are several types of glaucoma.

Etiology. One category of glaucoma is known as primary glaucoma, in which there is no other causative agent other than the glaucoma itself. Primary glaucoma is often inherited and may be classified as open-angle glaucoma or angle-closure glaucoma. In open-angle glaucoma, the aqueous humor can flow freely to the drainage apparatus (trabecular meshwork), but there is often a degenerative process of the drainage apparatus, resulting in reduction in aqueous drainage (Vaughn, Asbury, & Riordan-Eva, 1992). In angle-closure glaucoma, the peripheral portion of the iris blocks the drainage meshwork and prevents drainage of the aqueous humor from the anterior chamber (Newell, 1992). In both types, the increase of aqueous humor in the anterior chamber results in increased intraocular pressure. If the increase in intraocular pressure is permitted to progress, the optic nerve will be damaged, which will result in a loss of visual acuity or visual field or in blindness (Berkow, 1992; Martyn & DiGeorge, 1987). Congenital glaucoma, which is glaucoma occurring from birth, is considered a primary type of glaucoma. It is an autosomal-recessive trait.

Glaucoma may also develop as secondary to another eye disorder, such as uveitis or cataracts, or to disorders involving other organ systems. Glaucoma may be associated with other conditions (such as congenital infections like syphilis, toxoplasmosis, rubella, cytomegalovirus, or herpes) or with adventitious conditions like bleeding in the anterior chamber of the eye from trauma or tumors. Retinopathy of prematurity, some syndromes, and the overuse of topical eye corticosteroid medications are other possibilities. Secondary glaucoma is often caused by blockage of the flow of aqueous humor from any of these conditions.

Characteristics. The major signs of glaucoma in infants include eye enlargement, tearing, photophobia, corneal clouding, twitching of the eye muscles, intense eye pain, and decreased peripheral vision. After age 3 years, the sclera and cornea are less expandable, and signs of pressure elevation are different from signs in the infant and very young child. The older child, adolescent, or adult with glaucoma may have no symptoms until the pressure is high enough to cause visual loss. This is why regular eye examinations are recommended to screen for glaucoma. If left untreated, the optic disk will be damaged, resulting in a restricted visual field and eventual blindness. A unique characteristic of glaucoma, which may also occur with cataracts, is that the individual may describe seeing halos around lights. Cataracts may also develop in individuals with glaucoma.

Treatment. Surgical intervention is often necessary to clear the blockage or to enlarge the drainage system in primary glaucoma. Despite prompt medical treatment, it is estimated that over 50% of infants born with glaucoma will be legally blind (Hoyt & Lambert, 1990). This is due to irreparable damage to the cornea and optic nerve, early visual deprivation, and possible amblyopia. For individuals who have secondary glaucoma, the contributing condition should be treated if treatment is to be successful. In this case, medication and/or surgery may be used for treatment. Medications will help facilitate the drainage of the aqueous humor or decrease aqueous production. Adult-onset glaucoma and some juvenile cases are often effectively treated solely with medication, such as Timolol, given in eyedrop form.

Optical devices (for example, magnifiers) and sunglasses may be prescribed because photophobia and decreased visual acuity occur in glaucoma. Visual fatigue may occur in certain situations, such as during extended periods of reading, and these should be avoided. Vision may fluctuate if the medication level is changing (Bishop, 1986).

Disorders of the Lens

Cataract

A cataract is any opacification (clouding) of the lens of the eye. It may be present at birth (congenital cataracts) or may develop later in life.

Etiology. Cataracts may be caused by a wide range of diseases and disorders. They may be the result of congenital infections such as cytomegalovirus, toxoplasmosis, rubella, and herpes, or may be part of genetically transmitted syndromes (such as Trisomy 18, Trisomy 13, Down syndrome, or Cockayne, Crouzon, Refsum, and Usher syndromes). Cataracts may also occur from severe malnutrition, trauma, or drugs (steroids) and are associated with several metabolic disorders such as **diabetes mellitus** and other diseases like osteogenesis imperfecta. They also occur as part of the aging process.

Characteristics. Cataracts may appear as a white area in the pupil. A cataract's effect on vision varies, depending on the size, position, and density of the cloudy area. Some cataracts involve pinpoint areas that do not interfere with vision. Others result in decreased visual acuity with blurred vision. If the cataract is more centrally located, near vision may be affected and vision may be worse in bright light. Cataracts located in the outer portion of the lens may result in poor color discrimination due to the abnormal scattering of light rays (Jose, 1983). As a cataract progresses, it may become so dense that blindness results. No pain is associated with cataracts.

Treatment. When an infant has congenital cataracts, surgery within a few months of birth is often advised to allow for proper development of visual responses. Children born with cataracts due to maternal rubella usually must wait until they are 2 years of age because the live virus is still present several months after birth. However, even after surgical and optical treatment of binocular cataracts in infancy, 20 to 30% of children who have them are legally blind (Lambert & Hoyt, 1990). Possible complications of surgery include retinal detachments and glaucoma.

When cataracts develop in an older individual, frequent changes in eyeglass prescription may help maintain useful vision. When cataracts progress to the point that useful vision is gone, surgery is performed to remove the lens. After cataract surgery, the individual will need to wear glasses or contact lenses or may have a lens implant. These individuals usually have a good prognosis for useful vision.

If the cataract has not been surgically treated, lighting may be adjusted to reduce glare. Lighting should be provided from behind the individual to minimize glare. Also, if the cataract is positioned centrally in the lens, unusual head positions may be observed because the person is, in effect, looking around the cataract. This should be encouraged because the person is optimizing his or her vision. Occasionally, magnification may help improve vision (Bishop, 1986).

Disorders of the Uveal Tract

Uveitis

Uveitis is an inflammation of the uveal tract, which consists of the iris, ciliary body, and choroid. It includes iritis (inflammation of the iris), iridocyclitis (inflammation of the ciliary body), choroiditis (inflammation of the choroid), chorioretinitis (inflammation of the choroid and retina), and retinitis (inflammation of the retina). The term *posterior uveitis* refers to the last two conditions. (Although retinitis pertains to a structure posterior to the uveal tract, it is commonly included under uveitis).

There are two primary types of uveitis: *nongranulomatous* and *granulomatous*. The nongranulomatous type usually occurs in the anterior portion of the tract (iris and ciliary body) and is thought to occur as an inflammatory reaction. Granulomatous uveitis primarily occurs in the posterior portion of the uveal tract and is thought to be caused by infectious organisms (O'Conner, 1992).

Etiology. Uveitis may be caused by a physical or biological noxious stimulus, or it may be a result of a traumatic injury to the eye. Uveitis may also result from a bacterial, viral, fungal, or parasitic infection. Uveitis has been present in children with such congenital infections as herpes, rubella, syphilis, toxoplasmosis, and cytomegalovirus (CMV). Individuals with AIDS who have acquired one of these infections may also develop uveitis (Knox, 1987). Other infectious diseases that are associated with uveitis include childhood measles, mumps, tuberculosis, syphilis, and chickenpox. Certain chronic diseases such as juvenile rheumatoid arthritis are also associated with uveitis.

Characteristics. The characteristics of uveitis depend on the location and severity of the inflammatory process. Uveitis may be chronic or acute, often resulting in diminished or hazy vision. Black floating spots may be present, especially in posterior involvement. Severe pain, redness, blurred vision, and photophobia can occur in some cases. Complications such as cataracts, glaucoma, and retinal detachment may result, which can impair vision by leaving scars and scotomas (Berkow, 1992).

Treatment. Treatment of uveitis depends on its location and cause. Nongranulomatous uveitis often requires analgesics for pain and dark glasses for photophobia. The pupil is kept dilated, and steroid drops are usually prescribed. Systemic steroids may be given in severe cases. Granulomatous uveitis may be treated with corticosteroids (O'Conner, 1992).

Coloboma

A coloboma is a developmental abnormality of the uveal tract. A defect is present in the eye—a cleft, notch, gap, or fissure in the iris, ciliary body, choroid, and/or optic nerve. When the iris is involved, there is a visible gap in the iris.

Etiology. Coloboma occurs as a failure of the cleft to close during early prenatal development (about 6 weeks after conception), which prevents formation of an intact, complete eye. Coloboma may occur unassociated with other abnormalities or may occur in such conditions as Trisomy 13 and CHARGE Association. (CHARGE Association is the presence of several malformations. The acronym CHARGE stands for coloboma, heart disease, atresia choanae—closure between the nasal cavity and the windpipe—retarded growth, genital hypoplasia, and ear anomalies.)

Characteristics. If the retina or optic nerve is involved, there is usually a scotoma or field loss corresponding to the site of the defect (Apple & Rabb, 1991). Often the field loss is located in the upper fields of vision, which causes a person difficulty in seeing low, overhanging tree limbs, signs, or cabinets (Jose, 1983). There may be a decrease in visual acuity; additional visual abnormalities, such as strabismus or nystagmus, may occur.

Treatment. There are presently no medical or surgical treatments for a coloboma. To improve a person's appearance, cosmetic contact lenses may be used. Sunglasses may be prescribed for colobomas affecting the iris to decrease the amount of light entering the eye. Optical devices may help improve visual functioning (Bishop, 1986).

Disorders of the Retina and Macula

Retinal Dystrophies (Retinitis Pigmentosa)

Retinal dystrophies are a diverse group of inherited disorders that affect retinal cones, rods, pigments, or a combination of these. Some retinal dystrophies affect primarily the cones; some affect primarily the rods; while others affect both. Depending on the type of retinal dystrophy, the condition may be progressive or stationary. One of the primary types of retinal dystrophies is known as *retinitis pigmentosa* (RP). In retinitis pigmentosa, retinal degeneration occurs and melanin pigment cells migrate into the retina and are deposited there.

Etiology. Retinitis pigmentosa results from a wide variety of genetic disorders. The disease may be confined to the eye or may be part of a systemic disorder (Moore, 1990). Certain syndromes may have typical retinitis pigmentosa (for example, Usher syndrome) or have a different form of retinitis pigmentosa known as atypical retinitis pigmentosa. An example is Alstrom syndrome.

Characteristics. In typical retinitis pigmentosa, the condition begins as the rods are slowly destroyed, starting at the midperiphery. This results in night blindness and a progressive loss of peripheral vision. The process continues to worsen, leading to tunnel vision. Cone degeneration also occurs, and as it progresses, tunnel vision further constricts to the point that central vision is reduced and difficulties seeing in daylight occur as well. Both eyes are usually affected in this hereditary condition, and onset is between the ages of 10 and 20 years (Lucas, 1989). Vision loss is gradual; adolescents often have difficulty traveling at night, difficulty moving from outdoor to indoor lighting, as well as difficulty performing certain activities such as playing sports. As the condition progresses, total blindness can result later in life (Apple & Rabb, 1991).

Several atypical forms of retinitis pigmentosa have been found in which the symptoms and course of the condition are different from the form just described. In some forms of atypical retinitis pigmentosa, degeneration begins centrally. In these cases, the macula is involved, resulting in deficits of central vision, poor acuity, and color vision abnormalities. The condition may progress to the periphery and result in degeneration in that area as well.

Treatment. There is no effective treatment at this time for either typical or atypical retinitis pigmentosa, although considerable research is being done in this area. Regular eye examinations are needed to assess the rate of progression of this disease. To aid visual functioning, several optical devices may be helpful. Magnifiers, hand telescopes, closed circuit television (CCTV), and infrared devices to use at night (for example, "pocketscopes") are possibilities. Prism lenses may be helpful in increasing illumination (Bishop, 1986).

Detached Retina
When an individual has a detached retina, the retina separates from its supporting structures and atrophies.

Etiology. Retinal detachment may be caused by a wide variety of etiologies. Retinal detachment in children may occur from trauma (penetrating eye injuries, blunt trauma) or from other ocular conditions such as severe myopia, congenital cataract glaucoma, coloboma, retinopathy of prematurity, and optic nerve anomalies (Moore, 1990). Retinal detachments may also be associated with tumors (retinoblastoma), con-

genital infections such as toxoplasmosis, general physical conditions such as diabetes or head trauma, inherited disorders such as Marfan syndrome, or may occur following cataract surgery (Moore, 1990). If the individual is prone to retinal tears or detachment, rough physical activity, such as playing on a trampoline, must be avoided.

Characteristics. Depending on the cause of the detachment, the individual may see a bright flash of light and possibly floaters that look like black dots or spiderwebs. The detachment will usually progress as vitreous fluid accumulates under the retina and pushes it away from the choroid. A scotoma (blind spot) will develop in the field of vision corresponding to the area of detachment (Jose, 1983). When the detached retina passes over the macula, vision is blurred (Apple & Rabb, 1991). Detachment at the macula results in severe visual impairment or total blindness.

Treatment. When a retinal detachment occurs, surgery must be performed as soon as possible to avoid a permanent loss of vision or blindness. Often, cryotherapy or laser surgery is performed to reattach the retina. Prompt reattachment may result in minimal-to-no loss of visual function, but the child may have to avoid contact sports or strenuous activity to prevent further detachments.

Retinopathy of Prematurity (ROP)
Retinopathy of prematurity (previously known as retrolental fibroplasia) consists of an abnormal proliferation of blood vessels that occurs in the immature retina (Biglan, Van Hasselt, & Simon, 1988).

Etiology. In the 1950s, retinopathy of prematurity was thought to develop primarily in premature infants because they had been exposed to high levels of oxygen in incubators. However, the condition has also been present in premature infants who were not exposed to these oxygen levels (Berkow, 1992); other factors may be involved in the occurrence. Retinopathy of prematurity has been associated with very low birth weight, vitamin E deficiency, blood transfusion, pregnancy complications, respiratory distress syndrome, hemorrhage, and high light levels in the nursery (Moore, 1990). Children with retinopathy of prematurity have a higher risk of myopia, strabismus, and glaucoma.

Characteristics. About 90% of cases are mild, and spontaneous regression of these overabundant blood vessels may occur with minimal scarring and little-to-no visual loss (Flynn, 1987). In more severe cases, the abnormal blood vessels extend into the vitreous humor and may cause retinal detachment, severe visual loss, or blindness (Biglan, Van Hasselt, & Simon, 1988). This typically occurs in both eyes.

Treatment. Premature infants should be carefully monitored for this condition. Once identified, the child with retinopathy of prematurity should be monitored to determine whether regression or progression of the condition occurs. In the majority of cases, regression occurs. Progression of retinopathy of prematurity requires surgical intervention to reattach the retina. Although reattachment is possible in approximately 40 to 50% of cases, visual functioning may remain poor (Moore, 1990).

To improve visual functioning, optical devices such as magnifiers and telescopes may be prescribed. When myopia is also present, glasses may be prescribed. Often a high level of illumination is needed (Bishop, 1986).

Macular Dystrophies

Macular dystrophies refer to a wide variety of disorders in which there are macular abnormalities.

Etiology. Macular dystrophies may be divided into four groups. First, macular dystrophies may occur from a group of rare disorders that primarily affect the macula and not other systems, such as a genetic disorder known as Best's macular degeneration. Second, macular dystrophies may occur in rod-cone dystrophies, such as retinitis pigmentosa. Third, macular dystrophies may be associated with other ocular disorders, such as albinism and aniridia. Fourth, macular dystrophies may occur in several types of inherited systemic disorders, such as Batten's disease (Moore, 1990).

Characteristics. There is a wide range of characteristics of macular dystrophy, depending on the cause and severity. In some cases, visual acuity may be reduced; other cases may involve a serious decrease in or loss of central vision.

Treatment. There is a wide range in the rate of progression or degree of visual loss. The individual with a macular dystrophy will be carefully monitored as to progression or stabilization of the disorder. There is no effective treatment at this time. However, to improve visual functioning, some individuals may use eccentric viewing. Magnification may also help.

Retinoblastoma

Retinoblastoma is the most common malignant childhood tumor of the eye. It occurs in about 1 in 15,000 to 1 in 30,000 live births and is life-threatening (Berkow, 1992).

Etiology. Retinoblastoma may be inherited, or it can occur from nonhereditary causes in which there is a mutation in the retinal cells.

Characteristics. Retinoblastomas are present in the majority of cases before the child turns 3. The tumor is in both eyes in approximately 30% of the cases (Hardy, 1992). Retinoblastoma may go unnoticed until pupils appear white or until the child is examined for strabismus.

Treatment. Retinoblastoma is a life-threatening disease, but if detected early, the cure rate is 90%. Small retinoblastomas may be effectively treated with radiation, along with chemotherapy or cryotherapy. Larger retinoblastomas require removal of the eye (enucleation). This is successful if the cancerous tumor is confined to the eye and has not spread to other parts of the body. Although there is a high success rate, individuals with the hereditary form of retinoblastoma may develop a second tumor later in life and have a poorer prognosis (Hardy, 1992).

Disorders of the Optic Nerve

Atrophy of the Optic Nerve

Atrophy of the optic nerve is the most common disorder of the visual pathways. It is not a disease itself but a disorder that indicates the presence of some type of optic nerve disease that affects the functioning of the optic nerve.

Etiology. Optic nerve atrophy can be congenital or acquired. If congenital, it is typically hereditary and can be present in numerous diseases (such as Leber's disease). Optic nerve atrophy may also result from acquired causes such as tumors, hydrocephalus, and head trauma. It is sometimes associated with certain metabolic diseases such as diabetes.

Characteristics. Central vision loss and field losses are often present. The visual loss typically is roughly proportional to the amount of nerve atrophy. Depending on where the optic nerve is affected, hemianopsia may occur. If the optic nerve is affected at the optic chasm, bitemporal hemianopsia will be present, and total blindness can result (Berkow, 1992). Decrease in visual acuity and loss of color vision often occur (Chavis & Hoyt, 1992).

Treatment. Presently, there is no effective treatment because the degeneration of the optic nerve fibers is irreversible. However, when there are underlying causes, such as a tumor pressing on the optic nerve, early removal of the tumor may result in restoration of vision. Visual functioning may be enhanced by using high illumination and enlarged print.

Congenital Optic Nerve Hypoplasia

Another optic nerve disorder that causes visual impairment is *congenital optic nerve hypoplasia* (CONH or ONH). In this nonprogressive disorder, there is a diminished number of nerve fibers in the optic nerve.

Etiology. The exact cause of congenital optic nerve hypoplasia is uncertain. It is speculated that something happens prenatally to the visual system by the tenth week of gestation that results in the diminished number of optic nerve fibers. It may be associated with a variety of abnormalities. Congenital optic nerve hypoplasia has been associated with widespread brain maldevelopment, tumors, aniridia, and a negative environment, such as maternal diabetes, alcohol consumption, or the use of anticonvulsant drugs (Taylor, 1990).

Characteristics. A wide variety of visual impairments may be present in CONH. In some cases, bilateral congenital optic nerve hypoplasia may result in blindness with roving eye movements. Other individuals may have field defects; still others may have minor visual defects with good visual acuity.

Treatment. Careful monitoring of the condition by an ophthalmologist is warranted. There is no specific medical treatment.

Disorders of the Visual Cortex

Cortical Visual Impairment

Cortical visual impairment and *cortical blindness* are terms used to describe damage to the visual pathways or cortex of the brain. In these instances, the eye shows no pathology; however, the brain cannot process incoming visual information due to brain damage in the occipital lobe. The term *cortical blindness* is an older term that resulted in the misconception that all individuals with occipital lobe damage were blind. The term *cortical visual impairment* was introduced to refer to individuals who have occipital lobe damage and some remaining vision.

Etiology. There are several causes of cortical visual impairment, including closed head injury, drowning, prolonged tonic-clonic seizures, meningitis, metabolic disorder, and hypoxia resulting in brain damage. Depending on the etiology, visual improvement may occur over time. For example, untreated hydrocephalus may result in a visual loss, but visual status may improve after shunting (Buncic, 1987). (See Chapter 8.)

Characteristics. The resulting visual impairment may range from partial loss of visual acuity to blindness, depending on the cause, the location, and the severity of the damage. Visual field defects may be present as well. Usually, nystagmus is not present. Other conditions are often present in children with cortical vision impairment, including mental retardation, cerebral palsy, hydrocephalus, microcephaly, and seizure disorder.

A person with cortical vision impairment typically has fluctuating vision in which at one moment he or she can see an object, but a few minutes later he or she cannot see it. Many children can see better in familiar places and when they are told what to look for. Also, often they can identify objects more easily when they use touch to help them identify the objects, and often can identify colors more readily than shapes. Individuals with cortical visual impairment sometimes turn their heads while reaching for objects and sometimes see objects better when they are in motion rather than stationary (Jan, Groenveld, Sykanda, & Hoyt, 1987; Whiting, Jan, Wong, Flodmark, Farrell, & McCormick, 1985).

Treatment. Visual functioning may improve without medical treatment in cases that are transient in nature. Visual recovery is often slow; children may progress from having no light perception to regaining color vision, to regaining form perception, and eventually to having improved visual acuity. Residual perceptual difficulties in cases such as these have been found (Lambert & Hoyt, 1990). Vision stimulation (enhancement) activities may improve visual functioning. However, permanent cortical blindness also occurs in some cases without improvement of visual functioning. There is no specific medical treatment available at this time except treating underlying causes when possible. It is difficult to determine whether visual functioning in a particular child will improve or remain static.

EDUCATIONAL IMPLICATIONS OF VISUAL IMPAIRMENTS

The teacher must be alert for any indication of a visual impairment. Some examples are eye-squinting and head-turning. (See Box 16-1 for a list of possible behaviors indicating a visual impairment.) If a visual impairment is suspected, the child should be referred for evaluation.

Due to the wide variety of visual impairments and differing needs of children with these impairments, it is important that the teacher understand the student's individual needs. For students with very mild visual impairments, minimal adaptations may be needed on the part of the teacher. For students who are blind, the teacher may need to use several instructional modifications in order for the student to benefit most from instruction.

Meeting Physical and Sensory Needs

Vision teachers will typically help students with low vision to increase their visual efficiency. Certain strategies may be implemented, including (1) modifying the student's environment to enhance the visual characteristics of objects, (2) teaching the use of optical devices, and (3) stimulating or training the use of residual vision (Tavernier, 1993).

Five major environmental dimensions can be modified to help the student. These are (1) color (hue,

---

BOX 16-1

Screening Checklist

A. EYE APPEARANCE
_____ Eyes red
_____ One eye turns in, out, up, or down
_____ Eyes in constant motion (nystagmus)
_____ Tears excessively
_____ Eyelid crusted

B. VISUAL ABILITIES
_____ No blink reflex
_____ Pupils do not react to light
_____ Does not fixate on object
_____ Cannot track object
_____ Does not scan for object
_____ Cannot follow moving object toward nose (converge eyes)

C. BEHAVIORS
_____ Rubs eyes frequently
_____ Squints eyes
_____ Blinks frequently
_____ Closes one eye when doing certain tasks
_____ Does not look straight at an object (looks from side)
_____ Turns or tilts head
_____ Approaches items by touch rather than sight
_____ Holds items too close or far away

D. VERBAL COMPLAINTS
_____ Complains of eye pain, headaches
_____ Complains of seeing double
_____ Complains of not being able to see well

E. ACADEMIC WORK
_____ Cannot copy off blackboard
_____ Makes frequent errors when reading letters that are shaped similarly
_____ Rereads or skips words or lines when reading
_____ Uses hand to keep place
_____ Writes uphill or downhill on paper

■ VIGNETTE 1 ■

Rosario is a 6-year-old boy who is legally blind and has a right hemianopsia. To determine visual functioning, the vision teacher performed a functional visual assessment and recommended specific adaptations for the classroom. Rosario was placed close to the board in circle time, with his friends positioned to his left so he could see their interaction. Instructional items were placed on contrasting felt or a contrasting tablecloth. Glare often reflected off a calendar board the teacher used for instruction, so she tilted it slightly downward to significantly reduce the glare. Rosario was provided extra lighting, which significantly assisted him in seeing his work. The first time the light was provided, he said excitedly, "More light, more light, I can see!"

---

saturation, and brightness); (2) contrast; (3) time (frequency, duration, and speed of presentation); (4) illumination; and (5) space (size, pattern, distance, position, and detail) (Corn, 1983). The vision teacher and classroom teacher will need to assess the student to determine how to maximize visual functioning by modifying these environmental dimensions.

Teachers should take into account the colors of items being used in the classroom. Some students with low vision may be able to see brightly colored items with greater ease than other colors, while others may not see bright colors clearly. Students with color blindness may not benefit from the use of certain colors that appear to be the same shade of gray.

The use of contrast should be considered when teaching a student with visual impairments. Providing high contrast between an item and its background is often helpful because that makes the item easier to discriminate visually. For example, written material presented clearly and boldly on a contrasting colored paper (such as black print on white paper or black print on yellow paper) may help the student see the material better. If purple dittos are used, a piece of transparent yellow plastic (like that often used for report covers) can be placed over the printed page to enhance contrast for some students. When objects are used in instructional lessons, such as math manipulatives, it may be helpful to use a contrasting piece of felt under the objects to enhance contrast. This is especially the case when the tabletop is a color similar to the objects. Wall or carpet colors can also provide contrasting backgrounds. For example, when holding up a demonstration item, the background wall should be a solid, contrasting shade rather than a busy, multicolored bulletin board. Blackboards that are not erased and not washed well are often a poor contrast. Keeping the board clean, using a whiteboard, or giving the student his or her own board may be helpful modifications. The vision teacher can help the classroom teacher make the necessary modifications.

Some students with visual impairments will perform better if given more time to complete assignments. Students who read print often need one and one-half times longer to complete the assignment; braille users may need twice as long. When the student is using an optical device to read, more time is often needed as well. Some students will benefit if both speed of presentation of the teacher's lecture and length of presentation are altered. Many students with visual impairments tire visually. They may need breaks in tasks, or the teacher may consider providing a variety of instructional tasks with different demands, such as reading, followed by the use of tapes, followed by manipulatives.

Students may benefit from the use of additional lighting or reduced lighting in order to use their vision more efficiently. Some students with retinal detachments, for example, may benefit from increased illumination. Variable lighting or lighting from behind the student may be needed for students with intact cataracts.

Some students with visual impairments will perform better if there are spatial changes, such as moving to a different position in the classroom or changing the size of items. The student with poor distance acuity may perform better from the front row of the classroom. Students with field losses may do better if seated to favor their remaining fields. For example, a student with loss of the right field of vision may be better seated on the right side of the room in order to see classmates and material. Students with central field losses—as with macular dystrophy or certain kinds of cataracts—may need to use eccentric viewing to take advantage of peripheral vision.

Increasing the size of an item or the size of print may help improve some students' visual functioning. However, for students with a reduced field of vision, such as with retinitis pigmentosa or glaucoma, enlarging items may make it more difficult because they may not fit within the student's visual field. In some cases, students may benefit from the use of large print, but optical devices may have more applications.

A second major area is in the use of optical devices. Some optical devices, such as magnifiers and telescopes, enlarge images. These may give the student more choices of reading material and the ability to see items better that are not enlarged (see Figure 16-12). Some optical devices reduce items to make them more visible. When optical devices are prescribed by the low-vision specialist, it is important that the teacher

■ **FIGURE 16-12** Student using magnifier on a slanted desk

have a clear understanding of their proper use and be able to report to the vision teacher and the low-vision specialist any difficulties and problems with the use of the device. Systematic training by the vision teacher is needed.

Students with low vision may be trained to use their vision more efficiently through the use of vision stimulation programs or vision training programs. These programs are designed to use systematic presentation of stimuli and instruction to improve a student's visual functioning. These programs have been effective with young children and children with profound multiple disabilities. For children who are young and visually inattentive, these programs have been effective when used in the first few months of life when the eye is still developing; these programs should be used before age 6. Students with profound multiple disabilities may not use their vision functionally. Programs using operant conditioning techniques and employing highly contrasting stimuli have been effective (Tavernier, 1993). The

■ FIGURE 16-13 Student using a CCTV, which enlarges print onto a screen

vision teacher may include visual efficiency training in his or her goals for the student.

Meeting Communication Needs

Students with visual impairments or blindness may need modifications in written communication. The student with a visual impairment may use a larger size print, the same size print with an optical device such as a magnifier or CCTV that magnifies print placed under it, braille, or a combination of these (see Figure 16-13). Large-print textbooks are often used in the classroom, although use of an optical device or CCTV will provide the student with more choices of reading material because not all printed material is available in a large print.

Braille is a system of raised dots that is based on a cell made up of six possible dots (see Figure 16-14). Various configurations of the dots within each six-dot cell represent the letters of the alphabet, parts of words such

as "ch" or "ed," and whole words. For example, the letter "k" stands for the word "knowledge." The dots within each six-dot cell are combined to create words and sentences. Braille is read tactilely and is made easy by devices such as a brailler (see Figures 16-15 and 16-16). Braille is a very efficient means of written communication and may be used instead of print or in addition to it. The student should be assessed by the vision teacher to determine the most efficient medium and should be provided systematic instruction in its use.

When reading or writing print, special modifications may be needed. Young students with nystagmus, for example, may lose their place when they are reading print. The use of a typoscope (a card with a rectangular hole) or an underliner (a card with a line) may be indicated. Bold-line paper or raised-line paper may help some students with low vision write on the line.

Some students with visual impairments may be asked what is wrong with them. Often these questions come from confusion over why the student is blind but can still see the building. A simple explanation can be given: "My eyes don't work very well. I can see some things, but they are blurry" or "I can't see. I use my ears and hands to learn about things. Can you tell me what this game looks like?" Often, providing other children with blindfold experiences can help increase their understanding.

Meeting Learning Needs

Children with visual impairments may have normal intelligence or may have cognitive impairments. Infants and young children who are blind will achieve certain developmental milestones (such as walking) at slower or different rates than seeing infants and young children. This does not indicate mental impairment but is the effect of the visual impairment itself on posture and

There will be many children out on the playground this afternoon to watch the soccer game.

Uncontracted Braille

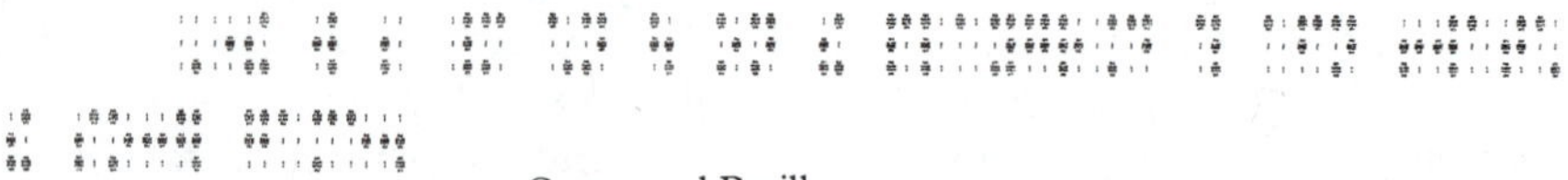

Contracted Braille

■ FIGURE 16-14 Uncontracted and contracted braille

■ VIGNETTE 2 ■

Terrill is a 7-year-old boy with a visual impairment who had been trying to read print with a magnifier. However, he read very slowly and after much effort he would fatigue. The vision teacher had been monitoring him closely, and after performing a learning media assessment, determined that Terrill would benefit from learning braille. This would give him the option of being able to use either print or braille, depending on the situation. Terrill was very excited about learning braille until he overheard a teacher saying that braille was a "last resort." He began to think that braille was somehow inferior to print. Fortunately, the vision teacher picked up on this early and talked with him and gave an inservice to the teachers about braille. He learned braille quickly and really liked using it. His classmates were impressed with this form of written communication.

on the dynamic movement used for exploratory movement. (See Chapter 2.)

Students with severe visual impairments or blindness may lack specific knowledge or concepts because much information is learned incidentally through visual experiences. Gaps in information or incorrect information may be present. For example, a blind child may think that cooking consists only of stirring because that is the only experience he or she might have had. Information about gathering, combining, and cooking ingredients is lacking—steps that a sighted child would see incidentally. A young child who is blind might have mistaken ideas. For example, when given an explanation of how people smile, the child may assume that birds also smile. Similarly, children who are blind who are given a feather to represent a bird may develop an erroneous notion of what constitutes a bird. Concepts such as color may not be understood. The teacher must take care to provide experiences that are meaningful and clearly connote the concept being explained.

With the use of computers in the classroom to aid learning, it is important that students with visual impairments not be excluded from using computers. Several different devices and programs are available that allow the student to access the computer. Screen enlargers make the print larger on the screen. Also available are speech synthesizers and programs that allow what is on the screen to be heard. The computer "reads" the printed material aloud. Braille printers can easily hook up to the computer. Computer programs are also available to convert print into braille. Special scanners also can "read" aloud printed material and have it recorded on a tape recorder or sent to the computer. Part of a student's education will be systematic instruction in the use of technology.

(a)

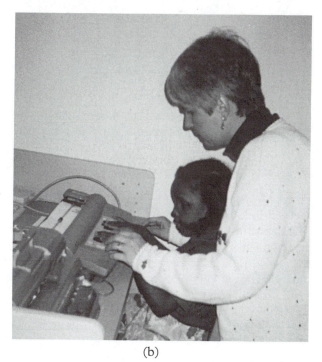

(b)

■ **FIGURE 16-15** Student using a standard Perkins brailler (a) and students using a Mount Batten electron brailler (b).

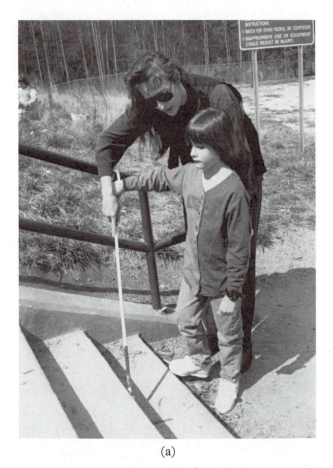

(a)   (b)

■ **FIGURE 16-16** Students learning cane (a) and precane (b) skills with orientation and mobility instructors

Meeting Daily Living Needs

Direct instruction in daily living skills is typically needed for students with severe visual impairment or blindness. Instruction is needed because students with very limited vision or blindness do not usually learn incidentally. Instruction often should include eating skills, table etiquette, personal grooming, clothing care, food preparation, house care, and shopping. Specific skills may need to be taught, such as judging the amount of food on a spoon by weight, determining if hair is in place by touch, labeling and storing clothes so they will match, labeling cans of food to specify what they are, having good organizational skills to assist with house care, and learning how to fold money

to indicate the denomination of the bills. Specific adaptations and strategies will need to be taught to the student by the vision teacher.

Orientation and mobility skills are also needed in order for the student to function independently. *Orientation* refers to the process of using one's senses to determine one's position in relation to other objects in the environment, and *mobility* refers to the ability to move about in the environment (Hill, 1986). An orientation and mobility instructor will teach the student the skills needed to move safely and independently in the environment (see Figure 16-16). This may include using another person (sighted guide), a specially designed cane, dog guides, a braille compass, electronic

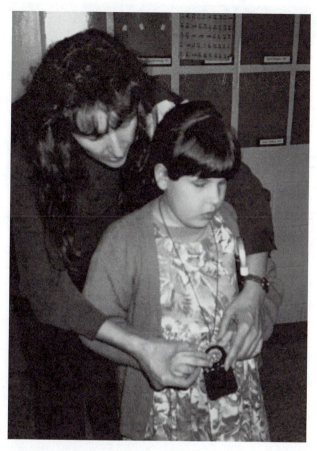

■ FIGURE 16-17 Student learning use of braille compass with orientation and mobility instructor

travel devices, or a combination of these (see Figure 16-17).

Meeting Behavioral and Social Needs

Students with severe visual impairments or blindness may exhibit stereotypic behaviors—typically motor behaviors such as body rocking and eye rubbing that are excessive, frequent, and intense. A careful assessment is needed to determine the extent to which these behaviors interfere with learning, inhibit social interaction, or cause physical damage to the student. The teacher may permit certain stereotypic behaviors to occur in certain locations, such as rocking in a rocking chair, but discourage others, such as eye rubbing. Stereotypic behavior may be managed in any number of ways, from simple verbal reminders to the implementation of a

behavioral plan that is agreed upon by the educational team to ensure consistent implementation across settings.

Students with severe visual impairments or blindness will need instruction to promote effective social interactions. Without useful vision, students will need instruction on smiling, facing the person who is talking, and other nonverbal forms of communication. Without intervention, other students may misinterpret the student's lack of smiling or other nonverbal behavior as a lack of interest, and they may not interact with the student. The teacher should facilitate interactions between students with visual impairments and nondisabled peers through mutual involvement in games and activities. Care should be taken that the teacher has provided peers with an understanding of the impact of visual impairments. This will promote better understanding on the part of the student. The teacher may use a buddy system to promote interactions. In one study (Sacks, 1992), most children with visual impairments needed adult guidance to initiate and maintain friendships. The teacher plays a critical role in helping the child develop socially.

SUMMARY

The term *visual impairment* refers to a wide range of vision losses, which can include deficits in how clearly a person sees (acuity), how much a person can see at one time (visual field), how well a person can move his or her eyes (motility), and a person's ability to distinguish colors (color blindness). A person's ability to interpret what is being seen can also be impaired if the brain is not functioning properly, as in cortical vision impairment. Several terms, including *legal blindness, blind, light perception only,* and *low vision,* describe distinct types of visual loss.

Several different types of disorders can cause varying amounts of visual impairment. Some of the ones we discussed in this chapter were keratoconus, glaucoma, cataract, uveitis, coloboma, retinal dystrophies, detached retina, retinopathy of prematurity, macular dystrophies, atrophy of the optic nerve, congenital optic nerve hypoplasia, and cortical visual impairment. Some of these eye conditions may develop gradually; hence, educators need to observe different types of behaviors that may indicate a visual problem. Once a visual impairment is identified, adaptations will be needed for the student to perform well in the school setting.

CHAPTER 17

Hearing Impairments

A wide range of disorders and diseases may cause a hearing impairment. If the hearing loss is severe enough, verbal communication may be affected and result in the need for adaptations and possibly alternate forms of communication. Having an understanding of how the ear functions, the common conditions causing hearing impairments, and their implications in the classroom will help the educator know how to best meet the needs of students with hearing impairments.

In this chapter, we will describe the major anatomical features of the ear, explain how the ear functions, define the terms used in the field, discuss common hearing impairments, and suggest educational implications.

DESCRIPTION OF HEARING IMPAIRMENTS

A number of terms are used to describe hearing impairments. Some of the most common terms are as follows:

1. *Deaf:* A hearing impairment so severe that an individual is unable to understand speech through hearing, with or without amplification. In the educational setting, the hearing impairment adversely affects the individual's educational performance.

2. *Hard of hearing:* A hearing impairment that adversely affects an individual's educational performance but allows some linguistic information to be processed by hearing, with or without amplification. This condition may be stable or progressive.

3. *Congenitally deaf:* Born deaf. Further classification may be made in terms of the age of onset of the hearing impairment. This has important implications because the earlier the hearing loss manifests itself in a child, the more difficult it will be for oral language to develop (Hallahan & Kaufman, 1988).

4. *Adventitiously deaf:* Deafness acquired after birth.

5. *Prelingual deafness:* Deafness occurring before spoken language develops.

6. *Postlingual deafness:* Deafness occurring after speech and language has developed. The age that differentiates prelinguistic from postlinguistic deafness has changed over the years because of the emphasis on the effect of receptive language. Presently, 18 months is commonly used as the dividing point, although some theorists argue that the age should be changed to 12 or 6 months (Meadow-Orlans, 1987).

7. *Stable hearing loss:* A hearing loss that does not increase in severity.

8. *Progressive hearing loss:* A hearing loss that increases in severity over time.

DYNAMICS OF HEARING IMPAIRMENTS

Before we discuss hearing impairments, a review of the auditory system is needed. The auditory system can be divided into four components: (1) the outer ear, (2) the middle ear, (3) the inner ear, and (4) the central auditory system. The structures of the ear collect sound waves and convert them into electrochemical impulses. These impulses exit the ear via the eighth cranial nerve (auditory nerve) and are transmitted to the auditory cortex of the brain. The type of hearing loss depends on where the disease, disorder, trauma, or blockage occurs.

The Outer Ear

The outer ear is composed of the auricle (pinna) and the external auditory canal (see Figure 17-1). The *auricle* is the visible, external part of the ear that collects sound waves and transmits them through the external auditory

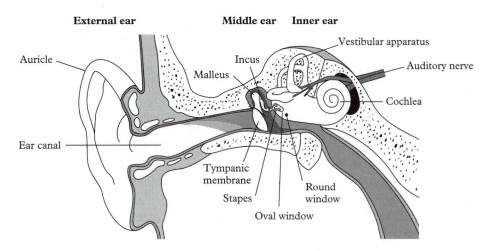

External ear　　　　　**Middle ear**　**Inner ear**

Auricle

Incus

Malleus

Vestibular apparatus

Auditory nerve

Cochlea

Ear canal

Tympanic
membrane

Stapes

Round
window

Oval window

■ **FIGURE 17-1** Anatomy of the ear

canal. The *external auditory canal* is lined by skin and contains hairs and cerumen (earwax). The cerumen helps prevent infection of the skin and protects the inner areas of the ear from foreign objects such as dust and insects. The hairs "wave" unwanted objects away and the bitter taste of the cerumen repels insects.

The Middle Ear

The middle ear is bordered on one side by the tympanic membrane (eardrum) and on the other by the oval window. Contained in this air-filled space within the temporal bone are three connected bones, or ossicles. They are the *malleus* (hammer), *incus* (anvil), and *stapes* (stirrup). The malleus is attached to the tympanic membrane, and the stapes is attached to the oval window; the incus is in between. When a sound is made, air vibrates away from it, and vibrations enter the outer ear and travel through the external ear canal; when vibrations reach the tympanic membrane, the membrane moves. The movement of the tympanic membrane causes the malleus, incus, and stapes to vibrate also, thus converting sound waves to mechanical vibrations. The vibrations of these three bones result in movement of the oval window.

Because the middle ear is filled with air, it is important that the air pressure in the middle ear be the same as the outside air. If the pressure inside the ear should become greater than the outside air pressure, as can happen in an airplane, the tympanic membrane could rupture. The eustachian tube maintains equal pressure. This tube runs between the middle ear and the pharynx (back of the throat). When a person swallows, the end of the tube located in the pharynx opens and causes air to move between the pharynx and the middle ear, equalizing air pressure (see Figure 17-2).

The Inner Ear

The inner ear (or internal ear) consists of two main sections. The first section is the *cochlea,* which is responsible for hearing. The second section is the *vestibular apparatus,* which is composed of three semi-circular canals, the utricle, and the saccule. The vestibular mechanism is responsible for the sense of balance. Together, the cochlea and the vestibular apparatus is referred to as the *labyrinth.*

The cochlea is a system of three tubes coiled side by side, which has the appearance of a snail shell (see Figure 17-1). These three coiled tubes are known as the *scala vestibuli, scala media,* and *scala tympani* (see Figure 17-3). The scala vestibuli and scala tympani are connected to each other at the end of the coil, and both are filled with a fluid known as *perilymph.* The middle coil (scala media) contains a fluid known as *endolymph.* The scala media and scala tympani are divided by a membrane known as the *basilar membrane.* Located on that membrane in the scala media is a structure known as the *organ of Corti* (see Figure 17-4). The organ of Corti contains about 20,000 auditory receptor cells, known as *hair cells* (Batshaw & Perret, 1992). Hair cells that are located near the oval window are connected to stiff, short fibers (basilar fibers) that react to high frequencies. Hair cells that are located near the tip of the cochlea are connected to fibers that vibrate at a low frequency (Guyton, 1991). As an individual ages, there is a loss of hair cells and damage to these supporting structures of the organ of Corti, which results in hearing loss of the higher frequencies. This is referred to as *presbycusis.*

The vibrations of the stapes produce movement of fluid within the inner ear. The vibrations travel through the scala vestibuli, pass through a small hole (helicotrema) at the end of the coil into the scala tympani,

Equal pressure

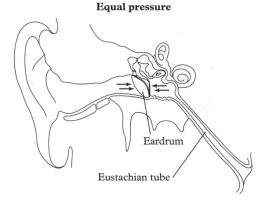

Eardrum

Eustachian tube

Outside pressure greater

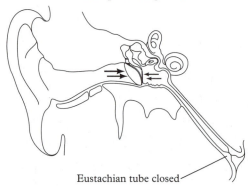

Eustachian tube closed

Pressure equalized

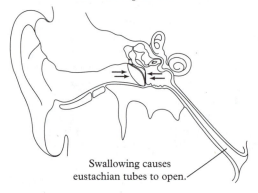

Swallowing causes
eustachian tubes to open.

■ **FIGURE 17-2** Eustachian tube

and travel through the scala tympani where they bounce against another membrane known as the *round window.* When the stapes moves inward, the round window bulges outward due to the movement of fluid. These vibrations result in a wave motion that moves the hair cells of the organ of Corti. High-frequency sound waves only move a short distance, stimulating hair cells near the oval window, while low-frequency sound waves

travel a long distance, stimulating hair cells near the end of the coil (see Figure 17-5). The loudness of the sound is communicated by an increase in the amplitude of the vibration, which results in an increased number of hair cells being stimulated and a faster rate of stimulation (Guyton, 1991).

When the hair cells are stimulated, they convert the vibrations into electrochemical impulses. These impulses then travel from the inner ear along the cochlear nerve, which joins with the nerve from the vestibular apparatus. The cochlear and vestibular nerves form the auditory nerve, also known as the eighth cranial nerve, which travels to the brain (see Figure 17-6).

The Auditory Cortex

The electrochemical impulses travel from the cochlea to the auditory cortex of the brain; their route is through several connecting neurons. The first interconnection (synapse) between neurons occurs at the brain stem. From this point, several of the impulses cross over to the other side, while others stay on the same side. This allows for stereophonic hearing. After several more interconnections at relay areas, the information is received in an area of the brain known as the *auditory cortex,* which is primarily located in the temporal lobe (see Figure 17-7). From here, other higher centers of the brain will process the sounds.

Hearing Loss

Various parts of the ear and related structures that affect hearing (such as the auditory nerve) may be adversely affected by a particular disease, disorder, or blockage, resulting in a hearing impairment. Disorder or abnormality of the outer or middle ear can result in a hearing loss. In these instances, sound waves are blocked from continuing to the other structures of the ear by some impediment in the outer or middle ear. This is called a *conductive hearing loss.*

Disease and disorders may also occur in the inner ear or auditory nerve. In these instances, the sound waves travel normally through the structures of the outer and middle ear but then are impeded in the inner ear or auditory nerve, which results in a hearing impairment. This type of hearing impairment is referred to as a *sensorineural loss.* If there is damage in the part of the brain that receives impulses from the auditory nerve, a *central hearing loss* is said to occur.

The severity of a conductive, sensorineural, and central hearing loss varies, as does the effect of the hearing loss.

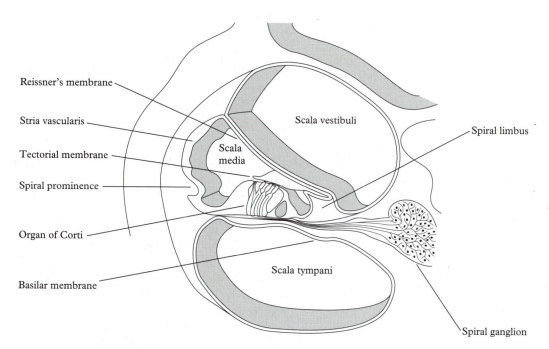

■ FIGURE 17-3 Section through one of the turns of the cochlea

Impact of Hearing Loss on Hearing Ability

The severity of a hearing impairment is often described in terms of *loudness* and *pitch*. *Loudness* is measured in decibels. Zero decibels (0 dB) corresponds to the smallest sound a person with normal hearing can perceive; normal hearing consists of the ability to hear sounds of between 0 to 15 dB. As the decibel level required for an individual to hear a sound at a certain frequency increases beyond 15 dB, the severity of the hearing loss increases.

Pitch (also known as frequency) refers to the number of repetitions of a complete sound waveform (cycle) per second. It is recorded as cycles per second (cps) or hertz (Hz). The lower the frequency, the lower the sound; the higher the frequency, the higher the sound. The amount of hearing loss may also vary across frequencies. A person may have a low-frequency hearing loss in which he or she is unable to hear low sounds or a high-frequency loss in which the person cannot hear high sounds. For example, a person with a hearing loss at or below 100 dB, 125 Hz, could not hear a truck going by

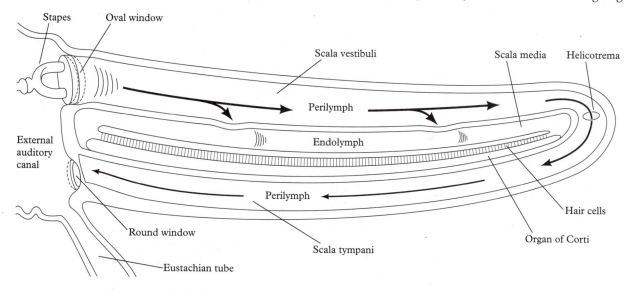

■ FIGURE 17-4 Uncoiled cochlea showing movement of sound

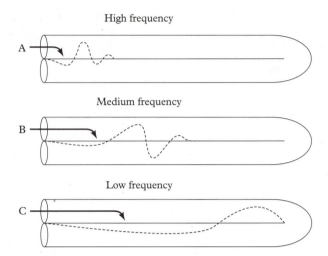

■ FIGURE 17-5 Example of high and low frequencies traveling in the cochlea (uncoiled)

(a loud, low sound). A person with a hearing loss at or below 55 dB, 125 Hz, could not hear an air conditioner (soft, low sound). A person with a hearing loss at or below 85–90 dB, 3,000 Hz, could not hear the ring of a telephone (a medium, high sound). Figure 17-8 shows a comparison of the frequency and intensity of various sounds. As seen in this figure, most speech sounds are contained in the area commonly referred to as the "speech banana," which is depicted as the banana-shaped line.

An audiometer measures hearing at varying decibel levels across low and high frequencies. Individuals are assessed across different frequencies and decibel levels to determine hearing ability. Severity of a hearing impairment may be classified according to the decibel level needed to hear a sound at a particular frequency.

1. *Normal:* Hearing level 0–15 dB
2. *Slight hearing loss:* Hearing level at 16–25 dB. Vowel sounds are usually heard clearly, but unvoiced consonant sounds may be missed. Individuals with slight hearing loss may have difficulty with fast-paced peer interactions, experience listening fatigue, and miss 10% of the speech signal.
3. *Mild hearing loss:* Hearing level at 26–40 dB. Individuals with mild hearing loss can hear some speech sounds but have difficulty hearing distant or faint sounds, unvoiced consonants, plurals, and tenses; they may miss 25 to 40% of the speech signal.
4. *Moderate hearing loss:* Hearing level at 41–55 dB. Individuals with moderate hearing loss miss most speech sounds at a normal conversational level. Articulation deficits are typically present, especially in persons who are prelinguistically deaf. These individuals may miss 50 to 80% of the speech signal.
5. *Moderate-to-severe hearing loss:* Hearing level at 55–70 dB. Individuals with moderate-to-severe hearing loss have delayed language and syntax development and

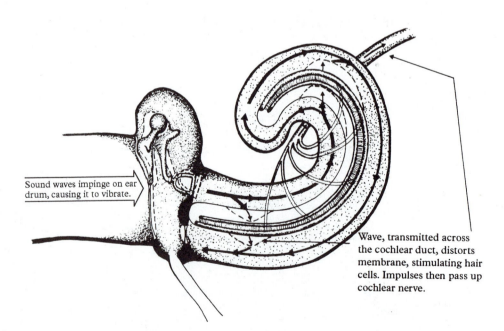

■ FIGURE 17-6 Cochlea with cochlea nerve

SOURCE: From *Handbook of Developmental and Physical Disabilities,* edited by V. B. Van Hasselt, P. S. Strain, and M. Hersen, p. 276, Simon & Schuster International Group, 1988.

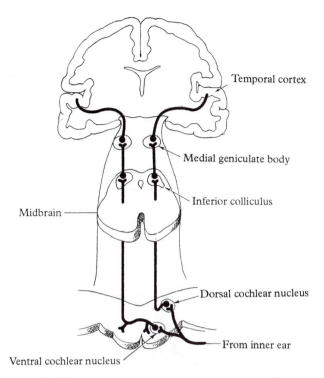

■ FIGURE 17-7 Auditory pathways from the inner ear to the brain
SOURCE: Langley & Cheraskin, 1965.

may have reduced speech intelligibility. They can miss most speech information.

6. *Severe hearing loss:* Hearing level at 71–90 dB. Individuals with severe hearing loss cannot hear speech sounds of normal conversation but may hear a loud voice at a distance of about 1 foot away and may be able to identify environmental noises. Severe speech problems are usually present, and often speech does not develop.

7. *Profound hearing loss:* Hearing loss greater than 91 dB. Individuals with profound hearing loss cannot hear speech but may react to sounds that are very loud, usually by feeling sound vibrations (Behrman, 1992; Hamre-Nietupski, Swatta, Veerhusen, & Olsen, 1986; Martin, 1994).

Results of a hearing test are usually displayed on an audiogram that shows not only the decibel level but the frequencies as well. An audiogram shows the decibel level on the *y* (vertical) axis and the frequency on the *x* (horizontal) axis (see Figure 17-9). When testing hearing through air conduction, an "X" on the audiogram indicates the left ear, and an "O" indicates the right ear. Hearing in one ear is compared to hearing in the other using headphones. In Figure 17-9, the person has hearing within normal limits across all frequencies. Figure 17-10 depicts a moderate hearing loss in the low frequencies and a severe hearing loss in the high frequencies.

Testing is also done to evaluate for bone conduction. In this test, a vibrator that makes tones similar to those of the air conduction test is placed on the bone behind the ear, or sometimes on the forehead. This test helps determine where the hearing impairment is located

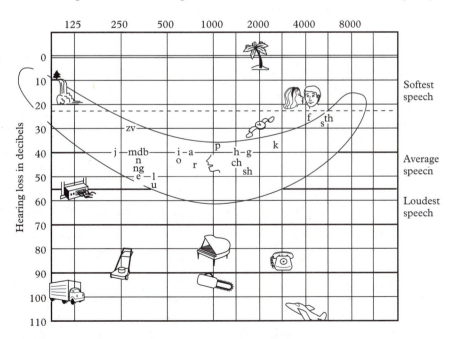

■ FIGURE 17-8 The frequency and intensity of various environmental and speech sounds
SOURCE: From *Graphics to Accompany the Ski-Hi Resource Manual,* by S. Watkins (Ed.).
Copyright © 1993 Hope, Inc. Reprinted with permission.

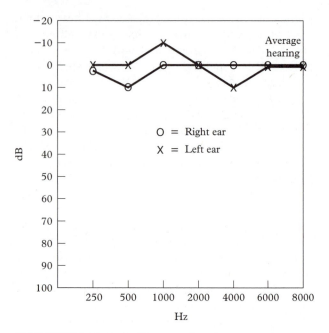

■ **FIGURE 17-9** Audiogram showing normal hearing

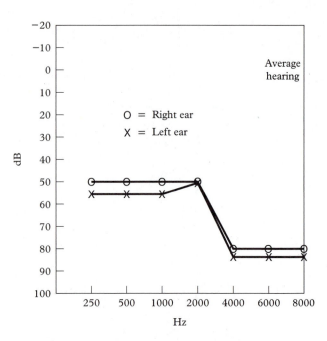

■ **FIGURE 17-10** Audiogram with moderate loss in low frequencies

because the test bypasses the middle ear and tests the inner ear. For example, if the bone conduction test shows normal hearing and the air conduction test shows moderate hearing loss, this indicates that the inner ear is working fine and that the problem is in the external or middle ear. The diagnosis would be a conductive hearing loss. This type of problem is illustrated in

Figure 17-11. If the bone conduction test and the air conduction test both show a moderate hearing loss, for example, this would indicate a problem in the inner ear. The diagnosis would be a sensorineural hearing loss, as depicted in Figure 17-12. If the air conduction test is worse than the bone conduction test, this may indicate a mixed loss.

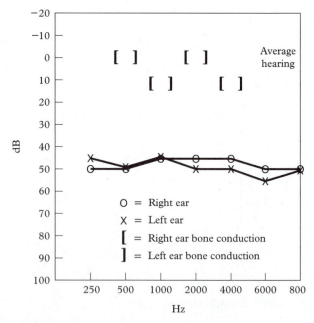

■ **FIGURE 17-11** Audiogram with bone conduction, moderate loss

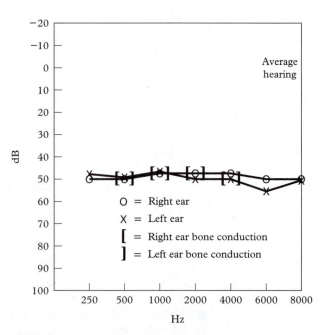

■ **FIGURE 17-12** Audiogram with bone conduction and air conduction loss

ETIOLOGY, CHARACTERISTICS, COURSE, AND TREATMENT OF COMMON HEARING IMPAIRMENTS

Several types of hearing impairments can be categorized as (1) disorders of the outer ear (conductive loss), (2) disorders of the middle ear (conductive loss), (3) disorders of the inner ear and eighth cranial nerve (sensorineural loss), (4) disorders of the outer/middle ear and inner ear (mixed loss), and (5) disorders of the central auditory mechanism (central loss). Each of these will be discussed in terms of etiology, characteristics, and treatment.

Disorders of the Outer Ear: Conductive Loss

Obstruction in the Outer Ear

When an obstruction in the outer ear affects hearing, it is classified as a conductive hearing loss.

Etiology. Several conditions can result in obstructions in the outer ear. There can be physical malformations, such as congenital atresia (absence or closure of the external auditory canal), or an obstruction in the external auditory canal from impacted cerumen (earwax), foreign bodies, or a tumor. Infections such as external otitis—an infection of the skin of the external auditory canal, also known as "swimmer's ear"—may also impede hearing because of secondary swelling of the canal and drainage of purulent material.

Characteristics. An obstruction of the external ear typically occurs in only one ear. The degree of hearing loss will vary, depending on how much the external ear is obstructed. The child will often turn the unobstructed ear to the side where conversation is occurring and may notice that he or she cannot hear as well through the obstructed ear.

Treatment. Treatment depends on the cause of the obstruction. Impacted cerumen, foreign bodies, or a tumor may be removed, which results in restoration of normal hearing. An infection of the external auditory canal is usually treated with medication given as ear drops. After the infection clears, if there was any loss of hearing, it returns to normal. Treatment of atresia of the external ear depends on the severity of the problem. If the canal can be surgically opened, doing so may result in normal hearing if there was no other damage to the structures in the ear.

Perforation of the Tympanic Membrane

The tympanic membrane (eardrum) between the outer and middle ear may become perforated, that is, get a hole in it.

Etiology. Perforation of the tympanic membrane may occur due to a middle ear infection, a blow to the head, or severe pressure change when diving.

Characteristics. Perforation results in a conductive hearing loss. Chronic perforation can lead to cholesteatoma (cystic mass in the middle ear), inflammation of the mastoid bone, brain ulcers, or meningitis.

Treatment. Depending on the size and severity of the perforation, the tympanic membrane will usually grow back together, although some scarring may result. In these cases, precautions are taken, such as keeping water out of the ear using cotton dabbed with Vaseline or ear molds. Surgical repair is necessary in some cases. If an infection causes the perforation, it should be treated with antibiotics and special ear drops.

Disorders of the Middle Ear: Conductive Loss

Otitis Media

One of the most frequent causes of a conductive hearing loss is otitis media, an infection of the middle ear. The eustachian tube and occasionally part of the temporal bone may also be infected.

Etiology. The infection may be bacterial or viral. Often there is an upper respiratory infection, and otitis media develops as a secondary infection. The eustachian tube may become obstructed and result in otitis media.

There are several different types of otitis media. In many types, fluid in the middle ear restricts movement of the tympanic membrane. This restriction of movement can result in a mild to moderate hearing loss and possible rupture of the tympanic membrane. This hearing loss is usually reversible after treatment. However, in some instances of untreated otitis media, a permanent conductive hearing loss can occur from complications (such as cholesteatoma or ossicular discontinuity).

Otitis media may occur at any age, although it is most common in infants and young children. After the age of 3 years, the eustachian tubes are mature enough to be better aligned, and this allows fluid to drain.

Characteristics. The first sign of otitis media is an earache. Temporary hearing loss may occur. Infants may show irritability and restlessness. In young children, fever up to 105° F, nausea, vomiting, and diarrhea may occur (Berkow, 1992). Older children may complain of dizziness and a headache.

Treatment. Antibiotics are typically prescribed to treat the infection. If the otitis media is persistent, a myringotomy (a small incision in the tympanic membrane) may be made and a small tube placed in the incision. This is commonly known as having "tubes in the ears." These tubes allow for the continual drainage of fluid from the middle ear, which restores hearing and assists with clearing up the infection. After several months, the tubes will typically fall out of the ear or be surgically removed, and the tympanic membrane will heal. Young children with chronic ear infections may need several sets of tubes. Prompt treatment with antibiotics for a designated treatment period and/or small tubes inserted into the tympanic membrane should clear the infection, allow drainage of built-up fluid, and permit the return of normal hearing.

Cholesteatoma

Cholesteatoma is a congenital or acquired cystic mass consisting of pockets of skin that can occur in the middle ear and in other areas of the temporal bone.

Etiology. Cholesteatoma typically develops as a complication of chronic or recurrent otitis media. The tympanic membrane is often perforated. A chronic perforation provides a greater risk of cholesteatoma formation, the dangers of which include the possible erosion of auditory or cranial structures (such as the anvil, malleus, and stapes) and an infection called mastoiditis—an infection of the cells in the mastoid bone.

Characteristics. Depending on the location and severity of the cholesteatoma, there may be no hearing loss, progressive conductive hearing loss, or sensorineural hearing loss and facial palsy (when a branch of the seventh cranial nerve is in the vicinity of the cholesteatoma) (Jerger & Jerger, 1981).

Treatment. Surgery is usually performed for cholesteatoma. Because this condition can spread and destroy other structures, surgery is usually performed as soon as possible.

Conditions Affecting the Ossicular Chain

Conditions affecting the ossicular chain (the three bones in the middle ear) include *discontinuity of the ossicular chain* and *malleus fixation*. Discontinuity of the ossicular chain refers to disruption of the connections between the malleus, incus, and stapes. Malleus fixation is an unusually firm attachment between the malleus and incus connections. Both conditions can interfere with the conduction of sound waves.

Etiology. Both conditions may occur from congenital defects, head trauma, middle ear disease, or other congenital or acquired causes.

Characteristics. Discontinuity of the ossicular chain results in a stable conductive hearing loss. However, in malleus fixation, there is typically a slow, gradually progressive conductive hearing loss. In individuals who acquire these conditions by traumatic injury, the hearing loss will typically be abrupt. Tinnitus (ringing in the ears) may also be present (Jerger & Jerger, 1981).

Treatment. Both conditions are usually treated surgically; hearing is restored following successful treatment.

Disorders of the Inner Ear and the Auditory Nerve: Sensorineural Loss

A hearing loss due to a dysfunction of the inner ear or the auditory nerve is referred to as a *sensorineural loss.* Sound reaches the inner ear or the auditory nerve but is not completely transmitted to the brain.

Etiology. Disorders of the inner ear and the auditory nerve that result in a sensorineural hearing loss may occur from congenital or acquired causes. Most babies born with a hearing loss have a sensorineural hearing loss. Congenital causes of sensorineural hearing loss include infections such as congenital cytomegalovirus (see Chapter 25), syndromes such as Usher's syndrome, and congenital malformations of the inner ear or auditory nerve. Acquired causes of sensorineural hearing loss include ototoxic drugs, trauma, loud noises, and infections such as meningitis (Ludman, 1988). Many of these conditions result in the destruction of the hair cells which, in turn, results in a hearing loss. In other cases, other parts of the cochlea or the nerve itself are damaged.

Characteristics. Individuals with sensorineural loss vary as to how well they can hear. The high frequencies that are needed to understand speech are usually affected. When sensorineural loss is due to congenital causes, both ears are often affected. This hearing loss may be constant or may progressively worsen.

Treatment. Treatment typically includes the use of hearing aids, which are of varying benefit. In some instances, a cochlear implant may be inserted surgically. A cochlear implant is a device that is surgically attached to the cochlea and serves as a substitute for the hair cells. The device stimulates electrochemical impulses, which travel through the auditory nerve to the brain. The effectiveness of cochlear implants varies greatly, from minimal improvement to a significant difference in hearing ability.

Disorders of the Outer, Middle, and Inner Ear: Mixed Hearing Loss

In some conditions and syndromes, conductive and sensorineural hearing losses are both present. This is referred to as a mixed hearing loss.

Disorders of the Central Auditory System: Central Hearing Loss

Hearing loss resulting from abnormalities in the auditory cortex or the neural pathways from the brain stem to the auditory cortex is called a central hearing loss.

Etiology.   A central hearing loss may be caused by a brain tumor, vascular changes in the brain, or congenital or acquired brain damage from congenital or acquired causes.

Characteristics.   In central deafness, the mechanics of the ear are working correctly, but the individual cannot interpret the auditory messages due to damage in the area of the brain that receives the transmissions (Beadle, 1982).

Treatment.   If there is an underlying cause, such as a tumor, surgery will probably be performed. Otherwise, there is no specific medical treatment at this time. Because there are many possible underlying causes of hearing loss, it is difficult to determine whether auditory functioning will improve or remain static.

EDUCATIONAL IMPLICATIONS OF HEARING IMPAIRMENTS

Several behaviors may indicate a hearing impairment. Examples include tilting the head toward a speaker and asking for frequent repetition (see Box 17-1 for more examples). The teacher should closely monitor students for these behaviors. If a hearing impairment is suspected, the teacher should notify the appropriate personnel—possibly the school nurse, audiologist, or other qualified person who does hearing screenings for the school system—for further investigation.

When a child has a hearing impairment, it is important that the teacher understand the student's needs. For students with slight or mild hearing loss, few adaptations may be needed in the classroom. For students with profound hearing loss, several modifications may be needed to help the student benefit most from instruction. The teacher certified in the area of hearing impairments will work with the educational team and provide information and guidelines regarding needed adaptations.

Meeting Physical and Sensory Needs

Students may benefit from several environmental and instructional modifications as well as from auditory devices. Environmental and instructional modifications include (1) modifications to the classroom, (2) seating placement of the student, and (3) modifications of materials used in instruction. The severity of the hearing impairment will determine the choice of modifications.

Classrooms often have background noise and poor acoustics because of the echo effect created when sound waves bounce off hard surfaces. Second or third sound waves pass through the room, causing distortions in sound (Gearheart, Mullen, & Gearheart, 1993). This may mean that residual hearing cannot be used as effectively as possible. To help improve acoustics, the classroom may be modified with carpeting, drapes, and sound-absorbing panels or ceilings.

Seating arrangements should be considered carefully when a child has a hearing impairment. Students should be able to see the teacher as well as classmates easily to allow for speechreading if necessary. Also, having unobstructed visual access to the teacher will allow the student to attend to body language and facial expres-

---

BOX 17-1

Screening Checklist for Hearing Impairments

APPEARANCE OF EARS
_____ Discharge from ear
_____ Excessive wax (cerumen) from ear

BEHAVIORS
_____ Doesn't respond when spoken to
_____ Doesn't turn toward loud sounds
_____ Closely watches person's face when spoken to and others' actions
_____ Turns one ear toward sound
_____ Doesn't follow oral directions well
_____ Volume of tape player or radio turned up high
_____ Misunderstands what people are saying and confuses similar-sounding words
_____ Articulates some words poorly
_____ Omits word endings
_____ Cannot hear soft sounds

VERBAL COMPLAINTS
_____ Complains of being unable to hear

ACADEMIC
_____ Doesn't follow oral directions well
_____ Frequently asks for directions to be repeated
_____ Response to visual directions faster than when given orally

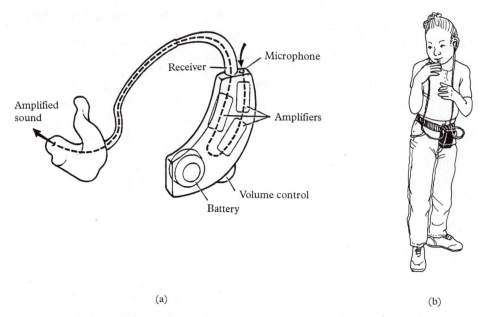

(a)   (b)

■ **FIGURE 17-13** Hearing aids
SOURCE: From *Children with Disabilities: A Medical Primer,* Third Edition, by M. L. Batshaw and Y. M. Perret, pp. 343, 460, 477. Copyright ©1992 Paul H. Brookes Publishing Co. Reprinted with permission of Dr. Mark L. Batshaw.

sions that can help him or her understand what is being conveyed.

If the student uses sign language, an interpreter will be needed in class. This person is usually positioned to the side of the person speaking, which allows the student to see both the interpreter and the speaker. The interpreter will repeat what the speaker has said by using sign language. There must be sufficient light on the interpreter so that he or she is visible to the student. (For example, if lights are turned off to show slides or a video, a small light must remain on the interpreter.)

Occasionally, the interpreter may need the teacher to slow the pace or momentarily stop instruction. This is particularly important if the interpreter must fingerspell words specific to a particular subject matter that are not part of the signing system. To facilitate the flow of interpreting, only one person should talk at a time because the interpreter cannot interpret several people at once. The teacher can help with this by being sure that the students speak one at a time. Also, to show respect for the student, the teacher and classmates should talk to the student, not to the interpreter. Another consideration is that the student with a hearing impairment will often need extra time to understand what is being said, as well as to see what is being demonstrated. The teacher should also be alert for signs of fatigue on the part of the student because attending to the interpreter, using residual hearing, and attending to the material may be

tiring. The student's schedule should have nonacademic subjects interspersed among the academic ones to avoid fatigue.

Materials may need to be adapted for the student with a hearing impairment. Use of tapes during class or in listening centers should be presented in written form for students who do not adequately hear speech. It is often helpful for the teacher to have written material available for the student in addition to what is being presented verbally. Outlines, summaries, written copies of verbal questions, and written assignments and homework are helpful. Other students can use carbon paper while taking notes and give a copy to the student with a hearing impairment.

Several types of assistive devices may be used to improve hearing. The most commonly prescribed aids are hearing aids. Hearing aids amplify sound. Although this does not usually correct the hearing impairment, the student often has improved amplification, which helps comprehension. Hearing aids consist of three main components: (1) a microphone to pick up the sound waves and change them into electrical signals, (2) an amplifier that increases the intensity of the signal, and (3) a loudspeaker that converts the signal to an amplified sound wave (Batshaw & Perret, 1992).

There are two main types of hearing aids: (1) ear-level aids, and (2) body aids (see Figure 17-13). There are different types of ear-level aids: behind-the-ear aids and in-the-ear aids. Behind-the-ear aids have a molded piece that is placed in the ear and is connected by tubing to a microphone, amplification device, a battery, and a volume control. This kind of hearing aid is worn behind the ear; it is quickly adjusted for volume, and the battery can be replaced quickly. An in-the-ear aid is smaller and more compact, and the entire aid is worn inside the ear. This type of aid appeals to some people because it is less conspicuous, but amplification is limited and the devices are more expensive.

Body aids have the microphone and amplifier worn on the body with wires running to the ear molds. Body aids are often used for children with malformed ears or for children with severe physical disabilities whose poor head control would interfere with ear-level aid placement. The body aid has the advantage of larger knobs that are easier for some people to adjust. However, since the microphone is often located at chest or waist level, sound cannot be localized. This is not the case with an ear-level aid.

The teacher must understand what to do if there is a problem with the hearing aid. In Box 17-2, common problems with hearing aids and possible solutions are provided.

Various aids and assistive devices can be used as auditory trainers, which transmit sounds directly to the student while minimizing background noises. Auditory trainers can transmit sounds by radio waves (FM systems), light waves (infrared systems), or magnetic field (induction loop systems). The most common of these are the frequency modulation (FM) systems. FM systems consist of the teacher wearing a microphone and a transmitter and the student wearing a radio receiver that is in an earphone or hearing aid (see Figure 17-14). The teacher's voice is transmitted to the student, minimizing background sounds. The FM system also allows the teacher to be at a distance from the student and still

■ **FIGURE 17-14** Teacher wearing an auditory trainer while teaching

turn away from him or her. The teacher often finds this system to be very advantageous; the only drawback is that the teacher may forget about the microphone and fail to turn it off when taking a break.

Teachers may also encounter students who have had a cochlear implant. Cochlear implants have been used in some children with profound hearing losses whose hearing has not improved with amplification (Kreton & Balkany, 1991). Cochlear implants stimulate the auditory nerve directly. Sound is received through a small microphone, which is usually hooked over the ear or attached to a magnet that has been surgically placed under the skin behind the ear. A wire connects this microphone to a small box that is often attached to a belt and contains a speech processor and transmitter. The transmitter sends the information to a receiver that is surgically implanted in the ear. By directly stimulating the nerve fibers, this device can improve hearing for some individuals. The child with a cochlear implant needs ongoing training and therapy to help him or her learn to use and interpret the new auditory information now available. When a student returns to school after receiving a cochlear implant, the teacher should be aware of any pain or infection in the area. Teacher training is necessary for use of the cochlear implant, as is true with other devices. Teachers should know how to care for the electrical pack and speech processor, as well as the microphone.

Some students may use tactile aids. Tactile aids are worn against the skin (tactile) or bone (vibrotactile) and are designed to provide information about sounds. This has been compared to "feeling the sounds." These devices have been used to teach speech as well as to improve receptive communication. Teachers should obtain information about the student's particular type of tactile aid and be familiar with its care.

BOX 17-2

Trouble-Shooting Hearing Aid Problems

WEAK, DISTORTED, INTERMITTENT, OR NO SIGNAL
Check battery placement
Put in new battery
Clean mold if earwax is present
Check that telephone switch (OTM) is in the *on* position (not *off* or in telephone position)
Call audiologist

SQUEALING OR WHISTLING
Reinsert ear mold
Push tubing between mold and aid together so it is tight
Call audiologist

Meeting Communication Needs

Communication needs may be met is several ways, depending on the severity of the hearing impairment and the philosophy of the team or school. Students with mild hearing loss will need speech therapy to improve articulation and syntax. Students whose hearing loss is more severe will be taught communication skills by the teacher of students with hearing impairments. This teacher and other educational personnel will use the commonly accepted approaches of auditory/oral, manual, or total communication. Because there are several approaches, educational personnel must know which method the student uses and understand any special modifications needed for maximum effectiveness of the method.

The auditory/oral approaches emphasize the use of amplification and residual hearing to develop oral language skills. These approaches have been used regardless of the severity of the hearing impairment. FM trainers are often used in conjunction with other devices to enhance hearing. Sometimes, the oral approach uses techniques such as feeling the individual's face to help with the comprehension and replication of what is being said. Also, the oral approach often teaches speechreading—formerly known as lipreading—which uses the position of the speaker's lips, face, and body posture to determine what is being said. Since it is difficult to identify many sounds in English that cannot be seen by lip movement, cued speech may be used also. Cued speech is the use of hand shapes and positions near the speaker's face to inform the student of which sound is being projected.

There are a few considerations for those who teach a student who uses the auditory/oral method. In regard to receptive communication, teachers must remember to face the student when speaking. This is especially crucial when the student is speechreading, or else information will be missed. Mustaches and beards may make interpretation difficult for some students; teachers have trimmed or shaved them off to assist students when necessary. Using visual cues when speaking is often helpful when the student is speechreading. The teacher should be in good light, but the light should not be directly behind him or her because this may strain the eyes of the student trying to speechread. When demonstrating or showing an item in class, the teacher should give the student time to look at the demonstration and to speechread. Both cannot usually be done simultaneously without information losses. The teacher should talk normally without exaggerating lip movements, which can cause confusion. Because some words look the same when spoken—words such as *pear* and *bear*, *pepper* and *paper*, for example—the teacher should

encourage the student to ask for clarification when needed. Students should know to do this. A teacher certified in the area of hearing impairments may show examples of how words look alike to help the student understand the difficulty of speechreading. Some students' expressive speech may be difficult to understand. Teachers should seek clarification of what the student is saying, rather than just pretending the speech is understood.

The manual approach uses a manual communication system. Manual communication means using the hands to communicate (see Figure 17-15). There are many different forms of manual communication. American Sign Language (ASL) is a commonly used manual signing system among individuals who are deaf. ASL is a language with its own structure and vocabulary. Some individuals refer to it as "the language of the deaf." There has been some dissatisfaction with ASL in the classroom because it does not correlate with English. Children who grew up learning ASL must also learn English when they begin to read and write. Alternate forms of manual sign language have been developed to more closely approximate English. Signing Exact English (SEE) is one example. These forms of sign language are commonly used in public school systems. A finger spelling system was also developed to allow for spelling out words.

Teachers must know what type of signing system the student uses. This will help the teacher plan an approach to teaching reading and writing. If the student learned ASL and does not know English, it will be more difficult at first for the student to learn the English language and the structure that is found in reading and writing. Teachers cannot assume that because a student knows a

■ **FIGURE 17-15** Student signing to another student

certain signing system, the signs in that system are the same across the county or the state. Certain signs in ASL are different in different locations. Clarification may be needed. If the teacher does not sign, an interpreter may be used. Teachers should be aware of the best positioning of the interpreter and the rate of delivery of instruction. When an interpreter is not available, students are encouraged to communicate in writing or to use alternative forms of communication.

Total communication uses both auditory/oral and manual forms of communication, as well as any other forms that are useful to the child, such as writing, finger spelling, gesturing, and so forth. This type of communication emphasizes using whatever is helpful to the student to assure success early in instruction.

Some children with hearing impairments may be asked by other children what is wrong with them. Simple explanations can be helpful. "I was born not being able to hear as well as you. You need to look toward me so I can see what you are saying" might be helpful. Providing simulation experiences with ear plugs can give the students some idea about hearing impairments. Also, explaining the different types of communication, including sign language, can be beneficial.

Meeting Daily Living Needs

Students with severe hearing impairments may use several different assistive devices to help with daily living needs. Teachers should know about these devices, where they can be obtained, and how they are used to be of most help to the student with a hearing impairment.

Some of these assistive devices include a closed-captioned television, a telecommunication device (TDD), specialized alarm clocks, and doorbells. A closed-captioned television is a television set with a built-in closed-caption decoder chip (or one that has been attached), which makes invisible captions visible at the bottom of the screen. These captions appear as subtitles and have both the narration and sound effects in print. Captioning is provided free of charge by the television companies, video industries, and the federal government.

A TDD is a device with a letter-based keyboard like a typewriter. It is about the size of an answering machine and hooks up to the telephone or plugs into the telephone jack. When using a TDD, the caller types out the message on his or her TDD. A printed message appears on a small screen or is printed out on a tape for the person with the hearing impairment to read. The person types a response. Communication with this device usually requires that each party have access to a TDD. A person without one can use number codes on a

---

■ VIGNETTE ■

Antwaun is a 10-year-old boy in fifth grade with many friends. He has a moderate bilateral sensorineural hearing loss. He wears ear-level hearing aids in both ears. His primary mode of communication is manual sign language. An interpreter is provided by the school system and is properly positioned to interpret what the teacher is saying. The teacher also provides Antwaun with written outlines and material. One classmate also uses carbon paper when taking notes and gives Antwaun the copies. When Antwaun is communicating with his friends, he will write out his messages when he is not understood verbally. Antwaun's friends write messages to him or use the signs they have learned to communicate to him. Antwaun has a successful school and social life with a few modifications.

---

regular telephone. For example, the instruction might be to push "4, 2" and "4, 3" to spell "hi." An alternative is to call a central number connected to an operator who relays the message to the person with a TDD.

Another assistive device is a specialized alarm clock. Students who are deaf cannot hear a regular alarm clock, but alarm clocks are available that work by vibrating. Part of the alarm clock is placed under the person's pillow, and it vibrates when it goes off. Other types vibrate and have flashing lights that help wake the person. Doorbells may also be attached to lights that flash to indicate the presence of someone at the door.

Just as individuals who are blind may have a guide dog to assist them, individuals who are deaf may have a hearing ear dog to assist them. Hearing ear dogs (also known as signal dogs or guide dogs for the deaf) are trained to listen for sounds, and when they hear specific sounds, such as a baby crying, to go to their master and take him or her to the source of the sound. In the case of a fire alarm, dogs are often taught to gain the master's attention, then drop to the ground and lie still as if to block their master's way (Gearheart, Mullen, & Gearheart, 1993).

Meeting Behavioral and Social Needs

Students who have hearing impairments often feel isolated from others who have normal hearing. When the hearing impairment is mild, there may be some misinterpretations of what is being said, which may result in exclusion or ridicule by other children. When the hearing impairment is severe and the student communicates by using signs, the student may not be able to communicate with hearing peers without an interpreter.

To promote social interactions, the teacher must create an accepting environment and educate peers about hearing impairments. Students can be encouraged to learn signs and other forms of communication. The teacher should encourage social interaction through activities and training.

SUMMARY

There are several different types of hearing impairments; these vary as to the extent of hearing loss they cause. Hearing loss can be recorded in terms of loudness (decibels) and pitch (hertz). Hearing losses may be categorized as slight, mild, moderate, moderate-to-severe, severe, and profound, depending on the decibel level loss. Hearing losses may also be categorized as having high-frequency losses (high pitch), low-frequency loses (low pitch), or a combination.

Hearing impairments that affect loudness and pitch may be classified as conductive, sensorineural, mixed, or central losses. Conductive hearing losses refer to impairments of the outer and middle ear. Sensorineural hearing losses refer to impairments of the inner ear and the auditory nerve. Mixed hearing losses refer to a combination of conductive and sensorineural hearing losses. Central hearing losses refer to impairments of the auditory cortex or the pathways from the brain stem to the auditory cortex. Several conditions may result in these types of hearing losses.

It is important that the educator be aware of the type of hearing loss the student has and whether or not it is progressive. To appropriately meet the needs of the student, communication strategies should be taught (either sign language or an auditory/oral method). Assistive devices, such as hearing aids, and adaptations will be needed.

PART VI

Major Health Impairments

CHAPTER 18

Congenital Heart Defects

When a child has been diagnosed as having a heart (cardiac) defect, much anxiety and misconception regarding this condition may result. Often, the assumption is made that a defect in the heart is always a life-threatening condition. Overprotectiveness may ensue at school, which can result in learned helplessness on the part of the student. Actually, there are many different types of **congenital heart defects,** and they range in severity and outcome. Some heart defects may cause no symptoms and resolve themselves, while others may be partially or totally incapacitating and require surgery to treat. Knowing how some of the basic types of heart defects affect the efficient operation of the heart will provide the teacher with a framework for understanding the educational implications of these conditions.

DESCRIPTION OF CONGENITAL HEART DEFECTS (CHD)

A *congenital heart defect* (CHD) refers to a variety of conditions in which the heart or the blood vessels in the heart are structurally impaired. Structural defects (such as a hole in one of the chambers of the heart, a malformed or defective valve, misplacement or lack of vessels of the heart, or other abnormalities) may be present. These structural abnormalities of the heart or blood vessels occur during fetal development. In some instances, the defect may not be structural but the structure of the heart is deviant due to the lack of closure of a blood vessel at birth.

ETIOLOGY OF CONGENITAL HEART DEFECTS

Congenital heart defects occur in approximately 1% of newborns. Approximately one-third of these babies require hospitalization the first year, one-third require

treatment later in life; and one-third will experience no significant consequence (Avery & First, 1994). Usually, the cause of the heart defect is unknown. Some cases may be attributable to genetic factors such as a single-gene defect. Certain chromosomal syndromes, such as Down syndrome or Turner syndrome, are associated with congenital heart defects. Other causes are associated with maternal infections (such as STORCH infections—see Chapter 25), drugs (such as certain anticonvulsant agents), or maternal disease (such as diabetes mellitus). There are also many cases of multifactorial etiologies.

DYNAMICS OF CONGENITAL HEART DEFECTS

Before we discuss the various forms of congenital heart defects, a clear understanding of the structure and function of the heart is needed. The heart is a muscle that pumps blood through the body when it is electrically stimulated to contract. Electrical stimulation of the heart through the vagus nerve occurs by a shift of ions that begins in the top part of the heart in a specific area known as the sinoatrial (SA) node and then follows a pathway down and around the heart to result in mechanical contractions.

The heart itself can be conceptualized as being divided into two parts: the right and left sides. The right side of the heart receives unoxygenated blood from the entire body through two large veins (the superior vena cava and the inferior vena cava) (see Figure 18-1). Blood that is unoxygenated (or more technically, oxygen-depleted because the body has used the oxygen) first enters the heart in the right atrium (top right chamber of the heart). As the top part of the heart contracts, the blood moves through a valve (tricuspid valve) to the right ventricle (bottom right chamber of the

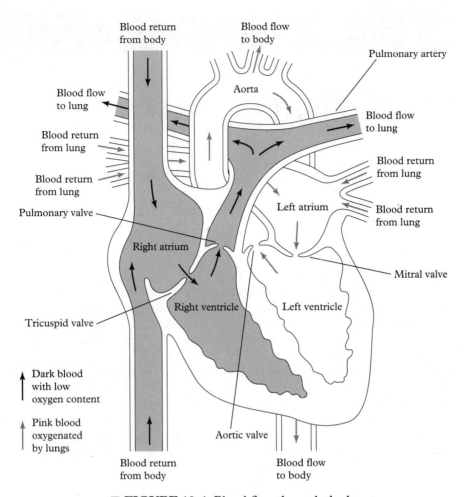

■ FIGURE 18-1 Blood flow through the heart

heart). As the bottom part of the heart contracts, the unoxygenated blood is pumped out of the heart through the pulmonary arteries to the lungs. As the blood reaches the lungs, a transfer of gases occurs in which carbon dioxide and other gases are transferred from the small blood vessels (capillaries) to the alveoli (air sacs) of the lungs. Oxygen and other gases are transferred from the alveoli to the capillaries. The newly oxygenated blood returns from the lungs to the left side of the heart via the pulmonary veins. Thus, the right side of the heart is responsible for pumping blood to the lungs and back to the heart.

As the oxygenated blood arrives on the left side of the heart, it first enters the left atrium (top left chamber of the heart). As the top part of the heart contracts, the oxygenated blood passes through the mitral valve to the left ventricle (bottom left chamber of the heart). As the ventricle contracts, it pumps the blood from the heart into the aortic valve, into the aorta, and on to blood vessels that supply the entire body. The function of the left side of the heart, therefore, is to pump

oxygenated blood to the body. Because the left side of the heart has to pump the blood so far, the muscle is thicker around the left ventricle and it pumps harder. This creates more pressure in the left ventricle.

When there is a congenital heart defect, the flow of blood through the heart may be affected, resulting in different types of medical problems and a range of symptoms. Most congenital heart defects are well-tolerated during fetal life; only after the maternal circulation is eliminated and the infant's cardiovascular system is independently sustained does the effect of the heart abnormality become apparent.

Congenital heart defects can be divided into two main categories: (1) congenital heart defects with little or no cyanosis (blue color due to lack of oxygenation), and (2) congenital heart defects with cyanosis. Congenital heart defects with little or no cyanosis typically continue to have oxygenated blood delivered to the body, although the heart may not be an efficient pump. A ventricular septal defect is one example. Congenital heart defects with cyanosis are usually associated with unoxygenated blood traveling back through the body, which results in cyanosis (for example, Tetralogy of Fallot). Several different types of congenital heart defects are found under each of the two main categories (see Figure 18-2). We will discuss only three of the most common congenital heart defects: *ventricular septal defect, patent ductus arteriosus,* and *Tetralogy of Fallot.*

CHARACTERISTICS OF CONGENITAL HEART DEFECTS

Congenital Heart Defect with Little or No Cyanosis: Ventricular Septal Defect (VSD)

Ventricular septal defect (VSD) is the most common of all congenital heart defects (Frontera-Izquierdo &

Heart Defect	Diagram	Category	Description
Ventricular septal defect	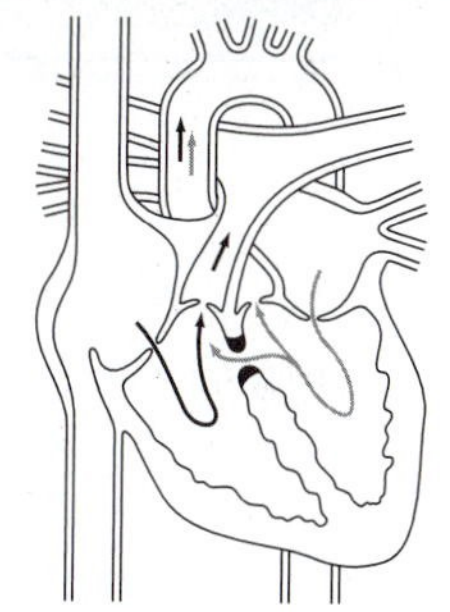	Little or no cyanosis	Hole in the septum between the ventricles
Patent ductus arteriosis	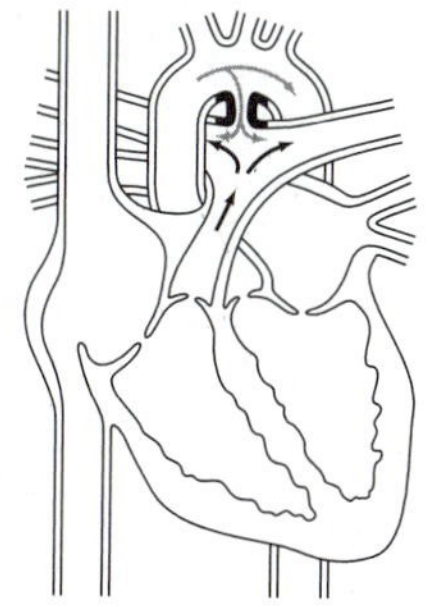	Little or no cyanosis	Ductus arteriosus remains open
Tetralogy of Fallot	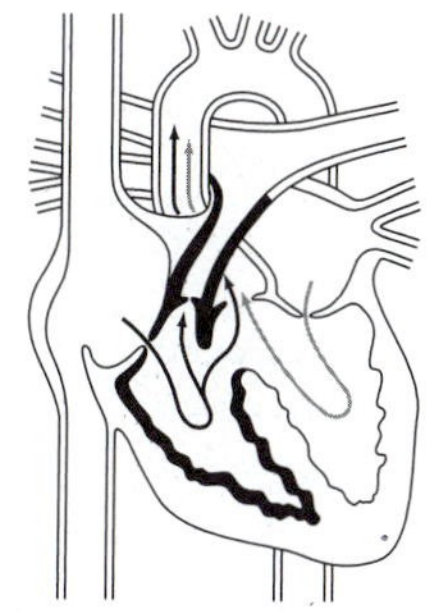	Cyanosis	1. Ventricular septal defect 2. Aorta malpositioned 3. Pulmonary stenosis 4. Right ventricle enlarged
Atrial septal defect	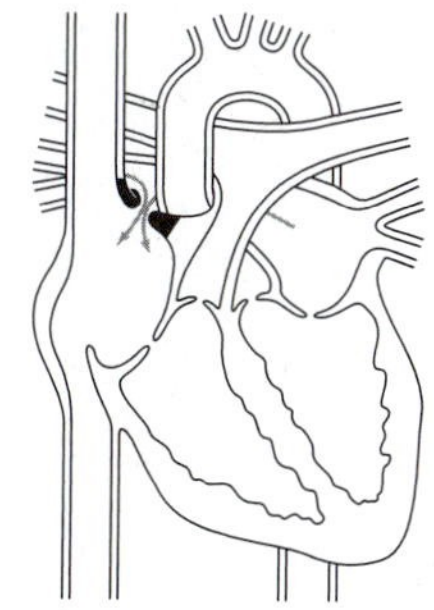	Little or no cyanosis	Hole in the septum between the atria

■ **FIGURE 18-2** Types of congenital heart defects

(Continued)

Cabezuelo-Huerta, 1992). Ventricular septal defect is a hole (or holes) in the wall (septum) between the right and left ventricles that allows blood to flow between the two ventricles. As we previously discussed, the left side of the heart has more muscle mass and is under higher pressure, so when there is a hole in the ventricular septum, blood moves from the left side of the heart to the right side.

The effects of this defect can best be understood by tracing blood flow through the heart (see Figure 18-3).

Blood enters the heart through two large veins (known as the superior and inferior vena cava). Blood flows through the right atrium and right ventricle and then flows to the lungs where it is oxygenated; it then returns to the left atrium. From the left atrium, blood enters the left ventricle where some oxygenated blood flows through the aorta and out to the body. The rest of the oxygenated blood flows through the hole in the septum to the right ventricle and back to the lungs. This type of defect is called a *left-to-right shunt* because blood flows

Heart Defect	Diagram	Category	Description
Transposition of the great arteries	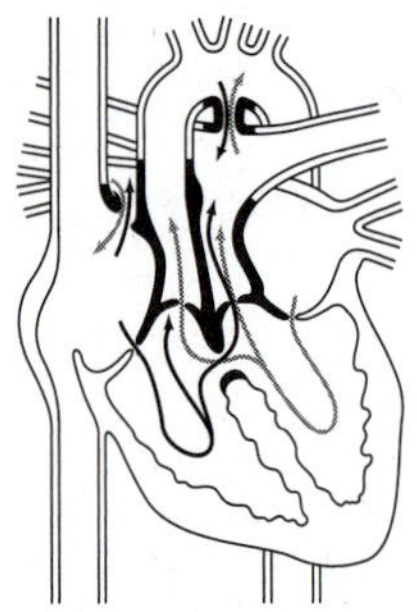	Cyanosis	Pulmonary artery is attached to left ventricle and aorta is attached to right ventricle
Aortic stenosis	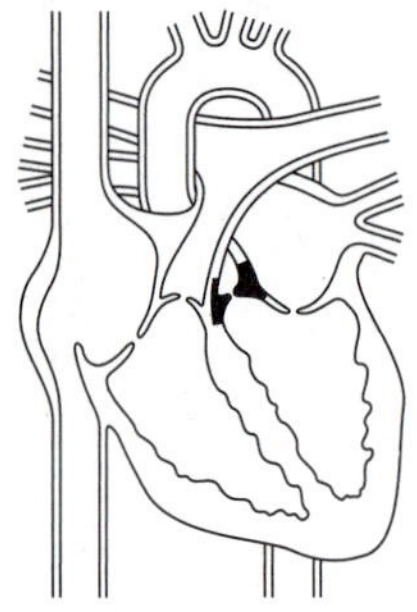	Little or no cyanosis	Narrowing at the aortic valve (valve at the entrance to the aorta)
Pulmonary stenosis	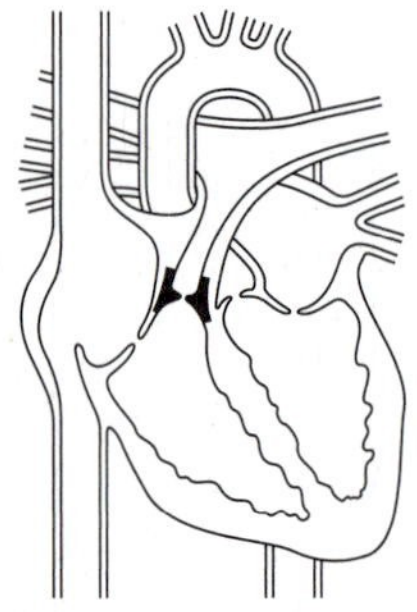	Little or no cyanosis	Narrowing at the pulmonary valve
Coarctation of the aorta	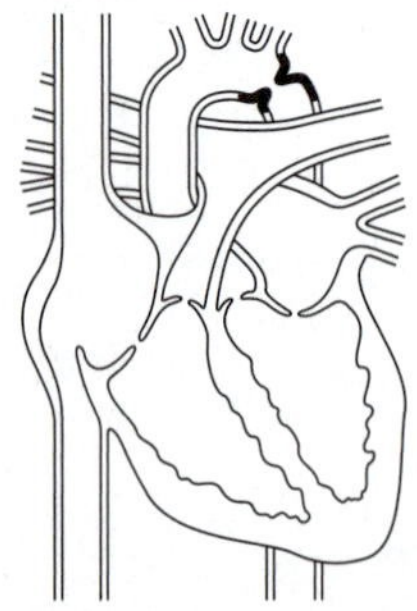	Little or no cyanosis	Narrowing of the large branch of the aorta

■ **FIGURE 18-2** (*Continued*) Types of congenital heart defects

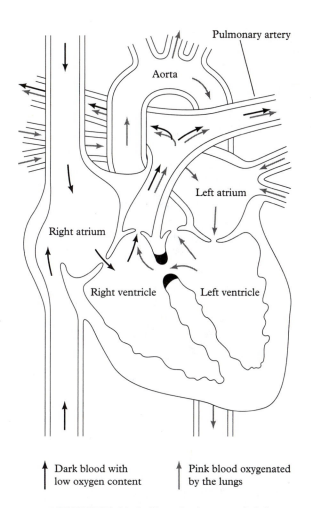

Dark blood with low oxygen content | Pink blood oxygenated by the lungs

■ **FIGURE 18-3** Ventricular septal defect

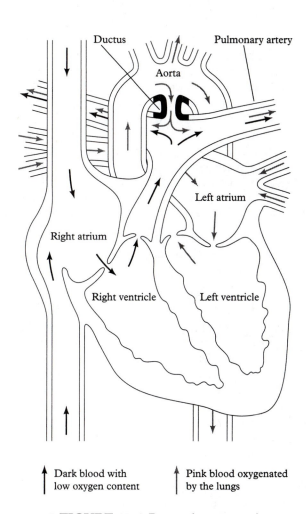

Dark blood with low oxygen content | Pink blood oxygenated by the lungs

■ **FIGURE 18-4** Patent ductus arteriosus

from the left side of the heart to the right. Only oxygenated blood goes to the body—hence, no cyanosis (blueness).

The size of the hole in the septum is one of the major factors that determines the severity of the symptoms. In some cases, the hole is very small and there are no clinical symptoms. According to Frontera-Izquierdo and Cabezuelo-Huerta (1992), 77% of a sample of children with ventricular septal defect were asymptomatic due to the small size of the defect. A large hole in the septum increases the amount of blood flow from the left to the right side of the heart. In large defects, shortness of breath (dyspnea), feeding difficulties, and poor growth may occur. Recurrent pulmonary infections and, in some cases, heart failure may occur in infancy.

Congenital Heart Defect with Little or No Cyanosis: Patent Ductus Arteriosus (PDA)

Patent ductus arteriosus is a heart defect that is common in premature infants, although it may occur in full-term infants as well. Unlike with other types of defects, there is no structural defect in the heart—no hole or mal-

formed valve or vessel. In patent ductus arteriosus, a blood vessel that normally closes shortly after birth remains open.

During **prenatal** development, the fetus receives oxygenated blood from the mother; because the fetus's lungs are not in use, blood does not need to be transported to the lungs. A small blood vessel called the *ductus arteriosus* connects the pulmonary artery and the aorta. In the fetal heart, blood usually travels into the right atrium to the right ventricle and out the pulmonary artery. Much of the blood then goes through the ductus arteriosus into the aorta and is pumped to the body (see Figure 18-4). After birth, the blood flows through the ductus arteriosus bidirectionally and then changes direction until the ductus arteriosus closes, between 8 hours to 72 hours after birth (Shiraishi & Yanagisawa, 1991). Over time, the ductus arteriosus tissue disintegrates.

In patent ductus arteriosus, the ductus arteriosus remains open (patent) after birth. With the ductus arteriosus patent, the direction of blood flow is reversed due to the increase in pulmonary resistance and pressure. Some oxygenated blood flows from the aorta to the pulmonary artery. Starting from where the blood enters the heart, blood flows through the right side of the heart, out the pulmonary artery, and on to the lungs. Oxygenated blood returns to the left side of the heart and flows out the aorta. At this point, some oxygenated blood flows from the aorta to the pulmonary artery, and some flows to the body. As with ventricular septal defect, patent ductus arteriosus is a left-to-right shunt defect. Only oxygenated blood flows to the body. A small patent ductus arteriosus will cause no symptoms. However, a large one will cause symptoms similar to those caused by a large ventricular septal defect, if not treated.

Cyanotic Heart Defects: Tetralogy of Fallot (TOF)

Tetralogy of Fallot is the most common cyanotic congenital heart defect (Karr, Brenner, Loffredo, Neill, & Rubin, 1992; Murphy et al., 1993). In Tetralogy of Fallot, there are four major abnormalities: (1) there is a ventricular septal defect, (2) the aorta is positioned over the ventricular septal defect, (3) the opening to the pulmonary artery at the tricuspid valve narrows (stenosis), and (4) the right ventricle muscle is enlarged (hypertrophied) because it must pump harder due to the stenosis (see Figure 18-5). This is a right-to-left shunt heart defect (cyanotic).

In Tetralogy of Fallot, blood enters the right atrium and flows to the right ventricle. It is then difficult for the blood to pass into the pulmonary artery because of the narrowed opening. Some blood can pass through the pulmonary artery, become oxygenated, return to the left side of the heart, and be pumped to the body in a normal manner. However, some of the blood is forced through the ventricular septal defect because there is less pressure in this area than at the narrowed opening to the pulmonary artery. This creates a right-to-left shunt. Unlike in the other two types of defects we mentioned, unoxygenated blood flows through the aorta and is circulated throughout the body.

One of the main characteristics of Tetralogy of Fallot is cyanosis, which is often not present at birth. However, as the child grows, the functioning of the heart may become further impeded and, later in the first year, cyanosis becomes apparent. Cyanosis usually appears on the lips, fingernails, and toenails.

Individuals with Tetralogy of Fallot may also have difficulty breathing (dyspnea) when exercising; the extent of exercise intolerance varies greatly. Some children with Tetralogy of Fallot may run around the playground for short periods of time, then sit quietly or lie down awhile. Other children with severe Tetralogy of Fallot may be unable to tolerate running and may need to stop and rest after walking short distances. To obtain relief, some children with Tetralogy of Fallot will

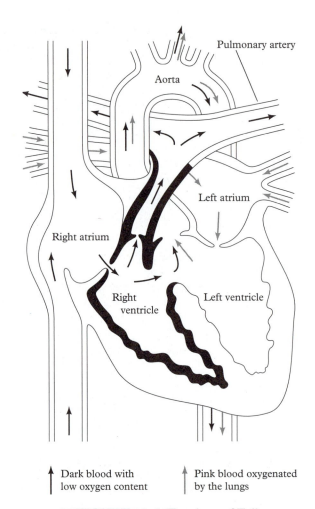

■ FIGURE 18-5 Tetralogy of Fallot

suddenly assume a squatting position after running or sometimes after walking (Avery & First, 1994).

A common and serious characteristic of Tetralogy of Fallot is cyanotic spells, known as *paroxysmal hyper-cyanotic attacks* or *blue spells*. These cyanotic spells may be accompanied by gasping, shortness of breath, and fainting. They frequently occur without any warning, although their onset may occur upon crying, feeding, or having a bowel movement (Kothari, 1992). Blue spells may last from a few minutes to several hours. Although these episodes are rarely fatal, the child may need oxygen and intravenous medication.

DETECTION OF CONGENITAL HEART DEFECTS

Congenital heart defects may be detected and assessed in several different ways. The physical examination includes observing for abnormalities, determining the heart rate, respiratory rate (breathing rate), and blood pressure, and listening for heart sounds. For children with congenital heart defects, this exam may show abnormalities in breathing (shortness of breath), abnormal heart sounds (that is, murmurs), abnormalities in the rate or rhythm of heartbeats, cyanosis, clubbing of fingers and toes (caused by changes in the soft tissue at the ends of the fingers and toes), or growth and development abnormalities.

Several tests may be used to confirm the diagnosis and assess the severity of the condition. A chest X-ray may be taken to show the configuration of the heart and lungs. An echocardiogram (ultrasound) is often used to visualize defects by using sound waves that bounce off the inner structures of the heart (Segni et al., 1988). An electrocardiogram (ECG or EKG) shows the electrical activity of the heart. A stress test may be given to determine the functioning of the heart during exercise. A cardiac catheterization may be performed in many instances to obtain further information, although an echocardiogram may be as effective in certain instances (Ge et al., 1993). Cardiac catheterization is a procedure in which a catheter (small tube) goes into the heart and a contrast dye is injected to make the inner chambers of the heart and blood vessel structure visible. Pressure and oxygen concentrations can also be measured to provide further information about the severity of the abnormality.

TREATMENT OF CONGENITAL HEART DEFECTS

Treatment varies according to the type of congenital heart defect and its severity. Treatment consists of monitoring the condition, providing medical management, providing surgical management, or a combination of these. In some cases, the child may need no intervention but will only require close monitoring. For example, in ventricular septal defect, there is a tendency in the majority of cases for the defect to diminish in size and to close without intervention (Papa, Santoro, & Corno, 1993). In other congenital heart defects, such as patent ductus arteriosus, the ductus arteriosus rarely closes after infancy and further treatment is often needed because symptoms may develop later in life.

The second type of treatment is medical management. In some instances, medical management may include fluid restriction and a low-salt diet in order to decrease the strain on the heart. Also, several different cardiac medications may be taken to control abnormal electrical rhythm, improve contractility of the heart, or affect other heart functions. Medications may also include diuretics, which increase urine excretion, and antibiotics, which are taken preventively to decrease the chance of an infection called bacterial endocarditis. Antibiotics may be taken routinely or before dental procedures. Medical management with medication is common in patent ductus arteriosus. Indomethacin is

a medication given intravenously to try to close the ductus arteriosus (Pongiglione et al., 1988).

For severe heart defects, surgery is necessary. Surgical candidates may include children with large ventricular septal defects who are symptomatic, children with patent ductus arteriosus, and those with various cyanotic forms of heart defects. In cases of ventricular septal defect and patent ductus arteriosus, surgery is done to close the hole or ductus arteriosus, thereby stopping the abnormal flow of blood. The time of surgery varies greatly, depending on the severity of symptoms; it may be done anytime from infancy to adolescence (Serraf et al., 1992; Yamagishi et al., 1993).

Surgery is typically the treatment of choice for individuals with Tetralogy of Fallot. There are temporary (palliative) procedures and definitive, totally corrective ones. Occasionally, surgery may be necessary in the neonatal period if the infant is experiencing severe symptoms and distress. However, in most instances surgery can be postponed until later in infancy or early childhood. Sometimes, correction has been postponed until adolescence or adulthood (Lukacs, Kassai, & Arvay, 1992). When surgery is delayed and symptoms are significant, growth and development may be delayed, and pulmonary infections and cyanotic spells may occur frequently.

COURSE OF CONGENITAL HEART DEFECTS

Children with small, uncorrected ventricular septal defects and patent ductus arteriosus may live a normal life span with minimal to no symptoms. If either type of defect is large and surgical correction is not obtained, the child is at risk for congestive heart failure (ineffective mechanical performance of the heart that results in an inadequate cardiac output to meet the body's needs) and possible death. The long-term prognosis after correction in uncomplicated cases is excellent.

In individuals with Tetralogy of Fallot, only about 5% can survive longer than 25 years without surgical intervention (Fernicola, Boodhoo, & Roberts, 1993). Another operation later in life (total corrective) may be needed after repair of Tetralogy of Fallot because of residual defects (Pome et al., 1992). Success in treatment of Tetralogy of Fallot depends partly on whether there are additional heart defects, other organ impairments, chromosomal abnormalities, or other associated risk factors (Allan & Sharland, 1992; Karr et al., 1992). For many individuals, prognosis after surgery is excellent for long-term survival, although the probability may be slightly lower than in the general population. Again, the results depend on the type of corrective surgery done and the type of congenital heart defect the person has (Murphy et al., 1993).

Terrill was a 15-year-old student with Down syndrome and ventricular septal defect. Although he showed no outward signs of a heart defect, he did have activity restrictions, which consisted of modified physical education. One day, Mr. Jones, Terrill's teacher, was taking a group picture of the class. Terrill stopped to tie his shoe while the rest of the class assembled for the group picture. Terrill took a little while to finish tying his shoe. When he was done, Mr. Jones yelled, "Come on, Terrill! Hurry over for this picture!" Terrill quickly ran over to the group. He was very short of breath, sweating, and appeared faint. Terrill said, "I don't feel good." Mr. Jones had forgotten that Terrill had a heart defect with activity restrictions. Mr. Jones quickly told Terrill to sit down and rest. Mr. Jones stayed with him, observing his breathing, coloration, and behavior. After a few minutes, Terrill felt fine and continued with the activity. Mr. Jones, however, felt terrible for forgetting his student's health needs.

EDUCATIONAL IMPLICATIONS OF CONGENITAL HEART DEFECTS

Teachers should understand each student's specific type of congenital heart defect and know what restrictions or adaptations may be needed. Although the precise educational implications will vary with each student, some general considerations will be taken into account to meet students' needs.

Meeting Physical and Sensory Needs

Students with congenital heart defects will vary in their need for adaptations in the school setting. Depending on the severity of the condition, some students may need significant modifications; others may need none. It is important that the teacher obtain specific guidelines from each student's physician regarding restrictions.

Students with mild forms of congenital heart defects will often have few or no limitations placed on their physical activity. In some cases, students can participate in all activities; in others, students may learn self-monitoring, and simply take breaks if necessary. This primarily applies to participation in physical education and recess when physical activity is at its maximum.

Students with more severe forms of congenital heart defects may have several kinds of restrictions. They may be unable to participate in activities that require much physical exertion. They may need minor modifications in physical education or may require an adap-

tive physical education program. Some students are advised not to participate in competitive sports; others may not be able to engage in isometric exercises. In extreme cases, some students can tolerate very little physical activity. These students may need to use elevators instead of stairs to get from one floor to another and may need more time to move from one class to another. In extreme instances, classes may be assigned based on proximity and on the amount of movement required to go from class to class. Students with severe heart defects may also need a shortened day or special rest periods.

Some students may need home-based (homebound) instruction because they are unable to tolerate a partial day of school or have extensive absences. Absences are more common in students with heart conditions in which blood flow to the lungs is increased (for example, patent ductus arteriosus, ventricular septal defect) and in some severe types of cyanotic heart disease because bronchitis and **pneumonia** are more prevalent in this population (Umbreit, 1983).

The teacher should follow activity restrictions strictly and be aware of any activities that may increase the workload on the heart. For example, taking a field trip to a park that is full of hills may be difficult for students with a significant heart defect unless there is plenty of time for them to go at their own pace. For some students, physical activity in the heat of a very warm day may be more difficult than it is when the weather is cooler. The teacher should be alert for signs that the student may be experiencing difficulty, including shortness of breath, faintness, unusual fatigue, cyanosis (blue color), fast heart rate, paleness, and sweating. Chest pain may occur but is a rare symptom in children. If these symptoms occur, the student should stop what he or she is doing and sit down and rest. If symptoms persist or worsen, the student's emergency plan should be followed, which may involve calling an ambulance and administering oxygen. Students with heart defects need to recognize these symptoms themselves and know what to do.

Meeting Communication Needs

Students with heart defects typically have no communication deficits. It is important to keep strong lines of communication open among the student, teacher, parents, and physician to ensure that everyone is clear about whether or not the student should be restricted and, if so, what those restrictions are. Emergency plans should be known to all members of the team and kept on file at school.

Students with congenital heart defects may need to explain their condition to peers. When this is the case, the student may say, "There are a lot of parts of your heart that work to make it run, sort of like a car engine. Some of the parts of mine don't work as well as others" (Association for the Care of Children's Health, 1982).

Meeting Learning Needs

Students with congenital heart defects do not usually have cognitive deficits unless the heart defect is part of a syndrome. Down syndrome, for example, is typically associated with ventricular septal defect, patent ductus arteriosus, and Tetralogy of Fallot. In these cases, the educator will need to provide the student with modification in instruction and curriculum to address any accompanying mental retardation. Also, the educator must keep in mind that these students may not necessarily self-monitor when they are in distress. The educator must monitor students closely. Compliance with fluid restriction may also be lacking and will require close monitoring.

As a part of their curriculum, students should be taught about the heart and about heart defects. Students with heart defects should be able to identify any symptoms indicating a need to stop or modify their present activity. Students also need to know their capabilities. They should be self-advocates and know when it is permissible to engage in physical activities because some teachers or others in authority may unduly restrict their activity or not make allowances for needed restrictions.

Meeting Daily Living Needs

Daily living needs can usually be addressed by the student. In extreme cases, the student may need a longer period of time to perform some activities. Modifications such as sitting in a tub chair during a shower may be used when showering after physical education class.

Teachers may need to monitor students who require a modified diet and restricted fluid intake. Younger children may need to be taught how much they can drink during a school day. Students on fluid restrictions are usually discouraged from drinking from a water fountain because it is difficult to measure how much a student drinks from a fountain. Minor adaptations, such as drinking out of a glass, are often used. Other school personnel should be advised about why the student who complains of being thirsty cannot have more water to drink.

Medications may also be taken at school and should be monitored. If the student is taking diuretics, he or she will need to go to the bathroom frequently throughout the day. The teacher must be sensitive to this and allow bathroom breaks.

Meeting Behavioral and Social Needs

Students with congenital heart defects may experience several behavioral or social difficulties. Often, students with this type of disorder are overprotected. They may not be allowed to participate in activities that other children typically do and may experience lowered self-esteem and learned helplessness as a result. This may negatively affect their social interactions with peers. Even after surgical correction, some studies have indicated that students are at continued risk of behavioral and emotional problems (Utens et al., 1993). Teachers need to be alert for possible social or behavioral difficulties and provide ameliorative techniques, such as providing books about children with congenital heart defects, providing self-esteem exercises, and listening. Psychological counseling may be indicated in some cases. Students should be encouraged to do as much as possible for themselves and to participate in activities with peers when possible. (See Chapter 3.)

SUMMARY

The term *congenital heart defect* refers to several different conditions of the heart or its blood vessels in which there is a structural impairment. This impairment occurs during fetal development or at birth. Heart defects may be divided into those resulting in little to no cyanosis (for example, patent ductus arteriosus and ventricular septal defect) and those resulting in cyanosis (for example, Tetralogy of Fallot). Students with a heart defect may experience no symptoms or may have extreme symptoms in which the student cannot walk more than a block or so without resting. Students with congenital heart defects are treated by monitoring the condition, receiving medical management (that is, medication, diet, fluid restriction, or all three), surgery, or a combination of these treatments. In some cases, the defect may close by itself, or surgery may partially or completely correct the defect. After treatment, many children live unrestricted lives. However, some students may not have the defect corrected or fully corrected. These students may need diet and fluid restrictions, activity restrictions, and medication. The teacher should monitor the student carefully for distress during exertion.

CHAPTER 19

Blood Disorders: Hemophilia and Sickle Cell Anemia

Two common diseases of the blood are **hemophilia** and **sickle cell anemia.** Although both diseases are inherited and are due to missing or defective blood components, they are very different in their characteristics, course, and treatment.

Hemophilia is the most common and serious bleeding disorder. The condition was described as early as 200 B.C.E. In the year 200 C.E., its transmission from mothers to sons only was noted by a medical rabbi and physician, Maimonides, who prohibited the circumcision of a child of a mother who had sons with hemophilia from a former marriage (Bleck & Nagel, 1982). Later in history, hemophilia was present in several royal houses of Europe, including those in England, Spain, Germany, and Russia (Umbreit, 1983). Hemophilia presently occurs in approximately 1 out of 10,000 births (Gomperts, 1990).

Sickle cell anemia, on the other hand, is one of the most common anemias. It was first described in the early 1900s. Although it is said to affect the black population in the United States, sickle cell anemia is found across several races and continents, primarily in areas of the world where malaria is common, such as Africa. Individuals who have sickle cell anemia have been found to be resistant to malaria and hence have a better chance of survival than those without it.

In both hemophilia and sickle cell anemia, the affected child has no outward symptoms of disease. However, both conditions may result in physical injury and life-threatening situations. It is vital that the teacher and child know exactly what to do when an emergency occurs in order to properly manage the situation.

Because the two diseases are different, each will be described separately in this chapter. At the end of the chapter, we will discuss both diseases together as they relate to the educational implications of blood disorders because there are commonalities in this area.

DESCRIPTION OF HEMOPHILIA

Hemophilia refers to a hereditary bleeding disorder in which there are inadequate amounts of clotting factor in the blood. Actually, several types of clotting factors are responsible for stopping bleeding when it occurs. When a clotting factor is missing or is in inadequate amounts, the person has excessive bleeding. Several different types of hemophilia are categorized according to which clotting factor is missing (see Table 19-1). The most common type is Hemophilia A, also known as factor VIII deficiency or classic hemophilia. In this type of hemophilia, there is not enough of clotting factor VIII. Approximately 80% of individuals with hemophilia are diagnosed as having this type. Hemophilia B, also known as factor IX deficiency or Christmas disease, is the second most common form of hemophilia and is characterized by an inadequate amount of clotting factor IX. About 12–15% of individuals with hemophilia have this type. The rarest type of hemophilia is Hemophilia C, also known as factor XI deficiency. This affects approximately 2–3% of individuals with hemophilia (Behrman, 1992).

ETIOLOGY OF HEMOPHILIA

Hemophilia is an inherited disorder. The two most common forms, Hemophilia A and Hemophilia B, are sex-linked recessive disorders. In these cases, there is a defective gene on the X chromosome. The disease is usually transmitted through mothers to their sons.

TABLE 19-1

Types of Hemophilia

Type	Deficiency	Chromosome Type
Hemophilia A (classic hemophilia)	Factor VIII deficiency	X-linked recessive
Hemophilia B (Christmas disease)	Factor IX deficiency	X-linked recessive
Hemophilia C	Factor XI deficiency	Autosomal-recessive

Women who are carriers of the defective gene (that is, women who have the gene but not the disease) have a 50% chance of passing the carrier state on to their daughters. Women who are carriers have a 50% chance of transmitting the disease to their sons (see Figure 19-1). Males who have the disease will pass on the carrier state to all daughters, while all sons will be totally unaffected (see Figure 19-1). In some cases, there may be a spontaneous mutation of the gene that results in hemophilia. When that is the case, males or females may have the disease.

Hemophilia C is the rarest form of hemophilia; it is an autosomal-recessive disease. In this instance, both parents must be carriers in order to transmit the disease. Since this form is not sex-linked, either a daughter or a son may have the disease.

DYNAMICS OF HEMOPHILIA

Blood is composed of several different components with diverse functions. The major cells in the blood are the *red blood cells* (RBC), *white blood cells* (WBC), and *platelets*. All of these are suspended in a fluid known as **plasma.** Red blood cells contain *hemoglobin*, which transports oxygen from the lungs to cells of the body and transports carbon dioxide from the body to the lungs. White blood cells fight off infection. Platelets are the smallest cells and assist with the coagulation (clotting) of blood. Plasma is a liquid that contains the various blood cells and the clotting factors, also referred to as *plasma proteins*.

Several internal processes stop the bleeding of a cut. First, the blood vessels that are damaged contract. Second, the damaged blood vessel wall containing collagen fibers and damaged epithelial cells is exposed to the circulating blood. A series of reactions cause the platelets that are circulating in the bloodstream to

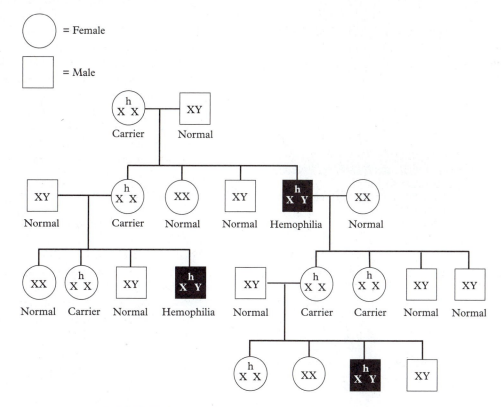

■ **FIGURE 19-1** Genetic transmission of hemophilia

adhere to the exposed collagen fibers. A chemical (adenosine diphosphate) is further released in the bloodstream, causing nearby platelets to stick to the platelets that are adhering to the blood vessel wall. The accumulation of platelets in this manner is called a *platelet plug*. If the cut is very small, the platelet plug can stop the bleeding and nothing further is needed. Typically, hundreds of tiny holes in blood vessels are closed by platelets each day. However, in larger cuts, a third process is also needed to stop the bleeding—plasma proteins must become activated to form a clot. Activation of these proteins to cause clotting occurs in two ways: (1) the damaged vessel sends out a chemical that activates the plasma proteins, and (2) blood vessel trauma or contact with collagen results in activation of the plasma proteins (Guyton, 1991). Through these two processes, the clotting factors become activated in a cascading fashion. All 13 plasma proteins are needed to form a strong clot. Each of these proteins is represented by a roman numeral and referred to as a *factor*.

In hemophilia, there is a deficiency of one of the clotting factors, which impedes the ability of the blood to form a solid clot to stop the bleeding. Very small cuts can be managed by the platelets, but larger cuts may continue to bleed without clotting because the clotting factor is missing.

CHARACTERISTICS OF HEMOPHILIA

The severity of hemophilia varies according to the individual. Severity depends on the amount of clotting factor that is present and is categorized as being mild, moderate, or severe. Hemophilia A and B have the same characteristics and are categorized the same way. As seen in Table 19-2, a person with mild hemophilia has

TABLE 19-2

Severity of Hemophilia A and B

Degree of severity	Percentage of clotting factor present	Symptoms
Mild hemophilia	6%–30%	Prolonged bleeding following dental work, surgery, or severe injury
Moderate hemophilia	1%–5%	Trauma may result in severe bleeding; may not bleed spontaneously
Severe hemophilia	Less than 1%	Severe bleeding; spontaneous bleeding; hemarthrosis

6–30% of normal clotting factor circulating in the blood. Mild hemophilia usually presents itself as prolonged bleeding during dental surgery, other surgery, or severe trauma (Suddarth, 1991). Individuals with mild hemophilia may not even realize they have the disease until they have a tooth extracted or have other surgery. Individuals with moderate hemophilia usually bleed only after injury or surgery. Even with 5% clotting factor, fatal bleeding can result after surgery if not treated properly (Berkow, 1992). Individuals with severe hemophilia (less than 1% of clotting factor) may bleed spontaneously without any injury. Diagnosis of the severe form of hemophilia is usually made within 12 to 18 months of age. Minor trauma may result in severe, prolonged bleeding, or bleeding in the joints may occur due to joint movement. Bleeding in the brain (**intracranial hemorrhage**) may occur as well.

Individuals with Hemophilia C usually do not bleed spontaneously but have continued bleeding after trauma and surgery. Those with Hemophilia C may also have blood in the urine (hematuria), nose bleeds (epistaxis), and increased amounts of bleeding during menstruation (menorrhagia) (Behrman, 1992).

Several major characteristics of hemophilia are usually present in the more severe forms. Individuals bruise easily and bleeding episodes are prolonged; often they do not stop without treatment. Blood may appear in the urine or in the stool, making stools appear black and tarry. Bleeding in the joints (**hemarthrosis**) is a common occurrence, especially involving the knees, elbows, ankles, and occasionally the hips. When bleeding occurs in a joint, the sensation is one of bubbling or tingling. This is usually followed by pain, swelling of the joint area, and warmth of the affected area. When the bleeding stops, enzymes are released into the area that clear away the blood in the joint, but they can also clear away some of the cartilage and bone. With repeated bleeding episodes in the same joint, there may be degenerative changes in which an arthritislike condition occurs, as well as contractures or limitations in joint movement, osteoporosis, and muscle atrophy. When bleeding occurs in the hip, it has been argued that Legg-Calve-Perthes disease or a similar hip disorder can occur (Pettersson, Wingstrand, Thambert, Nilsson, & Jonsson, 1990). (See Chapter 12 for a description of Legg-Calvé-Perthes disease.) Fortunately, there are now fewer orthopedic impairments from hemophilia because treatment has improved.

DETECTION OF HEMOPHILIA

Simple blood tests can show whether an individual has hemophilia. One blood test, known as partial thromboplastin time (PTT) will measure the clotting time. If the PTT is elevated, factor assays will be needed to make a diagnosis. Factor assays are blood tests that measure specific factors, such as factor VIII, and will be used to determine the type of hemophilia and its severity. Blood tests are also available to determine if a person is a carrier of the defective gene.

Prenatal diagnosis of hemophilia has been available since 1970. At that time, amniocentesis was done in the 16th to 18th week of gestation to determine the sex of the fetus; the implication was that if the fetus was a male, there was a 50% probability the child would have hemophilia. In 1979, advances in technology allowed for the sampling of fetal blood to determine clotting factors in about the 18th to 20th week. In 1985, chromosomal analysis of the fetus became possible in about the 8th to 10th week. The presence of hemophilia can be detected through examination of the amniotic fluid and tissue biopsy (Varekamp et al., 1990).

TREATMENT OF HEMOPHILIA

Prevention of trauma is an important aspect of care for the child with hemophilia. For example, use of a padded playpen for infants and avoidance of certain sports in older children will decrease the risk of a bleed. However, when a bleed occurs in an individual with moderate or severe hemophilia, the deficient clotting factor must be administered to stop the bleeding. For decades, technology has made it possible to separate specific components of blood (for example, red blood cells or plasma) to administer to individuals who need them. For persons with Hemophilia A, B, and C, plasma that contains the clotting factors may be administered. In order to get enough of the clotting factor, an exchange of plasma may be done. This is known as *plasmapheresis* and may be performed in severe, life-threatening bleeding, especially when the person has destructive antibodies or inhibitory factors to the administration of the clotting factor itself.

The most common treatment for Hemophilia A and B is the administration of the specific clotting factor—known as replacement therapy or factor concentrate—instead of using plasma. The factor may be derived from the donated blood of one individual (cryoprecipitate) or from the plasma pools of thousands of donors (for example, lyophilized factor VIII concentrate), depending on the factor type needed.

In a hospital setting, the clotting factor may be given by continuous intravenous infusion (Weinstein, Bona, & Rickles, 1991). Typically, however, the clotting factor is given in an intravenous injection over several minutes. Children and adults with hemophilia are taught how to reconstitute the clotting factor (infuse sterile fluid in the

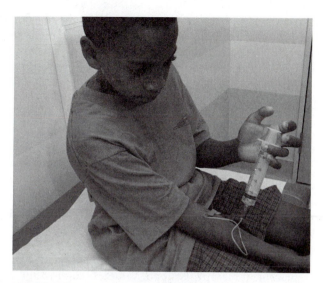

■ **FIGURE 19-2** Child giving himself coagulation medication

clotting concentrate medication bottle) and to correctly administer the clotting factor to themselves by intravenous injection in the home or school setting (see Figure 19-2).

Individuals with hemophilia are also taught how to tell when they need replacement therapy. Replacement therapy may be given in the case of injury, such as bleeding from a cut or because of a bubbling feeling in a joint. It may also be given prophylactically (preventively), before treatment by a dentist. By being taught how to properly identify the need for replacement therapy and how to administer their own clotting factor, persons with hemophilia will typically require fewer hospital visits, have a more normalized lifestyle, and have a feeling of control.

For individuals with mild Hemophilia A and in some moderate cases, replacement therapy may not be necessary. A medication known as *desmopressin acetate* may raise the amount of factor VIII sufficiently to stop bleeding. Besides replacement therapy, use of pressure and cold application may also control bleeding.

It should be noted that certain commonplace medications are contraindicated in hemophilia. Aspirin, for example, is an anticoagulant (blood thinner) that could increase bleeding time and provoke bleeding.

COURSE OF HEMOPHILIA

Advances in treating hemophilia have increased life expectancy from under 30 years of age in 1960 to presently being close to normal. Hemophilia can usually be kept under control by the prompt infusion of the needed clotting factor. Individuals with hemophilia have reported that they view the quality of their health as not really differing from the rest of the population (Rosendaal et al., 1990). However, life-threatening situations can arise, especially when there is trauma to the head or spine. Although rare, bleeding in the brain due to the birth process has occurred in newborns who have moderate-to-severe hemophilia; in one instance, it occurred spontaneously after cesarean section (Michaud, Rivard, & Chessex, 1991). These infants will often have recurrent bleeding episodes in the brain and may develop neurological deficits (Yoffe & Buchanan, 1988).

One of the most serious complications that can develop in the treatment of Hemophilia A is the development of inhibitors—antibodies that form against factor VIII coagulant and prevent the use of factor VIII replacement therapy (Gruppo, Valdez, & Stout, 1992). Little is known about inhibitors except that approximately 10–15% of infants and children with Hemophilia A will develop them. Inhibitors have not been found to be associated with the number of infusions; they could be genetically based. Several approaches are used to counteract inhibitors: the use of factor IX to activate clotting; using frequent, high doses of purified factor VIII concentrate (based on a concept of immune tolerance induction); and using porcine (animal) factor VIII. Each of these approaches has variable success; mild side effects such as fever, headache, and vomiting may be present (Bell, 1993; Gruppo, Valdez, & Stout, 1992).

Many individuals with hemophilia have contracted serious and fatal infections. If a blood donor has an infection in the blood, it can be transmitted to an individual with hemophilia who receives clotting factors or plasma. To produce most of the concentrated clotting factors, pools of thousands of donors are used. In the 1970s and 1980s, this resulted in an infected blood supply and the spread of such infections as Hepatitis B (HBV) and HIV, the virus that causes AIDS, to individuals with hemophilia. As early as 1982, three cases were reported of individuals with hemophilia contracting AIDS. By June 1990, 1,514 males and 32 females who had hemophilia were diagnosed with AIDS (Holman, Chorba, Clarke, & Evatt, 1992; Holman, Rhodes, Chorba, & Evatt, 1992). Screening of blood products began in an effort to keep the supply infection-free. New procedures were also developed, such as heating the blood, using heat in vapor, and using solvents and detergents. These methods decrease the incidence of hepatitis and, for the most part, inactivate HIV (Gomperts, 1990). At the present time, the blood supply is considered to be virtually free of HIV infection and Hepatitis B. (See Chapter 26.)

■ FIGURE 19-3 A sickle cell

DESCRIPTION OF SICKLE CELL ANEMIA

Sickle cell anemia (also known as sickle cell disease) is an inherited disorder in which chronic anemia is present. Instead of the normal disk-shaped red blood cells with pinched-in sides, some red blood cells are shaped like a sickle, hence the name (see Figure 19-3). These poorly formed, sickled red blood cells do not have a normal life span of an average of 120 days before being destroyed. The shortened life span of these red blood cells results in anemia.

Sickle cell trait refers to a condition in which the defective gene is inherited from one parent. Under normal circumstances, there are usually no symptoms present. Approximately 8% of the African American population in the United States have sickle cell trait (Behrman, 1992).

ETIOLOGY OF SICKLE CELL ANEMIA

In sickle cell anemia, an abnormal hemoglobin—hemoglobin S—is present. The production of hemoglobin S is a result of an abnormal autosomal gene that modifies the makeup of the hemoglobin. In order for an individual to get sickle cell anemia, both parents must carry the abnormal sickle gene, and it must be transmitted from both parents. This is known as *autosomal codominance* in which two genes of equal dominance from two parents determine the composition of the hemoglobin. When both parents are carriers of the abnormal sickle gene, there is a 25% chance of the child getting both abnormal sickle genes from the parents and having sickle cell anemia (Bleck & Nagel, 1982) (see Figure 19-4). Another name for sickle cell anemia is *homozygous hemoglobin S state,* because two identical defects of hemoglobin S are inherited.

When one of the offspring inherits one hemoglobin S and one normal hemoglobin, a sickle cell trait is inherited. This is known as *heterozygous state* because the hemoglobin genes inherited from the two parents are different. When both parents are carriers, there is a 50% chance that the offspring will be carriers of the sickle cell trait. However, there is a 25% chance that the offspring will have normal hemoglobin.

DYNAMICS OF SICKLE CELL ANEMIA

As we discussed earlier, several components make up the blood, one of which is the red blood cell. Red blood cells are produced by the bone marrow; almost all bones contribute to the production of red blood cells until the age of 5 years. After this time, the long bones begin to become fatty and no longer produce red blood cells. After age 20 years, the production of red blood cells occurs only in such bones as the breastbone (sternum), ribs, and the vertebrae (Guyton, 1991). Red blood cells live for about 120 days and then are destroyed, primar-

ily by the spleen. The bone marrow is constantly producing red blood cells to replace them.

The primary function of the red blood cells is to deliver oxygen to the cells of the body. In order for this to occur, the red blood cell must transport hemoglobin, which in turn carries the oxygen.

Several different types of hemoglobin may be inherited. Hemoglobin is typically composed of different combinations of protein chains. The most common form of hemoglobin is hemoglobin A, which is composed of two alpha chains and two beta chains, often referred to as *hemoglobin AA* (see Figure 19-5). The nature of the chains determines the ability of the hemoglobin to bind to oxygen.

In sickle cell trait and sickle cell anemia, the beta chains are affected. In sickle cell trait, only one of the beta chains has the abnormal sickle gene (hemoglobin S). This may also be referred to as hemoglobin SA. When this happens, there are no symptoms under normal circumstances. In sickle cell anemia, *both* beta chains are affected (referred to as hemoglobin SS), which results in changes in the structure of the red blood cell. These changes in structure typically occur during

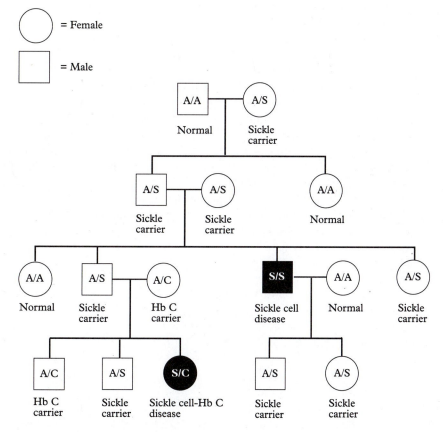

■ **FIGURE 19-4** Genetic transmission of sickle cell anemia

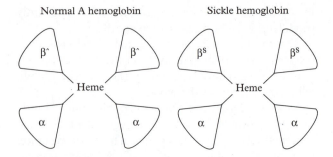

■ FIGURE 19-5 Normal hemoglobin and sickle hemoglobin

oxygen exchange in the capillaries when oxygen leaves the red blood cells to travel to the cells of the body. The decrease in oxygen in the red blood cells results in an abnormal bonding between the abnormal hemoglobin beta chains. As more bonding occurs, the hemoglobin forms a long crystal that distorts the cell membrane, resulting in the sickle shape (known as molecular polymerization) (see Figure 19-6). The sickled red blood cells then travel through the capillaries and veins to the heart and on to the lungs where they receive oxygen. Some red blood cells will revert to their normal shape after receiving oxygen—these are known as *reversible sickled cells*—and others will retain their sickle shape. These are called *irreversible sickled cells* (Zipursky, Chachula, & Brown, 1993). As the red blood cells travel through the arteries to the small capillaries, the reversible sickled cells tend to sickle again after they have exchanged oxygen to the cells of the body.

The sickled red blood cells are fragile and cannot withstand the mechanical trauma of circulation and often lack the ability to pass through small capillaries. The walls of the red blood cells then rupture, destroying the cell. In addition, cells may be destroyed through an autoimmune response in which the cells of the body attack the misshapen red blood cells because they do not recognize them as their own. Because sickled red blood cells last about 8 to 15 days instead of the typical 120 days, anemia results. This is a condition in which red blood cells or hemoglobin (or both) in the bloodstream are decreased.

Besides the chronic anemia that results from the decreased number of red blood cells, individuals with sickle cell anemia have intermittent, painful episodes referred to as *crises,* also known as sickling crises, painful crises, or vaso-occulsive episodes. In a crisis, the sickled cells become wedged in a small capillary due to their sickle shape. This can stop the flow of oxygen to tissues beyond the blockage. The lack of oxygen to the area can result in injury (ischemia) and death (necrosis)

of the affected tissue. Pain occurs because of the injury to and death of the tissue.

The exact mechanism causing the sickling crisis is not well understood. A repetitive cycle is precipitated by a sickling crisis—sickling results in further sickling of more red blood cells. As the sickled cells become wedged in blood vessels, further cell sickling tends to occur because oxygen is reduced in the affected area. Increased cell sickling results in a greater viscosity of the blood, which slows its flow and increases the probability of a "log jam," or a wedging of the sickled cells in small capillaries. However, the number of sickled cells may not contribute to the occurrence of a sickling crisis. Binding between the sickled red blood cell and the capillary membrane may be a major factor (Zipursky, Chachula, & Brown, 1993).

Several factors may precipitate a sickling crisis, most of which result in a decrease in oxygen. These factors include dehydration, trauma, strenuous physical exercise, extreme fatigue, cold exposure, infection, lack of oxygen (**hypoxia**), acidosis, or an altitude change (Suddarth, 1991). When the bone marrow slows production of RBCs, such as during an infection, a sickling crisis may result; this is referred to as an *aplastic crisis.* However, a sickling crisis often occurs without any apparent precipitating event (Behrman, 1992).

CHARACTERISTICS OF SICKLE CELL ANEMIA

The level of anemia varies among individuals with sickle cell anemia. Anemia limits the amount of oxygen that is carried to the cells of the body, so persons who are anemic may appear pale and experience fatigue, weakness, and limited exercise tolerance. Their ability to concentrate on tasks may be limited by fatigue.

Different parts of the body may be affected by chronic anemia. In an effort to deliver more oxygen to the body, the heart will work harder. Over time, this may

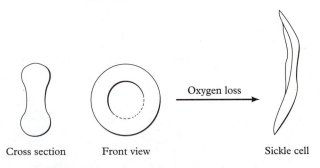

■ FIGURE 19-6 A red blood cell converts to a sickle cell shape.

result in an enlarged heart. In an effort to increase the numbers of red blood cells, the bone marrow will increase production. This results in changes in bone growth; a prominent forehead, high cheekbones, and long, thin legs and arms are typical (Bleck & Nagel, 1982). Individuals with sickle cell anemia also tend to have growth retardation; they are shorter and thinner than their unaffected counterparts. The exact reasons for this are not well understood. Inadequate food intake and vitamin E and C deficiencies have been found, but other factors such as oxygen deprivation to tissues and growth plates are also thought to be contributors (Chiu et al., 1990; Gray et al., 1992; Modebe & Ifenu, 1993). Puberty may also be delayed.

Individuals with sickle cell anemia may also appear jaundiced; that is, have a yellow color to the skin and especially to the sclera of the eyes. When red blood cells are broken down by the spleen, the liver metabolizes the resulting hemoglobin by-products. One by-product is called *bilirubin*. In sickle cell anemia, an increased number of red blood cells are destroyed. Cell destruction occurs faster than the liver can metabolize the by-products, resulting in an increase of bilirubin in the blood, which produces the jaundice. Liver and spleen enlargement may also be present. Eventually, the spleen may decrease in size and become less functional (because of cell destruction in the spleen).

One of the earliest overt signs of sickle cell anemia in infants and preschool-age children may be the occurrence of hand-foot syndrome (dactylitis). This syndrome consists of severe pain and swelling in the hands and feet, often with underlying injury and destruction of small bones. This is thought to be due to compression of the blood supply by the rapidly expanding bone marrow, which is trying to increase red blood cell production.

The major characteristic found in individuals with sickle cell anemia is pain resulting from sickling crises. The frequency and severity of these crises varies among individuals, and the characteristics associated with a crisis depend on where the sickling crisis is occurring in the body. Sickling often occurs in the bones, causing severe pain in the affected area. When a sickling crisis occurs in the abdominal (stomach) area, the individual usually has severe abdominal pain, usually due to a sickling crisis in the liver, spleen, or pancreas (Bonadio, 1990). The spleen is especially susceptible because it filters out the red blood cells. The spleen also produces lymphocytes, and if damage to the spleen results, the child will have an increased susceptibility to infections (Bleck & Nagel, 1992). Sickling crises can also occur in the kidneys and can eventually lead to chronic renal failure (Allon, 1990; Verani & Conley, 1991). (See

Chapter 23.) Sickling in the lung may result in pain, coughing, and shortness of breath. Especially serious is a sickling crisis in the brain, which can result in stroke (cerebrovascular accident or CVA), causing paralysis of legs or arms (hemiplegia) or other permanent damage.

Individuals with sickle cell trait do not usually have anemia or sickling crises. However, in extreme circumstances, such as when the person travels at high altitude in a plane that is not pressurized or goes scuba diving, a sickling crisis may occur.

Individuals with sickle cell anemia are usually of normal intelligence. However, subtle neuropsychological deficits have been found in children with sickle cell anemia. In one study (Wasserman et al., 1991), children with sickle cell anemia had significantly lower scores on the Wechsler Intelligence Scale for Children–Revised (WISC-R) than their siblings who served as controls in the study. On other tests, children with sickle cell anemia had scores lower than their counterparts, specifically in the areas of expressive speech, writing, reading, math, and memory. However, this was not found to influence academic achievement; those children's grades were comparable with those of the control group. The reason for the results is unclear, although it has been suggested that the children may have had small, undetected strokes or damage due to sickling crises. Absenteeism and the effects of chronic illness may also come into play. Whatever the reason for the differences found in psychological testing, the effects are mild.

DETECTION OF SICKLE CELL ANEMIA

Blood tests (such as sickle cell screen testing and hemoglobin electrophoresis) are available to determine whether an individual has sickle cell anemia. A diagnosis is confirmed in the laboratory by the presence of sickled cells and an absence of hemoglobin AA. A blood test (such as hemoglobin electrophoresis) can also be used to determine whether a person is a carrier and has the sickle cell trait. In these instances, hemoglobin A and S will both be present. Other tests, such as X-rays, can show bone changes, and liver enzyme tests will show liver damage. Prenatally, amniocentesis and gene mapping can be performed to determine whether or not the fetus has sickle cell anemia.

TREATMENT OF SICKLE CELL ANEMIA

There is presently no cure for sickle cell anemia. Treatment is aimed at preventing serious complications and relieving symptoms. Immunizations and the use of prophylactic (preventive) antibiotics are commonly used to prevent certain infections that could be life-threatening. Blood transfusions are only given to treat the anemia when it is extreme or to treat a severe crisis if indicated. In some instances, the person with sickle cell anemia may receive a partial exchange transfusion that replaces the abnormal red blood cells with normal cells (Piomelli, Seaman, Ackerman, Yu, & Blei, 1990).

Sickling crises are treated with pain medications (for example, acetaminophen or ibuprofen), oxygen, and fluids. Antibiotics are used as appropriate, and rest is often prescribed to decrease oxygen expenditure. A mild crisis can be treated at home, while more moderate or severe crises will require hospitalization so that intravenous fluids, injections of narcotics for severe pain, and blood transfusions can be administered if indicated.

Some experimental research has been done on administration of the medication known as *hydroxyurea* to individuals with sickle cell anemia. This medication increases the production of a different hemoglobin known as *fetal hemoglobin,* or hemoglobin F. Results have tentatively shown increases in the amounts of hemoglobin, decreases in red blood cell destruction, and subsequent decreases in the number of sickling crises (Goldberg et al., 1990).

COURSE OF SICKLE CELL ANEMIA

The effects of sickle cell anemia and its long-term outcomes vary widely, depending on where sickling crises occur in each individual. Although overall life span is decreased by complications from this disease, improvements in treatment have meant that most individuals with the disorder live past 40 years of age. Complications such as heart enlargement leading to cardiac failure can occur. Liver and spleen damage may result from excess iron absorption into the tissues from the destroyed red cells. Gallstone formation commonly occurs, with possible complications. Some potential causes of death include infections, multiple sickling crises in the lungs resulting in pulmonary emboli and death of tissue, heart failure, renal failure, and the occlusion of a blood vessel to a vital area such as the brain (Berkow, 1992).

EDUCATIONAL IMPLICATIONS OF HEMOPHILIA AND SICKLE CELL ANEMIA

It is important that the teacher understand hemophilia and sickle cell anemia so as to properly assist students with these disorders in the academic environment. Both diseases have acute crises—a bleed in hemophilia or a sickling crisis in sickle cell anemia—which the teacher needs to know how to manage. Between crises, the

---

■ **VIGNETTE 1** ■

Jerand is a 10-year-old boy with severe hemophilia. He has had several bleeding crises, primarily in the joints, and he can detect them himself and self-infuse the clotting factor. On Monday, prior to leaving for school, he felt a tingling in his knee. From instruction and past experience, he recognized this to be the early sign of a mild spontaneous bleed in the knee. He immediately infused himself with clotting factor and went on to school with no complications. On Friday, at school, he was on the playground and was hit in the head by a baseball. Jerand exclaimed that he didn't feel well. Following the emergency plan that called for an ambulance in case of injury to the head, the paramedics were immediately called. At the hospital, Jerand was treated for a subdural hematoma (compact mass of blood beneath the dura or membrane surrounding the brain). Due to the quick actions of his teachers, he sustained no permanent disability and was able to return to school the next week.

---

student may also need support and modification due to the processes of the diseases. Homebound programs may be instituted on a temporary basis for acute medical illnesses resulting from these two conditions.

Meeting Physical and Sensory Needs

When a teacher has a student with hemophilia or sickle cell anemia, it is imperative that he or she knows what to do if a bleed or sickling crisis occurs. In the case of hemophilia, the child will have been taught how to recognize a bleed and how to avoid significant trauma. If the student has other disabilities and no recognizable means of communication, the teacher needs to be alert for swelling, warmth in a specific area of the body, and the expression of pain. If the student knows how to give himself or herself the clotting factor concentrate, that should be done immediately. It is important that the medication be readily accessible. If the student does not know how to administer the medication, a plan must be in place in which either a nurse is responsible for administering it and for applying a cold pack and pressure over the affected area or the student is taken to the hospital. The parents should be notified immediately of the episode, and the student may require follow-up treatment by the physician, especially if the bleed occurred in a vital area. Bleeds that are caught early and are located in a nonvital area may not need further medical treatment except the infusion of the clotting

■ VIGNETTE 2 ■

Cansuala is a 7-year-old girl with sickle cell anemia. She attends a regular second-grade class. One day she had a substitute teacher, Mr. Marvin, who thought of Cansuala as a poor student because she seemed inattentive and fell asleep during reading. In the afternoon, she developed severe stomach pain. She told the substitute teacher that her stomach hurt and she needed to go home. The substitute teacher had not been informed that Cansuala had sickle cell anemia and told her it must have been what she had for lunch and that she needed to continue doing her math problems. Fortunately, her regular teacher had taught Cansuala to be a self-advocate. Cansuala explained that she had sickle cell anemia and should not continue doing math problems. Cansuala's mother was called. She went home and saw her doctor that day. She was having a sickling crisis and received medication to treat the symptoms.

---

factor. The student may continue in school. The emergency plan should provide specific guidelines.

In sickle cell anemia, a sickling crisis can occur almost anywhere in the body. In some instances, it is difficult to know whether the student is having a sickling crisis or whether pain is coming from some other cause. The student may have difficulty identifying a sickling crisis, especially if it occurs in a different location from one experienced previously. This is especially difficult because pain is the primary sign of a sickling crisis. The diagnosis should be made by the physician, so when a sickling crisis is suspected, the student will need to leave school to see a physician or go to the hospital. The emergency plan should provide guidance.

In both hemophilia and sickle cell anemia, there may be some restrictions on participation in physical education. Contact sports are prohibited for students with hemophilia due to the possibility of experiencing a blow to the head or neck that could be life-threatening. Physical education activities that might include jarring motions of the joints may also be contraindicated. In sickle cell anemia, strenuous exercise or trauma may precipitate a sickling crisis in some individuals. It may also be difficult for students to compete with their peers because they tire easily; physical education may need to be modified in these instances.

Meeting Communication Needs

Neither hemophilia nor sickle cell anemia affects the individual's ability to talk or communicate effectively.

Communication regarding the onset of a crisis should not be problematic for children who know the symptoms and have been instructed to tell the teacher or an adult when they occur. For students who do not effectively communicate due to young age or additional disabilities, the teacher will need to observe the student closely for nonverbal forms of communication that indicate a problem.

Children with hemophilia or sickle cell anemia may need to communicate to others about their medical condition. A child with hemophilia might say, "I have to be careful because I have hemophilia. You know how when you get a cut, it bleeds a little and then dries up? Well, my blood has a hard time drying up and I bleed a lot. It's not good to lose a lot of blood, so I have to be careful" (Association for the Care of Children's Health, 1982). A child with sickle cell anemia might say, "I have sickle cell anemia. I don't have as many blood cells as you so I get tired a lot. Sometimes my blood cells get stuck (like a clog in a drain) in different parts of my body and that hurts a lot."

Meeting Learning Needs

Students with either hemophilia or sickle cell anemia may have to be absent frequently. With prompt administration of medication, students with hemophilia tend to have less frequent absences. Students with sickle cell anemia may be absent for days or weeks when a sickling crisis occurs. Efforts must be made to help the student obtain any missed information.

In sickle cell anemia, some neuropsychological abnormalities have been found, especially after a clot has formed in the brain. This may or may not affect academic performance. However, the anemia will result in fatigue and a short attention span, which can negatively affect the student's performance. Planning the most difficult academic work early in the day and in short segments may be beneficial.

Meeting Daily Living Needs

Students with hemophilia or sickle cell anemia usually do not need to make major modifications in their daily lives. Activities that could cause injury may require extra care on the part of a student with hemophilia to avoid a bleed. Precipitating factors (such as dehydration, strenuous physical exercise, extreme fatigue, or cold exposure) may need to be avoided by individuals with sickle cell anemia. Home treatment with periodic assessment and counseling from a registered nurse is ideal management. It will help a child and family avoid major physical and psychological damage.

Meeting Behavioral and Social Needs

Students with hemophilia and sickle cell anemia may experience anxiety and stress over when the next crisis (bleed or sickling crisis) may occur. A positive, supportive environment in which the teacher is willing to listen to the student and provide emotional support is helpful. In some instances, counseling is needed.

When there are restrictions in activities, such as during physical education classes, as well as frequent absences, students with hemophilia or sickle cell anemia may have difficulty making friends. These students should be encouraged to join a club or to participate in other extracurricular activities. Peers need to be given information about these diseases so they can understand some of the manifestations and restrictions and know, for example, to avoid rough play with the child with hemophilia and to avoid thinking that the pain associated with sickle cell anemia is contagious.

SUMMARY

Hemophilia and sickle cell anemia are two inherited diseases of the blood. In hemophilia, the blood cannot clot normally, which results in abnormal bleeding. Hemophilia can be treated by infusion of a clotting factor. In sickle cell anemia, abnormal hemoglobin (sickle hemoglobin) causes the red blood cells to change into a sickle shape. This results in anemia when these red blood cells are destroyed prematurely. Painful crises occur when these sickle cells wedge into small capillaries, resulting in a lack of oxygen to the cells beyond. Treatment of sickle cell anemia is to alleviate symptoms because there is no cure.

Educators need to know the symptoms of a bleed for students with hemophilia and symptoms of a sickling crisis for students with sickle cell anemia. Prompt treatment and management is important to prevent further complications. Educators must also be aware of possible restrictions, especially in physical education classes. Learning may be interrupted by frequent absences. Students with sickle cell anemia may tire easily and have a short attention span, which can negatively affect learning. Social and behavioral issues need to be addressed in the educational setting as well.

CHAPTER 20

Asthma

Asthma is the most common pulmonary disease of childhood, but this disease can develop any time in life, from the first few weeks to adulthood. Although researchers used to think it was an emotional disorder caused by psychological reactions, asthma is now known to be a metabolic, biochemical, physical disorder. The child with asthma may be totally at ease at one moment, with no sign of disease, but may then start wheezing and need medication. Teachers who have students with asthma will need an understanding of how this disease occurs, what triggers an asthma attack, what to do when a student has an asthma attack, and how the condition affects the student's education.

DESCRIPTION OF ASTHMA

Because asthma is complex, has an uncertain etiology, and causes a great variety of symptoms, there is no single, standard definition of the disease. The most common descriptions refer to it as a lung disease with acute attacks of shortness of breath and wheezing due to airway inflammation and airway obstruction (Berkow, 1992; Morgan & Martinez, 1992). Some definitions also include the fact that the airway inflammation is a result of an increased airway responsiveness (or sensitivity) to a variety of stimuli that cause the airway to swell. Airway inflammation and obstruction are considered to be reversible to a significant degree.

ETIOLOGY OF ASTHMA

Asthma is a complex disorder that is not fully understood in terms of its etiology or dynamics. It has been linked to several exogenous factors (causes originating from outside the body) as well as to several endogenous factors (causes originating from inside the body). As seen in Box 20-1, exposure to viral respiratory infec-tions has been linked to asthma as an exogenous factor, especially when it occurs in the young child. Passive smoke exposure is also considered an exogenous factor (Duff & Platts-Mills, 1992). In one study by Weitzman et al. (1990), children from birth to 5 years were slightly more than twice as likely to develop asthma when their mothers smoked 10 or more cigarettes a day than were those whose mothers did not smoke. A third potential exogenous factor is allergen exposure (Larsen, 1992). Allergens are substances that produce immediate hypersensitivity (allergy), and they have been linked to asthma. Allergens such as house dust mites, cats, cockroach debris, and molds may be found indoors. Outdoor allergens include trees, shrubs, grasses, weeds, herbs, and molds (Duff & Platts-Mills, 1992).

Several endogenous factors are thought to play a role in the development of asthma. Endogenous factors include airway reactivity, allergy, family history of asthma, and gender (Morgan & Martinez, 1992). Increased airway reactivity and responsiveness and allergic sensitization have been targeted as playing a major role in the development of asthma. Individuals with asthma have antibodies (IgE type) against specific allergens, and when they are in contact with those allergens, increased airway reactivity and responsiveness may be followed by inflammation and obstruction.

Additional factors are also thought to contribute to the development of asthma. A significant genetic component has been established, for example. The precise relationship of genetics to asthma, allergy, and airway reactivity is not completely known. However, a difference in prevalence between the sexes has been noted; twice as many boys as girls typically have asthma (Morgan & Martinez, 1992). The reason for this is not well understood. Children who had respiratory distress syndrome as newborns are at greater

BOX 20-1

Exogenous and Endogenous Factors Pertaining to Asthma

EXOGENOUS
Exposure to viral infection
Exposure to smoke
Exposure to allergen

ENDOGENOUS
Initial airway reactivity
Immune response to infection
Allergy
Family history of asthma
Gender
Possible initial lung function
Possible immune response to infection

risk of developing asthma, as are children born with lower birth weight than normal (Chan et al., 1988).

DYNAMICS OF ASTHMA

The respiratory system is made up of a series of airways or "tubes." As seen in Figure 20-1, air first enters the nose or mouth when the diaphragm muscle (and other ancillary muscles) contracts, causing a negative pressure in the lungs. This negative pressure causes air to flow into the airway passages and eventually into the lungs. As the air passes through the nose and/or mouth, the air first travels down the large airway known as the *trachea*. At the end of the trachea, corresponding approximately to the end of the neck, the airway splits into two large tubes known as *bronchi*. (The singular form is *bronchus*.) The right bronchus goes to the right lung and the left bronchus goes to the left lung. The bronchi branch out into several smaller tubes known as *bronchioles*, which become smaller and smaller and end in small air sacs known as *alveoli*.

An exchange of gases occurs between the alveoli and the capillaries (small blood vessels) surrounding them (see Figure 20-2). During inspiration, the air from the environment travels to the alveoli, bringing in a high volume of oxygen and other gases the body needs in order to survive. This air is transported from the alveoli to the capillaries and the circulatory system to be distributed to the cells of the body. At the same time, a high volume of carbon dioxide and other gases that are waste products of the body cells have been transported to the capillaries surrounding the alveoli. These gases are transported to the alveoli to be expelled during exhalation. The diaphragm and other muscles then relax, creating an increase in positive pressure, and air is

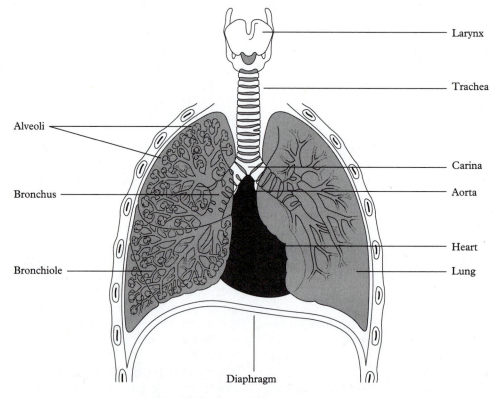

■ **FIGURE 20-1** The respiratory system

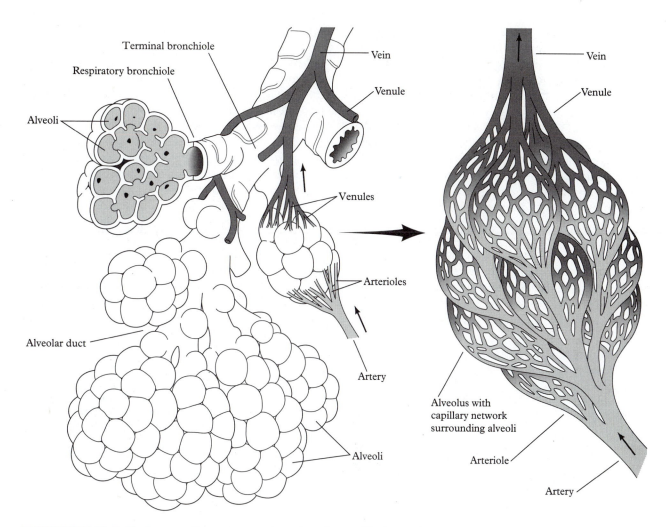

■ FIGURE 20-2 Exchange of gases occurs between the capillaries and alveoli of the lung.

forced to flow from the alveoli to the bronchioles, to the bronchi, up the trachea, and out the mouth or nose during expiration.

As a person breathes, large pieces of debris may be trapped in the nasal cavity and prevented from entering the trachea. However, small debris can enter the airway and result in coughing that clears the airway of the substance. Other mechanisms clear small debris from the airway and protect the lungs. The airway is lined with epithelial cells that form a protective barrier. On the epithelial cells of the trachea and bronchi are small, hairlike projections known as *cilia*. The cilia move back and forth and sweep debris and mucus up and out of the airway to keep it clean. In addition, epithelial cells are tightly joined together to prevent the debris from coming in contact with nerve receptors that lie under the cells.

For an individual with asthma, breathing is usually not difficult; nor are there any acute changes in the air-

way until the person comes in contact with a substance he or she is hypersensitive to. Then, the asthma attack is triggered. Substances or situations that trigger asthma attacks vary with the individual. Some of these include specific allergens (substances the person is allergic to), such as dust mites or pollen; respiratory infections; inhalation of irritating substances, such as fumes or gases; environmental factors, such as air pollution; exercise; aspirin; agents used as food preservatives; and emotional factors (Suddarth, 1991). An asthma attack may occur during sleep due to a change in breathing patterns and other pulmonary functions. This is known as *nocturnal asthma* (Hill, Szefler, & Larsen, 1992).

The reactions that occur during an asthma attack are triggered by an allergen in much the same way other allergic reactions, like hives, are triggered, except that the reactions are occurring in the pulmonary system instead of on the skin or in other bodily systems.

Individuals with allergies have an unusually large number of antibodies (known as IgE antibodies) that react to certain substances. These antibodies cause an allergic reaction when they come in contact with an irritating substance. In asthma, these antibodies aggregate along the bronchi and bronchioles by attaching themselves to cells known as *mast cells*. In an asthma attack, the substance to which the person is allergic enters the body and reacts with the antibodies on the mast cells (see Figure 20-3). This causes the cells to release several different substances (for example, histamine and serotonin) that cause (1) swelling of the small bronchioles, (2) secretion of thick mucus in the bronchioles, (3) spasm (tightening) of the smooth muscle of the bronchioles, and (4) inflammatory response (Guyton, 1991). As the bronchiole tubes swell and tighten, the passageways become narrow and partially occluded. This is aggravated when mucus blocks part of the airway system as well. Due to the extra pressure on the

bronchioles during expiration, the bronchioles tend to be further obstructed during exhalation, causing the person to have more difficulty breathing out than breathing in. A characteristic wheezing sound occurs as the individual tries to breathe out. Stale air becomes trapped in the alveoli, which results in ineffective air exchange and "air hunger"—the need to breathe. This process may reverse itself spontaneously, or medication may reverse it.

Additional processes have been identified as resulting in the narrowing of the airway passages. When the person with asthma comes in contact with stimuli such as viral respiratory infections or air pollutants, a nerve known as the *vagus nerve*, which partially controls the smooth muscle tone of the airway, is stimulated. This causes narrowing of the bronchioles and the increased secretion of mucus. Inflammation of the bronchial tubes with ensuing mast cell activation also occurs in these situations (Suddarth, 1991).

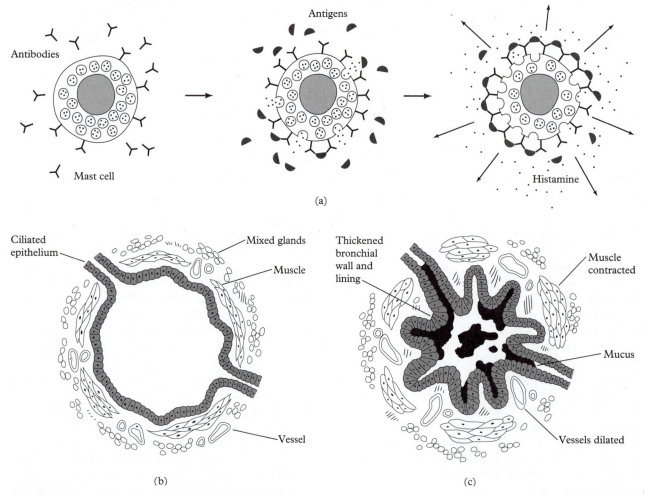

■ **FIGURE 20-3** As allergic substances interact with mast cells (a), the small, usually unobstructed bronchioles (b) swell and become blocked with mucus (c).

In some instances, hypersensitivity to certain substances may be cyclical. It has been proposed that repeated exposure to allergens in allergic individuals increases airway sensitivity (Cockcroft, 1983). Further exposure to the allergen may lead to increased airway sensitivity and obstruction, so stimuli that do not produce an asthma attack initially may begin to produce problems later (Hill, Szefler, & Larsen, 1992).

Although the overt symptoms of an acute attack can be relieved quickly with medication, days or weeks are needed for a total recovery because the inflammation process damages the epithelial lining of the airways. Time is needed for the epithelial lining to repair, for inflammation to totally subside, and for mucus transport to recover (Suddarth, 1991). Over many years, repeated attacks may result in permanent changes to the lungs.

CHARACTERISTICS OF ASTHMA

About 80–90% of children with asthma will experience their first symptoms before the age of 4 to 5 years. Young children may be more predisposed to asthma due to disproportionately narrow airways until they are 5 years old. They may have less smooth muscle surrounding the bronchioli, which results in less support, increased numbers of cells of the mucous gland in the major bronchioli, increased pulmonary resistance peripherally, and other differences (Behrman, 1992).

There are several different classification systems for asthma, usually based on what triggers the reaction. Some classification systems divide asthma into *allergic asthma* (those involving allergens) and *nonallergic asthma* (those involving everything else except allergens). A more extensive classification further divides asthma into six categories (see Box 20-2). The first category is *extrinsic asthma,* also known as allergic-type asthma. It includes stimuli that produce allergic reactions. As we discussed, allergic reactions consist of exposure to any substance to which the individual has an allergy and that results in the narrowing and inflammation of the airway passages. Smoke and pollen are two examples of triggers for this type of asthma. The second category is *intrinsic asthma,* which refers to asthma in which no identified allergen is found but may be triggered by viral respiratory infections (Cypcar, Stark, & Lemanske, 1992), or environmental stimuli such as air pollution. It should be noted that asthma has been associated with some types of air pollution, but this link is still being debated (Rossi, Kinnula, Tienari, & Huhti, 1993). The third category is *mixed asthma,* which combines extrinsic and intrinsic forms. The fourth type is *aspirin-induced asthma,* which results from taking aspirin or related compounds. The fifth

---

BOX 20-2

Classification of Asthma Types

1. Extrinsic asthma
   a. Inhaled allergens
   b. IgE antibodies
2. Intrinsic asthma
   a. Environment
   b. Infection
3. Mixed asthma
   a. Combination of extrinsic and intrinsic types
4. Aspirin-induced asthma
   a. Aspirin and related compounds
5. Exercise-induced asthma
   a. Asthma that typically begins after 5 to 20 minutes upon onset of exercising
6. Occupational asthma
   a. Industrial fumes and gases

---

type occurs from *exercise*. Its effects vary widely from slight chest tightness to significant respiratory distress. The final type is *occupational asthma,* which occurs from inhaling industrial gases and fumes. In some instances, coughing is present without the characteristic wheezing (Suddarth, 1991).

There are several characteristics of a typical asthma attack. Besides the characteristic wheezing, there may be coughing, shortness of breath, spitting up mucus, a gasping voice, paleness, a cold sweat, bluish nailbeds and lips, or feelings of chest tightness. Episodes may vary in severity. Mild asthma attacks usually have few symptoms and are not stressful to the individual. Serious asthma attacks may result in a feeling of being suffocated and the inability to speak more than a few words at a time. Symptoms may persist for a few minutes to a few days. Although it happens rarely, asthma can be fatal in extreme cases.

The overall severity of a person's asthma may be classified as mild, moderate, or severe. Classification is based on frequency, duration, exercise tolerance, nocturnal symptoms, and the amount of emergency care needed.

DETECTION OF ASTHMA

Asthma is often misdiagnosed in children as being bronchitis or pneumonia. Diagnosis is often difficult because of the variety of symptoms, which can change over time in the same child. Diagnosis is based on medical history, a physical examination, X-rays, laboratory tests, and pulmonary tests. The medical history will include noting when respiratory symptoms occurred, what treatment was given, and how the symptoms were alleviated. The information will be examined for any discernible pattern. The physical exam will focus on the respiratory tract, chest, and skin. An X-ray may be performed to examine the sinuses and lungs for any abnormalities. Laboratory tests can give specific information about the possibility of asthma and rule out other conditions. Blood tests will often be performed to rule out infection or anemia. Skin tests are typically performed for allergen sensitivity; others, such as immunoglobulin tests, help establish a person's allergic status. A sweat test may be done to rule out cystic fibrosis (Avery & First, 1994). Pulmonary function tests are commonly performed to evaluate lung disease and to provide information about lung capacity, flow rates, timed volumes, and airway reactivity (Mueller & Eigen, 1992). Exercise-induced asthma is evaluated by having the person exercise while their respiratory function is monitored.

TREATMENT OF ASTHMA

There are two major aims in the treatment of asthma: (1) preventing the occurrence of an asthma attack, and (2) treating an asthma attack when it occurs. Both require that the individual, parent, and educator have a good understanding of this disease and of how to treat it properly.

In order to prevent the occurrence of an asthma attack, the individual must know what can trigger an attack. A diagnostic skin test can usually identify any allergic substance(s). Once identified, proper management should begin with avoiding the allergen or irritating substance (Stempel & Szefler, 1992). When feathered or furry animals such as birds or dogs are the triggers, they can often be successfully avoided. However, when dust mites are the triggering substance, avoidance is more difficult. Strategies minimizing exposure to dust mites include substituting blinds for curtains, using mattress covers, using special vacuums that capture all dust, and using area rugs instead of wall-to-wall carpeting.

Allergy therapy, also known as allergy immunotherapy or hyposensitization therapy, may be given to decrease the person's sensitivity to the triggering allergens. In allergy therapy, the person is injected with very small amounts of the identified allergen; dosages are increased over a period of years. The body responds by producing certain antibodies that will make the person less susceptible to the effects of the allergen. Other preventive treatments include the daily use of a medication such as cromolyn sodium to reduce airway inflammation and hypersensitivity.

Although the person may comply with preventive measures, attacks will still typically occur, although they may not be as frequent or severe. Individuals with asthma are taught to identify the early onset of symptoms of an asthma attack and promptly administer medication. Medications to treat asthma attacks are aimed at opening up the airway passages to allow for easy breathing. This occurs by reducing airway swelling, relieving bronchospasms, clearing airway secretions, and reducing inflammation (Stempel & Redding, 1992). The most common categories of medications for treating asthma in this manner are known as *bronchodilators;* they dilate the bronchioles. As shown in Box 20-3, several types of medications are categorized as bronchodilators. They may be used for any type of asthma. Other types of medications include asthma inhibitors and steroids.

Medications that are taken at the onset of an asthma attack are typically administered in an aerosol form with an inhaler or nebulizer aerosol machine. The inhaler is a small device that delivers medication in a premeasured amount. The person places his or her mouth over the opening of the inhaler and presses the top while inhaling the medication (see Figure 20-4a). The nebulizer aerosol machine connects to a mask that fits over the mouth and nose or connects to a mouthpiece that is held in the mouth. The medication is placed in a little cup on the nebulizer, and the person having an attack inhales the medication (see Figures 20-4b and 20-4c). If either one of these steps is done incorrectly, the person may not get the full amount of medication.

Other supportive treatments may be prescribed as well. The student should drink plenty of fluids and breathe moist air to help rid the body of mucous plugs and ease breathing. If the person is congested, postural draining or clapping (pulmonary percussion) may help dislodge mucus enough that it can be coughed up and out of the lungs. During postural drainage, the person is placed in specific positions that allow gravity to assist in draining out the mucus. Clapping is a technique in which a cupped hand rhythmically and repeatedly strikes certain parts of the back, chest, and sides corresponding to certain parts of the lung. The technique helps to dislodge mucus and is not an uncomfortable procedure when properly done. In some situations, a mechanical vibrator, or vibratory technique applied to the back, is used instead of clapping. Other treatments, such as relaxation techniques, have helped decrease the anxiety that commonly occurs when an asthma attack begins.

COURSE OF ASTHMA

In most cases, asthma is adequately managed by avoiding the triggers of asthma attacks, using medication to avoid an asthma attack, and using treatment aimed at stopping an asthma attack. Although it is very unusual

BOX 20-3

Examples of Medications Used to Treat Asthma

Bronchodilators *(anticholinergic, beta-adrenergics, theophylline)* are medications taken to open the bronchial tubes (air passages). Bronchodilators relieve cough, wheezing, and shortness of breath by increasing the flow of air through the bronchial tubes.

BRAND NAME	GENERIC NAME
Atrovent	Ipratropium bromide
Brethine Tablets	Terbutaline sulfate
Bronkosol	Isoetharine
Choledyl Tablets	Oxtriphylline
Proventil Inhaler	Albuterol
Theo-Dur or Slobid	Theophylline anhydrous
Ventolin	Albuterol

SIDE EFFECTS OF BRONCHODILATORS (DEPENDS ON TYPE)

Most common: Restlessness, nervousness, hyperactivity, tremor, increased heart rate

Less common: Headaches, nausea, vomiting, drying of mouth, blurred vision, dizziness, abdominal pain

Asthma inhibitors *(chemical mediator inhibitors)* can be used to prevent bronchial asthma and bronchospasms. Used for intermittent and long-term management of chronic asthma.

BRAND NAME	GENERIC NAME
Intal Inhaler	Cromolyn sodium

SIDE EFFECTS OF ASTHMA INHIBITORS (VERY UNUSUAL TO HAVE SIDE EFFECTS)

Most common: Coughing, wheezing, oral thrush

Less common: Joint swelling, joint pain, throat swelling, urinary frequency, dizziness, nausea, nasal congestion, skin rash

Steroids, used as anti-inflammatory drugs, promote the healing of lung tissue.

SYSTEMIC STEROIDS

BRAND NAME	GENERIC NAME
Solucortef	Hydrocortisone
Deltasone	Prednisone
Aristocort	Triamcinolone

SIDE EFFECTS OF SYSTEMIC STEROIDS

Most common: acne, headache, abdominal pain

Less common (usually found with long-term use): growth suppression, electrolyte imbalances, myopathy, bone fractures, impaired wound healing, ulcer, increased eye pressure, cataracts, behavioral disturbances

INHALATION OF STEROIDS

BRAND NAME	GENERIC NAME
Decadron Respihaler	Dexamethasone sodium phosphate
Vanceril Inhaler	Beclomethasone diproprionate
Azmacort	Triamcinolone acetonide
Aerobid	Flunisolide

SIDE EFFECTS OF INHALED STEROIDS

Most common: Throat irritation, hoarseness, coughing, throat and mouth fungal infections

Less common: electrolyte imbalance, systemic abnormalities

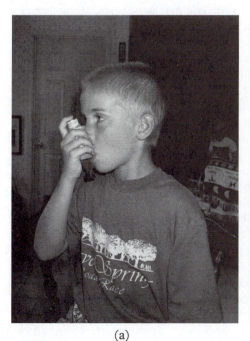
(a)

(b)

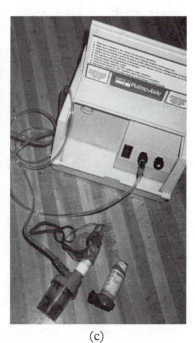
(c)

■ **FIGURE 20-4** Student who has asthma using his inhaler (a) and his nebulizer (b). Inhaler and nebulizer equipment (c).

for a child or adolescent to die from an asthma attack, there have been deaths from asthma (Stempel & Redding, 1992). This is attributed to undertreatment, or in some instances, a lack of compliance.

About one-half of the children diagnosed with asthma will outgrow the symptoms of asthma during their second and third decades of life. This supports the concept that some forms of asthma go into remission without intervention or change in environmental factors. However, almost one-half of these individuals may have recurrences of asthma when they are much older (T. J. Sullivan, 1992).

Some physical changes are associated with asthma. At one time, asthma and its treatment were thought to retard growth. However, we now know that asthma does not cause growth retardation, but it may delay puberty. This delay gives the impression that growth is slowing. After the onset of puberty, the person's growth catches up (Merkus et al., 1993; Reid, 1992). If the individual continues to have asthma, certain chronic pulmonary changes may occur. The chest may become permanently enlarged (known as a barrel chest) with an increase in the amount of air left in the lungs (residual capacity) after exhalation (Guyton, 1991).

EDUCATIONAL IMPLICATIONS OF ASTHMA

Asthma is a condition that is full of paradoxes. It is defined by its reversibility, yet in a few circumstances, it may be fatal. It occurs episodically, yet it is a chronic disease. Several medications are available, yet it is often undertreated (Bloomberg & Strunk, 1992). It is recognized as a disease, yet it continues to be perceived by many as an emotional or hysterical condition (which may contribute to its undertreatment). The teacher needs to have a clear understanding of the symptoms of this disease and its course for a specific child in order to respond properly across educational environments.

Meeting Physical and Sensory Needs

To properly attend to the physical needs of students with asthma, the teacher should be well-informed about the disease, including the signs of an acute attack and the administration of medication. The signs of an acute attack will vary among individuals, as will the severity of the attack. Some of these signs include coughing, wheezing, shortness of breath, labored breathing, flared nostrils while breathing, complaints of difficulty breathing, and any cyanosis (blue color) of the fingernails or around the lips. When an acute attack occurs, medication must be taken. The teacher and educational team will need to (1) have the medication in an accessible

■ **VIGNETTE** ■

Arun is an 8-year-old boy with asthma who is in regular education. Since he was 3 years old, his parents have taught him to recognize the signs of an asthma attack and how to take medication. One day during math, he began to wheeze and have shortness of breath. The teacher was well-informed about asthma and knew it was important to remain calm in order to help Arun remain calm and not panic over his being unable to breathe well. Arun was permitted to keep his inhaler with him in his backpack, which he carried from class to class. Arun pulled the inhaler from his backpack, administered the medication himself, and felt fine within a few minutes. He then continued working on his math problems.

location, (2) be aware of proper administration of the medication, and (3) know what to do if the medication does not relieve the attack.

Asthma has been considered a problem in the school setting when children are not allowed to keep their medication in the classroom but must ask permission to leave to go get it. This delays treatment and increases the possibility that the child may have to leave school because of asthma. This problem, along with discomfort that teachers may have about asthma, contributes to a high absenteeism rate (Bloomberg & Strunk, 1992). To avoid this problem, medication for asthma attacks must be kept in a location that is easily accessible to the student at all times so the attacks can be stopped quickly. Often, this means having the medication with the student. Younger students may need to keep it in the teacher's desk or nurse's office, but it should be quickly obtainable. When the student goes on a field trip or elsewhere outside the school, he or she should take the medication along.

In order for the medication to be effective, it must be properly administered. Teachers should be well-informed about the type of medication the student is taking and how it is taken. The use of an inhaler requires a specific technique of breathing slowly and deeply (as if sucking on a straw) and holding one's breath for 10 seconds. As presented in Box 20-4, there are several ways to use an inhaler *incorrectly,* such as not inhaling slowly, which will result in not receiving the proper amount of medication. The teacher should be alert for incorrect administration. If the student is not receiving relief from the medication due to incorrect administration, the teacher should help the student use the inhaler. The teacher will also need to contact the nurse and family so they, and the student, can receive additional instruction.

When asthma medication is taken correctly, it is usually very effective in stopping an asthma attack. However, in rare instances, the student may not obtain relief from the medication. All students should have an action plan should this occur. In some action plans, additional medication may be taken. If the attack is mild and the medication is not working, the parent or physician may be contacted. However, if the asthma attack is severe and involves shortness of breath, labored breathing, or cyanosis and there is no response from the medication, the student should be taken to a hospital emergency room. Whether the attack is severe or mild, the teacher should remain calm and try to keep the student calm; greater anxiety will often result in more difficulty in breathing. Usually, the student will want to be in a sitting position; this will allow him or her to breathe more easily than when lying down.

The nurse (or teacher) should share information about asthma and its treatment with other educational personnel so they will know what to do when an asthma attack occurs. It is especially important that the physical education instructor be informed when a student has asthma so any needed modifications can be made. For example, the physical education instructor should be sure there is always a warm-up period before exercise because this can reduce the risk of an asthma attack. Some students with asthma may have limited stamina, which may result in the need for the physical education instructor to modify the student's program. Although exercise is encouraged in most children with asthma,

some students may have exercise-induced asthma, which would exclude them from engaging in moderate-to-vigorous exercise. In these instances, activities such as track may be out of the question, but swimming, gymnastics, or wrestling may pose no problems. Extra medication may be taken prior to the exercise to help prevent or minimize reactions.

Teachers should be aware that no medications should be taken without the physician's permission. For example, aspirin should not be given because breathing could be affected and result in the onset of an episode of acute asthma.

Meeting Communication Needs

Typically, students with asthma have no communication problems. Communication may be impaired during a severe attack of asthma, thus requiring the teacher to be alert for signs of distress and to provide prompt treatment. Young students or those who have additional disabilities may require an observant teacher to recognize the nonverbal signs of distress as well.

Students with asthma will also sometimes need to communicate to peers and others about their disease. Some students may say, "I have asthma, and that means my lungs give me trouble sometimes. If the air is dirty and full of dust, I have trouble breathing, and I wheeze like this. As long as I take my medicine, I'm usually OK" (Association for the Care of Children's Health, 1982).

Meeting Learning Needs

It is important that the teacher know the type of medication the student is taking and its potential side effects. Bronchodilators may cause tremors that may result in sloppy handwriting. Bronchodilators also have been thought to subtly affect attention and behavior. Teachers should monitor for these side effects. If a decrease in attention span is noted, the teacher will need to modify the instruction by providing information in short, concise amounts and giving the student time to practice. However, in some studies, academic achievement among children with asthma who had used bronchodilators was not found to be affected (Lindgren et al., 1992).

Students with asthma will need to be taught about the disease and about which stimuli may result in an asthma attack. These should be avoided, as should rigorous exercise. Students with asthma will also need to be taught the signs and symptoms of an asthma attack and how to properly administer the prescribed medication. The student should know where the medication is kept and have easy access to it at all times.

BOX 20-4

Using an Inhaler

Proper use of an inhaler involves the following:
- Breathing in as if sucking through a straw when activating the inhaler
- Breathing in as slowly and deeply as possible
- Holding the breath for approximately 10 seconds after breathing in

Problems:
- Placing the inhaler in front of the teeth
- Directing the spray away from the mouth
- Exhaling instead of inhaling
- Breathing in too fast
- Not holding the breath after inhaling
- Not doing one spray at a time following the above recommended usage steps
- Not keeping the inhaler clean

Meeting Daily Living Needs

Daily living skills are not usually affected in a person with asthma. The student will just need to know whether to avoid certain triggers, such as dogs. The student should also understand that the use of blinds instead of curtains and area rugs instead of carpeting will help, if the asthma attacks are triggered by dust mites, and be prepared to set up his or her home accordingly if possible.

Meeting Behavioral and Social Needs

In some instances, asthma has been found to have an adverse effect on students' emotional and social life. Some students have felt restricted socially, have thought of themselves as being different, have been embarrassed about taking medication, and have been afraid of having asthma attacks. The fear of being different may contribute to noncompliance, especially during adolescence. Some of these students have been found to worry about death and about the side effects of medication (Bloomberg & Strunk, 1992). The teacher should be sensitive to these concerns and provide a supportive environment.

Social interactions may be adversely affected by peers' misconceptions about asthma, students' absenteeism, and students' possible restrictions on activity. Peers can be educated about asthma and other chronic illnesses as part of their curriculum on health. Because some students with asthma may feel socially isolated, social interactions should be encouraged. There are many clubs and school activities that students may enjoy and participate in easily, even when activity restrictions have been recommended.

If taking medication is embarrassing to the student, the teacher and student together can decide how to best accomplish medication administration. For students who must go to a nurse's office to take the medication, the teacher and student may decide that the student can get up and leave without interrupting the class. Students who keep their medication with them may either use it casually in class or freely go to a predetermined private location if doing so makes them more comfortable. As we said, it is important that the medication be taken promptly at the onset of an asthma attack. A method of doing so that causes the least embarrassment to the student and maximum compliance will be best.

In certain individuals, emotional upset may trigger an asthma attack. If a teacher knows this, he or she may try to avoid any unpleasant confrontations with the student, and the student may become manipulative. It is important that the teacher not treat the student with asthma any differently from others; the same classroom rules should apply to all students; rules should be obeyed, or the student should suffer the consequences. Equally important is that the teacher take seriously any complaint about difficulty breathing or about having an asthma attack.

Students with asthma may be overprotected or overly fearful about their disease. Asthma support groups for the student and the parents can be very beneficial. Additional counseling may be needed in certain circumstances.

SUMMARY

Asthma is a disease with acute attacks of shortness of breath and wheezing due to inflammation and obstruction of the airways. Asthma may be classified by what triggers the acute attacks: (1) extrinsic asthma, (2) intrinsic asthma, (3) mixed asthma, (4) aspirin-induced asthma, (5) exercise-induced asthma, and (6) occupational asthma. Regardless of the type of asthma a person has, the attacks may be very mild (and not even identified as asthma) or severe, causing difficulty breathing. Asthma attacks can usually be relieved by medications that are taken at the start of an attack. The student should have easy access to the medication and avoid any delay in taking it. A comprehensive management plan developed by a team including the physician, parents, student, nurse, and teacher is needed to address the student's physical, educational, and social needs. The teacher's attitudes, knowledge, and support can make a significant difference in the student's performance.

CHAPTER 21

Cystic Fibrosis

Cystic fibrosis is the major cause of severe chronic lung disease in children and has been the leading lethal genetic disease in whites since 1936. It occurs in approximately 1 out of 2,000 live births (Thompson, Gustafson, Hamlett, & Spock, 1992). Cystic fibrosis results in lung deterioration, and individuals will die from the disease and its complications at varying ages. Although coughing may be the most observable symptom, several other organs are involved. Students with cystic fibrosis who are receiving treatment may not look ill; hence, cystic fibrosis is often considered one of the "invisible" diseases. However, the gravity of this disease and its effect on the student's overall functioning requires that the educator be familiar with its characteristics and course and know how to provide appropriate support in the educational environment.

DESCRIPTION OF CYSTIC FIBROSIS (CF)

Cystic fibrosis (CF) is considered a disease of the exocrine glands—glands secreting through ducts. Although several exocrine glands are involved, cystic fibrosis primarily affects the glands of the respiratory, gastrointestinal, and reproductive systems. It results in obstruction of the airways, poor digestion, chronic diarrhea, an abnormally high concentration of salt in the sweat, and sterility.

ETIOLOGY OF CYSTIC FIBROSIS

Cystic fibrosis is a genetic disease. The defective gene that causes cystic fibrosis was discovered in 1989 on chromosome 7 (Rommens, Iannuzzi, & Derem, 1989). This defective gene is now commonly known as the *cystic fibrosis transmembrane conductance regulator* (CFTR) (Weinberger, 1993). Over 300 different genetic defects (mutations) have been identified; more than 200

of these changes are associated with the disease (Fiel, 1993; Tizzano & Buchwald, 1993). Identifying the CFTR gene provided new information regarding etiology and may lead to finding more effective treatments and possibly a cure.

Cystic fibrosis is an autosomal-recessive genetic disease. This means that both parents must be carriers of the gene for there to be a chance of their child's getting the disorder. As seen in Figure 21-1, when two parents who are carriers have children, there is a 25% chance that the child will have cystic fibrosis, a 50% chance that the child will be a carrier, and a 25% chance that the child will be totally unaffected. The odds of two carriers marrying are fairly high if testing to detect the gene mutation is not performed. In the United States, an estimated 5% of the white population, or 7 million individuals, carry the cystic fibrosis gene. Many of these individuals do not know they are carriers (FitzSimmons, 1993).

DYNAMICS OF CYSTIC FIBROSIS

Cystic fibrosis directly affects the exocrine glands, which are located throughout the body. These glands are composed of various-sized ducts that secrete fluid directly outside the body or to a body cavity that will empty to the outside. Because of this, these glands are known as *glands of external secretion,* as opposed to the endocrine glands that secrete internally. Examples of fluids produced by exocrine glands include sweat, saliva, tears, respiratory mucus, pancreatic fluid, and fluid from the glands of the digestive system, liver, and gallbladder.

In cystic fibrosis, almost all of the exocrine glands are affected to varying degrees by having abnormal electrolytes, abnormal amounts of mucus and protein secretions, or both. There is a characteristic increase of salt and chloride in the sweat, as well as in other exocrine

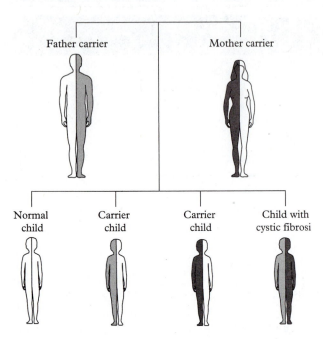

■ FIGURE 21-1 Genetic transmission of cystic fibrosis

respiratory system and in the digestive system that can result in obstructions and tissue damage. Each involved organ may become damaged due to the effects of the increased amounts of mucus, which leads to obstructions, infections, and other abnormalities.

In the normal respiratory system, a series of airways carry air from the environment to the lungs during inhalation and carry unwanted gases from the alveoli to the environment during exhalation. These airways consist of the trachea, bronchi, bronchioles, and alveoli (air sacs). (See Figure 21-2.) The cells of the trachea, bronchi, and bronchioles normally secrete mucus, which traps unwanted debris that enters the airway during breathing. Hairlike projections known as *cilia* sweep the mucus containing trapped debris up from the airways until it can be expelled or swallowed. In cystic fibrosis, the mucus is excessive and is unusually thick and discolored (yellow-green). The cilia cannot move the mucus effectively and the lungs have difficulty clearing it. The inability to properly clear out the mucus results in respiratory obstruction and infections, which are difficult to completely eliminate from the respiratory tract. If more mucus continues to accumulate in the smaller bronchioles, the bronchioles become partially obstructed (see Figure 21-3). This causes air to become trapped in the alveoli, which then overinflate. If the bronchioli become completely blocked, the air left in the alveoli will be absorbed into the body and the lung

glands such as the salivary gland. This electrolyte imbalance, however, does not usually impede normal bodily functioning. There are also increased amounts of secretions and abnormally thick, sticky mucus in the

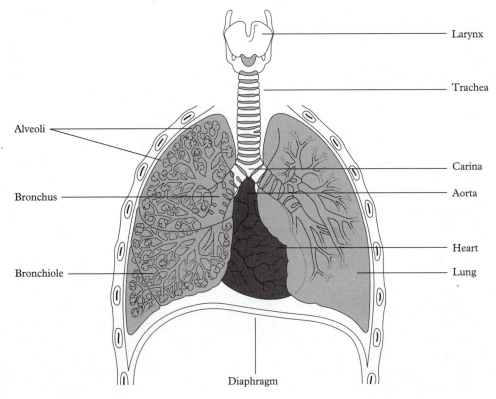

■ FIGURE 21-2 The respiratory system

alveoli will collapse. When this occurs over a portion of the lung, it is referred to as a *collapsed lung,* or **atelectasis.** Individuals with cystic fibrosis usually die as a result of respiratory infections and complications related to the damage described.

Cystic fibrosis affects other organs of the body. The pancreas contains several exocrine glands that produce important secretions for breaking down food into digestible parts. These exocrine glands consist of many small ducts that eventually merge and empty into the intestine. In cystic fibrosis, thick mucus blocks these small ducts. When the ducts become completely obstructed, the glands continue to secrete, swell, and then become cysts with scarred, fibrous tissue around them— hence the name, *cystic fibrosis* (Bleck & Nagel, 1982). Because there is a decrease in the amount of pancreatic enzyme secretions that reach the intestine, proteins, carbohydrates, and fats are not properly broken down. Although other enzymes from other organs will assist with the breakdown of food, the decrease or lack of pancreatic secretions can result in weight loss, chronic diarrhea, and poor nutrition. The liver may also be obstructed the same way the pancreas is, resulting in cirrhosis (liver disease). The intestines can become blocked with thick mucus; stools will be fatty. Women with cystic fibrosis may have thick cervical secretions but can still become impregnated. Men with cystic fibrosis may have obstructions resulting in the absence of sperm and are therefore sterile.

The mechanism that causes the abnormal electrolytes and increased amounts of mucus is now known. There is an abnormal transportation of chloride and increased permeability in the epithelial cells (chloride channels). Chloride cannot be transported to the cells normally and this affects sodium and water transportation. A lack of water in the mucus results in thick and viscous mucus. Abnormal chloride transportation and the resulting abnormal mucus may be due to a shift in the cellular fluid or to an abnormal metabolic process (Coutelle, Caplen, Hart, Huxley, & Williamson, 1993).

CHARACTERISTICS OF CYSTIC FIBROSIS

The characteristics of an individual with cystic fibrosis can vary widely, partially due to the different forms (mutations) of the cystic fibrosis gene. In some forms of cystic fibrosis (such as those with the common triangle F508 mutation), there is usually pancreatic insufficiency. However, about 15% of the cystic fibrosis population do not have pancreatic insufficiency; these individuals have a different type of mutation. Eventually, all individuals with cystic fibrosis will show the characteristic overproduction of mucus and the complications associated with the lungs, but this can vary as to

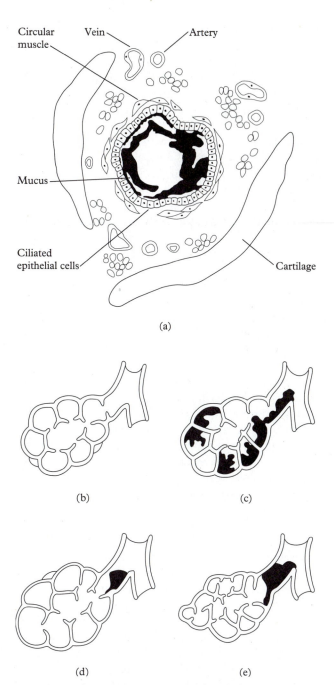

(a)

(b)   (c)

(d)   (e)

■ **FIGURE 21-3** In cystic fibrosis, there is an excess of mucus in the respiratory system that may cause the bronchioles to become partially obstructed (a). A normal alveoli (b) may become obstructed— especially during infection (c)—hyperinflate (d), and collapse (e).

its onset, duration, and severity. Some individuals will be born with the symptoms present; others will develop the symptoms during childhood. Some with cystic fibrosis die in childhood; others live into their thirties or forties and beyond. Even when the type of mutation has been found to be identical in individuals, significant differences in the characteristics and survival rates may still exist. This has been attributed to genetic factors (not including the cystic fibrosis gene), environmental factors (frequency of viral and bacterial infections), nutritional factors, and treatment (Fiel, 1993).

When symptoms of cystic fibrosis are present at birth, they usually affect the gastrointestinal tract. About 10–15% of infants with cystic fibrosis will be born with an obstructed bowel, a condition known as *meconium ileus*. This occurs because the meconium—a mixture of secretions of the intestinal glands and amniotic fluid in the intestines in full-term fetuses—becomes clogged in the loops of the intestines. When this occurs, the infant will usually have stomach **distention**, vomiting, and no bowel movements within the first 1 to 2 days of life. In these cases, testing for cystic fibrosis is indicated. Surgery or special medication will be given orally or by enemas to remove the blockage.

In some individuals, symptoms of pancreatic insufficiency will occur during infancy or in early childhood. For infants who did not have an obstructed bowel, the symptoms of pancreatic insufficiency may be the first indication that the infant has cystic fibrosis. Pancreatic insufficiency results in problems with digestion. For the infant or young child, there may be a failure to gain weight and growth may be impeded. In some instances, the infant or young child is emaciated. The infant or child may also have an enlarged abdomen due to distended intestines as well as a characteristic loss of muscle mass. Bowel movements usually occur frequently, and stools are large and fatty in appearance. Frequent gas may occur, and stools have a characteristic foul odor due to undigested fats in the stool. Since calories are being lost in the stool due to the decrease in pancreatic enzyme secretions needed for digestion, the infant or child may have a large appetite. High caloric intake is needed for proper nutrition.

Respiratory involvement may occur during the first few weeks of life or develop later in childhood. For some individuals, there may be no symptoms at first except that respiratory infections are of longer duration than usual or the child has frequent episodes of bronchitis or pneumonia. Many individuals will exhibit their first symptom of respiratory involvement as a cough. It may start as a dry cough, but eventually it will become moist and productive; that is, accompanied by mucus. Wheezing may be present as well, with 30–40% of individuals with cystic fibrosis developing an allergic component that may be manifested as an asthmatic condition. As the disease progresses, the lungs become increasingly damaged and scarred and the chest enlarges, a condition known as a barrel chest. The individual becomes unable to tolerate exercise and becomes short of breath. Frequent respiratory infections result in bronchitis and pneumonia. The individual will eventually die, usually from respiratory complications.

Individuals with cystic fibrosis have other characteristics. The liver may become affected due to blockages in the exocrine ducts, which may lead to cirrhosis. Besides the exocrine glands of the pancreas, the endocrine glands of the pancreas (islets of Langerhans) may also be affected, resulting in diabetes and complications caused by this disease. (See Chapter 22.) Other gastrointestinal complications may occur, such as gallbladder malfunction, gallstones, and distal intestinal obstructive syndrome. In sexual development, there is frequently a delay in puberty that is difficult emotionally for many adolescents. Males are essentially sterile because they lack sperm, but sexual functioning is unimpaired. Females can usually tolerate pregnancy if the condition of their lungs is good (Behrman, 1992).

DETECTION OF CYSTIC FIBROSIS

Cystic fibrosis has traditionally been diagnosed through the use of a sweat test. This painless test consists of stimulating a small area of the skin, usually on the forearm, to sweat with the use of a small electric current and medication (see Figure 21-4). The sweat is collected with filter paper or a capillary tube that is placed on the stimulated skin for about 30 to 60 minutes. The sweat is then analyzed for chloride (salt). If the chloride is over 60 mEq/L, the test is positive. Although a few other conditions may result in a high chloride measurement (for example, severe malnutrition, pancreatitis, hy-

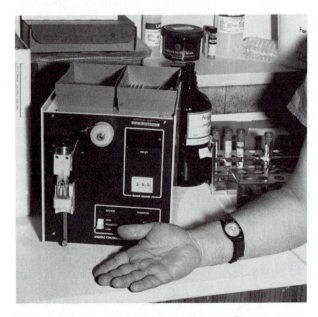

■ **FIGURE 21-4** Machine used to perform a sweat test

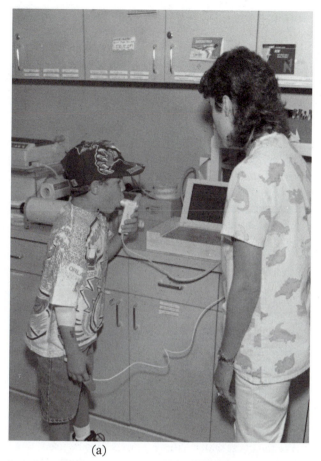

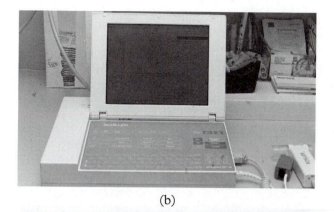

(b)

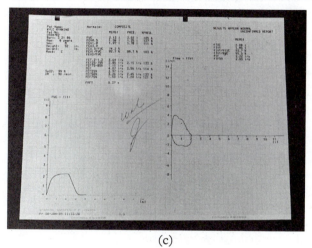

(c)

(a)

■ **FIGURE 21-5** A student having pulmonary function test performed (a) with a pulmonary machine (b), which displays a pulmonary function graph (c)

pothyroidism, and certain congenital conditions), they usually have very different characteristics. A diagnosis of cystic fibrosis is made when the sweat test is accompanied by pulmonary disease, pancreatic insufficiency, positive family history of cystic fibrosis, and genetic mutation analysis.

Additional tests can assist with the diagnosis. Pancreatic function may be tested by the analysis of stool samples or, less commonly, by more invasive procedures involving passing a tube into the upper small intestine where the pancreas empties its enzyme. The lungs and sinuses may be examined by X-rays. Pulmonary function tests that measure the amount of air exchange and capacity of the lungs may also be performed, along with blood oxygen analysis (see Figure 21-5). These supplementary tests may provide more information but cannot themselves diagnose cystic fibrosis.

With the discovery of the gene causing cystic fibrosis, **postnatal** and **prenatal** screening is now available for some of the genetic mutations causing cystic fibrosis. Early neonatal screening may be done for the most common cystic fibrosis gene mutation by using

a blood test that can be done when the infant is only a few days old (Green et al., 1994). Currently, this test is not sensitive enough or specific enough for mass screening, nor is it cost-effective. Until new treatments are available, early detection does not change the treatment regime. Prenatal diagnosis of cystic fibrosis has been made successfully when the entire family can also be analyzed (Behrman, 1992). However, because many individuals with cystic fibrosis may live until their thirties or longer, ethical questions are raised if the prenatal diagnosis is used to decide on an abortion. Carriers of the cystic fibrosis gene can also be detected for the most common types (Elias, Annas, & Simpson, 1991).

Although the sweat test is considered to be a very accurate test and the most reliable one, the results are occasionally in a moderately high range (40 mEq/L to 60 mEq/L) or are sometimes normal even when cystic fibrosis is present (Augarten et al., 1993). The test may indicate normality when cystic fibrosis is present when very young infants or individuals with a very mild form of cystic fibrosis are tested. In these instances, the sweat tests may be repeated later. Also, genetic testing may be more useful in determining a diagnosis.

TREATMENT OF CYSTIC FIBROSIS

Treatment has traditionally consisted of a combination of nutritional and respiratory therapy, as well as psychological counseling. For individuals with pancreatic insufficiency, pancreatic enzyme replacement medication is available. This medication is taken before each meal or snack, but it does not completely replace the loss of the child's natural pancreatic enzyme. Fats are not completely absorbed, so stools may continue to be somewhat fatty. Vitamin and mineral supplements are usually prescribed to aid with proper nutrition. Special low-fat diets used to be commonly prescribed, but some children became deficient in needed fatty acids (Behrman, 1992). With new pancreatic enzyme preparations, normal amounts of fats are usually recommended. Many children with cystic fibrosis require higher than usual amounts of calories because of calories lost in stools and the extra energy spent on breathing and fighting infections.

Weight loss is a common problem, especially when there are respiratory infections and chronic diarrhea. Children should be encouraged to eat and to take as many helpings as they want. In some cases, children may receive feedings at night through a high-calorie preparation (hyperalimentation) that runs into the circulatory system through a venous central catheter. A more common approach is for the child to receive a dietary supplement through a tube that empties directly into the stomach—either a nasogastric tube, gastrostomy tube, or jejunoscopy tube.

Respiratory complications are treated by several different approaches. Antibiotics are routinely prescribed when infection is present. Although antibiotics are often successful in treating the infection, bacterial infections are rarely completely eliminated. More resistant forms of infections make antibiotic therapy problematic. Presently, there is debate about whether oral antibiotics should be used prophylactically to decrease lung damage from chronic infection and decrease the risk of acute recurrences (Fiel, 1993). Other types of medications include bronchodilators, anti-inflammatory medication, and expectorants. Bronchodilators are used to increase the diameter of the airways to promote improved breathing. Anti-inflammatory drugs are used to decrease inflammation in the airways in an attempt to slow the lung damage. Expectorants facilitate the evacuation of mucus.

Standard respiratory treatment also includes the use of chest physiotherapy and exercise. Chest physiotherapy consists of several techniques used to remove excess secretion from the respiratory tract. One technique, known as postural drainage, consists of placing the child in several different positions to allow gravity to help move secretions out of the lungs. A qualified respiratory therapist, nurse, or trained family member will often perform clapping, or pulmonary percussion, in which the person uses a cupped hand to repeatedly strike the chest walls. Vibration may also be used. Fine, vibratory movements of the hand or a vibrator on the chest can be made over various parts of the lung to break up the mucus so it can be coughed up (see Figure 21-6). Usually, a combination of clapping or vibration and positioning is used to maximally benefit from this treatment. Postural drainage and clapping can be compared

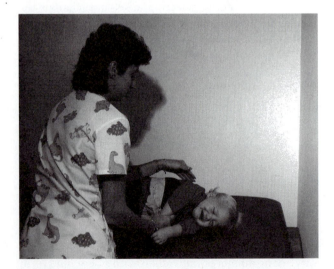
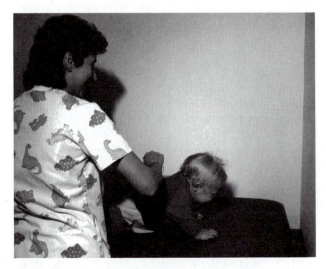

■ **FIGURE 21-6** A respiratory therapist performing chest physical (clapping) on a young child

to tilting and shaking or banging the back of a ketchup bottle to move the contents out (Bleck & Nagel, 1982).

Regular exercise is also beneficial to the child with cystic fibrosis. There is no indication that pulmonary function is improved by regular exercise, but it does improve oxygen use and perfusion, exercise tolerance, muscle tone, and psychological well-being (Fiel, 1993).

Several newer, experimental therapies are presently under examination to treat cystic fibrosis. New medications that manipulate the faulty chloride transportation occurring in the epithelial cells are under investigation. Also, anti-inflammatory medications, such as corticosteroids and ibuprofen, are being tried. Other medications, such as DNase and mucolytics, decrease the thickness of the sputum (Fiel, 1993). New passive immunotherapy that would deliver antibodies against the common infections found in the airways of individuals with cystic fibrosis are being investigated.

An exciting new area of investigation is gene therapy for cystic fibrosis. The aims of gene therapy may include correcting certain cells to function normally by replacing the affected gene by its healthy counterpart or adding the healthy counterpart to the affected gene. Laboratory experiments have shown some effectiveness of gene therapy in rats and humans on the airway epithelial cells (Coutelle et al., 1993).

A new, last-resort therapeutic option is a lung transplant for individuals who have advanced cystic fibrosis. This has been successfully done in the past few years for individuals with cystic fibrosis; the survival rate has been 60 to 80% (Caine et al., 1991). For surviving individuals, there has been no documented recurrence of cystic pulmonary fibrosis as yet. Although this drastic treatment is relatively successful, there is a danger of lung rejection. The individual must remain on constant medication with continuous medical supervision.

COURSE OF CYSTIC FIBROSIS

Cystic fibrosis continues to be a terminal illness at the present time. However, advances in identifying and treating the disease have resulted in a longer and better quality of life. In 1969, the median age of survival was 14 years, but in 1990 it doubled to 28 years, with some individuals living into their forties and fifties. Longevity continues on an upward trend, with 30 years being the median age of survival (Behrman, 1992). Early diagnosis has also contributed to longevity by allowing early treatment. Since 1990, the median age of diagnosis is 7 months of age (FitzSimmons, 1993). When cystic fibrosis is diagnosed and treated before significant lung disease develops, there is a 90% chance that the individual will live past 20 years of age (Behrman, 1992).

■ VIGNETTE 1 ■

Lakeisha is a 17-year-old girl with cystic fibrosis. She moved to a new school this year. Although the homeroom teacher received information on cystic fibrosis and discussed it with the parents, there has been some breakdown in communication among the school faculty. Lakeisha's peers tend to avoid her because of her coughing, even though she says she is not sick. She has begun to try to suppress coughing due to the stares of her classmates. She is embarrassed to use the restroom and has already been ridiculed. She is distressed that she has a terminal illness and is wondering why she should continue living.

For the most part, children with cystic fibrosis are fairly healthy during childhood and adolescence. During the course of the disease, complications such as intestinal obstructions, diabetes, and cirrhosis of the liver may occur. Respiratory infections are common. (Pseudomonas aeruginosa and staphylococcal aureus are the most frequently identified respiratory infections.) Over time, this progressive disease will result in increasing lung damage and, eventually, the damage will limit the individual's activity tolerance. The individual with cystic fibrosis usually dies from respiratory failure, which results in heart failure.

With the discovery of the cystic fibrosis gene and the new treatments being investigated, it is estimated that individuals with cystic fibrosis will continue to live longer and healthier lives. New treatments may eventually be found that will cure this disease.

EDUCATIONAL IMPLICATIONS OF CYSTIC FIBROSIS

Cystic fibrosis does not directly affect the student's academic achievement. However, the unique characteristics of the disease and the attending emotional stress mean that teacher and peer education is important. Some environmental changes may be needed to meet the student's physical needs. Because the characteristics of cystic fibrosis vary, teachers need to be well-informed about the disease and be able to educate others.

Meeting Physical and Sensory Needs

The most prominent symptom of cystic fibrosis is a frequent cough. The student may try to suppress the coughing due to social embarrassment, and classmates may avoid the student for fear of catching an infection.

The teacher should stress to students that coughing is an important mechanism for clearing unwanted secretions. The teacher should explain that not coughing when needed can be harmful because secretions would remain in the lungs and clog things up. This cannot be over-stressed. In the early 1980s, four to six children with cystic fibrosis died each year from taking cough sup-pressants (Umbreit, 1983). Because most individuals associate a cough with an infection, the teacher needs to teach others that the cough is not infectious. No one can "catch" the disease.

Students' gastrointestinal needs must also be met. Students with cystic fibrosis usually have large appetites due to the loss of calories in the stool and to high metabolic activity. It is important that the student be allowed to eat as much as he or she wants (second, third, or fourth servings) at lunch. Gaining sufficient weight is often difficult for some students, so it will not be harmful to eat a lot. The student may have a diet restricting fat, but this is unusual. Some students with cystic fibrosis may have diabetes and require special diets. The teacher should be well-informed about di-etary needs.

Students with cystic fibrosis also tend to have more bowel movements. The student may need to be allowed to leave class to go to the bathroom more frequently than other students. Bowel movements also tend to have a foul odor due to the undigested fat. Teachers should be sensitive to this because other students may make fun of the student. Arrangements to use the faculty restroom are often made to allow the student to feel more at ease; a deodorizer can be made available for the restroom.

Children with cystic fibrosis should be encouraged to exercise along with their peers. Some studies have shown that students with cystic fibrosis have a lower level of fitness than their same-age peers (Loutzenhiser & Clark, 1993). In some instances, the student with cystic fibrosis may not have the same stamina as the other students and may not be able to compete as well in strenuous sports. In other instances, the student with cystic fibrosis may have lacked fitness training and may have been socialized into a role of inactivity. Any activity restrictions or limitations should be directed by the physician and closely monitored. One caution regarding exercising in the hot summer months is that the student may lose a lot of salt in sweat, which disturbs the delicate balance of electrolytes in the body. This can be very serious and in some instances life-threatening. Students may need to take additional salt on those hot days when physical activity is expected to occur. The teacher should discuss this with the family or physician and have an understanding of activity restrictions and the need for salt tablets.

■ **VIGNETTE 2** ■

Tom is a 12-year-old boy with cystic fibrosis who attends regular classes at his local public school. He takes several medications a day to aid with digestion. He also has had frequent lung infections. His teachers are aware that he has cystic fibrosis and understand the characteristics and implications of the condition. Dur-ing health class, the teacher explained the function of coughing and how it is not always a sign of infection. (Each school year, a teacher does a unit on health, explaining the importance of coughing and how some people cough when there is no infection. This has helped Tom explain his condition to others.) When Tom coughs in class, the other students regard it as commonplace and ignore the behavior. Tom is allowed to use the faculty restroom to avoid peer teasing due to the odor of his bowel movements. The cafeteria staff has been informed that Tom should be allowed to eat all he wants, and he has a running joke with them about how much he eats.

The student with cystic fibrosis may be taking several medications. Several pills may be taken prior to each meal due to pancreatic insufficiency, along with antibi-otics, aerosol treatments, and other medication. It is important that the person dispensing the medication know what the medication is for and adhere to the time schedule.

Meeting Communication Needs

Cystic fibrosis does not affect the individual's ability to communicate, so there is no difficulty with speech. However, the student will need to communicate to peers about his or her condition and symptoms. Some stu-dents could explain, "I get this stuff in my lungs that makes me cough a lot—when I do cough it up, I can breathe better. I have stomach problems, but I take pills that help me digest my food" (Association for the Care of Children's Health, 1982).

Meeting Learning Needs

Students with cystic fibrosis are typically of normal intelligence. There is usually no mental retardation or learning disability associated with the condition. Cog-nitive disability may be present, as it is in the regular population, but not because of the disease. Advances in treatment have meant that most students live long enough to go on to college or to work.

Meeting Daily Living Needs

Daily living needs are similar to those of other students without disabilities. Modifications and adaptations are not necessary until the disease is far advanced, usually when the person is in his or her late twenties or early thirties. Lack of stamina usually becomes a problem then (Grunow, Azcue, Berall, & Pencharz, 1993).

Meeting Behavioral and Social Needs

As with all chronic diseases, it is important that the teacher be aware of the emotional and social needs of the student. The student may have a pattern of learned helplessness due to overprotection. The teacher will then need to help the student learn to be independent. The student may also have difficulties socializing because of the characteristics of the disease. Educating peers and providing a positive school environment will help address these needs. It is important that the parents, teachers, student, and medical personnel work as a team to address how to manage these issues.

Since cystic fibrosis is a terminal disease, the child or adolescent may be faced with questions about death or dying. Due to the advances made in the last several years, the student will not normally be faced with the prospect of dying until he or she is older. However, in some cases, the student may know the prognosis of the disease or may have an advanced case. In either case, the teacher should be available to provide support to the student, often in the role of a good listener. In some instances, the student may need psychological counseling. As we discussed earlier, some individuals commit suicide, although this is rare. Appropriate counseling and support should help the student lead a full, productive life, even when it is shortened. (See Chapter 9.)

SUMMARY

Cystic fibrosis is a terminal illness that affects the exocrine glands of the body. The respiratory system is affected, with increased amounts of mucus and subsequent obstructions and lung damage. The gastrointestinal tract is affected because it cannot break down food due to the lack of pancreatic enzyme secretions. Students with cystic fibrosis will present with frequent coughing and a voracious appetite. Advances have been made in treatment, with life expectancy now in the thirties and beyond. It is expected that life expectancy will further increase with new treatments. One day, a cure may be found.

CHAPTER 22

Insulin-Dependent Diabetes Mellitus

Diabetes is a condition that can affect individuals of any age. It may begin in infancy, childhood, or adulthood. For infants, children, and adolescents, it is estimated that diabetes may be present in 1 in 500 to 1 in 1,000 people (Kushion, Salisbury, Seitz, & Wilson, 1991). It is the most common endocrine/metabolic disorder of childhood and adolescence. With proper management, there are typically no outward signs of the disorder. This can make compliance with the treatment regime difficult for children and adolescents, often resulting in experimentation with the management program. Emergency situations can arise from noncompliance or from changes in the disorder. It is important that the teacher and the entire educational team understand diabetes and its proper management so they can provide support to the student and be alert to any emergency situations that may arise.

DESCRIPTION OF DIABETES

Diabetes refers to a condition in which there is an abnormally high amount of glucose (sugar) in the bloodstream (hyperglycemia) due to impaired secretion of **insulin**. This condition has been divided into several different subtypes: insulin-dependent diabetes mellitus (IDDM or Type I DM), non-insulin-dependent diabetes mellitus (NIDDM or Type II DM), malnutrition-related diabetes mellitus (MRDM), gestational diabetes mellitus, and other types (Hitman & Metcalfe, 1993). The insulin-dependent type of diabetes mellitus primarily begins in childhood and adolescence and was formerly called *juvenile-onset diabetes*. Non-insulin diabetes mellitus is most common in individuals over 30 and was formerly known as adult-onset diabetes. Non-insulin diabetes mellitus does not typically involve some of the severe reactions that can occur with insulin-dependent diabetes. The other subtypes of diabetes are due to rare disorders and those associated with certain conditions such as pancreatic disease, cystic fibrosis, malnutrition, pregnancy, drug use, or poisons. Because insulin-dependent diabetes mellitus is the type of diabetes primarily found in children, we will discuss this type further in this chapter. References to diabetes will be to this type.

ETIOLOGY OF DIABETES

Insulin-dependent diabetes is attributed to the destruction of the insulin-producing beta cells in the islets of Langerhans, which are located in the pancreas. The exact mechanism resulting in their destruction is not completely understood. It is hypothesized that a combination of environmental conditions and hereditary genetic factors result in the development of the disease.

Environmental conditions, such as those caused by viruses (possibly rubella or mumps) or by dietary proteins (possibly those found in cow's milk and certain chemical toxins), have been suggested as possible triggers for an autoimmune response in which the body destroys its own beta cells (Karjalainen et al., 1992; Pipeleers & Ling, 1992). In the diabetic autoimmune response, it is hypothesized that the beta cells of the islets of Langerhans change structure slightly due to the infection or response to the dietary protein. The body then perceives the islets of Langerhans to be foreign bodies and attacks them, thus destroying the cells that secrete insulin. It has been found that not all the beta cells are destroyed. However, when clinical onset begins in children under 7 years of age, the surviving beta cells disappear. Individuals with later onset often have survival of the remaining cells (Pipeleers & Ling, 1992).

Although diabetes has not been shown to be inherited, a genetic predisposition among family members has been found. Evidence of a genetic basis has been derived from population and family studies of the short arm of chromosome 6, which pertains to the genes involved in immunosurveillance and recognition of "self" and "nonself" (Hitman & Metcalfe, 1993). Apparently, in the case of diabetes, certain inherited **antigens** predispose the autoimmune system to fail to recognize its own cells and to destroy them. Thus, they destroy the body's cells that secrete insulin. Whatever the exact mechanism that results in this condition might be, we know that eating too much sugar does not cause diabetes. That is a myth.

DYNAMICS OF DIABETES

The endocrine system is made up of several ductless glands that secrete hormones directly into the bloodstream. As seen in Figure 22-1, there are several endocrine glands throughout the body. As these glands secrete their hormones, the hormones are transported by the blood to other sites where they exert an effect. The hormones are responsible for several diverse functions ranging from fluid balance to sexual maturation.

The endocrine gland known as the *pancreas* is located beside the stomach. In the pancreas are cells (beta cells of the islets of Langerhans) that are responsible for the secretion of insulin. When a person eats,

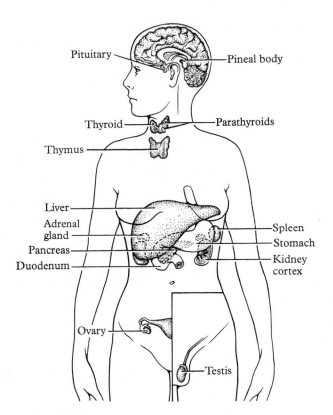

Pituitary
Pineal body
Thyroid
Parathyroids
Thymus
Liver
Adrenal gland
Pancreas
Duodenum
Spleen
Stomach
Kidney cortex
Ovary
Testis

■ **FIGURE 22-1** The endocrine system

food is digested in the stomach and some of the food is broken down into glucose (sugar), which is then absorbed into the bloodstream. The elevation in blood glucose stimulates the pancreas to secrete insulin into the bloodstream. Insulin is responsible for transporting the glucose from the bloodstream to cells in the body. Once in the cells, glucose serves as the main energy source for the cell (see Figure 22-2).

Since glucose is a major source of metabolic energy for the cells of the body, there are several mechanisms to ensure the proper maintenance of glucose concentrations. The release of insulin is the primary means of glucose regulation. Other means include the uptake of glucose by the small intestine, reabsorption of glucose by the proximal tubule of the kidney, and uptake, synthesis, and release of glucose by the liver (hepatic glucose). Insulin secretions inhibit hepatic glucose production (Pedersen, 1993).

The amount of insulin secreted is closely regulated to correspond to the amount of glucose in the bloodstream. This creates a narrow range of how much glucose remains in the blood; most is transported to the body cells. In diabetes, insulin is either diminished or missing in the bloodstream. The individual then has an abnormally high concentration of glucose in the blood and a lack of glucose in the body cells, which require glucose for energy. In an attempt to correct this, the liver will increase the amount of hepatic glucose production, but this usually worsens the situation due to unwanted by-products of the process.

CHARACTERISTICS OF DIABETES

Three early warning signs typically occur as a result of the lack of insulin and the subsequent rise in blood glucose. The first sign is polyuria, or excessive urination. When the body detects a high glucose concentration in the blood, the body tries to decrease the amount of glucose by excreting it in the urine as a waste product. The second sign is polydipsia, or excessive drinking. Due to the polyuria and subsequent dehydration, the person becomes thirsty and drinks excessively. The third sign is either polyphagia (excessive eating) or anorexia (lack of appetite). Because the body cells are not getting the energy they need, the person may become excessively hungry and eat in excess. Although this puts more glucose in the bloodstream, the cells are literally starving for glucose because it is not being transported into the cells due to the lack of insulin (Umbreit, 1983). For some individuals, anorexia (loss of interest in food) occurs instead of polyphagia. In both polyphagia and anorexia, there is usually weight loss. One reason is that 1,000 calories or 50% of the average caloric intake may be lost in the urine (Behrman, 1992).

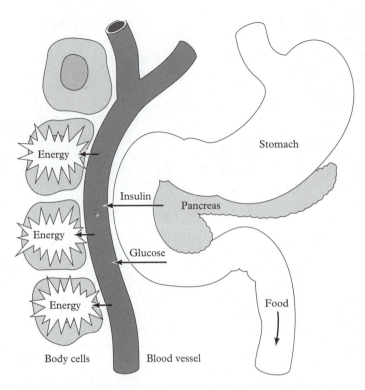

■ FIGURE 22-2 Insulin transporting glucose from the blood vessel to the body cells

When diabetes is not detected by the early warning signs, further symptoms will occur that have more serious consequences. As the body's cells continue to be deprived of glucose due to the lack of insulin, the body interprets that as a need for more glucose. The liver will break down fat to obtain more glucose. This process of hepatic production of glucose is usually suppressed by the effects of insulin, but without insulin, production is not controlled. The production of hepatic glucose results in a by-product of ketones, which are acidic. As the body cells continue to receive insufficient glucose, hepatic production of glucose increases, releasing a large quantity of ketones—too large a quantity for the body to dispose of in a timely fashion. This build-up of ketones and the other processes affected by it upsets the acid-base balance in the body, causing acidosis. This is referred to as ketoacidosis—accumulation of ketones resulting in acidosis. Initial symptoms of ketoacidosis include abdominal pain, nausea, and vomiting. If left untreated, ketoacidosis will progress and the individual may begin to have rapid, deep breathing with a fruity odor on the breath. (The fruity odor is caused by the excess ketones.) This may progress to drowsiness, unconsciousness, and coma; this is known as a *diabetic coma*. Ketoacidosis requires emergency treatment with fluids and insulin, as well as close monitoring to return the acid-base balance back to normal limits.

DETECTION OF DIABETES

A glucose tolerance test is the primary test used for detection of diabetes. In this test, the child ingests a chilled solution of flavored glucose, and blood samples are then taken at various time intervals to measure the amount of glucose in the blood. When this test is positive, it is often repeated to confirm the results.

Several studies have been conducted to determine whether the development of insulin-dependent diabetes can be predicted in individuals who are at-risk, such as those with a family history. Most findings show that the majority of individuals with high and persistent concentrations (titers) of islet-cell antibodies (which can be determined through a blood test) have been found to develop diabetes (Bosi et al., 1991; Christie et al., 1992; Karjalainen, 1990; Riley et al., 1990). However, some individuals meet this criteria and do not develop the disease.

TREATMENT OF DIABETES

Treatment of insulin-dependent diabetes consists of maintaining a balance of medication, diet, and exercise. Strict compliance to the prescribed treatment regime is necessary for optimal control of diabetes. Even with strict compliance, some individuals may have difficulty controlling the diabetes (and may be referred to as having "brittle diabetes").

Insulin

Insulin is the medication usually given to control diabetes. Several different types of insulin are available by prescription. For example, short-acting insulin preparations are known as *regular insulin;* insulin with extended action is known as NPH insulin. The type of insulin is carefully prescribed for the individual's specific need. Although adults who are diagnosed with non-insulin-dependent diabetes can often control the diabetes with oral medication, most individuals with the insulin-dependent type require insulin by injections. Individuals are taught to give themselves the injections (see Figure 22-3). Injections are administered beneath the skin (subcutaneously) in specific areas of the abdominal wall, arm, and thigh (see Figure 22-4). Injections are given one or more times a day. Since absorption rates of insulin vary according to site—the

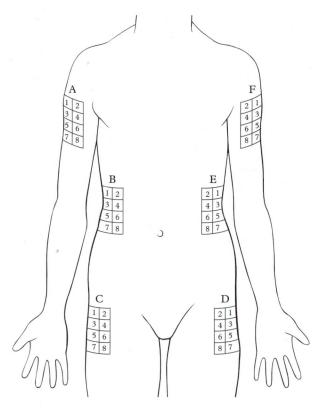

■ **FIGURE 22-4** Sites where insulin may be injected

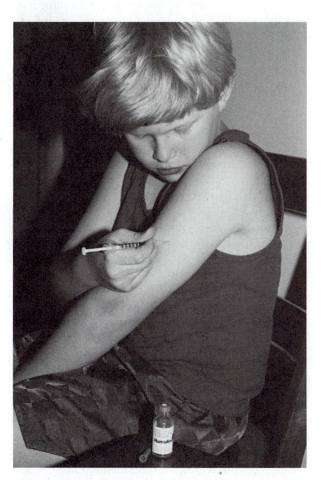

■ **FIGURE 22-3** A student demonstrating how to give an insulin injection

abdominal wall has the highest absorption rate and the thigh the slowest—some children are advised to use the abdominal area before meals and other regions for other doses to help maintain adequate glucose control (Heine, 1993).

An alternative to daily injections is an insulin pump, which has a reservoir that stores insulin and an insulin line that leads to a subcutaneous needle. Insulin is then delivered at an appropriate rate over a period of time. The advantage of the insulin pump is that insulin is absorbed faster and more predictably than when given by injection (Heine, 1993). This results in more balanced glucose levels. The disadvantage is possible displacement of the needle or infection at the infusion site (Levy, Borchelt, Kremer, Francis, & O'Conner, 1992). Another disadvantage is that it may alter body image and serve as a constant reminder of the diabetes.

In order to be sure that the proper amount of insulin is being administered, individuals with diabetes should monitor their blood glucose. The monitoring procedure consists of pricking a finger at specific times during the day to obtain a small blood sample and then placing it on a machine (glucose analyzer) that reads out the amount of blood glucose in the body (see Figure 22-5). The reading will inform the individual if the blood

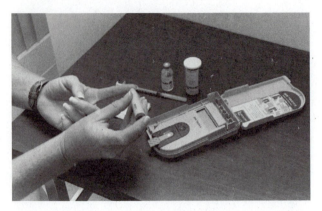

■ **FIGURE 22-5** Person drawing blood from finger to place on glucose monitoring machine to determine blood glucose level. The syringe on the table is used for giving insulin.

glucose level is within the expected range or if more or less glucose is needed with the next insulin injection.

Diet

The second major treatment area is diet. Individuals with diabetes need to maintain their diet so that the amount of glucose coming into the body is controlled. If sugar intake varies widely, the amount of injected insulin may not be appropriate and the individual may end up with too much glucose or too much insulin. A typical diabetic diet is one high in carbohydrates and fiber and low in fat, with avoidance of foods high in sugar and certain saturated fats. To help people with diabetes plan meals, exchange lists have been developed that are based on the calories, carbohydrates, protein, and fat content of food. These lists provide information about foods that will allow choice and flexibility in meal planning. A person can know which foods and in what quantities are appropriate for each meal (Holler, 1991).

It is important that the individual follow the meal plan and eat at regular times each day. A skipped meal or snack will result in too much insulin, which can have very adverse effects. In some instances, it may be important for the individual with diabetes to have snacks at certain times of the day to help achieve normal glucose levels. Weight must also be controlled because being overweight increases insulin needs and can complicate the management of diabetes.

Exercise

The third major treatment area is exercise. Exercise for the person with diabetes is not only good psychologi-

cally but may delay or prevent certain secondary conditions associated with diabetes such as cardiac complications (Armstrong, 1991). Exercise also affects the insulin-glucose balance by using up glucose and increasing the binding capacity of insulin receptors. Insulin is thus absorbed faster from the injection site, and the body needs less insulin (Armstrong, 1991). It is therefore important for individuals with diabetes to have a regular exercise regime. However, exercise can disrupt the insulin-glucose balance if the person exercises more than usual and has not adjusted the amount of insulin or food intake to match the exercise level. This would result in too much insulin in the body. More foods containing glucose, such as fruit and milk, will be needed to use the extra insulin and maintain the balance between insulin and glucose. If the person engages in prolonged exercise, carbohydrates and proteins will be needed. If the student knows that he or she will be exercising more, the quantity of insulin or food intake could be adjusted before exercising as prescribed by the physician.

A balance must be maintained between the food intake (glucose), amount of insulin, and quantity of exercise. Too much glucose and too little insulin could result in an emergency such as a diabetic coma. As we discussed, this happens when there is too much glucose and not enough insulin, such as when insulin is not taken or the amount prescribed is inadequate. A second emergency complication occurs when there is too much insulin in the body and too little glucose (hypoglycemia). In this instance, an insulin reaction could occur. This could happen if the person delays eating, skips a meal, or exercises more than usual. In an insulin reaction, the symptoms develop very rapidly, often in 15 minutes to an hour. Several possible symptoms include headache, dullness, irritability, crying, shaking, sweating, lightheadedness, behavior change, numbness of lips and tongue, paleness, moist skin, and weakness. Without intervention, the insulin reaction will progress to dizziness, slurred speech, double vision, confusion, unconsciousness, and death (Suddarth, 1991).

Blood glucose can be raised by drinking half a glass of fruit juice or nondiet soda, one glass of milk, sugar in any form, candy, any available food, or commercially available concentrated glucose. If there is no improvement, more food or sugar can be given in 15 minutes, provided that the person can swallow. If the person is unable to swallow or is confused or unconscious, an ambulance should be called immediately. Intravenous glucose will be given by the paramedics. When the reaction is over, often the person will need to eat food that is slowly digestible, such as bread, crackers, and milk, to prevent a second drop in blood glucose.

Pancreatic Transplant

Another possible treatment for diabetes is a pancreas transplant or transplantation of insulin-producing pancreatic islets (Landgraf, 1993; Milde, Hart, & Zehr, 1992; Pyzdrowski et al., 1992). Unlike certain types of transplants, a pancreatic transplant is not a life-saving measure but one to improve the quality of life. As we will discuss later, long-term diabetes can adversely affect the kidney, requiring a renal graph to improve kidney function. When this occurs, a simultaneous transplant of the pancreas may be performed. The surgical risks for organ transplants, such as infection and rejection, would be present for the kidney graph, and the surgical risks of adding a pancreatic transplant would be considered low (Markell & Friedman, 1992). Single pancreatic transplants are now relatively rare but are increasing, especially in cases in which it is difficult to control the glucose-insulin balance even with intensive treatment and complete compliance.

COURSE OF DIABETES

In most instances, diabetes can usually be well-controlled by keeping a balance of medication, diet, and exercise. However, some long-term complications can arise later in life. The precise mechanism that causes these complications is not known. The complications have been linked to hyperglycemia and to control of the diabetes. However, about 25% of individuals with diabetes do not develop these complications, no matter how well or how poorly hyperglycemia is controlled (Strowig & Raskin, 1992). This suggests that other factors are involved.

Complications may occur after the individual has had diabetes for many years. The complications typically involve damage to the large blood vessels such as those of the heart, small blood vessels such as those of the eyes and kidneys, and the nerves. There is a tendency for the person with diabetes to develop arteriosclerosis (thickening of the arteries), atherosclerosis (localized accumulations of lipid-containing material in the arteries), and microcirculatory lesions due to high levels of circulating cholesterols and lipids far more easily than the nondiabetic individual would (Guyton, 1991). The large vessels of the heart may become clogged, which results in an increased incidence of cardiovascular disease and heart attacks (Donahue & Orchard, 1992). Damage to the arteries in the feet can result in circulation problems and gangrene—tissue death due to lack of blood supply. There is also an increased incidence of stroke; that is, a blockage of a blood vessel in the brain.

Small blood vessels of the eye and kidney may be affected. Damage to the small blood vessels of the eye from diabetes is diagnosed as *diabetic retinopathy*, a progressive impairment in retinal circulation that progresses to bleeding in the vitreous humor, scarring, and retinal detachment. It is the most common cause of acquired blindness (Davis, 1992; Suddarth, 1991). When the small blood vessels of the kidneys are affected due to diabetes, a diagnosis of diabetic nephropathy is made. In diabetic nephropathy, the part of the kidney that filters the waste products (glomerulus) is damaged, resulting in chronic renal failure. As the chronic renal failure advances, dialysis will be needed. Diabetic nephropathy is one of the leading causes of acquired end-stage renal disease (Markell & Friedman, 1992; Suddarth, 1991; Viberti, Yip-Messent, & Morocutti, 1992).

Diabetic neuropathy is another possible complication of diabetes in which the peripheral and autonomic nervous systems are affected, producing a variety of syndromes and symptoms. Diabetic neuropathy is characterized by demyelination of some axons as well as a loss of some myelinated and unmyelinated nerve axons (Vink et al., 1992). Often, the nerves of the feet and legs are affected with numbness, tingling, and sometimes pain. When the autonomic nervous system is affected, there may be low blood pressure, sweating disorders, diarrhea or constipation, and/or impaired bladder and sexual functions (Berkow, 1992).

Individuals with diabetes who develop secondary complications are at risk of a shortened life span. Of the several possible complications, the two major causes of premature death in individuals with insulin-dependent diabetes are diabetic nephropathy and cardiovascular disease (Lloyd & Orchard, 1993).

EDUCATIONAL IMPLICATIONS OF DIABETES

In order to meet the physical needs of students with diabetes, the teacher and the rest of the educational team need to have a thorough understanding of the disease and of the child's specific needs.

Meeting Physical and Sensory Needs

It is important for the educator to understand the balance of insulin, food, and exercise. Although responsibility for compliance should be placed on the student, the teacher should be aware of the need for a diabetic diet and be sensitive to the student's needs if candy is brought into the classroom for parties or celebrations. Having alternative food available is helpful. If an extra snack is needed, the student must be given the opportunity to eat it when scheduled. The teacher should alert the parent and child to activities that include more exercise than usual, such as a field day, so that food intake or insulin dosage can be adjusted.

All teachers who are in contact with the student should know the signs and symptoms of ketoacidosis (hyperglycemia) and insulin reaction (hypoglycemia) (see Table 22-1). Usually, the student can detect a reaction and inform the teacher of its occurrence. However, onset can be so quick that the student delays in informing the teacher until he or she is incapacitated. If the student reports a reaction, the teacher should determine whether the student delayed eating, had unusually strenuous exercise, or took too much insulin. If one of these has occurred, the student is probably having an insulin reaction. In the event of insulin reaction, food or drinks high in sugar (or sugar itself) should be readily available for the student to take. The teacher should always have something available, and the student should always have something as well. If the student did not take insulin or there is a need for more insulin, which may occur during illness, the student may experience hyperglycemia and ketoacidosis. The student would then need insulin. A written plan of action should be available for the teacher to follow in either situation. This plan should be determined at the beginning of each year and planned with the parent, physician, school nurse, and the rest of the educational team. The plan should be available to, and understood by, other adults responsible for the student at school—instructional assistant, substitute teacher, adjacent classroom teacher, and so forth.

Students with diabetes, especially students with poor metabolic control, are often at-risk of poor school performance due to diabetes-related problems (such as symptoms of hypoglycemia or hyperglycemia) that interfere with performance. These students may need to have their glucose monitored and to receive insulin injections at school. Not only will blood glucose monitoring have a positive effect on the health of the student but it also can distinguish behaviors related to diabetes from those the student uses to avoid school work. When behaviors are identified as diabetes-related, treatment will improve the student's behavior and attention to the academic task because he or she will be feeling better. Also, school interruptions can be averted. Glucose monitoring can be performed by a qualified school nurse or other qualified nonhealth professional, such as an educator, who is trained and supervised by a nurse (Gray, Golden, & Reiswerg, 1991).

Meeting Communication Needs

Diabetes does not affect communication unless the student is experiencing confusion and subsequent unconsciousness due to an insulin reaction or hyperglycemia. In these instances, it is up to the teacher, nurse, or other school personnel to help the student as quickly as possible. The teacher will need to be alert for symptoms of hyperglycemia or an insulin reaction, especially in young students who have additional impairments that affect communication.

In some instances, the student with diabetes may have to communicate to others about his or her disease. The student could say, "I have diabetes—that means my

TABLE 22-1

Hyperglycemia and Hypoglycemia

Category	Possible symptoms	Cause	Treatment
Ketoacidosis; hyperglycemia (too much sugar)	Symptoms occur gradually (over hours or days): polyuria; polyphagia; polydipsia; fatigue; abdominal pain; nausea; vomiting; fruity odor on breath; rapid, deep breathing; unconsciousness	Did not take insulin; did not comply with diet	Give insulin; follow plan of action
Insulin reaction; hypoglycemia (too little sugar)	Symptoms occur quickly (in minutes): headache; dullness; irritability; shaking; sweating; lightheadedness; behavior change; paleness; weakness; moist skin; slurred speech; confusion; shallow breathing; unconsciousness	Delayed eating; participated in strenuous exercise; took too much insulin	Give sugar; follow plan of action

■ VIGNETTE 1 ■

Carlos has had insulin-dependent diabetes ever since he could remember. At 17, he is used to the regime of insulin, diet, and exercise. Although he had some difficulty with compliance as a young child at birthday parties and as a young teenager who did not want to deal with glucose monitoring or insulin injections, he is now more careful with his regime. One morning, while in his advanced chemistry class, he began to feel anxious and weak. He immediately recognized the symptoms of an insulin reaction and remembered how he had rushed out the door that morning without eating the breakfast he should have had. Carlos went to his backpack and gan to eat some crackers and drink a can of orange juice. His teacher was aware of Carlos's diabetes and casually walked over to ask if he was all right. Carlos felt fine after a few minutes and continued with his chemistry.

■ VIGNETTE 2 ■

Tonya is a 7-year-old girl with insulin-dependent diabetes that has been well controlled. While she was on a field trip with her class, she and her teacher forgot her midmorning snack, and lunch was delayed because of the timing of the elephant show. Tonya began to feel nauseated, weak, and anxious, and her skin was moist. Tonya did not want to interrupt the elephant show, so she didn't say anything. After about another 15 minutes, she fell out of her chair, had slurred speech, and was drowsy. Her teacher ran over and recognized the signs of an insulin reaction. Just to be sure, she smelled Tonya's breath for a sweet smell that would indicate ketones. The sweet smell was not present, which further confirmed insulin reaction, as did the realization that Tonya had not eaten. Because Tonya could swallow, the teacher began giving her the nondiet soda she had just bought. She also called an ambulance due to the severity of the symptoms and lack of response to the soda. The paramedics arrived quickly on the scene and tested the glucose level. An IV was started, and Tonya received glucose intravenously. She was stabilized at the hospital and felt fine afterwards.

body doesn't use sugar the same ways yours does. That's why I take shots and watch what I eat" (Association for the Care of Children's Health, 1982).

Meeting Learning Needs

Mental retardation or learning disabilities are not a characteristic of diabetes; individuals usually have normal intelligence. However, cognitive deficits may occur with severe episodes of hypoglycemia or repeated episodes of hypoglycemia in infants and toddlers. In these instances, infants and toddlers are unable to tell their parents when they are experiencing symptoms of hypoglycemia. Damage to the central nervous system may result when symptoms go unrecognized (Kushion et al., 1991).

For children and adolescents, hypoglycemia has been associated with a reduction in mental efficiency that can affect educational performance until it is corrected (Lloyd & Orchard, 1993). Academic achievement may also be affected, as with other students with chronic illnesses, due to missed school, others' attitudes, poor self-esteem, or feeling ill. (See Chapter 3.)

Meeting Daily Living Needs

Daily living needs are similar to those of other students except for the noted modifications in diet, the monitoring and administration of insulin, and the need to monitor exercise. Students will need to learn how to properly monitor their own diet and exercise, use the machine to measure the amount of glucose in their blood, and give themselves insulin injections.

Meeting Behavioral and Social Needs

Children and adolescents with diabetes may have difficulty coping with the disease. This may result in noncompliance, which can adversely affect their health. Students with diabetes or any chronic illness may feel different from their peers and lack self-esteem. Information about the disease and books about individuals with diabetes may be helpful, as can having other significant individuals with whom to discuss concerns. Social interactions may also be hampered when peers misunderstand the disease or the restrictions placed on the student. Peer education becomes important in providing a supportive environment. Diabetes can be discussed as part of a health class. A special assembly with a person from the American Diabetes Association can be arranged. (See Chapter 3.) Other possibilities include attending support groups or diabetes camp.

A high degree of responsibility for control of the disease is placed on the student and family. Compliance with the strict management regime may lapse if the person does not adjust to the disease. Family and social support, as well as educational level and age, may also influence compliance. Adjustment to the disease may be affected by knowledge of secondary complications and concern over the possibility of becoming blind or losing kidney function, regardless of how well the diabetes has been controlled. Counseling is very important when noncompliance is occurring in order to prevent life-threatening situations and decrease the probability of secondary complications. Overall, students may experience adjustment problems, but they are not necessarily prolonged.

SUMMARY

Insulin-dependent diabetes is caused by damage or malfunction of the beta cells in the islets of Langerhans in the pancreas, where insulin is secreted. With a lack of insulin, glucose cannot be delivered to the cells of the body for energy. Individuals will present with initial symptoms of polyuria, polydipsia, and polyphagia (or anorexia). More life-threatening symptoms of hyperglycemia will follow unless the condition is diagnosed and treated. Diabetes is treated by the administration of insulin as well as treatment of any secondary complications that occur. The student needs to maintain a balance of insulin, diet, and exercise to keep glucose at proper concentrations. Even when there is strict compliance, complications such as vision loss can occur later in life. If the student is not compliant with treatment, a life-threatening situation can occur. Teachers and the rest of the educational team should be supportive of the student and their treatment regime and be familiar with how to deal with emergencies related to diabetes.

CHAPTER 23

Chronic Renal Failure

In chronic renal failure, the kidneys no longer function properly, thus affecting the body's ability to regulate the composition of bodily fluids. The condition progresses to the point that the kidneys can no longer effectively filter out waste products—unusable end products of metabolism. This results in a life-threatening situation. Although individuals with chronic renal failure would have died several decades ago, now they lead productive lives with the use of dialysis or kidney transplants. Although the treatment for this condition is given primarily at home, in a dialysis unit, or in a hospital, physical and emotional side effects may affect school performance. The teacher needs a thorough understanding of the implications of this disease in order to effectively address the student's needs.

DESCRIPTION OF CHRONIC RENAL FAILURE (CRF)

Chronic renal failure (CRF) is a condition in which the kidneys are damaged and unable to function normally. Unlike in acute renal failure, which is usually reversible and is a temporary decrease of kidney function, in chronic renal failure there is destruction and damage to the kidneys that results in a progressive deterioration of renal function. This deterioration goes through a series of stages that ends with an excess of wastes in the blood, a condition known as *uremia*. Chronic renal failure is also referred to as *end-stage renal disease*.

ETIOLOGY OF CHRONIC RENAL FAILURE

Chronic renal failure in children has several possible causes. When the child is under 5 years of age, the cause is commonly due to congenital abnormalities in which there has been some malformation, underdevelopment,

or obstruction of the kidneys (Behrman, 1992). After 5 years of age, chronic renal failure is more typically caused by an acquired disease of the glomerulus, the filtering unit of the kidney. One of the primary causative diseases is glomerulonephritis, or inflammation of the glomerulus. The glomerulus can become diseased from viral or bacterial infections, drug reactions, or systemic diseases of the body such as arthritis. Other causes of chronic renal failure in children are vascular (blood) disorders, or hereditary disorders such as Alport syndrome—a hereditary disorder with hearing loss and renal failure occurring in the second or third decade of life. The most common genetic cause of chronic renal failure in children is *familiar juvenile nephronophthisis*, which is characterized by the development of cysts in the kidneys and renal failure around the age of 13 years (Behrman, 1992; Hildebrandt et al., 1993; Polito et al., 1991). Although rare, chronic renal failure may be caused by chemicals, animal venoms, certain foods and plants, disease, radiation therapy, and the misuse of drugs (Abuelo, 1990).

Although rare in children, chronic renal failure may also occur due to chronic high blood pressure and the complications of insulin-dependent diabetes. One common misconception is the role urinary tract infections play in chronic renal diseases. A urinary tract infection does not usually involve the kidneys, and hence, does not cause chronic renal failure.

DYNAMICS OF CHRONIC RENAL FAILURE

Each person has two kidneys that are located behind the intestines at the level of the lumbar spine. The kidneys regulate the composition and volume of body fluids. Essential substances and water are retained, while the kidneys filter out noxious substances through a process of urine formation. When urine is formed, it exits each kidney through tubes called *ureters* (see Figure 23-1). The ureters connect to the bladder. In the bladder, urine is stored until the person urinates; then the muscle surrounding the opening of the bladder relaxes, allowing urine to drain down the urethra and exit the body.

Each kidney is composed of approximately 1 million functioning units known as *nephrons.* The nephron is composed of three main parts: the *glomerulus, Bowman's capsule,* and the *tubules* (see Figure 23-2). The glomerulus consists of a bundle of capillaries covered with epithelial cells and encased by a capsule known as Bowman's capsule. Blood flows through the capillaries of the glomerulus; the glomerulus serves as a filter. Water and other substances in the blood (such as sodium, glucose, and urea) pass through the glomerulus into Bowman's capsule and continue into the connecting tubules. The remaining blood cells and blood proteins are too large to pass through the glomerulus, so they continue in the capillaries that flow into a small blood vessel and leave the glomerulus. They continue moving along the nephrons to the rest of the body.

Water, waste products, and other substances continue moving through the tubules. Water and substances such as glucose that are needed by the body are reabsorbed from the tubules into capillaries that sur-round them. Substances that are not needed by the body (urea and other metabolic end products) continue through the tubules. Other waste products are secreted into the tubules from adjacent capillaries. As the waste products are carried by the tubules, they flow into collecting ducts. The collecting ducts join into progressively larger tubules until they empty into the renal pelvis and flow into the ureter as urine.

Overall, the kidneys are responsible for filtering, reabsorbing, and secreting substances found in the blood. This process maintains the proper levels of certain chemicals (acids and bases) in the blood and, hence, in the tissues of the body. The body must maintain homeostasis (balance) between acids and bases, or death will occur.

Blood pressure control is another important function of the kidneys. Blood pressure is the force exerted by the blood against the walls of the blood vessels (Guyton, 1991). The kidneys directly contribute to the level of blood pressure through its regulation of sodium (salt) and water in the body. The glomerular cells of the kidney also produce an enzyme known as *renin,* which leads to the production of a chemical (angiotensin I and II) that can lead to increased blood pressure. Blood pressure must be maintained at a certain level. If it is too low, blood will not be circulated properly and shock could

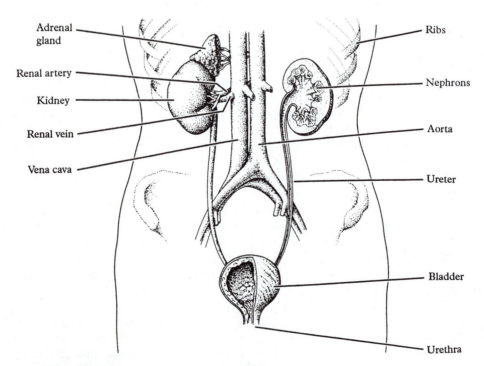

■ FIGURE 23-1 Anatomy of the urinary system
SOURCE: From *Physical Disabilities and Health Impairments: An Introduction,* by J. Umbreit, Ed., pp. 118, 123, 251, Merrill Publishing Co., 1983.

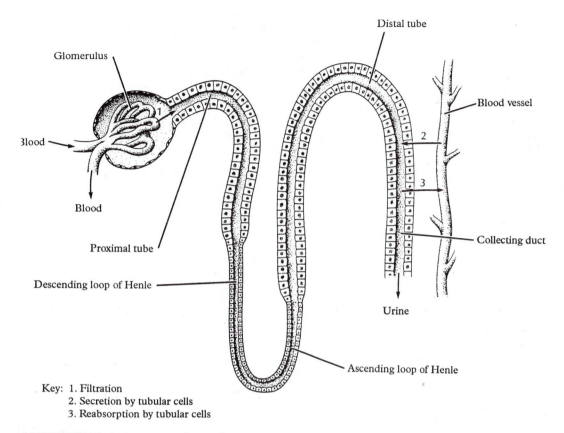

Key: 1. Filtration
      2. Secretion by tubular cells
      3. Reabsorption by tubular cells

■ **FIGURE 23-2** Anatomy of a nephron
SOURCE: From *Physical Disabilities and Health Impairments: An Introduction*, by J. Umbreit, Ed.,
pp. 118, 123, 251, Merrill Publishing Co., 1983.

result. If it is too high, the person is at-risk of having a stroke or other health problems. The kidneys also play a role in red blood cell formation. They produce a substance known as *erythropoietin,* which stimulates red blood cell production in the bone marrow.

How well the kidneys are functioning can be determined by calculating the filtration rate of the kidneys; this involves determining the amount of certain substances, such as creatinine, in the blood and urine. This is known as the *glomerulus filtration rate* (GFR). The GFR normally decreases as a person ages (DeSanto et al., 1991). Other decreases in GFR can be due to damage to the nephrons.

Nephrons can be destroyed any number of ways—by infections and diseases of the kidney, hereditary disorders, or toxins. When nephron damage occurs, several adaptational processes come into play to maintain as high a GRF as possible. For example, 75% of the nephrons can be destroyed, and a GFR of 50% of normal can still be maintained (Berkow, 1992). However, once a critical number of nephrons are destroyed, chronic renal failure occurs. In chronic renal failure, the remaining nephrons cannot filter out the waste products from the blood sufficiently. Progressive deterioration of kidney function is then inevitable.

Progressive deterioration of kidney function occurs in three stages: *diminished renal reserve, renal insufficiency (failure),* and *uremia.* In diminished renal reserve, a small increase in waste products, such as urea and creatinine, are found in the blood. Renal function continues to deteriorate until renal failure results, with fluid and acid-base imbalances. In uremia, effects of the malfunctioning kidney occur throughout the body. The manifestations of the uremic stage usually begin to emerge when the GRF drops below 20% of normal and there is a progressive increase of waste products, such as urea nitrogen and serum creatinine, in the blood.

CHARACTERISTICS OF CHRONIC RENAL FAILURE

The onset of chronic renal failure may begin with mild symptoms. In mild, diminished renal reserve, the child may have no symptoms, and only clinical laboratory testing would show the abnormality. As the disorder progresses to mild to moderate renal insufficiency, urination (or increased urination) at night (nocturia) may begin. Often, fatigue and decreased mental acuity, including a short attention span and the inability to concentrate, are the first symptoms of uremia. Other symptoms can involve most systems of the body. The urinary system may present with a decrease in urine output as the uremia progresses. The gastrointestinal system may be affected; the child may experience nausea and vomiting, which can progress to ulceration and gastrointestinal bleeding. Malnutrition is common. The cardiovascular system may be affected, resulting in edema (swelling) of the arms, legs, and face; in some instances, congestive heart failure may occur. The skin may have a yellow-brown discoloration from the increase in urea in the blood. Uremic frost may develop on the skin; this is when crystals are formed on the skin. In the neuromuscular and skeletal systems, muscular irritability and bone disease and deformity can result. In the neurological system, headaches, drowsiness, memory loss, slurred speech, muscle weakness, loss of sensation in the arms and legs, seizures, and coma may occur.

Some of the most common characteristics of chronic renal failure in children include high blood pressure (**hypertension**), anemia, and growth retardation. The kidneys play a central role in blood pressure control through the reabsorption of salt and water. High blood pressure may occur in chronic renal failure, especially as renal function declines. High blood pressure is not only a potential cause of chronic renal failure but is also a complication of renal failure as well (Drukker, 1991; Solhaug, Adelman, & Chan, 1992). Because the kidneys also produce the hormone erythropoietin (which is responsible for stimulating red blood cell production in the bone marrow), there is a decreased production of this hormone in chronic renal failure. Thus, fewer red blood cells are produced and anemia, with accompanying paleness and weakness, results. Anemia is par-ticularly severe in children with chronic renal failure (Navarro, Alonso, Avilla, & Espinosa, 1991). Growth retardation is also typically present; several factors, such as hormonal disturbances, malnutrition, acidosis, and defective bone formation (osteodystrophy), may cause children with chronic renal failure to be smaller and of shorter stature than others (Santos, Orejas, Rey, Garcia-Vicente, & Malaga, 1991).

DETECTION OF CHRONIC RENAL FAILURE

Chronic renal failure may be detected in an infant with severe abnormality of the kidneys or a hereditary disorder. Abnormalities pertaining to the kidneys may be suspected after birth when there is absent or diminished urination. When a hereditary disorder involving the kidneys is found in infancy, kidney disease is expected before any symptoms develop. In some hereditary disorders such as juvenile nephronophthisis, the gene responsible for the disorder has been identified or is in the process of being identified through genetic mapping, which may eventually lead to prenatal diagnosis (Hildebrant et al., 1993).

Chronic renal failure can be diagnosed by laboratory tests of the blood and urine to determine whether there are increases in waste products like urea nitrogen and creatinine (Berkow, 1992; Zaramella et al., 1991). Based on the findings of the various laboratory tests, the glomerular filtration rate will be determined; for example, by the creatinine clearance test on 24-hour urine collection. Laboratory blood tests, such as for electrolytes and blood cell counts, will also determine if acidosis and anemia are present, both of which are usually found in chronic renal failure. Other diagnostic tests, such as ultrasound, renal arteriography, special renal flow scans, or renal biopsy, may also be used to determine the etiology and extent of the chronic renal failure. Physical examination may reveal some abnormalities, and an electrocardiogram and a chest X-ray are often done to detect any additional abnormalities or complications.

TREATMENT OF CHRONIC RENAL FAILURE

Initial treatment for chronic renal failure often consists of close monitoring of the remaining kidney function and treatment of secondary symptoms. Dietary management is one important aspect of treatment, not only to prevent malnutrition but also because the ingestion of certain foods may produce noxious wastes that the kidneys cannot filter. In children with chronic renal failure, their growth rate can decrease when the GFR decreases to below 50% of normal. Dietary management often consists of increasing caloric intake to combat anorexia; increasing carbohydrates and fats by the use of jams, sugar, and special glucose (sugar) is common. Certain foods that are rich in protein that metabolizes into nitrogenous wastes are usually restricted. However, protein is needed for growth in children, so protein is encouraged in lowered amounts. Some studies indicate that a low-protein, phosphorus-restricted diet may slow the progression of renal failure (Mitch, 1991). Vitamins and minerals may also be prescribed due to inadequate dietary intake or to the loss of vitamins occurring during dialysis. In some instances, sodium may be restricted when high blood pressure, congestive heart failure, or edema (swelling) is present. Water is often restricted due to inadequate kidney function when renal failure develops.

Individuals with chronic renal failure may also receive medication in addition to dietary management to control the symptoms. Anemia is often treated with

■ FIGURE 23-3 A hemodialysis machine with a chair for student to sit in while procedure is being performed

intravenous injections of erythropoietin (Navarro et al., 1991; Suppiej et al., 1992). Blood transfusions are given only in extreme circumstances. High blood pressure and edema may be treated with diuretics, vasodilators, and other types of medications (Solhaug, Adelman, & Chan, 1992). Acidosis in chronic renal

failure may be treated with sodium bicarbonate tablets. Children may receive medication for other complications and symptoms.

As renal function continues to worsen and chronic insufficiency and uremia occur, along with increases in the levels of potassium (hyperkalemia), the individual must either undergo dialysis or have a kidney transplant. There are two main types of dialysis: *hemodialysis* and *peritoneal dialysis*. Hemodialysis involves the use of a hemodialyzer or "artificial kidney," which is a machine external to the body that filters out waste products from the blood (see Figure 23-3). Individuals receiving hemodialysis are usually connected to the hemodialyzer approximately 3 times a week for 4 to 6 hours. They undergo a minor surgical procedure that connects an artery to a vein, usually in the arm. This is known as an *arteriovenous shunt,* cannula, or fistula, depending on the type of connection (see Figure 23-4). In some instances, a catheter in the subclavian vessel (blood vessel by the collar bone) may be used. During dialysis, one tube is connected to the shunt so blood can leave the body and go to the dialyzer; a second tube is connected to the shunt to receive the cleansed blood from the hemodialyzer. As the blood goes through the hemodialyzer, it passes through artificial membranes that act as filters.

On the other side of the membranes is a dialyzing fluid, also known as a *dialysate fluid*. Waste products in the blood leave the blood and move to the dialyzing fluid in a process of diffusion. The dialyzing fluid also contains chemicals needed by the body; the concentration of the chemicals is adjusted in the dialyzing fluid to correspond to the needs of the body. For

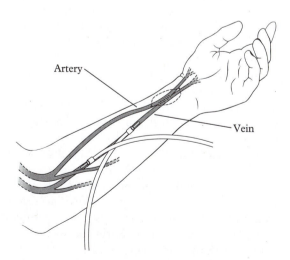

Internal fistula

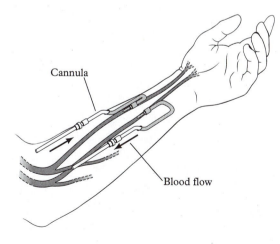

External shunt

■ FIGURE 23-4 Types of shunts used for dialysis

example, if there is an imbalance of certain chemicals due to disease, the dialyzing fluid will be adjusted so that more of these chemicals will be absorbed from the dialyzing fluid into the blood. If an excess of the chemical needs to be removed from the blood, the chemical is not added to the dialyzing fluid and it moves from the blood into the dialyzing fluid by diffusion (Kramer, 1980). Hemodialysis may be done in a dialysis center or at home with proper training, education, and equipment, and with nursing assistance as indicated.

Another type of dialysis is peritoneal dialysis in which a permanent tube (catheter) is placed into theperitoneum—a membrane lining the abdominal-

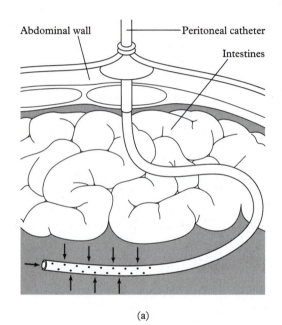

(a)

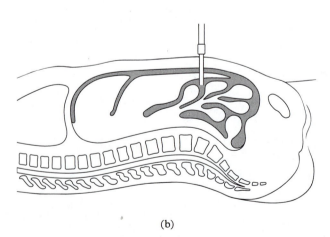

(b)

■ **FIGURE 23-5** The peritoneal cavity and a catheter inserted into the cavity for peritoneal dialysis

pelvic cavity below the diaphragm and above the pelvic floor (see Figure 23-5). A tube is attached to the external portion of the catheter. A bag with dialysate is raised to about shoulder level and infused by gravity into the peritoneal cavity—the space in which the liver, intestines, and other organs are housed. The dialyzing fluid remains in the peritoneal cavity for about 4 hours, which is referred to as *dwell time*. During dwell time, the waste products move from the uremic blood in the abdominal blood vessels to the dialyzing fluid, and needed substances move from the dialyzing fluid to the blood vessels. At the end of the dwell time, the fluid is drained into a bag and the process starts again.

Peritoneal dialysis is performed either as continuous ambulatory peritoneal dialysis (CAPD) or continuous cycling peritoneal dialysis (CCPD). In continuous ambulatory peritoneal dialysis, there are 4 to 5 exchanges daily, 7 days a week, with an overnight dwell time that allows the child to sleep without interruption. In continuous cycling peritoneal dialysis, 3 to 5 exchanges occur during the night using an automated peritoneal machine, and there is an extended dwell time during the day (Suddarth, 1991).

Continuous peritoneal dialysis has been successfully performed with infants under 2 years of age (Qamar & Balfe, 1991), and it has several advantages over hemodialysis. It is relatively pain-free, hospitalization is reduced, dietary restrictions are minimal, it costs less than hemodialysis, and is simpler technically. This simplicity allows the child to move about freely and there is less disruption of school and play. Also, the child or adolescent can be taught to do self-dialysis. The major drawback is the possible complication of peritonitis (inflammation of the peritoneum), infection, poor appetite, and poor body image. As with all home-based interventions, this one is a major responsibility for parents and may cause family psychological stress and social and marital disruption (Barakat, Savage, Burns, & Stewart, 1992).

Another option in the treatment of chronic renal failure is a renal transplant from either a live human donor or a cadaver. Individuals can live normal lives with one kidney, so live donors can successfully donate a kidney to give someone with chronic renal failure the chance to live a more normal life. Healthy organs are often viable for transplantation after a person is pronounced dead when organ donor cards have been signed or consent is given by relatives. Successful renal transplants are viewed as the best therapy for children with chronic renal failure. Early transplants are preferable in infants and young children because this prevents growth retardation and allows the child to have a normal life (Abitbol, Burke, Zilleruelo, Montane, & Strauss, 1991; Lerner et al., 1993). Although there has been much success with renal transplants, graft rejections still occur. Medications that suppress the immune system are used to decrease the likelihood of rejection, although this also increases the risk of infection. Individuals have died of severe infections as a result of immunosuppression therapy. Graft failure may also occur as long as 10 years after grafting due to chronic rejection (Donckerwolcke, 1991).

COURSE OF CHRONIC RENAL FAILURE

Hemodialysis and peritoneal dialysis can effectively filter out the waste products from the blood but do not replace all of the kidney's functions. Individuals on dialysis will typically need to continue with diet restrictions and medications. The management team should be alert for complications such as anemia and fatigue, gastrointestinal problems, bone problems, infection, and high blood pressure. Especially prevalent are psychosocial problems in which the child must cope with the physical and emotional dependence on dialysis. These problems include depression and, in some cases, suicide (Berkow, 1992).

Renal transplants have been found to be successful for children with chronic renal failure. Graft survival rates have been found to be comparable to those of older individuals; grafts received from a living, related donor have a longer life than grafts from a cadaver, especially when transplants are done after the recipient is 5 years of age (Leichter et al., 1992; McEnery, Stablein, Arbus, & Tejani, 1992). However, the survival rate of individuals with either type of graft does not compare favorably to that of the average population. Ten-year survival after transplantation has ranged between 57 and 89% (Donckerwolcke, 1991). Several major causes of death have been identified in individuals with renal transplants, including infection, cancer, heart attack, and liver failure. However, no single major cause of death has been identified in children and adolescents receiving renal transplants (Braun, 1990; Donckerwolcke, 1991).

EDUCATIONAL IMPLICATIONS OF CHRONIC RENAL FAILURE

The impact of chronic renal failure on the student's educational performance at school will vary. This variation is related to individual differences and to how the chronic renal failure is being treated. Students who have received a transplanted kidney will have few needs in the educational environment, while those who are undergoing dialysis will have several considerations that need to be met.

Meeting Physical and Sensory Needs

The student with chronic renal failure will have several physical needs that may have to be addressed at school, depending on how the chronic renal failure is being treated. Students undergoing dialysis typically have diet and fluid restrictions. Teachers need to understand these restrictions and help the younger student adhere to them. Older students should already understand the restrictions, but noncompliance has been documented, particularly with regard to fluid restriction. Members of the educational team should monitor the student's fluid intake closely and stress its importance to the student (Cohen, Kagen, Richter, Topor, & Saveedra, 1991). A dietitian may be a part of the educational team and can address the student's specific nutritional needs.

The student with chronic renal failure will typically be taking several medications. The teacher should be familiar with the medications and the possible side effects of each. Medication administration should be monitored and a form, such as the one in Chapter 27, can be used to document medication administration. If the student has received a transplanted kidney, he or she may be taking medication that suppresses the immune system. This causes the child to be more susceptible to infections. The teacher and school nurse should be alert for signs of illness in other children, and children who are ill should be sent home promptly to avoid spreading the infection to the more susceptible student.

Students who are undergoing dialysis may need to have their schedules arranged; for example, fatigue may be present in some students even after dialysis treatment and treatment for anemia has begun. More difficult academic work may need to be scheduled in the morning when the student is more alert, and allowances should be made for periodic breaks if needed. Scheduling should also take into account when a student goes for hemodialysis. Usually, every effort is made to schedule hemodialysis after school hours, but sometimes students may need to leave school early to go to a hemodialysis clinic. Scheduling should be done so that less important classes meet during that time. This will minimize the amount of work the student would need to make up. In the case of peritoneal dialysis, scheduling should accommodate the need to drain the dialyzing fluid and give a fresh bag. A time scheduled in the middle of the day may allow this to occur easily.

Younger students receiving peritoneal dialysis will need a nurse or trained school personnel to help them with the drainage of the fluid and the administration of a fresh bag. It is important that younger students be allowed to assist with this procedure so they can learn it themselves and become as independent as possible.

Students around 10 to 12 years of age, and sometimes younger, are usually able to perform the peritoneal dialysis on their own. At times, a private location will need to be provided, one in which a chair is available for the student to sit on.

Some physical disabilities may be present in individuals with chronic renal failure. Bone malformation may occur, as well as peripheral neuropathy resulting in "foot drop" (when the foot is in a downward position). Walking or stair-climbing may be hampered. In some instances, there can be some loss of grip strength, and handwriting can be impaired. This may be temporary until the student has had adequate dialysis, or there may be some long-lasting damage resulting in the need for adaptations (Parrish, 1980). Additionally, there may be a decrease in physical stamina, with shortness of breath after mild exertion due to anemia. Although adaptive physical education is not usually necessary, the teacher will need to check with the family and physician regarding any activity restrictions or modifications.

Meeting Communication Needs

Chronic renal failure does not affect the student's ability to communicate effectively. However, much misunderstanding can occur regarding this disease. The young child with chronic renal failure who receives hemodialysis may say to peers, "Kidneys clean your blood. Mine don't work well, so a special machine at a clinic cleans my blood every few days." A child who has peritoneal dialysis may say, "Kidneys clean your blood. Mine don't work well, so I have a special kind of water I add to my tummy that cleans my blood, and when it's done, the water is drained out. It's sort of like giving the inside of your tummy a bath."

Meeting Learning Needs

Students with chronic renal failure do not typically have mental retardation or learning disabilities any more frequently than in the general population. Modifications to the learning environment typically involve scheduling activities to compensate for fatigue (and in some cases a shorter attention span) as well as addressing missed work due to dialysis or hospitalization.

Meeting Daily Living Needs

Chronic renal failure does not have a significant effect on the student's performance of daily living skills. Modifications usually consist of diet, medication administration, and dialysis. The student needs to learn how to self-monitor fluid intake and dietary needs.

■ **VIGNETTE 1** ■

Kalid is a 16-year-old high school student. He was diagnosed with chronic renal failure at 8 years of age when he had a severe kidney infection that damaged his kidneys. Three times a week, after school, he goes to a hemodialysis center and receives dialysis for 4 hours. He is often physically and mentally fatigued during the day and is unable to participate in the usual sports activities after school. He sees his friends becoming more independent while he feels totally dependent on the dialysis machine. He feels he has little control over his life. Although the teachers try to provide Kalid with a supportive environment, he is depressed and rejects their efforts. He has been referred for counseling. He desperately would like a renal transplant if a suitable donor can be found. At this time, there is not a suitable donor. Several of Kalid's friends are concerned over his condition. Due to their increased awareness of chronic renal failure, several peers have decided to sign a card to be kidney donors when they die.

Eventually, the student will need to be responsible for medication administration. Dialysis usually becomes a part of the normal pattern of the student's life. When peritoneal dialysis is used, the main daily living concern becomes learning how to perform his or her own peritoneal dialysis correctly.

Meeting Behavioral and Social Needs

Students on dialysis may have difficulty coping with the disease, which may have a negative effect on the student's psychosocial adjustment. Altered body image, physical and psychological dependence on dialysis, hostility, depression, and feelings of uselessness may occur (Parrish, 1980). Children who have delays in growth may feel isolated and different from others. As with other chronic illnesses, students may have poor self-esteem and have difficulty coping with their disease. For some individuals, there may be negative reactions to dialysis because of the overwhelming feelings of dependence on the dialysis for survival. The teacher should provide a positive atmosphere of support and be a ready listener for the student. Also, the teacher should be alert for signs of significant emotional reactions, depression, or stress and refer the student to a counselor or psychologist as appropriate.

Delays in social development have been found in young adults who received dialysis or renal transplants as children. In one study (Reynolds et al., 1993), a lack

■ **VIGNETTE 2** ■

Lavonne is 10 years old and receives peritoneal dialysis for her chronic renal failure. She has learned the procedure herself. During school hours, a break has been scheduled to allow her to go to a private room and drain off the fluid after her dwell time and to administer new fluid. Her parents and teachers have provided a supportive environment in which she has been encouraged to try different activities. She is treated as a regular kid. She socializes well with her peers and jokes about the fluid in her stomach providing her with extra bounce.

---

of lifelong, close relationships was primarily attributed to general health problems. Also, there were limitations in social contacts and friendships for individuals on dialysis. However, this did not lead to an increase in distress over social circumstances or quality of life. It may be that those with chronic illnesses from childhood develop different expectations with regard to social and personal life than those without chronic illness.

Children who undergo a renal transplant have been found to be more socially adjusted than those who undergo dialysis, and those who receive peritoneal dialysis have been found to be better adjusted socially than those who receive hemodialysis (Brownbridge & Fielding, 1991). Individuals who have renal transplants early, before developing symptoms of uremia, may avoid developing a self-image as a "sick person with renal disease." Other advantages may include an avoidance of dependence on machine technology, avoidance of familial upset concerning dialysis, less interrupted school time, and maintenance of typical social patterns (Cole, 1991).

Teachers should help the student with chronic renal failure increase social contacts by encouraging participation in school activities and clubs. Group activities in the classroom may also enhance social interactions. Delays in social maturation may require role-playing to provide appropriate models of behavior. Explanations in health class to peers about the condition and its side effects may help improve understanding of the disease and increase acceptance of the student. The risk of isolation, especially when the student is receiving hemodialysis, should not be underestimated. Support may be needed in this area.

SUMMARY

Chronic renal failure is a condition in which the kidneys no longer carry out their functions efficiently. It progresses through three stages: diminished renal reserve, renal insufficiency (failure), and uremia. Initially, mild symptoms may occur with increased urination at night, fatigue, and difficulty concentrating. Other symptoms typically are present, including high blood pressure, anemia, and growth retardation. As toxic wastes accumulate in the blood, the condition can become life-threatening without treatment. Treatment consists primarily of dialysis, along with dietary restrictions and medications, or a renal transplant.

Teachers will need to consider the student's schedule due to the possibility of school interruptions for hemodialysis and the effect of fatigue. Some students may perform peritoneal dialysis at school, and time to perform the procedure must be scheduled into their school day. Teachers need to have a good understanding of chronic renal disease and its physical and psychosocial implications; they need to provide a supportive school environment.

CHAPTER 24

Childhood Cancer

Hearing that a student has cancer usually raises fears about death and dying. However, different types of cancer have differing prognoses. Some types of cancers, such as acute leukemia, have a high cure rate with the treatments currently available. Other types of cancers, such as brain tumors, have a more guarded prognosis. Although cancer does cause more deaths than any other disease in children ages 1 to 15 in the United States, it occurs in only about 14 out of every 100,000 children. Only about one-fourth of those children die from the cancer (Behrman, 1992). It is important for the educator to understand the different types of cancers, their treatments, and prognoses and to know how the student's educational progress may be affected.

DESCRIPTION OF CHILDHOOD CANCER

The term *cancer* refers to a large variety of diseases in which the cells have a unique capacity for unregulated, excessive growth and have the ability to invade local, or sometimes distant, tissues and organs in the body (Berkow, 1992). A proliferation of cells is often referred to as a *tumor* or *neoplasm*, meaning new growth. Tumors serve no useful purpose and are either malignant or **benign**. When a tumor is malignant (that is, cancerous), it usually has uncontrolled growth, lacks contact inhibition (grows regardless of tissue and cell boundaries), and has the ability to recur and spread to other, more distant sites. The malignant cells themselves often have a poorly differentiated structure. Tumors that are not cancerous are referred to as *benign*. They have more controlled growth, do not grow over boundaries, and are usually localized and not recurrent (Suddarth, 1991).

The many different types of cancers vary as to their location in the body and how they spread. The type of cancer will determine how it affects the body and the form of treatment. Children and adults typically get different types of cancer. Adults often acquire cancers of the lung, colon, or breast, while children tend to have acute leukemia and lymphomas.

ETIOLOGY OF CANCER

The development of cancer is thought to arise from environmental, genetic, and viral causes. Some individuals with high exposure to environmental factors such as radiation, sunlight, and asbestos have been found to have high incidences of certain forms of cancer. Some medications, such as those given to suppress the immune system after renal transplantation, have been associated with an increased risk of cancer. A higher risk of cancer has also been found in certain families, suggesting a genetic link. Cancers such as retinoblastoma (cancer of the eye) are thought to be associated with a defect on chromosome 13 (Behrman, 1992). Other chromosomal abnormalities have been found in several other cancers, including acute lymphoblastic leukemia. This may indicate that an abnormal chromosome pattern may be partly responsible for the development of cancer (Rubin & Le Beau, 1991). In animals, certain viruses have been associated with the transmission of cancer, such as feline leukemia (in cats). Some human viruses, such as the Epstein-Barr virus, have been associated with some types of cancer, such as **lymphomas** (cancer of the lymph nodes).

DYNAMICS OF CANCER

Billions of cells in the body make up the organs and tissues. As a child grows, the cells undergo a process of controlled cell division in which one cell divides in-to two cells. These two cells can, in turn, also divide.

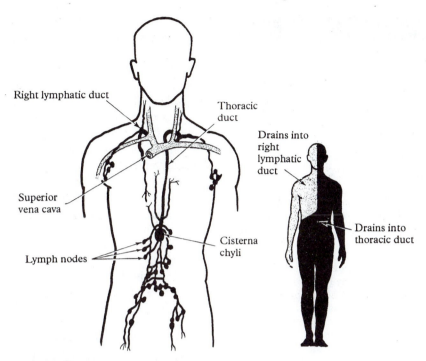

■ **FIGURE 24-1** The lymphatic system
SOURCE: Langley & Cheraskin, 1965.

This allows the organs and tissues to enlarge and grow. In an adult, cell division continues in order for old cells to be replaced by new cells. Also, if damage should occur, many cells will divide to repair the damaged area.

The primary difference between cancer cells and normal cells is the pattern and continued rapidity of growth. Normal cells divide in an orderly manner. Sometimes division may be accelerated, as when there is injury and the body is repairing itself. However, the accelerated division stops and returns to normal when additional cell structures are not needed. In cancer cells, some etiology triggers the cells to multiply uncontrollably. The cells proliferate and may compress or destroy surrounding tissues, which interferes with normal functioning of the tissue or bodily organ they are invading.

Cancer can also spread to other, more distant parts of the body. This spreading to other parts is known as **metastasis.** Cancer usually spreads one of two ways, either by way of the circulatory system or by the lymphatic system. The circulatory system is composed of a sophisticated network of blood vessels through which oxygen is delivered throughout the body and carbon dioxide is removed. Cancer cells can invade the circulatory system and travel to other areas in the body and begin to grow secondary tumors. The lymphatic system is a series of channels through which fluid can flow from the spaces between the cells and eventually into the blood (see Figure 24-1). This route allows proteins and large particulate matter, which cannot be absorbed by the small capillaries, to be carried away from the tissue spaces (Guyton, 1991). Along the channels are lymph nodes (small masses of lymph tissue) that are responsible for destroying foreign particles in the lymph fluid. Some cancer cells move into the lymph system and travel via this route to other parts of the body where secondary tumors are formed.

CHARACTERISTICS OF CANCER

Several types of cancers are named after the type of cell from which they originate or the individual who discovered them. Some types of childhood cancer are described in Table 24-1. We will now describe the more commonly encountered cancers in some detail.

Acute Leukemia

Leukemia, the most common form of childhood cancer, is cancer of the bone marrow. It can be classified into two main categories: *acute leukemia* and *chronic leukemia.* In this case, the terms *acute* and *chronic* do not refer to the severity of the disease or the life expectancy of the person but to the type or maturity of leukemic cells. The acute leukemias are more prevalent in childhood and have a more favorable prognosis with prompt treatment. Acute lymphoblastic leukemia (ALL) is the most common of the acute leukemias.

TABLE 24-1

Types of Cancer Found in Children

Type of cancer	Definition
Leukemia:	
a. Acute lymphoblastic leukemia (ALL)	Cancer of the bone marrow
b. Acute myeloid leukemia (AML)	
c. Chronic myelocytic leukemia (CML)	
Lymphoma:	
a. Hodgkin's disease	Cancer of the lymph nodes
b. Non-Hodgkin's disease	
Tumors of the central nervous system:	
a. Brain tumors	Cancer of the tissues of the brain
b. Spinal cord	Cancer of the spinal cord
Wilms' tumor	Cancer of the kidney
Retinoblastoma	Cancer of the retina of the eye
Bone tumor:	Cancer of the bone
a. Osteogenic sarcoma	
b. Ewing's tumor	
Soft tissue and muscle:	
a. Rhabdomyosarcoma	Cancer of the skeletal muscle
b. Other	Cancer of the connective tissue
Neuroblastoma	Cancer of the adrenal glands and sympathetic nervous system
Thyroid	Cancer of the thyroid gland
Melanoma	Cancer of the skin
Ovarian and testicular	Cancer of the sexual organs

In all types of leukemia, there is a proliferation of abnormal leukemic cells. These leukemic cells replace many of the normal blood cells that are formed in the bone marrow. This results in a decrease in numbers of red blood cells, white blood cells, and platelets. A decrease in the number of red blood cells is known as *anemia*. The child who is anemic will be tired, have a decreased appetite, and will often look pale. A decrease in the number of white blood cells will increase the possibility of acquiring severe infections. When infection occurs, fever is present. A decrease in the number of platelets (known as thrombocytopenia) will result in an increased likelihood of having bleeding episodes, such as nosebleeds, and of being easily bruised. Due to the involvement of the bone marrow with marrow cell death (infarction) and bleeding (hemorrhage), some children will have significant pain in their bones and joints; they rarely will have swelling.

In leukemia, the leukemic cells travel in the circulatory system. They can then spread to any organ in the body, causing damage and malfunction. Increased intracranial pressure can result in headaches, vomiting, and convulsions. Death is certain unless treatment is provided. With prompt, appropriate treatment, survival rates can be quite high, especially for those with acute lymphoblastic leukemia, the most common form of childhood leukemia. Survival rates for those with acute lymphoblastic leukemia are often approximately 85% (Barr et al., 1992). Other types of acute myeloid leukemia (AML) are reported to have about a 50–85% remission rate. Although rare, children who acquire a chronic form of leukemia, chronic myelocytic leukemia (CML), usually live only 4 years after diagnosis with traditional treatments (Marin et al., 1992).

When the leukemia has been treated successfully, some secondary effects have been found due to the drugs and disease, particularly in acute lymphoblastic leukemia. A small percentage of children who had acute lymphoblastic leukemia were found to have impairment in growth (height), while many children were obese. In some cases, children had impaired (smaller) head growth, which is considered to be a measure of brain growth. More advances in treatment may ameliorate impaired head growth (Dacou-Voutetakis et al., 1993).

Lymphoma

A lymphoma is a cancer of the lymph nodes. There are two main categories of lymphoma: *Hodgkin's disease* and *non-Hodgkin's lymphoma*. The exact characteristics of both types of lymphomas depend on which lymph nodes are primarily involved and where the cancer has spread. In Hodgkin's disease, children have enlarged, firm, and nontender lymph nodes in the neck, above the collar bone, and in the armpit area. This is often accompanied by fever, night sweats, easy fatigability, and anorexia. The disease may spread to other parts of the body such as the liver, lungs, and bone morrow, resulting in anemia and fatigue. Non-Hodgkin's lymphoma is more prevalent in young children. As with Hodgkin's disease, lymph nodes are enlarged, but non-Hodgkin's disease is more likely to involve other organ systems and to disseminate throughout the body. This lymphoma often spreads to the lungs, bone, bone marrow, bowel, and central nervous system. Also, certain conditions, such as AIDS, predispose individuals to the development of this type of cancer (Behrman, 1992). The prognosis for both categories varies as to the specific types of lymphomas and how far the cancer has progressed. Most children will be cured if treatment is begun in the early stages of the disease.

Tumors of the Central Nervous System

The most common tumors of the central nervous system in children are brain tumors, often occurring in the cerebellum and brain stem. Children with brain tumors may initially have no symptoms. As the tumor grows, intracranial pressure increases due to the tumor, and this can cause headaches, nausea and vomiting, problems in balance and coordination (ataxia), dizziness, cranial enlargement, or blurred vision (diplopia or strabismus). Other neurological signs include nystagmus (that is, dancing eyes), head tilt, uneven eye enlargement, seizures, and behavior and personality changes. Brain tumors are problematic even when they are benign because of the increased pressure they exert on the brain. Subsequent brain damage may lead to drowsiness (lethargy) and somnolence as well. Prognosis usually depends on the tumor's location, size, and growth and on when treatment was initiated. Fortunately, brain tumors do not usually metastasize outside the central nervous system.

Tumors of the spinal cord may also occur, although they are less common in infants and children than brain tumors. Children who have spinal cord tumors may have disturbances of gait and posture, pain, weakness in an arm or leg, changed reflexes, impaired bladder function, or sensory impairment. If the tumor progresses, paralysis can result.

Wilms' Tumor

Wilms' tumor is cancer of the kidney. This type of cancer has a higher incidence in certain syndromes such as Trisomy 18 and Beckwith-Wiedemann Syndromes and can be genetically based in families with autosomal-dominance. Usually only one kidney is affected, although both can be involved, especially if the cancer is hereditary. Children with Wilms' tumor may first notice a large mass in the abdomen. They may have no other symptoms, or pain and nausea may be present. In about 25% of the cases, there may be blood in the urine (hematuria). High blood pressure is a common finding. Prognosis varies depending on the type and extent of tumor present, but when the tumor is found early, the prognosis is usually very favorable.

Retinoblastoma

Retinoblastoma is cancer of the retina of the eye, which may occur in a hereditary (40%) or nonhereditary (60%) form. It may metastasize in any of four ways: through the optic nerve to the brain, from the optic nerve to the orbit of the eye, from the choroid circulation to other parts of the body (including the bone marrow, bone, lymph node, liver, and possibly the lung), and through the lymphatic system (Moore, 1990).

Retinoblastomas in children are often detected by parents who notice that the child has an odd appearance in the eyes or notice that when a picture with a flash is taken, something different occurs—the child has a white or cream-colored eye rather than the red eyes that are usually seen. The next most common sign is strabismus or a constant, one-eyed squint. A painful red eye may be present as well (Moore, 1990).

Without intervention, retinoblastoma, like the other cancers, results in death. However, there is a 92% survival rate for retinoblastoma that is confined to the eye (White, 1991). Prognosis for disseminated retinoblastoma is more guarded (Saarinen, Saroila, & Hovi, 1991).

Bone Tumor

Another form of cancer is cancer arising in the bone structure, not the bone marrow. There are several different types, with *osteosarcoma* being the most common in children. This type of cancer will first be detected when children have a painful swelling around a bone, especially the end part of the thigh bone (distal end of the femur) and the top ends of the arm bones (proximal ends of the tibia and humerus). Warmth, tenderness, and a firm mass may be felt. There may be limitations of motion, or, when the legs are involved, limping may occur. This form of cancer often metastasizes to the lungs, other bones, or to the central nervous system. Prognosis depends on whether or not it has spread; if metastasis has occurred, prognosis is usually poor.

DETECTION OF CANCER

Several tests may be used to detect cancer. These tests are designed to detect a tumor, determine whether it is **malignant** or benign, determine the type of cancer, and determine the size of the tumor and whether metastasis has occurred.

In adolescents and adults, several different types of screening procedures are routinely carried out during a physical examination. These include such tests as rectal and pelvic examinations, breast examinations, and mammography. However, because cancer is rare in children, there are usually no specific examinations for cancer other than the routine physical examination and routine laboratory tests. Usually, the diagnosis of childhood cancer is based on specific tests used to follow up on the physical symptoms the child is experiencing.

Routine blood tests, such as a red blood cell count, white blood cell count, and platelet count, will show decreased levels when a child has leukemia, although the white blood cell count may be normal or very elevated. Usually, microscopic examination of the blood smear will show leukemic cells. However, to confirm the diagnosis of leukemia or to detect the metastasis of cancer to the bone marrow, a bone marrow test is performed. In a bone marrow test, a needle is inserted into the bone of the pelvis and bone marrow is withdrawn into a syringe. The bone marrow is then analyzed for cancer cells.

When a mass is found on physical examination, such as an abdominal mass in the case of Wilms' tumor, or a brain tumor is suspected due to symptoms like severe headaches, several different types of X-rays or scans may be performed. In some types of X-rays, a radiopaque material (dye) may be injected to provide a better contrast in order to make the specific area visible. Some examples of tests using X-rays are intravenous pyelogram (X-ray of the kidney), gastrointestinal series (X-ray of the GI tract), lymphangiogram (X-ray of the lymph nodes), and arteriogram (X-ray of tissue that derives its blood supply from the artery into which radiopaque dye has been injected) (Bleck & Nagel, 1982).

Several types of scans may be used to visualize a mass or specific structure. Sonograms use the reflection of sound waves off a structure to generate an image of structures in the body. However, more sophisticated scanning procedures, such as CT (or CAT) scans and MRIs, are more typically used for the diagnosis of cancer. A CT scan (also known as computerized axial tomography, or CAT scan) uses multiple X-rays at slightly different angles to visualize the organ being studied. A CT scan can detect differences in structures and is excellent in determining differences in bone density. An MRI (magnetic resonance imaging) uses the magnetic resonance of atoms to reflect the magnetic differences in body tissue and provide clear images of certain tissues and organs. It is especially good in visualizing fat, marrow, white and gray matter, cerebrospinal fluid, vessels, **ligaments**, tendons, and muscles, while it visualizes bones and calcium poorly. The MRI is superior in detecting certain types of tumors; brain and spinal cord tumors are also better visualized with the MRI. However, renal tumors and metastasis to the lungs are usually visualized better with the CT scan (Behrman, 1992).

Other, newer scanning tests are available and are gaining widespread use. One of these is the positron emission tomography (PET) scan, which uses a radioactive chemical compound to study biological functions. For example, it has been used to study local glucose and oxygen utilization, blood flow, protein synthesis, and neurotransmitter uptake and binding in the brain. Studies of long-term survivors of childhood leukemia have used the PET scan to evaluate the metabolic rates of white matter. Although the PET scan may not contribute to the diagnosis of cancer, there may be a role for this type of functional imaging in evaluating any destructive effects of treatment on nerve tissue (Chugani, 1992).

When a tumor is found, a biopsy is performed to determine whether the tumor is malignant and, if so, the type of malignancy. A biopsy is the surgical removal of a few cells or the entire tumor, which will then be examined microscopically. A biopsy is performed to determine the best course of treatment and is usually done before the surgical removal of the tumor if surgery is indicated. In the case of a growing tumor in the brain, the tumor is usually surgically removed due to the increased pressure on the brain that the tumor exerts. After the tumor is removed, the biopsy is performed.

Other tests may be performed to see whether the cancer has metastasized to other areas. One example is the use of a lumbar puncture. In a lumbar puncture, the spinal fluid that flows from the brain around the spinal cord and back up around the brain is aspirated with a needle. The needle is inserted between the bones of the spine into the space around the spinal cord. The fluid is then analyzed for cancer cells.

TREATMENT OF CHILDHOOD CANCER

Several different medications and procedures can be used in the treatment of cancer. The three main types of treatment are *surgery, medication* (chemotherapy and steroids), and *radiation therapy*. The treatment modality depends on several factors, including the type of cancer or tumor and how far it has advanced. The goal of treatment is typically to cure, which is defined as a complete and indefinite remission—the disappearance of all clinical evidence of the disease. Treatment may result in only a reduction in the size of the tumor. This would prolong life, but the tumor would probably continue to grow. In some instances, there may be no response to treatment, which would indicate that the cancer would continue its course.

Surgery

Surgery is the oldest form of treatment for cancer. In curative surgery, the primary site of the tumor is removed, along with any adjacent lymph nodes to which the cancer may have spread. In the early stages of cancer, this type of surgery is often effective by itself. However, when the cancer has metastasized to several locations, additional treatment would be necessary. When the goal of surgery is cure, the excision of the tumor is most effective in cancers that are localized. For example, the use of surgery in Wilms' tumor or bone cancer to excise the localized tumor is an effective treatment; surgery is not used to treat leukemia, in which cancer is spread throughout the bone marrow. In some instances, surgery is the treatment of choice due to poor response to medications or radiation. However, successful surgical removal of the cancer may affect another structure. For example, removal of a bone cancer may entail amputation of the leg; removal of a retinoblastoma may mean removal of the eye.

Other types of surgery may be performed besides those aimed at curing the individual. Palliative surgery is used to treat the complications of cancer. For example, surgery may be done to remove an obstruction to the gastrointestinal tract or to relieve pain produced by a tumor that is compressing the surrounding nerves. Prophylactic surgery is used to remove lesions that are thought to develop into cancer if left in the body. Other types of surgery may also be performed to stop the spread of the cancer (Suddarth, 1991).

Medication

Chemotherapy is the use of antineoplastic (anticancer) medication. Several different types of chemotherapies are designed to attack the cancer cells and interrupt cell division. Chemotherapy may be used to cure cancer, control its spread, or prevent recurrence after surgical excision. Chemotherapy is used with other forms of treatment (surgery or radiation) or in some instances may be used alone. It may be given orally, intramuscularly (an injection in a muscle), intravenously (through a catheter in the vein, usually over a short period of time), or intra-arterially (through a catheter that is placed in a major artery and that may infuse medication over several hours or days). Chemotherapy has been used with many types of cancers, such as leukemia, Hodgkin's disease, Wilms' tumor, bone cancer, and lymphomas. Successful use of chemotherapy has also been achieved with certain types of brain tumors (Castello et al., 1990) and in some instances with retinoblastomas (White, 1991). Chemotherapy usually has several unpleasant side effects. The most common ones include nausea, vomiting, and hair loss. However, medications can be administered prior to the infusion of chemotherapy to counteract the nausea and vomiting. The complications of chemotherapy are related to the type of drug used and the general cytotoxic (deadly to certain cells) and immunosuppressive (decrease immune system) effects from the drug.

Other medication may be used in the treatment of cancer. Steroids are often used to decrease edema and thus relieve intracranial pressure from a brain tumor.

Some medications are under investigation, one of which is the use of immunotherapy. Immunotherapy uses substances to which a person has been sensitized to cause an attack on the cancer. This type of treatment, as well as others, may prove useful in the future treatment of cancer.

Radiation

The third common treatment of cancer is radiation therapy, in which radiation is directed toward the cancer cells to disrupt the structure of their atoms. It has been found to be successful in the treatment of Hodgkin's disease, non-Hodgkin's lymphoma, and as an adjunct to the treatment of leukemia. Radiation may be delivered by an external beam concentrated on the area where the cancer is located.

Another method is the use of implants. Implants may use an external mold placed directly on a cancer that is located on a skin surface, such as a skin cancer or shallow irradiation of eye cancer. Radiation may be implanted inside a cavity with the end of a catheter or a needle, tube, or wire that can be placed directly into tumor tissue. Some radioactive solutions can be taken orally or injected (Suddarth, 1991).

Side effects from the radiation treatment in children depend on the type of radiation, the strength of dosage, the administration site, and the child's health. Some short-term side effects include fatigue, malaise (achy feeling), nausea, vomiting, and dry mouth. Several long-term side effects have been attributed to radiation therapy, although this is not conclusive in many cases. Some of these possible side effects are musculoskeletal abnormalities (such as scoliosis for some children with Wilms' tumor), growth hormone deficiency, second tumors, learning difficulties, puberty and fertility abnormalities, and hypothyroidism (Crooks et al., 1991).

Other treatments may be used for specific types of cancers. One of these is the bone marrow transplant, which has been successful in the treatment of children with acute lymphoblastic leukemia whose cancer has recurred after remission (Alarcon et al., 1990). Bone marrow transplantation has also been used when cancer has disseminated to the bone marrow from other sites. One example is the successful use of high-dose chemotherapy, radiation, surgery (removal of the eye), and a bone marrow transplant in a 3-year-old child with retinoblastoma that had disseminated (Saarinen, Saroila, & Hovi, 1991).

COURSE OF CHILDHOOD CANCER

Without treatment, cancer will kill the individual because it is invasive and it disrupts normal body functions. How well cancer will respond to treatment depends on several factors. First, the type and histology of the cancer are important in determining the effectiveness of treatment. Some cancers are more responsive to treatment than others.

The second consideration is how far the cancer has progressed. The progression of some cancers is categorized by stages. Staging is a classification system based on knowledge of the natural history of a specific cancer, and staging varies with different types of cancers. Staging usually helps determine the appropriate treatment and may assist with determining prognosis. Stage I (or in some categories, A) usually represents the earliest form of the cancer. The final stage, often Stage IV or Stage V, usually represents very advanced or complicated disease. Children who are being treated in Stage I or II usually have a far better chance for long-term survival

---

BOX 24-1

Stages of Non-Hodgkin's Lymphoma

STAGE I

A single tumor (extranodal) or single anatomic area (nodal) with the exclusion of the mediastinum or abdomen

STAGE II

A single tumor (extranodal) with regional node involvement

Two or more nodal areas on the same side of the diaphragm

Two single (extranodal) tumors with or without regional node involvement on the same side of the diaphragm

A primary gastrointestinal tract tumor, usually in the ileocecal area with or without involvement of associated mesenteric nodes only, which must be grossly resected

STAGE III

Two single tumors (extranodal) on opposite sides of the diaphragm

Two or more nodal areas above and below the diaphragm

Any primary intrathoracic tumor (mediastinal, pleural, thymic)

Any extensive primarily intra-abdominal disease

STAGE IV

Any of the above, with involvement of CNS and/or bone marrow at time of diagnosis

---

SOURCE: From "Classification, Staging, and End Results of Treatment of Childhood Non-Hodgkin's Lymphomas: Dissimilarities from Lymphomas in Adults," by S. B. Murphy, 1980, *Semin Oncol, 7*, 332–339. Copyright © 1980 Semin Oncol. Reprinted with permission of W. B. Saunders Company.

BOX 24-2

Staging for Retinoblastoma

STAGE I

Solitary or multiple tumors, 4 disk diameters in size, at or behind the equator

STAGE II

Solitary or multiple tumors, 4–10 disk diameters in size, at or behind the equator

STAGE III

Any lesion anterior to the equator

Solitary tumors, 0.10 disk diameters, behind the equator

STAGE IV

Multiple tumors; some 0.10 disk diameters, any lesion extending anterior to the ora serrata

STAGE V

Massive tumors involving over half the retina

Vitreous seeding

SOURCE: From "The Practical Management of Retinoblastoma," by R. M. Ellsworth, 1969, *Trans Am Ophthalmological Society, 67*, p. 462. Copyright © 1969. Reprinted with permission of W. B. Saunders Company.

---

than those who are in Stage III or IV. Stages may pertain to the sites where the cancer has metastasized or to the size of the tumor. Two examples of staging classification systems that illustrate the different systems are shown in Box 24-1 for non-Hodgkin's lymphoma in childhood and in Box 24-2 for retinoblastoma.

Other considerations for determining the course of the cancer are individual factors and whether or not the cancer has been in remission. Individuals who are in poor health, for example, may not respond as well to treatment. Also, if the cancer has been in remission and recurs, this can indicate a poorer prognosis and makes remission difficult a second or third time.

EDUCATIONAL IMPLICATIONS OF CHILDHOOD CANCER

Teaching a student with cancer may be difficult for some teachers because they may feel disbelief, anger, or depression. As is true with degenerative disorders, teachers may have some emotional difficulty coping with a potentially fatal disease in a student. However, many cancers are curable. Even when the student may not survive, maintaining a supportive educational environment is paramount. For some students with cancer, going to school may be one of their primary goals and something to look forward to. The educator will be faced with the task of making the child's experience at school a pleasant and rewarding one.

Upon learning that a child has cancer, the educator needs to obtain specific information to meet the student's physical, communication, learning, daily living, behavioral, and social needs. Some of this information includes the type of cancer (including its prognosis), the type of treatment (including the side effects), the schedule of treatments and tests that require absences from school, a list of any physical limitations on the student's activities, and an understanding of what the child has been told about his or her disease (Umbreit, 1983). Open lines of communication between the teacher, parents, medical personnel, and the rest of the educational team are crucial to obtaining accurate information. As we discussed, many types of cancers have very favorable prognoses. Knowing what to expect not only with regard to the course of the disease but to the possible side effects of its management will allow the teacher to address the needs of the student with cancer more effectively.

Meeting Physical and Sensory Needs

The student with cancer who is undergoing treatment may have changes in physical abilities and endurance. The student may be tired from anemia when acute lymphoblastic leukemia is present or from other cancers and their treatment. Nausea and vomiting may be side effects of the cancer treatments as well. Students with cancer have good days and bad days; this will affect the child's ability to perform academically. Teachers should realize that when the student is feeling poorly, his or her performance may not be up to standard. Students who are feeling ill or who tire easily may need shorter assignments or more rest breaks. The teacher and educational team will need to determine the student's needs and be flexible in planning.

Because of treatment, side effects, or complications of the cancer, the child with cancer may have frequent absences from school or may have periodic hospitalizations. Hospital or homebound instructors will help the student in keeping up with school work. However, if the instructor is different from the student's regular classroom teacher, it is important that the regular teacher maintain contact with the student when he or she is at home or in the hospital. Aside from getting behind academically, some students fear returning to school after long absences because they fear rejection from peers and others or just because they feel they are different. The teacher can maintain open lines of communication and thus help make the student's transition back into the classroom an easier one. It is often helpful for the teacher to visit the student in the hospital, bringing cards and letters from classmates. Also, periodic visits allow the student to communicate any concerns regarding school to the teacher. Although the

teacher may not have the solutions for specific problems, the teacher can be a supportive listener and make an effort to address the student's concerns.

Some students who have cancer will have physical changes due to the cancer or its treatment. Students undergoing chemotherapy may lose their hair. This can be traumatic and can negatively affect body image. Some students will use wigs, scarves, or hats to cover their head. Usually, peer education is needed to provide information and sensitization so the student will have support. If the cancer is progressing, there may be physical deterioration and decreased activity in physical activities such as sports. Any limitations in activities should be ordered by the parent and physician. If limitations are present, or if they are self-imposed by the student, participation in more sedentary activities may be encouraged. Also, some treatments may result in physical disfigurement; amputation, for example, would require physical therapy, adaptations, an artificial limb, and emotional support.

Students who have cancer and are undergoing treatment are more susceptible to infections. This is the case in acute lymphoblastic leukemia as well as with other cancers in which there is a decrease in white blood cells. It is important that the educator send students home who are sick so the infection is not transmitted to the student with cancer.

Meeting Communication Needs

Unless the cancer occurs in the location of the vocal cords, there is no physical problem in communicating. However, children with cancer may need to communicate with their peers about their disease or their treatment. What is said about the cancer will depend on the type of cancer and how it is affecting the child. The child with leukemia may say, "My blood is sick and makes me feel tired. I take medicine to help it get better." Children may use the following explanation to explain hair loss: "I was really sick when I was in the hospital. The medicine they gave me for my cancer made my hair fall out. It'll grow back. I'll sure be glad when it does" (Association for the Care of Children's Health, 1982). It is important that the child stress that the cancer is not contagious; neither is having one's hair fall out.

Meeting Learning Needs

Students with cancer have no higher incidence of mental retardation or learning disability than the regular population. However, the treatment for cancer in children may make the child at-risk for learning difficulties. In one study (Kingma et al., 1993), MRI and neuropsychological assessments were performed on children with acute lymphoblastic leukemia who underwent brain irradiation and chemotherapy. Of the 35 children, 51% had abnormal MRI scans, most with white matter damage. As a group, the children had lower scores on neuropsychological assessments for intelligence, verbal auditory memory, visual motor integration, and fine motor functioning. No correlation could be found between the MRI results and cognitive functioning. However, there was a significant correlation between the lower scores and the higher dose of radiation at younger ages. Forty percent of the children studied were referred to schools or classes for students with learning disabilities. Other studies (Brouwers & Poplack, 1990; Williams, Berry, Caldwell, Zolten, & Spence, 1992) have found attention deficits in children who have been treated for leukemia, which may be associated with CT scan abnormalities or with significant levels of anxiety. If these learning difficulties arise, the regular teacher may draw from the expertise of a student support team or a special educator to provide strategies to help the student learn. If the student continues to have difficulties, the team may decide to pursue assessment and additional support from special education.

Meeting Daily Living Needs

Students with cancer can usually meet their own daily living needs. However, if the cancer is untreatable, there can be physical deterioration and disability that interferes with the student's normal functioning. If this occurs, adaptations, ancillary services, and support will be needed to help the student keep his or her dignity and independence.

Meeting Behavioral and Social Needs

Students with cancer often feel optimistic about their prognosis due to the advances in medical treatment. However, fears about the uncertainty of the prognosis or feelings of isolation may occur along with other emotional responses. The student may not feel comfortable sharing his or her thoughts with the family but would prefer to talk with the teacher or another member of the educational team. If the teacher suspects something is bothering the child, an informal invitation to the student can be made with such statements as, "If there is anything you would like to talk about at any time, I would be glad to listen and help if I can." The teacher should then take the time to really listen to the student. Often, having someone to talk with can help tremendously. Also, certain problems may arise, such as when the student is afraid of being teased about being bald. The teacher may be able to implement creative solutions with the student to address the specific problem.

■ VIGNETTE ■

Marcus is a 10-year-old boy who was diagnosed with acute lymphoblastic leukemia when he was 7 years old. At that time, he was informed of his diagnosis and the implications of chemotherapy and radiation therapy by his parents. His parents informed the teacher, who had noticed that Marcus seemed tired a lot and was getting occasional nosebleeds. Although Marcus was close to his family, he decided to approach his teacher about his leukemia. He was especially fearful about having his hair fall out with chemotherapy and about what the reactions would be from his classmates. The teacher and Marcus decided that a speaker from the American Cancer Association would come to a special assembly and tell the school about cancer and hair loss. Marcus felt that was helpful and found a really neat hat to wear. The teacher also found some books written by kids with cancer for Marcus to read. Mr. T (who is bald) became Marcus's idol. When Marcus's hair fell out, he and his friends were prepared. At present, the treatment for his cancer is successful and the cancer is in remission. Also, his hair has grown back.

Children with cancer may also feel isolated from their peers. Absences and changes in physical appearance may result in strained interactions or loss of friends. The teacher can promote peer interaction by first providing peers with information about cancer during a health class. A representative from the American Cancer Society can give a talk about cancer and provide the school with informational brochures and other media. The student with cancer may want specific information to be shared with the class. Peer interaction should also be encouraged by providing an avenue for peers to write, call, or visit the student during absences from school. Promoting continued interest in some of the activities that were popular before the illness will also help maintain friendships.

Although cancer is often curable, in some instances treatment may fail. When this occurs, the educator should have a good understanding of how to best support the student, the class, and herself or himself as a teacher. (See Chapter 9.)

SUMMARY

Cancer refers to a large variety of diseases in which the cells have unregulated, excessive growth and can invade other tissues. As the cancer cells proliferate, they may compress or destroy surrounding tissue, which causes a disruption of the normal function of the tissue or body organ. Cancer may occur at any age. Leukemia, lymphoma, brain tumors, and Wilms' tumor are just a few of the types of cancers that may be encountered in children. The type of cancer and its severity will determine the treatment. Primary treatment options usually consist of medication, radiation therapy, or surgery. Although prognosis is positive in many instances of childhood cancer (that is, a cure is achieved), death is still a possibility in some instances. The educator should provide a supportive environment that will meet the needs of the individual student.

PART VII

Infectious Diseases

CHAPTER 25

Congenital Infections

An infection is the invasion and proliferation of viruses, bacteria, or other microorganisms into the body. Infections may be transmitted in several ways, one of which is from the mother to the fetus. Although most infections the mother may acquire during pregnancy are harmless, there is a group of infections that, when transferred to the fetus, may result in multiple birth defects. These congenital infections are referred to by the acronym STORCH or TORCH.

DESCRIPTION OF CONGENITAL INFECTIONS

Congenital infections are infections that are present before birth or at the time of birth. Only a few infections that a pregnant woman may acquire can be transmitted to her fetus and result in congenital infections. Certain congenital infections have been grouped together because of their ability to result in birth defects. These infections are known as STORCH infections.

STORCH (or TORCH) refers to a group of congenital infections: syphilis, toxoplasmosis, rubella, other, cytomegalovirus, and herpes. (Sometimes the S is not included.) Unlike many other infections the mother may acquire during pregnancy, most STORCH infections can cross over the placenta to the fetus and invade the central nervous system and developing organs. These infections may be acquired prenatally (before birth) or perinatally (shortly before, during, or after birth). In this chapter, we will discuss only STORCH infections because of their potential effects on children.

ETIOLOGY OF CONGENITAL INFECTIONS

Each STORCH infection is caused by either a bacterium, a parasite, or a virus. Syphilis is caused by the bacterial organism *Treponema pallidum*. Toxoplasmosis is caused by the parasite *Toxoplasma gondii*. Viruses are responsible for rubella (rubella virus), cytomegalovirus (CMV), and herpes (herpes simplex viruses type 1 and 2) (Bale & Murph, 1992).

DYNAMICS OF CONGENITAL INFECTIONS

When a pregnant woman has a STORCH infection, the infection may be transmitted to the fetus. If that happens, the extent of the damage varies widely. There may be no clinical damage, or there may be multiple impairments. The extent of damage depends partly on the type of infection and the trimester in which the fetus was infected.

When an infection occurs early in pregnancy, it may interfere with the formation of the organs developing at that time. As seen in Figure 25-1, the heart, brain, eyes, and ears are primarily formed early in fetal development. Infection occurring early in fetal development is more likely to result in extensive damage to the developing fetal organs and nervous system (Andersen, Bale, Blackman, & Murph, 1986). Later in fetal development, many organs are already formed, with only minor parts left for development. Some congenital infections acquired in the third trimester when many organs are already formed may not result in extensive damage.

STORCH infections are transmitted either prenatally or perinatally. In prenatal transmission, the infection is in the maternal bloodstream and crosses the placenta into the fetal bloodstream. The infection may then infect fetal organs and the nervous system. Almost all STORCH infections occur through this mode of transmission. However, certain congenital infections are transmitted perinatally, such as herpes. As the infant passes through the birth canal, the infant acquires the

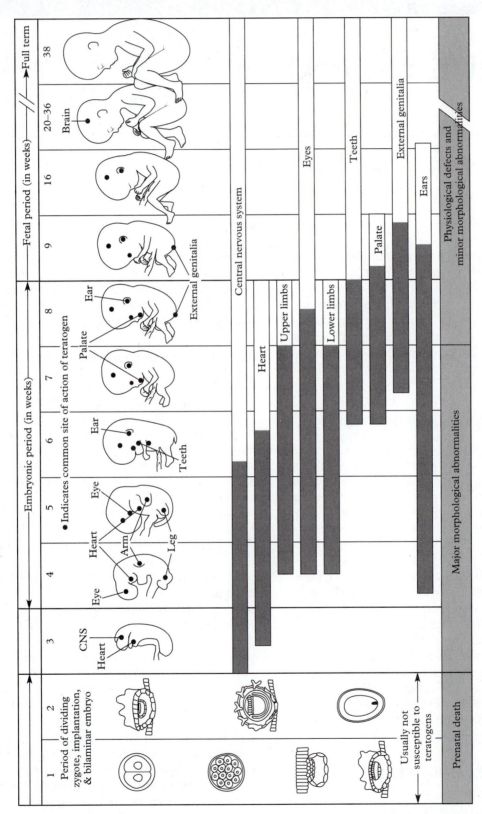

■ **FIGURE 25-1** Critical periods of human development

SOURCE: From *Before We Are Born: Basic Embryology and Birth Defects*, Second Edition, by K. L. Moore. Copyright © 1993 W. B. Saunders. Reprinted with permission.

TABLE 25-1
Frequently Found Impairments of STORCH Congenital Infections

	Syphilis	Toxoplasmosis	Rubella	CMV	Herpes
Eye/visual impairments	X	X	X	X	X
Ear/auditory impairments	X	X	X	X	X
Anemia	X	X	X	X	X
Brain calcifications		X		X	
Bone abnormalities			X		
Congenital heart defects			X		
Encephalitis	X	X	X	X	X
Hydrocephalus		X	X	X	X
Jaundice	X	X	X	X	X
Liver/spleen enlarged	X	X	X	X	X
Low birth weight	X	X	X	X	X
Low platelet count	X	X	X	X	X
Microcephaly	X	X	X	X	X
Pneumonia			X	X	X
Seizures	X	X	X	X	X
Skin rash	X	X	X	X	X

SOURCE: From "Etiologies and Characteristics of Deaf-Blindness," by K. Heller and C. Kennedy, 1994, *Etiologies and Characteristics of Deaf-Blindness*, p. 47. Copyright © 1994 Teaching Research Publications. Reprinted with permission.

infection. If not treated, extensive damage to the fetal organs and nervous system can result as the virus attacks the already-formed organs.

STORCH infections may result in organ and system damage. Some possible defects include heart defects, brain damage/malformation, visual and **hearing impairments,** and other severe impairments. Additional complications of these infections may also occur, some of which include mental retardation, poor body growth, motor abnormalities, endocrine disturbances (for example, thyroid abnormalities and diabetes mellitus), and a shortened life span. Several possible abnormalities that occur with many of the STORCH infections are listed in Table 25-1.

DETECTION OF CONGENITAL INFECTIONS

Diagnosis of STORCH infections is typically made by conducting laboratory tests such as blood titer analysis, taking a clinical history, and noting distinctive physical signs. In some instances, cerebrospinal fluid (CSF) may be analyzed and X-rays taken. Specialized examinations of various organs (such as the eye or heart) will often be done to determine organ involvement and the extent of damage. These tests include electrocardiograms, echocardiograms, and CAT scans. For a better understanding of these congenital infections, each infection will be briefly described.

CHARACTERISTICS, TREATMENT, AND COURSE OF CONGENITAL INFECTIONS

Congenital Syphilis

Characteristics
Congenital syphilis is an infection that is transmitted from the untreated, infected mother to the fetus. Although it is one of the oldest and most easily preventable infections of the STORCH group, there has been an increased incidence of congenital syphilis in the United States (Rolfs & Nakashima, 1991). In 1990, nearly 3,000 cases were reported (Bale & Murph, 1992).

Humans are the only natural host of this infection. The mother acquires it through sexual contact with another person who is infected. The infection progresses through a series of three stages. In the first stage (that is, in primary syphilis), a localized lesion develops at the site of the initial infection. Often, the pregnant mother who has acquired this infection does not realize the significance of the disease and may not seek treatment. If left untreated, the second stage, known as secondary syphilis, may develop. In secondary syphilis, the disease can extend to the skin, mouth, genital area, and central nervous system. The maternal infection may then progress into the third stage known as tertiary syphilis. In tertiary syphilis, the infection spreads to the adult's organ systems. During any of these stages, the syphilis infection can be transmitted to the fetus through the placenta, although the risk is greatest during the secondary syphilis stage (Bale & Murph, 1992).

When syphilis is transmitted to the fetus from the infected mother, the child will have congenital syphilis. There are two forms. In the first form, congenital syphilis may present at birth or in early infancy. This is known as *early congenital syphilis* or *infantile syphilis*. The infant may have skin lesions, lymph node enlargement, blood-stained nasal discharge, and an "old-man" look. Multiple organ involvement may be present, especially in the liver, lungs, bones, skin, and kidney. The central nervous system is usually involved as well (Regenbogen & Coscas, 1985; Williamson & Demmler, 1992). The most characteristic feature of congenital syphilis is the presence of skeletal abnormalities. Periostitis (inflammation of a specialized connective tissue covering the bones) and osteochondritis (inflammation of bone and cartilage) often affect the long bones and may inhibit leg movement and growth (Bale & Murph, 1992). Some infants also have seizures, hydrocephalus, meningitis, and mental retardation (Berkow, 1992). Visual impairments (chorioretinitis, glaucoma), hearing impairments (**sensorineural loss**), or deaf-blindness commonly occur. Approximately 25% of infants die in the first few months (Andersen et al., 1986).

Many infants born with congenital syphilis have the second, latent form of the disease in which symptoms are not present at birth. This second form is known as *late congenital syphilis* or *congenital syphilis tarda*. These individuals usually develop symptoms in childhood, adolescence, or early adult life. Symptoms may include dental abnormalities, skeletal changes such as bone thickening, visual impairments, progressive hearing loss, and neurological abnormalities (Behrman, 1992).

Treatment and Course

If the mother is diagnosed as having syphilis during pregnancy, treatment with antibiotics can eliminate the infection in the mother and the fetus. If treatment was not given during pregnancy, antibiotic therapy will be started once congenital syphilis is diagnosed. If organ damage has not occurred, the prognosis is usually good. However, if severe damage has occurred, treatment will not reverse the effects.

Congenital Toxoplasmosis

Characteristics

Toxoplasmosis is an infection caused by a parasite (*Toxoplasma gondii*) that infects most mammals. Domestic and wild cats are primary hosts for the parasite, and infected cats excrete the parasite in their feces. Pigs and cattle also host the parasite. The parasite is usually transmitted to humans by handling cat feces without proper hand washing or by eating undercooked, infected meat.

In the healthy adult, symptoms are very mild or nonexistent. However, if a pregnant woman contracts this infection, there is approximately a 40–60% chance of the infection being transmitted to the fetus, often resulting in serious damage. About 3,000 infants are born yearly in the United States with congenital toxoplasmosis (Bale & Murph, 1992).

The symptoms and severity of congenital toxoplasmosis vary according to when the disease was acquired. Congenital toxoplasmosis acquired during the first trimester of pregnancy may result in fetal death or severe impairments. When the infection is acquired during the first or second trimester, a classic triad of symptoms often occur, including eye abnormalities (chorioretinitis), hydrocephalus, and intracranial calcification. Other possible symptoms include seizures, cerebral palsy, psychomotor disturbances, and brain abnormalities such as microcephaly. Mental retardation is common. For children diagnosed with congenital toxoplasmosis, only 14% have been found to have an IQ of 90 or higher (Couvreur & Desmonts, 1962). Other abnormalities may include enlargement of the liver and spleen, anemia, and decreased numbers of platelets. Several eye abnormalities may be present, such as chorioretinitis, retinal detachment (Lucas, 1989), and cataracts (Martyn & DiGeorge, 1987). Sensorineural hearing loss may also occur, as well as deaf-blindness. Neurodevelopmental abnormalities from the infection may occur months or years after birth. On the other extreme, congenital toxoplasmosis contracted during the third trimester of pregnancy often results in the infant having no impairments or symptoms (Andersen et al., 1986; Berkow, 1992; Williamson & Demmler, 1992).

Treatment and Course

If blood analysis indicates that the mother has toxoplasmosis, medication will be given to reduce the risk of transmission to the fetus (Daffos, Forestier, & Copella-Pavlosky, 1988). Although medication will also be given to the infant with congenital toxoplasmosis to kill the organism and prevent further damage, impairments usually occur when the infection is acquired during the first trimester. Frequent vision and hearing tests will be necessary due to the risk of visual and hearing impairments developing later.

Other Infections

The *O* in the acronym *STORCH* stands for *other* infections that may cause severe congenital impairments when acquired prenatally or perinatally. Several viruses may fall into this category. When varicella zoster (which causes chicken pox and shingles) is acquired during pregnancy, it may be transmitted to the fetus prenatally, which can result in miscarriage, visual impairments, cerebral palsy, microcephaly, and/or organ involvement. Another virus in this category is the polio virus, which can cause miscarriage, deaf-blindness, and malformation (Andersen et al., 1986).

Congenital Rubella

Characteristics

Rubella, also known as German measles, was the most common viral cause of birth defects until a vaccination was developed and a vaccination program implemented, beginning in 1969 (Andersen et al., 1986; Ueda, Tokugawa, & Kusuhara, 1992). This virus is transmitted to individuals through the respiratory system by infected air droplets. In children and adults who have acquired rubella in this manner, only mild and transient symptoms are typically present. As with the other STORCH infections, this virus may be transmitted to the fetus across the placenta with adverse effects. There is approximately an 80% risk of transmission to the fetus during the first trimester, with the majority of the infected fetuses sustaining damage from the infection. The risk of severe impairment declines until after the 16th week. After this time, the fetus may acquire the infection but usually without sustaining disability. In 1990, more than 1,000 cases of rubella were reported (Bale & Murph, 1992).

Infants with congenital rubella may have no impairments, or they may have several abnormalities, including cardiac defects such as patent ductus arteriosus or ventricular septal defects. Also, visual impairments (such as cataracts, glaucoma, strabismus, pigmentary retinopathy, or optic nerve atrophy) may occur; hearing defects (sensorineural loss), deaf-blindness, and some organ involvement may occur as well. Additional symptoms and abnormalities may include low birth weight, liver and spleen enlargement, inflammation of the brain, microcephaly, decreased platelets (thrombocytopenia), jaundice, anemia, swelling of the lymph nodes (adenopathy), abnormalities of balance, inflammation of the lungs (pneumonitis), and abnormalities of the kidney, skin, and bones.

Children born with symptoms of the rubella virus often have long-term impairment. In addition to sensory impairments, children may have seizures, cerebral palsy, or both. Depending on the extent of damage, children with congenital rubella may have normal intelligence, mental retardation, or learning deficits.

Children who had no symptoms of the infection at birth may develop impairments long after the acute, original rubella infection is over. In some instances, children develop encephalitis (inflammation of the brain) with concomitant learning deficits and behavioral disturbances (Desmond, Wilson, & Vordeman, 1985). Other problems such as lack of motor coordination may occur; these impairments may not appear until the child is between the ages of 2 and 7 years. The impairments may increase in severity up to 12 years of age (Wolff, 1985). In some cases, hearing losses have been found to occur later in adolescence. Visual impairments have been found to progressively worsen. Close monitoring is necessary throughout the person's life for possible complications (Williamson & Demmler, 1992).

Treatment and Course

At this time, there is no effective antiviral treatment (medication) for congenital rubella. Children with congenital defects from the virus will continue to have lifelong disabilities. Treatment depends on the type of impairment. Medications are typically prescribed for seizures and leg cramps that may occur in cerebral palsy. Surgical intervention may be performed on the eye when cataracts and glaucoma are present. Heart defects may also require surgical intervention. Prescriptive lenses and hearing aids may be prescribed.

The infant with congenital rubella may excrete the virus for 6 months or much longer. The virus can then be transmitted to others through contact with the infected bodily fluids directly or through contact with the infected bodily fluids on environmental surfaces. Non-immunized pregnant women should be cautious around infants who are still shedding the virus. Prevention is the key to controlling the incidence of congenital rubella with the use of such measures as vaccinations.

Congenital Cytomegalovirus (CMV)

Characteristics

Cytomegalovirus is an infection that is commonly acquired with few or no symptoms by most healthy individuals before they are 50 years old (Andersen et al., 1986). However, when a pregnant woman acquires the infection, severe damage may occur to the fetus. There is approximately a 40% risk of transmission to the fetus. However, even upon transmission, the virus may or may not invade the fetal central nervous system and cause damage. The likelihood of fetal damage from intrauterine infection is thought to be greater the earlier in the pregnancy the infection occurs.

Congenital cytomegalovirus may present with varying severity and symptoms, ranging from no symptoms or impairments to severe or fatal involvement. Possible symptoms and complications include damage to numerous organs (including the brain, liver, spleen, heart, and kidney), decreased platelet count (thrombocytopenia), skin rash, and microcephaly (decreased growth of head and brain). Visual impairments (for example, retinitis, coloboma, cataracts), hearing impairments (mild-to-profound sensorineural hearing loss), or deaf-blindness may occur. Miscarriages and death shortly after birth can occur.

Children born with cytomegalovirus may have normal intelligence, a learning disability, mental retardation, motor abnormalities, seizures, cerebral palsy, vision impairments, hearing impairments, or deaf-blindness (Andersen et al., 1986; Conboy, Pass, & Stagno, 1986; Hanshaw et al., 1976; Williamson, Desmond, LaFevers, Taber, Catlin, & Weaver, 1982). Children who were exposed to cytomegalovirus congenitally but were born without symptoms are at-risk of developing problems later. Sensorineural hearing loss may develop after birth and continue to worsen through middle childhood. It has been suggested that many cases of sensorineural hearing loss with unidentified etiology may actually be due to congenital cytomegalovirus (Williamson, Demmler, Percy, & Catlin, 1992).

Treatment and Course

There is presently no effective medical treatment available for congenital cytomegalovirus. Antiviral medication may be prescribed to treat the infection, but it cannot correct the damage that has already occurred. Although surgeries may be performed to correct certain defects such as heart defects, children typically continue to have severe disability.

The virus may be shed by the infant and child with congenital cytomegalovirus for approximately 8 years. Cytomegalovirus may be present in the urine, saliva, blood, tears, stool, cervical secretions, and semen of infants and children with congenital cytomegalovirus. Unless proper infection control measures are used—hand washing, proper disposal of wastes, cleaning environmental surfaces—persons working with the infant or child may acquire the infection. If this occurs, symptoms will be minimal, but a pregnant woman may transmit the virus to her fetus.

Neonatal Herpes Simplex Virus (HSV)

Characteristics

Herpes simplex virus can cause serious illness in humans. There are two types of this virus: type 1, which causes most cold sores, and type 2, which results in most genital lesions. Both of these types can be transmitted to the fetus; approximately 80% of the neonatal herpes simplex virus infections are caused by type 2 (Berkow, 1992).

Most STORCH infections are acquired from the mother by transmission of the virus through the placenta to the fetus. In neonatal herpes, the virus is acquired either during birth as the infant passes through the infected birth canal or by the virus ascending to the fetus after the amniotic membranes have ruptured.

Symptoms of neonatal herpes simplex usually appear between the first and fourth week after birth. Initially, skin vesicles (blisters) usually appear, but approximately 45% of the infected infants will have no skin lesions. They will have a brain infection. A more serious form of the disease may follow unless treatment is begun. Other symptoms may include drowsiness, respiratory problems, hypotonia (low tone), hepatitis (inflammation of the liver), and diseases of coagulation. Seizures and coma are possible with brain involvement (Berkow, 1992).

Infants with this infection fall into three classifications. The first category is a localized form that consists of skin, eye, and mucous membrane involvement. The second category (another form of localized disease) consists of infants with encephalitis (inflammation of the brain), which usually has its onset several days after delivery. The third category consists of infants with the disseminated form with multiorgan involvement (Bale & Murph, 1992; Gammon & Nahmias, 1985).

Treatment and Course

Prompt treatment of this infection using antiviral medication increases the number of infants who will survive and develop normally from 10 to 35% (Berkow, 1992). Prognosis depends on the form and severity of the disease. About 80% of children with congenital herpes have the disseminated form. Some children with this form will have a 20 to 30% chance of having multiple impairments, including poor growth, mental retardation, and blindness (Andersen et al., 1986). A 50% mortality rate occurs when the central nervous system is involved. Neonatal herpes simplex can often be prevented if the infant is delivered by cesarean section within 4 hours from when the amniotic membranes have ruptured (Nahmias et al., 1971).

EDUCATIONAL IMPLICATIONS OF CONGENITAL INFECTIONS

Students with congenital infections represent a wide diversity of disabilities from no apparent symptoms to multiple and severe disabilities. As with other disabilities, each child will require that his or her educational needs be met on an individual basis.

Meeting Physical and Sensory Needs

Students born with one of the STORCH congenital infections are at high risk of having physical and sensory impairments. A team of individuals will be

■ VIGNETTE ■

While Ramona was pregnant, she contracted German measles. Her pediatrician informed her that her unborn child could be affected by the infection. When Ramona's daughter Alma was born prematurely, Alma had multiple impairments. Over time, Alma was diagnosed with a severe sensorineural hearing impairment, cataracts, hydrocephalus, severe mental retardation, and cerebral palsy. Despite the severity of her disabilities, Alma is doing well in elementary school with a functional curriculum that addresses her individual needs.

needed to optimize physical functioning and make any needed adaptations due to physical impairments. Because sensory impairments are common and may occur after birth, ongoing assessments of vision and hearing are needed to monitor any impairments in function. Also, the vision or hearing impairments (or both) resulting from the congenital infection can be progressive; regular, ongoing assessment is crucial.

In some infections, such as cytomegalovirus, the young child may continue to be contagious. It is important that the teacher implement proper infection control procedures in the classroom. These include proper hand washing and cleaning of equipment and environmental surfaces. (See Chapter 26.) Infection control procedures should be routinely performed, regardless of whether or not there is a known infection in the classroom.

Meeting Communication Needs, Learning Needs, Daily Living Needs, and Behavioral Needs

Because there is such a wide variety of impairments in students with congenital infections, educational interventions will vary greatly. For some students, communication may be difficult, and augmentative communication devices may be used. Cognitive impairments frequently occur, requiring the use of special instructional interventions. Sensory and physical impairments will require the use of adaptations and instructional strategies to meet the student's needs. Depending on the extent of physical and sensory impairments, students may require additional instruction in such areas as daily living skills. Behaviors vary widely, often requiring behavioral intervention. Specialized services (such as occupational therapy, physical therapy, orientation and mobility services, and audiology services) may be needed as well.

SUMMARY

Several congenital infections have the potential to result in severe disabilities. These include syphilis, toxoplasmosis, rubella, cytomegalovirus, and herpes. These are known by the acronym STORCH. The extent of damage caused by these infections varies widely. Educators need to be aware of the possible implications of these infections. Knowledge that hearing impairments can occur and may be progressive will alert the educator to observe the student closely for signs of this impairment. Visual impairments, physical impairments, and cognitive impairments may also occur and result in the need for adaptations and systematic instruction.

CHAPTER 26

Acquired Infections and AIDS

Individuals typically acquire many types of infections during their lives. Most infections will have no long-lasting effects. Some infections, however, may result in long-term disability or, in extreme cases, death.

Some of the acquired infections that may have severe consequences include infections of the nervous system (for example, meningitis and encephalitis), hepatitis, and the HIV infection that results in AIDS. Each of these infections will be described with regard to their etiology, means of transmission, characteristics, detection, treatment, course, and infection control. Overall educational implications will also be addressed.

DESCRIPTION OF ACQUIRED INFECTIONS

The term *acquired infection* refers to any infection that is not transmitted congenitally. The infection is acquired sometime during one's lifetime, but not prenatally (before birth) or perinatally (shortly before, during, or shortly after birth).

DYNAMICS OF ACQUIRED INFECTIONS

In order to have an understanding of how each infection is transmitted, it is important to know how infections are generally transmitted. In order for an infection to be transmitted to a person, three factors must be in place. The infectious agent must have (1) a means of escape from an infected host, (2) a means of transmission, and (3) a means of entry into the body (see Figure 26-1).

An infected host may be a person, an animal, or a nonanimal, such as garden soil. In order for the infection to be acquired, it must first have a way to leave the host. An infectious microorganism may escape from an infected host in several different ways; how it leaves depends on the type of organism it is and where it is located. For infections in the respiratory tract, infections may leave the host by a sneeze or cough. Infections in the gastrointestinal tract may leave an infected host through saliva or stool. Infections in the genitourinary system may leave an infected host through urine, semen, or cervical secretions. Infections in the blood may leave through open lesions, a needle stick, blood transfusions, or an insect bite.

After the infectious organism has left the infected host, it must next have a means of transmission in order to reach another person. Transmission may occur through one of four possible categories: (1) airborne transmission, (2) contact transmission, (3) vehicle route, and (4) vectorborne transmission. *Airborne transmission* refers to the organisms carried on droplets in the air or on dust particles or to organisms shed into the environment from skin or wounds. The second type of transmission is *contact transmission,* which may occur either directly or indirectly. Direct contact may occur person-to-person through sex, or fecal-oral transmission, or saliva-oral transmission. Indirect contact transmission refers to transmission through an inanimate object when the infectious organism is on the surface of an object. An example is a toy with saliva on it containing a microorganism. *Vehicle route* refers to the way the microorganism is transmitted in infected food, water, drugs, or blood. The last category—*vectorborne transmission*—refers to contaminated insects such as mosquitoes or ticks that may transport the infection. However, many infections that are present in blood cannot survive in a mosquito or tick (Suddarth, 1991).

Once an organism has left an infected host and has a means of transmission, it can only be contracted by another person if there is a means of entry. Infections that are airborne may enter another person through the

INFECTED HOST ⟶ NEW HOST

Human

Human

Animal

Nonanimal

Means of escape	Means of transmission	Means of entry
Respiratory tract	Airborne transmission	Respiratory tract
Gastrointestinal tract	Contact transmission	Gastrointestinal tract
Genitourinary tract	Vehicle route transmission	Genitourinary tract
Open lesion	Vectorborne transmission	Direct infection of mucous membranes; break in skin
Blood from insect bites, needles, or other		

■ **FIGURE 26-1** How infection is transmitted

respiratory tract. If the person breathes in an infected air droplet, he or she may acquire the infection. Examples of infections that are airborne include bacterial strep throat and viral respiratory illness.

Infections that are spread through contact transmission need a mode of entry past the natural barrier of the skin. Contact transmission may be achieved by an infection entering a break in the skin from a cut. Contact transmission may also occur by transporting an infection on one's hands (from touching infected saliva or stool, for example), then touching the mucous membranes of the mouth or eye. An example of this type of transmission is Hepatitis A. Contact transmission may also occur by infected semen or vaginal secretions entering another person during sexual contact. Syphilis can be transmitted in this way.

Infections that are transported by vehicle route transmission may enter a person through the gastrointestinal tract by eating or drinking an organism in infected food or drink. Diarrheal illnesses are commonly caused this way; an example is salmonella dysentery. Another vehicle route may be through infected blood. Before donor blood was screened, infections in the blood supply were obtained from blood transfusions; HIV is an example of this. Transmission may also occur by sharing needles infected with a virus, as in illegal drug use, or by hospital staff members who unintentionally prick themselves with a needle used on an infected patient.

Infections that are vectorborne may be contracted from tick or mosquito bites. For example, Rocky Mountain spotted fever and Lyme disease are acquired from infected ticks and encephalitis from infected mosquitos.

In order for infection to be transmitted, all three

elements must be in place. Someone who has an infection cannot pass it on to someone else unless there is a means of the infection leaving the body, a way to transmit the infection, and a way it can enter another's body. Even if the infection is transmitted to another person, the person's defense mechanisms may stop the infection. Some defense mechanisms include intact skin, secretions of the mucous membranes that have antimicrobial properties, the filter system of the respiratory tract (ciliary ladder), coughing, acid pH of the stomach and vagina, and antibacterial secretions in the gastrointestinal tract. The immune response of antibodies also resists and prevents infections (Berkow, 1992).

Although it is common for people to acquire infections all their lives, certain infections that teachers may encounter in the classroom could result in significant disability or death. Some of these infections include meningitis, encephalitis, hepatitis, and HIV.

TYPES OF ACQUIRED INFECTIONS

Bacterial Meningitis

Meningitis is an infection resulting in inflammation of the membranes (meninges) that cover the brain and spinal cord. Meningitis ranges in its effects from no permanent impairments to mild, severe, or profound impairments. In extreme cases, death can result. Meningitis can occur from viral or bacterial infections. The viral forms of meningitis usually have mild symptoms that pose no threat to healthy children. The bacterial forms of meningitis occur most frequently in young infants and children and can have serious consequences. Because bacterial meningitis is so severe, we will discuss it rather than the viral forms.

Etiology

Several different organisms can cause bacterial meningitis. Some of the most common types of bacteria that may result in meningitis are *Streptococcus pneumoniae*, *Hemophilus influenza* type B (HIB), and *Neisseria meningitidis* (meningococcus). For students who have a VP shunt (due to hydrocephalus), infection of the shunt may result in meningitis or encephalitis; in these cases, the *Staphylococcus* species are the most common (Bell, 1992).

Means of Transmission

Many of the bacterial microorganisms that cause bacterial meningitis are spread by respiratory transmission. Actually, many healthy children and adults normally carry the bacteria *Hemophilus influenza* type B in the back of their throats. These bacteria can be transmitted to susceptible individuals through transmission of respiratory secretions (Behrman, 1992).

Characteristics

One major symptom of meningitis is a stiff neck, which occurs due to the inflammation of the meninges in the cervical area. For children and adolescents, other symptoms may include a fever, sore throat, vomiting, headache, fever, lethargy, seizures, and sensitivity to bright light. A progression through irritability, lethargy, drowsiness, stupor, seizures, and coma is possible (Fishman, 1992). Sensory impairments may also occur. Cortical visual impairments may occur when neurological damage is present from a bacterial infection. A nerve that controls the lateral movement of the eye may be affected. Hearing loss occurs in approximately 10 to 20% of those who survive bacterial meningitis and is typically sensorineural in nature and is permanent (Andersen et al., 1986).

Detection, Treatment, and Course

Meningitis is diagnosed through physical signs and symptoms, laboratory tests, and lumbar puncture—a procedure in which cerebrospinal fluid is extracted and analyzed for infection. Once diagnosed, antibiotics and sometimes corticosteroids are used to treat bacterial meningitis (Quagliarello & Scheld, 1992). If seizures are present, antiseizure medications will be prescribed as well. Although antibiotics may be successful in treating the infection, some individuals may still have brain damage, mental retardation, seizures, deafness, blindness, deaf-blindness, and/or motor impairment.

Infection Control

Because many of the bacteria that cause meningitis transmit the infection through the air, infection control needs to be aimed at decreasing the risk of respiratory transmission. Students should be taught to cover their mouths when they cough. The use of tissues and the proper disposal of tissues should be taught. Students should also be taught how to wash their hands properly. Hand washing is the single most effective infection control procedure. The proper method is to wash one's hands under warm running water and use pump soap, which reduces the risk of infectious organisms growing on the soap. After wetting the hands and lathering well with soap, the hands should be rinsed and dried. Then, the water should be turned off by turning the handles with a paper towel to prevent reinfecting the hands with any microorganisms that may have been transferred to the handles (see Box 26-1).

Preventive infection control should occur as well. Infants and young children can be immunized with HIB vaccine, which should protect the child from developing HIB meningitis. If a student has had meningitis that was caused by *Neisseria meningitidis* or *Hemophilus influenza* type B, individuals with close contact to the student should receive antibiotics. Also, the parents of students at high risk for acquiring infections, such as those with sickle cell anemia or AIDS, should be contacted regarding the possibility of transmission (Fishman, 1992).

Encephalitis

Encephalitis is an inflammation of the brain. It may occur in one of two ways: (1) as the primary symptom of an infection, or (2) as a complication of another

---

BOX 26-1

Proper Hand Washing Techniques

1. Use soap and running water.
2. Rub your hands vigorously.
3. Wash all skin surfaces, including:

   - backs of hands
   - wrists
   - between fingers
   - under fingernails

4. Rinse well.
5. Dry hands with a paper towel.
6. Turn off water with a paper towel—not with your bare hands.

SOURCE: Adapted from guidelines provided by the Centers for Disease Control, Atlanta, GA.

infection, such as measles, chickenpox, mumps, or rubella.

Etiology

There are several causes of encephalitis, including viruses. Viruses causing encephalitis include those that spread person-to-person, such as mumps, measles, enteroviruses, rubella, herpes, and influenza. Also included are those viruses that are vectorborne (by mosquito or ticks) and viruses that are transmitted from warm-blooded mammals to people (rabies, for example). Encephalitis may also occur from nonviral means such as bacterial or fungal infections. Tuberculosis is an example of a bacterial infection. Encephalitis can also ensue from human slow-virus diseases in which the virus was acquired earlier in life but later causes a chronic neurological disease that results in encephalitis. HIV is such a virus (Behrman, 1992).

Means of Transmission

Depending on the etiology of encephalitis, transmission may occur in several ways. Although there are several etiologies, the most common causes of encephalitis are viruses, including the mumps virus, enteroviruses, arboviruses, and herpes simplex virus (Andersen et al., 1986). The mumps virus is contracted through respiratory transmission. Enteroviruses are viruses that are primarily transmitted through infected fecal material, although some of the enteroviruses may result in infectious respiratory secretions for a few days. Arboviruses are vectorborne; infected mosquitos and ticks carry the virus. Herpes simplex virus type 1 is transmitted primarily by saliva. Herpes simplex type 2 (genital herpes) is usually transmitted by direct sexual contact.

Characteristics

Symptoms of encephalitis vary. Typically, there is a headache, neurological signs, fever, and an altered state of consciousness (Fishman, 1992). At times, there may be a decrease in alertness. More severe symptoms may also be present such as seizures, paralysis of the arms or legs, or coma.

Detection, Treatment, and Course

Encephalitis may be diagnosed by physical signs and symptoms, laboratory tests, testing of the cerebrospinal fluid, and brain imaging techniques. Specific treatment will depend on the cause of the encephalitis, which should be determined upon diagnosis. Some children will respond to specific therapy, such as the administration of the medication acyclovir or vidarabine to individuals with herpes or varicella zoster encephalitis.

Most other viral causes do not have a specific treatment regime, but treatment is aimed toward controlling symptoms like seizures and increased cranial pressure and preventing complications.

Depending on the type of virus, the age of the person, and any underlying conditions, the prognosis for encephalitis varies. Even gravely ill individuals may make a complete recovery. Infants are most likely to have permanent effects. Permanent brain damage from the infection can result in mental retardation, learning disabilities, motor deficits, and seizures. In some cases, especially if untreated, children may die. Approximately 75% of individuals with herpes simplex virus encephalitis, for example, typically will die if not treated. Treatment may be postponed when the condition is not properly diagnosed (Cameron, Wallace, & Munro, 1992).

Infection Control

Infection control should be maintained to minimize the risk of infection. In the case of encephalitis, several means of transmission have been identified for some of the viruses that can cause this condition. To prevent the spread of mumps, which can result in encephalitis, infected students should be sent home. As with all airborne infections, it is important that the infected individual cover his or her mouth when coughing, use tissues and dispose of them properly, and use proper hand washing techniques.

To prevent the spread of enteroviruses that could cause encephalitis, proper hand washing and sanitary conditions should be observed. Teachers should teach students to wash their hands thoroughly after using the bathroom and before eating to prevent fecal-oral transmission. Proper diapering techniques should be used with infants to help prevent the spread of infection (see Box 26-2). This includes using a plastic-lined bag or receptacle for diapers, using proper hand washing techniques, and cleaning and disinfecting the diapering area. The proper disposal of fecal material is important in decreasing the risk of infection.

Viruses that are carried by mosquitos and ticks pose a difficult problem for infection control. Mosquito repellent is recommended for high-risk areas; screens over windows and appropriate clothing also aid in proper management (Gilmore & Gundersen, 1987). Any ticks spotted on students should be removed and reported to their parents.

Herpes type 1 is often transmitted by saliva. To decrease the risk of transmission, there should be no sharing of food or drinks. Each child should use his or her own cup. Teachers should not clean utensils or plates in the classroom, but they should be disinfected in

BOX 26-2

Proper Diapering Techniques

1. Check to be sure all necessary supplies are ready.
2. Place roll paper or disposable towel on diapering surface.
3. Lay the child on the diapering surface, taking care that the soiled diaper touches only your hands—not your arms or clothing.
4. Remove the soiled diaper and clothing.
   - Put disposable diapers in a plastic bag or plastic-lined receptacle.
   - Put soiled clothes in a plastic bag to be taken home.
5. Clean the child's bottom with a premoistened disposable towelette or a damp paper towel.
   - Dispose of the towelette or paper towel in the plastic bag or plastic-lined receptacle.
   - Remove the paper towel from beneath the child and dispose of it the same way.
6. Wipe your hands with a premoistened towelette or a damp paper towel.
   - Dispose of this towel in the plastic bag or plastic-lined receptacle.
7. Diaper or dress the child. Now you can hold the child close to you.
8. Wash the child's hands and return the child to the crib or group.
9. Clean and *disinfect* the diapering area and any equipment and supplies you touched.
10. Wash your hands.

SOURCE: Adapted from guidelines provided by the Centers for Disease Control, Atlanta, GA.

a dishwasher with a final rinse of 180° F. Personal care items such as toothbrushes should not be shared. Laundry should be done in a washing machine using hot water, and this is typically done at home.

Of paramount importance is the cleaning of environmental surfaces. Saliva on classroom items (from drooling on or mouthing items) can serve as a form of indirect contact transmission. Toys, mats, school supplies, environmental surfaces, and equipment should be regularly cleansed with a solution of 10 parts water to 1 part chlorine bleach. Teachers often mix this solution in a spray bottle, like a plant spray bottle or cleaning bottle, each morning in order to quickly and efficiently clean surfaces.

Herpes simplex type 2 virus is usually transmitted during sex. Proper education about transmission and prevention is important.

Hepatitis B

Hepatitis is an inflammation of the liver. There are several different types: Hepatitis A (infectious hepatitis), Hepatitis B (serum hepatitis), Hepatitis C, Hepatitis D, and Hepatitis E. Each has a different etiology and prognosis. Due to the prevalence of Hepatitis B and the presence of Hepatitis B carriers in individuals with disabilities, only Hepatitis B will be discussed.

Etiology

Hepatitis B is caused by the Hepatitis B virus (HBV). Groups of individuals who are at-risk of acquiring this disease are those who receive blood products, such as individuals with hemophilia, those who have been in accidents and need blood, and those undergoing certain surgical procedures. Also at-risk are those receiving dialysis, drug users, health care workers, and individuals with disabilities living in institutions, or those who have been deinstitutionalized. It has been proposed that Hepatitis B is an occupational hazard of special education teachers (Bauer & Shea, 1986).

Means of Transmission

Although the Hepatitis B virus is found in most bodily secretions, it has only been found to be infectious in blood, saliva, and semen (Bauer & Shea, 1986). The most common mode of transmission is through the blood. Hepatitis B can be transmitted through contaminated blood and blood products, although blood screening has greatly decreased this as a mode of transmission, and through intravenous drug use, in which an infected person's blood remains on unclean needles and is transmitted to another person through an injection. The virus can also be transmitted by way of a bleeding cut. For example, an unaffected person might get infected blood on a finger, then touch an open cut or a mucous membrane in his or her eye or mouth with that finger. Other possible modes of transmission include during sex or when saliva is transferred from one individual to another via direct or indirect transmission.

Characteristics

The symptoms of hepatitis vary greatly from no symptoms or those of a minor flu-like illness to fatal liver failure. This depends on the child's immune system response and other factors that are not well understood. Typically, the child will have fever, nausea and vomiting, weight loss, and an aching feeling. This is often followed by a rash, dark urine, and jaundice—yellowing of the sclera of the eye and skin (Berkow, 1992).

Detection, Treatment, and Course

Hepatitis B is diagnosed by physical symptoms and laboratory data. When there are no complications, there is no specific treatment. Infected individuals typically stay at home until the jaundice is resolved. A few individuals, however, develop complications such as acute fulminating hepatitis, which can cause death.

In some individuals, the symptoms of hepatitis disappear, but those individuals become chronic carriers of the infection. The Hepatitis B virus is found in their blood, saliva, and semen and can be transmitted to others if proper infection control procedures are not followed.

Infection Control

Proper infection control procedures need to be in place to prevent the spread of infection. Because blood is the primary mode of transmission, measures should be in place regarding contact with blood. As we discussed, proper hand washing is the single most important preventative measure. Gloves should be worn when handling a student's blood, as when a nosebleed or cut occurs. However, gloves do not substitute for proper hand washing. When the gloves are removed, the hands still need to be washed. Teaching students to wash their hands is important. Girls should be taught proper menstrual care and the proper disposal of menstrual care items because the virus is present in menstrual blood. Any open cuts on infected or uninfected students, teachers, or other school staff members should be covered by a Band-Aid or gauze to decrease the risk that an infectious agent will exit a host or enter a new host.

Because of the risk of transmission, the Centers for Disease Control and Prevention recommends the use of universal precautions. These precautions are aimed at protecting the health care worker in a medical setting. They primarily involve using barriers such as gloves or gowns to protect against contact with infected material. These precautions have been adopted in hospitals across the country.

Since Hepatitis B is also found in saliva, infection control measures should be aimed at preventing the sharing of food, drink, or personal care items. Proper cleaning of utensils and equipment is necessary to prevent transmission through indirect contact.

Proper cleaning of environmental surfaces and items in the environment is essential. This is usually done with 1 part chlorine bleach to 10 parts water. Inanimate objects that become contaminated with the Hepatitis B virus can transmit the disease for up to 1 week or longer if not properly cleaned.

Hepatitis B vaccine is available as a preventative treatment program for infants, children, adolescents, and adults. In many areas of the country, it is now given as a part of the regular immunization program.

AIDS

Acquired immune deficiency syndrome (AIDS) is presently the leading cause of death in individuals from 24 to 40 years of age (Centers for Disease Control and Prevention, 1993). AIDS not only infects adults but infants, children, and adolescents as well. It has been suggested that the virus that causes AIDS is the newest chronic illness of childhood and that it is more prevalent in children living in the United States than cystic fibrosis, hemophilia, deafness, acute lymphoblastic leukemia, chronic renal failure, or muscular dystrophy (Meyers & Weitzman, 1991).

Etiology

The human immunodeficiency virus (HIV) has been identified as the cause of AIDS. Several strands of HIV have been found; for example, HIV-1 and HIV-2 (Levy, 1990). When HIV enters the body, it typically invades the body by attaching to a CD4+ T-lymphocyte cell (CD4 cell, T-4 cell). The CD4 cell is part of the immune system that fights infection. When HIV invades the CD4 cell, HIV replicates inside the CD4 cell and then destroys it (see Figure 26-2). The multiplying virus spreads from CD4 cell to CD4 cell, increasing the numbers while decreasing the number of CD4 cells. This cripples the immune system and causes it to function ineffectively. In adolescents and adults, AIDS is diagnosed when the CD4 T-lymphocyte cell count (CD4 cell count, T4 cell count) drops to 200 or below. (Over 1,000 is normal in adolescents and adults.) For infants and children, normal CD4 counts are age-dependent, and the diagnosis of AIDS depends on certain laboratory tests detecting a low CD4 count for the age of the child, elevation of certain types of Ig (immunoglobulin) antibodies, physical symptoms, accompanying infections, and other abnormalities.

Means of Transmission

Risk of transmission of HIV is extremely low in the school setting. Although the virus has been found in several bodily secretions, it is only infectious in blood, semen, and cervical secretions (Lifson, 1992). Transmission typically occurs in three ways. First, HIV may be transmitted during sex. An increased likelihood of HIV

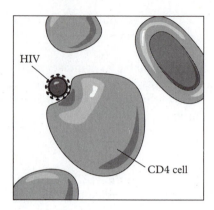

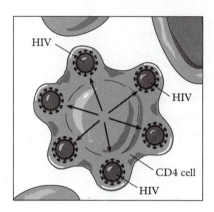

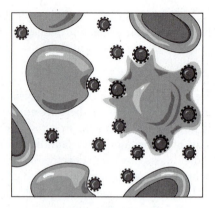

HIV invades the body. HIV enters the body and invades the CD4 cells.

Replication. HIV replicates inside the CD4 cells and then destroys the CD4 cells.

Takeover. The multiplying virus spreads to new CD4 cells and replicates again. The number of CD4 cells is decreased, and the immune system no longer functions effectively.

■ **FIGURE 26-2** How HIV cripples the immune system

SOURCE: From "The Spectrum of Adult HIV Infection," by K. Sessions, *Emory AIDS Training Network Training Material,* March 1993. Copyright © 1993 Emory AIDS Training Network. Reprinted with permission.

transmission has been reported with anal sex due to the possibility of small tears in the rectal area. However, transmission during vaginal sex also occurs. Some reports of transmission of HIV as a result of oral sex have been reported (Lifson, 1992). The number of sexual partners also increases the likelihood of infection.

Second, the HIV virus is transmitted in contaminated blood. This primarily occurred prior to blood screening, and those receiving blood or blood products, that is, those with hemophilia, were at special risk. Use of contaminated needles during intravenous drug use is also a common cause of transmission due to the sharing of needles. Third, transmission may occur congenitally; the infected mother may pass the infection to her baby.

AIDS cannot be transmitted by casual contact. One study examining preschool children with HIV found no transmission of the virus to their household contacts when sharing beds, toilets, utensils, or toothbrushes or by hugging or kissing (Roger, White, & Sanders, 1990). Other studies conducted over a span of a decade have not found one instance of transmission by casual contact (Berkow, 1992; Lifson, 1992).

Adolescents typically acquire the infection through sexual intercourse with an infected person or through contaminated needles typically used for illegal drugs. This is known as horizontal transmission. Because blood supplies used for transfusion purposes are now screened, a very small number of people have received the infection through contaminated blood.

The majority of infants or children under age 13 who have AIDS typically caught the virus from their infected mother as a congenital infection (Joshi, 1991). This is

known as vertical transmission. This transmission can occur in one of the following ways: (1) during gestation when the virus crosses the placenta, (2) during delivery by contact with maternal blood, or (3) by breast feeding. Other less common means of transmission in children under 13 are associated with contaminated blood in a blood transfusion and sexually related child abuse (Caldwell & Rogers, 1991).

Characteristics—Acquired AIDS in Adolescents and Adults

Individuals who acquire the HIV infection through horizontal transmission present with a wide range of symptoms and characteristics (see Figure 26-3). After the virus is transmitted to an individual, it takes from about 6 to 12 weeks for the HIV antibody test to become positive. This is followed by a chronic, asymptomatic (without symptoms) state in which the CD4 T-lymphocyte cell count is typically greater than 500. This state may continue for 6 months to more than 11 years. (It is important to note that the virus can be transmitted even when the person is asymptomatic.) This is usually followed by symptoms of HIV with a CD4 T-lymphocyte cell count falling below 500. If the CD4 T-lymphocyte count drops to 200 or below, a diagnosis of AIDS is made (AIDS Training Network, 1993; Volberding, 1992). .

Symptoms of AIDS usually reflect the injured immune system and may include fatigue, weight loss, intermittent fever, malaise, lethargy, chronic diarrhea, enlarged lymph nodes, dry cough, thrush, and a tendency to bruise easily. Other signs that reflect a chronic, symptomatic infection may include herpes zoster, thrush, skin problems, enlarged liver and spleen, and others.

Opportunistic infections usually occur in individuals with AIDS. These are infections that are not a threat to a healthy immune system but can be fatal to a person with AIDS because his or her immune system is impaired. Opportunistic infections may be bacterial, viral, fungal, or parasitic. These infections may be mild or severe. Cytomegalovirus and toxoplasmosis are two examples of opportunistic infections that typically have no significant consequence to healthy individuals when acquired after birth. However, if these are acquired by a person with AIDS, they may have devastating results, such as blindness, seizures, encephalitis, and death (Plona & Schremp, 1992; Schooley, 1992). The most common opportunistic infection is *Pneumocystis carinii* pneumonia (PCP), which is often fatal (Falloon & Masur, 1992).

Cancers (neoplastic disease) may also occur in individuals with AIDS. Kaposi's sarcoma is one of the most common forms of cancer that may occur in individuals with AIDS. Kaposi's sarcoma mainly affects the skin, mouth, and lymph nodes, although the intestines and lungs can become involved as well. Typically, individu-

als will die of opportunistic infections rather than the cancer (Safai & Schwartz, 1992). However, other forms of cancer, such as the lymphomas (cancer of the lymph nodes), frequently develop and can be fatal.

Neurological involvement may occur in individuals with AIDS. This may include a wide range of manifestations, some of which are seizures, hallucinations, and motor dysfunction, and changes in concentration, memory, and affect (Berkow, 1992). In some individuals, AIDS progressive dementia complex may occur in which there is a progressive cognitive decline, with no decline in level of alertness. This decline is usually accompanied by decline in motor function as well (Price, Brew, & Roke, 1992) (see Box 26-3).

Characteristics—Congenital AIDS in Infants and Children

There are some differences between congenital and acquired AIDS. The HIV infections in infants and children with congenital AIDS typically have a shorter incubation, and the disease typically progresses more rapidly in this population. If symptoms appear in infants less than 1 year of age, there is typically a development of opportunistic diseases at age 5 to 7 months and

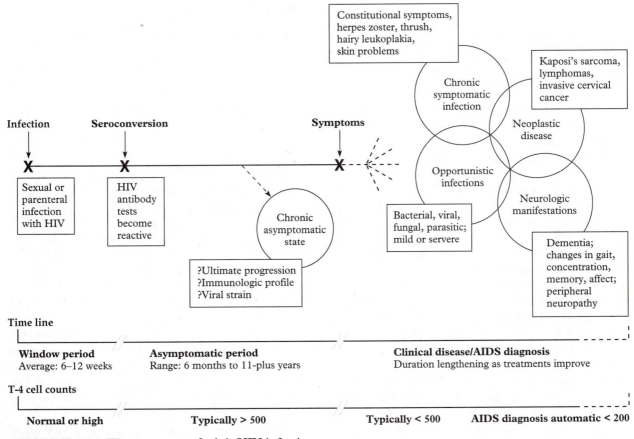

■ **FIGURE 26-3** The spectrum of adult HIV infection

BOX 26-3

Clinical Features of the AIDS Dementia Complex

Early Manifestations

Symptoms

COGNITION
Impaired concentration
Forgetfulness
Mental slowing

MOTOR
Unsteady gait
Leg weakness
Loss of coordination, impaired handwriting
Tremor

BEHAVIOR
Apathy, withdrawal, personality change
Agitation, confusion, hallucinations

Signs

MENTAL STATUS
Psychomotor slowing
Impaired serial 7s or reversals
Organic psychosis

NEUROLOGIC EXAMINATION
Impaired rapid movements (limbs, eyes)
Hyperreflexia
Release reflexes (snout, glabellar, grasp)
Gait ataxia (impaired tandem gait, rapid turns)
Tremor (postural)
Leg weakness

Late Manifestations

MENTAL STATUS
Global dementia
Psychomotor slowing: verbal responses delayed, near or absolute mutism, vacant stare
Unawareness of illness, disinhibition
Confusion, disorientation
Organic psychosis

NEUROLOGIC SIGNS
Weakness (legs to arms)
Ataxia
Pyramidal tract signs: spasticity, hyperreflexia, extensor plantar responses
Bladder and bowel incontinence
Myoclonus

SOURCE: From *Etiology, Diagnosis, Treatment, and Prevention,* Third Edition, by V. T. DeVita, Jr., et al. (Eds.). Copyright © 1992. Reprinted with permission of J. B. Lippincott Co.

---

encephalopathy at 9 to 15 months. Early mortality usually occurs. For children who do not develop symptoms during this time, survival usually extends beyond 5 years of age. In some instances, children have remained symptom-free for 10 years (Butler & Pizzo, 1992).

Infants and young children with AIDS who acquired the infection congenitally may have variable and nonspecific symptoms. These may include such symptoms as failure to thrive, developmental delay, enlarged liver and spleen, chronic diarrhea, lymphadenopathy, upper respiratory infection, ear infection, thrush, and recurrent pneumonia (Andersen et al., 1986).

Due to an inefficient immune system, infants and children with AIDS typically develop recurrent bacterial and opportunistic infections. Bacterial infections such as *Streptococcus pneumoniae* (strep) and *Hemophilus influenza* often occur. The most common opportunistic infections in children include *Pneumocystis carinii* pneumonia (PCP) and lymphocytic interstitial pneumonitis (LIP) (Caldwell & Rogers, 1991). Infections, such as cytomegalovirus and toxoplasmosis, may occur in the infant or child with AIDS and adversely affect various organ systems. For example, the eye could be affected, and blindness could result. Certain bacterial and opportunistic infections may be life-threatening (Levin et al., 1989; Mansour, 1990; Mitchell et al., 1990).

Children with AIDS often have central nervous system involvement. Some have microcephaly, progressive encephalopathy, movement disorders, ataxia, progressive dementia, and severe spasticity (Belman, 1992; Lyman et al., 1990; Rubinstein, 1989). Developmental problems such as mental retardation, developmental delays, cognitive deterioration, and other neurological impairments and motor abnormalities have been found in some children with AIDS, typically within the first 5 years of life (Diamond, 1989).

Every system can be affected by the HIV infection, including respiratory, cardiovascular, gastrointestinal, renal, hematopoietic, endocrine, locomotor systems, as well as the skin and the central nervous system. Table 26-1 shows the various signs and symptoms that can be associated with each organ affected.

The new 1994 classification system of HIV in children (Centers for Disease Control and Prevention, 1994) delineates HIV infection by infection status, immunological status, and clinical status (see Table 26-2). Infection status is reported as HIV-infected, perinatally exposed, or seroreverter—a child born to a mother with HIV who is HIV-negative and has no evidence of infection or an AIDS-defining condition. Immunological status is divided into three categories: no evidence of suppression, evidence of moderate suppression, and severe suppression. Levels of suppression are based on age-specific CD4+ T-lymphocyte counts and percentage of total lymphocytes. Clinical status ranges from no signs/symptoms to severe signs/symptoms. Box 26-4 illustrates the clinical categories.

Children with congenital AIDS are also at risk of acquiring infections from immunizations. This is because a child with AIDS is unable to mount a proper antibody response to immunizations. Therefore, immunizations do not afford protection from infections and can be detrimental. Certain minor illnesses, such as measles, can be fatal to a child with AIDS (Rubinstein, 1989).

Detection, Treatment, and Course

Diagnosis of HIV is made through clinical signs, symptoms, and laboratory tests. Several different analyses of blood samples are used to confirm the diagnosis. The ELISA is the standard screening test that is used to detect HIV exposure. The results of this test are usually confirmed by the Western blot assays, which test for IgG antibody (a type of Ig antibodies) response to specific HIV proteins (Sicklick & Rubinstein, 1992). For adolescents and adults, a diagnosis of AIDS is then made based upon the CD4 T-lymphocyte cell count. A new test that examines saliva to detect HIV infection is presently being tried.

Infants are usually more difficult to diagnose as having the HIV infection. Errors in diagnosis can occur when the infant is very young. False positive results may occur in the young infant because the mother's IgG antibodies cross the placenta and may persist in the child. The test results then reflect the maternal infection, not necessarily an infection in the child. False negative results may occur initially because the infant's immune system is immature. Because of this, there may be a deficient antibody response that results in an initial negative diagnosis. Other tests are often necessary to determine the correct diagnosis. Typically, by 3 to 6 months a correct diagnosis can be made (Sicklick & Rubinstein, 1992).

Several medications are used to treat individuals who are HIV-positive or have AIDS. AZT (zidovudine) and ddI (didanosine) are commonly used medications that slow the replication of the HIV virus. Medication used to prevent the development of *Pneumocystis carinii* pneumonia may be given as well. A study by Graham et al. (1992) has demonstrated that early treatment with AZT and medication to prevent *Pneumocystic carinii* pneumonia development slows the progression of AIDS.

TABLE 26-1
Signs and Symptoms of HIV Infection

Organ system affected	Signs and symptoms
General	Fever, malaise, failure to thrive, lymphadenopathy
Respiratory	Otitis, sinusitis, lymphocytic interstitial pneumonitis; pneumonias: bacterial, viral (CMV), protozoal (PCP), and fungal (*Candida* spp., *C. neoformans*)
Cardiovascular	Cardiomyopathy, pericarditis, arrhythmias, arteritis
Gastrointestinal	Anorexia, nausea, diarrhea, wasting, parotitis, oropharyngeal candidiasis, oral hairy leukoplakia, aphthous ulceration, gingivitis, HSV stomatitis, esophagitis (candidal, CMV, HSV), hepatitis, cholecystitis, pancreatitis, enteropathy, colitis (bacterial, viral, protozoal, fungal)
Renal	Nephrotic syndrome, acute nephritis, renal tubular dysfunction
Hematopoietic	Anemia, leukopenia, thrombocytopenia
Endocrine	Short stature, adrenal insufficiency
Central nervous	Loss of developmental milestones, impaired cognitive ability, acquired microcephaly, spastic paraparesis, extrapyramidal tract signs, aseptic meningitis
Ocular	Chorioretinitis (CMV, HSV, VZV, toxoplasmosis), cotton wool spots
Locomotor	Peripheral neuropathy, myopathy
Skin	*Infectious:* bacterial *(S. aureus)*; viral (HSV, VZV, *M. contagiosum*, warts); fungal (*Candida* spp., tinea corporis, tinea capitis, *Malassezia* spp.); infestations (scabies) *Inflammatory:* seborrheic, eczematoid, and psoriatic eruptions; drug eruptions
Recurrent bacterial infections	*Sites:* otitis, sinusitis, pneumonia, meningitis, osteomyelitis, bacteremia, urinary tract, cellulitis, bacterial colitis *Common organisms:* S. pneumoniae, H. influenzae, N. meningitides, Salmonella spp., atypical mycobacteria
Malignancy	Lymphoma, Kaposi's sarcoma, leiomyoma, others

SOURCE: From "HIV Infection in Children," by K. M. Butler and P. A. Pizzo. In V. T. DeVita, Jr., et al. (Eds.), *Etiology, Diagnosis, Treatment, and Prevention,* Third Edition, p. 291. Copyright © 1992. Reprinted with permission of J. B. Lippincott Co.

TABLE 26-2

Pediatric Human Immunodeficiency Virus (HIV) Classification[1]

Immunologic categories	Clinical Categories			
	N: No signs/ symptoms	A: Mild signs/ symptoms	B:[2] Moderate signs/ symptoms	C:[2] Severe signs/ symptoms
1: No evidence of suppression	N1	A1	B1	C1
2: Evidence of moderate suppression	N2	A2	B2	C2
3: Severe suppression	N3	A3	B3	C3

[1]Children whose HIV infection status is not confirmed are classified by using the above grid with a letter *E* (for perinatally exposed) placed before the appropriate classification code (e.g., EN2).

[2]Both Category C and lymphoid interstitial pneumonitis in Category B are reportable to state and local health departments as acquired immunodeficiency syndrome.

SOURCE: From the *Morbidity and Mortality Weekly Report, September 30, 1994,* Vol. 43, No. RR-12. Copyright © 1994 U. S. Department of Health and Human Services, Centers for Disease Control and Prevention.

No one has completely recovered from AIDS, although there have been some long-term survivors. Opportunistic infections are the cause of death in over 95% of individuals with AIDS (Berkow, 1992). Advances are being made in preventing the transmission of HIV (for example, through research in the development of vaccines) and management of opportunistic diseases. Research on the prevention and cure of AIDS continues.

Infection Control

Because HIV is transmitted by blood, semen, and vaginal secretions, infection control procedures are aimed at minimizing contact with these secretions. In the school setting, it is very difficult to acquire the infection. In health class, for example, the use of condoms may be discussed as a way to decrease the risk of transmission of the HIV infection during sex. The threat of acquiring AIDS during illegal intravenous drug use may also be discussed. If a student cuts himself or herself, gloves should be worn by anyone helping to bandage the wound. Getting blood on intact skin, however, will not result in transmission of the infection. After removing the gloves, hands should be washed. If HIV-infected blood drips on an environmental surface, it should be cleaned with a solution of 1 part chlorine bleach to 10 parts water. Surfaces should be cleaned with disposable material such as paper towels, which should then be placed in plastic bags, which are then tied shut.

Of paramount importance is to prevent infection transmission to the student with AIDS. The student who has AIDS is at far greater risk of acquiring infections from other individuals than others are at risk of acquiring the HIV infection from him or her. Because the student's immune system is impaired by HIV, infections are easily acquired from others, some

of which can be fatal. It is important that the teacher send children home who are sick. Infection control procedures should be in place to decrease the risk of infection for the student with AIDS.

EDUCATIONAL IMPLICATIONS OF ACQUIRED INFECTIONS

Teachers need to have a good understanding of infections, how infections may leave a host, the ways they can be transmitted, and means of entry into uninfected hosts. Even when there is no student known to be infected, teachers should use strict infection control procedures in the classroom.

Meeting Physical and Sensory Needs

To best meet the physical needs of students, the teacher should maintain control procedures to prevent the spread of infection. Teachers should follow infection control procedures for all students in the classroom because the teacher may not know whether a student has an infection or not. Infection control procedures stress proper hand washing, use of gloves when in contact with body fluids, proper disposal of wastes, and cleaning of environmental surfaces. Policies should be followed that determine when a student should be sent home due to illness, such as when running a fever. Infection control procedures are needed to protect students and teachers from acquiring an infection. This is particularly important to students at high risk who usually die from infections (for example, students with AIDS, muscular dystrophy, or cystic fibrosis).

The educator must also be aware that students with AIDS are often underweight and may develop wasting

BOX 26-4

Clinical Categories for Children with Human Immunodeficiency Virus (HIV) Infection

Category N: Not Symptomatic

Children who have no signs or symptoms considered to be the result of HIV infection or who have only one of the conditions listed in Category A.

Category A: Mildly Symptomatic

Children with two or more of the conditions listed below but none of the conditions listed in Categories B and C.

- Lymphadenopathy (≥0.5 cm at more than two sites; bilateral = one site)
- Hepatomegaly
- Splenomegaly
- Dermatitis
- Parotitis
- Recurrent or persistent upper respiratory infection, sinusitis, or otitis media

Category B: Moderately Symptomatic

Children who have symptomatic conditions other than those listed for Category A or C that are attributed to HIV infection. Examples of conditions in clinical Category B include but are not limited to:

- Anemia (<8 gm/dL), neutropenia (<1,000/mm^3), or thrombocytopenia (<100,000/mm^3) persisting ≥30 days
- Bacterial meningitis, pneumonia, or sepsis (single episode)
- Candidiasis, oropharyngeal (thrush), persisting (>2 months) in children >6 months of age
- Cardiomyopathy
- Cytomegalovirus infection, with onset before 1 month of age
- Diarrhea, recurrent or chronic
- Hepatitis
- Herpes simplex virus (HSV) stomatitis, recurrent (more than two episodes within 1 year)
- HSV bronchitis, pneumonitis, or esophagitis with onset before 1 month of age
- Herpes zoster (shingles) involving at least two distinct episodes or more than one dermatome
- Leiomyosarcoma
- Lymphoid interstitial pneumonia (LIP) or pulmonary lymphoid hyperplasia complex
- Nephropathy
- Nocardiosis
- Persistent fever (lasting >1 month)
- Toxoplasmosis, onset before 1 month of age
- Varicella, disseminated (complicated chickenpox)

Category C: Severely Symptomatic*

Children who have any condition listed in the 1987 surveillance case definition for acquired immunodeficiency syndrome (10), with the exception of LIP.

- Serious bacterial infections, multiple or recurrent (i.e., any combination of at least two culture-confirmed infections within a 2-year period), of the following types: septicemia, pneumonia, meningitis, bone or joint infection, or abscess of an internal organ or body cavity (excluding otitis media, superficial skin or mucosal abscesses, and indwelling catheter-related infections)
- Candidiasis, esophageal or pulmonary (bronchi, trachea, lungs)
- Coccidioidomycosis, disseminated (at site other than or in addition to lungs or cervical or hilar lymph nodes)
- Cryptococcosis, extrapulmonary
- Cryptosporidiosis or isosporiasis with diarrhea persisting >1 month
- Cytomegalovirus disease with onset of symptoms at age >1 month (at a site other than liver, spleen, or lymph nodes)
- Encephalopathy (at least one of the following progressive findings present for at least 2 months in the absence of a concurrent illness other than HIV infection that could explain the findings): a) failure to attain or loss of developmental milestones or loss of intellectual ability, verified by standard developmental scale or neuropsychological tests; b) impaired brain growth or acquired microcephaly demonstrated by head circumference measurements or brain atrophy demonstrated by computerized tomography or magnetic resonance imaging (serial imaging is required for children <2 years of age); c) acquired symmetric motor deficit manifested by two or more of the following: paresis, pathologic reflexes, ataxia, or gait disturbance
- Herpes simplex virus infection causing a mucocutaneous ulcer that persists for >1 month; or bronchitis, pneumonitis, or esophagitis for any duration affecting a child >1 month of age
- Histoplasmosis, disseminated (at a site other than or in addition to lungs or cervical or hilar lymph nodes)
- Kaposi's sarcoma
- Lymphoma, primary, in brain
- Lymphoma, small, noncleaved cell (Burkitt's), or immunoblastic or large cell lymphoma of B-cell or unknown immunologic phenotype
- *Mycobacterium tuberculosis*, disseminated or extrapulmonary

---

*See the 1987 AIDS surveillance case definition (10) for diagnosis criteria.

BOX 26-4 *Continued*

Clinical Categories for Children with Human Immunodeficiency Virus (HIV) Infection

- *Mycobacterium,* other species or unidentified species, disseminated (at a site other than or in addition to lungs, skin, or cervical or hilar lymph nodes)
- *Mycobacterium avium* complex or *Mycobacterium kanasii,* disseminated (at site other than or in addition to lungs, skin, or cervical or hilar lymph nodes)
- *Pneumocystis carinii* pneumonia
- Progressive multifocal leukoencephalopathy
- Salmonella (nontyphoid) septicemia, recurrent
- Toxoplasmosis of the brain with onset at >1 month of age

- Wasting syndrome in the absence of a concurrent illness other than HIV infection that could explain the following findings: a) persistent weight loss >10% of baseline OR b) downward crossing of at least two of the following percentile lines on the weight-for-age chart (e.g., 95th, 75th, 50th, 25th, 5th) in a child ≥1 year of age OR c) <5th percentile on weight-for-height chart on two consecutive measurments, ≥30 days apart *PLUS* a) chronic diarrhea (i.e., at least two loose stools per day for ≥30 days) OR b) documented fever (for ≥30 days, intermittent or constant)

SOURCE: From the *Morbidity and Mortality Weekly Report, September 30, 1994,* Vol. 43, No. RR-12. Copyright © 1994 U.S. Department of Health and Human Services, Centers for Disease Control and Prevention.

---

syndrome, in which there is a progressive weight loss. A nutritional program should be in place that helps the student.

If the student is left with physical or sensory disabilities from an infection, teachers will need to incorporate proper adaptations to allow the student to succeed in the classroom. A team approach will be needed to assess the student's needs and find ways to meet those needs.

Meeting Communication Needs, Learning Needs, and Daily Living Needs

Students with chronic infections should be given as accurate information about their illness as is appropriate to their age and cognitive level. This includes information about transmission, course, treatment, and prognosis. Information should be conveyed by the parents or physician in understandable terms and in a supportive manner. Part of the information should include what the student can do to prevent the spread of infection to others and to keep from acquiring another's infection. The teacher should routinely instruct all students on proper infection control procedures and self-help skills such as hand washing, using Band Aids, and covering the mouth when sneezing and coughing. Certain education classes should discuss preventative measures such using condoms and avoiding drugs.

Students who congenitally acquire the HIV infection are at-risk of developing neurological complications, including developmental delays and mental retardation (Diamond, 1989). It is important that these children be closely monitored for the development of any cognitive problems. Infants and children should be screened at 3- to 6-month intervals for cognitive, motor, and language function (Meyers & Weitzman, 1991). Students who are found to have developmental delays or problems in cognitive, motor, or language function will need to have a full assessment. A team approach is crucial in identifying and implementing proper programming and services to meet the individual needs of the student. Providing appropriate emotional support is also crucial when a student is undergoing a change in program due to a decrease in abilities.

Meeting Behavioral and Social Needs

Students with chronic health impairments such as a chronic infection are one and one-half to three times more likely to have behavioral and educational difficulties than their healthy peers (Cadman, Boyle, Szatmari, & Offord, 1987; Gortmaker, Walker, Weitzman, & Sobol, 1990; Haggerty, Roghmann, & Pless, 1975; Meyers & Weitzman, 1991). Students with chronic illnesses may have such behavior problems as depression, anxiety, and impaired self-images. These behaviors may negatively affect school performance. These problems arise not only from the student's perception of his or her illness but also from the reactions of teachers, staff, peers, family members, and people in the community (Meyers & Weitzman, 1991).

It is imperative that students receive the emotional support they need. The type of infection and the student's perception of the infection will determine the type of intervention needed. Students who are chronic carriers of Hepatitis B, for example, usually have very different concerns from students with the HIV infection. Students with the HIV infection are coping with a degenerative disease that typically results in death,

Mark, a 10-year-old boy with AIDS, has been receiving his education in a regular fifth-grade class with the other students. He is well-liked by his peers and enjoys sports. The teachers have received much information on AIDS and are supportive. They practice infection control procedures in class and try to minimize Mark's exposure to infections by sending sick students home, as outlined in their school policy. Mark is presently recovering from encephalitis and is being assessed for special education services due to resulting neurological damage.

about transmission and about the infection generally. Many teachers, for example, do not realize that the student with AIDS is at-risk of acquiring infections from the school environment that can have dire consequences and that infection control procedures are important in protecting the student with AIDS.

SUMMARY

There are many different types of infections, most of which do not pose a significant risk to the health and safety of the individual. However, some infections can result in disability and death; among these are meningitis, encephalitis, hepatitis, and HIV infection. Each of these has different forms of transmission, different characteristics, and different long-term implications. Students with the HIV infection, for example, have a terminal, degenerative infection that can affect cognition and behavior. Teachers need to provide proper educational and emotional support so the student can perform as well as possible in the school environment.

although there is always hope that an effective treatment will be found. Students with HIV infection may need someone to talk to about issues surrounding the infection as well as about death and dying. Teachers should make themselves available as nonjudgmental, supportive listeners. (See Chapter 9.) As always, teachers should maintain strict confidentiality.

Individuals with infections, especially the HIV infection, are surrounded with social stigma and hysteria. Although some studies have found special and regular educators willing to teach students with AIDS and not be biased toward educational placement, a need for more training and information about HIV and AIDS was also found (Evans, Melville, & Cass, 1992; Walker & Hulecki, 1989). Many misconceptions still exist

Teachers also need to have a good understanding of how infection is transmitted and how to provide proper infection control. Infections require three factors in order to be transmitted to another individual: (1) a means of escape from an infected host, (2) a means of transmission, and (3) a means of entry. In order to prevent the transmission of infection, the teacher needs to know such procedures as proper hand washing, disposal of wastes, use of gloves, and proper cleaning and disinfecting of environmental surfaces.

PART VIII

Meeting Educational Needs

CHAPTER 27

Multiple Disabilities

The term *multiple disabilities* refers to a combination of two or more disabilities, such as a combination of cerebral palsy and hearing impairments or a combination of severe spastic cerebral palsy, tonic-clonic seizures, mental retardation, ventricular septal defect, and low vision. Students with multiple disabilities present unique challenges to the educator due to the combination of their impairments. When teaching students with multiple disabilities, unique characteristics may be present that require dynamic interventions. Transdisciplinary team approaches become especially crucial in multiple disabilities in order to provide optimal intervention.

In this two-part chapter, we will describe the characteristics of students with multiple impairments, including the unique needs that arise when there is a combination of impairments. In the second part, we will provide an overview of general educational considerations that must be taken into account when educating students with multiple and severe disabilities. This second section will familiarize the teacher with certain key aspects of such areas as lifting and handling, assistive devices, and physical health care procedures.

DESCRIPTION OF MULTIPLE DISABILITIES

There is no single definition of the term *multiple disabilities,* nor are there common characteristics of individuals in this category. The term refers to the presence of two or more disabilities that significantly affect a person's ability to learn and function without the use of supportive adaptations. The disabilities combining to form a multiple disability usually create an interactional, multiplicative effect rather than a simple additive one (Hart, 1988). For example, an individual with multiple impairments who is deaf-blind would have many problems to overcome in several areas (such as communication, concept development, and mobility), which would present differently if the person had only one sensory impairment.

The term *multiple disabilities* does not include a major disability with minor impairments (Hart, 1988) nor a major disability with secondary conditions as part of the definition. For example, an individual with severe spastic cerebral palsy and a small ventricular defect would be categorized as having a primary impairment of cerebral palsy because this is the major disability causing functional impairment; the small ventricular defect is minor in comparison. A secondary disability is one that is causally related to a primary disability. By definition, the secondary condition would not be present without the primary condition (Pope, 1992). For example, cerebral palsy and scoliosis do not constitute a multiple disability since scoliosis is caused by the cerebral palsy. The person would be considered to have cerebral palsy with secondary impairments.

To illustrate which combinations of conditions may constitute a multiple disability, Box 27-1 contains various childhood conditions divided into six categories, including physical impairments, health impairments, sensory impairments, communication, cognitive impairments, and psychosocial (behavior/psychiatric) disorders.

The physical category typically contains disorders that affect the individual's ability to move. This includes neuromotor impairments such as cerebral palsy, muscular-skeletal impairments such as limb deficiency, and degenerative diseases such as muscular dystrophy. The second category is health impairments, in which chronic illness and conditions requiring health care procedures are found. Typically, chronic illnesses are conditions that change and can be life-threatening or life-limiting and that continue for a long period of time. These include such diseases and disorders as asthma,

351

BOX 27-1

Examples of Childhood Conditions

I. Physical impairments
 A. Neuromotor impairments (not including seizures)
 B. Muscular-skeletal impairments
 C. Degenerative diseases
II. Health impairments
 A. Chronic illness (including seizures)
 B. Physical health care needs
III. Sensory impairments
 A. Visual impairments
 B. Auditory impairments
 C. Other
IV. Communication disorders
 A. Language disorders
 B. Fluency disorders
V. Cognitive impairments
 A. Mental retardation
 B. Learning disabilities
VI. Psychosocial (behavior/psychiatric) disorders
 A. Behavior disorders
 B. Psychiatric disorders
  1. Childhood schizophrenia
  2. Neurosis and delusional disorders
  3. Other

cystic fibrosis, heart disorders, blood disorders, diabetes, kidney disorders, and AIDS. Students having such health care devices as a tracheostomy or colostomy or students requiring such procedures as sectioning, catheterization, tube feeding, ventilator care, or seizure control would be included in this category.

The third category, sensory impairments, refers to any significant disorder of the sensory system. This category typically includes visual impairments and hearing impairments, although tactile impairments may be included as well. The fourth category of communication disorders includes conditions such as language disorders (delayed language and **aphasia**) and speech disorders (articulation, stuttering, and voice).

The fifth category of cognitive impairments refers to impairments affecting learning and processing. In this category are such conditions as mental retardation and learning disabilities. The sixth category of psychosocial disorders includes an array of disorders dealing with behavior and psychiatric disorders.

The term *multiple disabilities* typically refers to two or more major disabilities. Categories from which multiple disabilities are traditionally drawn are among all the categories except health. Individuals may have two

or more disabilities across these categories, such as cerebral palsy and blindness or within one category, such as deaf-blindness. Although the health impairments category may significantly affect the student's life, these impairments have not traditionally been included in the designation multiple disabilities because their effects on learning and functioning are not typically as intrusive. For individuals with a physical impairment and a health impairment, for example, the health impairment is seldom considered the major impairment. Also, the combined effects of the two types of disabilities are usually additive rather than interactional as with multiple disabilities. However, when the health impairment is severe, it may be included as part of a multiple disability.

There are few statistics regarding the number of students with multiple disabilities. State departments of education do not usually differentiate more severe impairments from milder forms and most do not have a category of multiple disabilities. Students who are multiply disabled are typically categorized by making a judgment about which disability is more predominant. Students with multiple disabilities are then categorized under a single disability type. An exception is deaf-blindness, which is classified as a distinct area.

ETIOLOGY OF MULTIPLE DISABILITIES

Multiple disabilities have numerous etiologies and may be caused by prenatal, perinatal, or postnatal factors. Prenatal problems that can result in multiple disabilities include congenital infections, congenital abnormalities and neural tube defects, hypoxia, chromosomal and genetic defects, and parental alcohol and drug abuse. As we discussed in Chapter 25, the STORCH infections can cause several concurrent disabilities such as mental retardation, cerebral palsy, seizures, blindness, deafness, and heart defects. Congenital abnormalities and neural tube defects may result in limb deficiencies, spina bifida, anencephaly, and other structural abnormalities. These could occur in combination, which would result in multiple disabilities. A lack of oxygen to the brain (hypoxia) may result in damage to the brain and other organs. This can result in concurrent cerebral palsy, blindness, and other impairments.

Chromosomal and genetic defects may result in several different diseases and syndromes, which may result in a multiple disability. Genetic diseases such as muscular dystrophy and spinal muscular atrophy may exist in combination with other disorders, such as visual impairments, resulting in multiple disabilities. Other genetic defects may result in syndromes that have a cluster of impairments, such as Hurler's syndrome (Heller & Kennedy, 1994).

Parental use of alcohol and drugs, as well as malnutrition, may result in a child's having multiple disabilities. Fetal alcohol syndrome, for example, results from the ingestion of alcohol during pregnancy. Although the primary disability is usually mental retardation with minor structural defects such as facial abnormalities, multiple impairments such as mental retardation and behavior disorder may occur. Certain drugs taken by the mother during pregnancy have produced birth defects. Some of these include limb reduction malformations, poor perceptual and organizational skills, and social maladjustment.

Problems may occur during the perinatal period (the time shortly before, during, or after birth) and the postnatal period that can result in multiple disabilities. Problems during the perinatal period include intracranial hemorrhage, trauma, hypoxia, and infection. These may result in damage to the nervous system, which may result in neuromotor and neurocognitive impairments. Infants born prematurely and small for gestational age are also more likely to have multiple disabilities than full-term infants (Batshaw & Perret, 1992).

Postnatal problems that may result in multiple disabilities include trauma, tumors, drowning, poisoning, and infections. Psychiatric or behavioral conditions such as schizophrenia and behavior disorders may also occur during this time and be present with other disabilities.

DYNAMICS AND CHARACTERISTICS OF MULTIPLE DISABILITIES

Combinations of different disabilities from the six categories typically result in the designation multiple disabilities. Examples are cerebral palsy and blind, mental retardation and deaf, and deaf-blind. Several possible combinations may occur. Examples of multiple disabilities involving two disability areas are illustrated in Table 27-1. In some cases, there may be more than two combinations, such as children with the combined disabilities of cerebral palsy (physical), low vision (sensory), language impairments (although in this case communication deficits are related to the cerebral palsy), mental retardation (cognitive), and seizures (health impairments).

As we said, several different combinations are possible in the area of multiple disabilities. Often the combined impairments result in unique characteristics and educational challenges that would not be present in singular, severe impairments. To provide a better understanding of the effect of multiple impairments, we will briefly describe three of the categories: physical and sensory, cognitive and physical, and deaf-blind.

Physical and Sensory

Although there are several types of multiple disabilities with both physical and sensory impairment, there are some common characteristics among them. Students with physical and sensory impairments may have more difficulty accessing information, materials, and environments than would those with a single impairment.

The majority of information is learned through the use of distance senses (vision and hearing). When either one of these is impaired, learning may be affected. Individuals with physical disabilities may also have deficits in learning because they lack experiences. Limited mobility and a lack of tactile information may be responsible. When a person has a visual and physical impairment, information may be missed, or there may be difficulty in verifying the visual information if mobility or hand use is affected. When there is a hearing and physical impairment, auditory information may be missed or misinterpreted. The person may have difficulty verifying information, especially if communication is affected, as in such conditions as cerebral palsy. Accessing material, whether it is presented visually, auditorially, or physically, may pose problems, depending on the types of multiple impairments. This can affect performance of academic and daily living tasks due to the combined sensory and physical impairment. Moving from one environment to another may also pose challenges. Physical and sensory impairments may be combined with mental retardation, which could result in impaired learning of educational and daily living tasks.

Cognitive and Physical

Several types of multiple disabilities combine a cognitive and a physical impairment. Mental retardation is a common cognitive impairment present in many students with multiple disabilities. The mental retardation will affect learning in general, but the combined physical impairment will typically result in a lack of experiences and difficulty in accessing material. These students may take longer to learn specific tasks, and they may need unique adaptations.

Teachers will often need to devise unique adaptations for students with physical and cognitive impairments that will provide access to material and enhance learning. For example, switches may be used for students with severe physical impairments, but due to a cognitive impairment, additional instructional strategies may be

TABLE 27-1

Examples of Multiple Disabilities

	Physical	Health impairment	Sensory	Communication	Cognitive	Psychosocial
Physical	Cerebral palsy and spina bifida	Cerebral palsy and seizures	Cerebral palsy and low vision	Spinal cord injury and fluency	Cerebral palsy and mental retardation	Cerebral palsy and behavior disorder
Health impairment	Seizures and cerebral palsy	Seizures and asthma	Seizures and blindness	Seizures and fluency	Seizures and mental retardation	Seizures and behavior disorder
Sensory	Traumatic brain injury and blindness	Blindness and diabetes	Deaf-blind	Blind and apraxia	Visual impairment and learning disability	Visual impairment and behavior disorder
Communication	Apraxia and cerebral palsy	Apraxia and diabetes	Speech and deafness	Voice and apraxia	Language and mental retardation	Fluency and behavior disorder
Cognitive	Mental retardation and spina bifida	Mental retardation and seizures	Mental retardation and deafness	Mental retardation and language	Mental retardation and autism	Mental retardation and mental illness
Psychosocial	Behavior disorder and muscular dystrophy	Behavior disorder and asthma	Behavior disorder and deafness	Behavior disorder and fluency	Behavior disorder and mental retardation	Behavior disorder and drug addiction

used. Some may involve the use of antecedent or response prompts; for example, a switch might have a colored circle on it to draw the student's attention to the part of the switch to press. Partial physical guidance may be used in a time-delay strategy to teach the student how to access the switch (Snell & Brown, 1993).

Students with both mental retardation and a physical impairment such as myelomeningocele will also need to learn unique skills such as self-catheterization. Due to the mental retardation, the steps involved in the catheterization will typically need to be broken down into very small steps (that is, task analysis) with the use of systematic instructional strategies (for example, a system of least prompts) to assist the student in learning the task.

Deaf-Blind

The term *deaf-blind* refers to a combination of hearing and visual loss in which the combined impairment affects the individual more than either condition would singly. Children with deaf-blindness range in the severity of their vision and hearing loss. For example, children who are deaf-blind may be blind with a mild hearing loss, or deaf with low vision, or be profoundly deaf and have light perception only. However the combination of deaf-blindness occurs, its impact can be so severe that, without proper educational intervention, learning and performing daily activities can be severely affected. Because of the severity of this impairment, it is usually classified as a unique and distinct category in educational settings.

Because most information is learned through the distance senses of vision and hearing, the impairment in both areas can severely affect the person's functioning in several areas and require specialized instructional strategies. Some affected areas include communication, orientation and mobility, concept development, social behaviors, functional skills, and academic skills. Individuals with deaf-blindness typically have communication and language deficits that result in the need for specific training and development of communication systems (Mathy-Laikko, Iacono, Ratcliff, Villarruel, & Yoder, 1989; Rowland & Stremel-Campbell, 1987; Siegel-Causey & Downing, 1987). As we discussed earlier, a number of types of communication systems may be used with individuals with deaf-blindness. The type (or types) will depend on each student's needs and abilities.

Due to the vision loss, children with deaf-blindness often have difficulty in the areas of orientation and mobility, which is complicated by lost or diminished auditory cues that often help students find items or move to different locations. Orientation skills refer particularly to the process of using the remaining senses to establish position and relationships to all other significant objects and persons in one's environment (Gee, Harrell, & Rosenberg, 1987; Hill & Ponder, 1976). Mobility skills refer to the ability to navigate safely from one's present position to another part of the environment (Gee, Harrell, & Rosenberg, 1987). One of the fundamental goals for children who are deaf-blind is to help them get in touch with their environment and to increase their involvement with it (Rikhye, Gothelf, & Appel, 1989).

The combined sensory impairments also result in difficulties in concept development and in learning functional and academic skills. Children without sensory impairments typically learn about the world around them incidentally through the use of vision and hearing. Children with deaf-blindness have both distance senses (vision and hearing) impaired, and hence, are not able to pick up many concepts incidentally. Children with deaf-blindness will often use any residual vision and hearing, along with the near senses such as touch and smell. These near senses are not nearly as efficient as the distance senses in providing a total picture. Children with deaf-blindness may have misconceptions or incomplete ideas when they have come into contact with only part of an item or concept—or they may have received no information about it at all. Some concepts that cannot be touched, such as mountains, clouds, and colors, can be more difficult for some students with deaf-blindness to learn.

DETECTION, TREATMENT, AND COURSE OF MULTIPLE DISABILITIES

The detection, treatment, and course of multiple disabilities will vary according to the impairments involved. Often, due to the multiplicity of the impairment, diagnosis will occur in infancy or soon after onset. Any number of diagnostics can be performed, typically including the physical examination, laboratory tests, X-rays, or some type of scan such as a CT scan or MRI.

The treatment will typically involve several visits to doctors and possibly hospitalization. Frequent absences occur due to the treatment regime. A higher incidence of absences may also occur due to increased illness or to the impairment itself.

Often, a team of professionals is needed to meet the needs of the student who has multiple disabilities. It is common for students to have physical therapy, occupational therapy, and speech therapy. In some cases, additional instruction may be needed from the teacher of orthopedic impairments, or visual impairments, or hearing impairments to assist with adaptations or specific skills in that discipline. Teaching braille or sign language are two examples. Orientation and mobility instructors may also provide services to the student, depending on the disability. Often, parents have numerous specialized physicians and nurses with whom they must interact for evaluations and treatment. Some parents have as many as 50 professionals serving their child over the course of a few years.

EDUCATIONAL IMPLICATIONS OF MULTIPLE DISABILITIES

When students have multiple disabilities, there are often several areas of knowledge that a teacher and the team members will need in order to best meet the students' needs. In the remainder of this chapter, we will provide a brief overview of some of these areas, highlighting aspects of particular importance to team members. Many of these areas pertain to singular disabilities as well as to multiple disabilities. To have competence in these areas, the team member will typically need training by an individual who is qualified in the specific area.

Meeting Physical and Sensory Needs

Several major physical and sensory needs should be taken into consideration by members of the educational team before planning for the student's educational needs. First, the team will need to be sure that proper positioning and mobility are planned for; this will enhance motor performance and hence, academic performance. Second, the proper placement of material is crucial so the student can access it physically and/or visually. Third, proper lifting and handling techniques are crucial for the safety of the student and the adults doing the lifting. Fourth, the team needs to be sure that the student's adapted equipment, such as a brace or orthosis, is being worn correctly, with no skin breakdown. Fifth, adaptations and the use of assistive technology are often needed to allow the student to access material and to be as independent as possible. In each area, members of the team who have expertise in a particular area will provide help and information. For example, the occupational therapist may take the lead in determining appropriate placement of materials and discussing the use of adapted devices with the rest of the team; the physical therapist may take the lead in positioning the student and teaching proper lifting and handling techniques.

Mobility and Positioning Needs

Students with multiple disabilities often have mobility and positioning needs. For some students, their main mode of mobility may be a wheelchair. There are many different types of wheelchairs. Some are manual wheel-

■ VIGNETTE ■

Shraga is a 7-year-old boy with severe spastic cerebral palsy, bilateral congenital cataracts, and mild mental retardation. He also has a gastrostomy tube for tube feedings. Due to his multiple impairments, he has had difficulty in such areas as concept formation, learning daily skills, and accessing materials. He has most of his instruction in a regular classroom but also sees an orthopedic-impaired teacher for specific parts of the day and has an itinerant visual-impaired teacher. His educational team has made several adaptations and identified several crucial skills for him to learn. For example, the visual-impaired teacher has modified materials he is working with to enhance contrast and is training him in the use of a magnifier. The occupational therapist has assessed the best placement of materials for physical access in conjunction with the vision-impaired teacher for visual access (and the orthopedic-impaired teacher and regular education teacher for input into the types of materials he needs). The physical therapist has determined the type of positioning equipment needed, and his educational team has determined when and how the equipment can best be used. The speech and language pathologist and the educational team have assessed the type of communication device and are teaching him its use throughout the day, including the use of a switch that allows Shraga to scan the selections. The nurse is teaching Shraga how to perform tube feedings on his own with support from the orthopedic-impaired teacher and occupational therapist as to the types of adaptations needed. The regular education teacher and orthopedic-impaired teacher coordinate instruction to provide a smooth transition between classes. All members of the team have learned proper lifting and handling techniques. The educational team works together to meet his multiple educational needs.

chairs, which require the student or someone else to push it; others are motorized (see Figure 27-1). Some wheelchairs may have the capability of going from a sitting position to a standing position (see Figure 27-2).

To help achieve best positioning, wheelchairs may be fitted with pads, cushions, and straps (see Figure 27-3). The goal is to have the student in midline position with the ankles bent at 90°, knees bent at 90°, and hips bent at 90°. Guidelines for proper positioning in a wheelchair and possible adaptations are provided in Box 27-2. It is important that adaptations (for example, pads and headrests) are carefully assessed and used only when indicated. Students who can use their neck muscles to

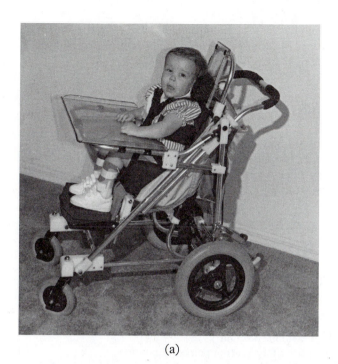

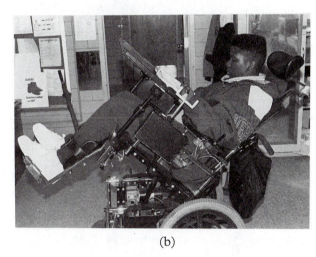

(a)

(b)

■ **FIGURE 27-1** Example of a manual wheelchair for a toddler (a) and an electric wheelchair that tilts back for comfort, positioning, and pressure relief (b)

support their heads, for example, could lose strength in their neck muscles if a headrest is used when it is not necessary. Also, when supports are placed incorrectly, such as a wheelchair tray placed too high, arm movement can be restricted.

Several other types of aids can assist with mobility, such as walkers, crutches, adapted bicycles, and scooter boards. Sometimes, toys may be used as mobility aids, such as hand-propelled carts. Motorized scooters may also be used (see Figure 27-4).

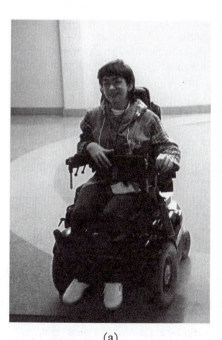

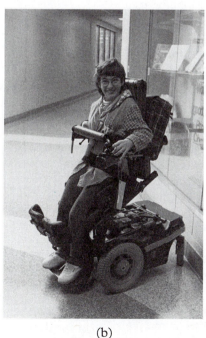

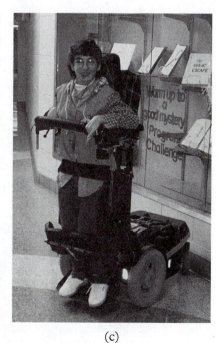

(a)

(b)

(c)

■ **FIGURE 27-2** Student with a motorized wheelchair that adjusts from a sitting position (a and b) to a standing position (c)

■ FIGURE 27-3 Student's wheelchair has shoulder straps to aid in correct positioning of student

Some students will need mobility training by an orientation and mobility instructor because of their visual impairment. Even when the child is in a wheelchair and has a visual impairment, techniques to assist the student in proper orientation should be used. For example, having the student feel landmarks while being wheeled or having the student trail the wall with his or her hand while being wheeled can help give the child an understanding of the surroundings. Mobility techniques for students with visual impairments can address the best ways to move about in a wheelchair. Special adaptations may be used, such as wheelchair bumpers, which decrease the possibility of injury to the foot if the student with a visual and physical impairment runs into a wall while in a wheelchair.

Other positioning devices may be used to promote movement, alignment, bone growth, or a combination of these. When positioning equipment is used correctly, it often provides alignment and stability of the trunk, which in turn promotes improved movement. Some positioning devices, such as wedges, may encourage head, arm, and trunk control; a sidelyer or roll can bring hands together (Orelove & Sobsey, 1991) (see Figure 27-5). Several positioning devices can be used to promote correct sitting, which in turn may promote arm movement. One example is a corner chair (see Figure 27-6). Some devices promote weight bearing, which improves bone growth. Example of these devices are the supine stander and the prone stander (see Figure 27-7). It is important to note that the student's positioning needs to be changed throughout the day. When there is a visual impairment, the student should be positioned to

enhance visual functioning. All of these positioning devices should be used during functional or academic activities and not as isolated events.

Placement of Material

After a student is in proper position, the optimal placement of the material needs to be determined. Due to a student's limited range of motion or limited vision, the placement of material becomes crucial if the student is to have access to it. Materials may need to be located to one side or another, or closer or farther away to

---

BOX 27-2

Guidelines for Positioning in a Wheelchair

HEAD AND NECK
Midline position
Face forward (not pointed up or down)
Adaptations: Headrest (maintain head alignment); head strap (to hold head back in headrest)

SHOULDERS AND ARMS
Shoulders in midline and neutral position (not hunched over)
Elbows flexed about 90°
Adaptations: Shoulder straps (to hold shoulders back); shoulder pommels (to hold shoulder back); wheelchair tray (to maintain alignment)

TRUNK
Midline position
Maintain normal curve of the spine
Adaptations: H-strap (to bring shoulders back and keep trunk up); scoliosis pads/side pads (to align trunk)

HIPS AND PELVIS
Midline position
Hips bent at 90°
Pelvis in back of the seat
Pelvis not tilted to one side
Adaptations: Seat belt across hips (to keep pelvis back of seat)

LEGS
Thighs slightly apart
Knees slightly apart
Knees bent at 90°
Feet directly below or slightly behind knees
Ankles bent 90° with feet on footrest
Feet facing forward
Ball and heel of foot flat on footrest
Adaptations: Adductor pads (to keep knees aligned when knees are too far out); abductor pads (to keep knees aligned when knees are too close together); footrest straps

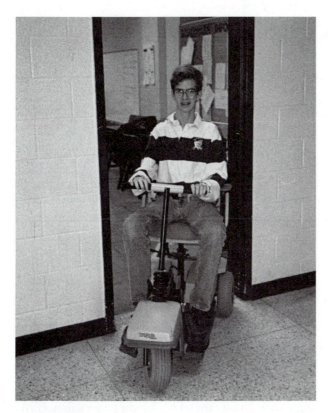
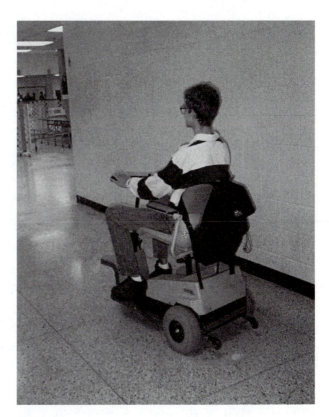

■ **FIGURE 27-4** Student using an electric scooter to get around

accommodate the student's range of motion. The team should work together to determine optimal physical placement of materials and how this varies depending on the positioning equipment being used. Students who have limited vision may need items to be closer, to be constructed of high-contrast material, or both. The vision teacher, in conjunction with the rest of the team, will determine optimal visual placement of material.

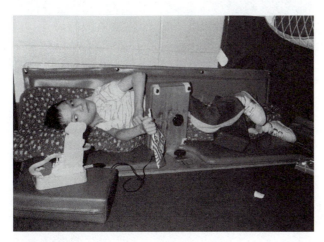

■ **FIGURE 27-5** Student squeezing a grasp switch to activate a toy while positioned in a sidelyer

Adaptations and Assistive Devices

Numerous adaptations and assistive devices may be used to help a child with multiple impairments accomplish specific activities, including work surface modifications, object modifications, and computer modifications.

In addition to assessing the best placement of materials, the work surface itself may need to be modified. Students in wheelchairs may need a cut-out table that a wheelchair can fit under so the work surface will be the proper height and in correct position. Work surfaces may need to be closer for students with low vision or students who are unable to reach down. Work surfaces may also need to be slanted to allow the student to reach the surface, or boundaries may be needed to prevent items from falling off the edge or moving out of reach. Boundaries can help students with visual impairments locate items. The boundary may be made of any material, including wood (molding, for example) or strips of Velcro. Adapted boxes may be used on the work surface to provide boundaries within which to search for material, such as in searching for a math manipulative.

Objects themselves may need to be modified to provide stabilization, improve grasping and manipulation, allow the student to use switches, or provide

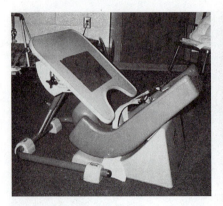
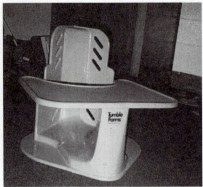

■ **FIGURE 27-6** Different types of adapted chairs that promote correct positioning for sitting

contrast (Corn, 1983; Schaeffler, 1988). Stabilization is important because students may have poor motor control and be unable to keep items steady. Objects may be stabilized in several different ways. They may be placed on dicem—a thin, plastic material that grips the object and prevents sliding. Also, masking tape, clamps, or Velcro can be used. Grasping and manipulation adaptations may be needed due to poor motor coordination and motor impairments. Often, building up the handle or shaft of the item will help, such as by wrapping clay around a pencil or spoon. Using adapted scissors that spring open may assist with cutting. Elongating items, such as by placing a dowel on a crayon, may allow the student to reach the paper to draw.

Switches may be used to activate items; that is, to turn on a favorite toy, turn on a tape recorder, or access a computer.

Switches are ideal for students who can make a voluntary motion with their bodies to access an item and thus gain control over their environment. A switch is a device that opens or closes an electrical circuit; it can be connected to an item such as a toy, tape player, or computer that turns on, off, or changes attributes in some way. The cursor on a computer screen may move, a toy may turn on, or the stations on a television set may change. The student activates the switch by some motor movement, such as pushing, pulling, grasping, blowing, moving toward, or by contracting a muscle (see Figure

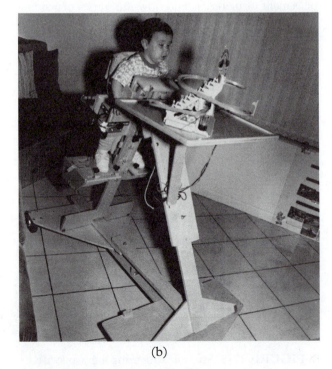

(a)   (b)

■ **FIGURE 27-7** Student using a supine stander (a); young child using a prone stander (b)

27-8). A switch may be constructed, including the part that fits between the batteries to access a battery-operated item, or may be purchased commercially.

As we discussed earlier, changing the size of items or using magnifiers or other optical devices to change the apparent size of an item may help some students with visual impairments. Also, the color and contrast of items and the lighting may need to be modified to make the best use of some students' visual functioning. (See Chapter 16.) When items have an auditory component, adaptations making use of the salient visual components should be made for students with hearing impairments.

Several modifications can be made to a computer to allow students to access it. Devices such as adapted keyboards, alternative keyboards, or devices to bypass the keyboard may be used. An adapted keyboard may include a finger guard to assist with isolated finger movements when typing or a protective guard with braille characters on it. Alternative keyboards can be of different sizes, which can make them easier to push and thus accommodate students' range of motion and

■ **FIGURE 27-9** Student using Intellikeys alternative keyboard to access computer with a large-screen monitor

■ **FIGURE 27-8** Teacher preparing switches to use with students *(pressure switch on left, wobble switch on right, and grasp switch in her hand)*

strength. Examples of these include the Unicorn Board and the Intellikeys board (see Figure 27-9). Devices to bypass the keyboard include using optical positing, switch use, speech recognition, an interface device (such as a communication device), or a combination of these (see Figure 27-10). Output devices may include a voice synthesizer so students can hear what is displayed on the screen or a braille embosser that prints out braille (Lewis, 1993).

Many other types of adaptations and devices may be used with students with multiple or severe physical impairments. Adaptations should be selected only when they are needed and faded out as quickly as possible when they are no longer needed. It is important to avoid overmechanizing a student. (See Chapter 28.)

Lifting and Handling

Some students will need partial or complete assistance in moving from one area to another. School personnel who are lifting students should have a good foundation in the basic principles of lifting and handling. The nurse and physical therapist are good resources for learning proper techniques. Some general principles of lifting are included in Box 27-3.

The person lifting should see whether more than one person is needed to lift the student. If that is so, help should be requested. Trying to lift the student alone when more than one person is needed will increase the risk of back injury and of dropping the student. Also, the student's arms or legs should never be used as handles because this increases the possibility of injury. When lifting a child, the lifter must provide a broad base

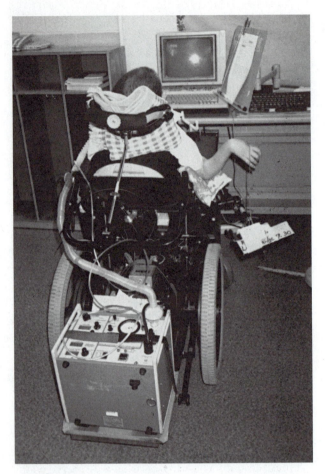

■ **FIGURE 27-10** Student using a pull switch with his right hand to activate the computer. He also is using a ventilator, which is mounted to the back of his wheelchair.

of support, with one foot ahead of another and the feet slightly apart. The person lifting should never bend down at the waist to pick up a child but should squat or kneel with their back kept as straight as possible. The large muscles of the arms and legs should be used to lift, not the small back muscles (Bigge, 1991). When carrying a child, the child should be held close to the person who is lifting rather than out in front. This maintains proper balance and decreases back strain. Finally, a person should never twist his or her back when moving a child. One's feet should always face in the same direction as the front of one's body. For example, when helping a child move from a wheelchair to a chair or toilet, adults often hold the child and turn without moving their feet in the same direction. This can result in back injury.

Several types of lifts may be used to move a student from one location to another. A one-person lift involves lifting a student by oneself, as explained in Box 27-4.

Adults typically injure their backs performing this lift if they (1) do not bring the child into sitting position before lifting them, (2) do not use proper body mechanics, or (3) carry the child far from their body. It is important that the student help keep himself or herself upright while being carried if this is possible. Carrying a child who has high (muscle) tone or low tone is different. The physical therapist can demonstrate the difference in proper carrying.

There are two basic types of two-person lifts: a side-to-side lift and a top-bottom lift. In a side-to-side lift, two adults stand on either side of the student. One adult places one arm under the child's arm and around his or her back and the other arm goes under one thigh (see Figure 27-11). The second person is in the same position on the other side. It is important that the arms and legs not be used as handles. The top-bottom lift involves having the tallest person behind the child, with the adult's arms going under the child's arms and holding the forearms crossed over the child's chest; the second person holds the legs. The person behind the child should not hold the child under the armpits because this can be injurious. The physical therapist will determine the best type of lift and provide demonstrations of these techniques (Finnie, 1974; Ossman, 1990).

Proper lifting technique is not only important for teachers who are lifting students, but for students who

---

BOX 27-3

General Principles of Good Body Mechanics

1. Have the child bear as much weight as possible and assist as much as possible or as much as is medically allowed.
2. Assess the child's weight to determine how many people are needed to lift.
3. Provide a broad base of support, with one foot ahead of another and the feet slightly apart.
4. Never bend at the waist to pick up a child, but squat or kneel with the back kept as straight as possible.
5. When placing a child in a wheelchair, do not bend at the back, but bend legs and keep back straight.
6. Use the large muscles of the arms and legs to lift instead of the small back muscles.
7. When carrying a child, hold the child close rather than out in front to maintain proper balance and decrease strain to the back.
8. Never twist your back when holding a child by having your feet pointed in a different direction from your arms.
9. Never use student's arms or legs as handles.

BOX 27-4

One- and Two-Person Lifts

ONE-PERSON LIFT FROM FLOOR
1. Bring wheelchair close to child and lock brakes.
2. Kneel on one leg next to child.
3. Bring child into a sitting position.
4. Place one arm under child's thigh and other arm around child's back.
5. Lift child up close to you.
6. Come to a standing position.
7. Slowly carry child to wheelchair and lower child into chair. Keep your legs bent and your back straight.
8. Properly position child in chair and put on seat belt and other positioning equipment.

TWO-PERSON LIFT FROM FLOOR
1. Bring wheelchair close to child and lock brakes.
2. A. Side-to-side method:
     a. Two adults kneel on either side of child.
     b. Bring child into a sitting position.
     c. One person brings one arm under thigh and other arm around back. Second person does the same on opposite side.
   B. Top-bottom method:
     a. One adult kneels at top of child and other kneels at side where child's legs are located.
     b. Bring child into sitting position.
     c. Top person brings arms under child's arms and around to front, holding child's crossed arms.
     d. Bottom person holds both of child's thighs.
3. One person says, "Lift on three. One . . . two . . . three."
4. Lift child straight up, keeping child next to body.
5. Together, the adults carry the child to the wheelchair.
6. Slowly lower the child into the wheelchair until he or she is on the seat
7. Place child in proper position and put on seat belt and other positioning equipment.

---

are lifting items during community-based vocational instruction. Students can easily injure themselves if they have not been taught proper techniques. Some students with physical impairments, such as severe scoliosis, may be unable to lift items from the floor; other students may be unable to lift items of medium weight. The teacher should have information about any restrictions to lifting that a student may have.

Checking Braces or Orthoses

During the school day, braces and orthoses may need to be removed and reapplied by the teacher. Proper appli-

cation of the device should be demonstrated by a therapist to ensure proper placement of the brace or orthosis. The teacher must be alert for any reddened areas that could indicate the beginning of skin breakdown. If a reddened area is present, the brace or orthosis may need to be removed and the physical therapist or nurse contacted.

Meeting Communication Needs

Students with multiple impairments may have difficulty communicating. Often, the student's attempts at communication are not understandable, such as when the student has severe spastic cerebral palsy. Due to additional cognitive factors, the student may use non-symbolic forms of communication. Behaviors such as screaming when seeing a wanted item or handing the teacher an empty cup meaning more is wanted are

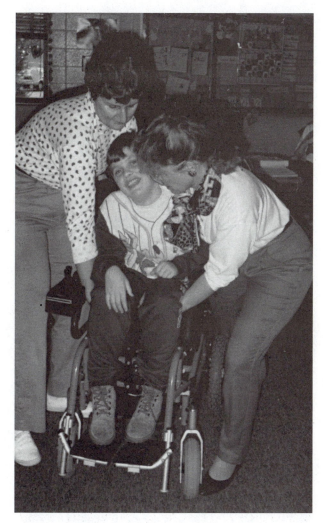

■ **FIGURE 27-11** A two-person lift using the side-to-side method

■ **FIGURE 27-12** Student with spastic cerebral palsy using her communication device

examples. The educational team will determine the appropriate form of communication and teach the student the use of augmentative or alternative forms of communication. Because communication occurs throughout the day, the teacher must provide communication opportunities throughout the day in functional or academic activities. This will allow the student to learn the effective use of a communication system.

Several forms of communication may be taught to students with multiple impairments. These systems can

be divided into those that are unaided and those that are aided (Lloyd, 1985). Unaided forms of communication refer to those in which the individual uses hand or body movements to communicate. Major types of unaided forms include movements, facial expressions, vocalizations, speech, gestures, and sign language. Sign language includes tactile signing; that is, signing with the student's hands over the communication partner's hands. The student who is deaf-blind can thus feel the sign. One major advantage of unaided systems is their portability; a major disadvantage is that they may not be understandable to communication partners who are unfamiliar with the system.

Aided forms of communication refer to those that require some type of device to communicate. Major types of communication systems include objects, pictures, drawings, and/or symbols. These forms of communication may be made larger, with highly contrasting colors, or tactual for students with visual impairments or deaf-blindness. Aided forms of communication may be presented singly or may be arranged on a nonelectronic or electronic communication device (see Figure 27-12). One major advantage of aided forms of communication is that they are easily understandable because they are labeled in print, or they have voice output. One major disadvantage is potential problems with portability across multiple environments and positions.

Due to the different environments that students are in, a combination of an aided and unaided system may be used. For example, deaf-blind students who have sign language as their major form of communication may also learn to use communication boards in the community so they can communicate with others (Heller, Ware, Allgood, & Castelle, 1994). (See Figure 27-13.) Careful selection of the type of system will need to be made by

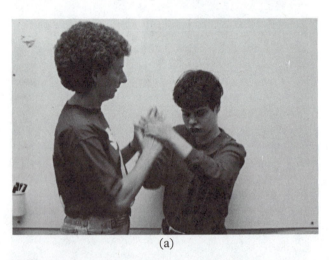

(a)

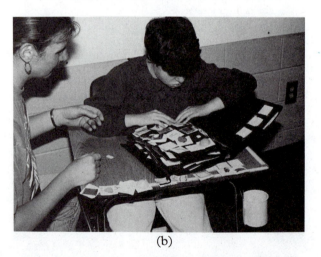

(b)

■ **FIGURE 27-13** A classroom intervener interprets spoken words into tactile signing to student with deaf-blindness (a), and the student communicates back by signing or using miniature objects in communication book (b).

MONTHLY MEDICATION REPORT

Student's Name: _____   Month: _____

Directions: Write in the medications/procedures, date and time for each week. Upon giving medication/procedure put time and initials under the current day of the week.

Medication and Procedure	Date	Time(s)	M	T	W	Th	F

Comments: _____

Medication and Procedure	Date	Time(s)	M	T	W	Th	F

Comments: _____

Medication and Procedure	Date	Time(s)	M	T	W	Th	F

Comments: _____

Medication and Procedure	Date	Time(s)	M	T	W	Th	F

Comments: _____

■ **FIGURE 27-14** Sample monthly medication report

(Continued)

Medication and Procedure	Date	Time(s)	M	T	W	Th	F

Comments:

■ **FIGURE 27-14** *(Continued)*

the team. In some instances, such as with students who are deaf-blind, both receptive and expressive forms of communication will need to be selected and taught systematically. Other major considerations for the use of augmentative communication will include means of accessing the communication system—pointing, eye-gazing, touching, scanning, or encoding—and vocabulary selection.

Meeting Learning Needs

Depending on the student's impairment, environmental variables, and psychological factors, there may be a significant impact on learning. Learning may be affected by such factors as severity of the impairment, fatigue, discomfort, absences, or self-concept. (See Chapter 3.)

When a student with a multiple impairment also has mental retardation, the teacher will need to use systematic instructional strategies (for example, prompting strategies). Curriculum will often include or focus on functional skills that will help the student in his or her home, work, community, and school environments. The team will need to coordinate instruction closely within functional contexts.

Meeting Daily Living Needs

Medications and Physical Health Care Procedures

Students with multiple impairments often require medication, physical health care procedures, or both, during school hours. These activities may be administered or performed by the teacher, nurse, or other trained, qualified individual. Whoever is the designated individual, it is important that the student's teachers have a good understanding of the implications of each procedure, including what to do when something goes wrong.

Many students with multiple impairments will be taking medications such as antiseizure medication or muscle relaxants. The teacher should know what type of medication is being taken and understand its side effects. The teacher will then be able to identify potential problems and notify the family, nurse, or physician. The person who is primarily responsible for giving the medication should also be familiar with its proper storage and administration. Medications should always be checked for color, consistency, and expiration date. Some medications need to be taken with food and are taken orally; others may be given topically (on the skin), through inhalation, rectally, or by injection. Medication must be administered properly. Some medication, for example, is time-released and should never be crushed for ease of administration. This would mean that the student gets medication that should have been released slowly into the system in a matter of minutes. Individuals who give medications should check carefully to see that the right medication is given to the right student. Using a medication/physical health care checklist like the one in Figure 27-14, will reduce the risk of missing a medication or giving it twice. The chart also provides documentation of administration. Having consent forms for medication use, as well as for physical health care procedures, should also be used routinely to ensure proper dosage of medication and correct administration.

Students with multiple impairments may also require several different types of physical health care procedures. When possible, these should be performed at home. However, some procedures must be performed at school, including tube feedings, clean intermittent catheterization, colostomy and ostomy care, and respiratory suctioning. The person who performs these procedures must have had extensive training in the rationale for the procedure, basic knowledge of the goals and implications of the procedure, step-by-step knowledge of how

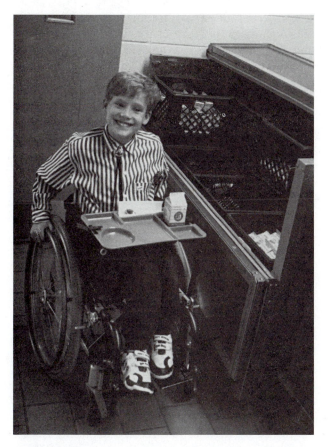

■ FIGURE 27-15 Student going through cafeteria line with an adapted lunch tray that attaches to his wheelchair with Velcro

to implement the procedure, side effects of the procedure, and specific problems that may arise. The person must know how to recognize and manage these problems and must also know how to alert others to possible problems with the procedure. Without this training, simple rules (like never to give a tube feeding to the student flat on his or her back) may be easily missed. An emergency situation such as vomiting and aspiration or a severe illness such as pneumonia could result. Training updates are needed to keep current and to verify that performance of the procedures is correct. Documentation of training and updates should be on file, and the physician and parent should be clear about who is performing the procedures. Signed permissions should be in place. Documentation of the procedure itself should also be done, just as for medications.

Eating and Self-Care Skills

Due to the severity of the physical or sensory involvement, some students will need instruction and support in the basic skills of eating and self-care. The goal is for the student to be as independent as possible in these areas. For some students, this may mean total independence; others may partially participate.

Students with physical impairments may need assistive devices or someone to help them eat. Some students may be able to eat independently but may need adaptations to allow them to go through the cafeteria line (see Figure 27-15). During meals, some students may be able to manipulate a spoon if it is bent to the side or has a built-up handle or a handle covered with Velcro. Feeding devices that use switches are available; they scoop the food and rotate the plate in order to help the

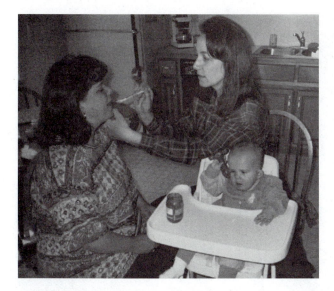

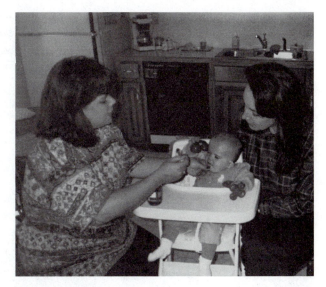

■ FIGURE 27-16 A physical therapist teaches a parent to use jaw support with her child, who has a physical disability.

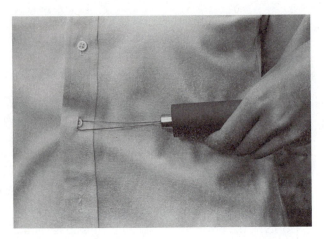

■ **FIGURE 27-17** Button aid

with physical impairments (see Figure 27-19). In all instances, the educational team will need to determine which modifications and devices will help the student and when using a person to provide support is necessary.

Students with severe visual impairment or deaf-blindness may need assistance in learning how to locate food and how to get the food onto the utensil when eating. Describing the location of food in a clock fashion, such as locating green beans at 2 o'clock, and using bread to push food onto a utensil are two techniques that may be used. In the area of self-care, having consistent locations for items is important; organizing things such as the toothpaste and being sure things are put back in the same position can make them easier to find next time they are needed. Labeling clothes and other adaptations is important to increasing independence.

Environmental Control

Due to the severity of their physical impairment, some students will have difficulty accessing such devices as light switches, radio or television controls, or microwave oven controls. An environmental control device is any device that allows access by another means (Bigge, 1991; Lewis, 1993). These can be simple devices that use mechanical switches to turn a toy on and off, to a more sophisticated device that uses electronics signals controlled by switches to turn on a television, change stations, turn on lights, and so on (see Figure 27-20). Environmental control systems can provide a student with choices and independence in school and home environments.

student eat. Some students will require physical assistance from a teacher or therapist. Due to the continuation of primitive reflexes and abnormal eating patterns, some students will need special feeding techniques such as those that require jaw control or lip closure to assist them in eating (see Figure 27-16). It is always important to let the student hold the utensil while eating when possible. Students should participate partially, even if they cannot do so fully.

In the area of self-care, several types of assistive devices or modifications may be used. Some students may use a button aid to assist with buttoning a shirt (see Figure 27-17). Other students may need the use of an adapted toilet so they can sit with support (see Figure 27-18). Bathrooms may need to be adapted for students

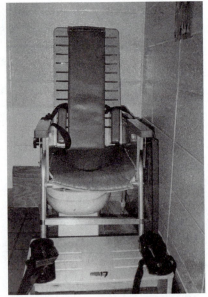

■ **FIGURE 27-18** Examples of adapted toilets

■ **FIGURE 27-19** Bathroom adapted for easy access to sink, with lever hooks to turn on water and pump soap; counter is adjusted for wheelchairs to fit underneath.

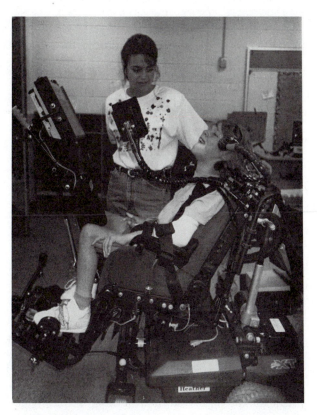

■ **FIGURE 27-20** Student using her environmental control device *(black center box)* to turn on her fan *(tube by her head)*. It also controls her augmentive communication device *(left)* and electric wheelchair. The student controls the environmental control with a switch by her left foot.

Meeting Behavioral and Social Needs

Students with multiple impairments may have several instructional needs within the behavioral and social domains. Psychological factors such as cognition, motivation, self-concept, social-emotional, and self-advocacy may affect learning and how the student behaves when alone and with others. Systematic instruction may be needed to help the student develop appropriate behavior and social interaction. (See Chapter 3.)

Students with multiple impairments may also be surrounded with technology and adaptations. A student with a ventilator, communication device, and adapted wheelchair may at first elicit reactions of fear and avoidance from peers and teachers. It is important that the student with multiple impairments not be forgotten amidst all the tubes and devices. Providing information about the devices and promoting socialization often are helpful to the student and to those around him or her.

SUMMARY

Students with multiple impairments present unique challenges to the educator due to the combination of impairments. *Multiple disabilities* is a term referring to students who have a combination of two or more disabilities that significantly affect their ability to learn and function. A multiple disability usually creates an interactional, multiplicative effect and hence, unique difficulties and adaptations. There are many possible combinations of multiple disabilities, such as having a physical impairment and a sensory impairment, physical impairment and cognitive impairment, and deaf-blindness. Each type of multiple impairment has unique characteristics and implications for the educator. Some general implications in physical and sensory considerations include mobility and positioning needs, placement of materials, adaptations and assistive devices, lifting and handling, and checking braces or orthoses. Other areas such as communication, learning, daily living needs, and behavioral and social needs may exist as well. A team approach is crucial in meeting the specific, individual needs of each student with a multiple disability.

CHAPTER 28

Classroom Adaptations

Students who have physical, sensory, or health impairments often require the systematic selection and implementation of classroom adaptations in order to function best in school settings. Although a multitude of information addresses adaptations for these students' physical, sensory, or health impairments, strategies and adaptations that include concomitant communication, learning, and behavior difficulties are typically not included. To help the teacher and the educational team select adaptations to meet these students' needs, a hierarchical decision-making model of adaptations for the student with physical, sensory, or health impairments is presented. Building a model of adaptations for students with physical, sensory, or health impairments requires examining four major areas: (1) identifying need, (2) determining the cause of performance discrepancy, (3) selecting the adaptation, and (4) evaluating its effectiveness (see Box 28-1).

IDENTIFYING NEED FOR ADAPTATIONS

Identifying the need for adaptations in a specific educational content area may consist of a three-part process. First, the exact skills needed for an individual without disabilities to successfully accomplish a task in a specific area of instruction are identified. Then, the student with physical, sensory, or health impairments is assessed as to his or her ability to perform these skills. Third, the differences between the performance of the student with an impairment and the performance of students without disabilities (the performance discrepancy or outcome result) are identified (Baumgart et al., 1982; Burnette, 1987; Wood, 1987; York & Rainforth, 1987). For example, if a student is incorrectly answering two-digit subtraction problems with borrowing, the teacher should delineate

the steps performed by students without disabilities, assess the targeted student's performance, and determine the performance discrepancy—that is, note the steps left out, steps incompletely performed, and steps incorrectly completed. The performance discrepancy can be caused by any number of problems. The next step is to identify those problems.

IDENTIFYING REASONS FOR PERFORMANCE DISCREPANCY

Students with physical, sensory, or health impairments often have not only the primary impairment but other associated problems. These may take the form of additional impairments or difficulties in communication, learning, or behavior. When a student is having a performance discrepancy, it may be due to (1) physical impairment, (2) sensory impairment, (3) health impairment, (4) communication difficulties, (5) learning difficulties, and/or (6) behavioral problems.

Physical Impairments
Students with physical impairments include those with neurological disorders, degenerative diseases, orthopedic disorders, and musculoskeletal disorders. A physical impairment implies involvement of the joints, bones, and muscles that interferes with an individual's motor movement. The educational performance of students with physical impairments may be affected unless adaptations are provided. Some performance discrepancies may be caused by the physical impairment when adaptations have not been adequately provided. For example, a student with severe spastic cerebral palsy may be physically unable to do the scratch work needed for borrowing when learning subtraction, or a student with muscular dystrophy may tire and miss a step of the problem.

BOX 28-1

Adaptation Model

Individual Adaptation Strategy

I. Identifying need for adaptation
  A. Select specific area of instruction
  B. Delineate skills
  C. Assess performance
  D. Identify performance discrepancy
II. Identifying reasons for performance discrepancy
  A. Physical impairments
  B. Sensory impairments
  C. Health impairments
  D. Communication problems
  E. Learning difficulties
  F. Behavior problems
III. Selecting adaptations
  A. Accessing the task
    1. Adapted devices/equipment
    2. Use behavior management
    3. Use person
    4. Modify physical environment
    5. Change student response
  B. Changing instruction of the task
    1. Modify instruction
  C. Altering the task
    1. Alter material
    2. Alter activity
    3. Alter curriculum
IV. Considerations of selected adaptations
V. Evaluation

SOURCE: Based on Heller, Alberto, and Romski, *American Journal on Mental Retardation, 99* (5) (in press).

Sensory Impairments

Sensory impairments can negatively affect performance and may be the cause of the performance discrepancy when adaptations are not suitable. Sensory impairments may occur separately or in combination with physical or health impairments. Students with cerebral palsy or spina bifida, for example, have an increased incidence of hearing and visual impairments (Rowley-Kelly & Reigel, 1993; Umbreit, 1983). Students with visual impairments may have difficulties because (1) the size of the problem does not permit adequate visualization; (2) the contrast is poor; (3) the student needs more time to complete problems when using large print; (4) the lighting needs to be enhanced or dimmed; or (5) the placement of materials is inadequate. Another example would be students with hearing impairments who have difficulty understanding directions on how to complete a math problem. Background noise, a soft voice, or other problems might be

the cause. Adaptations would be needed to accommodate the sensory impairment.

Health Impairments

The health impairment category refers especially to students who have major health impairments such as sickle cell anemia or diabetes. These conditions may interfere with academic performance due to fatigue, to inattentiveness, or to not feeling well. Students who have other physical impairments that require health care procedures, such as spina bifida students using catheterization procedure, will also fall under this category. Health care procedures include monitoring medication, observing the student's physical condition, providing rest, or providing physical health care procedures (Gearheart, Mullen, & Gearheart, 1993). Students in this category may require respiratory or nutritional support (that is, mechanical ventilators, suctioning, or tube feeding), or they may be dependent on such long-term devices as urinary catheters, colostomy bags, renal dialysis, or apnea monitors (Lehr, 1990). These students are technologically dependent and need to have their medical concerns met before they can benefit from education.

Many of these physical health care procedures must be provided in school. These procedures may result in a loss of independence for the student, as well as alienation from peers, and scholastic work can be adversely affected. For example, students with respiratory congestion may not perform their best because they do not feel well and their school day is interrupted for frequent suctioning. Students may not be able to go smoothly through the school day due to scheduled interruptions for clean intermittent catheterization or tube feedings. These can require more time to perform than the break given between classes or subject areas. Students' independence will be adversely affected when they must rely on others to help with the procedures if their physical impairments preclude them from performing the procedures themselves.

Communication Problems

Communication may also be impaired in students with physical, sensory, and health impairments and result in performance discrepancies. For example, students with cerebral palsy or stroke may have speech that is not understandable. Not only does this inhibit oral questioning by the student and receptive understanding by the teacher, but a lack of speech inhibits the student's learning through rephrasing or restating content to clarify or confirm information. Although other means of communicating may be available, the student may still be unable to clarify information satisfactorily due to limitations, such as the limited vocabulary available in the student's augmentative communication system. Additionally, students with conditions associated with hydrocephalus, such as spina bifida, may have cocktail party syndrome. In this condition, the student is verbose and uses jargon and clichés inappropriately. The student appears superficially skilled verbally, but actual performance is lacking (Rowley-Kelly & Reigel, 1993). This may impede socialization or even negatively affect receiving clarification of math calculations due to poor communication skills. Students with hearing impairments may miss what is being taught when the teacher moves her or his face away from the student's sight.

Learning Difficulties

Students with physical, sensory, and health impairments may also have learning deficiencies. Some learning deficiencies may be due to a lack of experience. This can occur when the effects of the physical and sensory impairment restrict movement and result in a lack of sensory information. Students may lack exposure to new experiences because of the impairment itself or because others are overly protective. Hospital interruptions may also result in irregular school attendance and difficulties staying on grade level due to the number of interruptions. Students with physical impairments often have delays in reaching cognitive milestones such as concrete and formal operations. Decreased opportunities to interact with the environment and fewer confrontational interactions with peers are possible causes (Yoos, 1987). Students with physical impairments may also show a pattern of underachievement when evaluated on normative tests (Pless & Pinkerton, 1975).

In addition to these factors, certain physical conditions are associated with mental retardation and learning disabilities. For example, cerebral palsy is associated with a higher incidence of mental retardation, and conditions such as spina bifida and cerebral palsy are associated with learning disabilities (Bleck & Nagel, 1982; Keele, 1983; Rowley-Kelly & Reigel, 1992; Umbreit, 1983). All of these cognitive and learning problems can result in the student not readily understanding the academic material being presented.

Behavioral Problems

Behavioral problems may prevent successful performance of a task and be the cause of a performance discrepancy. Behavior problems may include such difficulties as a lack of motivation, negative perceptions, attitudinal characteristics, poor self-concept, anger, grief, or sadness. Students may not be motivated to do the academic work when they do not feel well physically or as their condition worsens. Students who think that teachers react negatively to working with students with physical impairments may prefer not to work at all. Students may also have the attitudinal characteristics of

learned helplessness (a lack of persistence at tasks that could be mastered) and external loci of control (a feeling that success or failure is due to external factors). Both of these problems have been identified as negatively affecting achievement in school (Lefcourt, 1976; Tomlison, 1987). Students with physical impairments may also have difficulties interacting with peers. The effects of the physical illness may result in the student feeling markedly different from peers. Also, when there is a visible physical impairment, students may continue to experience grief, anger, and sadness (Yoos, 1987). These feelings can further impair academic performance.

Problems in any of the six areas (physical, sensory, health, communication, learning, and behavior) may result in poor academic performance unless adaptations are provided. The teacher needs to evaluate the student's performance to determine which area or areas may be the cause for a specific student in a specific learning task. Sometimes it will be hard to decipher whether the problem is due to a physical or learning difficulty, for example. Based on the information at hand, the teacher must go ahead and choose a discrepancy category and try adaptations in that category. If there is inconclusive information about which category to try first, the categories are in hierarchical order. Teachers should start at the top (physical) and then try other categories further down as needed.

SELECTING ADAPTATIONS BY DISCREPANCY CATEGORY

Several types of adaptations and strategies in each discrepancy category can be selected to help the student function optimally in school. These adaptations can be arranged hierarchically to assist in the selection of the appropriate adaptation. According to Schumm & Vaughn (1991), adaptations that require little individualized planning, instruction, and altering of the environment have been identified by classroom teachers as the most desirable and feasible. Teachers have identified adaptations pertaining to the social and motivational adjustment of the integrated student as among the most feasible, while adaptations in instruction and materials were rated as neither desirable or feasible. This agrees with Baker and Zigmond's (1990) findings that general education teachers do not view instructional or curriculum adaptations as feasible. Taking these findings into consideration, a hierarchy of adaptations can be devised that is based on ease of implementation and minimum intrusiveness or divergence into normalized scholastic routines and academic tasks.

Several types of adaptations may be used by the student with physical impairments. These can be hierarchically arranged from those that are least divergent from the academic task and require minimal teacher time to implement to those that are most divergent from the task and require considerable teacher time to implement. These include, first, adaptations that allow *access to the task*: (1) use of adapted device or equipment, (2) behavior management strategies, (3) use of person, (4) modification of physical environment, and (5) change of student response. Second, there are adaptations that *change how the teacher teaches a task* (teacher modifies instruction).

Third, there are adaptations that *change part or all of the task*; they (1) alter material, (2) alter activity, and (3) alter curriculum (Heller, Dangel, & Sweatman, in press).

Upon selecting a possible reason for a performance discrepancy, each one of these types of adaptations and strategies should be examined to determine their feasibility and their potential for success for the student Table 28-1 contains examples of adaptations for each type of adaptation across discrepancy categories.

TABLE 28-1

Types of Adaptations across Discrepancies

		Reasons for performance discrepancies					
		Physical impairments	**Sensory impairments**	**Health impairments**	**Communication problems**	**Learning difficulties**	**Behavior problems**
Types of adaptations	Adapted device/ equipment	Devices to compensate for physical disability (e.g., clay pencil)	Devices to compensate for sensory disability (e.g., magnifier)	Equipment used in care	AAC		
	Behavior management						Motivation strategies
	Person	Work in teams to assist with physical aspects of task	Work in teams to assist with sensory aspects of task	To direct; to assist with procedures	Sign language interpreter	Tutor	Dispel discrimination factors
	Physical environment	Modify to allow access to activities	Modify to allow access to activities	Secluded environment for privacy		Alter seating patterns	Seclude to decrease distractions
	Student response	Alternate response form (e.g., eye-gaze answer)	Alternate response form (e.g., braille, tape recording)		Use AAC	Simplify level (e.g., multiple choice)	
	Teacher instruction					Direct instruction; cognitive strategies	
	Alter material	Change material so student can physically use it	Change material so student can use it regardless of sensory loss			More concrete, experiential materials	
	Alter activity	Change activity to compensate for physical demands	Change activity to compensate for sensory demands			Simplify activity	Change to a more reinforcing activity
	Alter curriculum	Add to curriculum: teaching student use of adaptation	Add to curriculum: teaching student use of adaptation	Add to curriculum: how to do physical health care procedures	Add to curriculum: teaching students use of AAC device	Modify curriculum to align with cognitive abilities	Add to curriculum: advocacy

SOURCE: Based on "Effect of Object and Movement Cues on Receptive Communication by Preschool Children with Mental Retardation," by K. W. Heller, P. A. Alberto, and M. A. Romski (in press), *American Journal on Mental Retardation*.

■ VIGNETTE 1 ■

Sue is a first-grade student with spastic cerebral palsy and a left hemianopsia. In order to teach Sue to tell time, Ms. White will need to make some modifications so Sue can access the task. Sue uses a head pointer to move the hour hand into position, unless she tires and another student assists her. To get close enough to the clock, she uses a cut-out desk, which is at a height that her wheelchair can fit under. Material is positioned slightly to the right for optimum viewing due to her visual impairment. Sue often responds by pointing with her head pointer to the correct answer, and an assistant writes down the answer.

Adaptations for Performance Discrepancies due to Physical and Sensory Impairments

When performance discrepancies occur from physical or sensory limitations, adaptations may need to be used to compensate for the physical or sensory impairment. Several different types of adaptations may be selected that involve changing all or part of the task.

Accessing the task. The first type of adaptation in this category is the use of adapted devices or equipment that provides access to the task by compensating for the physical or sensory disability (Bigge, 1991). In this category, the adapted device allows the student to engage in the same task as his or her peers with no change in student response, instruction, or in the task itself. Students may use any number of adapted devices, such as book holders, clay-wrapped pencils, and magnifiers.

A second type of adaptation is the use of a person to help with physical or sensory components of a task. Peer assistance may be used to help the student with physical impairments on parts of a task. For example, a peer may help a student with limited head and arm use in the mechanics of frog dissection while they verbally rehearse, select, and plan the sequence of steps together. A second type of interaction is peer teaming, in which a cooperative arrangement exists. The student with physical impairments receives assistance to compensate for his or her physical or sensory impairment, but the student also helps the peer with different components of the task that do not require physical ability or sensory information. For example, the student with physical impairments may read the directions on how to dissect the frog to a peer who has dyslexia.

The third adaptation is to alter the classroom's physical environment to allow for access to the task. To allow access for a student in a wheelchair, chalkboards may be lowered, cut-out tables at the appropriate height may be used, and aisles may be widened. For students with visual or auditory impairments, blinds may be used to reduce glare, or preferential seating may be given to allow for easier visual access to the chalkboard or for easier speech reading.

Some students may be unable to respond to a task or activity the same way other students do because of physical or sensory impairments. In this situation, a fourth type of adaptation may be used that provides access to a task by changing the way the student responds to the task or activity. Students may use a different physical response to provide answers, such as an eye-gaze, or the student may use adapted devices or equipment, such as a braille writer (brailler). Unlike the first type of adaptation, which provides specialized equipment, these adaptations produce a different form of end product. For example, a student may be using eye-gaze to respond when the rest of the class uses oral responses, or the student may use a braille writer when the rest of the class is writing the answers. Other changes in student responses center around having the student respond to fewer questions on homework or tests to minimize fatigue. Modifying the response may also include extending the time limit for assignments for students who are physically slow or who are using large-print books, braille, or an interpreter.

Altering the task. Changing all or part of the task is the most divergent category because the change in the task itself involves using different materials, activities, or curricula (Schumm & Vaughn, 1991). Students with certain physical and sensory impairments may need task modification if they are to actively engage in learning. Allowing the student to make active responses with a high rate of success has been seen as a method that results in effective learning (Berliner, 1987).

■ VIGNETTE 2 ■

Sue needs different material to help her learn how to tell time. Because Sue is unable to draw the hands of the clock on worksheets, several drawings of clocks with different answers are placed in her field of vision, and she chooses her answer with her head pointer. One activity the teacher uses is having the class tell the time on the classroom clock when she intermittently says "Time." Sue has a modified activity in which she agrees or disagrees with the time identified by the class by looking at her own clock located at her desk.

To promote active participation, modifications in the materials may be needed. Students with physical disabilities who respond using an eye-gaze may need to have materials cut apart to allow responses using the eye-gaze or a scanning response. Students who are unable to circle the sentence they think provides the description of the story may need to have sentences numbered. To further identify the verb in the sentence, each word in the sentence may have a letter placed above it for identification. For example:

   A   B   CD   E   F GH   I
1. Mary went to the clothing store in the mall.
   A   B   C   D E F G   H   I
2. Mary liked the blue dress in the clothing store.

In this format, the student with cerebral palsy who has difficulty circling the correct answer or verbalizing the correct response may indicate the correct number or letter by typing out the correct response, pointing to the corresponding letter or number, or using some other means of responding. Students with visual impairment may need to have print enlarged or to have high-contrast materials used, such as light items on dark felt, or dark letters on white paper with yellow acetate on it. Students who are blind may need concrete materials or manipulatives or materials in braille. Students with auditory impairments may need materials that are on audiotape transcribed to paper.

Entire activities may need to be altered when the student cannot actively engage in them due to a physical or sensory impairment. For example, a student with physical impairments may be unable to dissect a frog but can place labels on the parts of a frog on a computer program. When demonstrating how plants grow, the student with a visual impairment can benefit from having the plant grow in water in order to feel the roots.

Students who are having difficulty solely because of their physical or sensory impairments will be able to study the same curriculum as their peers. However, additional information about the physical or sensory disability should be added to the curriculum. Students will also need to know how to manage their adaptations and any equipment they use.

Adaptations for Performance Discrepancies due to Health Impairments

For students with physical and health impairments to be educated at school, certain physical health care procedures may have to be performed during the school day (Heller et al., 1991). Adaptations will be needed with regard to available equipment, use of persons, and modification to physical environment. Additions to the curriculum will be needed as well.

■ VIGNETTE 3 ■

Janet has a myelomeningocele in the lumbar area. She is learning the CIC procedure, and this is one of her goals on her IEP. She is scheduled to do this procedure at certain times of the day. To perform this procedure, Janet is given a scheduled break before the lesson on telling time.

Accessing the task. Specialized equipment, such as catheters and colostomy bags, is needed to perform certain health care procedures. Another person may also be needed to perform the procedures or to teach the student how to perform them. A person who is knowledgeable about the student's disability and the necessary procedure may need to provide information and training to other school personnel. In terms of environmental adaptations, the selection of the location for the procedure may need to take into consideration both privacy and location. Effective time management will minimize interruptions in the student's schedule.

Altering the task. The student's curriculum may need to include information on how to do the procedure and how to identify problems and resolve them. Self-care and care of the equipment might be included. Students must learn to be self-advocates and to direct others to do the procedure if they cannot do it themselves.

Adaptations for Performance Discrepancies due to Communication Problems

When the student is not succeeding at a task because of a lack of appropriate communication, the adaptation involves providing an effective means of communication. This may affect access to the task and dynamics of the task.

■ VIGNETTE 4 ■

Mary, a first-grader with mixed cerebral palsy, uses an electronic communication device to communicate. Her device has been programmed by Ms. White and the speech therapist. Numbers and times correlate with the lesson on telling time so Mary can contribute orally by using voice output on her device.

Accessing the task. Students with discrepancies due to a lack of appropriate communication may use an augmentative communication system to interact in the classroom. Many different forms of augmentative communication may be used, including electronic or non-electronic communication boards, gestures, objects, and manual sign language. A person may be used as an interpreter for those who use manual sign language. The student response to the task may be altered when the student responds using the augmentative communication device. This occurs in instances when the student responds using the voice output of a device while other students are writing their answers.

Altering the task. Although there would be no alteration of curriculum, additional information will need to be added to the student's curriculum regarding the care and use of the augmentative communication system. How the student is to instruct others in its use may also be included.

Adaptations for Performance Discrepancies due to Learning Difficulties

Often, classroom achievement problems are due to a cognitive or learning impairment such as a learning disability, an intellectual disability, being a slow learner, or faulty concept development due to the physical or sensory impairments. The possible adaptations for these students are present in all main categories of the instructional model.

Accessing the task. Students who have performance discrepancies due to problems in learning the material may benefit from changes in how the material is accessed. Adaptations may be provided by using another person. Working with other students is a means of promoting academic achievement and social accep-

---

■ VIGNETTE 5 ■

Ms. White needs to make some instructional modifications for a student with physical impairments and learning problems, who wants to master telling time. She assigns Ralph, who has mild learning problems and cerebral palsy and tends to be uninterested in class activities, to work with Matt. Ralph seems to respect Matt. When the class works on learning to tell time, Ralph sits with Matt in a special study carrel; while Matt moves the hands of a small clock, Ralph indicates whether each hand is correctly positioned.

---

tance (Maddin & Slavin, 1983) for students with physical or sensory impairments and concomitant learning impairments. These options range from informal peer cooperation to more structured cooperative learning strategies and peer tutoring. In peer cooperation, all students support and encourage the work of classmates in such areas as reading and writing by being peer editors or reading partners, for example. In cooperative learning strategies (Johnson & Johnson, 1983; Slavin, 1990), a class is broken into heterogeneous groups of three to five students who work together as equals and receive group rewards while helping each other meet the class objectives. With peer tutoring, the student with a disability receives help either from classmates or from an older tutor (Jenkins & Jenkins, 1985). Peer tutoring can be used to promote basic skills such as writing. For example, two students might work together to review their spelling words or drill on math facts flashcards. They might review content areas, for example, by working together to prepare for an examination in social studies (Delquadri, Greenwood, Worton, Carta, & Hall, 1986; Maheady, Saac, & Harper, 1989).

Another type of adaptation is to modify the physical environment. Effective environmental design for the student with physical or sensory impairments and additional learning difficulties must include room arrangement as well as the design for presenting instruction and modifying the potential influence of distractors (Zentall, 1983). The room arrangement should provide the student with multiple instructional options, including close proximity to the teacher and use of large- and small-group formats.

Consider, for example, the need for environmental adaptations for a student with a physical impairment and learning difficulties that results in receptive and expressive language problems. A traditional seating arrangement of straight rows of chairs, in which students see only the backs of the heads of the students in front of them and the teacher in the distance, offers little assistance for a such a student. Rather, an arrangement in which students are seated in face-to-face clusters allows the student with language problems to see and to speak easily with other students as well as to see other students react to verbal and nonverbal messages from the teacher. Such an arrangement becomes a critical element in providing the needed adaptations for increasing language competence. A variety of large- and small-group formats provide enhanced opportunities for students to receive information from teachers as well as to participate in student-directed activities with classmates in practice sessions and reviews. Small-group arrangements might include a science and social studies center that offers hands-on participation, or

■ **VIGNETTE 6** ■

As Ms. White begins instruction in telling time at 5-minute intervals, she demonstrates the steps she goes through for Ralph. She says, "After I find the big hand, the minute hand, I count by fives while I touch each number. Five, ten, fifteen, twenty . . . Now everyone, count with me as you touch the numbers on your clocks." Then, when the group has been successful, she calls on individual students, especially on Ralph, to count while she monitors each student's accuracy.

listening centers, writing centers with word processing facilities, or free-time centers.

Students with physical and sensory impairments and concurrent learning difficulties benefit from modifications in the responses to the task that permit a high rate of correct, active responses to promote learning (Englert, 1984). A teacher provides this by requiring students to respond to instruction immediately. For example, the teacher might say, "This clock shows 8:15. Frankie, what time is it?" Clapping out the syllables of a word or actually touching objects when counting them are examples of dynamically responding to the task.

Another way to provide active, correct responses is by adjusting the response requirements, thus making the task more appropriate for students with learning difficulties. Response alternatives that require an identification response are typically the best responses for showing a student's mastery (Howell & Moreland, 1987). An identification response requires the student to choose the correct answer; it can be a yes/no response given verbally or a multiple-choice response. For example, rather than requiring a student to write (produce) the main idea of a passage, the teacher may adapt the dynamics of the response and ask the student to point to (identify) the topic sentence. For students at the secondary level, rather than being required to write "Legislative, Executive, and Judicial" for the branches of government, the response might be modified so that a student could point to the answer or indicate "yes or no" as the teacher gives each possible response. Finally, providing sufficient practice and drill (multiple task dynamics) are important steps for increasing fluency and automaticity—both of which are necessary for mastering the task (Rosenshine, 1986).

Changing instruction of the task. To provide maximal assistance to the student with physical or sensory impairments and learning problems in the mastery of the curriculum, the teacher may need to modify the way

she or he provides instruction to meet the needs of the student. Typically, a direct instruction format would be used in which the teacher demonstrates how to do the task, guides the students in their mastery of the skills and the content, and then provides ample independent practice (Smith, 1989). The key antecedent of teacher demonstration (or modeling) is the focal point of this approach.

Instruction in the task may involve changing the way in which information—a type of antecedent—is presented. Ms. White may want to write the daily schedule where the class can see it and place a clock face on the schedule that shows the time, as well as the time of each activity on the activity list. In this way, students can see, for example, what the clock looks like when it is time for arithmetic.

For students whose cognitive problems are relatively mild, instruction may also include developing learning and metacognitive strategies. Learning strategies consist of training a student to follow a set of prescribed steps to solve a particular problem. For example, the teacher has instructed a student with a reading problem to use the B-E-S-T strategy to decode an unfamiliar word in reading. That is, when the student comes to an unknown word, he or she is reminded to consider the Beginning sound, the Ending sound, whether the word makes Sense, and to go ahead and Try sounding out the word. Learning strategies may also include memory enhancement strategies, such as Pegword (Mastropieri & Scruggs, 1987); reading comprehension strategies, such as SQ3R—Survey, Question, Read, Recite, and Review (Robinson, 1964); Multiplass (Schumaker, Deshler, Alley, Warner, & Denton, 1982); and mathematics word-solving strategies. Metacognitive strategies may be used to plan and evaluate how to modify and successfully complete an activity. Such strategies include goal-setting (Schunk, 1985), self-instructions, and systematically evaluating the accuracy of a response (Graham, Harris, & Reid, 1992).

For students with more severe cognitive impairments, specialized instructional strategies will be used to aid in learning. Tasks are often taught by breaking them down into small steps. (For example, the first step in learning when lunch can be eaten at a community-based vocational job site is to identify the hour hand on the student's watch.) The teacher may use such strategies as intrastimulus prompts (also known as perceptual cues), in which a relevant aspect of the task is highlighted through the use of color, size, or other dimension. (For example, the hour hand and the numeral 12 may be highlighted in red.) Instructional prompts may be used to provide varying amounts of assistance to the student. These prompts include giving verbal instructions, demonstrating the task, matching a response to a sample

Ms. White decides to alter the task and only require Ralph to tell time to the hour rather than to the minute. She begins by only presenting times that occur during the school day so she can tie the times to specific activities.

(match to sample), and providing various levels of physical assistance. (For example, the student may carry a card that shows what "twelve o'clock" looks like and match it to the time on his watch.) Reinforcement (such as praise, tokens, favorite activities, favorite foods) may also be given when the student gives a correct response. This leads to an increase in the performance of the targeted behavior. (In this case, reinforcement occurs naturally because correctly identifying lunchtime results in the student's eating lunch.) (Snell, 1993).

Altering the task. Altering the task might involve changing the size for the instructional steps or, in the case of students with more severe learning problems, actually changing the task (Mercer & Mercer, 1989). An example of this would be the teacher who plans to teach her students how to tell time. She must consider whether to begin by teaching skills, such as identifying the hour and minute hands, or by developing concepts about when telling time is needed. A concept-related question would be, "How will you know when it's time to go to speech therapy? She needs to identify the elements of the task that are needed, such as recognizing the numerals 1 to 12, the vocabulary terms of hour, minute, o'clock, before and after, counting by fives, and so forth. She also must decide whether any components of telling time might need to be eliminated. For example, she may ask, "Should I teach both the analog clock face and the digital clock or just the one that will be most functional?"

Because more than 75% of students' instructional time is spent using educational materials (Bartel & Hammill, 1986), teachers must carefully select and modify materials to meet the unique needs of the student with physical and sensory disabilities. Instructional materials and devices are modified for students with physical and sensory disabilities, based on the extent to which these instructional tools are effective (Does it do the job?) and efficient (Does it require a minimum amount of time and effort?). For example, many students with physical or sensory impairments and cognitive difficulties may not reach the level of abstract thought required by the regular class curriculum. The

task might need to be altered so that it is more concrete. Thus, a teacher may need a way to counter the differences in real-world experiences that are typically more restricted for many students with physical impairments. This might be done by providing hands-on experiences with objects to increase mastery of mathematical concepts (Mastropieri, Scruggs, & Shiah, 1991) or, before having the student read a passage, making a special effort to activate the student's unique prior knowledge (Graham & Johnson, 1989). Activities may be modified to provide additional practice with concepts that are needed to ensure mastery of the targeted learning task.

Some students with physical or sensory impairments may not be able to function under the same curriculum as fellow students when they have a learning problem. Bigge (1991) suggests several curriculum options. In some instances, an identical curriculum is used, but with adaptations. A parallel curriculum might be appropriate for the student for whom the same goals and objectives as the regular curriculum are appropriate but whose attendance is not sufficiently regular to permit mastering all the components. A parallel curriculum would present the regular education goals and objectives at reduced levels of difficulty. For example, a teacher might give a student with learning problems a calculator to solve problems involving miles per gallon. A more extensive curricular modification would be to use the regular education curriculum for a lower grade level, thus treating the student with learning difficulties as a younger average learner. A practical academic curriculum would emphasize the same basic skills areas in the regular curriculum but would focus on these skills in the context of what is functional for immediate use. The life management curriculum offers those unique curricular objectives needed for each student, typically in the areas of physical self-care and family living, education, community leisure, work, communication, and social interactions.

Adaptations for Performance Discrepancies due to Behavior Problems

Students with physical or sensory impairments may have behavior problems that can be addressed by providing strategies in behavior management, use of people, and change of task.

Accessing the task. Behavior management strategies would include both the extrinsic and intrinsic techniques needed to promote student engagement and response to the instructional program. The elements of intrinsic motivation are seen as forming the foundation for school achievement (Deci & Chandler, 1986). The teacher who proactively provides students with learning problems with a sense of self-determination, compe-

While working with Josh, a student with a physical impairment and a behavior problem of not complying with her directions and not completing his work, Ms. White provides a group reward of extra time on the computer (which Josh enjoys) for Josh and three other students of his choice if he finishes within the specified time period.

tence, and relatedness will decrease the number of discipline problems and increase achievement (Adelman & Taylor, 1993). These factors have special significance for the student with physical impairments who may have a limited sense of self-determination due to a physical disability, along with restricted competence in academic areas and prerequisite skills. Therefore, issues of motivation require special effort on the part of the teacher to promote self-determination, competence, and relatedness.

For students with physical impairments who need more intensive classroom management than providing for intrinsic motivation, there is clear evidence that external contingencies promote the performance of students with learning problems in basic skill areas, such as arithmetic skills (Mastropiere, Scruggs, & Shiah, 1991) and reading skills (Graham & Johnson, 1990). At a more advanced level, specific training in self-regulation—including planning, self-monitoring, self-evaluation, and self-reinforcement—has been effective in developing greater independence for students with disabilities.

Other adaptations include getting advice from another person to be sure discrimination is not occurring. Specialists may give information about student disabilities and provide insight when teachers or other students may actually be the causes of behavior problems. Eventually, the student with a physical or sensory impairment will need to be a self-advocate and provide information.

Ms. White alters the task for Josh by initially having him recognize only those times that are important during his day at school. He knows when the clock in the front of the class indicates lunch time, time for speech therapy, story time, recess, and time for his bus to come. Additional times are added based on the task relevance to Josh, such as selected television shows.

Ms. Green's objective for her students in arithmetic class for the next several weeks is to teach the addition of fractions. Knowing from past experience that her students will be "turned off" by the presentation in the textbook because they won't see the relevance of the lessons, she chooses an alternative presentation. Her students learn about fractions by using simple recipes in a cooking project.

Altering the task. At times, the behavior problem may be due to uninteresting or inappropriate material. The task may be modified so that the material is more reinforcing.

Academic skills can be repackaged for unmotivated or uninterested learners by presenting the skills within the context of how they are to be used. This can be done by encapsulating a single skill in an example. The teacher might say, "When both the hour hand and the minute hand are on the 12, it is 12 o'clock, and we go to lunch." The teacher might also develop an experiential project to promote the motivation needed to facilitate learning a skill. "We are going to set up a school store to learn about counting coins and making change" is an example. Learning in context can be promoted by including students' input in choosing activities to facilitate learning, by providing clear feedback about successes, and assuring mastery of all elements of the tasks. Another modification would include self-advocacy skills in the student's curriculum.

CONSIDERATIONS OF SELECTED ADAPTATIONS

This adaptation model is designed to provide a framework for selecting adaptations needed for students with physical, sensory, or health impairments. There are several considerations for successful implementation. First, adaptations must be individualized for the student. Individualization of the adaptation is necessary to adequately meet the student's unique characteristics. Adaptations cannot be made for a group or category of students. Second, it is important for the teacher to be certain that technological devices and activities are not being misused as replacements for teacher-learner interactions (Garner & Campbell, 1987). Adaptations can hinder student progress when they supplant effective teaching practices. Third, adaptations need to be periodically reevaluated. Some adaptations may not be necessary any longer and can be eliminated; others will remain a permanent part of the task. If the student can function as well without the adaptation or can change to a simpler form that is more similar to what other students do, this should occur. Less complex adaptations are more likely to be systematically used and properly implemented. Fourth, adaptations must be reevaluated as students go to different environments. Changes from elementary school to high school involve differences in such areas as number of teachers and environments, space between classrooms, and more student ownership, which will need to be considered in the selection of adaptations. Fifth, sufficient time must be given to see whether or not an adaptation is effective. It is unlikely that an adaptation will be effective after one trial (Baumgart et al., 1982). The student may need some time to adjust to a new physical adaptation or to learn a cognitive strategy, for example. However, if no positive increase in the targeted behavior is seen after a sufficient period of time, the appropriateness of the adaptation will need to be enhanced. Sixth, the teacher will need to involve the related staff (occupational therapist, physical therapist, and speech and language pathologist), parents, and the student in selection of the adaptation as well as the evaluation of its effectiveness. A team approach will help with determining the appropriateness of the adaptation.

EVALUATION

After an adaptation is selected and implemented, its effectiveness must be evaluated with the systematic observation and collection of data. The effectiveness of the adaptation must be verified in the environment in which it will be used because different environments may result in different adaptations (Baumgart et al., 1982). If a least-divergent adaptation has not been successful after enough time has passed to assess its effectiveness, another type of adaptation in the same category may be selected or the teacher may need to choose a more divergent strategy. If many types of adaptations in one discrepancy category have been systematically applied with little success, reexamination of the possible cause of the discrepancy must occur. Another discrepancy category with differing types of adaptations may be selected.

Once an adaptation is in place, periodic reexamination of the adaptation is needed to determine whether the adaptation should be fazed out or whether it will remain permanently. As the student's skill changes over time, the adaptation may no longer be needed, or it may be supplanted by a more appropriate one.

SUMMARY

This hierarchical decision-making model of adaptations for students with physical or sensory impairments should assist the educator in systematically selecting appropriate adaptations. Due to the multiple categories of discrepancies and multiple adaptations that can ameliorate these discrepancies, the educator will need the contributions of related service staff, other teachers, parents, and the student. A collaborative approach will be more likely to ensure the success of selection, implementation, and evaluation of the adaptation.

CHAPTER 29

Collaborative Educational Teams and the Integration of Services

As the education of students with disabilities moves toward integration into community settings—neighborhood schools, supported employment settings, community leisure settings—and the use of environment-referenced curricula, the educational team working with these students must adopt a more integrated approach to service provision. Teachers, therapists, parents, and other professionals who make up the team need to actively pursue collaboration with one another if the student is to achieve optimal outcomes. In this chapter, we will define potential team members' roles, compare several team models, and describe strategies to facilitate collaborative teamwork.

TEAM MEMBERS

The composition of any collaborative educational team will vary according to the educational needs of the students they serve. The composition may change over time as students' needs change. An educational team may include both core team members and support team members. Core team members are those individuals who are directly involved with the design and implementation of students' educational programs. For example, team members for a junior high school student who has severe spastic quadriplegic cerebral palsy and visual impairment could include the student, family members, general education teacher, special education teacher for students with orthopedic impairments, the itinerant teacher for students with visual impairments, physical therapist, occupational therapist, speech and language pathologist, classroom teaching assistant, and community worksite representative.

Support team members typically serve on a consultant basis. Their roles do not directly support the student's day-to-day educational program. Examples of support team members could include the psychologist or social worker, audiologist, dietitian, nurse, and a physician. In some cases, when students have extensive medical needs, some of the support team members mentioned previously may become part of the core team. For example, if the student described here also had to begin tube feedings, the nurse would be more directly involved in the student's educational plan. The nurse would instruct the student and school personnel in proper implementation of the procedure and would become a more active part of the core team.

Students with multiple and severe disabilities tend to have a greater number of team members due to the severity and complexity of their impairments. As the number of team members increases, efficient coordination of team efforts tends to decrease due to the inability of all team members to schedule time to communicate with each other.

As students' needs change, the type and amount of an individual team member's participation should also change. For example, in the case of a student with severe physical disabilities who is transitioning from a preschool special education program into an integrated kindergarten, the team might decide that, during the first few weeks, the highest priority is that the child's basic physical needs be met. Therefore, the occupational therapist and physical therapist might initially follow the child intensely in the classroom and work with the teacher and teaching assistant on positioning, handling, and daily living activities such as feeding, toileting, and so on. Another important early role of the therapists might be to help the student acquaint classmates with his or her abilities and disabilities.

After almost daily involvement for the first few weeks of school, the occupational therapist and the physical therapist may adjust their schedules to weekly in-classroom consultation. At this time, the speech and language pathologist may need to increase classroom time to help set up a communication system. Schedules should be adjusted to avoid overwhelming the class-room teacher and to meet the student's prioritized needs, as determined by the total educational team.

All team members share some basic roles and respon-sibilities; those include participating in decision-making about each student's educational program, contributing problem-solving strategies to the student's educational program, sharing specific knowledge and skills to facili-tate understanding of the student's capabilities and needs, supporting the contributions of other team members, and supporting practices that facilitate the student's education and integration into the community (Orelove & Sobsey, 1991; Rainforth, York, & Mac-donald, 1992; Smith, 1990).

Each discipline also brings to the team its own set of knowledge and skills. These discipline-specific roles and areas of expertise are described in Chapter 1. Potential team members include the special education teacher, the student and family members, the regular education teacher, the special education teachers (for example, the teacher of students with orthopedic impairments and the teacher of students with visual impairments), the adapted physical education teacher, the physical thera-pist, the occupational therapist, the speech and lan-guage pathologist, the teaching assistant, the commu-nity service providers, the school psychologist, the school social worker, the orientation and mobility specialist, the audiologist, the school nurse, the nutri-tionist or dietitian, various physicians, and other medi-cal or nonmedical specialists.

While there are specific knowledge and skill areas inherent among different disciplines, there are also overlapping areas of knowledge and skill between disciplines as well. Furthermore, different individuals within the same discipline may not necessarily have the same knowledge and skills, based on their training programs and work experiences. When determining who is on the student's educational team, student needs must be matched with the potential team members who can contribute the necessary knowledge and skills, regardless of their title.

TEAM MODELS

Several team models are described in the literature (Orelove & Sobsey, 1991; Rainforth, York, & Mac-

donald, 1992; Smith, 1990). These models are ex-plained next (see Table 29-1).

Multidisciplinary Team Model

The multidisciplinary team model evolved from a medi-cal model of service delivery in which problems are typically isolated to one particular domain. In this approach, each professional evaluates and works with the student individually. No formal effort is made to prioritize the student's needs, and overlap among dis-ciplines is not considered. The professionals working with the student usually do not think of themselves as belonging to a team because they work in isolation.

In this model, professionals carry out their own assessment of the student according to their particular area of expertise. Assessments are typically conducted in isolation, outside the student's natural environment; for example, in a therapy room rather than a classroom. Because no individual can be an expert in all or even in several fields, no discipline's evaluation takes the whole student into account. Therefore, the likelihood of inac-curate or incomplete assessment results is increased. Recommendations based on these evaluations are also more likely to conflict with one another and be ex-tremely difficult for the teacher to synthesize and implement. For example, the speech therapist may recommend activation of a communication device using a movement pattern that the physical therapist recom-mends against.

Furthermore, in this multidisciplinary model, the assumption is that periodic and fragmented "treat-ment" of the student's problems will eventually result in improved performance that will automatically gen-eralize to a more meaningful everyday life. In this model, if improved performance is not achieved over time, students are judged "unable to benefit" and treatment is discontinued. Prior to the legal mandate for related services in education, therapy services for students were sometimes discontinued not because the students were unable to make improvement but be-cause isolated and periodic services failed to tap the students' potential.

The direct, isolated therapy approach discussed ear-lier is problematic because (1) when skills are not assessed in natural environments, the assessment out-comes may not represent what the student can actually do in these settings; (2) isolated skills, rather than the clusters of skills necessary in everyday activities, are frequently assessed; (3) remediation activities for teach-ers and other professionals are frequently not included; (4) collaboration with other professionals is hindered; and (5) opportunities for remediation of vital areas such as communication or motor abilities are diminished

TABLE 29-1

Team Models

	Multidisciplinary	Interdisciplinary	Transdisciplinary
Assessment	Separate by discipline.	Separate by discipline.	Team members conduct together.
Student/family participation	Family meets with individual team members and results are reported	Family meets with team as a whole and results are reported. Family provides input.	Student and family actively participate as members of the team.
Program plan development	Team members develop separate plans by discipline.	Team members share their separate plans with each other.	Team members (including student and family) develop a plan based on student and family priorities and resources.
Program plan responsibility	Team members are responsible for implementing their section of the plan.	Team members responsible for sharing information with each other and implementing their section of the plan.	Team members are responsible for how the primary service provider(s) implement the plan.
Program plan implementation	Team members individually implement their section of the plan.	Team members individually implement their section of the plan and incorporate other sections, when possible.	A primary service provider (or providers) implements the plan with assistance from other team members.
Lines of communication	Informal.	Periodic team meetings.	Regular team meetings, where transfer of information and skills occur.
Guiding philosophy	Team members recognize the importance of others' contributions.	Team members willing and able to develop, share, and take responsibility for services that are part of the total program.	Team members commit to team learning and work together to implement a unified program.
Staff development	Independent within each discipline.	Independent within/outside each discipline.	Integral part of team meetings.

SOURCE: Based on "Early Intervention Team Approaches: The Transdisciplinary Model," by G. Woodruff and C. Hanson. In J. B. Jordan, J. J. Gallagher, P. L. Hutinger, and M. B. Karnes (Eds.), *Early Childhood Special Education: Birth to Three*. Copyright © 1987 The Council for Exceptional Children. Used with permission.

because remediation is not carried out throughout the student's day by all parties interacting with him or her.

Interdisciplinary Team Model

The interdisciplinary team model represents a somewhat higher level in the evolution of team models than the multidisciplinary model. The interdisciplinary approach is similar to the multidisciplinary model in that assessments and the implementation of program goals are still discipline-specific and still carried out in isolation from other team members. However, the interdisciplinary model does provide a formal structure for interaction and communication among members of the team, which encourages a sharing of information. Programming decisions are made by group consensus and a formal method for communication among team

members is established by assigning a case manager or team leader for each student. This person coordinates services for that student.

However, as in the multidisciplinary model, the reality of the interdisciplinary model is that program planning and implementation are still separate. The isolated service delivery model described in this chapter is still the result of the interdisciplinary model with all its inherent problems.

Transdisciplinary Team Model

The transdisciplinary team model was introduced initially to serve the complex needs of high-risk infants. This model primarily recognized that the multiple needs of children are interrelated and that children do not perform skills in isolation; skills are directly related to function and occur in response to the environmental demands.

The transdisciplinary team model is characterized by sharing information and skills across discipline-specific boundaries. In this model, team members all provide information and teach intervention techniques to each other, thereby promoting consistency in program implementation for each student. The transdisciplinary approach may result in an indirect model of service delivery, in which one or two persons (usually the teacher) act as the primary program provider and other team members act as consultants. However, a combination of direct and indirect services is best used in the transdisciplinary approach.

Integrated Therapy

An integrated therapy approach is a vital part of the transdisciplinary team model. The three basic assumptions of an integrated therapy approach are that (1) assessment of a student's motor, sensory, and communication abilities can best be conducted in a natural environment such as in the home, classroom, or worksite; (2) students should be taught basic motor, sensory,

and communication skills, and these should be verified through age-appropriate and functional activities that relate to everyday life and occur in natural settings; and (3) therapy should occur throughout the day in situations and settings in which the student functions.

By providing therapy services in these real-life situations, the generalization of skills to relevant contexts occurs by design rather than by accident, and therapy services do not have to compete with classroom activities but rather support them.

As evidenced by the integrated therapy approach, there are several key concepts in the transdisciplinary team approach, including (1) shared goals—all team members' efforts, including those of the student and family members, are focused on jointly developing and implementing an overall set of objectives, as described in the student's IEP; (2) role release—the roles of each discipline become more flexible and some functions related to one's own discipline are "released" to be performed by another discipline or team member; and (3) an active and reciprocal learning process in which team members teach each other new skills and learn new skills from other team members as determined by student needs (see Figure 29-1).

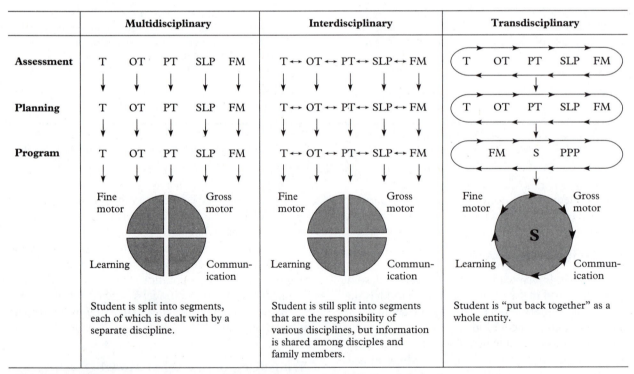

	Multidisciplinary	**Interdisciplinary**	**Transdisciplinary**
Assessment	T OT PT SLP FM	T ↔ OT ↔ PT ↔ SLP ↔ FM	T OT PT SLP FM
Planning	T OT PT SLP FM	T ↔ OT ↔ PT ↔ SLP ↔ FM	T OT PT SLP FM
Program	T OT PT SLP FM	T ↔ OT ↔ PT ↔ SLP ↔ FM	FM S PPP
	Student is split into segments, each of which is dealt with by a separate discipline.	Student is still split into segments that are the responsibility of various disciplines, but information is shared among disciples and family members.	Student is "put back together" as a whole entity.

Key   T = Teacher(s)   PT = Physical therapist
         FM = Family members and student   SLP = Speech and language pathologist
         S = Student   PPP = Primary program provider

■ **FIGURE 29-1** Example of team interactions
Source: Based on "Early Intervention Team Approaches: The Transdisciplinary Model," by G. Woodruff and C. Hanson. In J. B. Jordan, J. J. Gallagher, P. L. Hutinger, and M. B. Karnes (Eds.), *Early Childhood Special Education: Birth to Three.* Copyright © 1987 The Council for Exceptional Children. Used with permission.

STRATEGIES FOR FACILITATING COLLABORATIVE TEAMWORK

The information presented in this section describes strategies for facilitating transdisciplinary team service delivery that reflect educationally effective practices and can be used as a guide in planning and implementing this approach (Campbell, 1987; Orelove & Sobsey, 1991; Rainforth, York, & Macdonald, 1992). The three main areas within the educational setting that are most affected by choosing a transdisciplinary team model for educational services are assessment, development of instructional goals and actual delivery of instruction, and therapy services.

Assessment

The method used by an educational team to obtain initial assessment information about a student will affect all other subsequent programming for that student. Therefore, the educational team should share in the evaluative process from the onset, and the evaluation information should be obtained in settings that are natural for the student.

Several types of information can be obtained when assessing a student, and all are important for appropriate program development. These include background information, use of an ecological inventory, and utilization of discipline-specific information.

Important background information should be obtained by one or more team members from the student and the family, previous or current service providers, and the student's educational file. The following valuable information can be obtained through this process: current and previous educational goals; special learning characteristics or preferences; student/family/professional prioritization of needed skills; the student's preference for learning activities; materials, food, and so on; the student's communication mode; favorite or regular family activities; and medical problems and precautions. The general background information obtained should be shared with all team members.

Traditionally, assessment has been performed in isolation by each discipline, yielding diagnostic information on the student's current physical status and ability to perform certain isolated skills within individual developmental domains such as communication, motor development, and so forth. In the transdisciplinary model, team members jointly plan for and conduct the assessment that is carried out in the student's natural environment during regular daily activities. Information gleaned from this type of assessment allows the team to plan student goals that are age-appropriate, functional, meaningful to the student, and integrated with other aspects of the student's daily life.

The transdisciplinary assessment technique is referred to as an ecological inventory and consists of the following steps (Orelove & Sobsey, 1991; Smith, 1990):

1. Determine the environments in which the student currently functions or is likely to function in the near future.

2. Determine the activities and skills necessary to perform in those environments. Each activity is task analyzed or broken down into steps, and each step's requisite skills are delineated.

3. Determine the professionals who need to be involved in the various areas of the assessment. For example, for the skill of ordering and eating out in a restaurant, the communication therapist might be designated to assess how well a student can order food to determine the student's communication needs related to this activity. The occupational therapist may also be involved to assess the student's self-feeding to determine any needed interventions in the areas of positioning or adapted devices.

4. Conduct the actual environmental assessment: (a) designated team members go to the natural environments with the student; (b) team members record the student's responses during performance of natural activities; and (c) team members make notes on activities that require further assessment and potential needed adaptations or interventions.

Some team members may need to use discipline-specific information assessment strategies that are more traditional to their respective disciplines, in addition to the use of ecological assessment. Examples of this type of information, in the case of the physical therapist, might include specific measurements of joint range of motion or assessment of muscle tone.

Transdisciplinary assessment requires both additional discussion time among various members of the educational team and additional direct contact with the student in order to allow for problem-solving, consultation, and training among team members.

Developing Instructional Goals

Following the completion of the assessment process, the transdisciplinary team prioritizes the skills to be taught to the student and jointly writes goals that address these skills.

Prioritizing the skills to teach the student in the course of the school year can be a difficult task and must take into consideration the student's and family's preferences as well as which skills are necessary for educational, social, and vocational development.

The student's individualized education program (IEP) is developed by the transdisciplinary team. The goals and objectives on each student's IEP dictate the physical set-up of the classroom, the day's schedule, and the choice of instructional materials and strategies. Therefore, the manner in which the IEP is developed is critical to the success of the transdisciplinary model.

In the transdisciplinary model, members of each discipline do not write their own separate sections of the IEP. Such an individual approach would promote development of goals having no function in the real world and would exclude critical objectives related to multiple domains across school and community environments. Instead, the team develops goals that identify environments that are educationally relevant and specific activities to be performed within those environments. The related objectives that the team then develops include basic skills in the areas of the communication, motor, or sensory domains that are required to perform skill clusters that are part of the needed activities. These objectives are, therefore, activity-based and are taught in context, with the related service objectives being imbedded into the general student objectives. For example, in the case of an elementary student with severe physical impairments, instead of the physical therapist working on midline control of the head in isolation in the therapy room, the physical therapist, teacher, and communication therapist would develop an objective incorporating a midline head position to be used to control the student's switch-activated communication device in the classroom.

Delivering Instruction and Therapy Services

We have mentioned that in the transdisciplinary model an integrated therapy approach is utilized. The common features of this approach are that each discipline's planning and skills are applied to a common set of shared goals and that therapeutic techniques are implemented by all members of the team within functional instructional activities.

The process by which transdisciplinary service delivery takes place can be difficult to implement. In this section, we will provide suggestions for facilitating this process.

Block Scheduling

Members of the educational team cannot provide good information for planning, making recommendations, training and consulting with one another, designing adaptations, and evaluating the effectiveness of intervention unless they have adequate time to observe and work with the students and other team members in daily activities in natural settings.

Block scheduling is a strategy to provide large blocks of time for planning and consulting with other team members. Rather than working with one student for 30 minutes at a time twice a week, the therapist might see that student for 60 minutes one time per week. If several students are seen in one location and block scheduling is used, even larger blocks of time can be reserved for each student on a weekly basis, allowing the team members to better observe the student in multiple natural settings throughout the day, in school, in the community, and at home.

When scheduling is planned in conjunction with other team members, selected team members may block time periods to collaborate. The communication therapist, occupational therapist, and physical therapist could block time together to work with the student, the teacher, and the parent on developing a communication system and on planning and training for proper positioning, necessary adaptations, and functional vocabulary activities and settings.

Team Meetings

A system also must be implemented to ensure an ongoing exchange of information among team members, including family and community members. If face-to-face meetings are not always possible, communication forms and mailboxes for each team member may be set up to facilitate information exchange. A notebook may be sent to family members or worksite personnel for exchange of information between home or community sites and other team members.

Team meetings should also be scheduled on a regular basis to allow time for review and revision of a student's instructional program, for team problem-solving, and possibly to conduct needed team assessments. The frequency of the meetings is dependent on the school district's schedule. The best arrangement would be on a monthly basis. Team meeting agendas should be planned in advance and minutes should be kept. These should be shared with any members not present for the meeting and kept in the student's file.

Documentation

As we discussed earlier, the transdisciplinary approach does not eliminate the need for direct services to the student. A combination of direct and indirect consultation services is actually best for the student. However, all services provided to the student, whether direct or indirect, should be documented and retained as part of the student's file. Consultation and training to parents, community service providers, and other team members should also be documented and filed.

Training in any area should be provided by a qualified person. The task to be learned should be broken into steps, and the trainer should provide the instruction by demonstrating or modeling, observing the team member to be trained perform the steps, providing corrections and feedback on the performance of each step, leaving a written description of the procedure, and monitoring the team member's performance.

Each step of this training process should be documented to ensure a good teaching-learning process and also to protect the team members against any liability that might arise.

Barriers to Implementing Transdisciplinary Services

Implementing transdisciplinary services and an integrated therapy approach takes time and is a developmental process. Identification of barriers that impede the process is important for administrators and team members if they are to develop plans, procedures, and strategies for barrier removal.

Philosophical and professional barriers can impede the transdisciplinary process. Differences in professional orientation and training, use of too much professional terminology that impedes communication and understanding across disciplines, and the inability to "role release" can keep the transdisciplinary model from succeeding.

Interpersonal barriers emerge when individual members of the team feel threatened by training others or by being trained by them. Team members may be reluctant to surrender their roles because they feel personally and professionally threatened.

Administrative barriers can also emerge. Team members and administrators may lack knowledge or experience with the approach, may resist change, may have disputes about professional ethics and liability that are caused by an inability to role-release, and may argue over issues regarding traditional policies and procedures.

SUMMARY

There are several types of team models, including the multidisciplinary approach, interdisciplinary approach, and transdisciplinary approach (which includes the integrated therapy approach). Of these approaches, the transdisciplinary team model provides the most collaborative and consolidated services. This approach emphasizes (1) shared goals among team members, (2) role-release, in which roles of each discipline may be performed by another discipline, and (3) an active and reciprocal learning process across team members. To facilitate collaborative teamwork, areas such as assessment, development of instructional goals, and actual delivery of instruction need to be approached using a team framework. The use of collaborative teamwork should result in more effective, efficient planning and instruction for students with physical, sensory, or health impairments.

Glossary

abduction A movement of a body part away from the midline of the body.

acute The short and usually more severe course of a disease process.

adduction A movement of a body part toward the midline of the body.

amblyopia A loss of visual acuity that is not attributable to an organic cause. It can occur as a result of nonuse or visual deprivation, or when one eye sees a different image from the other.

ambulatory Describes a person who is able to walk.

amelia The category of limb deficiency describing a congenital, complete absence of one or more limbs.

amputation, acquired The removal of a limb or part of a limb either surgically or through trauma.

amputation, congenital The failure of a limb to grow or develop normally in utero causing a deficiency or absence of the limb at birth.

amputee A person who has either a congenital or acquired amputation of a part of a limb, a whole limb, or more than one limb. This person may also be said to have a limb deficiency.

anemia A broad term to describe conditions in which the erythrocytes (red blood cells) are decreased in number or quality.

aneurysm A sac or outpouching of a blood vessel that may rupture, resulting in internal bleeding.

aniridia A condition in which the iris is defective or absent.

anoxia The absence or a decrease of oxygen in body tissues. Prolonged anoxia results in tissue destruction and ultimately death.

anterior A term used in reference to the forward part of an organ or body, the face side of the body, or ventral (belly) surface of the body.

antibody An immunoglobulin molecule formed in response to a specific antigen. An antibody reacts only with a specific antigen and works to suppress the action of the antigen.

antigen A substance that produces an immune response and stimulates the production of antibodies. Antigens include toxins, foreign substances, bacteria, and tissue cells.

aphasia The loss of the ability to use written or spoken language (expressive aphasia) or to comprehend written or spoken language (receptive aphasia) due to damage to specific areas in the brain responsible for speech and language.

arthritis Inflammation of joints characterized by pain, heat, redness, and swelling, which may lead to disuse and/or deformity.

arthrogryposis A congenital condition characterized by multiple contracted and malformed joints (arthrogryposis multiplex congenita).

articular Refers to something that has joints or describes something pertaining to a joint.

asphyxia A severe lack of oxygen that can result in coma or death. Asphyxia is typically a more sudden and significant decrease in oxygen supply as compared to anoxia, although either can have the same sequelae if prolonged.

asthma A lung disease with acute attacks of shortness of breath and wheezing secondary to airway inflammation and airway obstruction due to allergies or infection.

astigmatism A condition in which there is an unequal curvature of the cornea or lens resulting in blurred or distorted images.

ataxia The inability to coordinate muscular control smoothly. A type of cerebral palsy.

atelectasis Either the incomplete expansion of the lungs at birth or the collapse of a lung.

athetosis A movement disorder caused by a brain lesion characterized by involuntary, slow, writhing movements that are nearly constant. A type of cerebral palsy.

atonia A decrease in muscle tone from normal tone or a lack of muscle tone.

atrophy The decrease in size or wasting away of a cell, muscle, or tissue.

autonomic nervous system (ANS) Regulates the functioning of internal organs as well as the internal environment (blood pressure).

benign Used to describe a condition that is not severe, does not cause deficits, or has a favorable chance for recovery. A benign tumor is not malignant and does not tend to spread or invade other body tissues.

brain stem The anatomical designation of the base of the brain that connects the cerebral hemispheres with the spinal cord and controls many autonomic vital functions (respiration, circulation, and alertness).

cataract Any clouding of the crystalline lens of the eye, either partial or complete.

catheter A tube used for withdrawing or inserting fluids into the body; most frequently used to describe the tube inserted through the urethra into the bladder to withdraw urine.

central nervous system (CNS) Consists of the brain and spinal cord.

cerebellum The portion of the brain below the cerebral hemispheres and behind the brain stem that functions to coordinate movements.

cerebral palsy A nonprogressive disorder of voluntary movement caused by damage to the motor centers of the brain before or during birth or within the first few years of life.

cerebral hemispheres These hemispheres form the *cerebrum*, the major portion of the human brain.

cerebrospinal fluid (CSF) The clear fluid that surrounds and helps protect the brain and spinal cord. It originates from ventricles in the brain and circulates between the meninges.

cerebrum Consists of the two cerebral hemispheres and makes up the main portion of the brain.

chemotherapy The treatment of a disease by chemical agents, often the use of antineoplastic medication, to treat cancer.

chorea The nearly constant occurrence of involuntary, jerky movements seen in a number of disorders.

chronic renal failure A condition in which the kidneys are damaged and cannot function normally.

chronic A disease process that lasts a long period of time.

congenital A condition present at birth.

congenital heart defect Refers to a variety of conditions in which the heart is structurally impaired at birth.

contracture A shortening of a muscle so that motion is limited.

cornea A transparent membrane that forms the anterior one-sixth of the outer covering of the eye.

cystic fibrosis An inherited disease of the exocrine glands affecting the pancreas, respiratory system, and sweat glands; glandular secretions are increased in amount and consistency causing obstructions and infections.

degenerative The process of becoming less functional.

diabetes mellitus A condition in which there is an abnormally high amount of glucose (sugar) in the bloodstream (hyperglycemia) due to impaired secretions of insulin.

diplegia A paralysis of both legs.

diplopia Double vision that can occur when one eye deviates from correct alignment.

dislocation The displacement of any body part, most typically the relationship of bones at a joint.

distal Far from the point of reference, as opposed to *proximal*, which means close to the point of reference.

distention The state of being enlarged.

dorsal A term used to denote a position more toward the back (posterior) surface.

electrolyte A substance that separates into ions when in a solution and then can conduct electricity.

encephalitis An inflammation of the brain.

epilepsy A chronic condition in which the person has recurring seizures (sudden, involuntary, time-limited disruptions in the normal function of the CNS).

equilibrium A state of balance or maintaining balance.

esotropia An impairment in eye muscle movements in which one or both eyes turn in toward the nose. Esotropia is a type of *strabismus*.

etiology The knowledge or study of the causes of a disease.

exotropia An impairment in eye muscle movements in which one or both eyes turn out away from the nose. Exotropia is a type of *strabismus*.

extension Refers to a body part being in a straight position.

febrile Pertaining to fever.

fetus An unborn baby after the embryonic period, which is the first 7 to 8 weeks of gestation.

fracture A break or disruption in a bone.

Friedreich's ataxia An inherited disease beginning in childhood or youth characterized by a hardening of the dorsal and lateral columns of the spinal cord. Symptoms include ataxia, problems with speech, scoliosis, paralysis (especially of the legs), and swaying, uncoordinated movements.

genetic Pertaining to birth or origin. It may also be used to indicate a condition that is inherited. (*Genetics* is the study of heredity.)

glaucoma An abnormal increase in intraocular pressure in one or both eyes that can damage the eye.

Gowers's sign A classic indication of Duchenne muscular dystrophy in which children use their hands to push up on their legs in order to get up from the floor to standing.

hearing impairments (HI) The term encompasses a wide range of disorders and diseases that may cause a variety of deficits in hearing and possibly communication.

hemarthrosis Bleeding in the joints—a common characteristic of *hemophilia*.

hemianopsia A visual field deficit in which one-half of the visual field is missing.

hemimelia A category of limb deficiency in which a part of a limb is absent.

hemiplegia A paralysis of the arm and leg on one side of the body.

hemophilia A hereditary bleeding disorder in which there are inadequate amounts of clotting factor in the blood.

hydrocephalus A condition characterized by an abnormal accumulation of cerebrospinal fluid in the brain, which may result in an enlarged head and pressure on the brain leading to brain damage.

hyperglycemia An abnormally high amount of sugar in the bloodstream; usually associated with *diabetes mellitus*.

hyperopia A deficit in visual acuity caused by a refractory error affecting near vision (farsightedness).

hypertension Abnormally high blood pressure.

hypertropia An impairment in eye muscle movements in which the eye deviates upward. Hypertropia is a type of *strabismus*.

hypoglycemia An abnormally low amount of sugar in the bloodstream. This is a complication of diabetes mellitus in which there is too much insulin and too little glucose.

hypotonia A condition of decreased muscle tone and decreased resistance of muscles to passive stretch.

hypoxia When the oxygen content of the blood and lungs is too low.

idiopathic Of unknown origin.

incontinent The inability to control secretions, most typically bowel and bladder functions.

inflammation A localized, protective response that occurs after injury or tissue destruction; characterized by pain, redness, swelling, and heat.

insulin The pancreatic secretion responsible for transporting glucose from the bloodstream to the cells in the body.

intracranial Positioned within the cranium or skull.

intracranial hemorrhage Bleeding within the cranium or skull.

intrauterine Within the uterus.

joint A point of junction between two or more bones, also called an *articulation*.

juvenile rheumatoid arthritis (JRA) A chronic arthritis disease (joint inflammation) present in a child before the age of 16. There are several different subtypes of JRA with differing characteristics.

kyphosis An abnormal curvature of the spine in which the upper back is excessively rounded forward.

lateral Pertaining to a side or away from the midline.

lazy eye An impairment in eye muscle movements (strabismus) that occurs primarily when the person's eyes are fatigued so that one eye deviates from correct alignment.

Legg-Perthes or Legg-Calvé-Perthes disease A degenerative disease affecting the head of the femur.

leukemia A progressive malignant disease of the blood-forming organs, in which blood is characterized by an increase in leukocytes (white blood cells).

ligament A band of fibrous tissue that joins bones or cartilage and gives more support to the junction.

limb deficiency Encompasses a wide range of skeletal problems, congenital or acquired, which include shortened limbs, absent limbs, and malformed limbs. (See also *amputations*.)

limb-girdle muscular dystrophy A type of muscular dystrophy that initially manifests as deterioration at the shoulders and pelvis.

lordosis A swaybacked posture in which the normal curvature of the spine in the lower back is increased.

lymphoma A general term referring to cancer of the lymph tissues.

malaise A nonspecific feeling of discomfort.

malignant Becoming progressively worse; often used in reference to tumors describing one that is growing and has a tendency to spread and recur (cancer).

medial The middle, or toward the middle.

meninges Three membranes that form a covering of the brain and spinal cord: the dura mater, pia mater, and the arachnoid.

meningitis An inflammation of the meninges (membranes surrounding the brain and spinal cord).

metabolize The process of chemically breaking down substances to provide nutrients.

metastasis The transfer of a disease from one body part to another part that is not in direct contact. Malignant tumors spread by metastasizing to other regions of the body.

multiple disabilities Two or more disabilities that significantly affect the person's ability to learn and function.

muscular dystrophy Any of a group of inherited diseases characterized by progressive weakness due to the degeneration of muscle fibers. Duchenne muscular dystrophy is one of the most common types.

musculoskeletal system Consists of the muscles, bones, tendons, and ligaments of the body and the systems that involve any of these entities.

myelin A substance that surrounds part of some neurons, which aids in transmitting information and maintaining the electrically charged environment of the neurons.

myelination The process of taking on myelin; also called *myelinization*.

myelomeningocele A form of spina bifida in which the meninges and spinal cord are pushed out through the malformed vertebrae, usually resulting in some degree of paralysis, sensory loss, or both.

myopathy A pathology or abnormal condition of the muscles.

myopia A deficit in visual acuity caused by a refractory error affecting distance vision (nearsightedness).

necrosis The death of cells or body tissues.

neonate A newborn infant. Infants are called neonates for the first 4 weeks of life.

nephritis An inflammation of the kidney.

neuron A cell of the nervous system that transmits electrical energy.

neuropathy A pathology or abnormal condition of the peripheral nervous system.

nystagmus The ocular movements consisting of involuntary, rhythmic eye movements (typically in the horizontal plane), which, when unelicited, are abnormal.

orthopedics A category of surgery that deals specifically with the musculoskeletal system.

orthotics Bracing or other types of external supports used to correct deformities, provide support, and increase function. (Practitioner is an *orthotist*; supporting devices are *orthoses*.)

otitis media An inflammation of the middle ear.

pathological A biological process that is not normal and causes injurious changes in body tissues or function.

pathology The changes in body tissues or structures that are caused by a disease process.

pelvis The large ring of bones at the base of the trunk that forms joints with the femurs (hip joints) and sacrum (end of the vertebral column).

perinatal The general period of time just before, during, and after birth.

peripheral nervous system (PNS) Consists of the nerves that connect the spinal cord to the rest of the body.

phocomelia A type of congenital limb deficiency in which the hands or feet are attached directly to the trunk, and the rest of the extremity is absent.

plasma The fluid part of the blood in which blood components are suspended.

pneumonia An acute inflammation of the alveoli of the lungs.

postnatal The period of time just after birth.

postural reaction The automatic movement a person makes in order to keep an upright position.

prenatal The period of time before birth (during gestation).

prognosis The estimate as to the probable outcome or chance of recovery from a disease or process that is based on the symptoms, response, and current knowledge.

prosthesis An artificial substitute for a body part.

proximal Close to the point of reference, as opposed to *distal,* which means far from the point of reference.

pseudohypertrophy An increase in size without an increase in muscle tissue; observed in the calves of boys with Duchenne's muscular dystrophy.

quadriplegia A paralysis of all four limbs (tetraplegia).

reflex An automatic, involuntary response to a stimuli.

relapse Used to note a recurrence of a condition after a period of improvement or stability.

remission A period in which the symptoms of a disease become much less significant or may abate entirely.

respiratory system The organs and structures concerned with air intake, output, and gas exchange. The lungs, bronchi, trachea, alveoli, nose, and mouth make up the respiratory system.

rigidity An abnormal increase in muscle tone in which resistance to passive movement is noted throughout the entire range of movement.

sclera The white outer covering of the eye.

scoliosis An abnormal side-to-side curvature of the spine, typically in an S or C pattern.

seizure disorder A chronic condition in which the person has recurring seizures (sudden, involuntary, time-limited disruptions in the normal function of the central nervous system).

seizure A sudden, involuntary, time-limited disruption in the normal function of the CNS, which may be characterized by altered consciousness, motor activity, sensory phenomena, or inappropriate behavior.

sensorineural hearing loss A type of hearing loss involving damage to the inner ear or auditory nerve.

shunting The process of providing an alternate route for the flow of body fluid.

sickle cell anemia A chronic, inherited anemia occurring primarily in the African American population, characterized by sickle-shaped red blood cells.

spasticity The abnormal increase in muscle tone (hypertonicity) often observed with persons who have neurological impairments. It is characterized by a hyperactive stretch reflex.

spina bifida A defective closure of the bony vertebral column that may or may not also involve part of the spinal column with resultant motor and/or sensory impairment.

spinal cord The part of the CNS contained in the vertebral column.

spinal muscular atrophy A group of degenerative diseases characterized by progressive weakening and atrophy of the skeletal muscles due to deterioration of motor cells in the spinal cord.

spinal cord injury Damage to the spinal cord caused by disease or trauma that results in symptoms ranging from weakness to total paralysis.

STORCH Acronym referring to a group of congenital infections: syphilis, toxoplasmosis, other, rubella, cytomegalovirus, and herpes, which, when acquired during pregnancy, can result in significant birth defects.

strabismus The condition of one or both eyes deviating from correct alignment.

teratogenic Producing abnormalities during formation, as when a substance produces a defect during gestation.

toxoplasmosis An infection caused by a parasite (*Toxoplasma gondii*), transmitted by cats and, although it causes mild symptoms in a healthy adult, is potentially very dangerous to a fetus.

trauma Any accident or abnormal occurrence that causes damage.

traumatic brain injury (TBI) A diagnosis that encompasses many types of injury to the brain; may also be referred to as *head injury.* TBI includes both *open head injuries* in which the skull has been penetrated, and *closed head injuries* in which the skull has not been fractured.

vertebral column The bones of the spine containing and protecting the spinal cord.

visual impairment Encompasses many types of vision loss, including deficits in acuity, field loss, ocular motility, or color perception.

References

Abithol, C., Burke, G., Zilleruelo, G., Montane, B., & Stauss, J. (1991). Clinical management of the pediatric renal-allograft recipient. *Child Nephrology and Urology, 11*, 169–178.

Abuelo, J. G. (1990). Renal failure caused by chemicals, foods, plants, animal venoms, and misuse of drugs. *Archives of Internal Medicine, 150*, 505–510.

Adachi, K., & Cole, R. (1990). Management of tracheal lesions in Hurler syndrome. *Archives of Otolaryngology Head Neck Surgery, 116*, 1205–1207.

Adams, R. D., & Victor, M. (1989). *Principles of neurology* (4th ed.). New York: McGraw-Hill.

Adamson, L., & Dunbar, B. (1991). Communication development of young children with tracheostomies. *Augmentative and Alternative Communication, 7*, 275–283.

Adelman, H. S., & Taylor, L. (1993). *Learning problems and learning disabilities: Moving forward.* Pacific Grove, CA: Brooks/Cole.

Aicardi, J., & Chevrie, J. (1970). Convulsive status epilepticus in infants and children: A study of 239 cases. *Epilepsia, 11*, 187–197.

Alarcon, P., Trigg, M., Giller, R., Rumelhart, S., Holida, M., & Wen, B. (1990). Bone marrow transplantation improves survival for acute lymphoblastic leukemia in relapse: A preliminary report. *The American Journal of Pediatric Hematology/Oncology, 12*(4), 468–471.

Alexander, M. A., & Bauer, R. E. (1988). Cerebral palsy. In V. B. Van Hasselt, P. Strain, & M. Hersen (Eds.), *Handbook of developmental and physical disabilities.* New York: Pergamon Press.

Alexander, R., Boehme, R., & Cupps, B. (1993). *Normal development of functional motor skills.* Tucson, AZ: Therapy Skill Builders.

Allan, L. D., & Sharland, G. K. (1992). Prognosis in fetal Tetralogy of Fallot. *Pediatric Cardiology, 13*, 1–4.

Allon, M. (1990). Renal abnormalities in sickle cell disease. *Archives of Internal Medicine, 150*, 501–504.

Alvarez, M. J., Espada, G., Maldonado-Cocco, J. A., & Gagliardi, S. A. (1992). Long-term follow-up of hip and knee soft tissue release in juvenile chronic arthritis. *The Journal of Rheumatology, 19*, 1608–1610.

American Optical. (1982). *The human eye: A course in programmed instruction.* Southbridge, MA: Optical Products Division.

American Spinal Injury Association Standards. (1990). Publication standards for neurologic classification of spinal injury patients. Atlanta, GA: American Spinal Injury Association.

Anastasiow, N. J. (1986). *Development and disability: A psychological analysis for special educators.* Baltimore: Paul H. Brookes.

Andersen, R., Bale, F., Blackman, J., & Murph, J. (1986). *Infections in children. A sourcebook for educators and child care providers.* Gaithersburg, MD: Aspen.

Anderson, M. S., & Kunkel, L. M. (1992). The molecular and biochemical basis of Duchenne muscular dystrophy. *Trends in Biochemical Sciences, 17*, 289–292.

Andersson G. B., Fasth, A., & Wiklund, I. (1993). Measurement of functional status in juvenile chronic arthritis: Evaluation of a Swedish version of the childhood health assessment questionnaire. *Clinical and Experimental Rheumatology, 11*, 569–576.

Apple, D., & Rabb, S. (1991). *Ocular pathology.* St Louis: Mosby.

Armstrong, J. J. (1991). A brief overview of diabetes mellitus and exercise. *The Diabetes Educator, 17*(3), 175–178.

Aronson, D. D., Peterson, D. A., & Miller, D. V. (1992). Slipped capital femoral epiphysis. The case for internal fixation in situ. *Clinical Orthopaedics and Related Research, 281*, 115–122.

Asbury, T., & Burke, M. (1992). Strabismus. In D. Vaughn, T. Asbury, & P. Riordan-Eva, *General ophthalmology.* Norwalk, CT: Appleton & Lange.

Asher, J., Morell, R., & Friedman, T. (1991). Waardenburg syndrome (WS): The analysis of a single family with WSI mutation showing linkage to RFLP marders on human chromosome 2q. *American Journal of Human Genetics, 48*, 43–52.

Association for the Care of Children's Health. (1982). *The chronically ill child and family in the community.* [Pamphlet.] Washington, D.C.: Author.

Augarten, A., Kerem, B., Yahav, Y., Noiman, S., Rivlin, Y., Tal, A., Blau, H., Ben-Tur, L., Szeinberg, A., Kerem, E., & Gazit, E. (1993). Mild cystic fibrosis and normal or borderline sweat test in patients with the 3849 + 10 kbc —>t mutation. *The Lancet, 342,* 25–26.

Avery, M. E., & First, L. R. (1994). *Pediatric care.* Baltimore: Williams & Wilkins.

Bagamato, S., & Feldman, H. (1989). Closed head injury in infants and children. *Infants and Young Children, 4,* 1–9.

Baker, J., & Zigmond, N. (1990). Are regular education classes equipped to accommodate students with learning disabilities? *Exceptional Children, 56,* 515–526.

Bale, J. F., & Murph, J. R. (1992). Congenital infections and the nervous system. *Pediatric Clinics of North America, 39,* 669–690.

Balkany, T., Simmons, B., & Jajek, B. (1978). Middle ear effusions in neonates. *Laryngoscope, 88,* 398–405.

Barakat, M., Savage, J., Burns, A., & Stewart, M. (1992). Efficacy of CAPD as the primary treatment for end stage renal failure in children. *Child Nephrology & Urology, 12,* 216–220.

Barnes, M. R., Crutchfield, C. A., & Heriza, C. B. (1979). *The neurophysiological basis of patient treatment: Vol. 2. Reflexes in motor development.* Atlanta, GA: Stockesville.

Barr, R., DeVeber, L., Pai, K., Andrew, M., Halton, J., Cairney, A., & Whitton, A. (1992). Management of children with acute lymphoblastic leukemia by the Dana-Farber cancer institute protocols. *The American Journal of Pediatric Hematology/Oncology 14,* 136–139.

Barrett, S. S. (1992). Comprehensive community-based services for adults who are deaf-blind: Issues, trends, and services. *Journal of Visual Impairment and Blindness, 86,* 393–397.

Barron, T. (1991). The child with spells. *Pediatric Clinics of North America, 38,* 711–724.

Bartel, N. R., & Hammill, D. D. (1986). Important generic practices in teaching students with learning and behavior problems. In D. D. Hammill & N. R. Bartel, *Teaching students with learning and behavior problems* (4th ed., pp. 347–377). Boston: Allyn & Bacon.

Barun, W. (1990). Long-term complications of renal transplantation. *Kidney International, 37,* 1363–1378.

Batshaw, M. L., & Perret, Y. (1992). *Children with disabilities: A medical primer.* Baltimore: Paul H. Brookes.

Bauer, A., & Shea, T. M. (1986). Hepatitis B: An occupational hazard for special educators. *Journal of the Association for Persons with Severe Handicaps, 11,* 171–175.

Baumgart, D., Brown, L., Pumpian, I., Nisbet, J., Sweet, M., Nessina, R., & Schroeder, J. (1982). Principle of partial participation and individualized adaptations in educational programs for severely handicapped students. *The Journal of the Association for Persons with Severe Handicaps, 7,* 17–27.

Beadle, K. (1982). Communication disorders: Speech and hearing. In E. Bleck & D. Nagel (Eds.), *Physically handicapped children: A medical atlas for teachers* (pp. 133–145). Orlando: Grune & Stratton.

Behrman, R. E. (1992). *Nelson textbook of pediatrics.* Philadelphia: W. B. Saunders.

Bell, B. A. (1993). A continuing challenge: Treatment of hemophilic children with acquired factor viii inhibitors. *American Journal of Pediatric Hematology/Oncology, 15*(1), 105–106.

Bell, W. (1992). Bacterial meningitis in children. *Pediatric Clinics of North America, 651*–668.

Belman, A. (1992). Acquired immunodeficiency syndrome and the child's central nervous system. *Pediatric Clinics of North America, 39,* 691–714.

Bennett, J. T., & MacEwen, G. D. (1989). Congenital dislocation of the hip: Recent advances and current problems. *Clinical Orthopaedics and Related Research, 247,* 15–21.

Benson, M. K. D., Fixsen, J. A., & Macnicol, M. F. (1994). *Children's orthopaedics and fractures.* Edinburgh: Churchill Livingstone.

Bergen, A. F., Presperin, J., & Tallman, T. (1990). *Positioning for function: Wheelchairs and other assistive technologies.* Valhalla, NY: Valhalla Rehabilitation Publications.

Berkow, R. (1992). *The Merck manual of diagnosis and therapy.* Rahway, NJ: Merck, Sharp & Dohme Research Laboratories.

Berliner, D. (1987). In pursuit of the expert pedagogue. *Educational Researcher, 15,* 5–13.

Berman, B., Vaughan, C. L., & Peacock, W. J. (1990). The effect of rhizotomy on movement in patients with cerebral palsy. *American Journal of Occupational Therapy, 44,* 511–516.

Best, A. B. (1992). *Teaching children with visual impairments.* Philadelphia: Open University Press.

Bigge, J. (1991). *Teaching individuals with physical and multiple disabilities.* New York: Merrill.

Biglan, A., Van Hasselt, V., & Simon, J. (1988). In V. Van Hasselt, P. Strain, & M. Hersen (Eds.), *Handbook of developmental and physical disabilities.* New York: Pergamon Press.

Bigler, E. (1987). *Diagnostic clinical neuropsychology.* Austin: University of Texas Press.

Billett, A. L., & Sallan, S. E. (1993). Autologous bone marrow transplantation in childhood acute lymphoid leukemia with use of purging. *The American Journal of Pediatric Hematology/Oncology, 15*(2), 162–168.

Binder, H., Conway, A., & Gerber, L. H. (1993). Rehabilitation approaches to children with osteogenesis imperfecta: A ten-year experience. *Archives of Physical Medicine and Rehabilitation, 74,* 386–390.

Binder, H., Conway, A., Hason S., Gerber, L. H., Marini, J., Berry, R., & Weintrob, J. (1993). Comprehensive rehabilitation of the child with osteogenesis imperfecta. *American Journal of Medical Genetics, 45,* 265–269.

Binnet, M. S., Chakirgil, G. S., Adiyaman, S., & Ates, Y. (1992). The relationship between the treatment of congenital dislocation of the hip and avascular necrosis. *Orthopedics, 15*(1), 73–81.

Bishop, V. (1986). *Selected anomalies and diseases of the eye.* University of Texas Press.

Blackman, J. (1990). *Medical aspects of developmental disabilities in children birth to three.* Rockville, MD: Aspen.

Bleck, D. (1982). Myelomeningocele, meningocele and spina bifida. In E. Bleck and D. Nagel, *Physically handicapped children: A medical atlas for teachers.* Orlando: Grune & Stratton.

Bleck, E., & Nagel, D. (1982). *Physically handicapped children: A medical atlas for teachers.* Orlando: Grune & Stratton.

Block, R., Saltzman, S., & Block, S. (1981). Teenage pregnancy. *Advances in Pediatrics, 28,* 75–98.

Bloomberg, G. R., & Strunk, R. C. (1992). Crisis in asthma care. *Pediatric Clinics of North America, 39*(6), 1255–1241.

Bly, L. (1983). *The components of normal movement during the first year of life and abnormal motor development.* Oak Park, IL: The Neurodevelopmental Treatment Association.

Bobath, B. (1967). The very early treatment of cerebral palsy. *Developmental Medicine Child Neurology, 9,* 373–390.

Bochmann, D. (1981). Prostheses for the limb-deficient child. In J. P. Kostuik & R. Gillespie (Eds.), *Amputation surgery and rehabilitation: The Toronto experience* (pp. 293–310). New York: Churchill Livingstone.

Bonadio, W. A. (1990). Clinical features of abdominal painful crisis in sickle cell anemia. *Journal of Pediatric Surgery, 25*(3), 301–302.

Bosi, E., Becker, F., Bonifacio, E., Wagner, R., Collins, P., Gale, E. A. M., & Bottazzo, G. F. (1991). Progression to type I diabetes in autoimmune endocrine patients with islet cell antibodies. *Diabetes, 40,* 977–984.

Bowen, J. R., & Choi, I. H. (1989). Lower limb lengthening. In A. Kalamchi (Ed.), *Congenital lower limb deficiencies* (pp. 180–210). New York: Springer-Verlag.

Braun, C., Baribeau, J., Ethier, M., Daigneault, S., & Proulx, R. (1989). Processing of pragmatic and facial affective information by patients with closed-head injuries. *Brain Injury, 34*(3), 5–17.

Briggs, A., Logan, K., & Alberto, P. (1994). Achieving educational change through technical assistance. *Journal of Visual Impairment & Blindness, 88,* 310–316.

Brill, R., MacNiel, B., & Newman, I. (1986). Framework for appropriate programs for deaf children. *American Annals of the Deaf, 131,* 65–77.

Brodin, J. (1990). Children with osteogenesis imperfecta and their daily living. *Handicap Research Group Report No. 4,* ED 331 195.

Brodin, J., & Millde, K. (1990). Three preschool children with osteogenesis imperfecta—Interviews with parents. *Handicap Research Group Report No. 5,* ED 331 196.

Brouwers, P., & Poplack, D. (1990). Memory and learning sequelae in long-term survivors of acute lymphoblastic leukemia: Association with attention deficits. *The American Journal of Pediatric Hematology/Oncology, 12*(2), 174–181.

Brown, J. C., Zeller, J. L., Swank, S. M., Furumasu, J., & Warath, S. L. (1989). Surgical and functional results of spine fusion in spinal muscular atrophy. *Spine, 14,* 763–770.

Brownbridge, G., & Fielding, D. (1991). Psychosocial adjustment to end-stage renal failure: Comparing hemodialysis, continuous ambulatory peritoneal dialysis, and transplantation. *Pediatric Nephrology, 5,* 612–616.

Browne, T. R., Dreifuss, F., Penry, J., Porter, R. J., & White, B. G. (1983). Clinical and EEG estimates of absence seizures frequency. *Archives of Neurology, 40,* 469–472.

Bruce, D. A. (1990). Head injuries in the pediatric populations. *Current Problems in Pediatrics, 20,* 63–107.

Brumback, R., Staton, R. D., & Wilson, H. (1987). Disturbances of personality, intellectual function, and psychosocial adjustment in myotonic dystrophy: Relationship to depression. In L. Charash, R. Lovelace, S. Wolf, A. Kutscher, D. Roye, & C. Leach (Eds.), *Realities in coping with progressive neuromuscular diseases.* The Charles Press.

Brzustowicz, L. M., Lehner, T., Castilla, L. H., Penchaszadeh, G. K., Wilhelmsen, K. C., Daniels, R., Davies, K. E., Leppert, M., Ziter, F., Wood, D., Dubowitz, V., Ott, J., Munsati, T. L., & Gilliam, T. C. (1990). Genetic mapping of chronic childhood-onset spinal muscular atrophy to chromosome 5q11.2-13.3. *Nature, 344,* 540–541.

Brzustowicz, L. M., Wilhelmsen, K. C., & Gilliam, T. C. (1991). Genetic analysis of childhood-onset spinal muscular atrophy. *Advances in Neurology, 56,* 181–187.

Buncic, J. (1987). The blind infant. *Pediatric Ophthalmology, 34,* 1403–1413.

Burnette, J. (1987). *Adapting instructional materials for mainstreamed students: Issue Brief 1.* Council for Exceptional Children, Reston VA (ERIC Document Reproduction Service No. ED 284 383).

Bushby, K. (1992). Recent advances in understanding muscular dystrophy. *Archives of Disease in Childhood, 67,* 1310–1312.

Bushby, K., & Gardner-Medwin, D. (1993). The clinical, genetic and dystrophin characteristics of Becker muscular dystrophy. *Journal of Neurology, 240,* 98–104.

Butler, K., & Pizzo, P. (1992). HIV infection in children. In V. Devita, S. Hellman, & S. Rosenberg (Eds.), *Aids: Etiology, diagnosis & treatment.* Philadelphia: Lippincott.

Byers, P. H., & Steiner, R. D. (1992). Osteogenesis imperfecta. *Annual Review of Medicine, 43,* 269–282.

Cabrera, M. E. (1990). Immunologic classification of acute lymphoblastic leukemia. *The American Journal of Pediatric Hematology/Oncology, 12*(3), 283–291.

Cadman, D., Boyle, M., Szatmari, P., & Offord, D. R. (1987). Chronic illness, disability, and mental and social well-being: Findings of the Ontario child health study. *Pediatrics, 79,* 805.

Caine, N., Sharples, L., Smyth, R., Scott, J., Hathaway, T., Higgenbottam, T. W., & Wallworth, J. (1991). Survival and quality of life of cystic fibrosis patients before and after heart-lung transplantation. *Transplant Proceedings, 23,* 1203–1204.

Caldwell, M. B., & Rogers, M. F. (1991). Epidemiology of pediatric HIV infection. *Pediatric Clinics of North America, 38*(1), 1–16.

Cameron, P. D., Wallace, S. J., & Munro, J. (1992). Herpes simplex virus encephalitis: Problems in diagnosis. *Developmental Medicine and Child Neurology, 34,* 134–140.

Campbell, P. (1987). Integrated programming for students with multiple handicaps. In L. Goetz, D. Guess, & K. Stremel-Campbell (Eds.), *Innovative program design for individuals with dual sensory impairments* (pp. 159–188). Baltimore: Paul H. Brookes.

Carlson, J. W., & Harlass, F. E. (1993). Management of osteogenesis imperfecta in pregnancy: A case report. *The Journal of Reproductive Medicine, 38*(3), 228–232.

Carpenter, M. B. (1985). *Core text of neuroanatomy.* Baltimore: Williams & Wilkins.

Carr, A. J., Jefferson, R. J., & Turner-Smith, A. R. (1993). Family stature in idiopathic scoliosis. *SPINE, 18*(1).

Cassella, J. P., & Ali, S. Y. (1992). Abnormal collagen and mineral formation in osteogenesis imperfecta. *Bone and Mineral, 17*, 123–128.

Cassidy, J. T., & Petty, R. E. (1990). *Textbook of pediatric rheumatology* (2nd ed.). New York: Churchill Livingstone.

Castello, M. A., Clerico A., Deb, G., Dominici, C., Fidani, P., & Donfrancesco, A. (1990). High-dose carboplatin in combination with etoposide (jet regimen) for childhood brain tumors. *The American Journal of Pediatric Hematology/Oncology, 12*(3), 297–300.

Cate, A., de Vries-van-der Vlugt, B. C. M., vanSuijlekom-Smit, L. W. A., & Cats, A. (1992). Disease patterns in early onset pauciarticular juvenile chronic arthritis. *European Journal of Pediatrics, 151*, 339–341.

Catterall, A. (1994). Legg-Calvé-Perthes' disease. In M. K. D. Benson, J. A. Fixsen, & M. F. Macnicol, *Children's orthopaedics and fractures* (pp. 443–457). Edinburgh: Churchill Livingstone.

Centers for Disease Control. (1990). Childhood injuries in the United States: *American Journal of Diseases of Children, 144*, 627–646.

Centers for Disease Control and Prevention. (1994). 1994 revised classification system for human immunodeficiency virus infection in children less than 13 years of age. *Morbidity and Mortality Weekly Report, 43*, 1–10.

Challenor, Y. (1992). Limb deficiencies in children. In G. E. Molnar (Ed.), *Pediatric rehabilitation* (2nd ed., pp. 400–424). Baltimore: Williams & Wilkins.

Chammovitz, I., Chorazy, A., Hanchett, J., & Mandella, P. (1987). In M. Ylvisaker (Ed.), *Head injury rehabilitation: Children and adolescents* (pp. 117–140). San Diego: College-Hill Press.

Chan, K., Koble-Jamieson, C., Elliman, A., et al. (1988). Airway responsibleness in low birthweight children and their mothers. *Archives of the Disabled Child, 63*, 905–910.

Charnas, L. R., & Marini, J. C. (1993). Communicating hydrocephalus, basilar invagination, and other neurologic features in osteogenesis imperfecta, *Neurology, 43*, 2603–2608.

Charney, E. (1992). Neural tube defects: Spina bifida and myelomeningocele. In M. Batshaw & Y. M. Perret (Eds.), *Children with disabilities: A medical primer.* Baltimore: Paul H. Brookes.

Chavis, P. S., & Hoyt, W. F. (1992). Neuro-ophthalmology. In D. G. Vaughn, T. Asbury, & P. Riordan-Eva (Eds.), *General ophthalmology* (pp. 262–300). Norwalk, CT: Appleton & Lange.

Chiu, D., Vichinsky, E., Ho, S., Liu, T., & Lubin, B. H. (1990). Vitamin C deficiency in patients with sickle cell anemia. *The American Journal of Pediatric Hematology/Oncology, 12*(3), 262–267.

Christie, M. R., Tun, R. Y. M., Lo, S. S. S., Cassidy, D., Brown, T. J., Hollands, J., Shattock, M., Bottazzo, G. F., & Leslie, R. D. G. (1992). Antibodies to gad and tryptic fragments of islet 64k antigen as distinct markers for development of IDDM. *Diabetes, 41*, 782–787.

Chugani, H. T. (1992). Functional brain imaging in pediatrics. *Pediatric Clinics of North America, 39*(4), 777–799.

Chung, S. M. K. (1986). Diseases of the developing hip joint. *Pediatric Clinics of North America, 33*(6), 1457–1473.

Churgay, C. A., & Caruthers, B. S. (1992). Diagnosis and treatment of congenital dislocation of the hip. *American Family Physician, 45*(3), 1217–1228.

Cockcroft, D. W. (1983). Mechanisms of perennial allergic asthma. *Lancet, 2*, 253–256.

Cohen, B., Kagen, L., Richter, B., Topor, M., & Saveedra, M. (1991). Children's compliance to dialysis. *Pediatric Nursing, 17*, 359–420.

Cohen, S., Joyce, C., Rhoades, K., & Welks, D. (1985). Educational programming for head injured students. In M. Ylvisaker (Ed.), *Head injury rehabilitation.* San Diego: College-Hill Press.

Cole, B. R. (1991). The psychosocial implications of preemptive transplantation. *Pediatric Nephrology, 5*, 158–161.

Cole, D. E. (1993). Psychosocial aspects of osteogenesis imperfecta: An update. *American Journal of Medical Genetics, 45*, 207–211.

Collins, M., Traboulsi, E., & Mamenee, R. (1990). Optic nerve head swelling and optic atrophy in the systemic mucopolysaccharidoses. *Ophthalmology, 97*, 1445–1449.

Conboy, T., Pass, R., & Stagno, S. (1986). Intellectual development in school-aged children with asymptomatic congenital cytomegalovirus infection. *Pediatrics, 77*, 801–806.

Connolly, B. H., & Montgomery, P. C. (1987). *Therapeutic exercise in developmental disabilities.* Chattanooga, TN: Chattanooga Corporation.

Conovan, W. H. (1984). Spinal cord injury. In W. Stolov & M. Clowers (Eds.), *Handbook in severe disability.* U.S. Department of Education.

Corn, A. (1983). Visual function: A theoretical model for individuals with low vision. *Journal of Visual Impairment & Blindness, 77*, 373–377.

Corr, C., Nabe, C., & Corr, D. (1994). *Death and dying; Life and living.* Pacific Grove, CA: Brooks/Cole.

Cosentino, C. M., Raffensperger, J. G., Luck, S. R., Reynolds, M., Sherman, J. O., & Reyes-Mugica, M. (1993). A 25-year experience with renal tumors of childhood. *Journal of Pediatric Surgery, 28*(10), 1350–1355.

Coutelle, C., Caplen, N., Hart, S., Huxley, C., & Williamson, R. (1993). Gene therapy for cystic fibrosis. *Archives of Disease in Childhood, 68*, 437–443.

Couvreur, J., & Desmonts, G. (1962). Congenital and maternal toxoplasmosis: A review of 300 congenital cases. *Developmental Medical Child Neurology, 4*, 519–526.

Cress, P. (1988). *Sensory assessment manual.* Monmouth, OR: Teaching Research Publications.

Crocker, A., Cohen, H., & Kastner, T. (1992). *HIV infection and developmental disabilities: A resource for service providers.* Baltimore: Paul H. Brookes.

Crooks, G., Baron-Hay, G., Byrne, G., Camerson, F., Hookings, P., Keogh, E., MacKellar, A., Prince, P., Stuckey, B.,

Campbell, S., & Willoughby, M. (1991). Late effects of childhood malignancies seen in western Australia. *The American Journal of Pediatric Hematology/Oncology, 13*(4), 442–449.

Crosley, C., & Vella, T. (1987). Physical education for children with muscular dystrophy: Current attitudes. In L. Charash, R. Lovelace, S. Wolf, A. Kutscher, D. Royce, & C. Leach (Eds.), *Realities in coping with progressive neuromuscular diseases.* New York: The Charles Press.

Curry, K., & Casady, L. (1992). The relationship between extended periods of immobility and decubitus ulcer formation in the acutely spinal cord injured individual. *Journal of Neuroscience Nursing, 24,* 185–189.

Dacou-Voutetakis, C., Kitra, V., Grafados, S., Polychronopoulou, S., Drakopoulou, M., & Haidas, S. (1993). Auxologic data and hormonal profile in long-term survivors of childhood acute lymphoid leukemia. *The American Journal of Pediatric Hematology/Oncology, 15*(3), 277–283.

Daffos, F., Forestier, F., Copella-Pavlosky, M. (1988). Management of 746 pregnancies at risk for toxoplasmosis. *New England Journal of Medicine, 318,* 271–275.

Daniels, R. J., Suthers, G. K., Morrison, K. E., Thomas, N. H., Francis, M. J., Mathew, C. G., Loughlin, S., Heiberg, A., Wood, D., Dubowitz, V., & Davies, K. E. (1992). Prenatal prediction of spinal muscular atrophy. *Journal of Medical Genetics, 29,* 165–170.

Daniels, R. J., Thomas, N. H., MacKinnon, R. N., Lehner, T., Ott, J., Flint, T. J., Dubowitz, V., Ignatius, J., Donner, M., Zerres, K., Rietschel, M., Cookson, W. O. C., Brzustowicz, L. M., Gilliam, T. C., & Davies, K. E. (1992). Linkage analysis of spinal muscular atrophy. *Genomics, 12,* 335–339.

Davis, M. D. (1992). Diabetic retinopathy: A clinical overview. *Diabetes Care, 15*(12), 1844–1869.

Day, S. (1990). Photophobia. In D. Taylor (Ed.), *Pediatric ophthalmology* (pp. 679–681). Boston: Blackwell Scientific Publications.

Deaton, A. (1987). Behavioral change strategies for children and adolescents with severe brain injury. *Journal of Learning Disabilities, 20,* 581–589.

Deci, E. L., & Chandler, C. L. (1986). The importance of motivation for the future of the LD field. *Journal of Learning Disabilities, 19,* 587–594.

Dekker, P. J., & Isdale, A. H. (1992). Sensorineural hearing loss in juvenile chronic arthritis. *British Journal of Rheumatology, 31,* 711–713.

DeLisa, J., & Stolov, W. C. (1981). Significant body systems. In W. Stolov & M. Clowers (Eds.), *Handbook of severe disability.* U.S. Department of Education Rehabilitation Services Administration.

Delquadri, J., Greenwood, C. R., Worton, D., Carta, J. J., & Hall, R. V. (1986). Classwide peer tutoring. *Exceptional Children, 52*(6), 535–542.

DeRuyter, F., & Donoghue, K. (1989). Communication and traumatic brain injury: A case study. *Augmentative and Alternative Communication, 5*(1), 49–54.

DeSanto, G., Anastasio, P., Coppola, S., Barba, G., Jadanza, A., & Capasso, G. (1991). Age-related changes in renal reserve and renal tubular function in healthy humans. *Journal of Nephrology and Urology, 11,* 33–40.

Desmond, M., Wilson, G., & Vordeman, A. (1985). The health and educational status of adolescents with congenital rubella syndrome. *Developmental Medicine and Child Neurology, 27,* 721–729.

Diamond, G. W. (1989). Developmental problems in children with HIV infection. *Mental Retardation, 27,* 213–217.

Diamond, L. (1982). Down's syndrome. In E. Bleck & D. Nagel (Eds.), *Physically handicapped children: A medical atlas for teachers.* Orlando, FL: Grune & Stratton.

Dixon, M. S. (1989). Pediatric screening and evaluation. In A. Kalamchi (Ed.), *Congenital lower limb deficiencies* (pp. 58–64). New York: Springer-Verlag.

Dodds, J. W. (1992). Sports and amputees. In L. A. Karacoloff, C. S. Hammersley, & F. J. Schneider (Eds.), *Lower extremity amputation: A guide to functional outcomes in physical therapy management. The Rehabilitation Institute of Chicago procedure manual* (pp. 183–196). Gaithersburg, MD: Aspen.

Donahue, R. P., & Orchard, T. J. (1992). Diabetes mellitus and macrovascular complications. *Diabetes Care, 15*(9), 1141–1155.

Donckerwolcke, R. (1991). Long-term complication of renal transplantation. *Child Nephrology Urology, 11,* 179–184.

Dorland (1988). *Dorland's illustrated medical dictionary.* Philadelphia: Saunders.

D'Ottavio, G., Tamaro, L. F., & Mandruzzato, G. (1993). Early prenatal ultrasonographic diagnosis of osteogenesis imperfecta: A case report. *American Journal of Obstetric Gynecology, 169,* 384–385.

Dreifuss, F. (1983). *Pediatric epileptology: Classification and management of seizures in the child.* Littleton, MA: PSG.

Dreifuss, F. E. (1989). Classification of epileptic seizures and the epilepsies. *Pediatric Clinics of North America, 36,* 265–279.

Driscoll, D. J., Michels, V. V., Gersony, W. M., Hayes, C. J., Keane, J. F., Kidd, L., Pieroni, D. R., Rings, L. R., Wolfe, R. R., & Weidman, W. H. (1993). Occurrence risk for congenital heart defects in relatives of patients with aortic stenosis pulmonary stenosis or ventricular septal defect. *Supplement to Circulation, 87*(2), 114–120.

Drukker, A. (1991). Hypertension in children and adolescents with chronic renal failure and end-stage renal disease. *Child Nephrology & Urology, 11,* 152–158.

Dubowitz, V. (1992). The muscular dystrophies. *Postgraduate Medical Journal, 68,* 500–506.

Dubowitz, V., Ignatius, J., Donner, M., Zerres, K., Rietschel, M., Cookson, W. O. C., Brzustowicz, L. M., Gilliam, T. C., & Davies, K. E. (1992). Linkage analysis of spinal muscular atrophy. *Genomixs, 12,* 335–339.

Duchowny, M. S. (1989). Surgery for intractable epilepsy: Issues and outcomes. *Pediatrics, 84,* 886–894.

Duff, A. L., & Platts-Mills, T. A. E. (1992). Allergens and asthma. *Pediatric Clinics of North America, 39*(6), 1277–1291.

Dunn, N. L., McCartan, K. W., & Fuqua, R. (1988). Young children with orthopedic handicaps: Self-knowledge about their disability. *Exceptional Children, 55,* 249–252.

Dunne, K. B., & Clarren, S. K. (1986). The origin of prenatal and postnatal deformities. *Pediatric Clinics of North America, 33*(6), 1277–1297.

Dvonch, V. M., Bunch, W. H., & Scoles, P. V. (1988). The hip. In P. V. Scoles, *Pediatric orthopedics in clinical practice* (pp. 140–158). Chicago: Yearbook Medical Publishers.

Dykes, L. (1986). The whiplash shaken infant syndrome: What has been learned? *Child Abuse and Neglect, 10,* 211–221.

Egbert, P. (1985). Cytomegalovirus ocular infections. In R. Darrell (Ed.), *Viral diseases of the eye* (pp. 97–111). Philadelphia: Lea & Febiger.

Eilert, R. (1989). Congenital short femur. In A. Kalamchi (Ed.), *Congenital lower limb deficiencies* (pp. 89–107). New York: Springer-Verlag.

Elias, S., Annas, G. J., & Simpson, J. L. (1991). Carrier screening for cystic fibrosis implications for obstetric and gynecologic practice. *American Journal of Obstetrics and Gynecology, 164,* 1077–1083.

Ellenberg, J. H., Hirtz, D. G., & Nelson, K. B. (1986). Do seizures in children cause intellectual deterioration? *The New England Journal of Medicine, 314,* 1085–1088.

Emery, A. (1991). Population frequencies of inherited neuromuscular diseases—a world survey. *Neuromuscular Disorders, 1,* 19.

Englert, C. S. (1984). Effective direct instruction practices in special education settings. *Remedial and Special Education, 5*(2), 38–47.

Epilepsy Foundation of America. (1994). *Seizure recognition and first aid.* Landover, MD: Epilepsy Foundation of America.

Erin, J. N., & Corn, A. L. (1994). A survey of children's first understanding of being visually impaired. *Journal of Visual Impairment & Blindness, 88,* 132–139.

Evans, E., Melville, G., & Cass, M. (1992). AIDS: Special educators' knowledge and attitudes. *Teacher Education and Special Education, 15,* 300–306.

Ewing-Cobbs, L., Fletcher, J., & Levin, H. (1986). Neurobehavioral sequelae following head injury in children: Educational implications. *Journal of Head Trauma Rehabilitation, 1*(4), 57–65.

Ewing-Cobbs, L., Miner, M., Fletcher, J., & Levin, H. (1989). Intellectual, motor, language sequelae following closed head injury in infants and preschoolers. *Journal of Pediatric Psychology, 14,* 531–547.

Falloon, J., & Masur, H. (1992). *Pneumocystis carinii* and other protozoa. In V. Devita, S. Hellman, & S. Rosenberg (Eds.), *AIDS: Etiology, diagnosis and treatment.* Philadelphia: Lippincott.

Fedrizzi, E. F., Botteon, G., Inverno, M., Ciceri, E., D'Incerti, L., & Dworzak, F. (1993). Neurogenic arthrogryposis multiplex congenita: Clinical and MRI findings. *Pediatric Neurology, 9,* 343–348.

Fernicola, D. J., Boodhoo, V. R., & Roberts, W. C. (1993). Prolonged survival (74 years) in unoperated Tetralogy of Fallot with associated mitral valve prolapse. *The American Journal of Cardiology, 71,* 479–483.

Fiel, S. B. (1993). Clinical management of pulmonary disease in cystic fibrosis. *The Lancet, 341,* 1070–1074.

Finnie, N. R. (1974). *Handling the young cerebral palsied child at home.* New York: Plume.

Fisher, A. G., Murray, E. A., & Bundy, A. C. (1991). *Sensory integration theory and practice.* Philadelphia: Davis.

Fishman, M. A. (1992). Infectious diseases. In R. B. David (Ed.), *Pediatric neurology.* Norwalk, CT: Appleton & Lange.

FitzSimmons, S. C. (1993). The changing epidemiology of cystic fibrosis. *The Journal of Pediatrics, 122*(1), 1–9.

Flavell, J. (1963). *The developmental psychology of Jean Piaget.* New York: Van Nostrand Reinhold.

Flynn, J. (1987). Retinopathy of prematurity. *Pediatric Clinics of North America, 34,* 1487–1511.

Fox, G. M., Flynn, H. W., Davis, J. L., & Culbertson, W. (1992). Causes of reduced visual acuity on long-term follow-up after cataract extraction in patients with uveitis and juvenile rheumatoid arthritis. *American Journal of Ophthalmology, 114,* 708–714.

Frank, B. B. (1985). Psycho-social aspects of educating epileptic children: Roles for school psychologists. *School Psychology, 14,* 196–203.

Fredlund, D. J. (1984). Children and death from the school setting viewpoint. In J. L. Thomas (Ed.), *Death and dying in the classroom: Reading for reference* (pp. 16–20). Phoenix, AZ: Oryx Press.

Friedmann, L. W. (1978). *The psychological rehabilitation of the amputee.* Springfield, IL: Charles C Thomas.

Friendly, D. (1987). Amblyopia: Definition, classification, diagnosis, and management considerations for pediatricians, family physicians, and general practitioners. *Pediatric Clinics of North America, 34,* 1389–1401.

Frontera-Izquierdo, P., & Cabezuelo-Huerta, G. (1992). Natural and modified history of isolated ventricular septal defect: A 17-year study. *Pediatric Cardiology, 13*(4), 193–197.

Fulford, G. E., Lunn, P. G., & Macnicol, M. F. (1993). A prospective study of nonoperative and operative management for Perthes' disease. *Journal of Pediatric Orthopaedics, 13*(3), 281–285.

Furumasu, J., Swank, S. M., Brown, J. C., Gilgoff, I., Warath, S., & Zeller, J. (1989). Functional activities in spinal muscular atrophy patients after spinal fusion. *Spine, 14,* 771–775.

Gadow, K. D. (1986). *Children on medication, Vol 2.* Boston: College-Hill Press.

Gallahue, D. L. (1982). *Understanding motor development in children.* New York: Wiley.

Gallo, A. M. (1990). Family management style in juvenile diabetes: A case illustration. *Journal of Pediatric Nursing, 5*(1), 23–32.

Galway, H. R. (1981). Recreational activities of juvenile amputees. In J. P. Kostuik & R. Gillespie (Eds.), *Amputation surgery and rehabilitation: The Toronto experience* (pp. 211–216). New York: Churchill Livingstone.

Galway, H. R., Hubbard, S., & Mowbray, M. (1981). Traumatic amputations in children. In J. P. Kostuik & R. Gillespie (Eds.), *Amputation surgery and rehabilitation: The Toronto experience* (pp. 137–144). New York: Churchill Livingstone.

Gammon, A., & Nahmias, A. (1985). Herpes simplex ocular infections in the newborn. In R. Darrell (Ed.), *Viral diseases of the eye* (pp. 46–58). Philadelphia: Lea & Febiger.

Gare, B. A., Fasth, A., & Wiklund, I. (1993). Measurement of functional status in juvenile chronic arthritis: Evaluation of a Swedish version of the childhood health assessment questionnaire. *Clinical and Experimental Rheumatology, 11,* 569–576.

Garner, J. B., & Campbell, P. H. (1987). Technology for persons with severe disabilities: Practical and ethical considerations. *The Journal of Special Education, 21(3),* 122–132.

Ge, Z., Zhang, Y., Kang, W., Fon, D., Ji, X., & Duran, C. (1993). Noninvasive evaluation of right ventricular and pulmonary artery systolic pressures in patients with ventricular septal defects: Simultaneous study of Doppler and catheterization data. *American Heart Journal, 125(4),* 1073–1081.

Gearheart, B., Mullen, R. C., & Gearheart, C. (1993). *Exceptional individuals: An introduction.* Pacific Grove, CA: Brooks/Cole.

Gearheart, B. Weishahn, M., & Gearheart, C. (1988). *The exceptional student in the regular classroom.* Columbus: Merrill.

Gee, K., Harrell, R., & Rosenberg, R. (1987). Teaching orientation and mobility skills within and across natural opportunities for travel. A model design for learners with multiple severe disability. In L. Goetz, D. Guess, & K. Stremel-Campbell (Eds.), *Innovative program design for individuals with dual sensory impairments* (pp. 127–157). Baltimore: Paul H. Brookes.

Geralis, E. (1991). *Children with cerebral palsy: A parent's guide.* Bethesda, MD: Woodbine House.

Gerring, J., & Carney, J. (1992). *Head trauma: Strategies for educational reintegration.* San Diego, CA: Singular Publishing Group.

Ghajar, J., & Hariri, R. (1992). Management of pediatric head injury. *Pediatric Clinics of North America, 39,* 1093–1125.

Giles, G., & Shore, M. (1988). The effectiveness of an electronic memory aid for a memory-impaired adult of normal intelligence. *The American Journal of Occupational Therapy, 43,* 409–411.

Gillespie, R. (1981). Congenital limb deformities and amputation surgery in children. In J. P. Kostuik & R. Gillespie (Eds.), *Amputation surgery and rehabilitation: The Toronto experience* (pp. 105–136). New York: Churchill Livingstone.

Gilmore, G., & Gundersen, C. (1987). Community-school collaboration for the control of viral encephalitis. *Health Education,* 28–31.

Godley, G., & Monks, K. (1984). A special report: Detecting early signs of scoliosis. *The Elementary School Journal, 84(3).*

Goetz, L., & Gee, K. (1987). Functional vision programming: A model for teaching visual behaviors in natural contexts. In L. Goetz, D. Guess, & K. Stremel-Campbell (Eds.), *Innovative program design for individuals with dual sensory impairments* (pp. 77–98). Baltimore: Paul H. Brookes.

Goldberg, C. J., Dowling, F. E., & Fogarty, E. E. (1993). Adolescent idiopathic scoliosis: Early menarche, normal growth. *SPINE, 18(5),* 529–535.

Goldberg, C. J., Dowling, F. E., Hall, J. E., & Emans, J. B. (1993). A statistical comparison between natural history of idiopathic scoliosis and brace treatment in skeletally immature adolescent girls. *SPINE, 18(7),* 902–908.

Goldberg, M. A., Brugnara, C., Dover, G. J., Schapira, L., Charache, S., & Bunn, H. F. (1990). Treatment of sickle cell anemia with hydroxyurea and erythropoietin. *The New England Journal of Medicine, 323(6),* 366–372.

Goldstein, F., & Levin, H. (1987). Epidemiology of pediatric closed head injury: Incidence, clinical characteristics, and risk factors. *Journal of Learning Disabilities, 20,* 518–525.

Gomperts, E. D. (1990). HIV infection in hemophiliac children: Clinical manifestations and therapy. *American Journal of Pediatric Hematology/Oncology, 12(4),* 497–504.

Good, W., & Hoyt, C. (1990). Corneal abnormalities in childhood. In D. Taylor (Ed.), *Pediatric ophthalmology* (pp. 178–198). Boston: Blackwell Scientific Publications.

Gordon, E. M., Mungo, R., & Goldsmith, J. C. (1993). Lingual hemorrhage in a patient with hemophilia as complicated by a high titer inhibitor. *American Journal of Pediatric Hematology/Oncology, 15(1),* 107–110.

Gortmaker, S., Walker, D., Weitzman, M., & Sobol, A. (1990). Chronic conditions, socioeconomic risks, and behavioral problems in children and adolescents. *Pediatrics, 85,* 267.

Gossler, S. (1987). A look at anticipatory grief: What is healthy denial. In L. Charash, R. Lovelace, S. Wolf, A. Kutscher, D. Royce, & C. Leach (Eds.), *Realities in coping with progressive neuromuscular diseases.* New York: The Charles Press.

Gothelf, C., Rikhye, C., & Silberman, R. (1988). *Working with students who have dual sensory impairments and cognitive disabilities.* New York: State Education Department Office for Education of Children with Handicapping Conditions Title VI-C.

Graham, N. M., Zeger, S. L., Park, L. P., Vermund, S., Detels, R., Rinaldo, C., & Phair, J. (1992). The effects on survival of early treatment of human immunodeficiency virus infection. *The New England Journal of Medicine, 326,* 1037–1042.

Graham, S., Harris, K. R., & Reid, R. (1992). Developing self-regulated learners. In E. L. Meyen, G. A. Vergason, & R. J. Wheylan (Eds.), *Educating students with mild disabilities* (pp. 127–149). Denver: Love.

Graham, S., & Johnson, L. A. (1989). Teaching reading to learning disabled students: A review of research-supported procedures. *Focus on Exceptional Children, 21(6),* 1–12.

Granata, C., Merlini, L., Magni, E., Marini, M. L., & Stagni, S. B. (1989). Spinal muscular atrophy: Natural history and orthopaedic treatment of scoliosis. *SPINE, 14,* 760–762.

Gray, D. L., Golden, M. P., & Reiswerg, J. (1991). Diabetes care in schools: Benefits and pitfalls of public law 94-142. *The Diabetes Annual, 7,* 33–36.

Gray, J., & Robertson, I. (1989). Remediation of difficulties following brain injury: Three experimental single case studies. *Brain Injury, 3(2),* 163–170.

Gray, N. T., Bartlett, J. M., Kolasa, K. M., Marcuard, S. P., Holbrook, C. T., & Horner, R. (1992). Nutritional status and dietary intake of children with sickle cell anemia. *The American Journal of Pediatric Hematology/Oncology, 14(1),* 57–61.

Green, C., & Reid, J. (1994). A comprehensive evaluation of

a train-the-trainers model for training education staff to assemble adaptive switches. *Journal of Developmental and Physical Disabilities, 6*, 219–238.

Green, M. R., & Weaver, C. T. (1994). Early and late outcomes of cystic fibrosis screening. *Journal of the Royal Society of Medicine, 21*, 5–10.

Green, M. R., Weaver, L. T., Heeley, A. F., Nicholson, K., Kuzemko, J. A., Barton, D. E., McMahon, R., Payne, S. J., Austin, S., Yates, J. R., & Davis, J. A. (1993). Cystic fibrosis identified by neonatal screening: Incidence, genotype, and early natural history. *Archives of Disease in Childhood, 68*, 464–467.

Griebel, M. L., Oakes, W. J., & Worley, G. (1991). The Chiari malformation associated with myelomeningocele. In H. L. Rekate (Ed.), *Comprehensive management of spina bifida* (pp. 67–92). Boca Raton, FL: CRC Press.

Grunow, J. E., Azcue, M. P., Berall, G., & Pencharz, P. B. (1993). Energy expenditure in cystic fibrosis during activities of daily living. *The Journal of Pediatrics, 122*(2), 243–246.

Gruppo, R. A., Valdez, L. P., & Stout, R. D. (1992). Induction of immune tolerance in patients with hemophilia A and inhibitors. *American Journal of Pediatric Hematology/ Oncology, 14*(1), 82–87.

Gullino, E., Abrate, M., Zerbino, E., Bricchi, G., & Rattazzi, P. D. (1993). Early prenatal sonographic diagnosis of neuropathic arthrogryposis multiplex congenita with osseous heterotopia. *Prenatal Diagnosis, 13*, 411–416.

Guyton, A. (1991). *Textbook of medical physiology.* Philadelphia: Saunders.

Hagberg, B., & Hagberg, G. (1984). Prenatal and perinatal risk factors in a survey of 681 Swedish cases. In F. Stanely & E. Alberman (Eds.), *The epidemiology of the cerebral palsied* (pp. 116–134). Philadelphia: Lippincott.

Haggerty, R. J., Roghmann, K. G., & Pless, I. B. (1975). *Child health and community.* New York: Wiley.

Hall, A. (1982). Teaching specific concepts to visually handicapped students. In S. S. Mangold (Ed.), *A teacher's guide to the special educational needs of blind and visually handicapped children* (pp. 10–19). New York: American Foundation for the Blind.

Hallahan, D., & Kaufman, J. (1988). *Exceptional children: Introduction to special education.* New Jersey: Prentice Hall.

Halle, J. W., Alpert, D. L., & Anderson, S. R. (1984). Natural environmental language assessment and intervention with severely impaired preschools. *Topics in Early Childhood Special Education, 4*, 35–56.

Haller, J. (1992). Congenital malformations of the central nervous system. In R. B. David (Ed.), *Pediatric neurology for the clinician.* Norwalk, CT: Appleton & Lange.

Hamre-Nietupski, S., Swatta, P., Veerhusen, K., & Olsen, (1986). *Teacher training modules relating to teaching severely handicapped students with sensory impairments.* Cedar Falls: University of Northern Iowa.

Hanscom, D. A., Winter, R. B., Lutter, L., Lonstein, J. E., Bloom, B., & Bradford, D. S. (1992). Osteogenesis imperfecta. *The Journal of Bone and Joint Surgery, 74*, 598–616.

Hanshaw, J., Scheiner, A., Mosley, A., Gaw, L., Abel, V., & Scheiner, B. (1976). CNS effects of "silent" cytomegalovi-

rus infection. *New England Journal of Medicine, 295*, 468–470.

Harcke, H. T. (1992). Imaging in congenital dislocation of and dysplasia of the hip. *Clinical Orthopaedics and Related Research, 281*, 22–28.

Hardy, R. (1992). Retina and intraocular tumors. In D. G. Vaughn, T. Asbury, & P. Riordan-Eva (Eds.), *General ophthalmology* (pp. 190–212). Norwalk, CT: Appleton & Lange.

Harley, R. K., & Altmeyer, E. A. (1982). Cerebral palsy associated visual defects. *Education of the Visually Handicapped, 14*, 41–49.

Harriman, D. G. F. (1984). Muscle. In J. H. Adams, J. A. N. Corsellis, & L. W. Duchen (Eds.), *Greenfield's neuropathology.* New York: Wiley.

Harrington, D., & Levandowski, D. (1987). Efficacy of an educationally-based cognitive retraining programme for traumatically head-injured as measured by LNNB pre- and post-test scores. *Brain Injury, 1*(1), 65–72.

Hart, K., & Faust, D. (1988). Prediction of the effects of mild head injury: A message about the Kennard principle. *Journal of Clinical Psychology, 44*, 780–782.

Hart, V. (1988). Multiply disabled children. In V. Hasselt, P. Strain, & M. Hersen (Eds.), *Handbook of developmental and physical disabilities.* New York: Pergamon Press.

Hauser, W. A., & Hesdorffer, D. C. (1990). *Epilepsy frequency, causes, and consequences.* New York: Demos.

Healy, G. B. (1982). Hearing loss and vertigo secondary to head injury. *New England Journal of Medicine, 306*, 1029–1031.

Hegel, M. (1988). Application of a token economy with a non-compliant closed head-injured male. *Brain Injury, 2*(4), 333–338.

Heine, R. J. (1993). Insulin therapy. *The Diabetes Annual, 7*, 284–302.

Heinrech, S. D., Missinne, L. H., & MacEwen, G. D. (1992). The conservative management of congenital dislocation of the hip after walking age. *Clinical Orthopaedics and Related Research, 281*, 34–40.

Heller, K., Alberto, P. A., Schwartzman, M., Shiplett, K., Pierce, J., Polokoff, J., Heller, E., Andrews, D., Briggs, A., & Kana, T. (1991). *Suggested physical health procedures for educators of students with special needs.* Atlanta: Georgia State University.

Heller, K. W., Alberto, P. A., & Romski, M. A. (1995). Effect of object and movement cues on receptive communication by preschool children with mental retardation. *American Journal on Mental Retardation, 99*(5), 510–521.

Heller, K. W., Dangel, H., & Sweatman, L. (in press). Systematic selection of adaptations for students with muscular dystrophy. *Journal of Developmental and Physical Disabilities.*

Heller, K. W., & Kennedy, C. (1994). *Etiologies and characteristics of deaf-blindness.* Monmouth, OR: Teaching Research Publications.

Heller, K. W., Ware, S., Allgood, M., & Castelle, M. (1994). Use of dual communication boards with students who are deaf-blind. *Journal of Visual Impairment and Blindness, 88*, 368–376.

Heubner, K. M. (1986). Curricular adaptations. In G. T.

Scholl (Ed.), *Foundations of education for blind and visually handicapped children and youth: Theory and practice*. New York: American Foundation for the Blind.

Hildebrandt, F., Singh-Sawhney, I., Schnieders, B., Centofante, L., Omran, H., Pohlmann, A., Schmaltz, C., Wedekind, H., Schubotz, C., Antignac, C., Weber, J., Brahdis, M., & Members of the APN study group. (1993). Mapping of a gene for familial juvenile nephronophthisis: Refining the map and defining flanking markers on chromosome 2. *American Journal of Human Genetics, 53,* 1256–1261.

Hill, E. W. (1986). Orientation and mobility. In G. S. Scholl (Ed.), *Foundations of education for blind and visually handicapped children and youth.* New York: American Foundation for the Blind.

Hill, E. W., & Ponder, P. (1976). *Orientation and mobility techniques: A guide for the practitioner.* New York: American Foundation for the Blind.

Hill, M., Szefler, S. J., & Larsen, G. L. (1992). Asthma pathogenesis and the implications for therapy in children. *Pediatric Clinics of North America, 39*(6), 1205–1225.

Hirtz, D. G. (1989). Generalized tonic-clonic and febrile seizures. *Pediatric Clinics of North America, 36,* 365–381.

Hitman, G. A., & Metcalfe, K. A. (1993). The genetics of diabetes: An update. *The Diabetes Annual, 7,* 1–17.

Hobbins, J. C. (1991). Diagnosis and management of neural tube defects today. *New England Journal of Medicine, 324,* 690–691.

Holler, H. J. (1991). Understanding the use of the exchange lists for meal planning in diabetes management. *The Diabetes Educator, 17*(6), 474–482.

Holman, R. C., Chorba, T. L., Clarke, M. J., & Evatt, B. L. (1992). Epidemiology of AIDS in females with hemophilia and other chronic bleeding disorders in the United States: Comparisons with males with chronic bleeding disorders and AIDS and with nonhemophilic female blood-transfusion recipients with AIDS. *American Journal of Hematology, 41,* 19–23.

Holman, R. C., Rhodes, P. H., Chorba, T. L., & Evatt, B. L. (1992). Survival of hemophilic males with acquired immunodeficiency syndrome with and without risk factors for AIDS other than hemophilia. *American Journal of Hematology, 39,* 275–282.

Holmes, G. L. (1992). The epilepsies. In R. B. David (Ed.), *Pediatric neurology.* Norwalk, CT: Appleton & Lange.

Horner, R., McDonnell, J., & Bellamy, T. (1986). Teaching generalized skills. General case instruction in simulation and community settings. In R. Horner, L. Meyer, & B. Fredericks (Eds.), *Education of learners with severe handicaps: Exemplary service strategies.* Baltimore: Paul H. Brookes.

Howell, K., & Moreland, M. K. (1987). *Curriculum-based evaluation.* Columbus, OH: Merrill.

Hoyt, C., & Lambert, S. (1990). Corneal abnormalities in childhood. In D. Taylor, *Pediatric ophthalmology* (pp. 319–332). Boston: Blackwell Scientific Publications.

Hsu, J., & Lewis, J. (1981). Challenges in the care of the retarded child with Duchenne muscular dystrophy. *Orthopedic Clinics of North America, 12,* 72–82.

Hu, S. S., & Cressy, J. M. (1992). Paraplegia and quadriplegia.

In M. Brodwin, F. Tellez, & S. Browdwin (Eds.), *Medical, psychosocial and vocational aspects of disability* (pp. 369–391). Athens, GA: Elliott & Fitzpatrick.

Hubbard, S., Bush, G., Kurtz, I., & Naumann, S. (1991). Myoelectric prostheses for the limb-deficient child. *Physical Medicine and Rehabilitation Clinics of North America, 2*(4), 847–866.

Hurley, A. D., Dorman, C., Laatsch, L. K., Bell, S., & D'Avignon, J. (1990). Cognitive functioning in patients with spina bifida, hydrocephalus, and the cocktail party syndrome. *Developmental Neuropsychology, 6,* 151–172.

Hutchison, H. T. (1992). Traumatic encephalopathies. In R. B. David (Ed.), *Pediatric neurology for the clinician* (pp. 169–184). Norwalk, CT: Appleton & Lange.

Iannaccone, S. T. (1992). Current status of Duchenne muscular dystrophy. *Pediatric Clinics of North America, 39,* 879–894.

Illingworth, R. S. (1987). *The development of the infant and young child: Normal and abnormal.* Edinburgh: Churchill Livingstone.

Ionasescu, V., & Zellweger, H. (1983). *Genetics in neurology.* New York: Raven Press.

Jacobsen, F. S., Crawford, A. H., & Broste, S. (1992). Hip involvement in juvenile rheumatoid arthritis. *Journal of Pediatric Orthopaedics, 12,* 45–53.

Jaffe, K. M., Fay, G. C., Polissar, N. L., Martin, K. M., Shurtless, H., Rivvara, J. M., & Winn, H. R. (1992). Severity of pediatric traumatic brain injury and early neurobehavioral outcome: A cohort study. *Archives of Physical Medical Rehabilitation, 73,* 540–547.

Jan, J. E., Groenveld, M., Sykanda, A. M., & Hoyt, C. S. (1987). Behavioural characteristics of children with permanent cortical visual impairment. *Developmental Medicine and Child Neurology, 29,* 571–576.

Jenkins, J. R., & Jenkins, L. (1985). Peer tutoring in elementary and secondary programs. *Focus on Exceptional Children, 17*(6), 1–12.

Jerger, S., & Jerger, J. (1981). *Auditory disorders: A manual for clinical evaluation.* Boston: Little, Brown.

Johnson, C. B. (1993). Developmental issues: Children infected with the human immunodeficiency virus. *Infants and Young Children, 6,* 1–8.

Johnson, D. W., & Johnson, R. T. (1986). Mainstreaming and cooperative learning strategies. *Exceptional Children, 52,* 247–252.

Jordan, F., Ozanne, A., & Murdoch, B. (1988). Long-term speech and language disorders subsequent to closed head injury in children. *Brain Injury, 2*(2), 179–185.

Jose, R. (1983). *Understanding low vision.* New York: American Foundation for the Blind.

Joshi, V. (1991). Pathology of childhood AIDS. *Pediatric Clinics of North America, 38,* 97–120.

Jourard, S. M. (1958). *Personal adjustment.* New York: Macmillan.

Jubala, J., & Brenes, G. (1988). In V. Van Hasselt, P. S. Strain, & M. Hersen (Eds.), *Handbook of developmental and physical disabilities.* New York: Pergamon Press.

Kalamchi, A. (1989). Congenital deficiency of the fibula. In A. Kalamchi (Eds.), *Congenital lower limb deficiencies* (pp. 128–139). New York: Springer-Verlag.

Karanjia, P., & Smigielski, J. (1988). Stroke. In V. Van Hasselt (Ed.), *Handbook of developmental and physical disabilities*. New York: Pergamon Press.

Karjalainen, J. K. (1990). Islet cell antibodies as predictive markers for IDDM in children with high background incidence of disease. *Diabetes, 39*, 1144–1150.

Karjalainen, J., Martin, J. M., Knip, M., Ilonen, J., Robinson, B. H., Savilahti, E., Akerblom, H. K., & Dosch, H. (1992). A bovine albumin peptide as a possible trigger of insulin-dependent diabetes mellitus. *The New England Journal of Medicine, 327*(5), 302–307.

Karr, S. S., Brenner, J. I., Loffredo, C., Neill, C. A., & Rubin, J. D. (1992). Tetralogy of Fallot. *American Journal of Diseases in Children, 14*(6), 121–124.

Keele, D. (1983). *The developmentally disabled child: A manual for primary physicians*. Oradell, NJ: Medical Economics Books.

Kennedy, C., & Freeman, J. (1986). Posttraumatic seizures and posttraumatic epilepsy in children. *Journal of Head Trauma Rehabilitation, 1*(4), 66–73.

Kingma, A., Mooyaart, E., Kamps, W., Nieuwenhuizen, P., & Wilmink, J. (1993). Magnetic resonance imaging of the brain and neuropsychological evaluation in children treated for acute lymphoblastic leukemia at a young age. *The American Journal of Pediatric Hematology/Oncology, 15*(2), 231–238.

Knights, R. M., Ivan, L. P., Ventureyra, E., Bentivoglio, C., Stoddart, C., Winogron, W., & Bawden, H. N. (1991). The effects of head injury in children on neuropsychological and behavioural functioning. *Brain Injury, 5*, 339–351.

Knox, D. (1987). Uveitis. *Pediatric Clinics of North America, 34*, 1467–1485.

Kopriva, P., & Taylor, J. (1992). Cerebral palsy. In M. G. Brodwin, F. Tellez, & S. K. Brodwin (Eds.), *Medical, psychosocial, and vocational aspects of disability*. Athens, GA: Elliott & Fitzpatrick.

Kothari, S. S. (1992). Mechanism of cyanotic spells in Tetralogy of Fallot: The missing link? *International Journal of Cardiology, 37*, 1–5.

Krajbich, I. (1989). Proximal femoral focal deficiency. In A. Kalamchi (Ed.), *Congenital lower limb deficiencies* (pp. 108–127). New York: Springer-Verlag.

Kramer, N. C. (1980). Hemodialysis—of machine and man. *Proceedings of Vocational Rehabilitation and End Stage Renal Disease Workshop*, ED260193.

Kreton, J., & Balkany, T. J. (1991). Status of cochlear implantation in children. *Journal of pediatrics, 118*, 1–7.

Kreutzer, J. S., Devany, C. W., Myers, S. L., & Marwitz, J. H. (1991). Neurobehavioral outcome following traumatic brain injury. In J. S. Kreutzer & P. H. Wehman (Eds.), *Cognitive rehabilitation for persons with traumatic brain injury: A functional approach*. Baltimore: Paul H. Brookes.

Kritter, A. E. (1989). Tibial rotation-plasty for proximal femoral focal deficiency. In A. Kalamchi (Ed.), *Congenital lower limb deficiencies* (pp. 152–162). New York: Springer-Verlag.

Kübler-Ross, E. (1969). *On death and dying*. New York: Macmillan.

Kushion, W., Salisbury, P. J., Seitz, K. W., & Wilson, B. E. (1991). Issues in the care of infants and toddlers with insulin-dependent diabetes mellitus. *The Diabetes Educator, 17*(2), 107–110.

Lambert, S., & Hoyt, C. (1990). Brain problems. In D. Taylor (Ed.), *Pediatric ophthalmology* (pp. 505–516). Boston: Blackwell Scientific Publications.

Landgraf, R. (1993). Pancreas transplantation. *The Diabetes Annual, 6*, 349–361.

Lansdown, R. (1994). Communicating with children. In A. Goldman (Ed.), *Care of the dying child*. Oxford: Oxford University Press.

Larsen, G. L. (1992). Asthma in children. *The New England Journal of Medicine, 326*(23), 1540–1544.

Laurence, K. M., James, N., Miller, M., & Campbell, H. (1980). Increased risk of recurrence of pregnancies complicated by fetal neural tube defects in others receiving poor diets, and possible benefit of dietary counseling. *British Medical Journal, 281*, 1592–1594.

Laxer, R. M. (1993). What's in a name: The nomenclature of juvenile arthritis. *The Journal of Rheumatology, 20*(40), 2–18.

Leary, B. B. (1987). Interactive place maps: A tool for tutor training. *Journal of Developmental Education, 10*(3), 8–12.

Lefcourt, H. (1976). *Loci of control*. Hillsdale, NJ: Erlbaum.

Lehr, D. W. (1990). Providing education to students with complex health care needs. *Focus on Exceptional Children, 22*, 1–12.

Leichter, H., Sheth, K., Gerlach, M., Franklin, S., Stevens, L., & Casale, A. (1992). Outcome of renal transplantation in children aged 1–5 and 6–18 years. *Child Nephrology and Urology, 12*, 1–5.

Lerner, J. (1988). *Learning disabilities: Theories, diagnosis and teaching strategies*. Boston: Houghton Mifflin.

Lerner, S., Grieffer, I., Taub, H., Greenstein, S., Schechner, R., Karwa, G., Melman, A., & Tellis, V. (1993). A single center experience with renal transplantation in young children. *The Journal of Urology, 149*, 549–552.

Levin, A., Zeichner, S., Duker, J., Starr, S., Augsburger, J., & Kronwitch, S. (1989). Cytomegalovirus retinitis in an infant with acquired immunodeficiency syndrome. *Pediatrics, 84*, 683–687.

Levy, J. (1990). Changing concepts in HIV infection: Challenges for the 1990s. *AIDS, 4*, 1051–1058.

Levy, R., Borchelt, M. D., Kremer, R. M., Francis, S. J., & O'Connor, C. A. (1992). Hemophilus influenza infection of an implantable insulin-pump packet. *Diabetes Care, 15*(11), 1449–1450.

Lewis, R. B. (1993). *Special education technology: Classroom applications*. Pacific Grove, CA: Brooks/Cole.

Lifson, A. R. (1992). Transmission of the human immunodeficiency virus. In V. Devita, S. Hellman, & S. Rosenberg (Eds.), *AIDS: Etiology, diagnosis, and treatment*. Philadelphia: Lippincott.

Lindgren, S., Lokshin, B., Stromquist, A., Weinberger, M., Nassif, E., McCubbin, M., & Frasher, R. (1992). Does asthma or treatment with theophylline limit children's academic performance? *The New England Journal of Medicine, 327*, 926–930.

Lloyd, C., & Orchard, T. (1993). Insulin-dependent diabetes mellitus in young people: The epidemiology of physical and psychosocial complications. *The Diabetes Annual, 7,* 211–244.

Lloyd, L. (1985). Comments on terminology. *Augmentative and Alternative Communication, 1,* 95–97.

Lockman, L. (1989). Absence, myoclonic and atonic seizures. *Pediatric Clinics of North America, 36,* 331–341.

Loder, R. T. (1992). Orthopedic aspects of children. *Journal of Pediatric Orthopaedics, 32,* 527–533.

Loutzenhiser, J. K., & Clark, R. (1993). Physical activity and exercise in children with cystic fibrosis. *Journal of Pediatric Nursing, 8*(2), 112–119.

Lovell, W. W., & Winter, R. B. (1986). *Pediatric orthopaedics* (3rd ed.). New York: Lippincott.

Lowe, T. G., & Peters, J. D. (1993). Anterior spinal fusion with Zielke instrumentation for idiopathic scoliosis. *SPINE, 18*(4), 423–426.

Lucas, D. (1989). *Ocular pathology.* Boston: Blackwell Scientific Publications.

Ludman, H. (1988). *Mawson's diseases of the ear.* Chicago: Yearbook Medical Publications.

Lukacs, L., Kassai, I., & Avay, A. (1992). Total correction of Tetralogy of Fallot in adolescents and adults. *Thoracic Cardiovascular Surgeon, 40,* 261–265.

Lyman, W., Kress, Y., Kure, K., Rashbaum, W., Rubinstein, A., & Soeiro, R. (1990). Detection of HIV in fetal central nervous system tissue. *AIDS, 4,* 917–920.

Maddin, N. A., & Slavin, R. E. (1983). Mainstreaming students with mild handicaps: Academic and social outcomes. *Review of Educational Research, 53,* 519–569.

Magill-Evans, J. E., & Restall, G. (1991). Self-esteem of persons with cerebral palsy: From adolescence to adulthood. *The American Journal of Occupational Therapy, 45,* 819–825.

Maheady, L., Saac, M. K., & Harper, G. F. (1988). Classwide peer tutoring with mildly handicapped high school students. *Exceptional Children, 55*(1), 52–59.

Mahon, D., & Elger, C. (1989). Analysis of posttraumatic syndrome following a mild head injury. *Journal of Neuroscience Nursing, 21,* 382–384.

Mansour, A. (1990). Neuro-ophthalmic finding in acquired immunodeficiency syndrome. *Journal of Clinical Neuro-ophthalmology, 10,* 167–174.

Marin, T., Butturini, A., Kantarjian, H., Sokal, J., Mickey, R., & Gale, R. (1992). Survival of children with chronic myeloid leukemia. *The American Journal of Pediatric Hematology/Oncology, 14,* 229–232.

Marion, M. S., & Hinojosa, R. (1993). Osteogenesis imperfecta. *American Journal of Otolaryngology, 14*(2), 137–138.

Markell, M. S., & Friedman, E. A. (1992). Diabetic nephropathy: Management of the end-stage patient. *Diabetes Care, 15*(9), 1226–1238.

Marshak, L., & Seligman, M. (1993). *Counseling persons with physical disabilities: Theoretical and clinical perspectives.* Austin: Pro-Ed.

Martin, F. N. (1994). *Introduction to audiology.* Englewood Cliffs, NJ: Prentice Hall.

Martyn, L., & DiGeorge, A. (1987). Selected eye defects of special importance in pediatrics. *Pediatric Ophthalmology, 34,* 1517–1542.

Maslow, A. H. (1954). *Motivation and personality.* New York: Harper & Row.

Mastropieri, M. A., & Scruggs, T. E. (1987). *Effective instruction for special education.* Boston: College-Hill Press.

Mastropieri, M. A., Scruggs T. E., & Shiah, S. (1991). Mathematics instruction for learning disabled students: A review of research. *Learning Disabilities Quarterly, 6,* 89–98.

Mathewson, C., Finley, M., & Reeves, J. (1994). *Care and treatment of the spinal cord injured.* Atlanta, GA: Shepherd Spinal Center.

Mathy-Laikko, P., Iacona, T., Ratcliff, A., Villarruel, F., Yoder, D., & Vanderheiden, G. (1989a). Evaluation of a training program to enhance social interactions between children with severe/profound multihandicaps and deaf-blindness and their caregivers. In M. Bullis (Ed.), *Research on the communication development of young children with deaf-blindness* (pp. 123–150). Monmouth, OR: Teaching Research Press.

Mathy-Laikko, P., Iacono, T., Ratcliff, A., Villarruel, F., Yoder, D., & Vanderheiden, G. (1989b). Training a child with multiple handicaps to use a tactile augmentative communication device. In M. Bullis (Ed.), *Research on the communication development of young children with deaf-blindness* (pp. 87–104). Monmouth, OR: Teaching Research Press.

Mayo, N. E. (1991). The effect of physical therapy for children with motor delay and cerebral palsy. *American Journal of Physical Medical Rehabilitation, 70,* 258–267.

McCormick, L. (1984). Perspective on categorization and intervention. In L. McCormick & R. Schiefelbush (Eds.), *Early language intervention.* Columbus: OH: Merrill.

McEnery, G., Borzyskowski, M., Cox, T. C., & Neville, B. G. R. (1992). The spinal cord in neurologically stable spina bifida: A clinical and MRI study. *Developmental Medicine and Child Neurology, 34,* 342–347.

McEnery, P. T., Stablein, D., Arbus, G., & Tejani, A. (1992). Renal transplantation in children. *The New England Journal of Medical, 326,* 1727–1732.

McEwen, I. R. (1992). Assistive positioning as a control parameter of social-communicative interactions between students with profound multiple disabilities and classroom staff. *Physical Therapy, 72,* 634–647.

McGuire, T., & Rothenberg, M. (1986). Behavioral and psychosocial sequelae of pediatric head injury. *Journal of Head Trauma Rehabilitation, 1*(4), 1–6.

McGuire, T., & Sylvester, C. (1987). Neuropsychiatric evaluation and treatment of children with head injury. *Journal of Learning Disabilities, 20,* 590–595.

Meadow-Orlans, K. (1987). An analysis of the effectiveness of early intervention programs for hearing-impaired children. In M. Guralnick & F. Bennett (Eds.), *The effectiveness of early intervention for at-risk and handicapped children* (pp. 325–362). New York: Academic Press.

Mennen, U. (1993). Early corrective surgery of the wrist and elbow in arthrogryposis multiplex congenita. *Journal of Hand Surgery, 18,* 304–307.

Mercer, C. D., & Mercer, A. R. (1989). *Teaching students with learning problems.* Columbus, OH: Merrill.

Merkus, P. J., van Essen-Zandvliet, E. E., Duiverman, E. J., van Houwelingen, H. C., Kerrebijn, K. F., & Quanjer, P. H. (1993). Long-term effects of inhaled corticosterioids on growth rate in adolescents with asthma. *Pediatrics, 91,* 1121–1126.

Merlini, L., Granata, C., Bonfiglioli, S., Marini, M. L., Cervellati, S., & Savini, R. (1989). Scoliosis in spinal muscular atrophy: Natural history and management. *Developmental Medicine and Child Neurology, 31,* 501–508.

Meyers, A., & Weitzman, M. (1991). Pediatric HIV disease: The newest chronic illness of childhood. *Pediatric Clinics of North America, 38,* 169–194.

Michaud, J. L., Rivard, G., & Chessex, P. (1991). Intracranial hemorrhage in a newborn with hemophilia following elective cesarean section. *American Journal of Pediatric Hematology/Oncology, 13*(4), 473–475.

Milde, F. K., Hart, L. K., & Zehr, P. S. (1992). Quality of life of pancreatic transplant recipients. *Diabetes Care, 15*(11), pp. 1459–1463.

Miller, F., Moseley, C., & Doreska, J. (1992). Spinal fusion in Duchenne muscular dystrophy. *Developmental Medicine and Child Neurology, 34,* 775–786.

Minear, W. L. (1956). A classification of cerebral palsy. *Pediatrics, 18,* 841–852.

Mira, M. P., & Tyler, J. S. (1991). Students with traumatic brain injury: Making the transition from hospital to school. *Focus on Exceptional Children, 23,* 1–12.

Mitch, W. (1991). Dietary manipulation and progression of chronic renal failure. *Child Nephrology and Urology, 11,* 134–139.

Mitchell, C., Erlich, S., Mastrucci, M., Hutto, S., Parks, W., & Scott, G. (1990). Congenital toxoplasmosis occurring in infants perinatally infected with human immunodeficiency virus 1. *The Pediatric Infectious Disease Journal, 9,* 512–518.

Modebe, O., & Ifenu, S. A. (1993). Growth retardation in homozygous sickle cell disease: Role of calorie intake and possible gender-related differences. *American Journal of Hematology, 44,* 149–154.

Molnar, G. E. (1992). *Pediatric rehabilitation.* Baltimore: Williams & Wilkins.

Monni, G., Ibba, R., Lai, R., Cau, G., Mura, S., Olla, G., Trosatelli, C., & Cao, A. (1993). Early transabdominal chorionic villus sampling in couples at high genetic risk. *American Journal of Obstetrics and Gynecology, 168,* 170–173.

Montgomery, F., & Willner, S. (1993). Screening for idiopathic scoliosis. *Acta orthopaedica Scandinavica, 64*(4), 456–458.

Moore, A. (1990). Inherited retinal dystrophies. In D. Taylor (Ed.), *Pediatric ophthalmology* (pp. 376–406). Boston: Blackwell Scientific Publications.

Moore, T. L., & Dorner, R. W. (1993). Rheumatoid factors. *Clinical Biochemistry, 26,* 75–84.

Morbidity and Mortality Weekly Report. (1992). Recommendations for the use of folic acid to reduce the number of cases of spina bifida and other neural tube defects. *MMWR, 41,* 1–7.

Moreno-Alvarez, M. J., Espada, G., Maldonado-Cocco, J. A., & Gagliardi, S. A. (1992). Long-term follow-up of hip and knee soft tissue release in juvenile chronic arthritis. *The Journal of Rheumatology, 19,* 1608–1610.

Morgan, A. (1987). Causes and treatment of hearing loss in children. In F. Martin (Ed.), *Hearing disorders in children* (pp. 5–48). Austin: Pro-Ed.

Morgan, W. J., & Martinez, F. D. (1992). Risk factors for developing wheezing and asthma in childhood. *Pediatric Clinics of North America, 39*(6), 1185–1203.

Morrow, G. (1985). *Helping chronically ill children in school: A practical guide for teachers, counselors, and administrators.* New York: Parker.

Mueller, G. A., & Eigen, H. (1992). Pediatric pulmonary function testing in asthma. *Pediatric Clinics of North America, 39*(6), 1243–1259.

Muller, B., Nordwall, A., & von Wendt, C. (1992). Influence of surgical treatment of scoliosis in children with spina bifida on ambulation and motoric skills. *Acta Paediatric, 81,* 173–176.

Murphy, J. G., Gersh, B. J., Mair, D. D., Fuster, V., McGoon, M. D., Ilstrup, D. M., McGoon, D. C., Kirklin, J. W., & Danielson, G. K. (1993). Long-term outcome in patients undergoing surgical repair of Tetralogy of Fallot. *The New England Journal of Medicine, 329*(9), 593–599.

Musselwhite, C., & St. Louis, K. (1988). *Communication programming for persons with severe handicaps: Vocal and augmentative strategies.* Boston: College-Hill.

Nahmias, A., Josey, W., Naib, Z., Freeman, M., Fernandez, R., & Wheeler, J. (1971). Perinatal risk associated with maternal genital herpes simplex virus infection. *American Journal of Obstetrics and Gynecology, 110,* 835–837.

National Heart, Lung and Blood Institute Expert Panel. An update on the diagnosis and management of pediatric asthma. *Nurse Practitioner, 18*(2), 51–62.

National Task Force on Special Education for Students and Youths with Traumatic Brain Injury. (1988). *An educator's manual. What educators need to know about students with traumatic brain injury.* Framingham, MA: National Head Injury Foundation.

Navarro, M., Alonso, A., Avilla, J., & Espinosa, L. (1991). Anemia of chronic renal failure: Treatment with erythropoietin. *Child Nephrology and Urology, 11,* 146–151.

Nealis, J. (1983). Epilepsy. In J. Umbreit (Ed.), *Physical disabilities and health impairments: An introduction.* Columbus, OH: Merrill.

Neidel, J., Boddenberg, B., Zander, D., Schicha, H., Rutt, J., & Hachenbroch, M. H. (1993). Thyroid function in Legg-Calvé-Perthes' disease: Cross-sectional and longitudinal study. *Journal of Pediatric Orthopaedics, 13*(5), 592–597.

Nelson, K. B., & Ellenberg, J. H. (1986). Antecedents of cerebral palsy: Multivariate analysis of risk. *The New England Journal of Medicine, 315,* 81–86.

Newell, F. W. (1992). *Ophthalmology: Principles and concepts.* St. Louis: Mosby Year Book.

Newton, V. (1990). Hearing loss and Waardenburg's syndrome: Implications for genetic counseling. *The Journal of Laryngology and Otology, 104,* 97–103.

Nicholson, A., & Alberman, E. (1992). Cerebral palsy: An increasing contributor to severe mental retardation? *Archives of Disease in Childhood,* 1050–1055.

Nixon, H. L. (1994). Looking sociologically at family coping with visual impairment. *Journal of Visual Impairment & Blindness, 88,* 329–336.

Noetzel, M. J. (1989). Myelomeningocele: Current concepts of management. *Clinics in Perinatology, 16,* 311–329.

Novack, T., Roth, D., & Boll, T. (1988). Treatment alternatives following mild head injury. *Rehabilitation Counseling Bulletin, 31,* 313–323.

O'Conner, G. (1992). Uveal tract and sclera. In D. Vaughn, T. Asbury, & P. Riordan-Eva, *General ophthalmology.* Norwalk, CT: Appleton & Lange.

Orelove, F. P., & Sobsey, D. (1991). *Educating children with multiple disabilities: A transdisciplinary approach.* Baltimore: Paul H. Brookes.

Ossman, N. J., & Campbell, M. (1990). *Adult positions, transitions, and transfers.* Tucson, AZ: Therapy Skill Builders.

Ostring, H., & Nieminen, S. (1982). Concept of self and the attitude of school age CP children towards their handicap. *International Journal of Rehabilitation Research, 5,* 235–237.

Page, C. P. (1993). An explanation of the asthma paradox. *American Review of Respiratory Diseases, 147,* 529–532.

Pang, D. (1985). Pathophysiologic correlates of neurobehavioral syndromes following closed head injury. In M. Ylvisaker (Ed.), *Head injury rehabilitation.* San Diego, CA: College-Hill Press.

Papa, M., Santoro, F., & Corno, A. (1993). Spontaneous closure of inlet ventricular septal defect in an infant with Down's syndrome and aortic coarctation. *Chest, 104*(2), 620–622.

Papini, M., Pasquinelli, A., Armellini, M., & Orlandi (1984). Alertness and incidence of seizures in patients with Lennox-Gastaut syndrome. *Epilepsia, 25,* 161–167.

Park, T., & Owen, J. (1992). Surgical management of spastic diplegia in cerebral palsy. *New England Journal of Medicine, 326,* 745–749.

Parmelee, D., Kowatch, R., Sellman, J., & Davidow, D. (1989). Ten cases of head-injured, suicide surviving adolescents: Challenges for rehabilitation. *Brain Injury, 33,* 295–300.

Parrish, A. E. (1980). Medical management of the ESRD patient: Hemodialysis—of machine and man. *Proceedings of Vocational Rehabilitation and End Stage Renal Disease Workshop,* ED260193.

Partridge, T., Cross, C., & Westminster Medical School. (1992). *Pathophysiology of muscular dystrophy.* London: Westminster Medical School.

Paterson, C. R., Burns, J., & McAllion, S. J. (1993). Osteogenesis imperfecta: The distinction from child abuse and the recognition of a variant form. *American Journal of Medical Genetics, 45,* 187–192.

Patton, J. G. (1989). Upper-limb prosthetic components for children and teenagers. In D. J. Atkins & R. H. Meier III (Eds.), *Comprehensive management of the upper-limb amputee* (p. 99–120). New York: Springer-Verlag.

Pedersen, O. (1993). Glucose transporters and diabetes mellitus. *The Diabetes Annual, 7,* 30–54.

Pellock, J. M. (1989). Efficacy and adverse effects of antiepileptic drugs. *Pediatric Clinics of North America, 36,* 435–448.

Penn, C., & Cleary, J. (1988). Compensatory strategies in the language of closed head injured patients. *Head Injury, 21,* 3–17.

Peoples, A. (1989). The juvenile amputee: Physical therapy and sports participation. In A. Kalamchi (Ed.), *Congenital lower limb deficiencies* (pp. 242–249). New York: Springer-Verlag.

Peregrine, J. G. (1992). Special considerations for the child amputee. In L. A. Karacoloff, C. S. Hammersley, & F. J. Schneider (Eds.), *Lower extremity amputation: A guide to functional outcomes in physical therapy management. The rehabilitation institute of Chicago procedure manual* (pp. 197–208). Gaithersburg, MD: Aspen.

Petersen, M. C. (1992). Tethered cord syndrome in myelodysplasia: Correlation between level of lesion and height at time of presentation. *Developmental Medicine and Child Neurology, 34,* 604–610.

Pettersson, H., Wingstrand, H., Thambert, C., Nilsson, I., & Jonsson, K. (1990). Legg-Calve-Perthes disease in hemophilia: Incidence and etiologic considerations. *Journal of Pediatric Orthopaedics, 10,* 28–32.

Phillips, D. P., Roye, D. P., Farcy, J. C., Leet, A., & Shelton, Y. A. (1990). Surgical treatment of scoliosis in a spinal muscular atrophy population. *SPINE, 15,* 942–945.

Physician's Desk Reference. (1995). Montreal, NJ: Medical Economics Data.

Pidcock, F. S., Graziani, L. J., Stanley, C., Mitchell, D. G., & Merton, D. (1990). Neurosonographic features of periventricular echodensities associated with cerebral palsy in preterm infants. *Journal of Pediatrics, 116,* 417–422.

Piomelli, S., Seaman, C., Ackerman, K., Yu, E., & Blei, F. (1990). Planning an exchange transfusion in patients with sickle cell syndromes. *American Journal of Pediatric Hematology/Oncology, 12*(3), 268–276.

Pipeleers, D., & Ling, Z. (1992). Pancreatic beta cells in insulin-dependent diabetes. *Diabetes/Metabolism Reviews, 8*(3), 209–227.

Pless, I. B., & Pinkerton, P. (1975). *Chronic childhood disorder: Promoting patterns of adjustment.* Chicago: Yearbook Medical Publishers.

Plona, R., & Schremp, P. (1992). Nursing care of patients with ocular manifestations of human immunodeficiency virus infection. *Nursing Clinics of North America, 27,* 793–805.

Polito, C., La Manna, A., Olivieri, A., Cartiglia, M., Bonomo, G., Di Tooro, A., Todisco, N., & DelGado, R. (1991). Progression of chronic renal failure. *Child Nephrology and Urology, 11,* 91–95.

Pome, G., Rossi, C., Colucci, V., Passini, C., Morello, M., Taglieri, C., Pezzano, A., Figini, A., & Pellegrini. (1992). Late reoperations after repair of Tetralogy of Fallot. *European Journal of Cardiothoracic Surgery, 6,* 31–35.

Pongiglione, G., Marasini, M., Silvestri, G., Tuo, P., Ribaldone, D., Bertolini, A., & Garello-Cantoni, L. (1988). Early treatment of patent ductus arteriosus in premature infants with severe respiratory distress syndrome. *Pediatric Cardiology, 9,* 91–94.

Pope, A. M. (1992). Preventing secondary conditions. *Mental Retardation, 30*(6), 347–354.

Porter, P., & Hall, C. (1987). The effects of teacher education on the classroom performance of children with Duchenne muscular dystrophy. In L. Charash, R. Lovelace, S. Wolf, A. Kutscher, D. Royce, & C. Leach (Eds.), *Realities in coping with progressive neuromuscular diseases.* New York: The Charles Press.

Price, R., Brew, B., & Roke, M. (1992). Central and peripheral nervous system complications of HIV-1 infection and AIDS. In V. Devita, S. Hellman, & S. Rosenberg (Eds.), *AIDS: Etiology, diagnosis, and treatment.* Philadelphia: Lippincott.

Pueschel, S. M., & Mulick, J. A. (1990). *Prevention of development disabilities.* Baltimore: Paul H. Brookes.

Pyzdrowski, K. L., Kendall, D. M., Halter, J. B., Nakhleh, R. E., Sutherland, D. E. R., & Robertson, R. P. (1992). Preserved insulin secretion and insulin independence in recipients of islet autografts. *The New England Journal of Medicine, 327*(4), 220–226.

Qamar, I., & Balfe, W. (1991). Experience with chronic peritoneal dialysis in infants. *Child Nephrology and Urology, 11,* 159–164.

Quagliarello, V., & Scheld, M. (1992). Bacterial meningitis: Pathogenesis, pathophysiology, and progress. *The New England Journal of Medicine, 327,* 864–872.

Rainforth, B., York, J., & Macdonald, C. (1992). *Collaborative teams for students with severe disabilities: Integrating therapy and educational services.* Baltimore: Paul H. Brookes.

Raney, R. B., Brashear, H. R., & Shands, A. R. (1971). *Shands' handbook of orthopedic surgery.* St. Louis: C. V. Mosby.

Rasmussen, T., & Milner, B. (1977). The role of early left brain injury in determining lateralization of cerebral speech functions. *Annals of the New York Academy of Sciences, 299,* 355–369.

Regenbogen, L., & Coscas, G. (1985). *Oculo-auditory syndromes.* New York: Masson.

Reid, M. J. (1992). Complicating features of asthma. *Pediatric Clinics of North America, 39*(6), 1327–1341.

Reynolds, J. M., Morton, M. J., Garralda, M., Postlewaite, R., & Goh, D. (1993). Psychosocial adjustment of adult survivors of a paediatric dialysis and transplant programme. *Archives of Disease in Childhood, 68,* 104–110.

Rheumatology and Ophthalmology Executive Committee. (1993). Guidelines for ophthalmologic examinations in children with juvenile rheumatoid arthritis. *Pediatrics, 92,* 295–296.

Rikhye, C. H., Gothelf, C. R., & Appel, M. W. (1989). A classroom environment checklist for students with dual sensory impairments. *Teaching Exceptional Children, 22,* 44–46.

Riley, W. J., Maclaren, N. K., Krischer, J., Spillar, R. P., Silverstein, J. H., Schatz, D. A., Schwartz, S., Malone, J., Shah, S., Vadheim, C., & Rotter, J. I. (1990). A prospective study of the development of diabetes in relatives of patients with insulin-dependent diabetes. *The New England Journal of Medicine, 323*(17), 1167–1172.

Robertson, I., Gray, J., & McKenzie, S. (1988). Microcomputer-based cognitive rehabilitation of visual neglect: Three multiple-baseline single-case studies. *Brain Injury, 2*(2), 151–163.

Robertson, W. L., Glinski, L. P., Kirkpatrick, S. J., & Pauli, R. M. (1992). Further evidence that arthrogryposis multiplex congenita in the human sometimes is caused by an intrauterine vascular accident. *Teratology, 45,* 345–351.

Robinson, F. P. (1964). *Effective study.* New York: Harper and Brothers.

Roger, M., White, C., & Sanders, R. (1990). Lack of transmission of human immunodeficiency virus from infected children to their household contacts. *Pediatrics, 85,* 210–214.

Rolfs, R., & Nakashima, A. (1991). Epidemiology of primary and secondary syphilis in the United States, 1981 through 1989. *Journal of the American Medical Association, 264,* 1432–1437.

Rommens, J. M., Iannuzzi, M. C., & Derem, B. (1989). Identification of the cystic fibrosis gene: Chromosome walking and jumping. *Science, 245,* 1059–1065.

Rooney, M. (1992). Is there a disease-modifying drug for juvenile chronic arthritis? *British Journal of Rheumatology, 31,* 635–641.

Rosa, F. W. (1991). Spina bifida in infants of women treated with carbomazepine during pregnancy. *New England Journal of Medicine, 324,* 674–677.

Rose, C. D., & Doughty, R. A. (1992). Pharmacological management of juvenile rheumatoid arthritis. *Drugs, 43*(6), 849–863.

Rosendaal, F. R., Smit, C., Varekamp, I., Brocker-Briends, A. H., Van Dijck, H., Suurmeijer, T., Vandenbroucke, J., & Breit, E. (1990). Modern haemophilia treatment: Medical improvements and quality of life. *Journal of Internal Medicine, 228,* 633–640.

Rosenshine, B. V. (1986). Synthesis of research on explicit teaching. *Educational Leadership, 43*(7), 60–69.

Rosenthal, A. (1982). Visual disorders. In E. Bleck & D. Nagel (Eds.), *Physically handicapped children: A medical atlas for teachers* (pp. 483–496). Orlando, FL: Grune & Stratton.

Ross, U. H., Laszig, R., Bornemann, H., & Ulrich, C. (1993). Osteogenesis imperfecta: Clinical symptoms and update findings in computed tomography and tympano-coclear scintigraphy. *Acta Oto-Laryngolica, 113,* 620–624.

Rossi, O. V. J., Kinnula, V. L., Tienari, J., & Huhti, E. (1993). Association of severe asthma attacks with weather, pollen, and air pollutants. *Thorax, 48,* 244–248.

Rotter, J. B. (1966). Generalized expectancies for internal versus external control of reinforcement. *Psychological Monographs, 1.*

Rowland, C., & Schweigert, P. (1990). *Tangible symbol system: Symbolic communication for individuals with multisensory impairments.* Tucson, AZ: Communication Skill Builder.

Rowland, C., & Stremel-Campbell, C. K. (1987). Share and share alike: Conventional gestures to emergent language for learners with sensory impairments. In L. Goetz, D. Guess, & K. Stremel-Campbell (Eds.), *Innovative program design for individuals with dual sensory impairments* (pp 49–76). Baltimore: Paul H. Brookes.

Rowley-Kelly, F. C., & Reigel, D. (1993). *Teaching the student with spina bifida.* Baltimore: Paul H. Brookes.

Rubin, C. M., & Le Beau, M. M. (1991). Cytogenetic abnormalities in childhood acute lymphoblastic leukemia. *The American Journal of Pediatric Hematology/Oncology, 13*(2), 202–216.

Rubinstein, A. (1989). Background, epidemiology and impact of HIV infection in children. *Mental Retardation, 27,* 209–211.

Russman, B. S. (1992). Disorders of motor execution. I: Cerebral palsy. In *Pediatric neurology for the clinician* (pp. 469–480). Norwalk, CT: Appleton & Lange.

Russman, B. S., Iannacone, S. T., Buncher, C. R., Samaha, F. J., White, M., Perkins, B., Zimmerman, L., Smith, C., Burhans, K., & Barker, L. (1992). Spinal muscular atrophy: New thoughts on the pathogenesis and classification schema. *Journal of Child Neurology, 7,* 347–353.

Saarinen, E. M., Saroila, H., & Hovi, L. (1991). Recurrent disseminated retinoblastoma treated by high-dose chemotherapy, total body irradiation, and autologous bone marrow rescue. *The American Journal of Pediatric Hematology/Oncology, 13*(3), 315–319.

Sacks, S. (1992). *The development of social skills by blind and visually impaired students.* New York: American Foundation for the Blind.

Safai, B., & Schwartz, J. (1992). Kaposi's sarcoma and the acquired immunodeficiency syndrome. In V. Devita, S. Hellman, & S. Rosenberg (Eds.), *AIDS: Etiology, diagnosis, and treatment.* Philadelphia: Lippincott.

Sanford, M. K., Kissling, G. E., & Joubert, P. E. (1992). Neural tube defect etiology: New evidence concerning maternal hyperthermia, health and diet. *Developmental Medicine and Child Neurology, 34,* 661–675.

Santos, F., Orejas, G., Rey, C., Garcia-Vicente, S., & Malaga, S. (1991). Growth hormone metabolism in uremia. *Child Nephrology and Urology, 11,* 130–133.

Sass, K. J., Spencer, D. D., Spencer, S. S., Novelly, R. A., Williamson, P. D., & Mattson, R. H. (1988). Corpus collosum for epilepsy II. Neurologic and neuropsychological outcome. *Neurology, 38,* 24–28.

Schaeffler, D. (1988). Making toys accessible for children with cerebral palsy. *Teaching Exceptional children, 20*(3), 26–28.

Schaller, J. G. (1993). Therapy for childhood rheumatic diseases. *Arthritis and Rheumatism, 36*(1), 65–70.

Schmidt, D. (1982). *Adverse effects of antiepileptic drugs.* New York: Raven Press.

Schmidt, R. (1985). *Fundamentals of neurophysiology.* New York: Springer-Verlag.

Scholl, G. (1986). What does it mean to be blind? In G. Scholl (Ed.), *Foundations of education for blind and visually handicapped children and youth: Theory and practice* (pp. 23–34). New York: American Foundation for the Blind.

Scholz, S., & Albert, E. D. (1993). Immunogenetic aspects of juvenile chronic arthritis. *Clinical and Experimental Rheumatology, 11*(9), S37–S41.

Schooley, R. (1992). Herpes virus infection in individuals with HIV infection. In V. Devita, S. Hellman, & S. Rosenberg (Eds.), *AIDS: Etiology, diagnosis, and treatment.* Philadelphia: Lippincott.

Schumaker, J. B., Deshler, D. D., Alley, G. R., Warner, M. M., & Denton, P. H. (1982). Multipass: A learning strategy for improving reading comprehension. *Learning Disability Quarterly, 5*(3), 295–304.

Schunk, D. H. (1985). Participation in goal setting: Effects on self-efficacy and skills of learning disabled children. *Journal of Special Education, 19,* 307–317.

Schuum, J., & Vaughn, S. (1991). Making adaptations for mainstreamed students: General classroom teachers' perspectives. *Remedial and Special Education, 12,* 18–27.

Schwartz, R., Eaton, J., Bower, B. D., & Aynsley-Green, A. (1989). Ketogenetic diets in the treatment of epilepsy: Short-term clinical effects. *Developmental Medicine and Child Neurology, 31,* 145–151.

Scoles, P. V. (1988). *Pediatric orthopedics in clinical practice.* Chicago: Yearbook Medical Publishers.

Scott, C. I. (1989). Genetic and familial aspects of limb defects with emphasis on the lower extremity. In A. Kalamchi (Ed.), *Congenital lower limb deficiencies* (pp. 46–57). New York: Springer-Verlag.

Scott, R. N. (1989). Biomedical engineering in upper-extremity prosthetics. In D. J. Atkins & R. H. Meier III (Eds.), *Comprehensive management of the upper-limb amputee* (pp. 173–189). New York: Springer-Verlag.

Scottish Rite Children's Medical Center. (1993). *Pediatric limb deficiency seminar.* Atlanta, GA: Author.

Segni, E. D., Bakst, A., Chetboun, I., David, D., Levi, A., Shapira, H., & Kaplinsky, E. (1988). Subcostal cross-sectional echocardiographic imaging of patent ductus arteriosus. *Pediatric Cardiology, 9,* 25–28.

Serraf, A., Lacour-Gayet, F., Bruniaux, J., Ouaknine, R., Losay, J., Petit, J., Binet, J., & Planche, C. (1992). Surgical management of isolated multiple ventricular defects. *Journal of Thoracic Cardiovascular Surgery, 103,* 437–743.

Setoguchi, Y. (1989). Evaluation of the pediatric amputee. In D. J. Atkins & R. H. Meier III (Eds.), *Comprehensive management of the upper-limb amputee* (pp. 92–98). New York: Springer-Verlag.

Setoguchi, Y., & Rosenfelder, R. (Eds.). (1982). *The limb deficient child.* Springfield, IL: Charles C Thomas.

Shaffer, D., Bijur, P., & Rutter, M. (1980). Head injury and later reading disability. *Journal of the American Academy of Child Psychiatry, 19,* 592–610.

Shapiro, B. (1992). Normal and abnormal development. In M. L. Batshaw & Y. M. Perret (Eds.), *Children with disabilities: A medical primer.* Baltimore: Paul H. Brookes.

Shaw, E. D., & Beals, R. K. (1992). The hip joint in Down's syndrome. A study of its structure and associated disease. *Clinical Orthopaedics and Related Research, 278,* 100–107.

Shelbourne, P., Davies, J., Buxton, J., Anvret, M., Blennow, E., Bonduelle, M., Schmedding, E., Glass, I., Lndenvaum, R., Lane, R., Williamson, R., & Johnson, K. (1993). Direct diagnosis of myotonic dystrophy with a disease-specific DNA marker. *The New England Journal of Medicine, 328,* 471–475.

Sher, J. (1990). Muscular dystrophy. In M. Adachi & J. H. Sher (Eds.), *Neuromuscular Disease.* New York: Igadu-Shoin.

Sheth, P., Abdelhak, S., Bachelot, M. F., Burlot, P., Masset, M., Hillaire, D., Clerget-Darpoux, F., Frezal, J., Lathrop, G. M., Munnich, A., & Melki, J. (1991). Linkage analysis in spinal muscular atrophy by six closely flanking markers on chromosome 5. *American Journal of Human Genetics, 48,* 764–768.

Shields, W. (1989). Status epilepticus. *Pediatric Clinics of North America, 36,* 383–393.

Shinnar, S., Vining, E. P., Mellitis, E. D., D'Souza, M. D., Holden, K., Baumgardner, R. A., & Freeman, J. M. (1985). Discontinuing antiepileptic medication in children with epilepsy after two years without seizures. A prospective study. *New England Journal of Medicine, 313,* 976–980.

Shiraishi, H., & Yanagisawa, M. (1991). Bidirectional flow through the ductus arteriosus in normal newborns: Evaluation by Doppler color flow imaging. *Pediatric Cardiology, 12*(4), 201–205.

Shurtleff, D. B., & Dunne, K. (1986). Adults and adolescents with meningomyelocele. In D. B. Shurtleff (Ed.), *Myelodysplasias and extrophies: Significance, prevention and treatment.* Orlando, FL: Grune & Stratton.

Sicklick, M. J., & Rubinstein, A. (1992). Types of HIV infection and the course of the disease. In A. C. Crocker, H. J. Cohen, & T. A. Kastner (Eds.), *HIV infection and developmental disabilities* (pp. 15–24). Baltimore: Paul H. Brookes.

Siegel, D. M., & Baum, J. (1993). Juvenile arthritis. *Primary Care, 20*(4), 883–893.

Siegel-Causey, E., & Downing, J. (1987). Nonsymbolic communication development to theoretical concepts and educational strategies. In L. Goetz, D. Guess, & K. Stremel-Campbell (Eds.), *Innovative program design for individuals with dual sensory impairments* (pp. 15–48). Baltimore: Paul H. Brookes.

Siegel-Causey, E., & Guess, D. (1989). *Enhancing nonsymbolic communication interaction among learners with severe disabilities.* Baltimore: Paul H. Brookes.

Sillence, D. O., Senn, A., & Danks, D. M. (1979). Genetic heterogeneity in osteogenesis imperfecta. *Journal of Medical Genetics, 16,* 101–116.

Simons, J. (1994). Practical issues. In A. Goldman, *Care of the dying child.* Oxford: Oxford University Press.

Sirvis, B. (1989). Students with specialized health care needs. Reston, VA: Council for Exceptional Children. ERIC: ED 309 590.

Slater, E. (1989). Does mild mean minor? Recovery after closed head injury. *Journal of Adolescent Health Care, 10,* 237–240.

Slavin, R. E. (1990). Synthesis of research on cooperative learning. *Educational Leadership, 48*(5), 71–82.

Smith, D. D. (1989). *Teaching students with learning and behavior problems.* Englewood Cliffs, NJ: Prentice Hall.

Smith, M., Alberto, P., Briggs, A., & Heller, K. (1991). Special educators' need for assistance in dealing with death and dying. *Division on Physically Handicapped Journal, 12,* 35–44.

Smith, P. (1990). *Integrating related services into programs for students with severe and multiple handicaps: Kentucky Systems Change Project.* Lexington: University of Kentucky, Interdisciplinary Human Development Institute.

Smith, R., Francis, M. J., & Houghton, G. R. (1983). *The brittle bone syndrome: Osteogenesis imperfecta.* London: Butterworth.

Smithells, R. W., Nevin, N. C., Seller, M. J., Sheppard, S., Harris, R., Schorah, C. J., & Wild, J. (1983). Further experience of vitamin supplementation for prevention of neural tube defect recurrences. *Lancet, 1,* 1027–1031.

Snell, M. (1993). *Systematic instruction of persons with severe handicaps.* Columbus, OH: Merrill.

Snell, M. E., & Brown, F. (1993). Instructional planning and implementation. In M. E. Snell (Ed.), *Instruction of students with severe disabilities.* New York: Merrill.

Sobsey, D., & Wolf-Schein, E. (1991). In F. Orelove & D. Sobsey (Eds.), *Educating children with multiple disabilities: A transdisciplinary approach* (pp. 119–153). Baltimore: Paul H. Brookes.

Sodergard, J., Jaaskelainen, J., & Ryoppy, S. (1993). Muscle ultrasonographys in arthrogryposis. *Acta Orthopaedica Scandinavica, 64*(3), 357–361.

Solhaug, M., Adelman, R., & Chan, J. (1992). Hypertension in the child with chronic renal insufficiency or undergoing dialysis. *Child Nephrology and Urology, 12,* 133–138.

Soueidan, S. (1992). Neuromuscular diseases. In R. B. David (Ed.), *Pediatric neurology for the clinician* (pp. 407–426). Norwalk, CT: Appleton & Lange.

Southwood, T. R., & Ryder, C. A. (1992). Ophthalmological screening in juvenile arthritis: Should the frequency of screening be based on the risk of developing chronic iridocyclitis? *British Journal of Rheumatology, 31,* 633–634.

Sprague, J. B. (1992). Surgical management of cerebral palsy. *Orthopaedic Nursing, 11,* 11–19.

Staheli, L. T. (1992). *Fundamentals of pediatric orthopedics.* New York: Raven Press.

Stark, A., & Saraste, H. (1993). Anterior fusion insufficient for scoliosis in myelomeningocele. *Acta Orthopaedica Scandinavica, 64*(1), 22–24.

Stempel, D. A., & Redding, G. J. (1992). Management of acute asthma. *Pediatric Clinics of North America, 39*(6), pp. 1311–1325.

Stempel, D. A., & Szefler, S. (1992). Management of chronic asthma. *Pediatric Clinics of North America, 39*(6), 1293–1309.

Strowig, S., & Raskin, P. (1992). Glycemic control and diabetic complications. *Diabetes Care, 15*(9), 1126–1140.

Suddarth, D. (1991). *The Lippincott manual of nursing practice.* Philadelphia: Lippincott.

Sullivan, J. (1992). Lids and lacrimal apparatus. In D. Vaughn, T. Asbury, & P. Riordan-Eva, *General ophthalmology.* Norwalk, CT: Appleton & Lange.

Sullivan, T. J. (1992). Is asthma curable? *Pediatric Clinics of North America, 39*(6), 1363–1383.

Suppiej, A., Montini, G., Casara, G., Polo, A., Zacchello, G., & Zacchello, F. (1992). Evoked potentials before and after anemia correction with recombinant human erythropoietin in end-stage renal disease. *Child Nephrology & Urology, 12,* 197–201.

Suzuki, S., Kasahara, Y., Yamamoto, S., Seto, Y., Furukawa, K., & Nishino, Y. (1993). Three dimensional spinal deformity in scoliosis associated with cerebral palsy and with progressive muscular dystrophy. *SPINE, 18*(15), 2290–2294.

Suzumori, K. (1992). The role of fetal blood sampling in

prenatal diagnosis. *Early Human Development, 29,* 155–159.

Swash, M., & Schwartz, M. (1988). *Neuromuscular disease: A practical approach to diagnosis and management* (2nd ed.). London: Springer-Verlag.

Swnak, M., & Dias, L. (1992). Myelomeningocele: Review of the orthopaedic aspects of 206 patients treated from birth with no selection criteria. *Developmental Medicine and Child Neurology, 34,* 1047–1052.

Takei, S., & Hokonohara, M. (1993). Quality of life and daily management of children with rheumatic disease. *Acta Paediatrica Japonica, 35,* 454–463.

Tavernier, G. G. (1993). The improvement of vision by vision stimulation and training: A review of the literature. *Journal of Visual Impairment and Blindness,* 143–148.

Taylor, D. (1990). Nystagmus. In D. Taylor (Ed.), *Pediatric ophthalmology* (pp. 595–602). Boston: Blackwell Scientific Publications.

Taylor, J., Passo, M., & Champion, V. (1987). School problems and teacher responsibilities in juvenile rheumatoid arthritis. *Journal of School Health, 57*(5), 186–190.

Temkin, O. (1971). *The falling sickness: A history of epilepsy from the Greeks to the beginning of modern neurology* (2nd ed.). Baltimore: Johns Hopkins University Press.

Teplin, S. W., Howard, J. A., & O'Connor, M. (1981). Self-concept of young children with cerebral palsy. *Developmental Medicine and Child Neurology, 23,* 730–738.

Theologis, T. N., Jefferson, R. J., Simpson, A. H. R. W., Turner-Smith, A. R., & Fairbank, J. C. T. (1993). Quantifying the cosmetic defect of adolescent idiopathic scoliosis. *SPINE, 18*(7), 909–912.

Thompson, G. H., & Leimkuehler, J. P. (1989). Prosthetic management. In A. Kalamchi (Ed.), *Congenital lower limb deficiencies* (pp. 211–235). New York: Springer-Verlag.

Thompson, R. L., Gustafson, K. E., Hamlett, K. W., & Spock, A. (1992). Psychological adjustment of children with cystic fibrosis: The role of child cognitive processes and maternal adjustment. *Journal of Pediatric Psychology, 17,* 741–755.

Thomsen, I. (1989). Do young patients have worse outcomes after severe blunt head trauma? *Brain Injury, 3*(2), 157–162.

Thurston, J. H., Thurston, D. L., Hixon, B. B., & Keller (1982). Prognosis in childhood epilepsy: Additional follow-up of 148 children 15 to 23 years after withdrawal of anticonvulsant therapy. *New England Journal of Medicine, 306,* 831–836.

Tizzano, E. F., & Buchwald, M. (1993). Recent advances in cystic fibrosis research. *The Journal of Pediatrics, 122,* 985–988.

Tomlison, L. (1987). *Locus of control and its effect on achievement.* ERIC Document Reproduction Service No. ED276965.

Truckenbrodt, H. (1993). Pain in juvenile chronic arthritis: Consequences for the musculo-skeletal system. *Clinical and Experimental Rheumatology, 11*(9), 59–63.

Turi, M., Johnston, C. E., & Richards, B. S. (1993). Anterior correction of idiopathic scoliosis using TSRH instrumentation. *SPINE, 18*(4), 417–422.

Ueda, K., Tokugawa, K., & Kusuhara, K. (1992). Perinatal viral infections. *Early Human Development, 29,* 131–136.

Ulchaker, M. M., & Sheehan, J. P. (1991). Iatrogenic brittle diabetes: The hold-the-insulin decision. *The Diabetes Educator, 17*(2), 111–113.

Umbreit, J. (1983). *Physical disabilities and health impairments.* New York: Merrill.

United Cerebral Palsy Association. (1993). *Cerebral palsy facts and figures.* Washington, D.C.: United Cerebral Palsy Association Press.

Utens, E. M. W. J., Verhurst, F. C., Meijboom, F. J., Duivenvoorden, H. J., Erdman, R. A., Bos, E., Roelandt, J. T. C., & Hess, J. (1993). Behavioral and emotional problems in children and adolescents with congenital heart disease. *Psychological Medicine, 23,* 415–424.

Uvebrant, P. (1988). *Hemiplegic cerebral palsy: Aetiology and outcome.* Goteborg: Department of Pediatrics, II, East Hospital, Goteborg.

Vanderheiden, G. C., & Smith, R. O. (1989). Application of communication technologies to an adult with a high spinal cord injury. *Augmentative and Alternative Communication, 6,* 62–66.

Vandvik, H. V., & Hoyeraal, H. M. (1993). Juvenile chronic arthritis: A biobehavioral disease. *Clinical and Experimental Rheumatology, 11,* 669–680.

Varekamp, I., Suurmeiher, T., Brocker-Vriends, A., van Dijck, H., Smit, C., Rosendaal, C., & Briet, E. (1990). Carrier testing and prenatal diagnosis for hemophilia: Experiences and attitudes of 549 potential and obligate carriers. *American Journal of Medical Genetics, 37,* 147–154.

Varni, J. W. (1992). Evaluation and management of pain in children with juvenile rheumatoid arthritis. *The Journal of Rheumatology, 19*(33), 32–35.

Vaughn, D. G., Asbury, T., & Riordan-Eva, P. (1992). *General ophthalmology.* Norwalk, CT: Appleton & Lange.

Verani, R. R., & Conley, S. B. (1991). Sickle cell glomerulopathy with focal segmental glomerulosclerosis. *Child Nephrology and Urology, 11,* 206–208.

Vetter, U., Pontz, B., Zauner, E., Brenner, R. E., & Spranger, J. (1992). Osteogenesis imperfecta: A clinical study of the first ten years of life. *Calcified Tissue International, 50,* 36–41.

Viberti, G., Yip-Messent, J., & Morocutti, A. (1992). Diabetic nephropathy: Future avenue. *Diabetes Care, 15*(9), 1216–1225.

Vink, A. I., Holland, M. T., Le Beau, J. M., Liuzzi, F. J., Stansberry, K. B., & Colen, L. B. (1992). Diabetic neuropathies. *Diabetes Care, 15*(12), 1926–1961.

Volberding, P. (1992). Clinical spectrum of HIV disease. In V. Devita, S. Hellman, & S. Rosenberg (Eds.), *AIDS: Etiology, diagnosis, and treatment.* Philadelphia: Lippincott.

Voutetakis, C., Kitra, V., Grafakos, S., Polychronopoulou, S., Drakopoulou, M., & Haidas, S. (1993). Auxologic data and hormonal profile in long-term survivors of childhood acute lymphoid leukemia. *The American Journal of Pediatric Hematology/Oncology, 15,* 277–283.

Wagner-Lampl, A., & Oliver, G. W. (1994). Folklore of blindness. *Journal of Visual Impairment & Blindness, 88,* 267–276.

Walker, D., & Hulecki, M. (1989). Is AIDS a biasing factor in teacher judgment? *Exceptional Children, 55,* 342–345.

Ward, M. (1986). The visual system. In G. Scholl (Ed.), *Foundations of education for blind and visually handicapped children and youth: Theory and practice* (pp. 23–34). New York: American Foundation for the Blind.

Wasserman, A. L., Williams, J. A., Fairclough, D. L., Mulhern, R. K., & Wang, W. (1991). Subtle neuropsychological deficits in children with sickle cell disease. *American Journal of Pediatric Hematology/Oncology, 13*(1), 14–20.

Weinberger, S. E. (1993). Recent advances in pulmonary medicine. *The New England Journal of Medicine, 328*(19), 1389–1397.

Weinstein, R. E., Bona, R. D., & Rickles, F. R. (1991). Continuous infusion of monoclonal antibody-purified factor viii. *American Journal of Hematology, 36,* 211–212.

Weitzman, M., Gortmaker, S., Walker, D. K., & Sobol, A. (1990). Maternal smoking and childhood asthma. *Pediatrics, 85,* 505–511.

Wells, D., King, J. D., Roe, T. F., & Kaufman, F. R. (1993). Review of slipped capital femoral epiphysis associated with endocrine disease. *Journal of Pediatric Orthopaedics, 13*(5), 610–614.

Wessel, H. B. (1989). Spinal muscular atrophy. *Pediatric Annals, 18,* 421–427.

Westcott, M. A., Dynes, M. C., Remer, E. M., Donaldson, J. S., & Dias, L. S. (1992). Congenital and acquired orthopedic abnormalities in patients with myelomeningocele. *RadioGraphics, 12*(6), 1155–1173.

White, L. (1991). Chemotherapy in retinoblastoma: Current status and future directions. *The American Journal of Pediatric Hematology/Oncology, 13*(2), 189–201.

White, P. H., & Shear, E. S. (1992). Transition/job readiness for adolescents with juvenile arthritis and other chronic illness. *The Journal of Rheumatology, 19*(33).

Whiting, S., Jan, J. E., Wong, P. K., Flodmark, O., Farrell, K., & McCormick, A. Q. (1985). Permanent cortical visual impairment in children. *Developmental Medicine and Child Neurology, 27,* 730–739.

Williams, J., Berry, D. H., Caldwell, D., Zolten, A. J., & Spence, G. T. (1992). A comparison of neuropsychological and psychosocial functioning after prophylactic treatment for childhood leukemia in monozygotic twins. *The American Journal of Pediatric Hematology/Oncology, 14*(4), 289–296.

Williamson, D., & Demmler, G. (1992). Congenital infections: Clinical outcomes and educational implications. *Infants & Young Children, 4,* 1–20.

Williamson, W. D., Demmler, G. J., Percy, A. K., & Catlin, F. I. (1992). Progressive hearing loss in infants with asymptomatic congenital cytomegalovirus infection. *Pediatrics, 90,* 862–866.

Williamson, W., Desmond, M., LaFevers, N., Taber, L., Catlin, F., & Weaver, T. (1982). Symptomatic congenital cytomegalovirus: Disorders of language, learning and hearing. *American Journal of Diseases in Childhood, 136,* 902–905.

Willing, M. C., Pruchno, C. J., Atkinson, M., & Byers, P. H. (1992). Osteogenesis imperfecta type I is commonly due to a COLIA null allele of type I collagen. *American Journal of Human Genetics, 51,* 508–515.

Wills, K. E., Holmbeck, G. N., Dillon, K., & McLone, D. G. (1990). Intelligence and achievement in children with myelomeningocele. *Journal of Pediatric Psychology, 15,* 161–176.

Wilson, S. R., Mitchell, J. H., Rolnick, S., & Fish, L. (1993). Effective and ineffective management behaviors of parents of infants and young children with asthma. *Journal of Pediatric Psychology, 18*(1), 63–81.

Wolff, S. (1985). Rubella syndrome. In R. Darrell (Ed.), *Viral diseases of the eye* (pp. 199–207). Philadelphia: Lea & Febiger.

Wood, J. (1987). Adapting the presentation of academic content. *Academic Therapy, 22,* 385–392.

Wyllie, E. A., Rothner, D., & Luders, H. (1989). Partial seizures in children: Clinical features, medical treatment, and surgical considerations. *Pediatric Clinics of North America, 36,* 343–364.

Yamagishi, M., Imai, Y., Hoshino, S., Ishihara, K., Koh, Y., Nagatsu, M., Shinoka, T., & Koide, M. (1993). Anatomic correction of atrioventricular discordance. *The Journal of Thoracic and Cardiovascular Surgery, 105,* 1067–1076.

Ylvisaker, M. (1986). Language and communication disorders following pediatric head injury. *Journal of Head Trauma Rehabilitation, 1*(4), 48–56.

Yoffe, G., & Buchanan, G. R. (1988). Intracranial hemorrhage in newborn and young infants with hemophilia. *Journal of Pediatrics, 113,* 333–335.

Yoos, L. (1987). Chronic childhood illnesses: Developmental issues. *Pediatric Nursing, 13,* 25–28.

York, J., & Rainforth, B. (1991). Developing instructional adaptations. In F. Orelove & D. Sobsey (Eds.), *Educating students with multiple disabilities* (pp. 259–296). Baltimore: Paul H. Brookes.

Yoshino, K. (1993). Immunological aspects of juvenile rheumatoid arthritis. *Acta Paediatrica Japonica, 35,* 427–438.

Yu, V. (1987). Neonatal complications in preterm infants. In V. Yu & E. Wood (Eds.), *Prematurity* (pp. 148–169). London: Churchill Livingstone.

Zambone, A. M., & Heubner, J. M. (1992). Services for children and youths who are deaf-blind: An overview. *Journal of Visual Impairment and Blindness, 86,* 287–290.

Zaramella, P., Zorzi, C., Pavanello, L., Rizzoni, G., Zacchello, G., Rubaltelli, F., & Cantarutti, F. (1991). The prognostic significance of acute neonatal renal failure. *Child Nephrology and Urology, 11,* 15–19.

Zentall, S. S. (1983). Learning environments: A review of physical and temporal factors. *Exceptional Education Quarterly, 4*(2), 90–115.

Zipursky, R., Chachula, D. M., & Brown, E. J. (1993). The reversibly sickled cell. *The American Journal of Pediatric Hematology/Oncology, 15*(2), 219–225.

Name Index

Subject Index